KINGS OF MERRY ENGLAND

By the Same Author

CHRONICLES

KING RICHARD THE THIRD
KING HENRY THE FIFTH

HISTORICAL NOVELS

THE HEART OF A KING
ALL THAT GLITTERS
THE NUTBROWN MAID
SHADOW OF THE RED BARN

all Howard Baker Books

Philip Lindsay

KINGS OF MERRY ENGLAND

from

EADWARD THE CONFESSOR

1042 – 1066

to

RICHARD THE THIRD

1483 – 1485

HOWARD BAKER, LONDON

Philip Lindsay

KINGS OF MERRY ENGLAND

© Copyright Philip Lindsay, 1936

Originally published in Great Britain by
Ivor Nicholson & Watson Ltd., 1936

First published as a Howard Baker book, 1969

SBN   09   304970 6

Howard Baker books are published by
Howard Baker Publishers Limited,
47 Museum Street, London, W.C.1

Printed in Great Britain by
Stephen Austin & Sons Ltd.,
Caxton Hill, Ware Road, Hertford, Herts

for
PETER LINDSAY

MY DEAR PETER,

There are two particular reasons why I offer you this book. Firstly, because, unlike so many relations, we have managed to forget that we are first-cousins and realise that we can be friends ; and secondly, because it is definitely a book that you should read. While retaining an interest in almost every subject under sun and moon, you have yet managed to keep whole the most astounding and abominable ignorance about England in the Middle Ages. It is not that you are bored by history or that you consider the Dark Ages something so dark that they aren't worth looking at, it is simply that you have never been shown a book that can both interest and instruct you. To-day scientists are giving us childlike résumés of the Einstein theory ; they are bringing the heavens into our hands ; they are explaining, revealing, but the historian stays defiant in his study and repudiates as " popular writing " any attempt to make history interesting. This is particularly true of the Middle Ages ; later periods have been retold without loss of scholarship, but the medieval period remains for the general public unexplored save by a very few.

I want you to look upon this book as a bridge to lead you to works of deeper scholarship. After all, I am a novelist, and perhaps for that reason, being interested in dramatic episodes and in the interplay of characters, my writing may have a particular appeal to readers like yourself who are scared by footnotes or by endless unbroken pages of small type. Please do not be satisfied with this one work, continue by studying detailed histories of particular episodes and periods. My space has been infuriatingly limited ; I have been able only to skip across the centuries, and there are innumerable and fascinating scenes I have been forced to ignore. As it is, too often have I been led astray down bypaths that have nothing to do with the main narrative, but the life of the people, social

DEDICATION

problems like the Black Death or the Peasants' Rising, and brilliant scenes like the murder of Becket, are literally irresistible to me, and whenever a battle comes, I must charge into it. Forgive my construction—or rather my lack of construction—but you who know me intimately will remember that my passion for this era is so very great that often I become incoherent and excitable from sheer love. Besides, this book is not a history: at the most I should call it a chronicle, for it is purely a narrative of the lives of nineteen men, a cavalcade of Kings. Novelist though I am, the details are as authentic as it is in my power to make them; nothing has been altered, nothing has been distorted, everything I quote—except when stated otherwise —is from old records, chronicles, letters, state papers, etc. You may accept the whole book, so far as it goes, as accurate.

I know that you have been looking forward to reading this—we have discussed it together so often—and I hope now that it is in your hands that you will not be disappointed. It is dangerous to talk about an unfinished work, as expectations are more easily raised than satisfied. But I am sure you will forgive the imperfections in these pages and will stifle any criticism because you know that they are offered to you as a kind of symbol of our deep friendship. That at least is not imperfect.

PHILIP LINDSAY.

London, N.W.

AUTHOR'S NOTE

TO ATTEMPT A BIBLIOGRAPHY for a book of this type is an appalling thought. The reading of a short lifetime has been packed between these covers, and I must ask the reader to accept on trust what I state or quote. He—or, of course, she—may rest assured that not a single detail has been altered or invented—at least, to my knowledge. If I have no space to mention the numerous modern works that have guided me, save in scanty wholly inadequate footnotes, it would be ungrateful if I did not speak of those kind friends who rescued me again and again when I despaired of a solution to various problems, who advised me, and who examined the proofs. I would therefore like to confess my debt to Mr. J. D. Griffith Davies, Dr. Saxon Barton, O.B.E., F.S.A. Scot., Dr. Philip Nelson, M.A., F.R.S.E., Mr. G. E. Manwaring, F.R.H.S., of the London Library, the Hon. George Rothe Bellew, M.V.O., Somerset Herald of Arms, Mr. Philip Owens, and my brother, Mr. Jack Lindsay. I would also like particularly to thank my brother for his aid in the translations from the Latin. Whatever help these friends have given does not by any means commit them to a single statement in this book, or hold them guilty of the smallest error. Often we disagreed on various points.

CONTENTS

CONTENTS

For God's sake, let us sit upon the ground
and tell sad stories of the death of Kings :
how some have been deposed ; some slain in war ;
some haunted by the ghosts they have deposed ;
some poison'd by their wives ; some sleeping kill'd ;
all murder'd : for within the hollow crown
that rounds the mortal temples of a King
keeps Death his court, and there the antick sits,
scoffing his state and grinning at his pomp,
allowing him a breath, a little scene,
to monarchise, be fear'd, and kill with looks,
infusing him with self and vain conceit,
as if this flesh which walls about our life
were brass impregnable and humour'd thus
comes at the last and with a little pin
bores through his castle-wall, and farewell King !

King Richard the Second.

PROLOGUE

KING EADWARD THE CONFESSOR 1042–1066 AND KING HAROLD THE SECOND ·1066

To be a medieval King was to know at their highest all the emotions that man can feel, it was to live either drunk with power or in dread of the assassin's blow, to see courtiers cringe before you, yet to walk in loneliness amongst thousands who aped the friend. Men would do murder at the least if they could steal that crown from you. It has been flung from hand to hand, from nation to nation ; on the heads of some it has weighed unbearably until they dreamed of cloisters and of the dark peace of a monk's dorter, it has been a featherweight upon the heads of others, it has been worn jauntily ; some have refused it, have put it aside, being contemptuous of a symbol that was mere show ; others have killed to reach it, others have been killed and have lost it. The crown of England with multi-coloured jewels for eyes that shone about the deadly golden lilies ! there has been blood spilt on it, yet the jewels have remained undimmed, dazzling ambitious men until they itched to take it, until they fingered the grips of polished swords and dreamed of murder. It has changed its shape ; from a circlet of gold, garlanded perhaps with living leaves, it has sprouted into golden leaves, until with the coming of the Lancastrians it was enclosed in more or less the modern form. Yet no matter how smiths hammered it, with trefoil or with strawberry leaves, whether they bent it to an arch or placed a cross atop, it remained the symbol of power which, with its glitter of jewels, drew men towards it and struck them silent as if it shone on them with the eyes of snakes.

Was it worth it ? was this leaved chaplet worth the pain of striving and the continual fretting once it was attained ? Only we of to-day with our desire for peace, with our humanitarian self-pities, would consider such a question. It would never occur to medieval men. They were braver than we, they strutted their brief hour and lived each second of it with tremendous gusto ; and there was hell at the end unless they could cheat the devil with sudden repentance or a huge donation to the Church. But the joys of living were to them worth the chance of hell. Most men would be in hell to greet you, they believed—your friends, the lusty women you desired, the knights who had been stifled or hacked in tournaments, the poets who trolled of limpid ladies in small gardens, the drinkers, the lechers, the lads like yourself. You might slither through into Paradise perhaps, for the Holy Mother had a kind heart and was gentle with sinners ; and if you wished, for a good sum down, you could buy your passport, the safeguard of the cowl : they even had a legal term for it, *ad succurrendum*—you pulled a cowl over your head when you were dying and sneaked into heaven as a monk or a friar. Let God wait, said they, while there were fierce joys to be possessed—there was always a fight somewhere, plotters were for ever plotting, women were kissable, and wine was strong. These men were not of the milky-watery chivalry of modern tales ; a Galahad who had the strength of ten because his heart was pure would have astounded the most honourable of medieval knights.

It is the intense humanity of the medieval ages that is their real fascination ; the people were not shameless, for that word in its modern puritan meaning was not understood ; they were frankly brutal, yet they strove to live up to the code that we now call chivalry. They stressed this code because it was necessary so as to attain some order amongst murderers ; for the same reason the Church stressed hell above heaven—as the only way of making the people keep their daggers in their sheaths and their hands from other men's wives. Chivalry was at first a religious movement, the spur to the Crusades, but later it developed into a cult of love, into the joyous art of Provençe. Murderers, poets, hermits sealed from life, monks quiet in the cloisters, friars stepping from lowly house to house, and the oppressed serfs—all beauty and all hell was in the medieval world ; and above everything, that symbol for which men would die, that coil of gold bursting into bejewelled leaves—the crown.

History flows without beginning or end, and it is difficult to know where to start. It is natural that we should date our modern England from 1066 when the great Norman culture fully arrived, but to understand the reign of William, we must go back, past Harold II, to the Confessor, even slightly beyond Eadward to Cnut, and to Æthelred II. Even then there is much that reluctantly we let slip, for of all stories there is none so enthralling, so inspiring and so exciting as history. But this book is not a history, it is the lives of nineteen men who wore the crown of England, a cavalcade of Kings, of heroes and warriors, of saints and rascals, of soldiers and statesmen, of fools and geniuses, of different types of men like ourselves, but of men who were raised to power and who found either that there was much to do or that the task was too great for their weak hands.

Pathetic Eadward starts the cavalcade. He is to be seen, big-eyed, white-bearded, on the Bayeux Tapestry. In his simple tunic and wearing his foliated crown he steps gingerly over the path of kingship, turning to gaze with longing towards the Holy Land which he was never to see. Harold, serious, a soldier, a plodder, follows Eadward, and is soon to be swept aside by the mighty William I. William would be in his coat-of-mail, a nut-shaped helmet on his head, his eyes bright each side of the nasal-guard. William II comes next, roistering, blaspheming, brave soldier and reckless politician ; he also would wear his hauberk mainly, it is difficult to see him unarmed and in the womanish garb of the period. Henry I, that cautious miserly law-giver, steps softly after his brother, holding his money-bags under his cloak. Stephen, poor wretch, has little chance to doff that heavy awkward hauberk ; he is always panting on horseback, lunging with a sword or swinging his giant Danish battle-axe ; he gazes stupidly at the circle of enemies, stout-hearted but flustered and trying to understand why men do not love him. In his short mantle, slovenly dressed, Henry II does not pause as he takes Stephen's place ; he has no time even to eat ; he darts from the battlefield to the council-chamber, from the mass to the hunt, and his son, Richard I, rarely sheaths the sword ; he would be lost without it, without the masses of steel rings about his body, without the helmet over his fair head and the din of battle in his ears ; while his brother, John, great soldier though he is, must be for ever plotting : he must put aside the war-harness and don long tunic and embroidered cloak. Henry III runs from the hauberk, he prefers to sit in churches or to chuckle to himself as he slithers from the grip of enemies and lets money drip between his fingers while he wails for more and more, for endless rivers of gold which he spends as quickly as he gains them. Edward I never cares for costume ; it is to him a waste of time when every second is precious, when there are laws to be reissued and battles to be won. Edward II takes more care of his appearance than his

2

father did ; he can fight when he wishes, but he would rather be with a good comrade and a stoup of wine than listen to the screams of wounded and feel the sweat between his fingers. It is different with his son Edward III : although he also likes to dress well, he prefers the coat-of-mail, yet he is happy almost anywhere ; he strides, a gaudy figure, amongst the women, or he leaps into battle with a yell of triumph ; he shines like a figure from a play, for he postures always before the mirror of other people's eyes, and dances a jig of chivalry. Rather sullen, frowning, brooding, his grandson takes the crown with its eight strawberry leaves alternating with tiny flowers ; it dazzles him a little and gives him fierce dreams of power as he looks upon his uncles and upon those who would drive from him the companions he loves—Richard II, in his beautiful tunic with its dagged sleeves that lap the ground, paces with secret hatreds until his cousin pushes him aside, and Henry IV seizes for an uneasy reign that golden symbol which rests next upon the dark head of brave Henry V, hero, statesman, fanatic, only to fall and almost crush the little figure of his son, poor troubled Henry VI, who wishes only to have peace with God and to look into the lovely eyes of his malicious wife ; that crown does not fit his bowed head, it hangs awry, it flops over his ears, it hides the pinched and frightened wondering face until burly, jovial Edward IV takes it from him and perhaps kills him and holds it until his death. And then, for a brief space, tragic Richard III wears it and struggles fiercely to keep it until it tumbles beside a hawthorn bush upon the field of Bosworth to be seized by a foreigner, by the Welsh usurper, Henry VII.

Nineteen Kings, lives of nineteen men who helped to mould this country. What they made, what they fought to create or to destroy, remains our heritage. To appreciate the present we must understand the past, we must study the gradual steps raised with such pain towards modernity.

And first comes Eadward III, whom the Church has reverenced as Confessor and saint.

IT was no peaceful country that Eadward was elected to rule. When he came to the throne the nation was more or less Danish, at least it was under Danish rule although Eadward himself was Anglo-Saxon. His mother was Norman, but through his father he had the blood of the race of Cedric ; he was a descendant of the handsome, brave, wise Ælfred. There was little of Ælfred in Eadward's character, he was in a negative fashion more like his father, Æthelred II, known as the Unredy, for " unredy " means without rede, or council, and Æthelred most certainly was that. A vacillating cowardly creature, he kept his throne only by paying for it ; he was weak, avaricious and cruel, and there seems not a good mark to be chalked on his side. It is true that he was sometimes capable of action, but it was usually at the wrong moment ; rather than fight he gave the invading Danes a " geld," a bribe, and they took the bribe and spent it, and then rowed back for more, until their leader, Sweyn, demanded the crown itself.

Æthelred ran at once to Normandy. He took with him his wife and two sons, the Æthelings—or royal princes—Ælfred and Eadward. His wife Emma was herself a Norman, but the English, unable to tolerate a foreign name, made her change it to Ælfgifu ; therefore the fugitive was more or less welcomed abroad, and he lurked there in resentment and terror until Sweyn suddenly dropped dead at Gainsborough. Even after that Æthelred waited until the witan—the council—invited his return, and " gladly was he received of all." For a very short time he kept the crown, then he died in London on Monday, April 23, 1016, and his place was taken by his son Eadmund, called the Ironside. This Eadmund was not the child of Emma-Ælfgifu ; he was born of another wife. We do not know this woman's name and in the lax morality of eleventh-century England we may well doubt if she were married ; that would not jeopardise Eadmund's claim to the throne, for illegitimacy was no bar to succession and even the law of primogeniture was not always followed amongst the Danes. He was elected King and proved a very different man from his unredy father ; he was brave and capable of withstanding the cunning of Cnut, son of Sweyn. And Cnut was a very great man indeed, a cold and merciless ruler never deceived by soft words or by the obvious ; he did not trust until he knew that trust was well founded ; affection could not move his will, clearly he saw ambitions and never deviated as he strode towards them. The tale that he sat in the ocean and ordered it to roll back as a rebuke to his courtiers is old enough to be authentic, and certainly it fits his character. Brave and wary though he was, he had a courageous opponent in Eadmund Ironside ; Cnut's claim to England was merely that of conquest while Eadmund's was heredity. Yet so troubled had been the reign of Æthelred, so leaderless and oppressed had become the people, that they were little more than a rabbl: lined against the disciplined Danish housecarls. Inspired, however, by their new King, they were prepared to withstand Cnut as he marched on London. Eadmund hastened to the city's rescue, and slowly he pushed Cnut back. Then while the race of Cedric seemed to have regained the strength of Ælfred, while the Ironside was proving himself a great soldier, a traitor came to smash what he was trying to build.

This traitor, Eadric Streona, has puzzled historians. Even the great Freeman [1] gives him up as too complicated a character to unravel, but the complications are not so much in Eadric's character as in the characters of the men who most strangely trusted him. He was probably a coward, he was certainly an ambitious rascal swift to take the hand of the first man who might advance him ; the only riddle to explain is, if the tales be true about him, why was Eadric ever trusted ? Again and again he proved himself disloyal until the record of his treacheries becomes so monotonous as to be incredible ; again and again he was forgiven only to turn traitor at the first opportunity. The truth, as suggested by Sir James Ramsay,[2] appears to be that he had become " the scapegoat of national vanity," that his name was seized by chroniclers only too eager to take any one to explain the collapse of England. Yet he had personal reasons for hating Eadmund. During the last years of Æthelred's reign, he and the King had plotted to steal the lands of two wealthy brothers who were then murdered by Eadric ; Eadmund frustrated the plot, he hurried after the widow of the elder brother and married her and thereby took her lands before his father and Eadric could seize them. For this, we may be certain, Eadric sought revenge, and only Eadmund's numerical weakness could have made him trusting enough to accept the rascal's proffered friendship—" the most ill-advised thing that ever was done."

During the great battle of Assandune in the flats of Essex, Eadric furled his banner and fled. At least he had the grace not to fight his own countrymen, but this sudden defection spread momentary panic. Eadmund cried that they were well rid of such cowards and he kept bravely on until after sunset ; un-

---

[1] *The History of the Norman Conquest of England*, by Edward A. Freeman, 5 vols. (Oxford University), 1867–76.

[2] *The Foundations of England*, by Sir James H. Ramsay of Bamff, 2 vols. (Swan Sonnenschein), 1898.

defeated though he was, the battle nevertheless was lost·and he drew back with the remnant of his troops to take refuge in Gloucestershire. Undaunted, he started to rebuild his army when Eadric again appeared. Surely, after Assandune, he could not have been trusted ? It seems more probable that he came now openly as Cnut's agent to arrange a peace, and there was little else that Eadmund could do at the moment but accept. He agreed to divide England, to take Wessex and let Cnut have Mercia and Northumbria. This treaty could have been meant for no more than a breathing-space, a pause in hostilities to give both parties time to recover. Conflict would have been inevitable had not death settled the question by taking Eadmund on November 30, 1016, and leaving Cnut in undisputed power.

We do not know how Eadmund died. Later chroniclers tell us that that superlative fiend, Eadric Streona, murdered him at the bidding of Cnut. Certainly his death was suspiciously opportune, but the race of Cedric was not physically strong, and Eadmund—despite his nickname—may have been exhausted by his fierce campaigns. Whether he died naturally or by poison or steel, dead without doubt was the brave Ironside, and Cnut possessed all England. Æthelred's other sons lived, but they were not at hand, they were in Normandy, and there was no longer, it appears, a loyal party. England was enfeebled after the weak reign of Æthelred and the fighting under Eadmund, the people were spiritless, tired of unceasing and apparently vain warfare. All the same, Cnut was taking no risks. Eadmund's two sons, Eadmund and Eadward, were shipped to Sweden with the natural but horrible request that they be efficiently murdered ; the King of Sweden refused to be another's executioner, and passed the boys on to Hungary.

Now that he was King, Cnut forgot that he was a foreigner. He became almost entirely English and many of his countrymen returned to Denmark in disgust ; curiously, instead of England under Cnut forming a part of the Danish empire, the Danish empire became a part of England. He settled himself to become as rapidly as possible a wise and just ruler, without prejudice of nationality. This was the type of King the country needed after the feeble reign of Æthelred ; an emotionless politician, never blinded by loves or hatreds, Cnut gradually welded a dispirited people into shape. He interfered with no good laws, he bowed to the clergy and he showed small favouritism to his countrymen. Honest men he raised to power, traitors he killed. One of the first to die was the scheming, vacillating Eadric Streona, for Cnut was far too intelligent to be swayed by gratitude. He knew the worth of Eadric and he repaid it as it deserved : he called the rascal to London and swiftly beheaded him.

With Eadric out of history, we find a new name rising into prominence, the name of Godwine. Where Godwine sprang from remains a mystery, but it seems that he was a Sussex man ; all that we actually know is that he was the son of Wulnoth. The difficulty is to discover which Wulnoth. The Anglo-Saxons had few names to distribute and for this reason their history is some-times a maze of apparent contradictions ; we come across numerous men and women with the same names who could not possibly have performed many of the actions credited to them. Whoever Godwine's father may have been, we can safely dismiss the romantic tales later woven about his birth : he came probably from good stock if not of the highest. Cnut gave him the un-precedented honour of the earldom of Wessex, over which he was probably appointed some kind of lieutenant, as this vast tract of country had never been anything but purely royal.

The rule of Cnut has remained with the English chroniclers as something to be remembered, whatever tales of cruelty we learn about him come mainly from the Danish writers. And for a conquered race to accept a usurper so wholeheartedly and with such genuine affection proves that he must have been a very great King. He decided to marry. His choice seems a peculiar one ; he took a widow far older than himself—he was probably about twenty-two at the time while she must have been over thirty—he married Emma-Ælfgifu, Lady of Æthelred the Unredy. When dealing with a man of Cnut's genius, one is liable to seek for pro-found motives, to be deceived by his passionless demeanour into believing him incapable of love. Yet it seems likely that he loved Emma. The suggestion that he married her to ingratiate himself with his new subjects is of little weight : Emma was as much a foreigner as he and was no favourite with the people. If we put the question of love aside, the only plausible reason for the match would be the hope of a Norman alliance. Yet again it is difficult to see what value such an alliance could have had for Cnut, although one chronicler gives us the amazing explanation that he admired the Normans very much because they were a conquering people ! Whether Cnut loved Emma or whether he married her for some obscure political purpose may remain a mystery, but we cannot doubt that Emma loved Cnut. She forgot Æthelred instantly, and no doubt was only too happy to forget him ; that is easily understandable, but the swiftness with which she not only forgot but even grew to dislike her children by him is less explicable. After her second marriage all her affection turned towards her new husband and the children she bore him. Ælfred and Eadward remained in exile.

On November 12, 1035, Cnut died at Shaftesbury, being little more than forty years of age. He left four children : by a presumed wife, Ælfgifu of Northampton, he had Sweyn and Harold, nicknamed the Harefoot ; by Emma-Ælfgifu he had Harthacnut and one daughter. Always cautious and far-seeing, he had carefully parcelled out his empire : to Sweyn he gave Norway, to Harthacnut Denmark, and to Harold Harefoot England. With the passing of this great King the empire crumbled, and the ambitious Emma strove to steal what she could for her son Harthacnut. Godwine was at her side, and he was powerful, cunning and brave. She demanded and got control of Wessex with Winchester as a centre, and had her son, who was eighteen, recognised as King, but Harthacnut was keeping a precarious grip on Denmark and was far too busy there to disturb his half-brother who reigned without real dispute, save for the invasion—if such it was—of Ælfred, the exiled son of Emma and Æthelred. The details of Ælfred's landing are conflicting but it seems most likely that he was enticed to England by false promises of the crown. One story tells us that Harold sent him forged letters that purported. to come from his mother, and another states that he came on a definite armed invasion and that his young brother Eadward arrived with him. For either reason, Ælfred sailed from Flanders and landed in England where he was met by Earl Godwine, whether by accident or arrangement is not certain. Godwine, until recently, had been on the side of Emma and Harthacnut, but being a shrewd ambitious man he now probably realised that he had backed the weaker candidate. That he surrendered the Ætheling to Harold cannot be denied, and even the inspired advocacy of Freeman fails to convince one that he was entirely innocent, that he was a rather naive good man who scarcely knew what he did. The later history of Godwine, the swift rise of his family from we know not what seed, is sufficient to prove that he was no guileless man. He met Ælfred at either Guildford or Gillingham and swore to become his man; he ate with him, had him lodged decently, and then when reinforcements arrived, attacked him during the night. The slaughter was horrible, all Ælfred's men were murdered or mutilated or sold as slaves, and the Ætheling himself was taken to London. Harold put out his eyes and sent him a prisoner to the isle of Ely. He was not fortunate enough to die at once; he was seen wandering pathetically about the island for some weeks or even months until the pain or, as some insist, starvation, removed one danger from the throne.

Harold next turned his hatred towards his stepmother Emma. She was alone, deserted by Godwine, and with her son Harthacnut still busy in Denmark. She was " driven out " of the country. What " driven out " exactly means is uncertain, but we know that it was a heavier decree than simple banishment and probably included being forcibly ejected from her home. She sailed to Flanders, not travelling as usual to Normandy, for that country was in a highly inflammable condition owing to the minority of William the Bastard.

These two acts—the maiming of Ælfred and the expulsion of Emma—are the only two charges that can be brought against Harold, and both were justified, both were according to the manners of the time. If not evil, neither was Harold good; a weak King, he could not control the nation, and he so loved the chase—for he was an active sportsman and thereby earned his nickname—that he could not keep from it even on Sundays. But he never was a pious man and rarely bothered to attend church services.

He died at Oxford on March 1040, and was buried at Westminster. Although married—he had an unnamed Lady, or Queen, whether churched or otherwise—he left no offspring, and the throne fell to his half-brother, Harthacnut, who sailed at once from Denmark to take the crown of England.

CHRONICLERS have striven to say pleasant things about this son of Cnut and Emma, but the best thing that can be said about him is that he resembled his father, at any rate in his father's worst qualities. The chroniclers' liking is easily understood—he was very generous to the Church, and most of the writers being monks, they naturally considered him a good King. In his recorded acts, however, we can find little for us to regret that his reign was brief. When he landed in England, he behaved like a conqueror to a stubborn foe. He called for the Dane-geld of the time of Æthelred so that he could pay his ships, and it was a particularly burdensome tax, for it came when corn was at a great height because of a hurricane that had destroyed the previous year's crops. The English almost revolted, and when two of his housecarls were murdered in Worcester while trying to raise the geld, Harthacnut sent Godwine and other earls to ravage the rebellious land and to tear down the minster in which the housecarls had taken refuge and from which they had been dragged. The earls did their task in the appropriate spirit : rich was the booty they carried back. Not content with wringing all the money he could from England, Harthacnut took spiteful revenge on his dead predecessor. The corpse of Harold was disinterred, it was beheaded and thrown into the Thames. Godwine took active part in this ghastly affair, but that did not save him from the new King's enmity. He was arraigned for the murder of Ælfrcd, and with the great men of England at his side he swore, and they swore with him, that the Ætheling had not been blinded by his advice or wish, and that all had been Harold's doing. This was the usual form of trial in those days ; if you could find influential men enough to swear your innocence you were acquitted, as Godwine was acquitted. But he had to pay heavily for his freedom. He presented Harthacnut with a ship almost incredibly magnificent.

Evidently Harthacnut despaired of having a son, for he sent abroad to Eadward to come to England. And for the first time the future King comes close to us. He landed with a horde of his beloved Normans, and was honourably received, perhaps was openly accepted as the heir to the throne that very soon became his.

Harthacnut died as he deserved : while guzzling wine at a marriage banquet he choked and dropped down dead. Then " before the King buried were, all folk chose Eadward to King at London."

AT last Eadward comes fully upon the scene, this frail creature whom the Church was to elevate to saintship as Confessor. He has been worshipped by the people, but his main saintlike quality is one of definite treachery towards England. He refused, we are told, to sleep with his wife. He did not like women about him, preferring the company of men or solitary communion with

God. Because of this, because he deliberately ignored the duty that was his, the Norman Conquest became possible. A King who wilfully refuses to procreate heirs is a King who has failed, who has acted the traitor, for he leaves his country open to any foreign invader or, at the least, to insurrection.

Eadward was possibly an albino. He was extremely tall and quite handsome and was noted particularly for the milky whiteness of hair and beard ; his face was red and plump, his hands lean and snow-white with long and almost transparent fingers. When he reached the throne in 1042, he was forty years of age, and the majority of those years had been spent abroad, amongst foreigners, therefore he despised things English and, until rebellion drove them from him, preferred Norman favourites to his own countrymen. He should have become a monk, most certainly he should never have been crowned King of so violent a realm as eleventh-century England that was still exhausted by its rush of murderous conquerors. And Eadward himself did not want to be King. When in exile he had sworn to travel to the Holy Land and the oath seemed to him of greater importance than the government of his country. Petulantly he tried to make his subjects allow him to leave England so that he could worship in the land of Our Lord, and a special mission had to be sent to Rome to beg absolution from his promise. It seems that for penance the Pope demanded the building of an abbey in honour of St. Peter. As he could not travel to the Holy Land, Eadward threw himself joyfully into the task of raising the church at Westminster where, in 969, King Eadgar had already built a place of worship in which Harold Harefoot had been buried. And this abbey, not England, became Eadward's lifework. Slowly the walls arose above Eadgar's small foundation, slowly the great abbey church was built that was to become the burial-place of Kings. To this turned Eadward's thoughts ; not to the prosperity, the well-being and security of his people, but to the building of a shrine at the order of the Pope.

THERE were three great men in England when Eadward was crowned King. These were Godwine, Leofric and Siward. All three, curiously enough, have been immortalised in English literature : Godwine by Lytton, Leofric in Tennyson's poem on Godiva—the Anglo-Saxon Godgifu—and Siward in *Macbeth*. Godwine has been set in a frame worthy of his genius, for despite its turgidity, Lytton's *Harold* has something epical in its emotional sweep, but Leofric is a poetic shadow in Tennyson, and Siward can barely be glimpsed in *Macbeth*. All three were great men, and Leofric deserves a nobler memorial than the probably fictional tale of his wife having once ridden naked through the market of Coventry, draped in her own long hair, unseen " except for her fair legs." The story is early enough to be genuine, but the first version tells us that the market-place was packed with the entire population, a second and chaster version of later date sends all the people indoors and locks their windows ; while a third version introduces Peeping Tom who was struck blind for having a lewd eye. We can at least be content, as remarked by Freeman, that Thomas was no English name and the rascal therefore must have been a Norman. Despite its antiquity, this story cannot be accepted, as we know that both Leofric and his wife Godgifu were exceptionally pious and charitable. He was neither the man to overtax his city nor to force his wife to parade her nakedness before a gaping people.

These three were the great men of England when Eadward became King. Godwine has a particular interest for us as being the father of the next King, Harold II, and Harold's life is so involved with Eadward's that they must be examined together. Godwine had been raised by Cnut to unprecedented power. He had five sons, Sweyn, Harold, Tostig, Gyrth and Leofwine, the last three being but children at the time of Eadward's coronation.

THERE was almost a year's delay between Eadward's election and coronation. Cnut's nephew, Sweyn, evidently believed himself the rightful heir, but he was at last made to leave the country with the promise of succeeding on Eadward's death ; yet even the candidature of Sweyn had probably no more force in the delay than Eadward's own objections. He dreamed of visiting the Holy Land, but Godwine insisted that he become King, promising help, warning him of the dangers to the country if the throne stayed vacant. Weakly, Eadward gave way, but he should never have let himself be persuaded. Yet he was very weak, strong only in the sudden angers of a feeble character, in abrupt gusts of rage and petty spite, similar to Æthelred's. Eadward resembled his father in a negative manner, but he lacked even the power of Æthelred, the power at least for evil. There was no strength in him, he was a toy for others, first for the Normans and later for Harold. As a King he does not exist, for during the last thirteen years of his reign Harold was the actual ruler. We have therefore to deal with Eadward purely as a man, rarely as a King. His administration does not concern us, to paint his portrait we must rely on stray anecdotes and on an occasional glimpse of a frail thin King with an old-fashioned beard lurking mistily behind the gestures of greater men.

Yet Eadward has been canonised and the Roman Catholic Church rarely canonises of its own accord. Usually its hand is forced by popular demand as with Thomas Becket and Jeanne d'Arc. The people choose their saints, such as Simon de Montfort, Thomas of Lancaster, Edward II, sometimes for political purposes, sometimes from mere sentiment, and the Church agrees only when public demand has grown too insistent to be denied. The people of England, not the Church, were the first to canonise Eadward, and within eight years after his death he was credited with having worked miracles and with having possessed the vision of a prophet. He could heal the sick, went the tales, and from his reign dates the belief of the King's touch having the power to heal scrofula. Eadward had cured a girl of suppurated glands in the neck and this appears to have formed the basis in the fable of the Kings' magic-working hands of Stuart days. He also, most peculiarly, cured a woman of barrenness, and others of blindness by merely letting them bathe their eyes with water in which he had cleansed himself. Our belief becomes merged with doubt when we learn that those who were healed became the King's pensioners. He could see into the future : on his death-bed he was shown a vision of divided England, but it scarcely needed a saint to prophesy disaster to a country that had no heir to reign over it. The strictly contemporary chroniclers are either silent or more or less sceptical about his holiness, yet the legends grew rapidly, and after the actual canonisation it became of course blasphemy to doubt them for a moment.

When we strip Eadward of the aura given him by hagiographers the result is not satisfying. It is true that he was pious, regularly attending mass and never speaking during service unless somebody spoke first ; he was always generous, regaling paupers on the royal bounty, and continually making offerings to the Church ; and he was gentle in manner, easy to approach, and so charmingly spoken that he could refuse a request without angering the suitor ; yet his temper was furious when roused. All these qualities are genuine, while one legend gives us a strange glimpse of him laughing aloud at a vision of destruction. Perhaps, however, this is only another example of that subtle sense of humour so stressed by Bishop Creighton.[1] The main example the bishop offers to prove this mythical humour is a tale that reveals only Eadward's quick and spiteful rage. It happened while he was hunting—a sport of which he was extremely fond. There is nothing out of the way in this, for sport was universal and beloved of many good churchmen, yet one is rather surprised and a little shocked to find the saintly Eadward joying in the death of animals. Besides, it is worthy of note that among the royal dues paid by Norwich are " a bear and six dogs to a bear," which suggests also a liking for bear-baiting. This day while hunting, Eadward had a quarrel with a peasant. The chronicle is rather vague, but Eadward turned for some such reason on the peasant with fury—in " noble wrath " says the chronicler—and cried, " By God and His mother, I will do you as bad a turn if I can ! " Bishop Creighton is kind enough to call this " a certain quaint humour, which men scarcely understood, but which impressed them and made them think ! "

Twice, as we shall see later, Eadward's temper became as violent and as dangerous as ever his father's had been, twice he would have brought anarchy into England if wise councillors had not restrained him.

But it is in Eadward's relations with his wife that his chief saintly virtue rests, and this is the most insoluble problem of all. He married Godwine's daughter Eadgyth, " a woman in whose breast was a gymnasium of all the liberal arts but small capacity in wordly matters," and we are informed that if she did not astonish you with her culture she would at least make you " admire her yearningly for her modesty of mind and beauty of body." If Eadward had been determined to remain celibate, as later chroniclers insist, why did he marry ? He never loved Eadgyth, he was only too delighted to get rid of her at the first opportunity, and they were more like father and daughter than husband and wife. She obeyed him meekly, followed him in his charities, giving always in his name and honour ; she called him " Father," and would always sit like a child at his feet except in church and during meals.

Contemporary chroniclers did not stress Eadward's celibacy. They refer to his chaste living, but only in terms that might be applied to any man who remained faithful to his wife ; Tostig, for example, is spoken of in almost the same fashion, and Tostig

---

[1] *Historical Lectures and Addresses*, by Mandell Creighton (Longmans, Green), 1903.

was no saint. Later grew the legend that Eadward swore a solemn oath never to defile himself with a woman's touch. Perhaps he remained childless because he was incapable of being anything else. The question cannot be answered, we can only move vaguely amidst conjecture, for the chroniclers themselves naturally knew but little more than we do to-day.

WHEN we leave myth for fact, we discover that a certain kindliness of manner, generosity—one tale relates that when Eadward trapped a thief in the palace he sent him off with a warning to be careful next time lest the treasurer catch him—profound belief in the Church, intense piety, a violent temper, a love of men favourites so profound that he believed whatever they told him, and a delight in hunting, are the main characteristics of Eadward III. His reign was comparatively bloodless, but any greatness of England must be placed to the credit of Godwine or Harold, not to the King himself.

Nevertheless, within a few years of his death, the people had canonised him, and his supposed chastity alone is not enough to justify such worship. The true reason is not difficult to find. During a period of stress, a nation, like the individual, gazes at the near past with regret ; days that in themselves were little better than the present become ennobled and seem more beautiful in retrospect ; even the cut of yesterday's clothes, of the speech and manners of our grandparents, take on a rarefied half-comical sweetness when we look back after contemplating a to-day of violence or despair. So it was in the years that followed Eadward's death. The Normans had conquered England, and to whom could the people turn ? what man could they lift out of the past, rebuilding their shamed nationalism with a memory of splendour ? Eadward was the last of the English, their symbol of freedom ; his old-fashioned courtly manners, his long beard worn at a time when the Normans were clean-shaven and the English had only moustaches, and the whiteness of that beard and of his slender hands, his obvious dislike of women and his passion for the Church, all combined to weave around a feeble yet charming creature an aura of saintliness. His actual bad qualities, his weak-mindedness and ultra-amiability, helped to swell the legend until it grew so rapidly that within a very few years it had become an established fact and the Church was busily consolidating what the people had built and for which they demanded recognition.

Once the myth had started, the hagiographers dug up tale after tale, they invented and glorified ; under their pens Eadward changed into a visionary, a prophet, a healer, and miracles sprang from his tomb. Now could the oppressed English look back with yearning to the days of the good Saint Eadward the Confessor as in earlier times they had looked back towards the truly great days of their good King Ælfred.

ONE of Eadward's first acts as King was to despoil his mother. She had been niggardly, he complained, doubtless recalling how she had preferred his half-brothers to him and Ælfred ; she " had been too hard with him and had done less for him than he would, both ere he was King and ckc since." Eadward himself, with Godwine, Leofric and Siward, rode armed to Winchester and seized Emma's goods, leaving her to exist on a small income. No matter whether Emma deserved this fate or not, it was an inauspicious opening for the reign. Yet the English must have been more troubled to see the Norman followers of their new King.

Earl Godwine was now the greatest man in England ; with his sons he held vast tracts of territory, and his daughter was the Lady of Eadward. We cannot believe that Eadward liked Godwine, perhaps he was afraid of him. All his affections went to the foreigners he brought from Normandy and whom he installed in important posts, making one Archbishop of Canterbury and another Bishop of London. Nevertheless, despite the growth of Norman power, there seemed no chink in Earl Godwine's strength until his eldest son Sweyn ravished the Abbess of Leominster. There is still doubt about this affair ; we are uncertain if it was the frolic of a moment's lust or whether Sweyn really loved the woman. The latter seems the truth, and certainly it appears that she was no unwilling victim. One story relates that Sweyn ordered her to be brought to him, and that he kept her " while him listed, syne let her fare home," but a second, more pleasing and more probable tale says that he intended to marry her but was forbidden, and therefore fled the land to seek adventure in warring Denmark. Two years later, in 1049, he came back only to find that his possessions had been divided between his brother Harold and his cousin Beorn, and neither would surrender to him an inch of his land. King Eadward did his best for Sweyn, but against the determination of Harold and Beorn no generous arguments could prevail, and disgusted, Sweyn returned to his ships and sailed for Bosham. At this point the story becomes a trifle complicated. An English fleet lay at Sandwich, and two of the commanders were Harold and Tostig ; it sailed to Pevensey, and here for some reason Harold was taken from his post and the command was given to Beorn. Sweyn arrived from Bosham, had a talk with his father and cousin, and persuaded them of the injustice of his exile. From this it would seem that Harold rather than Beorn was the stumbling-block ; at any rate, Beorn was so affected by Sweyn's pitiful tale that he agreed to see Eadward, offering to ride immediately to Sandwich to plead with the King. Sweyn went with him, but they never reached Sandwich. They turned westward to Bosham, Sweyn explaining that he feared his crews might desert unless they were heartened by the sight of Beorn and the knowledge that his suit progressed. Unsuspecting, Beorn galloped into the trap, and it was not until the last moment that he realised the truth, it was not until Sweyn strove to entice him aboard one of the ships. Then Beorn knew that it was revenge not justice Sweyn desired. He was bound, thrown into a boat, and rowed to the ships ; his corpse was left for burial at Dartmouth.

When this treacherous and almost insane revenge became known, Sweyn, by order of the King and the army, was declared a *nithing*, a word of such incredible degradation that we have to-day no equivalent that could possibly express its full shame. That word alone was sufficient to drive men to diabolic rages or to awful terrors ; it was worse than the horrors of excommunication, and now it was sufficient to cause most of Sweyn's followers to desert at once. Only two vessels remained loyal to him, and these were soon captured by the men of Hastings, the crews were killed and the ships taken to port, but somehow Sweyn managed to escape and hurry to Flanders.

The peculiarity of this tale rests chiefly in its sequel. It is possible to understand that a man, driven half-insane by brooding on his wrongs, might seek so horrible a revenge ; but it seems scarcely credible that that same man should the following year be forgiven his crimes and restored to his earldom. Such indeed happened to Sweyn ; the attainder was reversed at the witenagemót—the assembly of the witan, the national council of the Anglo-Saxons—and in 1050 Sweyn came home exactly as if he had never ravished an abbess and cold-bloodedly murdered his cousin.

How many Normans were with Eadward it is impossible to tell, but they were numerous enough. Already the conquest of England, later made actuality by William the Bastard, was beginning : Norman manners, Norman thought was seeping through the Anglo-Saxon country under a King who was himself half-Norman by birth and wholly Norman by desire. Constant must have been the irritations, the slights, the menaces that existed at court, but they did not burst into fire until the summer of 1050 when Eustace of Boulogne came to England. His visit passed amiably until he sought to leave the country and reached Dover. His men he quartered where he wished in true Norman fashion ; in England, however, these rights of chivalry were little known : if all men were not considered equal, they at least had rights of their own of some kind. Therefore this high-handed manner of Eustace infuriated the Dover men, and one unknown and courageous householder strove to stop the foreigner entering his house, and killed a Norman. At this to him incredible insolence, Eustace leaped upon his horse and charged the house, murdering the Englishman ; he turned his haughty rage against others, riding through the streets and slaughtering at his will. Then he hurried back to the King and demanded justice. When Eadward heard the story of how upstart burghers had dared attack a Norman lord who was his guest, his kingly rage was great and he called for Earl Godwine, Dover being in Godwine's district. This was a ticklish corner that Godwine found himself pushed into : already he had probably suffered much from Norman hauteur, and now was demanded from him retribution on men who had only acted within their rights. To the undying credit of Godwine he took the weaker and the nobler side ; when Eadward commanded that he wreak all the horrors of Norman justice on Dover—such as he had once wreaked on Worcester—Godwine refused. Eadward, knowing the futility of trying to force Godwine's hand, decided on a subtle course— he impeached Godwine for the murder of the Ætheling Ælfred, an alleged crime for which Godwine had already been acquitted under Harthacnut.

When commanded to attend the witenagemót at Gloucester, Godwine knew that his enemies were prepared to bay him down, and he was too astute to walk into the trap. With his sons he gathered an army at Beverstone while the King's men trooped armed to Gloucester. Again it seemed that civil war would come to England, the long smouldering outburst of Anglo-

Saxon hatred and fear of the encroaching Norman. Godwine, however, could dictate, and he did not want to fight. He demanded an audience for himself and his sons, and offered to swear a second compurgation on the charge of murdering Ælfred. Eadward refused, and Godwine took a high hand ; he ordered the surrender of the more truculent French. This, too, was refused, and he decided that further negotiation was useless ; he marched against his King. Eadward might flounder amongst terrors, his favourites might urge the cry of instant battle, but at the King's side were loyal Englishmen who dreaded the return of civil war. Leofric asked that all quarrels cease, that both parties disband their armies and let the question be settled at the next meeting of the witan which should be adjourned to meet again after hot blood had cooled. This seems a purposeless suggestion although both parties adopted it ; Leofric, wise and good man though he was, must surely have realised that more than a few weeks would be needed to calm a quarrel that had been maturing for years. The only result of such an adjournment was to give the King time to gather a stronger force than Godwine and thereby overpower him at the witenagemót ; Godwine refused to appear unless he and his sons were given safe-conducts and even hostages. Eadward's answer was a demand for bail as surety of good behaviour ; Harold's thegns complied, but Sweyn—who presumably had an obstinate as well as a dangerous temper—refused and was promptly outlawed, evidently on the almost forgotten charge of ravishing the abbess. Only the river divided the two parties, the King being at London, Godwine in his Southwark house.

When Godwine was told that his safe-conducts were refused, he leaped so quickly to his feet that he overturned the table ; then he sprang on his horse and with his sons galloped to safety, for he knew that he was doomed, that the Normans would assuredly drag him down. Next morning at the witenagemót he and his sons were formally outlawed. They had already outlawed themselves, Godwine was sailing to Flanders with Sweyn and Tostig and Gyrth and families, Harold and Leofwine were off to Ireland.

Whether deliberately or not, Godwine had become the leader of the Danish-Anglo-Saxons. Freeman makes him act as a conscious fighter for the rights of the people, as the defiant unselfish patriot ; perhaps there is a certain truth in this, but Godwine was a miserly man who, to gain his own ends, was capable of turning against the English as he had done at Worcester ; this time his own ends coincided with the demands of the people. We cannot tell what slights he had had to undergo in Eadward's Norman-speaking court where his daughter was the despised Lady ; he could have been no welcome visitor, this man of ambition who had built his power upon nothing but his own sword and quick mind ; the Normans with their culture, their southern graces and songs, their richer clothing and more fastidious manners, must assuredly often have made Godwine seem an outcast barbarian. The insults, slowly gathered, had borne fruit after the Dover fight ; Godwine was battling for the English, but as the most powerful of the earls he was also battling for himself against the foreigner.

WITH Godwine at last out of the country, Eadward's first act was to get rid of his Queen. " Lest, forsooth," as William of Malmesbury tells us, " while all her relatives were yearning for the homeland, she alone might snore in down [*in a down-bed*]," she was packed off to the royal monastery of Wherwell. There is even a suggestion of a divorce but this apparently was not carried out. Eadward satisfied himself by removing Eadgyth from his sight and by seizing all her goods, real and personal.

His joyous freedom was brief, for the Godwine family was preparing to return. But meanwhile another figure steps on to the stage, the great William the Bastard. Son of Robert the Devil and Arlette the tanner's daughter, William had gradually built his ducal throne secure amidst factions and treachery. Starting as a minor to be cheated and bullied, he had begun the moment he was old enough for action to draw the country to one united people. The details of those early days we had best leave until later when William will be treated fully. It is sufficient now only to state that he was a very great and powerful duke indeed when he landed in England. He was not the kind of man to waste his days in idle visiting and his arrival in England therefore must have been for some purpose, and without doubt that purpose was the desire to steal the throne. Eadward was childless and certain to remain childless ; the sons of Eadmund Ironside were in distant Hungary and must have been almost forgotten, and Eadward's nearest relatives were his two nephews, neither of whom had any strong chance of succeeding. Therefore the crown of England was suspended aloft, liable to fall on any side, and here was the fair head of William the Bastard eager to feel its weight. He had no actual claim, merely a vague descent from Eadward's mother, but that would not trouble him, few others having a better claim.

When Godwine ran from England, William landed, and there is something in this landing that is almost sinister to us who know so well the sequel. In later times, William proclaimed that Eadward now promised him the crown. With Norman favourites on every side, men of William's race, it is not difficult to believe that the weak-willed King would promise anything to one of his beloved Normans.

WILLIAM left England before Godwine's return. Harold and Leofwine sailed from Ireland with nine ships, and as they voyaged around the coast, seeking to meet their father, they ravaged the land like enemies and not like Englishmen returning to their own people. Father and sons met at Portland and the combined fleet turned east until it anchored off Southwark below London Bridge. The spirit of the people had changed during the twelve weeks of Godwine's absence, and now he had almost all the whole land behind him while Eadward found himself wellnigh alone facing an armed avenger. But Godwine did not wish to remain armed, he and his sons asked pardon " and that they might be held worthy of all these things that from them unrightly had been taken." Eadward had lost the love of his people for the time, but the Norman favourites still were around him, striving to give him strength enough to defy Godwine. Yet what could Eadward do? his troops were not loyal, for they thought it a pity " that Englishmen should destroy one another to make room for foreigners " ; he had to give in, but he did so as reluctantly as possible. Immediately his Norman favourites ran for their lives.

GODWINE had conquered without a blow. In the morning at the witenagemót he laid his axe at the feet of the King and knelt in homage, pleading for the right to clear himself of the crimes laid to his name. His plea was answered by a general shout from the people, and the witan reinstated him in full in all his rights while " the Frenchmen who had reared up bad law and judged unjust judgments and counselled evil counsel in the land " were banished, but affection for Eadward was strong enough for the saving and peculiar clause to be added that those were excepted " whom the King liked and who were true to him and all his folk." Unwillingly Eadward reinstated Godwine. He returned him his axe of office and afterwards in the palace " when his heat of mind had lessened, calmed, he took counsel with his wise men and offered a kiss to the earl." Not only must Eadward accept Godwine, but Godwine's daughter must be taken from her monastery to become again his Lady.

One of Godwine's sons was absent from the triumph—Sweyn. He had left England with his father but he had not returned. Stricken with remorse for the rape of the abbess and for the murder of Beorn, he had set out barefoot to seek penance in the Holy Land. He died fourteen days after his father's triumph at the witenagemót, while struggling homeward, his vow fulfilled. Exhaustion, cold, and exposure dragged him to an unknown grave in Lycia.

And Godwine himself had not long to live. He grew ill shortly after his return to power but he refused to give in to the tugging of a wearied body. During the Easter festival at Winchester, 1053, he sat eating at the King's table with his sons Harold, Tostig and Gyrth, when suddenly he lurched and fell from his seat. He did not speak or move again. They carried him into the King's own bower and for three days he lay in a state of semi-death. Norman writers seized this chance to show how the hand of God worked, striking down the murderer of Ælfred in his hour of glory. They said that he died while in the very act of praying that God might choke him if ever he had done harm to Ælfred or the King. The picturesque touch is added of Harold dragging his father's body from under the table. This is not an unusual legend : it has been tagged on to others beside Godwine.

GODWINE and Sweyn both dead, Harold automatically became leader of the family, the unacknowledged King of England. The vague figure of Eadward begins to disappear even farther from us, while Harold grows stronger, taking shape as the true leader of the country, as its uncrowned King. " For virtue of body and mind he stood before the people as another Judas Maccabeus." The Bayeux Tapestry depicts him as tall and handsome, with long moustaches and hair cut to a fringe, and his strength was evidently very great even in those days of strong men. Norman writers assure us that he was " foul as to lewd living," but only the story of Eadgyth Swanneshals—Edith Swan-Neck—remains to show that he loved women, and one mistress is surely little enough with which to damn a man as "unchaste"? We find references to his concubine or to his Danish wife, but almost no facts. Apparently she was from Norfolk—but we are confused by two Eadgyths, very likely the same woman—and she bore all Harold's children save Wulf and Harold.

Tostig was well-beloved of Eadward. Something in the appearance or the character of this bad-tempered arrogant man appealed to the frail King. He was the only one of Godwine's family towards whom Eadward showed the least genuine affection ; his association with Harold might breed respect for a capable man, but we glimpse no love in it.

The earldom of Northumberland was vacant ; this was a vast space of England, stretching from the Humber to the Tweed, too dangerous an earldom it would have seemed for one man to possess. It should have been split, and would have been under any cautious King, yet this earldom, at the pleading of Harold and Eadgyth, was given to Tostig who already controlled Huntingdonshire and probably Northamptonshire. All England was falling into the grip of the Godwine brood ; Harold guided the King, his sister was Eadward's Lady, and his own and his brother's lands stretched for amazing extents on every side.

Eadward, as well he might, was presumably troubled by thoughts of the succession. Harold was at hand, but Harold came from common stock, and across the Channel William the Bastard was waiting patiently. Then Eadmund Ironside, King Eadward's half-brother, was remembered, and his two sons far away in Hungary. The eldest of these sons was dead, but the second, Eadward, was asked to return. He landed in England in 1057, bringing with him his wife, his son Eadgar and his two daughters. The Ætheling was forty-one, his wife was a foreigner, and he probably knew but few if any words of English. He had been reared abroad as the present King himself had been reared, but in a land even farther removed than Normandy. Yet any resentment his foreign manners might have aroused was soon removed ; he died almost immediately after reaching London and even before meeting Eadward. This end is sudden and suspicious, but there is no reason whatever to link Harold's name with his death. The Ætheling might have been exhausted by his journey, we have no contemporary suggestions of murder, and it is more than likely that Harold had as yet no thought of demanding the throne. If the Ætheling was murdered, William the Bastard is the more probable culprit.

The Ætheling left one son, Eadgar, a feeble lad who showed no signs of courage or capability. With the death of the Ætheling, it is probable that Harold first realised that the throne might become his. Already he possessed with his brothers almost the entire country except for a few shires in the centre ; the royal line, never a physically strong one, was dying rapidly. Eadward would leave no children, Eadmund Ironside's two sons were dead, only remained the Ætheling's son Eadgar, a child and almost a foreigner with no hold on English love. Oversea, however, was William the Bastard, with no real claim except the alleged promise of Eadward. But as Eadward had brought the Ætheling from Hungary to be his successor, it does not appear that he held himself bound by that promise.

LIKE so many others of that time, like Cnut, like Robert, father of William, Harold decided to travel to Rome on pilgrimage to the tombs of the apostles. For lack of definite evidence we place this journey after the death of the Ætheling, but we are not certain of the date. It was no idle religious pilgrimage. Harold examined the policy and events in France as he passed, and the suggestion has been made that it was now that he gave his famous oath to William. That oath, if ever given, must, I feel, be placed at a later time than this. The year 1064 is almost a blank in the Saxon chronicles and it is therefore the most probable time to accept for Harold's oath, if we accept it at all. Yet it must be accepted although our only actual proof of it is a negative one : when William proclaimed the story Harold did not deny it.

Not only are we unaware when Harold became William's guest, we are also unaware how he ever reached Normandy. One tale records that he was dispatched on an embassy by Eadward to offer William the crown, but that is obviously a Norman lie ; if William ever was promised the crown it must have been during his visit in 1051. A second tale states that Harold visited Normandy on his own affairs, to negotiate the freedom of his youngest brother Wulnoth and his nephew Hakon, who were held as hostages by William ; but we have no proof whatever of this, and it seems unlikely that the fact of such important hostages at this time would not be recorded. The third and most possible tale says that the visit was an accident. Harold was on a pleasure-trip with friends and with perhaps some of his family when he was caught in a storm and driven over the Channel to fall prisoner to Guy, Count of Ponthieu. His adventures before and afterwards are clearly depicted on the famous Bayeux Tapestry.[1] We see Harold leaving white-bearded Eadward, and we see him sailing merrily across the Channel with no suggestion of a storm ; the storm would naturally not be shown as this is a Norman work and the Normans insisted that the visit was a friendly one. Hawk on wrist, Harold is conducted dolefully by Guy's men to Beurain. Then come hurrying messengers from William of Normandy ; the Tapestry shows them arguing, expostulating, but it tells us nothing of the huge ransom William paid so that he could capture so miraculous an opportunity in the person of Harold. We see Harold conducted to Normandy and received royally by William in his palace. There is no suggestion that he was a prisoner. William was too cunning to treat him in any other way than as a most honoured guest ; besides, there was as yet no words of rivalry between them. Harold was merely a great earl, he was not the heir of England ; all the same, each must have been conscious of his unspoken ambitions and each must have played warily with the other.

Harold was accepted as one of the family, he was fondled and given every possible mark of honour, and in respect for Norman customs he actually shaved off his long moustaches. William often went early to bed and left his guest with his duchess, Matilda, talking until a late hour. Yet for all the deference and kindness, Harold must have known that he was a prisoner ; otherwise it is difficult to understand why he wasted so long a time in Normandy when England needed his strong hand. He rode with William to the Breton war and distinguished himself, as shown in the Tapestry, by lifting soldiers from the quicksands of the Coesnon—no small feat, for these men were armed, and mail was heavy. When the war ended, William knighted Harold. On the Tapestry we see the Norman duke with one hand placing a nut-shaped helmet on the head of his comrade-in-arms, and with the other hand fastening the straps of Harold's hauberk or

[1] The authenticity of the Bayeux Tapestry has for many years been a battleground for scholars. Each scholar has proved his case in a most convincing fashion and has juggled the Tapestry from date to date, from century to century. I have no space to add my full arguments to the gigantic mass of words, but I feel that it must be very near-contemporary. The costumes alone convince me of it.

shirt-of-mail. Now occurs the oath-taking, if ever it did occur.
In Bayeux, Harold gave his oath to William, but the contents of
that oath are still a matter of doubt, the so-called authorities do
not agree on its exact terms. It appears that Harold promised
to marry one of William's daughters and to give his own sister to
an unnamed Norman noble, to become William's man, to accept
William as King of England on Eadward's death, to surrender
immediately the castle of Dover and to receive a Norman garrison
in it, and to build further castles garrisoned by Normans on
English land wherever William might desire them ; in return,
he was promised great favours on William's accession, even to
the offer of half of the kingdom. To something of the kind,
at least to some formal oath of allegiance, Harold must have
sworn that day in Bayeux. Later writers were to extol the
cunning of the duke above the simplicity of the Englishman
because William tricked Harold into swearing upon most sacred
relics. The Bayeux Tapestry shows two boxes on altars, Harold
with a hand on each, but there is no attempt to hide the relics,
nor does it sketch Harold's terror when the cloths were removed.
This rather contradicts the tale, which is, however, far from
contemporary.

Whether Harold actually swore on thrice-precious relics does
not matter to us, but it did at the time. Superstition would
convince the people that the saints, on whose bones Harold had
sworn, would be made to fight against him. There was a great
deal of magic in medieval religion, exorcisms and other conjura-
tions were of more importance than the moralities ; so long as you
kept to the outward form, surrendering your money to the Church,
crossing yourself before images, muttering prayers that were
little more than magic formulas to ward off evil, you were safe,
you could murder and buy pardon from God with a few pieces of
silver. The saints were always ready to return to earth, to
defend their followers or to strike down their blasphemers. If
Harold actually had sworn, and we cannot doubt that he did,
the people of the time would believe the saints so outraged in their
celestial dignity that they would gallop out of heaven because
their names were taken in vain.

AFFAIRS in England were reaching a dangerous pitch. Harold
maintained the strength of Eadward in battles with Welsh and
Scots, and he proved himself a brave leader. He made his
soldiers dress lightly, and himself put aside the cumbersome

hauberk and wore a jerkin of toughened leather—probably of cuir bouilli, the boiled leather so popular in later days. This, of course, was not leather brought to boiling-point, it was taken from the pot when warm and plunged into oil or melted wax to keep it firm yet supple.

Harold was a brutal fighter, he slaughtered without mercy, but that was the common method of the time. One regrets, however, to find that he boastfully erected monuments on the various battlefields with the inscription, *Here Harold conquered.*

TOSTIG did not possess Harold's charm or his tact and cunning although his biographer speaks of him as " a man of rather grave and sagacious self-control, but a little harsher than Harold in following out his feuds, endowed with manly and unshakable constancy of mind." Far from revealing sagacity and self-control, his rule in Northumberland became tyranny ; he over-taxed, he passed unjust laws, he robbed God—a peculiar charge against otherwise a pious man—he stole land and he murdered : such were the indictments that the people of Northumbria brought against their earl when they rose in arms. They told of horrible injustice, of how Tostig had once lured two thegns into his house and had most treacherously murdered them ; it was also charged that the Lady herself, at Tostig's instigation, had assassinated a thegn in the King's very court. He was deposed at the York germót in October 1065, and was declared outlaw, and Morkere, son of Ælfgar, was elected in his place. One would expect Harold to stand beside his brother in such a crisis, but he was too great a man to let affection blind him to ambition. Tostig could not be reinstated without civil war and without Harold himself being reviled and perhaps destroyed. Then would die for ever his hopes of gaining Eadward's throne, as England would be against him. For this treachery to family pride, Tostig was never to forgive Harold. They were enemies, and the most bitter of enemies, from that moment.

OF these two brothers the chronicler tells us that " each was sufficiently endowed with beauty and physical charm, and, as we conjecture, with not unequal strength of body, nor were they ill-matched in courage. But Harold, the elder by birth, was taller in stature, and like his father in endless toilings, in vigils and fasts, in great mildness of temper and in even more quick-witted sagacity." To find a portrait of Tostig, we must reverse this description of Harold. He was selfish, ambitious and cruel, and the power of his family did not matter against his own foiled vanity and egotism.

When the Northumbrians rose against him and chose Morkere for earl, Tostig was absent, he was at court delayed by Eadward's love and the settling of palace-affairs. These affairs apparently included hunting, and while Tostig roved the forests with Eadward, Harold was riding to Northampton. He commanded that the rebels lay down their arms and bring their grievances to a lawful germót. The Northumbrians would not listen. If Eadward, they told Harold, did not banish Tostig and elect Morkere, they would secede and become a kingdom. No arguments could shift them, and Eadward was forced to relinquish his sport and take some interest in his kingdom. Hurriedly he gathered a witan to discuss the matter ; discussion became argument, some insisted that Tostig was guilty of cruelty and avarice, others that Harold had instigated the revolt. This is a queer charge, for Harold could have had no possible reason for wanting Tostig deposed. Tostig himself apparently charged Harold with this treason, and Harold solemnly denied it upon oath. But squabbling did not settle the question—what were they to do ? was Tostig to be deposed or was Morkere to be fought ? Harold stood for peace, but Eadward was for battle. The King fumed to see his favourite insulted. " Having called on God to witness, with heavy sorrowing, he complained that he was deprived of the true obedience of his own people for the purpose of crushing the insolence of the wicked. Then he implored the vengeance of heaven on their heads." As in the time of Godwine when his beloved Eustace was attacked at Dover, now did Eadward demand the slaughter and wreckage of England because his new favourite was insulted. But the men around him, probably led by Harold, restrained his wrath ; they pointed out that it was winter when fighting was almost impossible because of the cold and the difficulty of gathering supplies, and they added that they had not time in which to collect an army strong enough to defeat the rebels. Eadward insisted on immediate war ; but if his followers could not ignore the royal command, they could at least frustrate it by delay.

So great was Eadward's fury that he became ill. Shortly, however, his rage quietened. He had not the strength to sustain emotion, it wilted after the first uprush, and soon Harold was permitted to manage things his own way, the right way. He

determined to yield to Northumbria's demands, to banish Tostig
and to confirm Morkere's election.   Tostig never forgave Harold.
He bade farewell to King and sister, to wife and children, and
left England to seek exile in Flanders, brooding continually on
dreams of revenge.

EADWARD was dying.   He never recovered from the illness that
struck him in the height of his rage and he barely managed to
linger on until his life's work was completed—the building of
St. Peter's at Westminster.   That great abbey was his ambition
and it was his one achievement.   It may have made him worthy
of canonisation by the Church but it most decidedly does not
make him worthy of canonisation by England.   Luckily he had
strong and just men at his side ; if unworthy men had been his
councillors one dreads to think of the injustice, the tyranny that
would have made his name hated for ever.   As it was, under the
guidance of Harold, the nation remained comparatively at peace,
leaving for later generations a heritage about which to dream
and by which to elevate a feeble childlike creature to goodness
and greatness.   The days of St. Eadward became to future
Englishmen days of freedom and plenty ; easily they might have
become instead a memory of horror and destruction.   In his
last moments it seemed that the knowledge of his own irresponsi-
bility came to Eadward.   He saw a vision of two monks he had
known in youth in Normandy, and these monks warned him
that the great men of England, both lay and clerical, were in the
eyes of God ministers of the fiend and that God had put a curse on
the land and would deliver it to its enemy.   Within a year and a
day of Eadward's death, they said, demons would plunder and
murder throughout England.   There was no possibility of
evading God's revenge, even repentence was hopeless.   Yet " in
a day," the monks told Eadward, " when a green tree shall be
cut away from the midst of its trunk, when it shall be carried away
for the space of three furlongs from its root, when without the
help of man it shall join itself again to its trunk and shall
again put forth leaves and bear fruit in its season.   Then first
shall be the time when the woes of England shall come to an
end."

Six days after the consecration of St. Peter's, Eadward's voice
had begun to fail and he could scarcely be heard.   He lay
exhausted until on the seventh day he sat up suddenly in bed.
Harold and others were at his side, his Lady sat on the ground

pressing his naked feet into her bosom. Eadward spoke, he told of his vision of the monks and of their awful warning of destruction. Then he gave orders for his burial, telling his friend not to weep but to rejoice at his deliverance, and he begged the prayers of all his people. And he mentioned Eadgyth ; perhaps remorse drove him to speak of her with tenderness as a loving daughter, saying that she would be rewarded by God. But there were those around him impatient to know whom he nominated as successor. Eadward might die but England lived, a troubled England to which he left no son. He stretched forth his hand. " To thee, Harold," he said, " my brother, I commit my kingdom," and he added with almost tragic lack of humour certain rules that Harold must follow in statecraft. Then he begged that his favourites be not hurt : the Lady was commended to Harold's protection and " equally those who left their native land for the sake of my love and who have so far faithfully followed me."

Earthly matters over, Eadward asked that his body be buried in the minster he had built, and added—wisely enough—that the news of his end should not be hidden from the people. While he spoke, the Lady rubbed his feet into her breasts as if to warm life into them, and he turned to her and said, " Fear not, I shall not die, but by God's grace I shall soon arise to better health." He received the host, and slowly died.

" Then," we are told, " there was to be seen in the defunct body the glory of the soul migrating to God : when manifestly the flesh of the face glowed like the rose, the fallen beard glistened like the lily, the hands set out in the natural order were living-white, and the whole body declared itself surrendered not to death but to auspicious sleep."

EADWARD the Saint was dead but Harold lived. On January 5, 1066, Eadward breathed his last and on the same day the witan formally elected Harold. Voices, we are told, were raised for Eadgar, grandson of Eadmund Ironside, but the common cry was for Harold. England chose him. He was crowned on January 6, the same day that King Eadward was carried for the last time into that minster it had been his life-work to complete.

Harold came to a precarious throne. There was no tradition behind his race, he was an Englishman who by his own genius and the genius of his father had reached the greatest possible power and honour in the land. Yet there is no talk of insurrection at his becoming King, even the unruly north agreed that he was necessary to England.

Though there might be peace at home, there were dangers abroad. Tostig was ready to avenge his honour, William was preparing to stake his claim. William sent an embassy to Harold as was necessary before declaring war ; he demanded the crown, we presume, but we have no knowledge of what his ambassadors asked.

Harold decided to marry. His choice was not that Eadgyth of the Swan's-Neck who had borne his children. He married for political reasons, and chose Ealdgyth, widow of the conquered Welshman, Gruffyd, whom he had defeated and who had been murdered by his own followers. Ealdgyth was also the sister of Tostig's opponents Morkere and Eadwine. Of Ealdgyth we know practically nothing, but we are safe in presuming that she had little love for her husband as she did not help him to a close alliance with her brothers.

IMMEDIATELY after depicting the coronation of Harold, the Bayeux Tapestry rushes us with the startling rapidity of a cinematographic cut into a scene that reads ISTI MIRANT STELLA— ' They wonder at the star." This design is as vivid as any modern impressionist could conceive ; huddling in a narrow room, gaping and goggling, five Englishmen point upwards in terror, while from the window a sixth turns aghast as if to prophesy calamities following in the wake of that ball of coloured flame which streaks into the border of the Tapestry like some gigantic Chinese kite. It was Halley's comet. Actually it did not appear so shortly after Harold's coronation—January 6 ; it was seen just after Easter, being most brilliant from April 24 to May 1. Every seventy-five or seventy-six years it burns across the heavens, but to the men in 1066 it was an omen of disaster, they gazed horror-struck upon " the comet star which men call the hairy star." Almost every chronicler noted it, even writers in China lifted their heads from the contemplation of beautiful things and thought it worthy of a scribble on paper. In Western Europe few doubted that the blow was meant for England, or, at least, as a warning of destruction to some great man. Old hermits blind with vision saw in it the finger of God, magnificent lords in their castles, workmen, serfs, knights and priests, all gazed upwards and crossed themselves as the comet flamed through the sky. In Malmesbury, old Æthelmær—he who had striven to fly like a bird and was crippled because of it—cried that the star would drag tears from mothers, that he had seen such a one before, and that now it had been sent to bring overthrow upon his country.

For whom did that star raise its fiery mane? for Harold or for William? To both it must have brought more dread than hope, to both it must have presaged a conflict in which either might die.

THE Tapestry rushes us to Harold. He listens in horror to the news of a messenger who is perhaps gasping about the comet. From Harold we run to a ship sailing to Normandy, warning William of Harold's coronation. The Tapestry moves more quickly; William and his half-brother Odo, Bishop of Bayeux, hear the news and instantly trees are chopped down, smoothed with the bulky adze, ships are built, hammered and adzed, they are hauled to the sea, and arms are carried aboard—bundles of spears, hauberks with poles through the sleeves—and a cart with a truly gigantic cask of wine is dragged over the sands. William is now aboard, he crosses the Channel, his ships laden high with men and cheerful horses; then Pevensey is reached.

Quickly, too quickly, the Tapestry dashes through events, it gives no suggestion of the worries of the Norman duke, of his efforts to inspire his men and to build an army. We must leave the Tapestry's thrilling story and turn to the slow chaos of the chroniclers. We learn here, in the *Roman de Rou*, that William was preparing for the hunt when the news came of Harold's coronation. He was about to give his bow to a page when a man-at-arms from England arrived and after greeting William, took him aside to whisper the news—Eadward was dead, and Harold was King. Like a man gripped with sudden rage, William rode from the hunt; he spoke to none and none dared speak to him, and as he went, he constantly laced and unlaced his mantle. He passed over the Seine in a boat, and when in his hall, he sat on a bench and was not able to keep still, he turned from one side to the other while his head rested against a pillar and his face was covered by his mantle. The courtiers remained apart until William's seneschal entered, humming a tune, and as he passed, those in the hall asked if he knew what ailed the duke. William heard their voices, and lowered his mantle and looked up. His seneschal—William Fitz-Osbern—told him that it was useless to remain silent for all Rouen rang with what had happened, and

William answered that he sorrowed equally for the death of Eadward and for the treachery of Harold. Fitz-Osbern rallied him, he bade him not mourn but to rise to immediate action.

WILLIAM's task must have seemed to many wellnigh hopeless. He had no claim to England save the stories of Eadward's promise and of Harold's oath ; his blood-claim was of the vaguest. Emma-Ælfgifu, wife of Æthelred and mother of Eadward the Confessor, had been William's grandfather's sister. He could have no partisans in England save a few powerless Norman friends of the late King, therefore, if he succeeded, it could only be by invasion, by leading a foreign army. It is doubtful if Norman feudal tenure included oversea-service, and even if it did, William would have had little or no hope of succeeding with an army of conscripts, the men must follow him enthusiastically of their own accord. He realised that the strongest appeal was the appeal of religion, if he could manage to create a crusade against England, not only Normandy, but all Europe, would follow him. Probably the courageous and cunning Lanfranc was the inspiration behind William here, it smacks of Lanfranc's casuistry that a Norman duke should use the Church for personal gain. He was a very great man, this Lanfranc, Prior of Bec : a scholar, a theologian and a diplomatist, he could argue with the most skilled of dialecticians and he knew the laws of Rome and the examples of the Church by heart. He was sincere, but like many such men, he was capable of distorting his own sincerity, hiding the greedy truth beneath a self-hypnotic attitude. We realise his genius guiding William, teaching the pupil subtleties that he was avid to learn and could appreciate.

William never obtruded the fact that his only right to England was the right of conquest. He asked the Pope to give him England ; he spoke of his kinship with Eadward, of his love for him, of Eadward's promise, and of Harold's broken oath. Even had all these arguments been true, they were worthless—at least in England where a King must be elected by the witan, by the voice of the people. William never mentioned the grandson of Eadmund Ironside. He also never mentioned the fact that English law forbade the giving of the crown by any one except the witan.

Religion was the most powerful ally he could invoke, but he urged other reasons on men with more ambition than faith.

There was plunder to be got in England, and there was land to steal. Men rallied to the banner of the Norman, fired by ambition or piety. The Pope was eager to help, for in Rome was that genius, one of the most extraordinary men of the Middle Ages, Hildebrand, later Pope Gregory VII. Hildebrand was a fanatic in the worthiest sense, all his energies were fused into one ambition, into building the Church of Rome to incalculable power, into dragging the temporal Holy Roman Empire under the domination of the Holy Roman Church. When William and Lanfranc pleaded their cause before him, Hildebrand saw his opportunity. England's Church had retained its independence, English law made small difference between the status of lay or clerical, priests could be punished like ordinary men, they could be deposed by the witan as if they were earls. To Rome this was heresy, yet even Eadward had never dared interfere ; now William came and offered to Hildebrand exactly what Hildebrand desired : let William conquer the people, he said, but he must surrender the Church to Rome.

A crusade was preached against England as if it were a pagan land.

ROME behind him, William had yet his own duchy to convince. When the assembly met, the barons asked time to consider the question. Fitz-Osbern pleaded with them, he called upon their feudal loyalty, he threatened them with shame if William failed because of their cowardice. Then he turned to William and, in the name of all, promised obedience. The barons immediately disowned his pledge. They bellowed so loudly that not a word could be understood, and the assembly broke up, cursing Fitz-Osbern.

It is quite probable that William desired the assembly to break up. If the barons had united against him he would have been doomed, but now each man could be argued with separately, and it was a very different matter defying your duke with an assembly behind you from defying him when alone in his chamber. One by one the barons gave in before William's threats and pleadings, and slowly the great army of conquest was built.

NORMANDY was not Harold's one enemy. Tostig, his brother, remained, eager to seek revenge for the loss of his earldom. He left Flanders for Normandy to urge on William what William fully intended, invasion of England, then he set out on an invasion of his own and ravaged the coast before deciding to seek help in Norway. Norway was then ruled by Harold Hardrada who had spent most of his time fighting his enemy Sweyn of Denmark. When Tostig arrived, however, Hardrada was luxuriating in an unaccustomed peace, and—according to the Norwegian sagas— Tostig suggested that he take the English crown as other North- men had done before him. Hardrada, probably already wearying of his peace, agreed to everything Tostig suggested, and Harold had therefore two enemies to face—Norway in the north, Nor- mandy in the south.

Harold Hardrada struck before William. He struck at the coast of Cleveland, and after a sturdy fight burned Scarborough. His intention was to march on York, and with Tostig he landed on the left bank of the Ouse. Morkere raced to hold him back, but was defeated at Fulford, and shortly afterwards York sur- rendered. Hardrada was received as King, the Northumbrians agreeing more or less under compulsion to follow him against the south.

King Harold was not idle. So swiftly did he ride that when Hardrada saw in the distance the steam rising from the sweating horses, the glare of shields and the ripple of hauberks, he turned to Tostig and asked idly what host this could be. Tostig answered that they might be some of his kinsmen, but that he rather feared they were enemies. Soon there was no need to ask who led that host ; the English steel shone, we are told, like sunlight flashing from a glacier.

Harold parleyed before sounding the battle-horn. He offered Tostig a third of his kingdom if he would swear peace. " What then," asked Tostig, " shall King Harold of Norway have for his trouble ? " And Harold of England answered, " Seven foot's room, or as much as he needs, for he is taller than other men ! " All that day the battle continued, but at last King Harold broke the wall of Norwegian shields by pretended flight. As the enemy left its ranks in triumph to pursue him, Harold turned with arrow and javelin. Hardrada stood by his standard as he fought, chanting of the glories of Norway, but when he saw defeat upon him, he lifted his gigantic two-handed sword and charged. None could withstand the fury of that sword ; then as he ran forward an arrow pierced his throat and tumbled him amongst the corpses. The battle paused when the giant fell, and Harold again pleaded with Tostig. But Tostig had caught Hardrada's standard and had taken Hardrada's place as leader ; he cried that he would rather die than surrender.

The battle continued until Tostig fell like his ally.

Such is the tale given by Norwegian sagas. Much without doubt is poetic invention and the English chroniclers are maddeningly vague or silent. Here and there the saga is obviously inaccurate, and the famous story of Harold's retort of seven feet of earth for Hardrada is, I regret to say, most probably mythical. It is recorded as having been said by other men. But lacking absolute fact, we must accept the saga where it does not conflict with what we know to be truth.

After this battle—called the battle of Stamford Bridge—we see a noble side of Harold. He had won splendidly, and although Hardrada and Tostig were dead, the Norwegian fleet remained, but Harold did not press the victory. He offered peace, accepted hostages, and permitted the remnant of the invaders to sail and row safely back to Norway. These negotiations absorbed valuable time, they left the southern coast open to the Normans. Two or three days after Stamford Bridge, Harold wasted at York, then during the Banquet of Victory a messenger arrived with the expected but terrible tidings that Duke William had reached the coast of Sussex and had landed at Pevensey.

Scarcely had he fought one battle, had he beaten back one invader, before Harold had to move his broken army south, gathering recruits by the way, preparing to meet such a foe as had not been seen in England for many years.

If the winds had not kept the Normans in port, it is likely that the battle with William would have preceded the battle of Stamford Bridge. Harold must have relied on the weather as protection, for he had disbanded his southern army. But William had luck behind him ; after waiting for a month futilely in the Dive he moved his fleet to St. Valery near the estuary of the Somme, and here at last the south wind came to blow him gently, with the loss of only two ships, across the narrow Channel that barred him from his goal.

It is difficult to estimate the exact number of William's fleet, one chronicler soaring to 3000, but Wace, who had the details from his father, tells us that it was 696. William's own vessel was a gift from his duchess, for some reason called the *Mora*, and she had on her prow the bronze figure of a boy aiming with his bow an arrow towards England. You can recognise this ship easily in the Tapestry, she is one of the two that carry no horses or mules. To the sounds of zithers and pipes, to the scream of cymbals, the dulled clatter of drums and the blast of trumpets, the troops of Normandy lost all order when the south wind came ; they scrambled amongst each other, they fought each other, struggling to be first aboard the ships. Lugging their heavy mail, pulling at carts laden with spears and wine, they waded aboard while masts were heaved up and sails unfurled. It was very dark, and William ordered each ship to bear a light, the great lantern on the *Mora* to be a signal for all. From his ship he cried his last commands before sailing. In that moonless starless night, lit only by the lamps in the rigging, the voice of the Norman duke called to his men. His ships were to remain close together, he cried, they were to rest when out at sea, and were to steer by the lantern on his mast-head. Trumpets sounded and the fleet set sail ; it paused in mid-channel, as William had ordered, then it continued through the darkness, like a handful of stars rocking above the waves.

When dawn came, William found that the *Mora* was alone. Breakfast was eaten, yet still the skyline stayed unbroken. A seaman crouched on the *Mora's* mast-head, and soon he shouted that four ships were dipping up over the horizon. Then so many were the ships he decried that they seemed like a forest rising miraculously out of water. Lanterns were no longer needed. The chequered sail of the *Mora* was beacon enough.

Nine o'clock on the morning of Thursday, September 28, 1066, Duke William the Bastard set foot again on English earth.

WILLIAM was the first to land. So eager was he that he slipped and fell sprawling with both hands on the ground. At this evil omen the Normans wailed in horror, but William cried, " By the splendour of God, I have taken seizin of my kingdom, the earth of England is in my two hands ! " And a soldier, as quick-witted as his duke, tugged some thatch from a cottage. This he placed in William's hand as seizin, not only of English earth, but also of all that stood upon that earth. " I accept it," said William, " and may God be with us."

First landed the archers, then followed knights in hauberk and helm ; they mounted their horses as if ready for battle. But no enemy came, for Harold was still at York, resting after the

victory of Stamford Bridge and negotiating with the conquered.
Leaving a small garrison, William marched from Pevensey on the
second day to Hastings. From here he conducted a campaign of
such plundering and burning that it seems purposeless unless we
believe it done to entice Harold south. William did not want to
march inland through hostile country, he wished to draw the
English to him, to make them battle on a ground he could fortify.
In its cinematographic fashion, the Tapestry whirls us from the
crossing of the Channel to the disembarkation ; we see the horses
leaving the ships, then the march to Hastings. From dinner, the
Tapestry next flings us into a scene of William in conference with
Odo and his other half-brother, Count Robert of Mortain. The
walls of the house are pulled away for our convenience, and we
see William, sword raised, arguing with Odo, while Robert
plays with the pommel and blade of his sword. Conference
ended, the scene shifts quickly to the building of earthworks,
from this to a messenger gasping to a stern William his news of
Harold, then to the burning of a house. There is no pause after
this, we are whirled to the evacuation of Hastings, to the march,
to William questioning one Vidal about Harold's position. Not
until now is there a hint of Harold's movements. One would
think, judging by the Tapestry, that he did not even know that
his enemy had landed until after Hastings had been left. Yet,
at the moment of William's leaving Hastings, Harold was bringing his men to battle. When he heard the news of the landing,
he was feasting at York. Immediately he called a council of
his leaders, and each man shouted that he would die rather than
accept any King but Harold. After thanking them for their
loyalty, Harold began his march to London, bidding Morkere
follow. Morkere never followed. Perhaps he hoped that
William would be more pliable than Harold and might agree to
a division of the kingdom.

Before leaving London, Harold went on a pilgrimage to
the minster which he had founded at Waltham, and there he
offered God the sacred relics of his own chapel. Before the
altar of the Holy Cross he vowed that if heaven give him victory
he would present the minster with further gifts and land and
would increase the convent. And one story tells us that in return
the Holy Cross prophesied his imminent doom.

Messengers were travelling between Harold and William.
It is said that when William demanded the crown, Harold's anger
was so great that he would have killed the envoy had not his

brother Gyrth restrained him. William had succeeded in his plan. He remained by the coast and drew his prey to him, he lured Harold to battle instead of risking an invasion into dangerous territory. It is said that Gyrth strove to dissuade Harold from the march, pleading with him to remain in London to recuperate from the northern campaigns while himself led the army : be-sides, added Gyrth, the oath did not bind him, he could fight without saints battling on the other side. All who listened to Gyrth's speech agreed that it was true counsel, that Harold should not risk his life and the chances of his kingdom on one throw ; but Harold would not agree. He said that this war was his, and that he would never permit others to face perils from which himself drew back.

Six days were spent in London to gather troops, then he could wait no longer for the men of the north under Morkere to arrive. He had promised William to fight on Saturday and he was determined to prove his word.

The battle took place on Saturday, October 14, beginning at 9 a.m.

OUR details of the great fight give no clue to the exact formation of Harold's army ; William had archers—far superior to the English—in the front rank, mailed infantry in the second, and chivalry in the rear. Of the English we can only state that, while the Normans relied a great deal on horses, they remained on foot.

Harold was encamped about seven miles from Hastings, on the edge of the forest of Anderid. William, fearful of sudden attack, decided to strike first blow. After mass, he draped around his neck some of the relics on which Harold was said to have sworn, and rode to the heights above Telham. From here he would get his first glimpse of the English who, we are told by the Norman writers, had spent the previous night in heavy drinking. At sight of the enemy, Harold led his troops to a small hill and awaited the attack, and so crowded were his men that in the ensuing fight the wounded and dead could not fall, but were held up by the pressure of living comrades. The Tapestry here comes to our rescue, showing the English fighting in two directions. It has been suggested that this was the wedge formation, but a triangle would have been dangerous to make on a rectangular hill, as it would leave room for the Normans to get a hold. Probably the English were formed into rough squares, Harold being in the centre of one with his brothers ; above him curled the Dragon of Wessex, the royal standard, and beside it was his personal banner, glittering with jewels, showing a fighting man advancing to battle.

WILLIAM called for his harness. Somehow in the excitement of that moment the hauberk was pulled on back-the-front. William was quick to interpret the omen as before when he had fallen at Pevensey. Like his own hauberk, he said, he was being turned back-the-front, being changed from a duke into a King. The hauberk donned, falling to his knees, and the pointed helmet with its broad nasal-guard upon his head, William called for his destrer, the war-horse that was never ridden save to battle. To one man there at least, he seemed the equal of no knight ever seen beneath heaven.

A spy told of Harold's position, of how he stood in the midst of his followers, and William cried that if God gave him victory over that perjured usurper, he would build upon the spot where now the English standard rose, a great minster ; and a monk who heard him, asked that it be dedicated to St. Martin, apostle of the Gauls.

William did not have with him that famous bow which no one other than himself could bend, but which he, giving his horse free rein, could even curve with his feet ; he carried no spear or sword, but wielded instead an iron mace, the only possible weapon against the terrible two-handed axe of the English. His half-brother, Odo, also carried a mace, but there was another purpose in this ; it was the churchmen's especial weapon, for it saved them from being damned as " men of the sword." Odo was this morning at William's side, with William's other half-brother, Robert of Mortain ; above them was lifted the consecrated banner.given by the Pope.

AT prime, three hours before noon, the trumpets screamed for the advance and the Norman archers pulled on their bow-strings. A troubadour known as Taillefer, Cleaver of Iron, had begged from William the honour of striking first blow. Alone against the might of England he rode, singing of Roland and of Charlemagne. Three times he held his lance by the end of the shaft, three times he flung it into the air and caught it by the pointed tip ; then he hurled it and struck down an Englishman. His sword next he drew, and this he held by the grip, tossed it three times into the air and caught it by the blade. Then he charged to his death.

First reckless blood to the Norman ; now came the foot-soldiers, clambering up the rise towards that wall of steel, the shield-wall of the English. That wall could not be broken ; it might sway and give, but it would not break. " God help us ! " was the Norman battlecry and the English answered from behind their shields, " Out ! Out ! " They shouted also their battlecry of " God Almighty ! " and Harold's cry of " Holy Cross ! " The Norman foot-soldiers slid back before those axes, before that unbroken wall of shields, and their chivalry swept up, knights upon horses, wielding lance, spear, sword, or mace. Up the hill they charged with their duke ; but like the infantry before them they could not pierce that wall, they fell before the swing of the giant axes. Many fled, some Bretons on the left ran, and against the strict orders of Harold, his men broke their ranks and followed. The panic spread. So quickly after the first blow it seemed that England had already won. The Normans were flying, pursued, when William and Odo raced furiously after them. You can see William in the Tapestry, he is lifting his helmet by the nasal-guard to prove that he lives, for cowards or traitors have shouted that he is dead. He is turning on his horse, pressing against the cantel, as he rallies his troops. A chronicler records that he did not merely lift the nasal-guard but actually tore the whole helmet from his head, and shouted, " Look here on me ! I live, and will conquer with the succour of God ! What madness lures you to flight ! " With a spear that he must have borrowed from a comrade, he stood in the way of the Bretons " and barred their flight, beating and threatening them." The Tapestry shows us Odo also at this task, but the Tapestry inevitably pushes Odo to the front—as well it might, for he was Bishop of Bayeux. The brothers stemmed the panic, they inspired their men with new courage so that they turned and massacred those English who still pursued.

But the shield-wall glistening in the sunlight stayed unbroken, Harold's banner of the Fighting Man yet waved defiantly beside the Dragon of Wessex. William deliberately sought for Harold, knowing that if he died his followers would lose heart, and once he almost met him, but Gyrth sprang forward and flung a spear that killed William's great Spanish charger. William leaped to the ground, he struck with his mace, and Gyrth was slain. Almost in the same moment it seems that another brother,

Leofwine, died at the hand of a nameless Norman. Harold alone remained, last of the family of brothers who had appeared unconquerable when they had stood beside their father, Godwine, in the past days of Eadward.

William was still on foot, and he demanded the horse of a follower. The coward refused, so William struck him from the saddle. That horse also was killed and William claimed a third, this time it was given him at once, by Eustace—he who had quarrelled with the burghers at Dover. Fight like a demon though he might, encouraging his troops by the most splendid example, still William could not break that wall of shields, and he was forced again to draw back down the hill.

To continue seemed hopeless, but if William could not win by courage, he could win by craft. He remembered how, when the Bretons had fled, part of the English had run after them ; he determined to break the shield-wall by a feint of panic, and succeeded perfectly. The right wing of the English charged down exultantly only to be drawn out of the battle and slaughtered ; William charged up as they charged down. He struck into the gap and forced his way towards the standard. . . .

The story of that great fight comes to us through the pens of Norman writers or through the needlework of Norman ladies. Those of the English who are spoken of as doing great deeds remain unknown, and of Harold we learn almost nothing save that he was " wont to strike at any foe approaching to battle-distance, so that no one neared him with impunity, but at once with one blow, horse and rider were struck down." Of William and particularly of Bishop Odo we hear many deeds ; of Harold, last King of the Anglo-Saxons, courageous fighter and wise ruler, we know but little how he bore himself that day. Yet we need not doubt that few other axes in the army did the havoc of that giant axe of his ; the man who single-armed could lift mailed warriors out of quicksands must have had gigantic strength. He fought magnificently at Senlac, but he fought in vain.

It was late in the afternoon, twilight was setting in, when William gave the command to loose arrows into the air so that they would fall upon the heads of the English. Under this winged hail, the English could do practically nothing ; they lifted their shields to protect their faces and their bodies were bared. Suddenly on the Tapestry we see the figure of Harold, his hand is lifted striving to wrench an arrow-head from his right eye. An arrow had fallen, aimed by some unknown hand, and struck into his eye. In torment he snapped the shaft, the axe slid from his fingers, and Harold himself fell at the foot of his standard in ghastly agony. The Tapestry sweeps us from Harold clutching the arrow-shaft to a figure, undoubtedly also of Harold, falling beneath the sword of a mounted Norman. Twenty knights had sworn to tear down the English standard, sixteen died in the attempt, but the remainder won through just as Harold fell. The man slashing Harold on the Tapestry must be one of that group ; perhaps it is Eustace of Boulogne seeking revenge for the indignity put upon him by the burghers of Dover. Eustace was one of the four who kept their word. They recognised the English King lying in torment and they mauled his body. One lunged through his shield into his chest, a second jabbed his sword-point up under the chin beneath the fastening of the helmet, and a third transfixed the dying man with his lance, while the fourth hacked off his leg. This last man William degraded for such bestiality ; the chroniclers are generous enough not to tell his name.

WHERE the English standard had stood was raised the consecrated banner of the Pope. William had sworn to build a religious house on this spot and he kept his word. Battle Abbey was raised to commemorate the victory. The English nobility had not run, it had been hacked down around the standard, and William now had the ground cleared. He was determined to spend that night on earth wet with the blood of the conquered. His comrades tried to dissuade him, pointing out that many of those who lay nearby were only wounded and might kill him in the night. But William had placed his trust in God, and God had fought for him. Night was drawing in upon the battlefield, and William gazed at the heaps of dead and dying with pity and sorrow. He knelt where Harold's bloodied standard was trampled into the ground and gave his thanks to God while the Pope's banner was lifted above his head. Then he commanded that the bodies be carried away, and his tent pitched. He pulled the helmet from his sweaty head and the hauberk from his body. Steel might be dented and snapped but the limbs of William were unharmed. He was not wounded, and while his troops shouted his name, calling him a second Roland and Oliver, he knelt again to pray before food and drink were brought.

By the campfire on the hard-fought-for hill, the conqueror

of England quietly ate and drank, watching the slain being carried to nameless graves.

WOMEN from the countryside begged for the corpses of their men. William permitted them to carry away any bodies they liked except the body of Harold. This must not be given Christian burial, for it was the remains of an excommunicate and a usurper. The most that William would permit was for a cairn to be built on the ocean-side as a monument to the last of the Anglo-Saxon Kings.

Amongst so many dead, who could recognise the body of Harold ? Two priests, who had followed the army, searched, but searched in vain. " Lacking all his beauty," mangled, smashed, the body of the King lay unknown amongst his comrades. Then the priests remembered that there was one person living who might recognise their lord, " a certain woman by name Eadgyth, of shrewd mind." Eadgyth came to this final and horrible task of love " because she might handle the spoils more kindlily, in that she had loved him the more closely and known him the more fully, seeing that it was commonly agreed that she had been present more freely at the secrets of his bed." The face of Harold was broken beyond recognition, but there were " certain signs " known only to Eadgyth, for with Harold she had " been admitted to the final intimacies of secret things."

Thus, by the love of a woman, was the corpse of Harold recognised and laid reverently under its cairn. Later, it was taken—one story tells us—and was translated to his own beloved minster at Waltham. Of this we cannot be certain. To-day we do not know where lies the body of this last of our Anglo-Saxon Kings.

I

KING WILLIAM THE FIRST

1066–1087

THE CONQUEST OF ENGLAND did not end with the battle of Senlac, it merely began. William had a gigantic task before him ; he had to force the whole country to accept him, and few men could have succeeded as he was to succeed. He had been well trained for the task. A bastard and a minor, with rivals bobbing up on every side, he had yet held firmly to his duchy and by just laws had welded a disrupted land into prosperity and freedom. He was curiously passionless although sometimes capable of awful bursts of rage, but in his dealings with men we usually find an almost Solomon-like sense of right and wrong, of temperate justice, of unyielding severity to the guilty, yet a strange dislike of executing his enemies. That he loved his wife is beyond question, and we have no hint that he ever cared for any other woman. In fact, his continence aroused suspicions in his followers and they suspected him of impotence. " In addition to his other virtues," says a chronicler, " especially in earliest youth he esteemed chastity to such an extent that publicly it was believed certain that he could do nothing in a woman." He was devout without a trace of hypocrisy, and utterly unscrupulous in the means he took to gain an end. Avaricious, drawing cruelly all money he could from the people, arrogant and wrathful, according to an English chronicler, yet as both statesman and soldier few kings in our history can equal let alone surpass him.

When William reached the throne of England he was nearly forty years of age. He was of good height and physically very powerful, as witness his unique bow and the ease with which he could bend it even with his feet, possessing " huge strength in his arms." He was clean-shaven, according to Norman custom, and partially bald in front, fair skinned, and although the Tapestry shows him slim enough, he was apparently rather fat. He grew enormously fat before his end.

ABOUT the conception and birth of William, many legends have arisen. There is some truth in them, without doubt, and it seems indisputable that his mother was a tanner's daughter of Falaise. One story remarks that Robert—William's father— saw the girl at a dance, another tells that he noticed her while she was scrubbing linen in the beck that ran by her father's tannery at the foot of the castle. Her name is variously spelt as Arlette and Herleva. When William was born, at the very moment of birth, he seized the straw on the chamber floor, so that all knew at once that he would grow into a conqueror ; another legend tells us that Arlette, on the night that Robert first embraced her, dreamed that a tree sprouted from her body and overshadowed all Normandy and England.

William's father, Robert, was called the Devil, but he was also called the Magnificent. There seems little cause for the first nickname, as he was not a particularly violent man—apart from the suspicion that he murdered his elder brother—and whatever sins he might have committed he expiated by a pilgrimage to Rome. This pilgrimage was a risky venture, as his son could have been little more then seven years of age at the time. Robert did what he could to ensure peace during his absence, for he had neither brother nor legitimate child to succeed him. Others were gazing hungrily at his duchy : there was his uncle, Robert, Archbishop of Rouen, who was also Count of Evreux. Like many other churchmen of that time, Archbishop Robert lived two lives : he was an archbishop and a count. As archbishop he remained celibate, as count he had a wife called Herleva and children by her. He was not the only candidate for Normandy. There were also Robert the Devil's nephew, Guy of Burgundy ; his cousin, Alan of Brittany ; and his two half-brothers, Malger—who later succeeded Archbishop Robert in the see of Rouen—and William, who held Arques, near Dieppe. None of these claims were very strong ; as a churchman, Robert would have had difficulty in being accepted, Alan and Guy could claim only through female descent, Malger and William of Arques were illegitimate. This illegitimacy did not debar a candidate from succession, William himself was illegitimate, but it made Malger and William of Arques' claims no stronger than his.

WHEN Duke Robert decided to start on his pilgrimage he called together the great men of his duchy and told them that he wished the problem of his succession to be decided at once. The assembly retorted that he should remain at home, but Robert was determined to leave ; he said that he wanted William of Falaise acknowledged as his heir. The boy was little, he told them, but he would grow, and his overlord the King of the French had promised protection. The Norman lords could not evade so direct a command. They did not want a young master and many probably objected to his low birth—it is curious that the title of Bastard should stick to William when it was not usually considered derogatory—and besides, Archbishop Robert was present, and the archbishop had his eye on the duchy for himself. But there was no evasion possible. Sullenly the lords swore fealty to the little Bastard, and the grandson of a tanner was acclaimed the future Duke of Normandy.

Having settled this problem, Robert set out on his pilgrimage, only to die at Nikaia within a few months. Immediately there was rebellion ; if not open rebellion, there was at least a slackening of fealty. Castles rose on every side, barons turned robbers, men murdered each other ; it was a state of anarchy astonishing even in that brutal time.

For guardians William had Alan of Brittany—himself a possible candidate to the dukedom—one Thurcytel or Thorold, the seneschal Fitz-Osbern, and Count Gilbert, both relatives. He managed to live through those dangerous years by some miracle while his guardians paid the penalty of loyalty amongst thieves. Alan was poisoned, Gilbert was assassinated, and Osbern was killed in young William's own bedchamber, the boy himself being rescued by his maternal uncle Walter. These were fierce times, battle succeeded battle, the Norman dukes fought for themselves and were united only in hatred of William.

Somehow, through this passion of murder and intrigue, William grew up. It seems incredible that he was not assassinated. The culmination of treachery came in 1047 when he became of age and had the strength and the right to avenge his friends and to punish rebels. Now was the final blow struck, the blow that raised him to full power. The battle of Val-ès-Dunes made William truly Duke of Normandy.

WITHIN the next two years after this victory, he was to find the two people who had the greatest influence on him and who helped to mould his character into the ambitious, just, courageous and crafty hero he became. One of these was a woman, Matilda, the other a man, Lanfranc of Pavia.

Lanfranc must come first. Because of him, William was to capture Matilda, the woman he loved. He came from the Lombard city of Pavia and was of good family ; his father was a lawyer, and on his death, Lanfranc took his place. He made a detailed study of civil law and could speak the Greek tongue. At first he had no inclination for the Church ; he was a lawyer, a scholar, inspired only by a passion for knowledge, and it is difficult to understand why he ever left his cultured home to adventure into the violent and ignorant land of the Normans. Perhaps their very ignorance was an inducement ; here was a country that might be moulded to greatness, and he had heard that the young duke was eager to encourage learned men. With a large following of disciples, Lanfranc opened a school at Avranches, and it was now that grace came to him, that he woke from the secular world to see before him the vision of a glorious spiritual future. He looked upon his fame with disgust, his one desire was to escape the world and to lurk in some small convent where he could remain unknown. But he was so famous that it was difficult to find a hiding-place ; eventually, however, warning no one of his departure, he wandered forth alone until he reached the small monastery of Bec, ruled by the childlike Abbot Herlein. The abbot received him as a monk, but even these lowly walls could not satisfy Lanfranc's lust for escape, he longed for actual wildernesses where he could discover solitude as the old saints had discovered it ; his abnegation was profound and, in its own way, the result of an overwhelming vanity. Herlein very sensibly forbade his leaving for the deserts of renunciation, and soon he was advanced to the position of prior. Nothing, not even the humblest monastery walls, could dim the genius of Lanfranc ; his fame spread, pilgrims came from far lands to hear his teachings and to offer gifts. Simple and great, lords and scholars, wandered to the tiny convent and listened in awe to the wisdom of its prior.

William heard of his learning, and Lanfranc went back into the world. He had found a man worthy of him, a man to whom he could play the Machiavelli to perfection. There was a third party to William's genius, another person who helped create him—Matilda, daughter of Baldwin, Count of Flanders. We cannot state definitely when this romance began, our first authentic knowledge of it comes when the marriage was forbidden by the synod of Rheims of 1049 because of consanguinity, for which there seems little evidence ; Wace, however, places its beginnings earlier, before William's visit to England in 1048.

When William first presumed to look so high as the daughter of the Count of Flanders, he was already a great figure. At Val-ès-Dunes, with the aid of Henry, King of the French, he had, by splendid personal heroism, helped defeat the rebels. He aided his overlord, Henry of France, against Geoffrey, Count of Anjou—who called himself Martel because of the vigour of his battle-strokes—and on one occasion the King was forced to restrain William's rashness, to warn him that his life was too valuable to risk in personal exploits. Later, William was to learn the virtue of restraint. Much as he might glory in the exultant power of war, much as he might feel ecstasy in hand-to-hand fighting, he was to school himself so that he dared nothing that he could not perform, and never acted rashly.

He besieged Domfront in which the rebels were defying their overlord, he challenged Geoffrey to a duel to which Geoffrey did not turn up, and he then besieged Alençon. Here we discover that, although William might be prepared to forgive the conquered, there were certain things his proud spirit could not overlook. Alençon was separated from his army by a bridge over the Sarthe, and the defenders beat skins and leather coats, yelling, " Hides, hides for the Tanner ! " Insults to the dignity of a King or lord were unforgivable ; William swore his favourite oath—" By the Splendour of God ! "—and vowed that those who jeered at him would be treated like the branches of a tree snipped by the pollarding-knife.

When the city fell to his sword, thirty-two of the jesters were dragged before him, their limbs were chopped off and were thrown into the castle as a warning of its fate. The garrison surrendered immediately.

THEREFORE no penniless duke sued for the hand of Matilda of Flanders. Son of a tanner's daughter William might be, but he was also the victor of Val-ès-Dunes and the conqueror of Alençon and Domfront. It was necessary that he marry, that he produce an heir, and after long discussions with his assembly it was decided that Matilda would suit both him and Normandy. Not only was she beautiful—probably a small consideration—being " very elegant of body and liberal of mind," but an alliance with Flanders would have been most valuable as it was rich borderland close to Normandy. Matilda's father was Count Baldwin V, and her mother was Adela the sister of the reigning King of France, Henry I ; she had two brothers, Baldwin and Robert, both of whom were later to rule Flanders ; her aunt Judith had been the wife of Tostig.

Matilda's value as a wife makes us suspect William's affection for her. It is probable that he at first desired her for political purposes, but later, understanding her charm and quick intelligence, grew to love her. Certainly there is never a genuine hint that he cared for another woman ; he and Matilda became the ideal couple, untouched by proved slander. There is, however, one slander that still clings to Matilda, but it is undoubtedly a myth. In the days of King Eadward, runs the tale, an Englishman called Brihtric came as ambassador to Flanders, and Matilda offered to marry him but was refused. Then when William conquered England her vengeance fell upon him who had scorned her : Brihtric was seized at his home, taken to Winchester and died in prison. The only possible basis for this tale is that Matilda did receive most of the lands of a Brihtric who had territory dotted from Worcestershire to Cornwall. This we find recorded in Domesday. The story, however, is of later date and it certainly does not fit into our knowledge of Matilda's character. It might, of course, be true, but it must be treated at least with the greatest suspicion.

Of William's courtship of Matilda we hear romantic and amusing tales. We are told that he kicked and beat her, that he actually dragged her to the floor by the hair. These stories we can afford to ignore, together with the stupid anecdote, which William of Malmesbury doubts even as he repeats it, that in later life William took for mistress the daughter of a priest and that Matilda discovered the liaison and had the girl hamstrung. There are so many tales about the pair that their very volume defeats their purpose. Are we seriously expected to believe that before leaving for England William kicked Matilda in the breast with his spurs ? This tale carries its own refutation by adding that Matilda died of the wound. It has about as much truth in it as the story of Harold kicking his mother when she begged him not to fight at Senlac.

LEAVING myth—whether based in truth or otherwise—we find that suggestions about the vicissitudes of the courtship rest purely in the fact that the marriage was forbidden by the Church. Many

5

are the reasons stated for this refusal. The common argument—the one given by the Pope—was that William and Matilda were related, yet they were not related within the canonical restrictions for there was no community of descent. Matilda's mother, before wedding Baldwin, had been married to the brother of William's father. Roughly we might call them distant cousins, they had no blood relationship whatever. All the same, Pope Leo IX forbade the marriage and probably had obscure political reasons for the ban. William knuckled under to the prohibition until fate gave him the opportunity to defy it. The Normans were conquering southern Italy ; Leo was reckless enough to fight them and was captured and imprisoned. With the Pope out of the way and in the hands of men of his own race, William decided to ignore the papal ban : in 1053, he married Matilda at Eu.

In thus defying the Pope, William risked the anger of his people, and he had subjects brave enough to rebuke him. His uncle Malger, Archbishop of Rouen, has come down to us with a peculiar reputation as a debauchee, for which there seems little cause. We certainly now find him standing for the rights of his Church and daring to threaten excommunication of William. The excommunication may even have been proclaimed. William did not forgive his uncle ; two years after the marriage he arranged for Malger to be deposed from his see ; he was banished to the Isles of the Côtentin—our present Channel Isles—and after arousing a deal of scandal by interest in magic, he fell into the water and was drowned.

A greater opponent than poor Malger rose against William. Lanfranc himself, now Prior of Bec and a favourite with William, rebuked his master openly. William was unable to restrain his anger. For years he had waited to embrace this woman and he was now exasperated by opposition from relatives and friends. He not only banished Lanfranc but he sacked and burnt a part of the abbey of Bec itself. Again, the scholar set out on his pilgrimage, deserting the good things of life. Could it have been by accident that he met William and adroitly talked himself back into favour ? had he deliberately arranged the meeting and made it appear a coincidence ? It seems that the first gush of ecstasy had left the Prior, that his old dreams of a solitary life as hermit no longer thrilled him, for after receiving the kiss of peace from William, he agreed to help him about the marriage which himself had denounced and to see if he could not argue the

Pope into withdrawing the ban. In this he succeeded ; a dispensation was granted by Pope Nicholas II in 1059–60 on condition that two monasteries were founded, one for nuns to be raised by Matilda, one for monks to be raised by William. Work started immediately ; Lanfranc became the first abbot of William's foundation of St. Stephen's ; Matilda's foundation of the Holy Trinity was not completed until four years later. Both monasteries were at Caen.

WILLIAM had attained his bride but his duchy was not yet at peace. His old ally and overlord, Henry of France, had watched apprehensively the growth of the young Bastard ; seeing him steal from Normandy into Flanders, he now strove to humble him by instigating rebellion, and at last actually led troops against his ambitious vassal. Here William was at a disadvantage, for he was loyal enough not to wish to fight his King. While permitting others to go to battle, himself always turned aside.

GRADUALLY Normandy soaked into the rest of the Frankish states. It was creeping into Anjou. King Henry allied himself with Geoffrey Martel. They entered Normandy from the south in 1058, and William retreated before them. He permitted the enemy to ravage his country, letting them march farther and farther into his territory until he could surprise them. His opportunity came at Varaville while the French army was crossing the Dive, half being on one bank, half on the other. William swept down on the rear and slaughtered it, he pushed it to the banks of the river, and into the river. The Dive was thick with bodies and armour, and dark with blood. Not one man escaped. And impotently from a hill on the opposite side King Henry watched the carnage.

He gave up all further hope of subduing Normandy after this defeat. He made his peace with William, and two years later was dead—killed, went the report, by poison drunk by accident—leaving his throne to an infant son, Philip I, who was placed in the guardianship of Baldwin of Flanders. At about the same time died William's other enemy, Geoffrey Martel.

Now begins William's great war with Maine, a kind of prelude to the conquest of England. The existence of Maine had always been a troubled one, lying as it did between Normandy and Anjou.

The Angevins had constantly fought to steal it, and Geoffrey Martel had driven the heir, Herbert, from the country on the death of Herbert's father, Count Hugh. Herbert wandered to Normandy, and William was only too delighted to accept him as a guest until the opportunity should arrive when the lad might be of use. That opportunity came on the death of Geoffrey in 1060. Herbert swore to become William's man if he would help him win back his lands, he promised to keep Maine as a fief of Normandy and to marry one of William's daughters while his own sister Margaret would marry William's son Robert. If Herbert died without an heir, it was agreed that the country should become William's. Therefore William held every card ; a descendant of his, no matter what happened, would rule in Maine.

Herbert died within two years, before his betrothed was of age to marry, and William asked for Maine according to the bargain, adding that with his last breath Herbert had proclaimed him heir. Exactly as later he was to demand England, William demanded Maine, but the people were by no means eager to accept him. He had to use force. First he ravaged the countryside, cutting off supplies from the chief city, Le Mans, until it was forced to surrender and the people's claimant had submitted. This was Walter, husband of Herbert's aunt and nephew of Eadward the Confessor. Both Walter and his wife disappear almost immediately afterwards. It was said that William poisoned them, but it is difficult to believe that a man of his piety and justness would resort to such an unknightly trick to rid himself of enemies.

It is about this date, after the conquest of Maine, that we must place Harold's visit and the Breton war. Harold, as we have seen, aided William in this war. Duke Conan of Brittany challenged William and besieged Dol, which was held by one of William's allies. William and Harold charged to the rescue and Conan ran away so fast that he didn't stop until he had shut himself into his own castle of Rennes and left his country open for William to capture and pillage.

This war is of little importance. It is time that we left Normandy and took up the threads severed by the opening of this chapter. We must deal with William no longer as mere Duke of Normandy but also as King of England.

HAROLD was dead and his army defeated, but England itself remained unsubdued. The victory of Senlac was but an overture to the gradual conquest. William slept that night on the hill, on the blood-soaked ground, and in the morning he rose to face a task more gigantic than ever he had faced before.

He was conqueror but he was not King. And the country did not surrender at once, it remained defiant although Harold lived no more. Morkere lived. He who should have been at Harold's side at Senlac now marched from the north and sent his sister, Harold's Lady, to Chester in fear lest William seek vengeance on the dead King's wife. The lords of England were merging on London, and there they hurriedly collected a witan which consisted mainly of sailors. There seemed no candidate to raise who would be strong enough to defeat William. We cannot doubt that if there had been another Harold the Norman invasion would have perished at Senlac. But who was there to choose ? Harold's sons were the children of the Swan's-Neck, and therefore illegitimate, but although that was not really important, they were young ; the witan did not even mention them. Harold's brothers were killed, brave Gyrth and Leofwine, either of whom might have been capable of holding England. Morkere and his brother Eadwine were ready to accept the power, but it was not offered them. Instead, the witan decided on the Ætheling Eadgar, grandson of Eadmund Ironside. Morkere and Eadwine were presumably satisfied by merely accepting Eadgar's election ; they had no intention of helping their new King to maintain his throne. They returned to the north and left the south to take care of itself. After this act of treachery, the south was doomed. The flower of its men had died at Senlac, it had no leader, no army. It crumbled before the advance of William. Opposition ceased to exist, but William did not march direct on London. He had learned the value of patience, he knew that the kingdom was leaderless and he thought to strike terror and to make the people call to him of their own will.

For five days he remained at Hastings in expectation of an embassy from London, then he marched to Romney where some of his stragglers were killed. William realised that he must show no sign of weakness ; his policy was to be merciless to those who resisted but gentle to those who surrendered. He took vengeance on Romney, then marched to Dover which surrendered at once. Towards Dover, because of its submission,

he showed nothing but kindness as a contrast to his treatment of
Romney. He wished England to understand and value his
attitude. When some of Dover was accidentally burned by
his troops, he indemnified the owners. That was his policy :
clemency mixed with retribution. He drew towards London.
Canterbury opened its gates and here he was smitten by a strange
illness. The story is told that Harold before Senlac was suffering
but refused to recognise the truth, hardening his spirit against
the weakness of the flesh ; here we find the tale repeated about
William. Yet it was serious enough to detain him for a month
in and near Canterbury while his captains carried on the task of
conquest, gradually cutting London off from England. On
December 1, William himself set out on the task of frightening
the city into submission ; killing, burning, ravaging, he descended
on Southwark, destroyed it, passed along on the west bank of the
Thames, crossed the river at Wallingford and reached Berkhampstead in Hertfordshire. He had no need to go farther. London
gave in.

An embassy waited on him and it included Eadgar the elected
King. Oaths were sworn, homage was paid, and William gave
to Eadgar the kiss of peace. At first he showed a certain reluctance to take the crown. He called his officers to him and discussed the question : should be accept while so much of England
held out against him ? Besides, he added, he would like to
postpone the coronation until his duchess—now regent of Normandy—could be crowned beside him. This is a charming
and undoubtedly sincere touch ; William had fought and had
conquered and now he wished to lay his spoils in the lap of the
woman he loved, to share with her this triumph and this glory.
For a moment he becomes human ; the machine-like intensity
of the man, the cold-bloodedness of his ambition, the fox and the
lion that together made his character—all go, and we see such a
one as ourselves, a man who does not struggle forward from mere
insatiable greed—he struggles to pluck riches for a woman as
men still do to-day. It is a gentle touch that makes one love the
Conqueror, we see him unarmed, without the snakish rings of
mail on his plump body, we see tenderness in his eyes and the
thought of a woman making his conquest worthy and splendid.

William might be swayed by sentiment for the moment, but
his council decided that he must accept the crown immediately,
and he realised the strength of their arguments. To continue
the war without consecration would mark him as an invader,

while to be crowned King would give him an august right, it would make traitors of those who defied him. The coronation therefore was fixed for Christmas.

On December 25, 1066, he walked into the West Minster as Harold had done before him ; he walked through a guard of Norman soldiers, behind the bishops and the clergy with their crosses ; the Te Deum was sung and the people were asked if they would accept William as King. For the first time in history the question was asked in a new language, it was not spoken in English alone—it was spoken also in French. " Yes, yes," came the answer, " King William ! "

The uproar excited the Normans outside the minster. They believed, we are told, that their duke was being murdered and therefore pillaged and burnt the surrounding houses, but if they thought their leader actually in danger, surely they would have rushed to his rescue instead of running wildly about outside ? No matter what caused the riot, the Norman troops behaved in a disgraceful fashion, yet William did not stir. The others ran from the minster to rescue their goods or to join in the fight ; alone with the officiating prelates and the abbey-clergy, William remained until the ceremony was concluded, until he had taken the oath to give justice and mercy to all his people and to rule as well as his predecessors ; he stayed until the holy oil was poured upon his hair, the rod and the sceptre given into his hands, and the new crown of gems lifted and placed around his brow.

GRADUALLY he won the country for there was no leader capable of standing against him, he had to fight only the sullen resistance of a nation that feared yet respected him. Gradually he conquered ; but this man who had kept so steadfastly towards his ambitions, permitting no sentiment or thought of vengeance to draw him from the path, was doomed to die in terrible unhappiness, to see his life-work in danger of being broken, to be hated by one who should have loved him most.

We need not list all William's children as we are uncertain not only of the dates of birth but of the existence of some of his daughters. He had four sons : Robert, born perhaps in 1056 ; Richard, born perhaps in 1058 who died suddenly while hunting in the New Forest : William, the third son, was also to receive an arrow in his eye while hunting here ; it seemed that a doom hung over the ground to clear which William had demolished churches and homes and had let good arable land sprout trees and bushes to help sport. This third son was called William after his father and was nicknamed Rufus because of his red face ; he was born perhaps in 1060. The youngest, Henry, the only son born in England, in 1068, was to earn the title of Beau-Clerk because of his learning.

WE must skip a great many years, jumping over the slow sub-jugation of England, the suppressions of isolated risings, ignoring the battles in the fens with Hereward the Wake and the election of Lanfranc to the archbishopric of Canterbury, until we reach the approximate year of 1077 when William's eldest son, Robert, was beginning to grow troublesome.

Nominally, Robert had been associated with his mother in the rule of Normandy during William's absence in England, and twice he was acknowledged Count of Maine by the counts of Anjou, as he had been promised this heritage by his betrothal to Margaret, now dead. When he came of age—which was probably in 1077—he expected to be formally given his lands. That caused the trouble.

In appearance, Robert resembled his father. He was fattish, short, and round-faced, and was nicknamed *Gambaron* or *Curt-Hose*. He was a brave lad, a clever archer, and generous and frank in manner. This generosity of his, one of the essential qualities of a perfect knight, had dragged him heavily into debt, and William was probably slow with his allowance. Robert, at any rate, was wearying of being the hard-up son of a great man and began to desire the honours rightly his and a little more money to distribute. He demanded a share of England or at least the possession of Normandy and Maine, Maine being rightly his and Normandy having been promised him by his father before the invasion of England. The chronicler gives us a long dialogue between William and Robert on this question and he stuffs it with the usual scriptural and classical tags, but it con-cludes, as it is likely the real dialogue concluded, by Robert crying, " My lord the King, I did not come here to hear sermons of which my tutors gave me more than enough when I was learning grammar ! "

Rebellion did not follow at once. Robert retired to sulk and scheme amongst his favourites. At this time William was carry-ing on a war with Rotron, Count of Mortagne, in Perche, and while advancing towards his enemy's territory he took with him his three sons, Robert, William Rufus and Henry. Rufus and

Henry were lodged in one house, Robert in another ; the younger boys visited their elder brother and went into the solar—the sun-room built above the living quarters. Here they played at dice until, wearying of annoying each other, they emptied water into the yard in which Robert was strutting with his comrades. At this insult, Robert lost his temper, ran upstairs and would have taken a brutal revenge if the King had not calmed the uproar. It was a small matter, one would think, to take seriously ; brothers have always fought and played tricks on each other. Robert, however, believed his dignity so hurt that he decided to run away and capture his father's castle at Rouen. In this he was foiled and at the head of a troop of discontented young rascals he harried his father's lands ; William seized the castles of Robert's adherents, took their money and with it hired mercenaries to fight them.

Others were quick to help Robert in his disobedience. Even King Philip of France was discreetly on his side, but all hopes of rebellion on a large scale were soon quashed by William. He pounced on Robert's most powerful protector, Aimeric of Villerai, had him captured and thrown across a horse " like a hog." After that, Robert became a homeless wanderer, trailing from court to court, flinging to his favourites and wenches the bounty of others. Now, worse even than the rebellion of a son, William had to suffer the knowledge that his wife was disobeying him. Matilda was woman enough to retire from William's ambitions when those ambitions chafed her love for the children. She sent secretly to Robert what money she could gather. When William heard of this, he commanded that she stop at once, pointing out that the money she sent made his enemies more powerful and might cause his own death. But Matilda answered that if Robert were stretched beneath seven feet of earth, she would surrender her blood to bring him alive. William lost his temper. This happy couple, whose ambitions before had always coincided, now quarrelled ; yet William loved Matilda too greatly to be strict. Instead, his fury fell upon her agent, a Breton named Samson, whom he commanded should be blinded. Samson was warned and escaped in time ; as the only safe way of remaining out of William's clutches he turned monk.

ROBERT was becoming really dangerous. Philip of France, who feared the King of England as his neighbour the Duke of Normandy, now presented Robert with the castle of Gerberoi in

Beauvais, near the border of Normandy and France. Disgruntled Normans and soldiers-of-fortune rushed to aid the son against the father. This was too close to William's lands to be ignored. The father had to turn against his son. He hardened his pity, ignoring the natural love of a parent and the pleadings of Matilda. Above all, above even father and husband, he was Duke of Normandy. Inside his lands there must be peace, love must not interfere with law.

Robert awaited him in Gerberoi. It is a simple matter for historians to damn Robert as the ungrateful child of a famous man, but the child of a famous man, if he would keep intact his own ego, must rebel. Only by rebellion can he assert the uniqueness of his personality. To be bred as the eldest son of a conqueror, as the prince who would be given by hereditary and without effort the spoils of a parent, must have been torment to a proud and sensitive soul. Robert cannot be blamed. William was not the father to breed affection in his children, he ruled them probably as he ruled his duchy ; certainly he gave Robert little that the lad could call his own, merely a few titles without the power or the money to make those titles more than words. Inevitably, Robert revolted. He threw away in scorn the paltry drops of gold he could squeeze from his parent, he defied him bravely. He demanded his rights, not only the rights of power and territory, but the right to be an individual, to be a personality apart from the father. William more than Robert must take the blame for this rebellion ; if he had been kinder, more understanding, it would probably never have taken place.

WITH a mixed army of English, Norman and mercenary, William set out to conquer Gerberoi. It seems that his overlord, Philip of France, was with him—Philip, who was secretly aiding Robert, having given him this very castle they were about to besiege.

For the second time after so many years of warfare, William lost a battle—he had been defeated by France and Brittany once at Dol—and he fled, not from the army of a brave nation, but from the walls of a small border fortress, from the troops of a rebel, his son. For nine hours the conflict raged. Rufus was with his father. They struggled about the walls, striving to make a breach ; then Robert and his father met suddenly in the mêlée. Robert hurled his spear, a comrade loosed his bow-string. The steed of William was struck by the arrow and the bulky Conqueror was flung to the ground. He would have died then under the hand of his son if an Englishman had not darted forward and offered him his horse. This Englishman had no sooner leaped from the saddle than a crossbow-shaft struck him dead. William however, was mounted again, mounted but wounded. He had no heart to carry on the fight, he called his men and drew back, leaving Robert victorious, victorious over the great Conqueror who had only once known defeat before that day. Rufus, too, was wounded, and Rufus was to prove himself probably the greatest soldier of his time, the equal almost of his father.

At Rouen, William brooded over his defeat. Surely he must have felt a certain pride even in his shame? Robert had left Gerberoi, he had wandered to Flanders. The suggestion that his troops deserted him after the battle seems of little weight ; it would be purposeless for them to disband after such a victory. It is more possible that Robert felt remorse. He had shown his father that he was a man capable of great deeds ; swiftly must have followed the reaction, the horror of a son who had been close to parricide. Besides, Robert had little ability for sustained action. He was probably bored with fighting.

Neither party suggested carrying on the war. The Normans merely debated how best to heal the quarrel. At first William would not listen to their pleas. He said that he had suffered both as prince and father, that no Duke of Normandy had ever been so wronged as he, and he added that particularly he could not forgive Robert for conspiring against him with foreign enemies. But his lords pleaded, his Lady added the sorrow of a mother in the scales of his pity, and William relented. He promised to receive Robert.

After that, there was peace for a time. Robert was reinstated in all his old honours and was sent on an expedition against Scotland in 1080, in which he fought no battle but founded a castle as guardian of the marches. This was to become Newcastle-upon-Tyne. After being a dutiful son for a time, Robert once more quarrelled with his father. We do not know the cause of the quarrel, but soon he was again a rebel, exiled in France.

THESE were tragic days for William. The brilliant youth who had schemed and toiled to greatness, who had seized England and who had made the power of Normandy a terror to France, had grown to attain all his ambition only to find despair at the end. He held his conquests, but all the things he loved were fading. His eldest son had rebelled and one of his daughters had died, it is said in terror at the thought of a marriage with Alfonso of Spain—when her body was taken to Bayeux for burial, her knees were found to have grown calloused because of constant prayers ; his second son Richard also died about this time, killed in the New Forest ; and now the wife he adored was to follow daughter and son. Matilda died on November 3, 1083.

She had long been ill and perhaps her sickness had been made stronger by quarrels in the home. For the first time she and her husband had fought against each other ; now she was dead and William was alone with the memory of those last bitter years. She died piously and was buried in her own monastery of the Holy Trinity at Caen where her eldest daughter was a nun and was one day to become abbess ; this daughter William and Matilda had offered to God before the invasion of England.

UNTIL he died, William remained a man of sorrow. Life had lost all beauty to him with the loss of Matilda, and the only task of happiness remaining was to give money and lands to the Church so that masses might be said for the soul of his Lady.

He had little time to ponder on his grief. Wars distracted him, fighting in Maine, in Scotland, Wales ; then began that great work of administration, the creation of Domesday Book. This book was a survey of England, giving the names of the men who had held land under Eadward and of those who held it now under William, the value of their land, and the possibilities of increasing its value.

Fighting with enemies, sending commissioners throughout England, William had yet other affairs which he must handle. His son had turned traitor and now he found a second traitor in his own half-brother, Odo. William gave him many honours after the conquest, appointing him regent of England when himself was absent. The rule of Odo had been little more than tyranny, it grew so violent that William had to suppress it. Odo must have become almost insane with ambition ; he executed without mercy, made innocent men pay bribes for freedom, and now his vanity drove him to a dangerous peak, he dreamed of attaining the papacy itself. Some prophet had once said that the successor to Gregory VII would be an Odo or an Otto ; that was sufficient to make Odo of Bayeux quite certain that he was meant. He bought a palace at Rome, he threw away his money to bribe votes and he even thought of crossing the Alps with an army. Just as he was about to set out on this adventure, William forbade his going. Before the assembly, William impeached his half-brother, saying that Odo's rule in England had been tyranny, that he had oppressed the poor, despoiled the Church, and had enticed William's knights, needed so badly at home, to cross the Alps with him in a hopeless attempt to steal the papacy. What justice should be meted out to such a man?

No one dared obey the King when he commanded the arrest of Odo. He was forced with his own hands to take his half-brother. Odo cried that he was a clerk and that it was not lawful to condemn a bishop without the command of the Pope. Prompted by Lanfranc, William answered grimly, " I meddle not with clerks and prelates. I do not seize the Bishop of Bayeux but I do seize the Earl of Kent. I seize my earl whom I set over my kingdom and I demand of him an account of the stewardship which I committed to him." As Earl of Kent, the bishop could not retort. He was imprisoned at Rouen, and even the protests of Rome could not move William to release him.

In William the lust for conquest was like a disease. He turned now hungrily towards that strip of land, the Vexin, which separated Normandy and France. This had once been Norman territory but during William's childhood it had been taken back by France. William demanded its return, and he backed up his demands with the threat of an army.

He could threaten and demand, he could send his troops against Philip, but he was growing too sick and fat to lead the troops himself. Philip jeered at his grossness, he said that the King of England was with child and was lying at Rouen where there would be a great glittering of candles at his churching. William could never bear a taunt, his dignity was so great that an insult must be revenged at once. He swore by the Resurrection and the Splendour of God that when he rose again and went to mass, he would light a hundred thousand candles at the expense of Philip. Those candles were lit. Fearfully the vengeance of William fell upon his enemy. He led his troops into the harvest, he despoiled everything, he burnt the crops and demolished homes. All fell before him. The candles burned brightly, candles of death, of flaming homes, of slaughtered men and ravished women. Into the country charged William on this work of destruction, he lit candles all the way to Mantes, letting no mercy soften the rage of his pride. Mantes fell before him, it was razed to the ground ; the candles guttered to the last spark, until there was not a house or church standing, not a man living, a woman unravished. Even the holy recluses who disdained to desert their cells were burned to death by the bright candles of William's vengeance.

He gloated on the sight, he shouted to his men to lay on tinder so that the flames could be fed to greater glory. He rode about the falling city, exultant, until suddenly on the edge of a ditch, his horse slipped, and he was flung against the arçon of his saddle.

The blow was so violent that he called for the retreat to be sounded. That gross belly of the Conqueror had wrought his death.

He lay in agony at Rouen until the noise of the palace so irritated him that he was moved to the priory of St. Gervase on a hill overlooking the city from the west.

Around the bed gathered abbots and bishops, eager to offer consolation ; but the man whom William most desired to see, the saintly Anselm, was absent. He had hurried from Bec at William's request and had himself fallen sick on the road ; William had to give his soul's passage into the hands of others. He died repentant. He asked that his treasures be offered to the poor ; money, books, gems were to be distributed amongst the churches of England and an especial sum must be given for the rebuilding of the churches he had demolished at Mantes. The rule of Normandy he gave, as was only right, to his eldest son Robert to be held as a fief to the King of the French ; to England, William dared appoint no ruler. He realised at this last awful moment that he had stolen the country, that it was not his to give to anyone ; he had been cruel to the conquered, he said, he had robbed them of their country and had killed them by hunger and the sword. He dared give England to no one save to God. At the same time, even amidst the remorse and terror of his last hours, he remained King enough to wish that his second living son, William Rufus, might succeed him. He dared not give the command, he could but plead that Lanfranc should offer Rufus the crown if he believed that Rufus should have it.

Rufus, who had always been a most loyal son, was at the bedside with the youngest boy, Henry. Robert was still a rebel and was far away. Henry the Clerk, the only son born in

England, now begged a heritage. " And what do you give me, my father ? " he asked. " Five thousand pounds of silver from my hoard," said William. " But of what use is a hoard to me," asked Henry, " if I have no place to dwell in ? " " Be patient, my son," said William, " and trust in the Lord and let your elders go before you."

He dictated a letter to Lanfranc, sealed it and gave it to Rufus with his blessing ; then kissing his son for the last time he bade him hurry to England. Rufus went at once. Henry soon followed his brother, leaving presumably to gather his legacy and hide it. William had now no kin beside him, and the lords and prelates begged him to release his prisoners. To this he agreed, all should be released except his half-brother Odo. For the safety of his people, Odo must remain in prison. Odo's brother, Robert of Mortain, begged of him to relent, the others added their entreaties, and against his better judgment, William gave way. He freed Odo on condition that those present gave their promises that he would behave himself.

It was on the morning of Thursday, September 9, 1087, that the dying King heard the tolling of the minster-bell. He asked why it sounded and those around him said that it was the hour of prime—6 a.m., the opening office of the day. William raised his hands and cried, " To my Lady Mary, the holy Mother of God, I commend myself that by her holy prayers she may reconcile me to her dear Son our Lord Jesus Christ."

And while he prayed, death came to the Conqueror.

WHEN they knew without doubt that their King was dead, the lords and prelates fled that chamber. They realised that with the lifting of the strong hand there would be anarchy ; the people, leaderless and unprotected, would be ravaged by outlaws and ambitious lords. They must all hide in their homes, they must lock their gates and conceal their treasures. With lords and prelates fled, the servants sacked the royal chamber, stealing even the bed and pushing the Conqueror's body to the floor. There, half-naked, he lay until a simple knight, Herlwin, offered to have the body washed, anointed and embalmed and carried to the monastery of St. Saviour's at Caen.

When William had been crowned at Westminster the buildings outside had been lit by his soldiers ; now as his body was carried into the monastery, a house caught fire and the flames ran quickly through the town. People deserted the dead King to rescue their goods. The monks alone continued, waving their censers, singing the office for the dead. Prelates from all parts of Normandy had hurried to be present and were in the monastery, Odo amongst them ; of William's sons, Robert was still in France, Rufus was in England, but Henry the Clerk was present, as was also the good Anselm.

When the office concluded, when the bishop called on all to pray for William's soul, asking their forgiveness for his sins, a knight called Asselin suddenly jumped up on a stone and cried, " This ground where you stand was the site of my father's house which the man for whom you pray, while he was but Count of Normandy, took forcibly, and in spite of law and justice, built this church upon it by his might. I therefore claim the land, I challenge it as mine before all men, and in the name of God I forbid that the body of the robber be covered with my earth or that he be buried within the bounds of my inheritance ! " The voice of the bishop had ceased at this outcry and those present agreed that Asselin spoke truth, that this was stolen ground. The body of him who as a baby had gripped the straw in his fists and who as a man had taken England, was about to be covered in earth he had filched from another. Hurriedly, with the agreement of Henry, sixty shillings were paid Asselin for the seven feet of grave-length.

Even after this, the corpse of William was not to be buried in peace. The careless workmen had made the stone coffin too small for his huge bulk, and as they tried to push it into the narrow space the skin burst. The stink was so ghastly that the remainder of the office was run through as quickly as possible and all fled the church.

Amidst a flaming city, in ground that was disputed as stolen, with his own body bursting at the last moment, the corpse of William the Conqueror went to its final rest.

II

KING WILLIAM THE SECOND

1087–1100

A BLASPHEMER, A DEBAUCHEE, A TYRANT, King William II of England—called Rufus—was nevertheless almost the perfect knight of chivalry. There has been a great deal of sentiment written about chivalry. The word itself means no more than a man-at-arms on horseback ; chroniclers never use it in any other sense and it seems that the modern abstract meaning did not appear until the eighteenth century. Yet taking that abstract meaning and applying it to the truth of the eleventh and twelfth centuries, we find that this chivalry was a vastly different thing from what the dreams of a William Morris or a Hewlett would make one believe. Our present conception dates, I suppose, mainly from the glorious *Morte Darthur*, a fifteenth-century work, but the ideal had been created long before then. Chaucer jeered merrily at it in his pretty-pretty *Tale of Sir Thopas* ; and in the *Knightes Tale* gave one of the most beautiful examples of it in literature. An ideal of some kind was essential in the world of might that was medievalism. In this world the Roman Church strove to carry on the task of the Roman Empire, it strove to retain what Rome had built—order on an insane earth. And it succeeded, it held back inevitable chaos, it kept man human.

Confused with the Church's teaching grew up the doctrine of what to-day we entitle " chivalry "—the doctrine of the perfect knight, courteous, generous, loyal to God, his lord and his lady, a man who never broke his oath or injured a conquered equal. It was an aristocratic code, it built one law for the gentleman and another for the simple. Save in his lack of reverence for God, William Rufus, the new King of England, was very nearly a perfect knight of chivalry.

He has been damned by history. Men of his own time deplored his reign, later writers have united to execrate him. It is true that he was not a good King but he had little time to be anything except à warrior, and he was forced to use his country

6   81

as a machine to produce money with which to arm soldiers. Those soldiers were cruel as were all mercenaries ; being without a sense of patriotism, it was natural that they should consider any land their prey. The soldiers of William behaved brutally, but against William himself it is difficult to find any specific act of cruelty. If we strip him of the numerous legends, take into consideration the fact that he was the enemy of churchmen and that churchmen usually wrote history, we might discover that William the Red King was not such a bestial lord as we have been told.

It is a simple matter to label Kings either *good* or *bad*, to place them neatly in their separate boxes, and then discuss history on an abstract constitutional plane. We are not interested in constitutional or political history, we are striving to understand the characters of the men who ruled this country. William II was not a good man, he was not a great King, but he was also not the beast he has been made to appear. I for one refuse to believe that men are either *good* or *bad* ; and there was a great deal of good in William Rufus.

IN appearance he was somewhat like his father but he was not so tall, being squat and with a prominent belly. The redness of his complexion earned him the nickname Rufus ; he had yellow-red hair and a speckled roving eye. Physically he was extremely powerful, capable of great exertion and courage : he believed it shame if another was armed before him or if another was first to give the challenge or to overthrow an enemy. He stuttered, spoke in sudden jerks, and was often quite witty—usually when explaining his own actions. His temper was great and swift, as was his merriment.

This is the exterior of the third son of the Conqueror, the man whom history has found cause to condemn almost without a hearing. There is a particular reason for this hatred—apart from William's contempt for religion—and the reason is one for which William cannot for a moment be held to account. In these days of psychological research, when the so-called base impulses of man have been studied with sympathy and not, as in the past, been taken as examples of deliberate bestiality, we should feel understanding for William. He was homosexual. This aroused horror at the time and it has aroused horror in nearly every historian since. Because of it, the Red King has been pushed aside as contemptible, as something too evil to be called human.

No woman's name was ever linked with his and the men of his court dressed in ultra-feminine garb which was spoken of with horror by the holy Anselm. They let their hair grow and curled it and bound it with ribbons like girls, no longer cropping it as in the days of the Conqueror, while the toes of their shoes sprouted until they seemed the fangs of scorpions, a fashion introduced from France. Not only did they grow their hair and dress foppishly, the men of the Red King imitated the mincing walk of ladies ; they spent their days in sleep, their nights in drinking, dicing and vain talk.

This is the black sin marked against Rufus; and there is another sin that has caused historians to loathe him. William had the utmost contempt for religion, but his blasphemies probably seem more horrifying to us than they did to the men of his time. The puritans were the first to give importance to the rule not to take the name of God in vain. In medieval times, nearly all men blasphemed. Chaucer notes that the Host of the *Canterbury Tales* suspects the Poor Parson of being a Lollard because he was revolted by oaths. It was " God this " and " God that " in the Middle Ages. God was a personal figure, He was painted to be seen vividly on the walls of churches ; and He was treated, if with great reverence, yet with a familiarity amazing to us. Medieval Christianity had much of the Roman religion sticking to it. God, Christ, and later the Virgin, were not abstract words, they were living people swayed by the jealousies, the desires, the revengeful habits and the compassions of human beings. Therefore William's blasphemies were a personal matter ; he defied God as he would defy an enemy on the other side of the lists, with a certain jovial comradeship about it. Rufus was a vain man, and this arrogance was his worst failing ; it dragged God down to his level instead of raising him towards heaven. Rufus felt that he was an opponent of whom the Lord should take heed. Being almost an equal, he had a perfect right to insult Him.

It was this gigantic arrogance that made William capable of converting Christians to Judaism. He had become to himself almost a god and he had a subtle and slightly diabolic sense of humour. He must have enjoyed the scandal he created. Having himself no trust in God's judgment, he liked tormenting the trust of others.

That he was blasphemous, abnormal sexually, a reckless soldier and an oppressor of his people cannot be denied. But his blasphemy certainly did not harm his kingdom, and his private affairs are not to be judged by historians whose own lives are probably not always blameless ; he fought because it was necessary to fight, because he was the son of his father, and he acted within the strictest rules of honour. On the charge of oppressing his people William must stand convicted. Yet he was certainly not the only King who behaved in the same way ; King Richard I had even less interest in his subjects, but many historians have treated him almost with reverence. William's taxation and his acceptance of bribes were usually in order to raise men to fight for him.

There is one point in his character that must be understood and which arouses a certain sympathy. William the Conqueror was a harsh father. If his sons—except for Robert—had not been strong-willed men the greatness of the father would have destroyed whatever initiative they possessed. With the utmost reluctance William had permitted the eldest a small show of power ; to the others he gave nothing. All his possessions, his huge wealth, his lands, must be held by himself alone. He could not bear the thought of sharing an inch of earth with anybody except his wife. If he had trained his sons to carry on his task, much that was difficult in their characters would very likely not have existed. Robert revolted during the Conqueror's life-time, Rufus was subdued until his death, his revolt came later.

As a matter of fact, Rufus was an extraordinarily dutiful son. There is no suggestion that he ever disobeyed the Conqueror for a moment ; it was at his father's side that he received his wound at Gerberoi. This submission without doubt weakened his character. He was capable of splendid action, he was a brave soldier, but always he lost interest in his struggles ; something seemed to snap suddenly inside him ; his energy would die, and restlessly he would turn his quick mind and nervous strength towards a different ambition. The strong will, if not broken, was at least bent by the harshness of the father. Yet he could stick to some things : he never forgot an injury ; he was determined, courageous, yet curiously weak ; at the moment of triumph his arm was often enfeebled by the inferiority thrust upon him by his father's greatness. And scornfully he would mock at holy things, raging within himself at his own weakness. It was this sense of inferiority that frustrated him, that swept his genius into futile bypaths, into revilings of God, into the prodigality with which he threw away the fortune his father had amassed.

Very true to William is the psycho-analytic rule to look towards the father if you would understand the son. With this humour, this strength, this ability to rule wisely, ran through William II that undercurrent of hatred for the things his father had treasured ; his bursts of irreligion were aimed more at the memory of the Conqueror—that symbol of God—than at God Himself. It was the father who destroyed Rufus, and unknowingly, it was the father at whom he raged and jeered.

To me there is something very tragic in this man. He never asked for sympathy, he would have scorned all pity. Ruthless and splendid, he ran his course and dazzled the men who watched. Of few Kings are so many tales recounted, few Kings so startled their contemporaries and drew from them either admiration or hatred. He could have been a great man. Deliberately, defying the memory of his father, he chose to become otherwise.

WHEN his father died, he must have been from twenty-seven to twenty-nine years of age. He was highly respected as a soldier, and we are told that his brilliance would already have raised him high in the people's eyes had it not been dimmed by the Conqueror's genius. The moment he had the note for Lanfranc he sped to Winchester to see if his father's treasure was safe ; being assured of this, he went to Canterbury and showed Lanfranc the letter. No time was wasted. He was crowned at Westminster on Sunday, September 26, 1087, seventeen days after the death of William I. It is said that he swore to Lanfranc to rule with justice, mercy and equity, to keep peace, to uphold the Church, and to obey Lanfranc in everything. These promises—except for the last—are too similar to the usual coronation oath to be taken as a sign that the archbishop doubted the good faith of his young King.

No one thought of returning to the old dynasties, of suggesting the claims of Eadgar the Ætheling, of Ulf the posthumous legitimate son of Harold, or of Wulnoth the brother of Harold. Rufus was the choice of the English. They were only too delighted to have a King of their own, one who was separate from Normandy. He solemnly carried out his father's wishes. He gave vast sums away as the Conqueror had demanded ; every church in England received its payment for masses, and in every county £100 was given to the poor.

The English might acclaim Rufus, but the Normans in England

were far from satisfied. Many of them possessed land in both countries and the last thing they wanted was a division of the empire into the old order of the kingdom of England and the duchy of Normandy. Their only hope of stopping the division was to set up one King over both lands, and the obvious man to choose was Robert, the eldest son. When told of Rufus's accession and urged to demand his rights, he had replied scornfully that even if he were as far away as Alexandria the English would not dare crown his brother and his brother would not dare accept the crown. Yet both events took place, and Robert, to his own amazement, was left in France. He had good friends in England, however, and chief amongst them was the man whom the Conqueror had realised was the most dangerous in his kingdom—that ambitious fighting prelate, Odo, Bishop of Bayeux. Odo detested Lanfranc, and he must have seen in the young Rufus signs of the iron will of the father. Besides, Rufus had ignored his claims to be given first place in the council and had chosen instead William of St. Carilef, Bishop of Durham.

The outbreak of the plot seems to have been caused by this bishop. Rufus was never the type to remain idle amongst plotters and he probably knew the treason meditated. The Bishop of Durham became his first victim. Rufus outlawed him on the excuse of his leaving the court without leave. Shortly afterwards the conspirators crept from their burrows and strode with fire and sword into the open. In all parts of England they bobbed up, Normans prepared to resist separation from Normandy. For his army, Rufus had to rely mainly upon the English. This civil war became almost a second battle of the Conquest, the English against the Norman, the English prepared to resist any further invasion from oversea.

Rufus sent forth a written declaration, calling himself King of the English, and it is more than probable that he had it inscribed in the Anglo-Saxon tongue. He swore that the wrongs committed in the reign of William the Elder would be redressed in the reign of William the Younger, he would make the best laws the country had ever known, he would be another Eadward or Cnut or Ælfred, no longer would taxation be heavy, no longer would lands be seized for royal hunting. . . . Many and reckless were the promises he made the English ; but, as himself remarked afterwards to Lanfranc, a man can't keep all his promises.

Even if the people did not believe everything he said, Rufus was at least an unknown quantity ; too well they knew the injustice and cruelty of Odo, of Rufus they knew as yet nothing. The troops gathered in London were only too eager to revenge themselves on the Normans even if they were to be led by a Norman. And Rufus had another most powerful ally in the Church. Durham was the only English prelate to join the traitors, Lanfranc and those of his order stood firmly behind the King.

Against Odo, Rufus concentrated all his strength and skill. With Odo in his hands, the conspiracy would collapse. And the centre of Odo's territory was Rochester. Here seemed the obvious point of attack, but Rufus was too good a general to fight without having cleared danger from his rear. Before besieging Rochester, he must take Tunbridge, and he stormed and captured the castle. Then he moved direct on to Rochester only to learn that Odo was lurking in Pevensey ; he changed his course at once and was soon besieging the castle there. This was a harder task than Tunbridge and for six weeks Odo held out. During those six weeks a Norman fleet sailed to the coast but was beaten back. Robert had foolishly remained in Normandy : he sent a leaderless host that was not even permitted to land.

After this failure of the relief, with starvation coming inevitably upon them, the besieged at Pevensey were forced to surrender. We do not know what terms Rufus granted the others, but we do know that he forgave Odo on condition that he left England for ever and arranged for Rochester to be delivered without fighting. Being a man of his word in all matters of chivalry, he never doubted Odo's good faith. He sent his uncle ahead with a small guard and himself followed leisurely, with the result that when Odo appeared before Rochester to plead with the defenders, the defenders sallied out and carried him back inside their walls. This was against the code of chivalry in which Rufus had such belief. The word of a knight given to a knight should have been surety against any bad faith ; perhaps he had forgotten, as his father had not forgotten, that Odo could be two people at will : he might give his oath as Earl of Kent, then quite as freely break it when he changed into the Bishop of Bayeux.

Rufus sent forth a proclamation calling the English to his standard. He revived the ancient form and swore that all who did not come to him were *nithings*. The threat of that word was enough to make any Englishman take up his sword at once. Before long, Rufus had a mighty army girdling the walls of

Rochester. The besieged had no hope of relief, both Pevensey and Tunbridge were in the hands of the King, Robert's fleet had been driven back. Starvation came, followed by a plague of flies. Again Odo had to beg for terms. Yet he was still insolent. He and the others promised to deliver the city if Rufus would reinstate them in their old honours. This was too much for Rufus, he cried that he would grant no terms, he could take the castle when he willed and he would hang all the traitors on gibbets when he caught them. His comrades pleaded with him to restrain his fury ; as the son of his father, they said, he must show mercy, that noblest attribute of a conqueror. Rufus answered that he feared that by being merciful he might also be unjust ; by sparing thieves and liars he might injure the peace of the innocent. In reply it was argued that Odo was his uncle, his father's half-brother and comrade-in-arms, he was also a bishop beyond lay justice ; Rufus had shown, they said, how greatly he outshone his enemies in power, wealth and valour, let him show also how he surpassed them in mercy and greatness of soul. Always swayed by chivalry, eager to act the noble part, Rufus gave his word that the garrison would not be hurt if it came forth with arms and horses, but all must leave the realm. Odo pleaded for one last favour. Would his nephew forbid the playing of trumpets when he rode forth ? Rufus denied him this, so that when Odo at last crept from the castle the trumpets brayed at him and the soldiers yelled contemptuously, " Halters ! bring halters ! hang up the traitor bishop and his friends on the gallows ! " They implored Rufus to take revenge, saying, " Mighty King of the English, let not the stirrer up of all evil go away unharmed. The lying murderer whose craft and cruelty have taken away the lives of thousands of men should not live any longer ! " But Rufus had given his knightly word, from that he would not shift. Odo left England for ever, without the justice he deserved.

THE rebellion was now at an end and an exchange of lands took place. The estates of some of the traitors were given to those who had been loyal ; many of the traitors, however, were presumably allowed to keep their old rank and places of honour. Rufus's reckless prodigality stretched to giving away what belonged to others. Either now or later he presented a comrade with the property of his brother Henry, some of the estates of Brihtric which Matilda had bequeathed to her youngest son.

Henry, being a careful rather miserly man, decided to claim his heritage.

These three brothers were different in character yet somehow one feels a peculiar similarity between them. Robert, being the eldest,· had suffered more than the others from the weight of his father's greatness and it had destroyed all initiative in him. He was a brave man who nevertheless preferred to let God settle matters rather than himself take action. It is more than probable that if he had led his own troops and had joined Odo in ·the rebellion, he would have succeeded in defeating Rufus. But he was incapable of sustained effort. Under his careless rule, Normandy degenerated into anarchy. He was too good a fellow, too amiable, to bear resentment or to seek revenge. Debauchery, easy living, contented him except when occasional outrageous insults stirred him to a moment's fury. The Conqueror had destroyed whatever will poor Robert ever had.

We have seen what effect the Conqueror had upon his third son, William Rufus. While not utterly breaking him, he had nevertheless managed to soften a great deal of Rufus's strength. His effect on the youngest boy, Henry, was slight. He bequeathed to him his cunning but not his genius. Henry was a scholar, a glorified money-lender, a lawyer more than a soldier, and a debauchee.

In physical appearance, all three were alike, being dumpy men.

ROBERT was always pressed for money. He tried to borrow from Henry, but Henry was cautious and refused to lend without security. Robert then offered to give the Côtentin and Avranchin in exchange for £3000. Henry closed with this at once and then decided to visit England to claim his mother's estates. There is a certain confusion about these estates. Presumably Rufus either gave them back to Henry or promised to give them back and later stole them again ; there was no quarrel, at any rate, as there certainly would have been if Rufus had refused his brother at this point. Already Henry was automatically imitating his father and acquiring lands ; he did not as yet try to steal by force, he bought what he needed and was entitled count, possessing—through his exchange with Robert—quite a slice of territory which he governed wisely.

When Henry went back to his possessions he was captured even before he could leave his ship. That rascal Odo now had his talons into Robert and was whispering of meditated treachery, of a union between Rufus and Henry against Normandy. Henry was fettered, imprisoned, and placed in the charge of Odo. Before long, all Normandy was alight with civil war. Odo never could resist meddling and in the happy-go-lucky duke he had found the ideal tool. He lectured him gravely before his nobles, speaking of his misgovernment, pointing out how his border fortresses were in the hands of rebels and demanding that Robert march against them, particularly against Earl Roger of Bellême. The son of this Roger was a prisoner of Robert's, having been captured with Henry, and with drawn sword the father was fighting for his son's release. There was not only Bellême to destroy, insisted Odo, but Robert must fight to hold Maine, which was slipping from him. After the Conqueror's death, the Angevin Count Fulk had turned towards Maine and the only method Robert could devise of keeping his lands was to swear fealty to Fulk.

As Rufus is our main problem we must ignore Robert's battles to maintain his duchy. It is sufficient to state that he was successful and that eventually Henry was liberated. Henry returned to the Côtentin, muzzling his fury, and his first acts were to strengthen his castles, to bribe adherents and to purchase mercenaries. He was too cautious to begin a war ; he had learned the golden rule of his father, that by waiting all riches flutter to the spider.

LANFRANC died on May 24, 1089, and with his death a strong hand was lifted from the passions of King William. Lanfranc had become to Rufus the symbol of his father ; he may never have liked the stern prelate but he respected and feared him. From now on, the Red King stood alone, parental authority shed from him. Although he never exactly defied the Church, save in his later quarrel with Anselm, he no longer showed any reverence for it. His father had introduced the Jews into England and Rufus found them valuable. They stored the money for him to borrow. Christians were forbidden by the Church to be usurers, therefore the trade fell to the Jews, who demanded what rates of interest they liked, and often these rates were so gigantic that the debtors rose and murdered the usurers, as in the massacre of York of 1189. The popular conception of the medieval Jew cringing before the hectoring Christian is certainly not borne out by history. The Jew, with his terrific arrogance, never did—and undoubtedly still doesn't—feel anything but contempt for the Gentile. When his opportunity came he treated Christians with a scorn that drove the crude medieval man into a fury that only blood could satisfy. The Jews asked for many of the pogroms by their infuriating air of superiority and by the crippling interest they demanded ; they built splendid homes and kept them garrisoned against the mob, and often they could not resist jeering openly at the Christian faith. Never did they attempt to show deference to the beliefs of others, they secretly carried on thier own religion, and the simple medieval man began to conceive that the most diabolic acts of witchcraft were going on behind locked doors.

Under Rufus, the Jew in England had a merry time because Rufus, being reckless with largesse, was always in need of money. Besides, his strange humour delighted in tormenting Christians by fondling the Christians' enemy. He did not fondle the Jew unless the Jew could be useful to him ; his tolerance was a reaction from his hatred of God the Father. He once forced the bishops of England to argue with the Jewish rabbis, promising to take whichever religion won the contest. Later in his reign, when the Jews were troubled by the amount of renegades, he promised, on the gift of a large sum, to entice the converts back to the old faith, and by threatening and bullying he usually managed to carry out his bargain. We have one anecdote about a failure. A certain Jew was baptized and called himself by the name of Stephen ; his father begged the King's help and struck a bargain of sixty silver marks in return for which Rufus agreed to drive the lad back to Judaism. When argued with, Stephen replied that surely his King was jesting ; Rufus lost his temper and threatened to tear out the boy's eyes. All failed, arguments and hectoring, Stephen remained Christian, and naturally the father refused to pay. Rufus insisted that he had done his best and the pair wrangled until at last it was settled that half the sum should be paid.

Whether such tales be true is unimportant. They show that Rufus was accepted as the friend of the Jews, than which nothing more diabolic could be named against a medieval man. Yet most peculiarly he was never excommunicated. although he scorned God openly. After a trial by ordeal, when some deer-stealers underwent the ordeal of hot iron and when their hands were unbandaged after three days and were found to be un-scarred, Rufus cried that either God did not know the deeds

of men, or else He weighed them in an unfair balance. On
another occasion he swore that neither St. Peter nor any other
saint had the ear of God, and that he would call on none of them.

Now that Lanfranc was dead, Rufus no longer attempted to
restrain his contempt for religion. And, noting the feeble
grip of Robert in Normandy, he turned his restless eyes towards
his father's duchy. All his life, Rufus was to be spurred on by the
lust to recover what his father had held, and this ambition
pricked him until he was not satisfied unless he could conquer
France as well as Normandy and Maine.

The wars of other Kings, of Edward III, of Henry V, have
been accepted by most historians as noble efforts ; even the
senseless fighting of Richard I is coloured with glamour. Yet the
wars of Rufus have often been passed over hurriedly as a stain
on English history. Yet Rufus was only carrying on what his
father had planned. The wars of later Kings were commonly
deliberate acts of foreign aggression ; Rufus was himself a Norman,
and he was merely trying to hold his own people, to take them
from the misrule of his brother and to press upwards into France.
Unlike Richard I, he did not forget England. It is at this period
that the new title of King of England was creeping into vogue,
and it fits Rufus to perfection. He may not have deserved the
old title of King of the English, but definitely he was King of
England. England remained his base, he had men of England
fighting under his standard. Of the great empire he strove
strenuously to build, London was to be the centre. Even his
father had been more Duke of Normandy than King of England ; Rufus thought first of England and of Europe
afterwards.

We must strip him of the rancour of historians, we must
ignore his sexual life and his blasphemies ; they are nothing
whatever to do with him as King and soldier. As a King he was
an oppressor, but as a soldier he was often superb. Before detail-
ing the campaigns, perhaps it would be best if we examined these
oppressions of Rufus. In the first place, he broke his oath ; he
did not carry out the promises made when gathering an army to
fight the rebels. They would have been almost impossible to
carry out, and any man, pressed dangerously, would promise
the world if he might triumph. That he was reckless with money,
is another charge—he dragged gold from the people and threw it
away. We have many examples of this. It was said that the

merchant could ask any price for his goods and that the soldier could demand any pay for his services. Rufus once angrily refused a pair of boots because they had cost only three shillings—the price of an ox—but was satisfied when his chamberlain gave him instead a pair no better than the first which he was told cost a mark—13*s*. 4*d*. For treasurer he had a rogue named Randolph Flambard, an expert at hooking money, who apparently packed the courts with his hirelings. There was certainly oppression on the land. " In his days," moans the chronicler, " ilk right fell and ilk unright for God and for world up-rose." It was Flambard who suggested to the King the cunning trick of leaving bishoprics vacant as long as possible so that the crown could draw the revenues, with the result that many parts of England had no spiritual pastors, and when the offices were at last sold, not the worthiest but the wealthiest men clambered into power.

Against Rufus himself we do not find any actual examples of deliberate cruelty, but the mercenaries he was forced to employ were given entire freedom, for which he must take the blame. They " snatched the very morsel from people's mouths " ; during a progress through England they took what homes they liked and sold or wasted what they could not use ; they insulted their hosts, ravished the women and washed their horses' legs in wine. His reign was remembered as one of torment ; he strengthened the forest laws of his father yet he reprieved many a condemned criminal who had money enough to bribe justice.

All these sins must stand recorded against Rufus. He had a demon in him, the demon of chivalry that could not understand that simple people were more worthy of love than wolves or cattle. In the code of chivalry, knights and ladies alone were respected ; others could be tortured, used, or killed. People of simple birth were to the knight somewhat as heretics were to the Church, with this difference—the Church hated and burnt the heretics, the knight considered himself too strong and perfect to bother even to notice the simple.

IT is this oppression that damns William's reign, an oppression not of conscious cruelty but of sheer carelessness, of a lack of interest in anything outside his own ambitions. But we must not forget that when he died his kingdom was great, he was lord from Scotland to the Maine, he had made England a power in Europe, he had stretched its borders into Scotland and into Wales.

The money wrung from the people and flung into the hands of merchants, Jews and soldiers, was not entirely wasted. Rufus built a wall around his father's Tower of London, he placed a bridge across the Thames and erected the new Hall at Westminster.

In the Easter witanagemót of 1090 William spoke of his brother's treason, of how Robert had stirred up rebellion ; this alone, he said, would not force him into battle, but Robert had proved himself incapable of ruling justly. Normandy was in chaos, it needed a strong grip to bind it together as in the days of his father. He called upon all those who held fiefs in Normandy to follow and rescue the duchy. Yet of his own will he could not declare war, the assembly must decide. The assembly decided at once, war was declared. Yet Rufus waited a year before crossing the Channel, he wanted the Normans themselves to become so weary of Robert's rule that they would accept the King of England for overlord. His treasury was full, and those he could not cajole, he could buy. Gradually his intrigues spread through the duchy, they seeped into Rouen itself, castle after castle becoming his in spirit if not in fact. The wealthiest man in Rouen was one Conan ; he agreed to sell his city to Rufus, being tired of the rule of his " drowsy lord," and a day was fixed on which Rouen would declare for the English King.

Robert called on his brother Henry to help him against a common enemy. We cannot suspect Henry of any affection for Robert ; he sided with him because he feared that the precedent of Rouen might affect his own lands, and besides, his ambitions were strong. If Robert was pushed out of his duchy, Henry would have no hope against the strength of Rufus of expanding, of stealing more land from Robert. He went to his brother, to stand beside him at this danger-point.

With disaffection in the city, with his subjects openly pledging themselves to desert him, Robert was besieged inside his own walls. Henry had the cooler mind and he probably distrusted Robert's recklessness. He stayed in the tower with his brother while comrades fought their way into the city. Immediately there was confusion, the citizens who had boasted of betraying their duke were struck with terror now that the duke's friends were amongst them, slaughtering, burning. Conan was captured. Henry took him to the top of the tower and bade him gaze upon the splendid landscape. Detail by detail, he pointed out the charms of scenery, tormenting the wretched traitor. From the landscape he turned his prey towards the city and bade him look on that, on the city he would have stolen. In terror, Conan begged his life, he offered everything, his own riches, his friends' riches, if Henry would spare him. But there was no mercy in Henry. " By the soul of my mother," he cried, " there'll be no ransom for the traitor but rather a quickening towards the death he deserves ! " If his life was to be robbed from him, at least, implored Conan, give him time to save his soul, to be houselled. But even that solace Henry would not permit. With his own hands he lifted Conan up and hurled him down; Conan died, it was said, before he reached the ground.

By quick action Henry had saved Rouen, by a merciless vengeance he had warned others of their fate if they rebelled. Robert, however, was not vindictive, he would have pardoned the citizens if his allies had let him : this they refused, but they submitted enough to his weakness not to maim or kill their captives ; they enslaved them instead.

For a moment the machinations of Rufus were defeated, but Normandy was by no means at peace under Robert. Rufus decided himself to lead his army ; and almost immediately on landing, men ran to serve beneath his standard. Those who visited his camp at Eu swore that the King of the English was far richer and more generous than any of their own princes. Robert, almost completely deserted, could not fight, he could only beg for terms, and a treaty was signed at Caen in 1091. He surrendered to his brother all those places that had already declared for him, " a great part of Normandy " pressing down on Rouen from north and south ; he also agreed to expel not only the Ætheling Eadgar from Normandy but also his late ally Henry from the Côtentin and to share Henry's possessions with Rufus ; in return, Rufus guaranteed Robert's power in Normandy and Maine and promised to help him recover Maine. And it was agreed that if either Rufus or Robert died without lawful issue, the survivor should succeed to both dominions.

They now turned against Henry who was quite ready for them ; his lords, however, deserted his standard before the great English force, and he found himself practically alone, stranded on the island fortress in the Bay of St. Michael. Only at high tide could this be called an island, at low tide it stood amongst sands, those treacherous sands from which Harold had once rescued the men of the Conqueror. Rufus and Robert did not invade the island by ships. They stayed on the mainland to starve Henry out. One day Rufus, on a horse recently bought for fifteen marks silver, gallantly charged the enemy. Presumably he was alone and reckless in the true chivalric fashion. His horse was killed and Rufus was dragged to the ground, almost to the enemy lines. " Hold, rascal," he shouted at a man about to strike, " I am the King of England ! " The man was so amazed that he drew back, and Henry's soldiers actually gave Rufus a fresh horse ; in full mail, he sprang into the saddle. " Who un-horsed me ? " he asked. " I," said the man, " I who took you not for a King but for a knight." Pleased with the brave retort, Rufus cried, " By the face of Lucca[1] you shall be mine, your name shall be written in my book, and you shall receive the reward of good service."

This tale throws an extraordinary sidelight on medieval warfare. Henry's men had Rufus at their mercy, on foot and alone, yet they not only gave him a horse but apologised for daring to harm him. The tale is repeated as an example of Rufus's magnanimity ; the chronicler takes it for granted that a knight would not possibly injure a King, he is only surprised into admiration because Rufus forgave the man who struck him, and then took him into his service. It is an amazing scene, if it be true, and one cannot help respecting Rufus ; alone he had charged the army, and when unhorsed he had not given a wink of fear, he had taken immediate command of the situation, becom-ing instantly the King.

He was never a man to show fear and he was always quick-witted. During this same siege, when his saddle-girth broke in the midst of a battle, he seized the saddle and fought his way out, saying to those who laughed, " By the holy face of Lucca, one must be able to hold one's own. It would be shame to lose what one can defend. The Bretons would have bragged had they taken my saddle ! "

We have a third story of this siege, and one that does not show him in the same heroic light. It reveals the darker side of chivalry. Henry had meat enough but little water. He begged permission to have his casks refilled, reminding his brothers that though they might use force, they had no right to deprive him of

[1] His favourite oath. It does not refer to St. Luke but apparently to the image of Christ on the wooden cross which Nicodemus is alleged to have made after the crucifixion.

those gifts of providence free to all human beings. Robert ordered the sentinels to let the water-carriers pass. When Rufus jeered at him for this, he answered, " Shall we let our brother die of thirst ? Where shall we find another if we lose him ? " " A fit one you to conduct war ! " laughed Rufus. " How shall we conquer if we indulge our foes with meat and drink ? "

The line between the magnanimity of pardoning the knight who dared strike him and the cruelty of permitting his brother to die of thirst is not so broad as might be supposed. Both were typical of chivalry. On his death-bed, Richard I was to forgive the archer who killed him because he had spoken bravely and had shown no fear, yet this same Richard could butcher innocent prisoners ; the Black Prince pardoned the French knights who fought against him, but he slaughtered the helpless women and children at Limoges when they implored mercy. There were these two sides to the perfect knight, the black and the white, no greys between. When the Italian Geoffrey Malaterra writes at about 1100 of the Normans swarming in the south, he sums them up as being " evenly balanced between greed and avarice." The point of this jeer lies in the fact that an even balance was not a perfect balance, but was one veering up and down. The perfect knight veered up and down, he who could commune with God must be able to grovel in the mud. When Rufus forgave the knight for not killing him, he was behaving in a chivalric manner, acting the part of magnanimity ; when he refused his brother drink, he was also acting chivalrously, he was taking advantage of the fortunes of war. If Henry had appealed to him according to the code, if he had stood unarmed in front of him, Rufus would have behaved magnanimously ; instead of that, Henry was foolish enough to appeal to the affections and to humanity. There was none of that in war, there was only honour and ruthlessness.

AFTER fifteen days of thirst, Henry gave in. He offered to surrender if promised a free passage for himself and troops. To this Rufus agreed ; then apparently, he and Robert cut up Henry's land between them as had been arranged.

Shortly afterwards Rufus returned to England. We are not surprised to find Robert going with him as his guest, but our first feeling is one of amazement when we discover Henry going as well. But we are only amazed because instinctively we judge these men by our modern standards. As medieval knights who

7

had fought honourably together there was not the least reason why they should feel rancour. Each would be on the alert to cheat or—if need be—even kill the others ; that would not disturb their affections. As brothers they were probably happy together ; but being also great lords they must sometimes fight. The two points should not be confused. The enemy of one day in the Middle Ages was very often the beloved comrade of the next.

It was not long before Rufus and Robert quarrelled again. It seems that Rufus had not acted up to the promises given in the treaty of Caen. Here, once more, we find that dividing-line of chivalry. When he acted as a knight, Rufus never broke his word ; as King, he believed himself to have every justification to say one thing and mean another. Before Christmas 1091, Robert left England and took Eadgar, the grandson of Eadmund Ironside, with him. Henry probably went at the same time ; he made for the Vexin, that dividing land between France and Normandy. Here he lived quietly with only a few friends and servants, for a time. Robert returned with Eadgar to his own duchy of Normandy.

ANOTHER character must now step upon the stage, a character strange in contrast to the violent blasphemous Red King. This is the kindly modest Anselm, Prior of Bec, the lover of animals. His father had been a Lombard, his mother a Burgundian, and from an early age Anselm had revealed a deep love of letters ; in youth it seems that he abandoned himself to lively joys, but his pious mother restrained him and set him on the road towards holiness. When she died, Anselm determined to leave his tyrannical father, and for three years he wandered through Burgundy and France, undecided whether or not to take shelter at Bec. He frankly tells us that what made him at first avoid Bec was the fear that the learning of Lanfranc might overshadow his own merits. This pride he conquered, and like Lanfranc, whose pupil he became, he attained at Bec the position of prior. Anselm was in every way a good man, one who was never distracted from his beliefs by worldly affairs. Before everything he placed his Church ; in this he was different from his master : Lanfranc was more statesman than churchman, Anselm was wholly churchman.

Lanfranc had been dead for three years and during that time the archbishopric of Canterbury had remained vacant and its lands had been farmed out to the highest bidder. When invited by a friend to England, Anselm refused, suspecting he might be nominated to the vacancy ; he would not go until his monks at Bec commanded him to inquire into the heavy taxation of their English property. With reluctance, fearing the worst, Anselm sailed for the fourth time to England.

Rufus received him kindlily. He rose from his seat, met the prior at the door, gave him the kiss of peace, and conducted him to a chair. Anselm asked that all save himself and the King withdraw, and when they were alone together he spoke plainly to Rufus. We have no knowledge of the words he used, but they are not difficult to imagine. And William's good humour gave him patience to bear the lecture with meekness and to part amiably with the good prior. That he bore no malice is shown by the fact that shortly afterwards he stopped Anselm from leaving England, evidently weighing the question of appointing him to the archbishopric of Canterbury. Anselm's election was the wish of the people, but Rufus did not want to surrender so valuable a property. When the witan gathered at Christmas 1092-3, it humbly petitioned Rufus to allow prayers to be said in every church towards a future appointment to Canterbury. " Pray as you will," said Rufus, " I shall do as I think right, no man's prayers will do anything to shake my will." Nevertheless the prayers were given and were, in fact, drawn up by Anselm himself. But Rufus would not surrender the wealthy see. When an over-bold courtier hinted that Anselm was a man who loved only God and desired nothing from this world, Rufus retorted, " Not the archbishopric of Canterbury ? " The courtier answered that this was the very last thing Anselm desired. " Indeed ! " scoffed Rufus, " I well know that if Anselm thought he had the faintest chance of getting Canterbury he would rush to embrace me, clapping hands and feet for joy," and he added jovially, " By the face of Lucca, he and every other man who seeks the archbishopric may this time give way to me, for I will be archbishop myself ! " The jest so amused him that he kept on repeating it. He would probably have continued repeating it until the end of his reign if he had not been struck with sickness.

Even Rufus's bold spirit quailed when he saw death close. In his awful terror he promised anything—perhaps recalling his own words that a man can't keep all his promises ; he agreed to whatever Anselm suggested, he swore to mend his ways, to rule his kingdom mildly and justly. A proclamation was sent to the people embodying all these promises : Rufus would keep good laws, would heed the right, would examine wrongs, he would hold no vacant benefices, he would free all prisoners . . . he would, in fact, do anything and everything if only God would make him well.

Even more valuable than these vague promises was Rufus's agreement to make the Prior of Bec Archbishop of Canterbury. He sat up in bed and pointed at Anselm. " I choose this holy man Anselm," he said. The excitement was almost lunatic. Anselm, who at his age—he was sixty—shrank from so great a post, himself wrote amusingly to Bec that " whether they were madmen dragging a sane man or sane men dragging a madman might well be doubted." He implored the bishops to leave him in peace. They would not listen ; they dragged him forcibly to the King's bed to take the staff, they held out his arm but the old man kept his fingers so tightly clenched that when they were squeezed open he screamed with the pain.

RUFUS got well. With the shedding of sickness he shed his repentance. He felt that God had cheated him into weakness of will by weakening his body ; to Rufus, it appeared that God had acted the part of traitor. " The Lord will get no good of me," he said, " for the ill He sent me." He quarrelled with Anselm, being determined to retain some of the Canterbury lands and Anselm being equally determined not to give them up. When this squabble was concluded, Rufus having to back down, he started another squabble. He was about to invade Normandy again, and demanded money from Anselm. This smacked of simony to the good archbishop, but his friends insisted that he must pay something. He offered £500. Rufus rejected the sum with scorn, demanding £1000. " My lord," replied Anselm, " do not refuse the offering of your archbishop. If it be his first gift it will not be his last gift to you. Better to take a little of freewill than much under slavery." Rufus was tired of arguing. " Keep your money and your jaw to yourself," he cried, " I have enough of my own. Get you gone."

Rufus had little time to trouble about Anselm. The lust for conquest was working in him and he was determined to return to Normandy. Robert was demanding that he keep to the oath sworn between them at Caen ; if Rufus failed in this he was, said Robert, false and forsworn. Rufus's retort was a declaration of war and the gathering of men and supplies for a second invasion of Normandy. By February 1094 he was at Hastings with his army and here he again quarrelled with Anselm. The archbishop had recently preached a virulent sermon against the vices and fashions of the court and he refused his blessing and the Easter sprinkling of ashes on the head of any man who wore his hair long and beribboned in girlish fashion. Rufus had no objection to the sermon, but Anselm's sense of duty drove him to arguing personally with the King on the subject ; he asked permission to hold episcopal synods. " I will see to the matter when I think good," answered Rufus, " I will act, not at your pleasure, but at my own. And pray, when you have got your synod, what will you talk about in it ? " Anselm told him bluntly—the reformation of the terrible sins in England. " And what may come out of this for you ? " jeered Rufus. " For me, nothing," replied Anselm, " for you and for God I hope much." The subject was brushed aside, and Anselm argued about a second question : he wanted the vacancies in the Church filled. This meant the King having to surrender one of his main sources of revenue, and Rufus began to lose his temper. " Are not the abbeys mine ? " he cried. " Tush, you do as you like with your manors, shall I not do as I like with my abbeys ? " Anselm strove to argue, but Rufus cried : " Understand that your words offend me. Your predecessor would never have dared speak to my father as you have spoken to me. Rest assured I will do nothing for you."

Anselm departed humbly and a little afraid ; he wrote asking to be taken back into favour and offering to mend any offence he might have committed. Rufus replied that Anselm had not offended him but he refused to take him back into favour, " because," he said unanswerably, " I don't see why I should." The archbishop's friends suggested that Rufus probably wanted money, but the saintly Anselm abhorred the very thought of bribes, besides, he would not tax his tenants any further. They had been stripped to the skins, he said, must he now flay them alive ? When Rufus was told of this remark, he said that yesterday he had hated Anselm, that to-day he hated him, and that he to-morrow would hate him even more, and so on, every other day ; never would he consider Anselm father or archbishop ; he cursed his blessings and prayers. Eadmer, Anselm's friend and biographer, writes that after this " we departed from the court with speed and left him to his will."

THE second invasion of Normandy was very brief. Rufus met Robert, but neither would come to a decision ; they asked the guarantors of the treaty to give a verdict and their verdict went against Rufus. When Rufus refused to agree to their ruling, Robert called for help from his overlord, Philip of France, but Rufus was quick enough to bribe Philip to remain neutral and himself then called on Henry for aid.

Before his brother could join him, Rufus had hurried back to his own kingdom, leaving the command to Henry. Anselm was becoming a nuisance again. He could not consider himself truly archbishop, he insisted, unless he followed the usual tradition and went to Rome to receive the pallium—the woollen vestment of metropolitans, symbol of papal confirmation—from the hands of the Pope. The difficulty was that there were three Popes at the time and Rufus had never bothered to recognise any one of them ; therefore when Anselm asked permission to receive the pallium from the Pope, Rufus asked, " Which Pope ? " " From Urban," answered Anselm, for Urban was the accepted candidate in Italy and Gaul. Rufus retorted that he did not accept Urban, obviously speaking from a moment's spite against the archbishop ; he probably wished to force him to resign. Councils were held, the question was argued and re-argued until the cunning Rufus decided to outwit his enemy. He would himself secretly approach Urban and ask for the pallium ; with this in his hands, he could give it to any man he liked, and that man was not going to be Anselm. His trick worked splendidly at first. The pallium arrived in England, and immediately that Rufus possessed it, he publicly proclaimed Urban as Pope and then told the legate to depose Anselm, adding gold to his arguments. But the legate could not be bribed. Rufus was beaten by his own cunning ; he made a last effort to gain something and asked Anselm to pay for the cost of bringing the pallium from Rome. Anselm refused. On every side the Red King was defeated ; he had proclaimed himself a man of the Pope, he had taken the trouble to bring the pallium to England, and now his enemy was more powerful than ever. Himself had gained nothing but a still worse reputation out of the whole affair.

MEANWHILE there was rebellion in England and fighting in Wales. The rebellion was crushed at last, and its main importance to us lies in the change we find in Rufus's character. Before, after Odo's conspiracy, he had treated the conquered almost with kindness ; this time his vengeance was particularly brutal. His prisoners were mutilated and executed. The whole campaign gives little credit to Rufus, there was nothing heroic in it. Altogether, the conspiracy was a queer affair, the work of a few dissatisfied nobles without the backing of the people ; much as they may have detested Rufus the people remained loyal. And Rufus for once was revengeful. He refused gigantic bribes for the life of one of the traitors. Chivalrous sentiments did not stir him now, he probably feared that he was losing the love of England and thought to strike terror into any possible future conspirators.

THEN came the crusades. Alexis, Emperor of Constantinople, sent his appeal into the Christian world for help against the infidel, and Pope Urban took up the cry. The empire of Constantinople was mutilated, he cried ; men must come to the rescue of the Holy Land. Robert, weary of his quarrels with Rufus, decided to adventure to the East, but he needed money. He offered to pledge Normandy with Rufus for 10,000 marks. This was too splendid an offer to ignore, it was almost throwing Normandy away. Yet it was a vast sum to raise in a hurry and Rufus had to resort to the most cruel and unjust taxation. Raised the money was at last, and Normandy was pawned to him for three years.

Another crusader, besides Robert, rode out of William's life. This was Odo, Bishop of Bayeux, and also he rides out of English history. He died at Palermo in February 1097. A third crusader was the Ætheling Eadgar, another one of Rufus's troubles. He followed Robert, with whom he was very friendly.

RUFUS appeared to be getting rid of all his troubles, but Anselm remained. And Rufus's hatred of Anselm seemed uncontrollable. He now complained that the contingent sent by the archbishop to the Welsh wars had been worse than useless ; so badly equipped were the knights that instead of owing Anselm thanks, Rufus owed him the opposite. We do not know if the complaint was justified ; even if it were, even if these knights were useless, the archbishop can scarcely be blamed, he surely could not be expected to examine the harness and ability of his military tenants ? Rufus demanded that the archbishop attend his court for judgment.

Already Anselm was wearying of England, of his continual

friction with the King ; his was not the character for such an important post ; he was a scholar who should never have meddled with lay affairs, and himself was aware of it. There was nothing of the Lanfranc or Thomas Becket in him. He was a tired old man, a dreamer who loved all living creatures, who yearned only for communion with God and nature, and who desired merely to obey the Church in everything. At this last attack from Rufus he pleaded for permission to leave England. He wanted to throw aside his burden, and we cannot blame him for it. The people, however, did blame him. In his request many of them saw cowardice, desertion. When he had stood up against the King on the question of the pallium, England had stood behind him ; this time he was practically alone. Rufus jeered at his messengers. " Certainly not," he answered. " Anselm is not such a sinner as to need apostolic absolution. If he talks about advice, he is better fitted to counsel the Pope than the Pope to counsel him."

The trouble about the contingent was apparently dropped, Rufus probably being afraid of driving Anselm out of the country. He did not want the world to know that so saintly a man could leave him in despair and rage. Anselm, however, was persistent. The idea of going to Rome had become an obsession. At last, his patience dying, Rufus threatened that if he left England his archbishopric would be seized. At this outburst some of the assembly cheered the King, others cheered the archbishop.

The trouble dragged wearily. Rufus tried to be subtle, he strove to put Anselm in the wrong, he said that the archbishop had worried him, embittered him, tormented him with complaints ; he said that Anselm had not kept his promises, for he had sworn to obey the laws and customs of the realm and now he threatened to go to Rome without permission. When informed of this message, Anselm went and sat beside the King and began to argue. The assembly broke into an uproar, and at last Rufus shouted, " This is a mere sermon ! " After a few further words Anselm left and sat outside the chamber. A messenger came telling him to leave England but to take with him nothing that belonged to the King. " So be it," said Anselm. " Horses I have, also clothes and goods, which some perhaps might say were the King's. But if I have to go naked and on foot, I will yet go." After his first burst of petulance, Rufus grew ashamed of himself : he said he would give the archbishop what was needful, but that he must leave by the eleventh day.

This was Anselm's one desire and happily he returned to see Rufus and asked if he might give him his blessing. Rufus was gracious enough not to insult the old man. He bowed his head, and with his right hand, Anselm made the sign of the cross.

With the departure of Anselm, Rufus had lost all those he hated or feared. His ambitions were now to be satisfied as he willed. And the gentle old archbishop travelled slowly to Rome to do for Rufus his last good service. When the Pope would have excommunicated the Red King, Anselm implored his indulgence, and won it.

ROBERT was no longer in Normandy, he had pledged it to England and Rufus hurried over to govern his new possession. He decided to add Maine and even France to the empire. Maine had been given to the Conqueror but it had slipped back after his death and was now controlled by a brave soldier, Hélie of La Flèche, a descendant—on the female side—of the old counts of Maine. He had taken the cross and when William demanded Maine he retorted by pleading immunity from assault, for he was under the protection of the Church as he was about to set out for the Holy Land. " Go where you please," said Rufus, " but give up Maine to me. My father held it at his dying day, I also will have it." Hélie offered to refer the question to the peers of France or to any other tribunal, but Rufus answered that he would " plead only with sword, spear, and sheaves of arrows." Hélie then swore that, as he dared not take off his cross, he would cover his arms with it, and would fight with it behind him. The chivalrous side of Rufus saved Hélie ; this man who cared nothing for cross or for any symbol of religion, turned from Maine and charged instead at France. " I make no war against crusaders," he cried, " yet I shall have the city my father took. Lose no time in repairing its walls and moats, hire workmen and stone-cutters, I shall send waggon-loads of bolts and arrows and shall come myself with a hundred thousand lances to your gate. Le Mans I will have ! " The threat was sufficient to keep Hélie at home, wary and afraid. But Rufus, the knight, had proved stronger than Rufus the conqueror.

Towards the Vexin he now turned his army, and the lords there were uncertain which side to take. Their King, Philip, was a lazy gourmand who was under the ban of excommunication because he had married a woman while both her husband and his own wife were alive (need I add that the bishop who performed the ceremony was Odo of Bayeux?), and his son Louis was as yet scarcely capable of action. Louis found that most of his men deserted him, but he fought as well as he could with few men and less money.

For some reason Rufus returned to England. It was a queer trait in his character that suddenly he seemed to lose interest in affairs, often as now when they were most favourable to him. He was soon, however, back on the Continent, lured by an opportunity of seizing Maine. His excuse was the election of a new bishop to the vacant see of Le Mans ; Rufus insisted that this was an infringement of his rights and prepared for war whether Hélie was a crusader or not. Then good fortune came to Rufus. His ally, a scoundrel called Robert of Bellême, managed to ambush and capture Hélie.

Rufus acted the part of the perfect knight. He was most courteous to Hélie but he kept him well guarded at Rouen. The fighting continued furiously, Maine now being commanded by its overlord, Fulk Réchin of Anjou, who started to attack the fortress of Ballon. Fulk must have kept the most amazingly lax watch, for while he was at dinner he was surrounded by men from the castle and himself barely managed to escape, most of his army and all his wealth falling into the hands of the enemy. When Rufus arrived after some time, the prisoners were evidently lined up in triumph for him to see. As he approached, they wailed, " Noble King William set us free ! " An appeal to Rufus's chivalry never passed unanswered ; he freed the knights on their parole until a good dinner should be cooked for them. When his friends suggested that they might escape, Rufus retorted, " Far be it from me to doubt the word of true knights who, if they broke their word, would be for ever afterwards held in contempt."

For a time, after the taking of Ballon, there was peace in Maine. Rufus and Fulk met, and Rufus was accepted as count on condition that he released Hélie and other prisoners. Unshaven and dirty, Hélie was brought before Rufus. " I have you now, sir ! " cried Rufus. " Evil fortune has put me in your power," answered Hélie, " yet if I were free, I would know well how to bear myself," and he begged of Rufus to admit him to his household. Rufus rarely doubted a man's word but his councillors, fearful of another gaining influence, suggested that all Hélie desired was an opportunity to act the traitor, to creep into favour only to learn secrets and later to rebel. Rufus therefore refused the petition. Again Hélie asked, again he was refused. "Willingly would I have served you, Sir King," said Hélie, "if it had been your pleasure, willingly would I have earned favour in your sight. But now I pray you, blame me not if I take another course. I cannot bear patiently to see my inheritance stolen from me. All right is denied me by over-whelming violence, therefore let no man wonder if I renew my claim, if I fight with all my strength to win back the honour of my fathers." At this defiance, Rufus lost his temper. Stuttering with rage, he cried, "Scoundrel, what can you do? Get out, march, fly! I give you leave to do all you can. And if you conquer me, by the holy face of Lucca, I will ask no grace in return for my favour to-day!"

Hélie was brave enough to ask for a safe-conduct, and Rufus was knight enough to give it.

Rufus returned to the Vexin. In his usual manner, he left the conquest of Maine unfinished; then after further fighting, he left the conquest of the Vexin undecided.

Hélie did nothing while Rufus was on the Continent, he waited for him to go back to England, which the King did in the spring of 1099. Hélie instantly returned to the conflict and after hard fighting managed to capture Le Mans. The forts, however, still held for Rufus, and the garrison, by throwing down torches and cinders, managed to fire the houses and burn the city to the ground. Rufus was hunting in the New Forest when the tidings reached him. All he said was, "Let us go beyond the sea and help our friends." Those with him strove to restrain his impatience. "I will see who will follow," answered Rufus. "Do you think I shall be left without men? I know well the youth of my lands, they will run to me even at the risk of shipwreck." Then without another word, he dug his spurs into his horse and made direct for Southampton. Only one crazy old ship was in port but Rufus trusted in his destiny. A storm was on the Channel, the sky was cloudy, the waves huge, the wind against him; even the sailors dreaded the attempt and begged their King to wait. "I never heard of a King being drowned," cried Rufus. "Make haste, loose your cables, you will see the elements combine to obey me!" Next morning he was at Touques. He wasted no time on explanations but taking the first horse he saw—a mare belonging to a priest—he galloped to the nearby castle of Bonneville. As he rode up the hill to the castle, his people cheered him, as well indeed they might.

Soon he was leading an army south and Hélie fled at his approach. Rufus was capable of this magnificent burst of speed, but in his peculiarly futile manner he did not carry the war to its conclusion. He fought for a time and then seemed to weary of it. Once he had retaken Le Mans, his interest in warfare flagged, for Le Mans was his father's especial city. For that reason, it was of inestimable value to Rufus. Otherwise Maine did not excite him very greatly. It is said that he grew afraid during the siege of Mayet, but this I doubt. If so, it was the first time in his life—save on his sick-bed—when he knew fear, and the fact that a stone just missed him and killed the man at his side seems scarcely sufficient to make him abandon the war. As the man fell crushed, the besieged shouted from the walls, " Lo, the King's now got fresh meat, let it be taken to the kitchen and prepared for his supper ! "

Such an insult as this was more likely to drive Rufus to fury than to scare him. Nevertheless, he did withdraw from Mayet, and shortly afterwards returned to England.

As swiftly as Rufus tired of one war, he hurled himself into another. Although none of his campaigns were ever actually decisive, gradually he had built a vast kingdom. He had more or less forced Scotland and Maine to accept him, he had pushed his way into southern Wales, and he still had ambitions to take Ireland and France and was now negotiating for Aquitaine. His dreams were too enormous. England at least was tired of them, she was tired of having to pay continually for conquests that never seemed to come to anything.

Then, in May 1100, the King's nephew, Richard, natural son of Robert, was killed while hunting in the New Forest. A bolt from a cross-bow accidentally struck him down. He was the second of the race of the Conqueror to die amidst these glades. The bolt, aimed at a stag, had missed the beast and struck the man ; terrified, the slayer turned monk to escape vengeance. The first of the race to die here had been the Conqueror's third son, also a Richard ; what had caused his death we do not know. Legend tells us that he struck his jaw on the branches of a tree. The people took this second death as a portent of evil and, longing for wonders, they descried apparitions on every hand. The Conqueror had demolished churches to create this forest and there was a doom upon it, they said. A puddle of blood was found in Berkshire ; the devil appeared and discussed the King's affairs with quite a few people ; unholy births took place, and queer dreams were dreamt. Not only Satan was met, but a glorious virgin appeared to an abbot. These tales were invented later perhaps ; yet in the chronicles they appear, spreading an air of doom, of constricting terror, about the year 1100, the year in which the Red King died.

HE was hunting in the New Forest as his nephew had hunted, and like his nephew he was struck dead. His brother Henry was with him, and many others, scattered here and there at the sport.

It was near sunset when the arrow came.

Beyond that, we know nothing. We do not know who killed Rufus. Walter Tirel has been blamed for the deed, but Tirel denied it stoutly " when he had nothing to hope or fear." The chroniclers are maddeningly vague ; if the Red King died by treason the facts have been well concealed. We shall most probably never learn the truth.

THE courtiers fled at the King's death. They deserted the corpse and raced for their homes, each eager to barricade his castle in preparation for the usual outburst of anarchy.

Peasants lifted the plump body and placed it in a cart. As well as they were able, they draped the limbs with cloth, and, still dribbling blood, the remains of the Red King were jolted to the gates of Winchester.

When the fat lax body was lowered into its grave in the minster, no bell tolled, no mass was said, no offerings were given to help the soul through its perilous journey. There were no tears at the Red King's funeral.

A few years later the tower under which the body lay yielded and fell. Men only shrugged at the news. What could one expect ? Even stone must decay, they said, with so vile a body at its root.

III

KING HENRY THE FIRST

1100-1135

ONLY ONE KING could follow William Rufus to the throne, and that was Henry, fourth son of the Conqueror. Robert, the eldest son, was away fighting the infidel, yet even had he been in England his election would have been doubtful. His rule—or rather misrule—of Normandy gave little promise of his making a good King of England, and the people badly needed a good King. No longer was there any suggestion of electing a man outside the house of the Conqueror. Eadgar, grandson of Eadmund Ironside, was at any rate far away with Robert and his nephew was in Scotland. The succession rested between Robert and Henry. Robert was a bad ruler and he was absent ; Henry had shown wisdom in the management of his small dominion and he was on the spot. Robert, of course, had the treaty of Caen to back his pretensions, the treaty by which he and Rufus had promised on the event of either's death to let the other have both England and Normandy. Such a casual manner of treating the throne had never been understood in England ; it was considered the property of the people, not of the King. Henry therefore was the only possible choice.

There is another reason why Henry's pretensions were popular. He was indeed the Ætheling, the only son of the Conqueror born in England, and, what is more, it is said that he could read the ancient tongue. He was presumably a scholar, and later generations dubbed him the Clerk or even the Beau-Clerk, and also the Lion of Justice. He was continually turning to books for solace or education, and one of his favourite remarks was that " a King without letters was an ass with a crown." It appears that he could read and could possibly write French and a little English, but it reveals more the ignorance of the period than the attainments of Henry when the fact that he could comprehend a letter from Philip of France was considered remarkable.

In appearance, he followed his family. He was thick-set, of average height, and plumpish. His eyes were kindly, his hair black and falling over the forehead. Like others of his family he loved the chase, but he had not the chastity of his father or the inversion of his brother Rufus ; sexually he was more like Robert, he was normal enough—if the term may be used—to have mistresses of almost every possible nation he could pick from. He had British mistresses and English and French and Norman, and he probably had many others. There was the Welsh Nest —a ward he ravished—the two English Eadgyths, an unknown French lady, and the Norman Isabel. Others are unnamed, but we have the story of Anfrida who must have been English like the Eadgyths. Her husband had been imprisoned by Rufus, who had then seized his lands which should have become the property of her son. She was sensible enough not to appeal to Rufus, she appealed to Henry ; Henry did not return her her lands, probably not having the power to do so ; he presented her with another son instead.

This young King—he was thirty-two at the date of his coronation—was a great lover of women and he was evidently an amusing companion, serious during business but ready to jest afterwards. He neither ate nor drank to excess, but slept heavily and snored. He was, all the same, by no means lazy like Robert ; when occasion demanded action, he could be as swift as the Conqueror or Rufus. Unlike the Conqueror and Rufus, however, he had control of his temper and rarely showed his feelings ; so well placed was this mask of his that the chronicler bewails that he was inscrutable, a man of unfathomable dissimulation ; and we have a rather unpleasant glimpse of him from a bishop who was out of favour : when the bishop was told that Henry spoke kindlily about him, he wailed, " The King never speaks well of a man unless he intends to ruin him ! "

Henry seems at first glance a cold politician, but there were human feelings in him. The man who could be so great a lover of women could not have been a passionless machine—we cannot accept the chronicler's excuse that he was " led by feminine charms not for the gratification of lust but for the sake of issue," he had issue more than enough ; besides, he disliked bloodshed, apart from the chase. He still kept the brutal Forest laws and maimed any dog within the verge except his own, yet he was fascinated by living creatures and erected a vivary in which were camels, lions and a porcupine.

That he was selfish cannot be denied, but his people honoured him as the Lion of Justice. His justice was heavy but impartial, it fell on high or low, on English or Norman ; he revoked many of his father's too strict laws against capital punishment and hanged any thief of any class, he mutilated false coiners and restrained the licences of his own household. Of his reign the chronicler writes : " Good man he was and mickle awe was of him. Durst none man misdo against other in his time. Peace he made for man and deer." Yet again we are told that " no man in his dominions was equally wretched, equally wicked." And a Welsh writer speaks of him with such awe that he firmly believed that he was one " with whom God alone could fight."

A man who could so impress his contemporaries must have had greatness in him. And without doubt there was greatness in Henry : his quarrel with Anselm and the Pope was managed with extraordinary cleverness. Had it not been for his continental ambitions it is likely he would have anticipated even more fully the reforms later made by Henry II, but during the last years he was fighting continually abroad and was rarely at home ; the justice he meted out was harsh but perhaps necessary ; the wise laws he made were mainly a recapitulation of the ancient ones. Yet in his organisation of the exchequer, his taking of the power from earls to sheriffs, and in the creating of itinerant justices, he cannot be too highly praised.

One chronicler accuses him of cruelty, avarice and treachery, and he must stand convicted on all three counts, on cruelty and treachery perhaps less than on avarice. He was rarely cruel without purpose, as when he hurled Conan from the tower at Rouen ; but he possessed that form of cruelty which, if not sadistic, is at least inhuman. He could be cold and harsh beyond all pleading when harshness was demanded. And he was avaricious : " a slave to his cupidity, he lived in alarms. He was reckoned the most fortunate of Kings but truly he was the most miserable." Heavy were the taxes he laid upon the people so that he might carry on his wars, but he was never foolish enough to make them too heavy. Always he strove to find the mean point in everything. The charge of treachery is a common one of those days and it sticks less to Henry than to most others.

When all is examined, all the comments of writers and the proof of Henry's actions thoroughly looked into, our respect and admiration for him must be high. He was a man of acute intelligence who strove always to be impartial and just. Perhaps he was a tyrant, but a wise tyrant on the throne is better than a foolish King.

HENRY'S coronation was hurried through as quickly as possible. The Red King had died on August 2, 1100, and Henry was crowned on August 5. Quickly after the coronation came his famous charter, " the parent of all later charters," the precursor to the one sealed at Runnymede. We must pause to examine it briefly ; although it was scarcely more than a revival of old laws, it has been acclaimed as an example of Henry's genius. Our chief interest lies in the fact that it reveals the abuses that flourished under Rufus ; these laws were passed not so much as innovations as efforts to check present evil.

FIRSTLY, Henry promised not to " sell nor farm out nor, on the death of archbishop or bishop or abbot, accept anything from the demesne of the church or from its feudal-tenants until a successor has been inducted to it " ; secondly, wards of the crown would not have to redeem their property at a vast price " as they did in the time of my brother," but should pay a just relief ; thirdly, " so that it be not to one of the King's enemies," girls and widows could be married to whom they pleased without cost ; fourthly, children could be kept as wards by the widow or kinsmen, not by the Crown ; fifthly, the coinage was to return to the days of King Eadward, and false coiners would be punished ; sixthly, all Rufus's debtors would be relieved from payment, except for such debts as arose from rent and just obligations ; seventhly, a man could bequeath his goods as he liked ; eighthly, if any of the King's men incurred forfeiture or amercement— for petty offences as opposed to treasons or crimes—he should only be fined ; ninthly, all murders up to the day of coronation were forgiven, those incurred after that date should be paid for " in accordance with the law of King Eadward " [1]; tenthly,

[1] Murder here must not be taken in the modern sense. It refers to the *murdrum* fine, money demanded by the Norman Kings from every hundred or other district in which a corpse not English was discovered and the slayer unknown. It was a protection against secret revenge by the conquered race. The puzzle about Henry's oath is that it speaks of " the law of King Eadward," which is contrary to the accepted view that the *murdrum* fine was introduced by William I. The fine may have been an English law to stop killing in general, and William may have narrowed it to include only foreigners. Otherwise it is difficult to believe that the lawmakers of 1100 were not so wise about their own affairs as modern scholars and that they could have been

8

Henry refused to surrender the forest-lands, keeping them by his barons' consent ; eleventhly, knights who held lands on military tenure were to be " quit of all gelds and non-military service " so they might " effectually provide themselves with horses and arms for my service and the defence of my kingdom " ; twelfthly, peace would be established in future throughout the kingdom ; thirteenthly, " I restore to you the law of King Eadward, with those amendments which my father made with the consent of his barons " ; fourteenthly, indemnity given for acts of spoliation committed between the death of William II and the coronation of Henry I. These were the promises of Henry that Stephen Langton was to produce as a basis on which to work. And the oath bears in it the same weakness as John's charter. Promises are given but no method is ensured to see that those promises will be fulfilled. It was not so much something with which to bind the King as something with which to threaten him ; as with a great deal of modern justice, the law was made to hang the criminal, not to prevent crime. And there is one point that must not be overlooked. In all the fifteen clauses nothing is said of the people of England. A hasty glance might lead one to assume that they constitute justice for all ; examination reveals that—apart from clauses 12 and 13 which are vague enough to be worthless—these clauses promise no justice or relief for the people as a whole, they are merely a sop to the barons and—in clause 1—to the Church.

WHEN Henry agreed to put away his brother's evil government, he fully meant what he said, and he began by imprisoning the Treasurer Randolf Flambard in the Tower of London ; then he followed this by the decision to marry. He had a great many children already, but slowly the law was gaining force that only legitimate sons could succeed the father. Apart from this, Henry was actually in love with the woman he proposed to marry. She was Eadgyth, daughter of Malcolm III King of the Scots by the sister of Eadgar the Ætheling. And, despite the stupid later legends woven about this marriage, it is more than likely that Eadgyth loved Henry.

ignorant of what did or did not constitute law before 1066. The law may now have been expanding to include bodies of any nation, as perhaps it had under Eadward ; the usual date given for this is the Assize of Clarendon in 1166, but the appearance of a law as law does not always mean that it had not been operating unofficially for some time.

Apparently she was attractive in appearance; when she was twelve years of age she was said to be beautiful, but William of Malmesbury will give her no further praise than that of a "not to be despised appearance." She was intelligent, extraordinarily pious—it was said that she wore a hair-shirt next to her skin—a scholar, not very well off financially but of good descent. At any rate, Henry loved her, and that was the main point; and it seems that she loved Henry in return. They had probably known each other for some time, as from her childhood Eadgyth had lived in English nunneries, first at Wilton and later at Romsey, while the King's brother Robert had been her godfather.

The marriage was popular, but there was a hurdle to surmount that nobody realised until the Church discovered it. Eadgyth, said the Church, was a consecrated virgin and therefore it would be sacrilege for her to marry. She had, it was alleged, taken the veil at Romsey. The question was referred to Anselm who had been recalled by the new King. Already Anselm was insisting on the rights of the Pope, struggling to bring the English Church under the domination of Rome, and Henry was doing his best to stand against him. To a man of Anselm's gentle character, the character of one born only to obey, it was incredible that the world could not understand that the Pope held the keys of St. Peter, that he was God's proxy on earth. He had left Rufus in sorrow, not in anger; when news reached him of the Red King's sudden end he burst into tears and his companions in surprise asked why he wept. Sobbing he answered that he would rather have died himself than that Rufus should be struck down unhouselled, being thereby smitten direct to hell.

Anselm arrived in England and soon found that again he had to quarrel with an English King. Henry asked him to do the customary homage for his archbishopric. Anselm refused. The Lateran Council had condemned the old English law according to which Church appointments were controlled by the King; Rome decreed that Rome and Rome alone should hold them in future. Anselm added to his refusal that if Henry dared appoint any one to a vacant see he would not speak to him again. "If the King will not obey the Pope," he said, "I need not tarry in England." Henry could not defy Anselm lest he transfer his allegiance to Robert who was now home and clamouring for the crown. He suggested therefore that the question be put aside until after Easter and quickly wrote to the new Pope Pascal II asking him to accept the ancient customs of England.

It was at this point, while King and archbishop were momentarily at peace, that the marriage problem cropped up. Was Eadgyth a consecrated virgin ? Anselm summoned a synod of ecclesiastics to Lambeth and debated the question. Eadgyth was questioned. She said that she had worn the veil only to hide from the lust of the Normans, that her aunt had made her wear it, and whenever her aunt's back was turned she said she had torn it off and trampled on it ; investigations were also made in the monastery. Anselm left the gathering to discuss the problem alone, and it was decided that Eadgyth had never formally taken the veil but that she had worn it at times to escape unwanted love-approaches. Anselm did not agree with the verdict, but he gave in to it, probably disliking the thought of a virgin—whether consecrated or not—surrendering her jewel of maidenhood to any human man. Eadgyth heard the finding with a delighted air and offered to give her oath that she had spoken truth ; she added that she did not fear she would be disbelieved but she wanted no one to have the opportunity to doubt. Anselm told her that this was not necessary, he gave her his blessing and sent her off, yet he regretted to see one who might have been · God's bride being placed in a carnal bed. Before celebrating the wedding on November 11, 1100, he mounted into his pulpit and repeated the whole discussion, asking any one who could object to the marriage to stand forth. No one stood forth, and the marriage was celebrated.

It was probably at this point that Eadgyth changed her name and from now on we must call her Matilda. We have seen that an earlier Matilda changed her name to Ælfgifu when she married an English King ; times had altered since then. Now an English lady had to change her English name to please the Normans. Apparently it did not please the Normans, they jeered at the couple, calling them Godric and Godgifu. For a while Henry forgot the light ladies of his bachelor days, he settled down to become a perfect husband. The regeneration did not last long. Matilda—to give her new name—may not have actually taken the veil but she was eminently suited for a nunnery. Beneath that royal gown with its long sleeves and tight bodice was concealed, we are told, the hair-shirt that chafed continually against her flesh. With so saintly a woman for wife, one need not be surprised to discover further illegitimate children born after Henry's marriage; Matilda did not seem to bother about his absences, being quite " satisfied with a child of either sex " for herself. Nevertheless she did not hide from the world, she had constant visitors to her home—she lived usually at Westminster—and often took a hand in public affairs. Not only was she virtuous and pious, she was cunning enough a scholar to be able to write to Anselm and the Pope, and she loved music and poetry so greatly that to pay her troubadours and lavish charity she was forced to overtax her lands. Good Queen Mold—for Maud—she was called, and good she was in every way—as wife, as Queen, as Christian. Her goodness as a Christian, however, may have lessened her qualities as a wife, for her brother once jeered at her, asking whether King Henry liked to kiss the mouth that had kissed the ulcers of lepers. William of Malmesbury assures us that this was no unfounded jeer; Matilda did like to kiss the lepers' sores and to wash the feet of the poor : she tried to entice her brother to do the same, but the brother refused and laughed as he left her amidst her leprous gathering.

ROBERT was home from the Crusades. This lazy Duke of Normandy had become a hero : he had been one of the first to break into Jerusalem and had fought magnificently at Ascalon ; it was even said that he had been offered the crown of the Holy City, but that is doubtful. He had won something far more valuable than a crown on the journey home—a beautiful, wealthy and intelligent wife. This was Sibylle of Conversana, and her dowry would have been sufficient to redeem Normandy ; Robert spent every penny of it before he returned. The chroniclers unite to speak gloriously of Sibylle as if dazzled by her beauty and culture. Unfortunately for Robert, she did not live long ; one story says that she died giving birth to his son, William, another tells us that she was poisoned by a rival who loved the duke. The first seems the more probable.

Robert came back in September 1100 to a duchy that was little more than a land of bandits. He was received blithely, being an ideal ruler for bandits, and was forced immediately to fight the few English garrisons that remained. His pledge to surrender the duchy died with William as it had been a personal matter ; Henry could make no claim through that.

Very likely if he had been left undisturbed Robert would

never have made any pretensions towards his brother's throne, but discontented Normans in England were intriguing to make him King, being tired of the too strict rule of Henry. Their leader was a notorious traitor, a man who seemed incapable of remaining true to anybody, even to himself, Robert of Bellême. Then Rufus's treasurer, Randolph Flambard, escaped from the Tower of London. He called on Robert and incited him against Henry. The English rebels were powerful ; Henry to oppose them had only his mercenaries and the people of England, but the Church was on his side. He waited at Pevensey for his brother's fleet to appear, but Robert landed instead at Portsmouth and moved towards Winchester ; hearing of this, Henry galloped to meet him. At Winchester lay Matilda expecting her first child, and Robert was too chivalrous to attack ; he said that it would be the deed of a villain to besiege the city at such a time.

When Robert approached Alton, news was brought that Henry's army awaited him beyond a wood, and he paused. Neither brother wished to fight, they decided to discuss their troubles friendlily, and met between both armies ; they embraced and kissed each other. Subtle Henry soon had Robert's pledge to surrender his claim on England in exchange for Henry's dominions in Normandy—excepting Domfront—and a large pension. Robert went gaily home and Henry could now take revenge upon his rebellious nobles. He fought Bellême and his brothers, he chased them until they surrendered and were banished.

In this war there is one incident of importance, showing that the wishes of the barons were by no means the wishes of England. While Henry was besieging Bridgenorth his barons pleaded for Bellême. Since the desertion of Robert, the nobles had not dared take up arms, but secretly they were in sympathy with the rebels, for they desired anarchy in which they could do as they liked. Henry listened to the plea for mercy from these, the chief men of his kingdom ; he, one against so many, might have given in to their demands, but the army was not deceived. The English army shouted, " Hearken not to the traitors, O King ! " and Henry refused the petition.

After this there was peace in England for the rest of Henry's reign of thirty-three years, " nor in all those years durst any man hold a castle against him." He had acted quickly and astutely and had broken the barons who, if they had united, could have crushed him.

THE quarrel with Anselm was not yet settled. Henry had written to the new Pope Pascal asking for the recognition of the ancient English custom of allowing the King's right of investiture (which did not mean the right of ordination), but he must have done so only to temporise, knowing that the Pope would never agree to letting any power slip from him. The Pope almost took such a request as an insult. Henry wasted more time by sending a second embassy. When the Pope answered this with two letters, one to Henry, one to Anselm, Henry hid his letter and prompted the envoys to deny Anselm's letter and to say that the Pope personally had told them that so long as Henry was a good man he could keep the right of investiture. Anselm's envoys insisted that Pascal had said nothing of the kind. Therefore a third message was sent to Rome. When the answer was received to this, Anselm delayed opening the letter until he could do so before the King. He asked for permission, but Henry cried, " Certainly not. What has the Pope got to do with my rights ? That which my predecessors in this realm had is mine ; whoever tries to deprive me of those rights shall learn that he is my enemy." He knew that further lies were useless but he could not bully the frail old man who had stood against the fury of the Red King. Anselm did not give back a step in his determination to obey Rome. Then Henry suggested that the archbishop himself go to discuss the problem with the Pope, and Anselm was forced to agree. He left England on April 27, 1103.

Altogether, Henry's diplomacy shows well in this affair. He had not broken off negotiations yet he had not retreated from his demands.

WHEN Robert of Bellême was banished from England he went straight to Normandy and before long he had conquered almost the whole duchy. He was a terrific scoundrel, this Bellême, and a most capable one. The tales of his villany are almost incredible. He kept his wife—an heiress—chained in a dungeon from which she was at last lucky enough to escape. His favourite sport was the art of impaling, of driving a pointed stake clean through a man or a woman's trunk ; and sometimes he rejected ransom for his prisoners so that he could keep the delights of torturing them. A most ghastly story relates his treatment of his own godchild. He pushed a hand up the boy's cloak and tore out his eyes with his finger-nails. This was the ruffian who now marched into Robert's lands. Robert could do nothing to stay him. He was penniless ; on one occasion, we are told, he was unable to get out of bed until after midday because his whores and drunken comrades had stolen his clothes. He had to give in before Bellême and ceded Argentan to his demands.

Henry took this opportunity to lecture his brother, then decided himself to go to Normandy and deal with Bellême. He went to Normandy three times and before long, between the opposing forces fighting over his duchy, the wretched Robert was almost squeezed out of it. He was tossed from side to side and sometimes it is difficult to know why he was on either side at all. He besought his brother to make terms. Henry refused, wanting to seize all Normandy. Things at last reached a head when Robert's army faced Henry's before Tinchebrai. Henry won that battle, although the clergy strove to make him come to terms ; Bellême escaped, but Robert became his brother's prisoner.

Robert had never really wanted to fight. Now he surrendered Falaise and offered his brother the charge of his little son, William ; this was too great a responsibility to accept, and Henry wisely passed the child into the keeping of that brave man, Hélie of Saint-Saens.

Normandy was now falling straight into Henry's hands. That rascal Flambard saw which way the wind blew and offered to surrender Lisieux. Henry took Lisieux and forgave Flambard, but he never trusted him. Then it was Bellême's turn to give in after vainly trying to make Hélie into a traitor. Henry also forgave Bellême, it was safer to keep him near at hand than to force him to remain an open and revengeful enemy.

The only one of the three who came really badly out of the affair was poor Robert. He was put into various prisons and never freed again. It is a relief to know that Henry did not treat his brother badly ; he permitted him to have every pleasure he wanted except freedom. Very probably Robert was delighted. He lived for another twenty-eight years with as many women and as much liquor as he might desire. And that was about all he ever did ask from life, except peace. Now he was given that as well.

NORMANDY was Henry's, and soon he won another victory. The Pope was forced to give way before him in diplomacy. When Anselm reached Rome he found that Henry's envoy had got there before him, and during the debate, when Pascal had almost decided to excommunicate the King, the envoys warned him that Henry would rather surrender his crown than his rights. Pascal feared that he might lose everything if he remained firm. The King of the English had proved himself subtle and stubborn and dangerous. Pascal forced himself to write a friendly letter to Henry ; Anselm had lost on every hand. The Pope might confirm him in his rights, but he remained an exile. The English envoy warned him that Henry would not have him back in England unless he bowed to the King's will. " What ! have you nothing more to say to me ? " cried poor Anselm. " Nothing more," said the envoy, " a word to the wise."

For over a year the problem remained in the same suspended state. Henry enjoyed the Canterbury revenues, Anselm remained in exile. Pascal decided to take action again and he forbade any man who had accepted investiture from Henry to enter a church. The time appeared to be growing close for Henry's excommunication, and Anselm, who had implored pardon for the Red King, seemed strangely delighted at the prospect of his new enemy being struck with the same doom. He was travelling north, from Lyons to Rheims, when he heard that the King's sister, Adela, Countess of Blois, was very ill, and decided to visit her. Perhaps it was a plan of Henry's to soften Anselm ; at any rate, Adela had quite recovered when Anselm saw her and she managed to inveigle him into meeting Henry at Laigle. Nothing definite came from the meeting— that was scarcely possible—but Henry did calm the exile and they agreed once more to apply to Pascal.

Another year was bridged, another year passed during which the threat of excommunication was lifted ; and this threat was an important one in those days. Constant misuse had not lessened its power, as it was to lessen it in later times ; an excommunicated King was cut off from all hope of heaven. With troubles in Normandy to be rectified, Henry could not afford to allow his enemies any excuse to turn against him.

The Pope gave way completely. We do not know what caused him to surrender so suddenly, but he left the unfortunate Anselm with almost no weapons whatever. Henry surrendered a few points on the right of investiture but he kept the important right to appoint bishoprics and abbeys. Anselm went back to England and within two years he was to die, still fighting courageously, attacking the married clergy and the King's own household, and asserting the supremacy of Canterbury over York. He was seventy-six when he died, and his dream had not matured—that dream of enslaving the English clergy, of making them a Roman colony from which the Pope could draw the Church's revenues and send his foreign ecclesiastics to rule English dioceses. It had been a hopeless battle because Anselm was not a fighter ; yet it had been easier for him to stand against the bull-like fury of Rufus than against the cunning of Henry. Anselm was too honest a creature to understand intrigue. He died embittered, a scholar who had been forced into action, a lover of all living things who had been made to hate his fellow-men. He had fought and shouted in a vacuum. The only matter on which he ever succeeded was the suppression of married clergy and even there his success was only partial ; so long as priests were human it was impossible to stop them from maintaining " spiritual sisters." Anselm himself was of the flesh of saints which does not comprehend desire because it has never suffered it. As a scholar he will be remembered for ever ; as a churchman he is a tragic and rather pathetic failure.

THE power of England was now so great that its King could betroth his daughter to the Emperor Henry V of Germany— although at the time Henry was merely King, not having yet been crowned. This girl, or rather child—she was only eight— was named Adelaide, and on April 10, 1110, she was formerly betrothed to Henry at Utrecht, the marriage itself being con-'summated on January 7, 1114, when the bride was twelve. Like her mother, she was forced to change her name to Matilda, and as such she was ever afterwards known, even when she was eventually crowned Queen of the English during the reign of Stephen.

Henry's power grew every year. He was seeping his kingdom into Wales, England was quiet, Normandy was his, the Pope had bowed before him, and his daughter was betrothed to a future Emperor. Yet great as was his power, it was no simple matter to hold it firmly with rebels and jealous enemies on every hand. There was trouble once more in Maine. Hélie died and Fulk V of Anjou seized the country. At the same time France was quarrelling because Henry had not destroyed the castle of Gisors in the Vexin as he had promised. Then a third trouble occurred. Robert of Bellême was preparing to rebel so that he could place Duke Robert's son William in power. France was met first. Henry strove to negotiate with King Louis, and at last was saved from invasion by the French having to turn to fight rebels of their own. Bellême was foolish enough to appear at Henry's court as an envoy from Louis. It was the last appearance he ever made. He was condemned to perpetual imprisonment, and was sent over to England to be locked into Wareham Castle. This sudden collapse of the conspiracy frightened the rebels in Maine. Count Fulk rendered homage to Henry, and also the Count of Brittany rendered homage in return for Matilda, Henry's natural daughter, to be given as a bride to his son.

With his continental possession quietened, Henry returned to England and charged once more at Wales, that danger-spot on the side of England that never would give in. But Henry was gradually driving his fortresses deeper over the marches, slowly gaining ground. Soon, however, he had to race back to Normandy. There were spurts of rebellion on every side, but the rebels could not concentrate, they lacked a leader. Nevertheless, they kept their duke busy, they kept him darting here and there, pushing down one uprush only to have to spring round to push down another ; and at the same time Henry had to keep one hand free lest King Louis sprang over his border.

Henry had little peace, never a moment for relaxation. And then his Queen died. He had once loved Matilda, but as we know that natural children were born to him after his marriage, it is doubtful if his love were lasting. Matilda had done her task, she had given him a legitimate son. Probably her death had little effect on the King. He was too busy stopping up the spurts of rebellion to mourn anybody.

WE approach one of the really horrible episodes in this reign, and it gives us a peculiar window into Henry's character. It reveals that inhumanity of his of which some complain, the inhumanity that, because of a principle, would sacrifice anything, even life or honour.

Henry's illegitimate daughter Juliana had married Eustace of Breteuil, who had succeeded to his father's lands. In these lands stood the border castle of Ivry commanded by Ralph Harenc. It was too important a garrison to give away ; Henry could not bear to part with it, but at the same time he did not wish to anger Eustace. He made what was for him an extremely stupid compromise. To prove his good faith he made Harenc give his son as hostage to Eustace and Eustace surrender his two daughters to Harenc. This seems very pointless, and becomes even more pointless when Eustace—prompted by rascals who wanted him to fight Henry—blinded Harenc's boy and sent him back to his father. Harenc rushed to Henry, he demanded vengeance, and we really cannot blame Henry for giving permission, although these hostages were his own granddaughters. Justice demanded that Harenc take revenge, and undoubtedly Eustace and Juliana had relied on Henry's love to let them act as brutally as they pleased. They had forgotten that he was the Lion of Justice. I feel that, far from blaming him, we should rather pity him at this moment. The eyes of the two girls were pushed in, their noses were cut off. Eustace and Juliana declared war. They had no right to be outraged, they had acted first. Henry marched to subdue them. Juliana was in command at Breteuil and she begged to speak with her father. Unsuspectingly, Henry rode to meet her, and Juliana—for, says the chronicler, " there is no wickedness like the wickedness of a woman "—aimed a cross-bow at her father. She failed in her revenge and very soon the castle had to surrender. Those historians who have spoken of Henry's brutality in this transaction forget that when he had every chance of being cruel to his daughter he treated her mildly. At the command of justice he had mutilated his grandchildren, and now at his mercy he had the woman, his daughter, who had forced him to that horrible mutilation and who had tried herself to murder him. Although the revenge he took was cruel and subtle, one can hardly call it brutal. He degraded his daughter's pride, he made her suffer a little, but he did her no actual harm. He commanded that she wade through the icy waters of the half-frozen moat and that she perform the penance naked from the waist down.

TROUBLES on every hand, little rebellions, little outbreaks to be patted into place. And there was Louis fighting over the Seine, stealing into the continually disputed Vexin. Henry quietly bought allies, built castles. Then he married his son William to Matilda of Anjou, the daughter of Fulk. More fighting, until came the great victory of Brémule. Henry was mainly a diplomatist, but when argument was useless he could prove himself as great a soldier as his father or his brother Rufus. His tactics at this battle appear to be an innovation, although he had already used them to a certain extent before. He placed the chivalry under his natural son Robert—it was a hundred strong —while himself and the remainder of the army dismounted. The chivalry were to use shock-tactics, to fight where and when Robert thought best ; the main battle was to be the foot. The French horsemen were routed badly ; although Henry himself received a clout on the head, the victory was his. He made the French King ride so fast that he lost himself in a wood and had to be shown the way home by a peasant, while the royal standard fell to Henry.

It seemed that all was indeed well with the kingdom of Henry. He had built magnificently, he had reconquered his father's possessions and had added to them ; England was at peace, and he had settled the Flems in Wales to hold back the native British ; Scotland had rendered homage. Then came the heavy blow, the tragedy that wiped away the foundations of all he had built, that dashed in ruins the fabrics of a mighty empire, leaving it worthless, turning it to an idle ambition that must gradually die.

Henry's only legitimate son, William, was drowned in *La Blanche Nef—The White Ship.*

WILLIAM had just passed seventeen, and although one chronicler at least might suspect him of being proud and insolent, that is too often only the natural arrogance and vitality of youth. There are hints that he might have imitated his uncle Rufus sexually, and some commented on the disaster as an act of God. Wrote William of Huntingdon—" my soul used to whisper to me ' this boy, so delicate as he is, is being nourished as food for hell-fire.' " From the vague statements of medieval writers, however, eager to trace the finger of God in everything from a thunderstorm to the falling of a sparrow, we must be careful to draw no theories. The hauteur of young William and the alleged vices of his companions might have been an exaggeration un-consciously supplied to explain why God should strike *The White Ship.* There was no such thing as an accident in the Middle Ages, the winds blew, the waves rose, only at the bidding of God ; if a ship sank, God wanted it to sink, ergo there must have been something wrong, not with the ship itself, but with its living cargo.

We are, at least, certain that that living cargo was abomin-ably drunk when it clambered aboard *The White Ship.* It was so drunk that wiser travellers drew back : Theobald, Count of Blois, the King's nephew, pleaded an attack of cholic, and his brother Stephen—later King of England—frankly refused to journey with such dangerous companions. The man who steered the vessel claimed to be son of the pilot of the Conqueror's *Mora* ; one chronicler quickly notes this as most suggestive of something, but of what it is difficult to decide.

King Henry sailed from Barfleur on the evening of Thurdsay, November 25, 1120, reaching England next day after an absence of four and a half years ; he expected his son and friends to follow immediately in this *White Ship*, a newly built craft of fifty oars. There were a great many people with young William, " several noble women with no small number of the King's children." Before setting out, William and his rowdy companions made the crew drunk, with the result that when they attempted wildly to overtake Henry's vessel and reach England before him, they struck a rock about a mile and a half from port, and all went down. From two hundred to three hundred died that evening, and only one was saved. A young lord and a butcher gripped the yard-arm ; it was cold and the lord's fingers began to freeze, he dropped off, but the butcher wore a sheepskin jacket and managed to keep alive until rescued. William of Malmesbury alone gives a pretty story that may be true : he states that the Ætheling William made off in a boat, but when he heard the wailing of his deserted half-sister, Matilda, he put back to rescue her, and died. I would like to believe the tale, it certainly refutes the hints of the other chroniclers about the selfish arrogance of William.

What seemed to horrify the people of the time more even than the loss of William, Henry's only legitimate son, was the fact that so few of the bodies were recovered. Unhouselled, drunk and reckless, the youth of England and Normandy died without Christian burial.

FOR a whole day none dared tell the King about the disaster. At last a boy was deputed to break the news, and it is said that Henry fainted at the shock. If some accounts be true, he never really recovered and was melancholy ever afterwards. And well he might, for with the drowning of William were drowned all his hopes. There was no one to whom he could leave his throne, his conquests ; the father of so many children had no child to succeed him. There was only Robert's son left, another William, and apparently Henry detested the lad : he was, at any rate, determined never to let him be King of England or Duke of Normandy.

Henry's will was indomitable. God might strike at him but He could not destroy him. If one son was taken he could yet create other sons, he would marry again. He was still strong and in late middle age, being fifty-two, and it did not seem possible that after producing such an innumerable brood of children he would fail now when the need for a son was so vital a link in the chain of his ambitions. On January 6, 1121, he told his council in London that he must marry a second time and that his choice was Adelaide, daughter of Godfrey, Count of Louvain and Duke of Lower Lorraine. Adelaide was rushed to England and on the 29th she married Henry at Windsor,[1] her " beauty dazzling her diadem."

During the hallowing on the following day a peculiar incident occurred. The archbishop was about to begin when he noticed that Henry was wearing his crown. Henry should never have put it on himself, that was the archbishop's prerogative. The whole affair is most mysterious, Henry himself did not trouble to explain it, but the archbishop firmly untied the chin-straps, took off the crown and replaced it before continuing the service.

Perhaps the miserable King had worn it unthinkingly. There could have been no reason to insult the archbishop. And it is not difficult to understand the impulse to hold the crown upon his head, the crown that could be passed to no heir, that must die with him.

MAN may struggle against God with all his strength, but he is fighting a treacherous enemy that strikes when he is unprepared, that cheats at the last moment. This hurried marriage, last defiance of God, came to nothing. The father of uncounted children failed to produce the son he demanded and needed. Adelaide remained barren.

The inevitable rebellion drew Henry back to Normandy. There was a growing movement to give the duchy to Robert's son William, and Henry was most firm on that question, he was

---

[1] It may be of interest to note that this is our present Windsor, and the court was first held there during Whitsun, May 29, 1110. It was called New Windsor. Old Windsor was about two miles lower down the Thames and was of great antiquity.

determined not to surrender his dominions to a child of his elder brother. We find growing in him now a harshness that he did not have before ; his cruelty had been only the concomitant of his justness. After putting down these rebellions, however, we find him unjustly brutal—yet can he be blamed ? He had risen to mighty power, but in the end he had lost everything. His power was worthless. It was inevitable that a little bitterness, a certain resentment of God, must come with the passing of tragic years.

He forgave the leaders of the rebellion, but on three others fell his vengeance. Against two of these his command to have them blinded seems purposeless, they had committed no particular crime, certainly they had done nothing worse than the men he pardoned ; his judgment, however, of the third prisoner is understandable. There was one thing that no medieval King could possibly forgive, and that was ridicule. This third prisoner was a troubadour, Luke, Lord of La Barre-en-Ouche, who—in the words put into Henry's mouth—" Never did me homage [*that is, never broke his oath of allegiance to Henry as the others had done*], but he stood in arms against me at Pont-Audemer, and although when making peace I forgave all forfeitures, he again joined my enemies. Besides, he sang scurrilous verses on me and made me a jest to his comrades." Because of this, Henry decreed the blinding of the troubadour. Luke would not suffer the agony. He wrenched himself from the grip of the torturers and dashed out his own brains against the wall.

THE pretensions of Robert's son William were growing, he was becoming dangerous. He was about to marry the daughter of Fulk of Anjou who would have brought him vast possessions, but Henry proved that they were within the forbidden grounds of consanguinity and the betrothal was set aside. Fearing that Adelaide would never conceive after five years of marriage and disappointment, Henry began to scheme new ways of avoiding the loss of his kingdom. He decided on the unprecedented step of forcing England to accept a woman-ruler. This was something entirely unknown in either England or Normandy,[1] and it is

---

[1] The only previous Queen of England in her own right that we know of, is the doubtful Sexburh, who is supposed to have reigned over Wessex from the death of her husband Cenwalh (? 673) to the accession of Æscwine (674–676). Bede, however, tells us that the kingdom was disrupted during this period, and her name may only have been given for the sake of convenience,

interesting when we glance back only a few years to see how rapidly the ideas of men had changed, how swiftly the world was turning towards modern conceptions of heredity. At one time illegitimacy had been no bar to succession, yet Henry never for a moment thought of making the English accept any of his natural children. He understood fully that they were ruled out. The abruptness of this development is startling, and was based on the growing respect for property. The crown of England was becoming private property, it was no longer the jewel of the people to be given of the man of their choice. Harold would have had no chance of taking the crown in Henry's time. Although illegitimacy was becoming the bâton sinister that deprived a child of his or her full rights, it was not considered shameful as it is to-day. Medieval people were at least intelligent and humane enough never to look on a bastard as some kind of a disgraceful accident that could be mentioned only in whispers. To be descended from a great man, whether by bâton sinister or not, was naturally something of which to be proud. It deprived you of no respect.

Henry's daughter Matilda—once Adelaide—was a widowed Empress, and Henry called her to him. She was popular in Germany and was thoroughly enjoying herself, but the commands of her father had to be obeyed. She arrived in England with Henry, who had met her in Normandy, on September 11, 1126 ; and during the Christmas gemót at Windsor, before the great men of the land, both spiritual and temporal, the King insisted on his daughter being accepted as his heir. He made those present take an oath to accept her as Lady of the English and the Normans —curiously enough there is no mention of her being Queen or duchess. Three of those who took the oath must be mentioned : David, King of the Scots, Matilda's uncle and England's most important vassal ; Stephen, Count of Boulogne and Mortain, the King's nephew ; and the King's illegitimate son, Robert, Earl of Gloucester. David first took the oath amongst the laity, then Stephen and Robert quarrelled as to who should be next. Stephen, it was decided, had the better claim. He then swore fealty to Matilda, and after him, Robert—the loyal heroic Robert

to cover what would otherwise have been a gap. She can scarcely be taken as a precedent for the election of Matilda. It is worth noting, in passing, that women at this date could succeed to property and therefore were not quite the chattels that many writers make them out to be ; besides, a Queen could be regent in her husband's absence.

9

of later days—swore to honour the Lady he was to follow until he died.

It was argued later that those who took the oath did so only on the understanding that Matilda would not marry without the consent of the barons. This story appears to smack of late invention, it seems a hurried explanation to excuse treachery. The King, if he had made such a promise, was not the kind of man to break it. He was far too intelligent to give the lords any reason to turn against Matilda, and when he decided to marry her to Geoffrey of Anjou, although " it liked neither French nor English, but the King did it to have sib of the Earl of Anjou and for help against his nephew William," we are not told of any protest from the barons or clergy. The protest appears to have come from Normandy where the Angevins were detested.

WE have passed over, in the importance of Matilda's succession, the tale of Henry's last battle with Rome. He had always refused to allow papal legates to enter England to try to enforce the rule of the Pope. But suddenly, in 1124, he changed his mind. He agreed to let Calixtus send John of Crema with a commission extending over Scotland and England. This would seem weakness on Henry's part but undoubtedly it was cunning. He hoped to trap the legate in some way, and he succeeded.

John de Crema was received with great pomp and then infuriated the English clergy by celebrating high mass at Canterbury, which he had no right to do, being not even a bishop. Wherever he went, at Henry's orders, he was offered gifts " mickle and mair than mickle," until he appeared at the Westminster Abbey synod on September 8, 1124. He had wanted to issue the summonses for the assembly, but this he was not allowed to do, either in his own or in the Pope's name, nevertheless he made a great stir at the synod, particularly in his denunciation of married clergy. How could they dare, he asked, rise from the couches of their wives to consecrate the Body of the Lord ? Three times he asked, " Are ye content ? " and as none dared confess that they were not content, he said his " Amen," and retired well satisfied. That very night, the chronicler tells us, " this cardinal, who in the sacred council inveighed against the wives of priests, saying that it was pollution for one to rise from a woman's bed and straightway consecrate God's Body," was discovered in his own bed with a woman, " having himself that day elevated the holy host. The fact could not be denied. And it was not right it should be hidden." The legate left England shamed and ridiculed, and Henry remained in a more secure position than ever. If it was an accident, it was an extremely lucky one.

WHEN the Normans heard that their future ruler was to be a woman, and the wife of a hated Angevin, they decided to take Robert's son William for duke. Louis presented him with his own Queen's half-sister for wife and gave him the French Vexin ; shortly afterwards, the Count of Flanders was murdered in a church in Bruges ; Louis gave William Flanders as well.

On August 26, 1127, Henry landed in Normandy to settle the nuisance, but already William had been fighting with Stephen of Boulogne and had been almost assassinated at Ypres; then came the end of this son of Robert, this William the Miserable as he was truly called. During a battle, a spear-head was jabbed through the palm of his hand and ran into his wrist. For five days he lived in torment, then knowing that he was doomed, he decided to turn monk. This was a common trick to make the Almighty accept you straight into heaven, which, if the Almighty had any compassion, He most certainly did on July 28, 1128, when William died.

WITH William at last out of the way, Henry's main trouble was to settle his daughter's matrimonial uproars. Young Geoffrey of Anjou—he was not fourteen—threw his twenty-five-year-old wife out of his home and sent her to Rouen. Matilda had a most haughty temper and one can scarcely blame Geoffrey ; even the prospect of getting England evidently did not weigh against the terrors of that virago. He took her back, however, after a time, and on March 25, 1133, was born their son, called after his grandfather, Henry.

The King in August decided to see the child for himself, but he delayed his passage because of the extraordinary portents that struck the heavens. It was on the anniversary of the death of Rufus when, Henry being about to set out, the skies turned black at midday, and the stars could be seen to shine. In other words, there was a total eclipse of the sun. And as if this were not sufficient to prove that God was preparing something particularly awful with which to startle humanity, there was an earthquake two days later. William of Malmesbury assures us that he felt the house rock beneath him. In defiance of these portents, Henry sailed, and he never returned to England. There was trouble in Wales, and he was not by to suppress it. His son-in-law was becoming so obstreperous that Henry dared not leave him alone. Geoffrey wailed for money, he wailed for castles, he began fighting another son-in-law of Henry's. He became the centre of the inevitable plots and the King began to grow exasperated. He even thought of taking Matilda away and depriving Geoffrey of every hope of England.

It was said that a dish of lampreys killed the Lion of Justice. He who had withstood intrigue and battle was dragged to his death-bed by a cooked eel-like fish that had always disagreed with him. Henry was no glutton, and this surfeit could not have been too large a quantity. It is more than likely that he died from ptomaine poisoning. At the age of sixty-seven, he died at his favourite hunting-seat in the Forest of Lyons. He ended well, confessing his sins, ordering his debts to be paid, arrears of salary to be settled, and his treasures to be given to the poor. From one who was not present at the time, we learn that he repeated his desire for Matilda to succeed him, but he did not mention her husband. His dominions were for his daughter, to become her personal property, and Geoffrey could look after himself.

The first English-born King of the new race was dead. Yet through Matilda he was to bring to fruition the prophecy of the dying Eadward. Through her the green tree was to return to its home by Henry II, to dig its roots fast into the soil of England.

IV

KING STEPHEN 1135–1154 AND
QUEEN MATILDA 1141

WHEN NEWS REACHED ENGLAND of Henry I's death the first
thing that the people did was to raid the deer-parks. Then the
late King's favourite nephew, Stephen, Count of Mortain and
Boulogne, hurried over the Channel and demanded his uncle's
crown. Stephen had as good a claim as any other man, better
than most. He was of direct descent from William I, for his
mother had been William's daughter Adela, and his wife was
the granddaughter—spindle-side again—of King Malcolm of
Scotland and Queen Margaret, the granddaughter of Eadmund
Ironside and sister of the Ætheling Eadgar. He possessed large
estates in England and was very popular ; more important than
any claim he could put forward was the country's dislike of the
Angevins. Hatred of the Angevins more than love for Stephen
won him the throne.

We are not certain of his age, but he was born some time
before 1100 and must have been still a boy when his uncle took
him into favour, knighted him and made him Count of Mortain.
By marriage he had become Count of Boulogne. Undoubtedly
when the Ætheling William went down in *The White Ship*—a fate
that Stephen himself almost shared—he must have believed that
the crown of England would become his, and his disappointment
must therefore have been intense when Matilda was brought from
Germany. Nevertheless, he fought with Robert of Gloucester
for the honour of being the second lord to swear fealty to her,
an oath which even at the time he could scarcely have intended
to keep. His usurpation was too sudden not to have been planned.
Scarcely was Henry dead before Stephen was sailing the Channel,
Matilda being safe in Anjou and her champion, Robert of
Gloucester, being busy with affairs in Normandy.

OF Stephen's personal appearance we know nothing, but tradition
states that he surpassed all his contemporaries in manly beauty.

His intelligence, to the misfortune of England, cannot be rated so highly. He was a mild, kind, impulsive man with no evil in him ; he would have made a brave and good soldier if he had had a capable leader to tell him what to do. There certainly could never have been a worse choice made for King. The barons were not blind to his weaknesses, they knew that he was amiable, and for that reason they expected an amiable reign. Naturally the opposite was the result. To maintain a country at peace needs a strong hand, the hand of a William I or a Henry I. Stephen was not in the least like either grandfather or uncle, he was more like that other uncle Robert. He lacked Robert's vices, however ; we hear of no debaucheries except for a few illegitimate children—they were by no means anything unusual and Stephen cannot be condemned because of them. The really difficult point to explain in his character is how he ever summoned ambition enough to usurp the throne.

His wife may have given him the courage. Matilda of Boulogne is a charming and brave creature ; she shines with beauty beside the malignant figure of that other Matilda, the daughter of Henry. Stephen himself, once the throne was his, merely stuck to it out of mulish determination. " Why did they elect me ? " he cried when his partisans began to desert him. " By God's birth, they shall never call me a dethroned King ! " He had that stubbornness of a weak man, that futile pride which will allow itself to suffer and a country with it rather than confess defeat. He was only too conscious of his futility. He would sometimes weep, moaning that his own behaviour had brought anarchy into England. Weep though he might, he never did the one sensible and decent thing he might have done—that is, to leave the country for ever. No ! he struck to his throne and he defied his enemies, smiling pleasantly in the hope that everybody would smile back at him.

" The traitors understood that he, mild man was, and soft and good," says the chronicler, " and no justice did." He is the perfect retort to those tender-hearted historians who bewail the cruelty of stronger Kings. Henry I has often been written of with horror for putting out the eyes of Juliana's daughters ; if he had weakened, as these writers wish he had weakened, he would never have become the great King that he did become. Strength to hurt oneself, to trample on the thing one loves, to remain dispassionate, putting aside the weak affections that turn other men to cowards—that is what is needed in a King. He must be a miniature god, inhuman, the personification of justice, never being swayed by fears or loves or hates from the small light of truth ; he must be cruel to his people, to that vast mass of vaguely thinking souls who would disintegrate if their wills were their own. To all who shut their eyes in disgust at the brutalities of great Kings, imploring a little human weakness, Stephen stands on the pages of our history as the perfect and final retort. Here is your good King, your tender husband, your man who dislikes evil and desires affection ; an athlete, beautiful, gentle, self-pitiful, and therefore the worst possible ruler a country could possess. He drove England straight to anarchy.

DOVER repelled the usurper, Canterbury kept him out, but London flung open its gates and welcomed him. Stephen swore to be a good King, and as proof of his intentions he darted out and destroyed a gang of robbers lurking in the neighbourhood. With the backing of London, he hurried to Winchester to see his brother, Henry of Blois. Henry interviewed the keeper of the Royal Treasure, and the hoard was given to Stephen. The excuse for everybody ignoring Matilda was that she had been married without their consent, and now the legend was invented that with his last words the King had decided against his daughter. The Angevins were not liked, and Matilda, with her arrogant temper, was not the kind of woman to be popular. Besides, it was repugnant to men even to consider bowing under female rule. Stephen was at hand, brave and friendly, and—important point of the ecclesiastics—he would be ready to grant Rome all that his uncle had refused. Therefore, before he would hallow Stephen, the Archbishop of Canterbury, William of Corbell, insisted that he give the Church her " liberty." Stephen agreed, of course ; Stephen was the kind of man who would agree to anything.

This " liberty " of the Church is a vague enough phrase to make one intensely suspicious. It could mean a vast number of things—whatever any ambitious churchman had the power to demand. Later, in the days of John, Stephen Langton was to give it just such a meaning—an illimitable one.

Stephen was crowned exactly three weeks after Henry's death, on Sunday, December 22, 1135. As we learn that, apart from the officials necessary to such a function, " there were no abbots present and very few lay magnates," it appears that his accession was by no means as yet accepted. All the same, he was crowned, and after being crowned he issued a charter. He repeated the laws of his uncle and of King Eadward, as was customary. Later, he gave out another charter which is of more interest. It was obviously drawn up by the Church. Its very opening is significant. Unlike Henry who had merely styled himself, " Son of King William, by the grace of God, King in succession to his brother William," Stephen ignored all ancestry, relying wholly on Rome's support—" By the grace of God elected King of England by the assent of clergy and people, consecrated by William, Archbishop of Canterbury and legate of the Church of Rome, and confirmed by Innocent, pontiff of the see of Rome." He had surrendered his throne utterly, the throne for which his uncle had fought so gallantly to keep control. This was the price that Stephen paid for England. Bishops were to have exclusive jurisdiction over ecclesiastics and their goods, with sole control of their property after death, and were to retain the wardship of church lands. In fact, by merely placing the crown on the head of an amiable fellow, the Church was to get at last all that it had striven vainly to steal from Henry. His usurpation therefore cost Stephen nothing, it cost England a great deal. He bought it from the Church at the cost of weakening the throne itself.

THE embalmed corpse of Henry was laid in his own foundation, Reading Abbey, on January 4, 1136. As yet, England had not rallied to support its new King, and Matilda was entering Normandy. She had no possible hope of winning the duchy's allegiance ; apart from the medieval man's natural objection to being ruled by a woman, she was the wife of the detested Angevin. The barons ignored her pretension and were about to elect Stephen's elder brother Theobald when news came of Stephen's coronation. That settled the question. Stephen became duke and both Matilda and Theobald were put aside. Meanwhile Count Geoffrey was behaving in his usual reckless manner. He led his troops over the border and permitted them to do what they liked, with the result that instead of appearing as a peaceful candidate he was looked upon as a dangerous enemy. Matilda did not give up hope. She sent to Rome, putting forward her case.

With everything comparatively quiet, Stephen decided it was time that his wife was crowned Queen, and it was a particularly splendid coronation. Henry had always had a touch of the miser about him, but he had gathered his hoard only to have it flung high-handedly about by Stephen. The show of jewels and plate at this feast was unknown before, it dazzled everybody. Stephen hoped to bribe loyalty, he gave gold expecting love to be given in exchange. Naturally, the return was either contempt or dislike. Outwardly the nobles bowed to Stephen and scooped up the gold, inwardly they jeered at him and romped brutally about the countryside as if each were a little king in his own right.

Then Pope Innocent II confirmed Stephen in his usurpation, the claims of the Empress being put aside because—against the judgment of Anselm—it was declared that her mother had been a nun and herself was therefore illegitimate. It was natural that Innocent should support Stephen ; he was a personal friend of Stephen's brother the Bishop of Winchester, and besides, being a good churchman, Rome must come first. Stephen had promised liberty to the Church, Matilda was haughty and would most likely cling to every privilege.

At this blow to the hopes of the Empress, it was decided that cunning must be used, that England must be stolen if it could not be won. Robert of Gloucester, natural son of Henry I, left Normandy and returned to England. He came apparently as a friend but secretly as a traitor. It was not a task that Robert liked, but as the loyal follower of his half-sister he forced himself to stifle his good conscience and ape the traitor. He did homage to Stephen and was accepted. It must have seemed then to Stephen that all the country was his, that ahead of him stretched a reign of peace and joy. He was soon disillusioned. Rebellion broke out here and there, little risings that presaged war ; then Devon rose, led by Baldwin of Réviers—Redvers as the English called him—who seized Exeter Castle. Stephen arrived just in time to save the city from burning, but Baldwin held the castle, or rather Baldwin's wife held it, and she kept the King at bay for nearly three months. It was a powerful castle, one of the four important ones in the kingdom, and Stephen could not break the walls. He drove the garrison back into its inner defences, he smashed the drawbridge and built great towers of wood and hides to overtop the walls. There were traitors in his own camp. Baldwin's comrades drove thousands of cattle through the King's lines, passing unsuspected into the castle on the pretence of bringing provender for the royal camp. A monk carried the news to the castle and the garrison sallied out and drove the cattle in. " It is good," said Stephen, " that all our enemies be in one place." The garrison might have food enough but it had little water, the men were forced to drink only wine ; they baked bread with wine, they boiled their meat in it ; they must have grown to loathe its very smell, until even this began to run out. Barefooted, with ashes on her unbound hair, Baldwin's wife came weeping to Stephen. At first he would not listen, but the traitors implored mercy. Stephen gave in when he should have been strong. Thus, at the very beginning of his reign he showed that he was quick to forgive. The garrison marched out, not only unhurt and with all its goods, but with freedom to join any lord it pleased. If Stephen had driven these men as his uncle would have driven them, if he had shown that he would give no mercy, it is probable that his long and ghastly era of rapine and murder would never have happened. He did not draw men to him by being merciful, instead he gave courage to future rebels.

South Wales, which Rufus and Henry had fought and schemed to hold, was rising, murdering the Flemings, the English, the Normans. Stephen sent troops of mercenaries, men with no heart save for plunder, who did not care if they lost a battle so long as themselves remained unhurt and had booty to throw across their saddle-bows. They were defeated, yet Stephen made no move. He let Wales slide from England with scarcely a blow struck to retain it. And there was also Normandy calling to him ; it was stirred to rebellion, invaded by Anjou. Stephen hurried over the Channel, did homage to the King of France, and marched against his enemy. His troops were Norman and Fleming, with the result that there was more fighting in his own ranks than in pitched battles. And traitors were at work. Robert of Gloucester, who had aped the friend, now gradually drew men from loyalty. Stephen found that he was deserted by his own vassals, with his army quarrelling and apparently determined to fight only amongst itself. He was forced to agree to a two years' truce ; then Robert of Gloucester returned, promising to be Stephen's man again.

Scarcely had Stephen started once more to breathe freely, to return to his past optimism, than he involved himself in a quarrel about lands he wished to offer a friend. He was giving England to almost anybody, breaking up the royal revenues by creating earldoms, in a feverish desire to purchase loyalty, peace. He created only jealousies ; where so much was to be cajoled from an amiable King, each man lusted for more. By creating an earldom of Bedford for an old comrade, Stephen infuriated the man who already held the lands. A five weeks' siege was the result.

Then the Scots poured over the marches. Stephen had offered King David more than he could ever give. David, old man though he was, led his troops to take by force what had been promised. The English chroniclers repeat abominable tales of the behaviour of these Scots—they slashed the stomachs of pregnant women, it was said ; they impaled children on spear-points, they cut the heads from images and pushed them into the bleeding necks of the dead. These tales were probably true of many of the army, but David was exonerated from any share in such abominations. The English and Normans themselves were no better ; when the real civil war started the tale of their atrocities is almost incredible.

Three times the Scots came to England ; they retreated on the first occasion without a blow being struck ; Stephen dared not follow, there was the threat of rebellion in his own camp to hold him back. Two months later, David again crossed the Tweed, but, like Stephen, he was forced to return at the rumour that the Picts in his army were considering ways of murdering him. He waited for about another two months, then once more passed the Tweed. This time it was not Stephen who sent him home ; the northern barons gathered at the call of Archbishop Thurstan who preached a Holy War against the invaders, promising absolution to all who would fight. Under the thrill of the archbishop's courage and enthusiasm, the barons called out their men and beat the Scots so magnificently in the fight recorded by history as the Battle of the Standard that David was dragged off the field by his own guard, terrified lest their King be killed.

It was no peaceful throne that Stephen had taken. Often he must have been puzzled by the hatred he aroused, by the jealousies about him, the feuds that could not be suppressed. He was eager to rule kindlily, he wanted to be popular and would have bought popularity if he had been able. He must have wondered at the insurrections when he remembered the harsh laws of Henry and the comparative peace of his reign ; himself did so want to please everybody, and that was why he failed.

There was no cruelty in him ; yet Wales was tearing itself from the kingdom, Normandy was in continual revolt, Scotland was rushing furiously over the Tweed ; not only had he these wars with which to contend, but amongst those who should have been his allies were only continual plotting and treachery. There was only one person he could trust wholly, his wife Matilda. In the bloodshed of this reign, through the years of dreary fighting and repetitions of disloyalty, it is with relief that one turns to Matilda and sees that gentle woman standing nobly by a man weaker than herself. We do not know a great deal about her. She was merely the perfect wife who gave everything to her lord— affection, sons and loyalty. The eldest son had died in childhood ; the second, Eustace, had been recognised by Louis as Duke of Normandy ; William came third, then Matilda and Mary.

About the Queen's married life we hear practically nothing apart from the silly fable that Stephen had once loved that other Matilda, the Empress. We know, however, that he was not faithful to her, as we have the names of one or two of his illegitimate children, but he was probably as faithful as most other princes of the time. Few had the chastity of a William I.

Matilda was capable of action, she could lead her troops in person ; and she was capable also of arranging treaties of peace. After the defeat of the Scots, while the northern barons were about to follow up their victory, and while both Stephen and David were stubbornly refusing to discuss terms, Matilda brought husband and uncle together. The treaty was made by her, and afterwards she took with her to court David's son, Henry, now Earl of Northumberland. She was in every way a good woman; the tragedy is that her husband was a feeble King.

FEEBLE as a King Stephen might have been, yet it is impossible not to sympathise with him. He had taken on a task that was too great for his handling. Worried and lonely, he lived in continual fear of being dethroned, he forgave his prisoners when he should have executed them, and he made vast promises he could never fulfil. He was no coward, he could fight and fight well, but he dodged from battle to battle leading armies that were fully prepared to stab him in the back at any moment. He had no one to trust except his wife ; even his own brother was to turn against him.

So far he had found little peace, but these opening years were tranquil compared to those that were to come. Scotland, Wales, Normandy, and a few rebels had been his enemies ; from now he was to suffer a different war, an invasion by a woman who many believed was England's rightful Queen.

ROBERT of Gloucester gave first warning of the coming danger. He stepped into the open and no longer pretended to be Stephen's friend. While the Battle of the Standard had been fought, Robert was in Normandy, and from there he formally renounced the homage he had twice paid the King ; he said that Stephen was a usurper and that he had broken promises. Bristol and Dover were in Robert's hands, but he had friends scattered all over south and west England, men who were itching to fight. Stephen marched on Bristol where Robert's adherents had gathered in force, malcontents, general rascals who wanted plunder and fighting. Already an attempt had been made on Bath, but Robert's captain who led the attack was caught and released again after the most simple trick. His men asked to parley with the Bishop of Bath, the simple bishop walked out to discuss matters and was immediately seized and exchanged for his own prisoner. With its mixture of childish cunning and childish faith, that trick was typical of the medieval times.

Stephen found that his attack on Bristol was to be no simple matter. Plans were discussed only to be rejected ; someone suggested damming the Avon and flooding out the rebels, someone else thought a blockade would be simplest. In the end, nothing was done. Stephen began to fight lesser towns, concentrating on Shrewsbury. Here we discover that he was wearying of mercy. He hanged the captain of Shrewsbury with ninety-three of his men, and the effect was soon felt. Town after town gave in at once. Soon only Bristol remained defiant. Stephen could pause for a moment and attend a grand council at Oxford on June 24, 1139. It would have seemed that peace was not far off, but in his tactless manner he was about to turn against him those who had been his staunchest allies, the churchmen. Already he had angered his brother, the powerful Bishop of Winchester, by refusing him the archbishopric of Canterbury. Why Stephen, usually so generous, should suddenly take a stand against the brother who had won him his throne is impossible to explain. The bishop, an arrogant, ambitious man, may have been asserting too blatantly his power ; he may have irritated Stephen as so often great men irritate their Kings. Even Stephen, merciful and eager to please, must have had some strength ; otherwise he would have never pounced on the throne in the first place.

Already he had turned this most powerful supporter, his brother, against him when the grand council met at Oxford. Next he was to quarrel with an equally important ally, Bishop Roger of Salisbury. Bishop Roger was perhaps the wealthiest man in England ; under Henry I he had amassed honours and built castles. With jaundiced eyes the barons watched, asking, " What business had bishops with such castles ? " Stephen at first had refused to listen to their whispers, but the poison remained. He grew suspicious, and a weak man who begins to doubt is dangerous, his reactions are so swift, and his anger is great because it is anger against himself, against his own credulity.

Bishop Roger had started life as a clerk but Henry I raised him to the chancellorship and later made him Bishop of Sarum, next he became treasurer with power over all fiscal matters, he examined the revenue and judged legal suits about land, wardship, and such. His nephew Nigel succeeded him in this last post, but his own position then, if vague, became even greater, he was a sort of personal adviser to Henry. When Stephen was crowned he made the bishop's son, Roger, his Chancellor and retained Nigel as treasurer. " By God's birth," Stephen once cried—this was his favourite oath—" I would give him half England if he asked it—until time went." Time went quickly. Roger the elder, no longer in office, forgot his clerical place and turned baron. He built castles such as England had not known before, and this castle-building was a serious menace. Castles were things in which to hide, they were walls behind which you could bolt when the dogs were after you. What did a bishop need with castles ? what did any true man need with castles ? This passion for building seems to have come from the East, brought by the Crusaders struck to wonder and envy by the walled cities of the pagans. A mania for lurking behind stone ran through Europe. The great men had found a way of defying their King, by hiding from him. The history of medieval England is the history of Kings against castles, of Kings standing alone against fierce barons. Under Stephen, the castles rose as if bursting from the earth, and soon the danger was to come to a violent head at Runnymede, and at last to die when the great

Earl of Warwick the Kingmaker was destroyed by Edward IV in the fifteenth century.

STEPHEN listened to the words of men about him, he looked upon the castles of Bishop Roger, and he began to fear the power of the man. Few actions ever sprang from Stephen's own will ; he was like a puppet twirling on the strings of other men's desires. All contemporary chroniclers, even when they condemn the reign, pardon the King. His " advisers " did this or that, we are told—his " rebels." Now, these advisers turned him against Bishop Roger. His Queen we know had been a partner in refusing Henry of Winchester the archbishopric of Canterbury ; perhaps after all she had been the inspirer of that insane move. Now Stephen was told that Bishop Roger and family were intriguing with the Empress Matilda, and the tale might have been true. It is difficult to believe the good faith of any man of that time.

When the bishop set out for the Oxford council he knew what to expect. Whether spies had told him of the King's anger or whether it was intuition alone or merely bad conscience is not explained, but William of Malmesbury tells us that himself heard the bishop cry, " By my lady St. Mary, I don't know why, but my heart turns from this journey. Of this I am certain, I shall be as much use at court as a foal in a battle." At Oxford there was a quarrel about lodgings, a quarrel more than probably engineered by the King. The bishop's retainers were attacked during dinner by Alan, Earl of Richmond ; several were wounded, one killed, and a nephew of Alan's wounded near to death.

When the uproar was reported to him, Stephen decided that the bishop was the aggressor, the fight having occurred in his lodgings. He demanded the keys of his castles, which were of course refused. The bishop and his son were imprisoned, with the bishop's nephew, Alexander, Bishop of Lincoln. His other nephew, Nigel the treasurer, managed to escape to Devizes, which was held by his uncle's mistress, Maud of Ramsbury. Stephen decided to win by cunning ; he sent the two Rogers and Alexander to Devizes, placing the bishop in an ox-crib and his nephew in a hovel, and led the son with a rope about his neck before the castle, threatening to hang him if it was not delivered. Alexander was starved, placed on a daily reduced diet, and shown to the defenders of Newark. The bishop fasted voluntarily, despairing at the thought of his son's death.. But the boy's mother was in Devizes. She, unlike so many mothers of the time, thought children more difficult to produce and more worthy of love than any mound of stone. Devizes was surrendered, and Newark, too, surrendered at the sight of Alexander losing his flesh ; other garrisons also soon gave in.

Stephen had thrown his predecessor's money about with wide-open hands, and this fresh wealth came when the treasury badly needed it. Money he might have gained, but he lost things of greater value. He had placed a bludgeon in the hands of his enemies. For just such a chance as this, his brother of Winchester had waited, brooding over the loss of the arch-bishopric ; to console him, the Pope had made him legate and this gave Henry extraordinary powers. He denounced his brother at the synod of Winchester, August 29, 1139 ; he asked for advice, hinting that he was prepared to excommunicate the King if necessary. Stephen's chamberlain retorted that Bishop Roger had started the quarrel at Oxford, that he had been intriguing with the Empress and was prepared to join her the moment she landed. And he rounded his arguments with the Conqueror's attack on Odo of Bayeux—Roger had not been arrested, he said, as the bishop but as the King's servant. This was quickly answered : Roger held no position under Stephen, he drew no pay from him.

For two days the synod was adjourned, then Stephen had a better advocate in his friend, the Archbishop of Rouen. The archbishop attacked the assembly on its own ground, he demanded warrant to be shown from the canons proving that churchmen had the right to maintain castles. That finished the synod. The legate bowed before Stephen, imploring him not to break with the Church, but the most the King would do was to perform a small penance, which did not satisfy the bishops.

Stephen had made a great many powerful enemies at the moment when he needed friends, for the Empress was preparing to land in England.

From Bristol the mercenaries of Robert had roved the surrounding country, ravishing, plundering, burning. All over England there were tiny barons acting in this manner, like robbers. The cry that rises from the pages of the chroniclers is a cry of intense misery, of hopelessness, as from men surrounded by wolves. These castles were springing up everywhere, and

" when the castles were made, they filled them with devils."
Castles ! that is the wail of torment ; castles in which to house
devils, castles in which murderers lurked " and oppressed the
wretched." From end to end of Stephen's reign, gradually
becoming louder, more terrible, there is heard this cry of despair.
" Castles, castles ! They filled the land full of castles ! "

The anarchy of this reign is incredible. Each lord became
a petty, ruthless King ; he captured men and women and ransomed them and tortured them. " Never were martyrs so
tortured as they were. They hanged them up by the feet and
smoked them with foul smoke, they hanged them up by the
thumbs, or by the head, and hung fires on their feet, they put
knotted strings about their heads and writhed them so that it
went to the brain. They put them in dungeons in which were
adders and snakes and toads, and killed them so. Some they
put in a *crucet hûs*, that is, in a chest that was short and narrow and
shallow, and put sharp stones therein, and pressed the man
therein, so that they brake all his limbs." There were other
instruments used, there was the *lâð and grim* made of " neck-
bonds, of which two or three men had enough to bear one. It
was so made that [it was] fastened to a beam, and they put a
sharp iron about the man's throat and his neck, so that he could
not in any direction sit or lie or sleep, but must bear all that iron.
Many thousands they killed with hunger ; I neither can nor may
tell all the wounds or all the tortures which they inflicted on
wretched men in this land ; and that lasted the nineteen winters
while Stephen was King : and ever it was worse and worse.
They laid imposts on the town continually and called it *censerie*.
When the wretched men had no more to give, they robbed and
burned all the towns, so that thou mightest well go all a day's
journey and thou shouldst never find a man sitting in a town, or
the land tilled. Then was corn dear, and flesh and cheese and
butter, for there was none in the land. Wretched men died of
hunger, some went seeking alms who at one while were rich men,
some fled out of the land. Never yet had more wretchedness
been in the land, nor did heathen men ever do worse than they
did, for everywhere at times they forbore neither church nor
churchyard, but took all the property that was therein, and then
burned the church and altogether. Nor forbore they a bishop's
land, nor an abbot's, nor a priest's, but robbed monks and clerks,
and every man another who anywhere could. If two or three
men came riding to a town, all the township fled before them,

imagining them to be robbers. The bishops and clergy constantly cursed them, but nothing came of it, for they were all accursed and forsworn and lost. It was ploughing the sea, the earth bare no corn, for the land was all fordone by such deeds, and they said openly that Christ and his saints slept. Such and more than we can say, we endured nineteen winters for our sins."

Such also, can we say, is the result of having an amiable and weak ruler. Yet Stephen, when he struck at the Bishop of Salisbury, struck at the basis of his whole misrule, at the castle-building. Unfortunately he had not the strength to carry out his intentions. He made this one splendid effort at exactly the wrong moment, when allies were needed.

After giving wild promises in his hunger for the crown, Stephen naturally discovered, as perhaps he had always known, that he could never keep his word. A subtle King like Henry I would not have offered so much nor have reacted so abruptly and with so little proof of treason. Stephen had declared that he would disafforest the large tracts of land that the Conqueror and Henry had taken for royal parks and in which not only the deer but wild beasts, wolves and bears, were given freedom. No man without royal licence could enter these forests save at the risk of death or mutilation, and they were a strong grievance with the common people. Stephen swore to stop this grievance, yet in the year following his coronation we discover him hunting at Brampton near Huntingdon and holding a Forest Assize, which appears to mean that he now resumed forests after swearing to disclaim them. In a small matter such as this he could not stand by his oath, and on the larger question, the freedom of the Church, he behaved in exactly the same way. He had dared arrest a bishop, he had thereby insulted the power of Rome.

His kingdom in a state of utter anarchy, his people weary of his too-generous rule and the Church moving sullenly away, Stephen prepared his forces to withstand the invader, his cousin, the Empress Matilda.

HE concentrated on Corfe Castle in which lurked his old enemy Baldwin of Redvers ; it was suggested that his time might be better used by supervising the coasts in preparation for Matilda's landing than by taking Baldwin. Off bolted Stephen on this new track, leaving Baldwin untouched. The Empress with

Robert of Gloucester were by now already in England and were guests of the Queen Dowager Adelaide—Henry I's second Queen—and her new husband William of Aubigny at Arundel. Stephen moved on to Arundel, but Robert slipped away at his approach and reached Bristol. Here was Stephen's opportunity, now he could have clenched his fist around the whole conspiracy, he could have cornered and captured Matilda in Arundel. He dashed first after Robert, then decided that Matilda would be a more useful capture, and turned towards Arundel. His behaviour now becomes so stupidly chivalric that it amazed even the men of his time. When Adelaide heard that he was marching to the attack she grew afraid and almost promised to surrender her royal guest ; but Stephen became suddenly preposterously noble. He refused to take a woman captive when she was at his mercy. Not only did he give Matilda freedom to leave Arundel, he also gave her a safe-conduct to Bristol. His position was certainly a troublesome one : he could not execute Matilda and he could not imprison her. Apart from the chivalric standpoint, either act would have been dangerous policy. To execute her would have been to make her a martyr ; to imprison her would give cause for schemes for her rescue : either way, many men, blinded with their noble reverence for distressed womanhood, would take Matilda's banner. His only course was to expel her honourably from the country. That would have been generous, noble, and sane. Instead, he freed her unconditionally and gave her the courage to continue, and also he made his own followers despise his weakness.

MATILDA at Bristol made herself an unacknowledged Queen. Men came to join her, yet there were others who, while in secret sympathy with her cause, were cautious enough not to be open in their treachery. They advised Stephen, which was safer and probably more useful than fighting against him.

Instead of riding to Bristol and defeating his enemies once and for all, Stephen attacked Wallingford Castle, only to give up the siege for no particular reason and to ride against Trowbridge where further Matilda-adherents defied him. This siege also came to nothing. He darted here and there, attacking, fighting, yet achieving nothing. As a soldier he was courageous, as a leader he was worthless ; suggestions from his " advisers " distracted him from his purpose, he raced away from what was almost in his hands to start something entirely different which, in its turn, was never to be finished. Up and down England he went, darting here and there like a man chased by hornets, swinging wildly and futilely on every side, instead of turning to smoke out the entire nest at Bristol.

Month followed month of fruitless fighting, either side avoiding the other, the months spread to a year, to well over a year, and still the different armies swung away from each other, striking at little towns, taking small castles, executing, ravaging. There was no battle, there was but a series of minor conflicts. Stephen and Gloucester edged apart, like two boxers feinting and hitting into the air, each frightened of a definite blow lest it miss its aim and leave him at the other's mercy. They struck at the people of England, at the peasants, the merchants ; no land was tilled and prices rose to above starvation-point while the currency was debased until it was almost worthless. Yet the two enemies, panting and raging, chased aside from battle to strike into the air. Their mercenaries found good spoil, liquor and women and what gold they could dig from buried hoards ; it was like a plague on the country. Christ and His saints were asleep, without doubt, and the devil had free hand, until England was like a desert, an unpeopled arena for two armies that dared not meet, that pounced on lesser adversaries, defiant both and yet afraid of decision, afraid of the gamble of a pitched battle where a cause could be lost so very easily, by the chance of a traitor's unexpected blow, by a slip of the leader's foot to cause an evil omen and to terrify his men. England was trampled on heedlessly, was drenched with the blood of harmless peasants. Good spoil, good fighting for the mercenaries ; for England all the evils of hell unloosed.

Then at last, no matter how the enemies might feint, the day was forced upon them when they must meet and stake everything on a few hours.

During February 1141, while besieging the garrison at Lincoln, King Stephen was hearing mass when the ceremonial wax taper in his hand suddenly snapped and went out ; and it was said that the pyx on the altar, that body of our Lord, turned over and fell down. The King's attendants were struck with horror at this omen, but Stephen was not afraid. He knew that Robert was approaching to relieve the garrison with a large army, and the need for action killed all terrors in him. Whatever contempt we may have for Stephen's weakness of will, his dilatory tactics and stupid faith in councillors, we must admit his personal courage and swiftness of movement. Until the final moment, he could act splendidly, but something watered in him, left him helpless, when the first bravado had passed. Now not waiting even to conclude the feast of purification—tactlessness in a medieval general, particularly after such an omen—Stephen called out his troops to fight the enemy.

Robert had difficulty in passing the Witham, for the rain had been heavy and the river was high and rushing dangerously ; he led his men across a most treacherous swamp, exultant at having cornered Stephen. " He cannot fly," cried Robert, " we must win."

OUTSIDE the walls of Lincoln, to the north, the armies at last faced each other. Both leaders used the same formation, the common medieval one of three battles : Stephen, superior to Robert in cavalry, drew up his two front ranks with mounted men, himself commanding the rear of dismounted men-at-arms ; Robert's forces were superior in numbers to Stephen's, but we are uncertain how many of his troops were mounted, his front rank certainly must have been. In this rank, he wisely placed Stephen's most furious enemies, the rebels who had been disinherited for loyalty to Matilda ; his Cheshire and Welsh troops formed the second rank ; himself commanded the rear.

After the usual speeches—of interest only because we learn that Stephen's voice was too weak to be heard and he was forced to use a deputy—the battle started. Stephen's men had little to fight for, they were led by a King whom many despised, and fighting was to them but a kind of glorified tournament in which themselves remained unhurt while the common soldiers were slaughtered. This time, however, they were fighting men driven desperate by the thought of what little mercy they could expect from Stephen, men chased from their homes, exiles, fearless knights who would prefer death to the torture that their captivity would probably mean. Before these troops, the chivalry of Stephen was broken. His knights charged amidst " blast of trumpets and trampling of horses," their lances poised only for the gentlemanly prick, for not dangerous but honourable war ; and against them rushed the fury of Robert's troops, men careless for the moment of honour, determined only on victory. Before that rush the surprised knights of Stephen were slaughtered as if they were but common men unworthy of ransom ; they found not single-handed jovial encounters, but a sweep of furious enemies intent on killing. Flemings and Bretons gave way first, they tried to run, and their panic spread panic amongst the others. " Some were slain, some captured, some chased from the field." Alone to withstand that impact stood the King with his infantry. " The enemy pressing as if assaulting a castle, the battle waged terribly around this citadel," this citadel of kingship. Surrounded, beaten inwards, Stephen and his men stood firm. There was "no pause nor breathing for any." The King's sword shivered and broke, so he snatched up a Danish battle-axe, a fearful weapon, that was pushed towards him by a Lincoln burgher. No man could come within reach for a final thrust, he held them at bay with that axe, until someone—his name we do not know—flung a stone and struck him down. One William de Cahaigne took his chance. He shouted, " Here ! here ! I have the King ! " and leaped on the stunned man, pinning him to the earth.

LINCOLN fell as booty to the conquerors. Harmless burghers and their wives and children were slaughtered like cattle, many escaped by way of the Witham, but others were drowned by over-crowding the boats. The casualties were heavier in the city than in the field.

Taken to the castle, King Stephen was disarmed, and those near him wept openly as he bewailed his shame and said that for his sins he deserved all sorrows, adding that " such as had sworn fealty and done him homage had been guilty of heavy crime." And what he said was true—he had been defeated by traitors, but a greater general would not have been so reckless and so trusting.

A week later he was taken to Gloucester and shown to the Empress. Now, at last, the throne was hers, Stephen was in her hands, his cause was lost. She sent him to Bristol and herself made for Winchester where the royal treasure lay. On reaching Cirencester negotiations were started with Henry of Winchester, Stephen's brother. He demanded gigantic powers for the Church, greater powers even than he had wrung from Stephen. In mist and rain, at Wherwell near Andover, at a meeting with Henry in the open air, Matilda agreed to give full liberty to the Church and promised that " all matters of importance, especially the bestowing of bishoprics and abbeys, should await his

[*Henry's*] decision if he, with holy Church, would receive her as sovereign and be true to her."

The following day she entered Winchester, and the city was delivered to her, together with the royal crown and royal treasury that was "small in amount." Then she proclaimed herself "Lady and Queen" of England.

At a Winchester synod, April 8, 1141, Henry spoke to the clergy in public, calling on them to swear allegiance to Matilda, recalling the oaths sworn to her in her father's reign. Himself, he said, had bowed to Stephen because Matilda had delayed in Normandy, and then Stephen had promised to "honour and advance holy Church, uphold good and abrogate evil laws, yet it grieves me to recall, it shames to me say, how far justice failed and prosperity ended almost within the year. Then were the bishops captured, their possessions seized, abbeys sold, churches robbed, the counsels of the wicken taken, and of the virtuous despised. . . . I should love my brother in the flesh, but as the greatest duty I must sustain the cause of my immortal Father. And as God, without my help, has judged my brother, I, by virtue of my legation, invite you to deliberate lest for lack of a ruler the realm should decay." Yesterday, he said, he had talked the matter over with the greater part of the clergy, "to whom mainly the election of a King appertained," and knowing their opinion there was no need to call for votes, therefore he declared "the daughter of that most peaceful and glorious, that good and, in our time, incomparable King as sovereign of England and Normandy, and promise her loyalty and support." He concluded by remarking that he had sent for the Londoners to attend, for they, because of the importance of the city, were ranked as magnates.

When the Londoners arrived next day, Henry found that they were not so eager as the Church to take Matilda for Queen. "On the part of the fraternity, as they call it," says William of Malmesbury, who was present, they demanded the freedom of Stephen. Not expecting this, Henry had no arguments ready ; he could only repeat his yesterday-speech, merely adding "that it did not become the Londoners who were considered the chief people of England" to stand against the Church. Then one called Christian—"if I rightly remember," say, William of Malmesbury—gave Henry a paper which the bishop read and thrust aside, shouting, "It is informal !" But Christian would not be put aside like his paper. If Henry would not read what was written, he himself would read it aloud, which he did, saying that " the Queen implores the clergy, particularly the Bishop of Winchester, her lord's brother, to restore the King to his kingdom, wicked men, his own liege subjects, having thrown him into bonds." The wretched Henry was evidently incapable of making an impromptu speech ; he repeated for a third time his speech in favour of the Empress.

On the next day the synod was dissolved, the Londoners, still unconvinced, going home with vague menaces.

MATILDA was determined to be crowned in Westminster and therefore London must be conciliated. Slowly she began her progress towards the great city while efforts were made to force it to accept her. Already, however, the Empress was showing that as a ruler she would be even worse than Stephen. Robert of Gloucester struggled to please everybody ; he promised, cajoled, threatened, but whatever good he did was undone by the imperious manners of Matilda. She would listen to no advice and would herself decide whatever was best ; all that Stephen had enacted she reversed ; and when refusing a request she did it in the crudest possible manner ; even her friends, even men like King David of Scotland and Henry of Blois, when they approached her bowing, were treated with contempt : Matilda did not rise to acknowledge their courtesies.

Between the two evils, between the gentle amiability of Stephen and the cold harshness of Matilda, England could find little to choose. In their opposite ways Stephen's and Matilda's manners were equal, both were the extremes of bad kingship.

LONDON at last gave in, and in June the Empress entered the city. But her triumph did not lessen her arrogance ; two requests from Henry were rejected although she had sworn to obey him, and spitefully she turned against the city that for two months had refused her homage. She demanded from London, " not with gentle courtesy but in an imperious tone," a vast sum of money. The citizens pleaded with her, explaining that they had suffered by the recent wars, but she would not listen. " Without any of the gentleness of her sex, she burst into insufferable rage, while she answered with stern eye and frowning brow that the Londoners had often paid large sums to the King, that they had pulled wide their purse-strings to strengthen him and to weaken her, that they had long been confederate with her enemies for her harm, that they had no claim to mercy or to have the tiniest part of the fine remitted. Hearing this, the citizens returned to their homes, sorrowful and unsatisfied."

London, she felt, must pay for having hurt her dignity. When the citizens begged that she gave them back the laws of Eadward, as those of her father were too harsh to bear, she refused at once.

Stephen's Queen, that other Matilda, tried pathetically to win the Empress's sympathy, pleading for her husband's release or for her son's heritage of Boulogne and Mortain ; Henry added his word to his sister-in-law's : at least, while Stephen was in prison, he said, his boy Eustace should possess his lands. The Empress would not listen. The Queen wrote that if only her husband were released she would see that he relinquished his claim to the throne and she promised to make him turn monk or pilgrim. Securities were offered by the nobles. Still the Empress, in her awful pride, would not listen, would give no mercy to the man who had permitted her unconditional liberty when he had trapped her at Arundel.

THE loyalty of Queen Matilda, Stephen's wife, was only equalled by her swiftness to take action. When she realised that nothing could be gained by further entreaty, she brought her troops, with her uncle, her brother and true noblemen, out of Kent, and marched on London. The city came to her aid. The Tower was besieged, and its captain, the notorious Geoffrey de Mandeville, was quick to shift his allegiance. He became one of the Queen's party, as Henry of Blois had already done.

At the hour of dinner St. Paul's great bell was tolled. The Empress was somewhere in Ludgate about to begin her meal, when " like swarms of wasps " the citizens raced from their homes to capture her. With her friends, many of whom dropped from her as she rode, the Empress raced to Oxford.

LONDON was Stephen's again, won by his Queen ; it might be prepared to fight for him but it could not rescue him. He was safely shut away in Bristol, that stronghold of the rebels.

The Empress did not give up hope. So long as she could hold the King, England would stay rulerless ; and she decided to add the King's brother, Henry, to her hostages. She entered Winchester and commanded Henry to appear before her. The legate did exactly what anybody other than Matilda might expect him to do—he fled, telling the messengers, " I will prepare myself." The comrades he left behind fired the city so that they could clear themselves from the risk of ambush. The minster escaped the flames, but the Conqueror's palace was burnt with over forty churches. Then the besiegers suddenly found themselves the besieged, Henry sent troops to his friends' succour and the Queen came from London with Geoffrey de Mandeville and a thousand men.

Robert of Gloucester, holding off the enemy, thought only of his half-sister. He managed to arrange her escape while himself protected her, fighting his way to Gloucester. So exhausted became the Empress that she could not sit her horse, she had to be strapped on to a litter. Bravely, Robert kept the enemy back until, outnumbered, weary with riding and fighting, he was captured as he crossed the Test.

THE Empress held Stephen, and the Queen held Robert. Surely an exchange could be made? It was thus that everybody reasoned, but Robert himself stood in the path of any proposal. He was only an earl and an earl was not equal to a King ; if all the prisoners of his party were thrown into the balance, he suggested, the weight might be equalled. This was impossible ; the prisoners were too valuable as ransom to be given away even for the return of Stephen, gold came before loyalty to the great men of England. Efforts were then made to force Robert to turn traitor, to shift his allegiance from the Empress to Stephen, to make his own terms for freedom ; he would not listen. Threats followed : they would imprison him for life in Boulogne. Let them, he answered, then his Empress would imprison Stephen for life in Ireland.

The Queen bore no malice towards this brave man : " though she might have fettered him as he had fettered her lord, she would not let a bond of any kind be put upon him, nor presumed on her power to treat him dishonourably." She gave him complete freedom when at Rochester, permitting him to talk with anybody, even when only herself was present. And after she had left Rochester, he was still allowed the same licence ; we are told that with money sent him by his Kentish vassals he bought some valuable horses " that were useful to him later."

Negotiations dragged on, but at last details of the exchange were made final. Both sides were so suspicious that they dared not let their hostages go ; the Queen and Eustace went to Bristol on November 1, then Stephen left on the first stage, wife and son being taken in his place. Robert was at Winchester and was released when the King arrived ; but he left his son William to be kept until the Queen and Eustace were released.

" THE English people rejoiced on recovering their King." So one chronicler tells us, but we may doubt the statement. Stephen again in power meant only the renewal of the civil war. He reached London in December to be met with great enthusiasm, for London at least stood by him until the end.

Henry of Winchester called a synod at Westminster to explain why he who had crowned Stephen, then uncrowned him, and now wanted to crown him again. He began by reading a letter from the Pope who insisted on Stephen being released, and continued by boldly stating that he had only accepted the Empress—" Countess of Anjou," we now find her discreetly called—because she had forced him to against his will ; she had broken all her promises to the Church, he said, and had even attempted to murder him ; he concluded by calling on all to swear allegiance to Stephen, the King chosen by Rome, while the supporters of the Countess of Anjou would be laid under ban and cut off from the society of all Christian people.

Meanwhile, Stephen had entered the synod in no happy mood. He grumbled about the indignities he had suffered ; his own men whom he had never deprived of justice had dared fetter him, he said. He was then re-elected, and at Canterbury was once again crowned King of England.

FOR a moment there was peace ; that is to say, there was no civil war. England could never be at peace while the castles remained, those adulterine—or unlicensed—fortification, nests of wolves, bolt-holes from justice. They must remain while Stephen was King and Matilda was ambitious. The barons, we cannot doubt, desired no peace : with the country at war, they had leisure for plunder and for every conceivable brutality.

Again the civil war started. Robert of Gloucester had left for Normandy to seek help from Geoffrey of Anjou ; Geoffrey was too busy to go himself, but he sent his son, little Henry, a boy not yet ten. Stephen too was busy. He concentrated on Oxford in which the Empress lay. No longer was Stephen the chivalrous knight who would not harm a woman ; he had suffered at Matilda's hands and no longer had such idiotic delusions, therefore he was determined to catch her now while Robert was away. For three months, the Empress kept her enemy outside the walls, then she managed to escape. It was winter, December 1142, with snow on the earth, snow making all clear even at night. Matilda dressed herself and three or four others in cloaks the colour of the landscape ; like figures of snow they crept over the frozen moat, passing a sentry they had bribed, and were soon galloping freely to Abingdon.

Oxford gave in, but that was a worthless capture after the escape of the Empress.

ROBERT was back in England, little Henry remained for a short time at Bristol under the charge of a tutor, and the old adversaries began the game of hitting into the air and trying never to meet. Fighting here, fighting there, the civil war continued, with the combatants keeping apart and slaughtering only lesser enemies. And while the conflict—if such it can be called—went on, England lay depopulated, famine-struck ; whole towns were emptied, those not killed fled abroad or hid in huts in some sanctuary which even these ruffians dared not defile with blood and rape. Mercenaries in both armies enjoyed themselves while England it seemed was doomed, for neither party made a sign of giving in.

Stephen was once nearly captured, but not in battle. The Earl of Chester, a rebel, came to court and sued for pardon. To prove his words, he captured a town as a gift to the King and helped build a stockade. Then he suggested that Stephen come to Wales and help fight the Welsh. The mere sight of such a King, suggested the earl, would mean success. Stephen agreed and actually would have gone had not his councillors—true for once, but probably not wishing him murdered as that would stop the war — suggested that in exchange for the King the earl give hostages. As he refused to do this, he was seized and imprisoned. And the war continued.

The war continued. It seemed that it would never stop, that it had become a part of the affairs of England. Each party was struggling to grip that crown, that bauble which meant torment and loneliness and treason, but which also meant power

—power, to be the King, the lord, even if you were friendless amongst traitors ! And Stephen also had his pride, he had sworn not to die dethroned. Let England be broken, let men perish by the thousands, let not a virgin be left in the country, Stephen would yet be King although his kingdom might be penniless, depopulated. The crown, the sense of power—what else mattered to these strong medieval lords ? Let there be leisure for hunting of man or beast, leisure for drink and women, for torture and for occasional singing of gay songs ; but above all, let there be power, let men tremble when you step into the room, let the women droop in their skirts and crumple to their knees before you ; let there be bloodshed and laughter, let there be death and the doom of everlasting hell, all for the brief candle of a man's lifetime glory, for the light of your power reflected in the abject eyes of men and women. . . . That was sufficient.

Yet Stephen was no cruel man, he was kind, he was generous ; how could such a man as this be driven by such fury towards the desolation of a country merely that the crown could remain his property ? We cannot tell. Perhaps his wife may have had great longings for the bejewelled bauble. Even in the weakest and kindliest of men lives this flame that would turn him murderer and criminal if opportunity arrived. Stephen had seen the opportunity, he had grasped at it and had held it in a shaking hand, yet only blood was squeezed from its majesty, only the blood of others, of the people of England who turned dreaming towards the past, towards the days of good King Eadward, even towards the days of the harsh Conqueror and his sons Rufus and Henry. Then there might have been oppression, but also there had been justice. The ploughman had not been harmed, merchants could sell their goods, and women could go to bed at night and know that that bed was for them alone if they wished it.

Of what worth was this crown ? What could it bring except suffering, distrust, despair ? Those were small matters to value against the crown itself, against that symbol of power. No medieval man would have considered the argument. Let churchmen quarrel about right and wrong, let them brandish the key to heaven, earth was man's property, it was man's to take with both hands, to possess utterly.

At first sight one is puzzled by these two apparently irreconcilable halves to the medieval character—intense piety and intense ruthlessness. Yet they are not irreconcilable. Apart from the fact that the doctrine of predestination was vaguely believed in, man's faith in God—particularly in the Virgin—was so great, equalled only by his own arrogance, that he rarely doubted his chance of slipping into heaven somehow. It was only when he fell dangerously ill, when sword and horse were taken from him, that the terror of hell came ; lying in bed, priests nagging at him on every side, he could not escape the sense of inevitable doom. We have seen this in Rufus. While life was in him, while he was bounding joyously from battle to council-table, he had little time for God ; in bed, God caught him, shook him, and terrified him. It was the same with Henry II, a greater man than Rufus. He could swear by the Eyes of God and avoid mass, but on the sick-bed his sins took shape and haunted him. The very narrowness of the Church produced its own reaction ; besides, by dedicating your children to God in a monastery at great expense, by founding an abbey, or by leaving a fortune to have illimitable masses said for your soul, you could evade God's justice. He would realise that a man who would give money away must be truly repentant, and repentance was what God desired. He did not object to sin if repentance followed. There would be time for repentance, said the medieval man, but let that time wait. Like many others, William, son of Robert Curt-Hose, was buried in monk's garb ; no matter what his crimes, this sudden repentance would give him his passport to paradise. Therefore if God could be bribed at the last moment, let the devil have power while you lived. The only thing that really shook these knights was the awful fear of dying unhouselled—then, of course, you went direct to hell without hope of crawling out again. Before going to battle, it was the custom to take the last sacrament ; if this was impossible, you tasted the earth, as the English did before Agincourt. This was considered to be almost as valuable, no priest being near.

They were reckless men because they had a trick up their sleeves which would pull them out of the devil's hands at the last moment. That last moment seemed æons off ; for the present there were good foods to be had, and warm wines and warmer women, there was blood to be spilt, there was the crown that might be seized and held.

Brutal, fearless, the nobles of England jeered when told that Christ was asleep. They deliberately separated Stephen and

Matilda. They wanted no peace to be sealed, for anarchy meant power, it meant freedom.

Yet all must end, even the violent joys of life. The civil war petered out for a time ; Matilda wearied of it and left England, and, shortly afterwards, Robert of Gloucester died.

WITH Robert dead and Matilda out of the country, Stephen had an opportunity for another quarrel with the Church in which he was badly beaten ; then for the third time young Henry Fitz-Empress, son of Matilda and Geoffrey of Anjou, entered England.

Henry was now twenty years of age ; his father's death had made him Count of Anjou, Touraine and Maine ; by right of his mother he was Duke of Normandy ; and through his wife, Eleanor —divorced consort of the King of France—he was Duke of Aquitaine. Already he had fought bravely against France and against Stephen's son Eustace, now he turned towards England.

Miracles are said to have taken place at his landing. He came within the octaves of the Epiphany—January 6-12, 1153— and going into a church " to pray for a space, after the manner of soldiers," he entered at the exact moment that the priest opened the office of the mass with the words, " Behold there cometh the Lord, the Ruler, and the kingdom is in his hand."

Stephen rode to the rescue of Malmesbury which was besieged by Henry. He had little enough to fight for. His last quarrel with the Pope had lost him his greatest ambition. The Pope had refused to recognise his son Eustace as heir of England ; then at a London council, Stephen had tried to defeat Rome by ignoring its ban ; he insisted that Eustace should be recognised as heir and be crowned immediately, a custom new to England but common enough in France. The bishops objected. Not only had the Pope refused to " hallow and confirm " Eustace, he had forbidden the English bishops to do so, Stephen having " snatched the crown in violation of his oath." It was rather late in the day to bring this up, but the King had really behaved in a most obstreperous manner, treating bishops as his private property, refusing to let them go abroad and deposing them from their sees. Stephen was weary of argument with churchmen who always knew the right things to say ; he called out his troops, surrounded the building and threatened to imprison every bishop unless they agreed to elect and crown Eustace. The clergy refused, and Stephen knew that he was helpless. The crown would die with him.

This Eustace was certainly no king to be desired. One friendly chronicler does his best to make him appear amiable, but the most he can do is to talk vaguely about his gravity, his skill in war, his generosity and his likeness to his father. The other chroniclers are definite enough. " He was an evil man," says one ; " he did more evil than good." " He spoiled the lands and laid on heavy taxes." " Fond of low company, dissolute." " He brought his wife to England. She was a good woman but she had little happiness with him." " A good soldier but an ungodly man. . . ." No, the bishops showed true judgment when they abided by the Pope's command.

WHEN Stephen charged to the rescue of Malmesbury he charged straight into a storm. Henry " had the wind at his back and it struck Stephen in the face "—it struck with sleet and with ice. The cold was unbearable, and the Avon barred his path, its banks swollen with rain. Stephen, in his typical manner, returned to London, and Malmesbury surrendered to Henry.

Wallingford was the next point of war. As Stephen rode to the field, it was noted that he fell three times from his horse— a bad omen which terrified his men. Besides, the barons did not want a battle, they feared victory for either party, and it was decided that Stephen and Henry should talk together. Separated by a branch of the Thames, the King and the duke parleyed, shouting at each other from bank to bank. A truce for five days was agreed to by both.

Then in a manner that nobody expected, the civil war abruptly ended. It was finished by an accident. Eustace, outraged by his father even daring to discuss matters with Henry and fearful that he might lose his heritage, wandered from the royal camp. He went to Cambridge and then to Bury St. Edmunds. Here he demanded money, and, being refused, decided to reap the abbey crops. But St. Laurence foiled him, for this was St. Laurence's day, August 10 ; the saint struck Eustace dead a week afterwards.

Now that Eustace was removed, there was no cause to hold off peace. Stephen had two other sons, but his wife was dead, her counsel lost, and probably he felt for the boys' own sake it would be best to deny them England.

Henry of Winchester, who seemed to enjoy passing round the crown, offered to mediate. After two months it was decided that

Stephen should remain King until his death, then Henry Fitz-Empress would succeed him.

And at last there was peace in England.

THE remaining year of Stephen's reign passed in efforts to reduce the adulterine castles ; spurred on to the task by a rebuke from Henry, he managed to travel north, enjoying the first peaceful progress of his reign.

For nineteen years he had striven to hold the country, he had spun around it as if on a top, at every moment seeming about to be thrown off yet clinging to the throne with a tenacity astonishing in so weak and casual a man. To the last moment he clung there, dizzied perhaps, but triumphant. He had sworn not to die dethroned and he kept his oath. His life had been violent, friendless, and pathetic, but he kept his word, he held the crown to the end. And he died with it. Evidently it was some bowel trouble that killed him. He was at Dover when he was dragged to his bed, to end a weary and futile life on October 25, 1154, in the priory of St. Martin. The body was taken to Canterbury and then to Faversham, where it was buried beside his wife and Eustace in the church of the monastery of the Holy Saviour which himself had founded.

We have no details of his funeral. He died as he had wished, as King, but facts about the funeral are lacking. Unrecorded, he was carried to lie beside his wife and to-day we do not know even the exact spot where he was buried. After so turbulent a career, he disappears from history with only a casual mention, as if the corpse that went to Faversham was the corpse, not of a King, but of any common baron. Poor Stephen ! To keep the honours of royalty he had striven so hard, it seems scarcely fair that he should have been cheated of the most solemn honours of all at the very end.

V

KING HENRY THE SECOND

1154–1189

WHEN HE WAS ONLY TWENTY-ONE YEARS OF AGE, Henry FitzEmpress
—nicknamed Curtmantle because of the shortness of his Angevin
mantle compared to the long fur-lined cloaks of English and
Norman—was not only King of England, he was also Duke of
Normandy, Count of Anjou, Maine, and Touraine, Count of
Poitou, Duke of Aquitaine, and suzerain lord of Britanny.
Broadly built, of middle-height, Henry II had a round fair face,
freckled, and with prominent grey eyes that could be mild as a
dove's when he was tender, or as brilliant as fire when he was
in an Angevin rage. His hair was red and cropped close for
fear of baldness, his voice was loud, harsh and cracked. With
bull-neck and broad shoulders, with long powerful arms and with
legs arched by continual riding, this first of our Angevin Kings
had something "lion-like" in his face. A man of gigantic
energy, of swift moods and clerkly cunning, no King could have
been better suited than Henry for the task of hammering into
shape the chaos of Stephen's reign. He set about it firmly,
without impatience, being a man sure of his own strength and of
his magnificent destiny.

He laughed at God when the mood was on him ; he could
fondle with one hand and whip you with the other. He feared
nothing except his own ungovernable fury that occasionally
burst through his strong will and turned him to a maniac who
grovelled on the ground and bit the straw. Only by the greatest
effort could he restrain his fingers from tearing out the eyes of
men he hated. And he was sometimes unable to hold back his
lust ; his son's betrothed he stole and bedded, he broke a sacred
knightly duty and seduced a hostage. His own wife he hated,
as she deserved ; she had cheated and left the King of France,
her first husband, but Henry soon pushed her into prison and kept
her there.

A man ruled by both body and mind, in whom the physical lusts were in conflict with a sane well-balanced judgment, he could be brave, patient, murderous, spiteful or cunning ; all vices, all virtues, fought in Henry, moulding him into a ruler such as was needed for a broken country like England after the civil wars.

His energy was so terrific that few could keep pace with him. He rarely sat except when eating or in the saddle ; food he despised, and gulped it in sparingly only to keep the body active. With filthy hands, scarred and stained from the kill, he would sit at table ; he was the plainest dressed man at court, for he despised the childish emblems of power and vanity. A great King indeed, a splendid soldier, a law-giver and a statesman. Brutal when the mood took him, " he was more tender to dead soldiers than to the living, and found more sorrow in the loss of the slain than in the comforting love of those who remained." There was no leisure in his court, when not busy about affairs he was hunting in the forests, leading " unquiet days," rushing home to supper yet scarcely sparing time for food, driving his courtiers to exhaustion by not bothering to sit, although his own feet and legs were chafed and broken with sores from riding, and he suffered from at least one ingrowing toenail.

A pathetic letter has come to us that tells the sorrows of a man attached to Henry. His courtiers, we learn, " know neither order nor reason nor measure in their meals, or in their ridings abroad, or in their nightly watchings. Court chaplains and knights are served with bread hastily made, without leaven, from the dregs of the ale-tub—leaden bread, bread of tares, bread unbaken. The wine is turned sour or mouldy ; thick, greasy, stale, flat, and smacking of pitch [*from the caulking of the barrel*]. I have sometimes seen even great lords served with wine so muddy that a man must needs close his eyes and clench his teeth, wry-mouthed and shuddering, and filtering the stuff rather than drinking. The ale which men drink in that place is horrid to the taste and abominable to the sight. There also (such is the concourse of people) sick and whole beasts are sold at random, with fishes even four days old, for the servants reck not whether an unhappy guest fall sick or die, so that their lords' tables be served with a multitude of dishes ; we who sit at meat must needs fill our bellies with carrion, and become graves (as it were) for sundry corpses. . . . Yet even so, if the court dwell longer than usual in any town, some courtiers are ever left behind to die. I cannot endure (to say nothing of others) the vexations of the royal stewards—fawning flatterers, wicked back-biters, unprincipled extortioners : wearisome with their importunities for gifts, ungrateful for benefits received, malignant to all such as are loth to give again and again. . . . This again addeth to the courtiers' misery, that if the King have promised to stay anywhere, and especially if the herald have publicly proclaimed this as the royal will, then be sure that he will set out at daybreak, mocking all men's expectations by his sudden change of purpose. Whereby it cometh frequently to pass that such courtiers as have let themselves be bled, or have taken some purgative, must yet follow their Prince forthwith without regard to their own bodies, and, setting their life on the hazard of a dice, hasten blindfold to ruin for dread of losing that which they have not, nor never shall have. Then may ye see men rush forth like madmen, sumpter-mules jostling sumpter-mules and chariots clashing against chariots in frantic confusion, a very Pandemonium made visible. Or again, if the Prince have proclaimed his purpose of setting out for a certain place with the morrow's dawn, then will he surely change his purpose ; doubt not but that he will lie abed till midday. Here wait the sumpters standing under their loads, the chariots idly silent, the out-riders asleep, the royal merchants in anxious expectation, and all murmuring together : men flock round the court prostitutes and vintners (a kind of courtiers who often know the palace secrets) to get tidings of the King's journey. For the King's train swarms with play-actors and washerwomen [*for some reason, often synonymous with whores*], dicers and flatterers, taverners, waferers [*wafer-makers, also for some reason with more than doubtful reputations*], buffoons, barbers, tumblers, and all birds of that feather. . . . Yet when our out-riders had well-nigh or fully gone the whole day's journey, then again would the King change his purpose and lodge elsewhere, having perchance a single house and victuals enough for himself alone, whereof no other might share : yea, and I verily believe (if I may dare so to speak) that he hath found in our anguish a keener zest to his own pleasures. We therefore, wandering for three or four miles through unknown forests, and oftentimes in the black darkness, esteemed ourselves fortunate if perchance we fell upon some vile and sordid hovel. Oftentimes the courtiers would fight bitterly and obstinately for mere huts, and contend with drawn swords for a lair which had been unworthy of contention among swine. How we and our beasts fared meanwhile on such a night may well be imagined : I myself was so divided from my train that it was scarce possible to collect the scattered remnants within three days. Almighty God on high, Thou who are King of kings and Lord of lords, and terrible with the kings of earth, Who takest away the spirit of princes, Who givest health to kings, in Whose hand is the King's heart and Who turnest it whithersoever Thou wilt, turn now and convert the King's heart from this his pestilent custom, that he may know himself to be but a man, and may learn by use to show the grace of royal liberality and the kindness of human compassion to those men who are drawn after him not by ambition but by necessity ! " [1]

While deploring the trials of good Peter of Blois, we should certainly give him our gratitude for this extraordinarily vivid picture of Henry's court. There was no comfort to be found in it, no leisure, courtiers were dragged forward willy-nilly by this King who would not believe himself a man, who ignored cushions and down-beds, who took no notice of the fatigue in his own limbs, the sores on his legs.

There was no etiquette in his court, Henry behaved like any other man, all talked openly together ; " he does not presume to be haughty," says Walter Map, " nor speak with a proud tongue, nor exalt himself over any man."

His temper was diabolic. The legend of the demon-ancestress of the Angevins was accepted ; Henry's son, Richard I, boasted of it during the crusades. Henry's grandmother—goes the tale—was a beautiful demon who would seldom go to church and then could not " abide the secrets of the Mass. The earl her husband took her and was ware of that doing, and ordained four knights to hold her in church ; and she threw away her mantle that she was y-holden by, and left there her two sons under her right side of her mantle, and with her other two sons that she had under the left side of her mantle she flew out at the window of the church in sight of all men, and was never y-seen after that time."

It is true that Henry and his sons, Richard and John, had such temper that it was maniacal. This alone, perhaps, restrained Henry from becoming the very greatest of our Kings. In all else, he seemed the perfect ruler. And added to his strength of

[1] From the extract in *Life in the Middle Ages*, by G. G. Coulton, vol. iii. (Cambridge), 1929.

will and his contempt for fatigue and his filthiness of manner, we learn that queer other side of him, his reverence for scholarship. His knowledge of law must have been extreme, and he knew " almost all histories and [had] experience of all things ready to his hand." He liked to have around him wise men, and enjoyed talk on serious matters, being for ever urged on by an insatiable curiosity. We are told that he understood all the languages from Gaul to the Jordan, but spoke only French and Latin. " The King has always in his hands bows and arrows, swords and hunting-spears, save when he is busy in council or over his books. For as often as he can find breathing-space amongst his business-cares, he uses his time in private reading or troubles to work out some intricate questions with his clerks. . . . With the King of England there is school every day, continual conversation of the finest scholars and discussions of problems."

He was for ever busy and grudged a second away from action or learning ; eating he grudged, and even services to God. He did not attend confession until extremely ill, and during mass he talked or arranged business, wrote or drew pictures. Yet he could be devout when struck with sudden superstition or when terrified by prophecies.

In every way a complex character, yet undoubtedly a great ruler, Henry II was crowned King of England on December 19, 1154, at Winchester, about six weeks after the death of Stephen.

When told of Stephen's end he had been besieging a castle in Normandy ; friends urged him to race to England lest the barons revolt, but he merely remarked that they wouldn't dare and continued with the task at hand. That was typical of Henry, the opposite in every way to Stephen. Cruel, just, brutal, violent, patient, learned, active, politic and courageous, he was, like most of the Angevins, feared more than loved. Of him St. Bernard once said, " From the devil he came and to the devil he will go."

GEOFFREY PLANTAGENET,[1] the father of Henry, would seem at the first glance to be the perfect knight, but in him the acts of knight-

---

[1] The title Plantagenet has been taken very loosely. Geoffrey is the only true Plantagenet, so-called because he wore a sprig of broom—*genet*—in his cap. It was a personal nickname, such as Henry's "Curt-mantel" and Robert's " Curt-hose." Soon this nickname habit was to die, to be replaced

hood were on the surface only, springing from the mind and not the heart. He postured as the gallant before the mirror of his own admiration ; having read all the histories of every nation, he knew fully the ideals of knighthood—courtesy, generosity and smooth speech—and he acted them whenever possible. As a boy he had been lettered enough to be able to converse as an equal with so cultured a King as Henry I, and when he rode to battle, a learned man rode at his side. This passion for knowledge he passed on to his son Henry, together with his violent Angevin temper ; unfortunately, he did not add his extreme good looks, he gave instead a more valuable heritage—a charm of manner that could lull the most vindictive enemy.

Of Henry's upbringing we know very little. He lived sometimes with his father, sometimes with his mother, sometimes with the gallant Robert of Gloucester. From the age of fourteen—when first he invaded England to fight King Stephen—he was a soldier, and his days were spent either in learning or in battle. When his father died suddenly on September 7, 1151—after riding hard he swam to cool himself and caught fever—Henry was already a duke, powerful enough to invade England. Soon he added to his power by marrying the divorced wife of King Louis VII of France, Eleanor, the Duchess of Aquitaine and Gascony. She was a very beautiful woman, strong-willed and passionate ; she was cultured, able to read and write, and could compose and sing the troubadour lyrics, the chansons and tensons of Provençal poetry. Such a woman as this, gay, clever and ambitious, was a strange creature at the gloomy court of Louis and there could have been no happiness in such a marriage. Cruel as Eleanor was, rapacious and domineering, it is impossible not to respect her vitality and learning. As the Queen of any other King than Henry her effect on history might have been great ; but she comes to us as being of no importance save as the mistress of vast territories that passed to France, and from France to England.

It was weakness in Louis that made him divorce her. He was a saintly man who sacrificed his curls, his beard and moustaches, in penitence to God ; this was no husband for the gay and pas-

---

by names taken from one's birthplace, such as Thomas of " Woodstock," Thomas of " London," etc. The name Plantagenet was revived by Richard, Duke of York, father of Edward IV, and used by him for a surname : of his line, all were wiped out by the Tudors. After 1499, not one of the whole legitimate male issue of Count Geoffrey remained.

sionate Eleanor who mocked at his smooth face, saying that he was a priest and not a man. Louis found escape the only solution to his matrimonial problems ; it was a feeble act, to surrender for comfort his Queen's mighty possessions. He dared not divorce her until his father's old minister, Suger, had died ; immediately he summoned a church council and pleaded that he and Eleanor were within the prohibited degrees of consanguinity. This was the time-honoured plea, and if the Church had really acted on it, scarcely a royal family in Europe would have existed, for the papal ban stretched to the most distant blood-connections. What was the exact relationship between Louis and Eleanor is unknown, but it was certainly no closer than Eleanor's relationship to her next husband.

Already Eleanor had decided to marry the young Count of Anjou, but she was too valuable a commodity to travel Europe without risk. Twice she was nearly trapped by hopeful suitors, but at last reached her own country and from there wrote to Henry, offering herself and her lands to him in marriage. This was too good an offer to miss ; Henry started off to her at once and married her at Poitou, " without the pomp or ceremony befitting their rank," two months after the divorce. At this time she must have been about twenty-seven years of age, he was nineteen.

THE life of Henry falls into two parts—his conflict with Thomas Becket [1] and his conflict with his sons. It was a life of such enormous activity that it is impossible to compress it even slightly into so small a space as this. His administration of England, Poitou and Normandy, and his conquests of Wales, Ireland and Brittany, must be more or less ignored while we examine those two dramatic episodes which most clearly reveal his character.

The quarrel with Thomas reminds one of Henry I's quarrel with Anselm ; it reminded the antagonists themselves of it ; Thomas tried to have Anselm canonised and it is obvious enough that he imitated his great predecessor, wishing to equal him. He failed. When Henry I and Anselm fought, they fought with dignity ; there was no dignity in the later quarrel, both King

---

[1] It is difficult to know what to call Thomas Becket, for surnames were haphazardly used in the twelfth century. His contemporaries usually called him " Thomas of London " or " Thomas of Canterbury," and I have followed them by taking " Thomas " alone as being the most accurate. How, why or when that " à " ever cleft his name is a mystery.

and archbishop lost their temper, both were vindictive, stubborn.
On either side there was right, and on either side there was wrong ;
they over-acted their parts. Thomas particularly always held
the mirror before himself, whatever he did he saw reflected
gloriously before his eyes. Theatrical, flamboyantly distorting
the quiet courage of Anselm, he gains little sympathy, while
Henry with his spite and awful rages gains no more than Becket,
yet often when Henry would have given in, Thomas refused to
listen to one word of reason.

HENRY's task was not so great as one might think when he was
crowned King of England. Stephen had reduced many of the
adulterine castles during the end of his reign and even the barons
were beginning to tire of slitting each other's throats. The new
King's main task was to set in order the administration of Henry I,
and he appointcd Thomas Becket, Archdeacon of Canterbury,
his chancellor. This was a most important position, a kind of
secretary of state ; the chancellor presided at all councils, he
sealed the royal edicts, received the incomes of vacant bishoprics,
abbacies and baronies, and was a general factotum of the
King.

The man who rose to this high post, and who was to rise yet
higher, was not of noble birth. His mother was a native of Caen,
his father of Rouen, but they had settled in London before the
birth of Thomas. At one time the father, Gilbert Becket, had
been port-reeve—a sheriff, an important position. The tale was
later given that Thomas's mother was the daughter of a Saracen
emir who had captured Gilbert while he was on a pilgrimage to
the Holy Land, and that the pagan girl had so loved the Christian
that not only did she help him to escape but followed him to
London. This story is entirely fallacious.

Thomas was well educated. At the age of ten he was at
school under the canons of Merton Priory in Surrey, then he was
taught at London and later studied theology at Paris ; but when
he returned home at the age of twenty-two he found that his
father's fortunes had ebbed and he was forced to become a
notary. A family friend rescued him from a commonplace
future, he introduced Thomas to Archbishop Theobald. From
that date, Thomas's rise was swift, and he studied canon law at
Bologna and Auxerre ; his qualities were soon noted ; in 1151
Theobald sent him to Rome on the important task of persuading
the curia not to saction the coronation of Stephen's eldest son,

Eustace. Probably his success here made him a favourite with
the Angevins ; they certainly did not forget him when Stephen
was forced to surrender to their invasion. The Thomas then became
Archdeacon of Canterbury in 1154 ; and when Nigel, Bishop of
Ely, was removed from the chancellorship to the exchequer
within a month or so of Henry's accession, Thomas was appointed
to his place.

Great must have been the ambition and the genius of Thomas
Becket that could lift him from a middle-class environment to
this high position. He was an extraordinary man, in many
ways similar to the King ; he had the same energy, the same
strong temper, the same conscientiousness, clinging stubbornly
to a task until it was achieved, the same courage in battle and
the same graciousness of manner. He has been accused of
ambition and of insincerity ; ambitious he decidedly was, but
so are most great men, and it is no crime that the humble Thomas
should wish to become mighty in the world. That he was
insincere I do not for one moment believe. The volte face of
his change from chancellor to saint has so puzzled many writers
that they have been unable to explain it except as hypocrisy—
either the chancellor or the archbishop was a hypocrite, they
state. Yet surely it is understandable that a man can become so
absorbed in his present task that his entire character can alter,
that Thomas with his terrific energy could not remain passive
in any post ? that whatever was his duty he would perform it
fearlessly ? that he would battle against his King if need called
as in the old carnal days he had battled with living enemies in
warfare ?

Yet the feeling remains that Thomas was always more the
chancellor than the archbishop. The second rôle did not fit
him so neatly as the first. He had not the beautiful passivity of
the saint, the gentle forbearance before anger, the will to remain
silent under insult. He was no Anselm. He was a man of the
world who discovered himself a churchman and who determined
to be a churchman in every respect.

Even when he was chancellor, however, he remained a strict
celibate. In that profligate court, this man, sworn never to
marry, was able to stand outside innumerable temptations. His
worldliness showed itself in his extravagance, in his gaudy
clothes, and in his love of dining in state ; he was never a
debauchee, but the tale of Henry and the cloak proves that he
was not made of the charitable stuff of a true churchman. One

winter's day the King and his chancellor were riding through London when they noted a poor man shivering by the wayside. " Would it not be a worthy act," said Henry, " to give that poor old man a warm cloak ? " Thomas agreed and Henry cried, " Then you shall have the merit for this goodly act ! " and after a tussle wrenched Thomas's splendid fur-lined cloak from his shoulders and flung it to the beggar.

They were great friends, these two. Henry would often call unexpectedly on his chancellor, would ride into his hall and gulp a cup of wine, or would vault the table and sit beside him, laughing at the luxury which he denied himself. Thomas's luxury was greater than that of any other man at court : gold and silver shone on his board, earls and barons sat there daily ; and it is remarked that every morning the hall pavement was strewn with fresh hay and straw in winter, or with fresh rushes and green leaves in summer, so that the knights could lounge anywhere without soiling their gorgeous clothes. When Thomas was sent on an embassy to Louis of France, the description of his entourage reads like the list of a travelling circus. First marched serving-men and lackeys—two hundred and fifty of them—singing English songs, then came huntsmen, gaily dressed, tugging at the leashes of harriers and greyhounds ; six giant waggons followed, drawn by five splendid chargers, each led by a groom and guarded by a mastiff : in these waggons was laid the necessities of the chancellor's household, one was his chapel, another his chamber, a third his kitchen, the other three held food and iron-hooped barrels of English ale as gifts for the French ; then came pack-horses bearing the church ornaments, furniture, clothes, boxes of money, and plate : on each horse crouched a groom with a long-tailed monkey chattering on top of each load ; squires followed, bearing their masters' shields, leading their chargers, or holding hawks on fists ; officers of the household came next, knights and clerks, riding two and two ; and lastly rode Thomas himself on horseback amongst his friends.

This over-rich display was a matter of policy designed to dazzle the French, yet it was typical of Thomas who dressed in scarlet and furs, with gold-work on his clothes. Hunting he liked, and hawking and chess. The King and his chancellor were continually together, at sport, at business, in church or in battle. Under this exterior of jovial worldliness no man could have suspected that a saint was living ; Henry cannot be blamed when he appointed his friend Archbishop of Canterbury.

In appearance Thomas—sixteen years older than Henry—
was tall and handsome. He was over six feet, dark-haired,
with heavy eyebrows and strong jaw, his nose was long, and he
stuttered a little in his speech. No man, we are told, unless he
was a determined enemy, could withstand Thomas's fascination,
his smile, his charm of manner.

JUST before his consecration, Thomas swore allegiance to Henry's
eldest son, also named Henry ; then on June 3, 1162, he was
fully consecrated and he ordained that for ever after this day
should be held a festival in honour of the Holy Trinity. He
showed that he was determined to change his character, he
wasted little time, and almost immediately resigned the chancellorship. This was the last thing that Henry desired. He
had expected to keep the friendship and counsel of Becket,
together with the power of the Church ; yet disappointed though
he must have been, Henry did not show his feelings. When he
landed at Southampton in January 1163, he gave his old comrade
a friendly kiss and embraced him.

Whatever Becket's intentions might have been about the
future, he could not relinquish the secular pomp of his early
days. Being archbishop, he had in his care the second sons of
nobles, the King having the first, and these lads formed a gay
household ; his table remained as rich as ever, but instead of
knights, clerks now jostled for place beside him, and particular
prominence was given to the distribution of alms. Before
Thomas would sit down to eat—and now he ate very little—
twenty-six poor men must be served with the best ; whatever
remained after the meal was offered in charity. A man of
Thomas's vitality could never become lazy ; what minutes were
left him from public affairs he spent in feverish study, ashamed
of his lack of sacred knowledge ; when riding he would slip a
book from his sleeve and peruse it, and at Canterbury he sought
always the quietest corners and read in peace.

When chancellor, he had been never idle, he had thrown
all his abilities into the task ; now his task was greater, he had
the Church and not the state for which to fight, and he was
determined that every ounce of his strength would be exerted
in the inevitable conflict. He had warned the King. " Our
friendship," he had said, " will turn to bitter hate. I know
your plans for the Church, you will assert claims that I as archbishop must oppose, and when the breach is forced, jealous

hands will make certain that it is never joined again." But Henry refused to realise that Thomas was sincere. Others also could not believe it. The honest clergy suspected their new archbishop, dishonest ones were jealous of his rise, ambitious ones disdained his low birth ; only a few friends stood beside him. " The King has wrought a miracle," jeered Gilbert Foliot, Bishop of Hereford, " out of a soldier and a courtier he has made an archbishop." The jeer was soon proved to be truth, much to Gilbert's own embarrassment. He was one of the most intelligent of the clergy, and in the ensuing conflict between Thomas and Henry found himself in a dangerous position—his good sense demanding a calm mediation, triumph by strong passivity, and his love for the Church forcing him against his will to stand often beside his archbishop.

Gilbert was not the only one of the clergy to find himself in this awkward situation. Except for a few faithful friends, none really believed in Thomas save the people of England. The bishops, who should have been his brothers-in-arms, were so outraged by his methods that they were made to relinquish his aim which was also their aim—the complete freedom of the Church.

THE conflict between Henry and Thomas, apart from a few minor troubles, was based on the legal rights of Church and state. The Church had its own court separate from the lay court : here were judged clerks who had committed breaches against the King's peace. Murderers and thieves, even of the lowest church orders, could commit their crimes and escape scot free except to suffer degradation or, at the most, confinement. This power of the Church had been wrung from Stephen, and Henry was determined that it should be recovered by the crown. In the eight years of his reign, it was claimed, one hundred murders had been committed by clerks—beside lesser crimes of theft and mayhem and such—and the offenders had escaped all but the lightest punishment. England was therefore split into two, lay and ecclesiastical : the churchmen relied on their own courts, made their own laws, and their tribunal of appeal was always to Rome.

When Henry argued with Thomas, telling him of his wish, all that the archbishop would answer was—" I will render unto Cæsar the things that are Cæsar's, and unto God the things that are God's." Henry found that argument was useless, he decided to act. In July 1163, his opportunity came. A clerk named Philip de Broi had been tried in the Bishop of Lincoln's court for murder and had been acquitted. Henry demanded that he be re-tried by a lay court at Dunstable, but Philip refused to plead and scoffed at the judge. At this insult, Henry swore " by God's eyes "—his favourite oath—that the clerk would suffer for both murder and contempt, although Thomas insisted that the trial must take place, not in the King's court, but at Canterbury. Henry was forced to agree and once again Philip was acquitted of murder, but for insulting a king's officer he was sentenced to a public flogging and a forfeiture of the whole of his income for the next two years. Henry was not satisfied ; he insisted that the punishment was too light and cried that the bishops had perverted justice to shield their order.

The only way that Thomas could find of calming the King merely outraged him the further. A clerk convicted of theft was branded as well as degraded, and another was banished. These judgments seemed to Henry an encroachment on the royal prerogative : he did not want harsh measures from spiritual courts, he wanted the spiritual courts abolished. He demanded that the charter of Stephen he ignored and that the Church return to its old position, that it become as it had been under Henry I. He brought the question before a great council at Westminster on October 1, 1163. The arguments continued until late at night, the bishops trying to evade a direct answer, the King insisting. Bishops, he said, must be more strict in searching out criminal clerks, and when captured, those clerks, besides being convicted and degraded, should be passed on to temporal justice to be dealt with as they deserved.

Thomas tried to force an adjournment until the morning, but Henry would not back an inch and at last the archbishop retired to discuss the matter with his suffragans. He returned to state that what the King demanded was inacceptable, the only point on which he would give way was to agree that if a clerk, once degraded, should commit a second crime he might then be treated as a layman. And whenever Henry pressed him, asking if the bishops would obey the King, always Thomas gave the evasive reply—" Ay, saving our order." Henry's Angevin temper grew uncontrollable. He abruptly strode from the room and spurred for London ; next day, Thomas was summoned to surrender some honours he had held as chancellor and which he still retained ; the King's eldest son, Henry, was also taken from his charge.

His first rage over, Henry tried again to negotiate. In a field near Northampton, King and archbishop met on horseback only to quarrel furiously. Henry then tried persuasion through others : he sent commissioners, Gilbert Foliot and the papal nuncio amongst them, to force Thomas to withdraw his reservation of " saving our order " to the King's demands. Thomas now found himself almost alone ; those who should have been fighting at his side were pleading with him to surrender. Weakly, he gave in. He said that he would accept the " ancient customs," but Henry doubted his old friend's good faith. A verbal promise was not enough, he must have Thomas's seal to the charter, he must have it indisputably stated. He summoned a great council to meet at Clarendon in January 1164.

None of the clergy realised what they were to face at this council. They expected merely a vague oath, a promise to confirm to " ancient rights," which could be squirmed out of later. Henry was too shrewd to risk any such thing, he wanted those " ancient customs " of the reign of Henry I written down and sealed. He reiterated his demand that criminal clerks should be judged also by lay courts, and added that appeals should go to no one but the King, thereby cutting off appeals to Rome, also no ecclesiastic was to leave the kingdom without royal licence, no tenant-in-chief should be excommunicated or have his lands laid under interdict without the King's permission, pleas touching advowson should be given to the royal courts, and the sons of villeins should not be ordained without their lords' permission.

These demands were too great. The clergy, with Thomas for spokesman, repudiated them utterly ; to condemn a clerk by a lay court was, he said, " to bring Christ before Pilate a second time." Bishops and earls implored him to turn from so direct an answer, they dreaded an open quarrel. Thomas strove to hold out, but at last, exhausted by their importunity, he cried, " If the King insists on my perjuring myself I must do it and must hope to cleanse away the sin by future penance." Then before Henry he swore to accept the " ancient customs " " honestly, in good faith and without deceit." This was the only time that Thomas was to weaken, but he hoped by clerkly casuistry to evade the consequences of his oath ; he forgot that he was dealing with a King as cunning as Henry. A verbal oath was not sufficient, the King produced a written copy of the customs and asked for Thomas's seal to be placed upon it. Thomas still tried to escape the issue ; he said that a priest's word was as good as any oath, and while not sealing the customs, he was weak enough to accept a copy.

Immediately after leaving Clarendon, Thomas bitterly repented having given way, and without doubt much of his stubbornness in the later stages of the quarrel can be traced to this one act of weakness. He could never forgive himself for the humiliation ; it haunted him, it drove him to extents to which probably he would never otherwise have gone. In shame he suspended himself from the performance of church services until he received absolution from the Pope. Towards the Pope both parties turned for a final arbitration, Henry, with astonishing optimism, expecting the pontiff to ratify the ancient customs, and asking him to make the Archbishop of York legate for all England. To the second request Pope Alexander III agreed, but he made it pointless by exempting Thomas from the legate's power ; furiously, Henry rejected the letters of legation, he sent them back to the Pope.

Thomas, eager to be absolved of his oath to the King, decided to visit Alexander at Sens, and one of the articles to which he had sworn forbade any ecclesiastic leaving England without the King's permission. But Thomas no longer considered his oath of importance as he would shortly be absolved from it ; the winds and the boatmen's terror of Henry's vengeance stopped him leaving the country. He crept back to Canterbury, and when a servant arrived to close the gates of the deserted palace he found his master sitting like a beggar on the steps, weary and in despair.

Finding that he could not leave England, Thomas besought another interview with Henry, who received him at once and treated him kindlily. The last thing that Henry desired was Thomas to leave the country and become a tool for Louis of France ; he dreaded lest the Pope pronounce an interdict against England—a terrible thing, for it would mean that in all the country no church office would be given and the sacrament would be denied the people. Few medieval Kings had the power to fight so dreadful an attack. Therefore Henry was pleasant with Thomas, asking merrily " whether the archbishop did not think the realm was wide enough to contain them both ? " But merrily though the King might speak, Thomas knew him too well not to realise that the old friendship was gone for ever.

The quarrel soon broke out again. John, the King's marshal, had a suit in Thomas's court concerning a manor, and, having lost his claim, he appealed to the King, which was permitted according to the Clarendon articles. Thomas was called to answer the claim. He was very ill at the time, too ill to move, and sent essoiners to explain his absence in a legal manner, adding a written protest at the suit being taken elsewhere because John had committed perjury, having sworn not on the Gospels but on an old song-book which he had sneaked into court. Henry would not listen to the essoiners ; he swore furiously that Thomas was lying, that he was not ill, and named another day, October 6, for hearing the suit. So enraged was Henry that he could not dictate even the usual formal salutation of affection to his old friend ; instead, therefore, of being summoned to the new hearing in a manner befitting his rank, Thomas was commanded to attend by a sheriff, and on his arrival the King refused him the kiss of peace.

When at last the suit was heard, Thomas's arguments were ignored and he was sentenced to a fine of five hundred pounds for his alleged contempt in not appearing before the previous court. Henry, now that Thomas was at his mercy, was not satisfied with this one judgment : he demanded a further three hundred pounds as the revenue of certain estates that Thomas had retained since his resignation as chancellor. Still, Henry was not content : now five hundred marks were demanded as an old debt of their friendship days ; but the final blow was too heavy for Thomas to bear—Henry asked for a complete statement of all the revenues of vacant sees, baronies and honours that Thomas had managed during his chancellorship. Thomas was beaten. He fell at the King's feet and implored mercy. "By God's eyes," swore Henry, he would have a full accounting of every penny that Thomas had handled.

The strain had been too great ; there was no longer any hiding of the King's purpose : he intended to break Thomas for ever, to ruin him. Thomas collapsed and he had to beg for a day's adjournment ; then while he lay in pain and despair a warning came to him that if he appeared at court he would be executed or imprisoned unless he surrendered entirely to the King. At that, Thomas swore he would appear if he had to be carried in a litter.

He prepared for the conflict, determined on a final settlement, no matter what the end might be. Early in the morning

12

he celebrated the mass of the proto-martyr Stephen with its prophetic introit—" Princes have sat and spoken against me." He was evidently quite certain that he was to be murdered, and perhaps welcomed the idea of martyrdom. He decided to walk barefooted to court, dressed in full canonicals, and carrying his own cross ; his friends, however, managed to dissuade him from this ostentatious defiance and he rode to the castle in his usual manner ; but now he did not have with him his splendid troupe of clerks and knights, only the common people followed, imploring his blessing.

Thomas was determined not to be deprived of the full drama of the situation. His friends had restrained him from walking barefoot, but he decided that at least he would carry his own cross. He took it from its usual bearer and, lifting it high before him, strode into the hall amongst the bishops and barons. His friends were aghast, for this taking of the cross was a direct defiance of the King ; it meant that Thomas appealed from royal injustice to the protection of God. Thomas refused when his followers besought him to be meek. He told them that " he would not lay down his standard, he would not part with his shield." Gilbert Foliot shrugged and turned aside : " He always was a fool," he jeered. Save for his two friends, FitzStephen and Herbert of Bosham, Thomas now sat quite alone, the others recoiling from this open challenge to the King.

There was no possibility of any compromise with Thomas determined on martyrdom. Henry sent the Earl of Leicester to pronounce sentence. What that sentence was we will never know. Before the earl could proceed beyond the word " judgment," Thomas sprang up, raised his cross and forbade him to utter another word, appealing to the protection of the court of Rome as being above the court of Henry. The earl departed ; and saying, " I too will go, for the hour is past," Thomas walked steadily from the hall, still upholding his defiant crucifix.

When his back was turned, the courtiers howled after him, the squires and servitors echoed their insults. Thomas stumbled against a heap of faggots placed ready for the fire. A knight shouted at him, " Traitor ! Traitor ! " and the King's half-brother, Count Hamelin, added his voice to " Traitor ! Traitor ! " Thomas turned on him. " Were I a knight instead of a priest," he cried, " this hand would prove you liar ! "

With the crowd yelling at him, he strode into the courtyard

and sprang on to his horse, taking Herbert up behind. The outer gate was locked, but a squire found the keys and opened it. There could have been no intention of imprisoning Thomas, the locked gate must have been an accident, for already, having heard the uproar, Henry had sent a messenger to command that the archbishop be neither insulted not interfered with.

Out of the gates rode Thomas, away from the jeering courtiers, and in the streets he met a vastly different reception. The people crowded about him, wailing for his blessing, kneeling and weeping.

His household had left him, save for a few faithful ones, and as he sat at supper that evening, considering what next to do, an omen decided him to fly the country. In the evening lection occurred the phrase : " If men persecute you in one city, flee unto another."

When Henry heard next day the news of Thomas's flight, he cried, " We have not done with him yet ! " and commanded that all ports be sealed against his passage, and sent messengers to the Pope. Then he turned to other affairs, to the invasion of Wales.

After racing about the country seeking a ship, Thomas at last managed to make sail and reach Soissons, to ask the protection of Louis, who was delighted to help him. From Soissons Thomas hurried to Sens to lay at the feet of Alexander his copy of the Constitutions of Clarendon. Henry's messengers had reached the papal court already, but the Pope would not listen to their arguments. He read the constitutions and condemned them, and, safe at last, Thomas took refuge in the Cistercian abbey of Pontigny in Burgundy.

THE first stage of the quarrel was over. For six years Thomas was to remain in exile, and to follow the arguments further would be tedious. There were messengers from Henry to the Pope and pleas from Thomas, but the Pope was unable to answer definitely. Naturally, he had to protect the archbishop, who was in voluntary exile as a result of fighting for his Church's rights, but at the same time he dared not break finally with Henry by laying England under an interdict. At the moment there was an anti-Pope supported by Italy and Germany, and if Henry were to acclaim the anti-Pope, Alexander might never succeed to Rome. Therefore he strove to temporise, to calm the fiery Thomas. That was impossible. Thomas hurled ex-

communications against his enemies in England, he wrote
insulting letters, he pleaded with Alexander to denounce Henry.
The quarrel became almost childish, for again and again efforts
were made vainly to patch it. Thomas had become a nuisance
to everybody.

The Church naturally agreed with all his demands, but the
intelligent English ecclesiastics, such as Gilbert Foliot, realised
that more could be gained by apparent submission and by a
gradual encroachment into Henry's rights than by open defiance.
Even Thomas's main disciple, Herbert of Bosham, who revered
Thomas and stood beside him in his greatest dangers, summed
up the situation as : "Both parties had a zeal for God, but
which zeal was according to knowledge, His judgment alone
can determine."

From a matter of principle, the quarrel had degenerated
into almost a personal affair, and for this reason Thomas's main
following was amongst the people who did not understand
involved questions of right and wrong but who revered him as
wellnigh a saint. Henry strove to make peace, but Thomas
would not listen ; he threatened an interdict, he hurled further
excommunications against his enemies. Efforts were made to
stop these excommunications entering England, all people who
might have come from Thomas were searched on landing, but·
many bulls were sneaked in and were given to the victims ;
while Gilbert Foliot one day stood before the high altar of his
cathedral church, a paper was pushed into his hand : it was a
papal brief giving Thomas a commission as legate for all England.
It was impossible to keep the indefatigable exile's missives
out of the country. At one time Henry was almost forced to
join the anti-Pope, but in the midst of the negotiations he shifted
the answer aside by rushing into a war with Wales.

With Thomas hurling denunciations from the Continent,
Henry continued at his task of holding his vast empire, arranging
marriages for his children and invading Wales. His eldest son
Henry did homage to the King of France for Anjou and Maine
and Brittany, Richard did homage for Aquitaine and was
granted the hand of Louis's daughter Alais. For his children's
sake, to consolidate them in their countries, King Henry himself did homage to Louis as his suzerain.

There was one thing that Henry greatly desired—the crowning
of his eldest son as King of England in his own lifetime. This
was often done on the Continent, and Stephen had tried to have

it performed for Eustace. But the King of England must be crowned by the Archbishop of Canterbury, and the Archbishop of Canterbury was at that moment in a gigantic temper, eager to frustrate Henry at every point. Henry took a spiteful and inexcusable revenge, which was also extremely stupid for so cunning a man. He insisted that the Cistercian monks eject Thomas from his refuge. Thomas instantly ran to the King of France.

Efforts were continually made to arbitrate. The Pope dispatched legates to Henry, but he sent them off, crying, " I hope I may never set eyes on a cardinal again ! " It was hopeless waiting for Thomas to surrender. If the Archbishop of Canterbury refused to live in England, then the Archbishop of York must crown the young King. Henry had years ago managed to obtain a grant from the Pope authorising York to perform the ceremony ; this he now produced. Immediately, Thomas wrote to the English bishops commanding that the lad—he was sixteen— must not be crowned. These letters were kept out of the country until the young Henry had been acclaimed King of England at Westminster on June 14, 1170.

Almost immediately afterwards the reconciliation took place. There had already been promising negotiations, although Thomas had refused to listen ; but at last, on June 22, 1170, the two enemies who had once been such dear friends met at Fréteval. Henry was in a happy mood as he rode to meet Thomas ; he doffed his cap and smiled, then the two went apart from the others. Thomas immediately attacked Henry about the coronation and Henry answered with feeble references to historical precedents and showed the papal letters granting the Archbishop of York the right to perform the ceremony. These letters were dated many years back and had been given while the primacy was vacant, after the death of Theobald and before the consecration of Thomas. Henry promised vaguely to do justice in the affair and said that he would return Thomas all the possessions he had held three months before his exile and would take him and his friends back into favour. Thomas got from his horse and knelt on the ground, but, leaping from his saddle, Henry raised him and held his stirrup for him while he remounted.

On one point Henry was stubborn. He had sworn not to give Thomas the kiss of peace, and this he would not do. He offered to kiss " his mouth and his hands and his feet a hundred times," but the kiss of peace he would not give. Thomas tried to cheat the King by stealing into the chapel during mass, for in the

service Henry would have to give the pax ; Henry was warned in
time.   He commanded the celebration of a mass for the dead,
in which the pax was not given.

" WE are going to England," Thomas told the King of France.
" So I see," replied Louis ; " and if you will take my advice, you
will not trust yourself in the power of a King who refuses you the
kiss of peace.   Stay where you are.   As long as I live, the wines,
the bread, the abundance of France are yours." Thomas answered
quietly : " God's will be done."

In this spirit he returned to claim his archbishopric.   Henry
was unable to escort him owing to trouble in Auvergne, and in
the company of John of Oxford, Dean of Salisbury, Thomas set
out.   Thomas and John were not friends, and the archbishop
grumbled because he was placed in the care of a man who should
have been honoured to have even a place in his suite.   On landing
at Sandwich, the archbishop was received with insults and threats,
but John restrained the fury of Thomas's enemies ; in the name of
the King he commanded that the archbishop be not harmed.
Knights who held the Canterbury lands might be eager to kill the
returning exile, but the common people waded into the sea to
greet him—they lined the streets, imploring the blessing of " the
father of orphans, the judge of widows."

Thomas discovered that his lands were almost ruined, the
rents had been collected ahead, manors had been plundered and
burnt, crops had been gathered.   He could not as yet retort, he
contented himself by telling the prelates who visited him that he
could not lift the ban of excommunication from their masters as
the Pope had reserved the case for himself.   Furious at this,
three of the bishops sped to Normandy to see the King.   Thomas
had always loved Henry's eldest son, now the young King.   The
boy had been trained in his household and he wished to see him
again.   He sent young Henry three splendid chargers gaily
caparisoned and followed his gift to court, taking with him some
five or six men-at-arms for protection against enemies.   This
small troop was magnified into a vast army and he was told to
" go back and mind his own business at Canterbury."

Sadly he returned.   Men hated him ; the de Brocs—who had
taken many of his lands—now captured a ship with a cargo of
wine sent him by Louis ; they killed some of the sailors and
imprisoned the rest ; they fought his servants, they hunted in his
woods, on Christmas Eve they stopped his packhorses and

lopped the tails of a horse and a sumpter-mule. It was impossible for Thomas to remain silent under these insults. On Christmas Day, 1170, he preached a sermon from St. Luke's text, "On earth peace to men of good will," then he spoke of his inevitable martyrdom. After that he excommunicated Robert de Broc and many others.

When the news of this reached King Henry at Bur-le-Roi, near Bayeux, following so swiftly on Thomas's refusal to absolve the excommunicated bishops, he lost his temper. The Angevin demon burst through his reserve and he shouted the words which he was for ever to regret. "What sluggards and knaves," he cried, "have I fed in my house that they are faithless to their lord and let him be tricked so infamously by one upstart clerk ! "

Four knights, William de Tracy, Hugh de Moreville, Reginald FitzUrse, and Richard the Breton, were present when Henry spoke those rash words. They thought to win favour and perhaps to gain private vengeance by taking advantage of the King's notorious temper, that awful fury which could crook his fingers to tear out men's eyes, which could hurl him to his bed to bite the straw and rushes, or to tear his clothes to rags. Never did the Angevin demon-ancestress do her work so thoroughly as she did that day when Henry asked if his men were sluggards that they dared not kill one upstart clerk.

The four knights saddled their horses and made for the coast ; it is said that they left by different ports and met in England at Randolph de Broc's castle. The tale went that as they plotted they extinguished the candles so that they would not see their own faces. In the darkness, with subdued whispers, they planned the murder. The following morning, orders were issued in the name of the King for a troop of soldiers to be levied. Then they galloped to the abbey of St. Augustine outside the walls of Canterbury.

THE three o'clock dinner was over in the great hall of the archbishop's palace. Thomas was in a small chamber, sitting on the bed as he chatted with his friends when the four knights entered the hall ; they had left their weapons outside and had covered their hauberks with civil dress, with gown and cloak, as if they came upon some peaceful mission. "They scorned the food, thirsting rather for blood," and strode on until at the foot of the staircase leading to the archbishop's apartments they met

William FitzNigel, Thomas's seneschal. He knew them well and greeted them with a kiss before, not knowing their intent, he led them to the archbishop's chamber. " My lord," he said, opening the door, " here are four knights from King Henry who wish to speak with you." " Let them in," said Thomas.

The steel links of their hauberks hidden under silk and cloth, the four knights entered, and Thomas did not even glance up at them. Leaning on the shoulder of a friend, he went on with the interrupted conversation while the knights pushed through the clergy and sat on the floor at his feet. Then Thomas looked at them, gazing from man to man silently, until at last he called on Tracy's name. Tracy did not answer, but Fitz-Urse cried, " God help you ! " and Thomas's face grew scarlet. FitzUrse went on : " We have a message from the King over the water [*young Henry was in England*], tell us whether you want to hear it in private or before these others." " As you wish," said Thomas. " Nay, as *you* wish," said FitzUrse. " Nay, as *you* wish," said Thomas, nevertheless he nodded for his friends to depart ; but they were suspicious enough to leave the door ajar so that they could overhear what was said. Scarcely had Fitz-Urse begun again to speak before Thomas realised that these men carried no peaceful message from Henry. " This must not be told in secret ! " he cried and ordered the doorkeeper to recall his friends. The murderers had been alone with their destined victim. They thought of killing him with his own cross-staff that lay at his feet, for they had left their weapons outside. But even as the thought came, it was too late. The monks returned. FitzUrse continued with Henry's complaints against Thomas ; the archbishop, he said, wished to take away the young King's crown (" I would give him three or four," said Thomas) ; he had raised disturbances in the country and must answer for them in the King's court (" Never again," said Thomas, " shall the sea come between me and my church unless I am dragged away by the feet ") ; he had excommunicated bishops and must absolve them (" Not I," said Thomas, " but the Pope ").

Both parties began to lose their temper, and when the knights leapt up, exasperated by Thomas's arguments, he asked, " Do you come to kill me ? " The knights could barely resist attacking him, they twisted their long gloves and lifted their arms menacingly above their heads. Cried FitzUrse, " You threaten us, you threaten us, are you going to excommunicate us all ? "

" You threaten me in vain," answered Thomas, springing to his feet.

These knights had come with the deliberate intention of either abducting or of murdering the archbishop, yet they had left their swords outside and had stopped to parley. Perhaps they wished to justify their act by working themselves into a fury ; if that were so, they certainly succeeded. Men of the arch-bishop's household had run to the chamber when they heard the uproar, and now they grouped themselves about their master. " You who are on the King's side," said FitzUrse, " and bound to him by your allegiance, stand off ! " None moved. Fitz-Urse turned with his companions towards the door. " Guard him," he said, " stop him from escaping." " I shall not escape," said Thomas. Protected as he was by his household, he could not be harmed for the moment, so the knights departed to seek their weapons ; they were determined that Thomas, not they, should be in the wrong and FitzUrse could not resist saying at the door, " It is you who threaten," and muttering under his breath a warning to the monks not to let their archbishop escape. Hitting himself on the neck as if to show them where to strike, Thomas answered, " Here, here you shall find me ! " He could have escaped, his friends besought him to escape : he would not listen. They wanted him to seek refuge in the church, but as his friend and biographer, Grim, tells us, " he who had long sighed for martyrdom now saw that the time would likely come, and he dreaded lest he delay it or avoid it altogether by going into the church . . . he feared lest reverence for the sacred place should deter even the impious from their purpose and cheat him of his heart's desire." His friends tried to drag him out and he struggled with them. One cried that the knights were arming. " Let them arm," said Thomas. Outside they heard the knights smashing at a wooden partition, and the monks fled. " Fear not," said Thomas, " all monks are cowards." His friends then argued that it was now five o'clock and vespers were be-ginning, his duty demanded his attendance ; at last, half-resisting, Thomas let them pull him along, but he noticed that his cross-staff was not borne before him and cried that they must bring it.

At last they dragged him into the church. He could have hidden in the crypt or in the loft, but he refused. The knights were now in the cloisters, their mail hauberks clattering to below their knees, their helms over their heads, the broad nasal-guards

shadowing their faces. FitzUrse led them, wielding an axe
and a sword, and yelling, " Here, here, King's men ! " When
the monks would have barred the door into the church, Thomas
commanded them to desist, saying that he would not have
God's house turned into a castle. Then bravely he awaited
death.

His friends still pleaded with him. All had fled save three—
Robert, Canon of Merton, FitzStephen, and Edward Grim—
and they half-dragged him towards the steps leading to the
quire, believing that he would be safer in the most sacred part
of the church. It was very dark in the transept, and night was
drawing in. Only the altar-lamps and the grey twilight lit the
dark cavern, glancing on the huge pillars, making the roof
mysterious and seeming endlessly black ; into the silence, into
the gloom, strode the knights, their steel shirts flapping and
clacking about them, their steel shoes clashing on the floor.
They could not see Thomas who was half-way up the stairs
leading to the quire : the central pillar hid him from them.
FitzUrse, sword in one hand, axe in the other, sprang to the right
of the pillar ; his three companions turned to the left. Ahead
they could make out the pale figures of the archbishop and his
three disciples, blurred shadows on the darkness. One of the
knights cried, " Stay ! " and another : " Where is Thomas
Becket, traitor to the King ? " There was no answer. FitzUrse
pushed his way forward, fell against a monk in the darkness,
grappled him and cried, " Where is the archbishop ? " Quietly
Thomas answered from the stairs, " Reginald, I am here : I
am no traitor, I am the archbishop and priest of God.
What do you want ? " and he walked down to meet his
murderers.

Surprised, FitzUrse sprang back and Thomas walked past
him and stood between the central pillar and the wall. Before
them he stood, his cloak and hood thrown from his shoulders to
reveal the white rochet. The knights crept towards him and one
said, " Absolve the bishops you excommunicated." " I cannot
do other than I have done," answered Thomas ; then he turned
to FitzUrse to add, " Reginald, you have had many favours
from my hands, why do you come armed into my church ? "
FitzUrse lifted his axe and placed it against Thomas's breast.
" You shall die," he told him, " I will tear out your heart,"
while another, touched perhaps with pity or remorse, slapped
Thomas on the back with the flat of his sword, saying, " Fly.

You are a dead man." " I am ready to die," answered Thomas,
" for God and the Church, but I warn you in the name of
Almighty God to let my men go free."

Even these rascals did not wish to add sacrilege to murder.
Already they had broken God's law by bringing arms into a
church, and they meditated killing God's representative ; yet
such were small matters compared to spilling blood on the holy
pavement itself. FitzUrse put aside his axe and caught Thomas
by the collar of his long cloak, trying to drag him outside. " Come
with us," he shouted, " you are our prisoner." But Thomas
was determined to be killed in his own church, he struggled
out of FitzUrse's grip, cursing him ; the others caught their
victim, but the archbishop, once a warrior, was no weakling.
He leaned against the pillar and beat them off as they strove to
heave him on to the back of Tracy ; Grim came to his aid and
held him with both arms. So strong was Thomas that he lifted
Tracy in his great coat-of-mail and hurled him to the pavement.
The knights drew back. There was no other course open to
them save murder in this sacred dwelling.

Naked sword raised for a blow, FitzUrse led his men while
Thomas reviled him, calling him " pander " and worse. Stung
to fury, FitzUrse waved his sword above the archbishop's head
and yelled, " Strike ! strike ! " but his rage blinded him and
the blow went wide, merely knocking off Thomas's cap. Meekly
Thomas lowered his head as if in prayer, saying, " I commend
my cause and the cause of this church to God, to St. Denis of
France and to the saints of the Church." Tracy, after his fall,
had thrown away his hauberk lest it impede his agility, and
perhaps in fear of bruises from a second throw, he struck with
his sword, but Grim with his bare arm tried to ward off the
blade. " Spare this defence," cried Thomas, as the sword,
almost breaking Grim's arm, glanced on to Thomas's own skull.
Then another hit him on the head with the flat of his sword,
and, dizzied, Thomas staggered back, lifting his hands in the
air. He wiped the blood from his face and gazed on it where it
stained his arm. " Into thy hands, O Lord, I commend my
spirit," he said as Tracy struck again, knocking him to his knees.
Yet his hands were still clasped in prayer, and he whispered,
" For the name of Jesus and the defence of the Church, I am
willing to die," as slowly he sank forward and lay upon his face,
falling so gradually that not a fold of his cloak was out of order.
Richard the Breton struck next, shouting, " Take this for love

of my lord William, brother of the King ! " [1] and so furiously did he strike that his blade lopped the crown from Thomas's skull and snapped when it jarred on the marble floor, " so that the blood white with the brain and the brain red with blood dyed the surface of the virgin mother church with the life and death of the confessor and martyr in the colours of the lily and the rose."

To a fourth man, Hugh of Horsea, subdeacon, and otherwise unknown to history, remained the final and most ghastly act of all. He stood with one foot on the neck of the corpse, then jabbed his sword into the open skull to spill the brains about the marble pavement.

" Let us go, let us go," he cried when the vile act was done, " the traitor is dead. He will rise no more."

WHEN the news reached Henry he was in council. Already he suspected that the four knights meant harm to Thomas and had vainly sent messengers to stop them leaving for England. As he sat in council a messenger arrived with the terrible tidings. The King wailed aloud, he dressed himself in sackcloth and ashes ; for three days he kept to his chamber, and when he was not crying he " became stupid," dulled with the horror of the murder, with a knowledge of the consequences it must bring upon him. The stupid phase would pass and once again he would scream as if tormented by demons. His courtiers feared that he was mad.

While Henry lay in torment behind his shut door, already the people of England were beginning their sanctification of Thomas. On the night of the murder the terrified monks crept back into the church and turned the body of the dead archbishop so that it lay upon its back. There was a gentle smile on the lips and the eyes were closed as if in sleep. Under the body they found FitzUrse's axe and a small iron hammer. To prove the martyr's saintliness, one of Thomas's oldest friends showed the doubting monks that beneath his rich clothing was a monk's

---

[1] At the very outset of his quarrel with the King, Thomas had forbidden Henry's brother William to marry the wealthy Isabel of Warenne because they were within the prohibited degrees of consanguinity. William died shortly afterwards, and it was commonly believed at the time that he died of a broken heart and that Thomas was therefore his murderer. Isabel then married Henry's half-brother, Hamelin, bastard of Geoffrey. Far from feeling gratitude, Hamelin was one of those who insulted Thomas at Northampton— see p. 178.

habit and a hair-shirt ; all further doubts vanished when it was discovered that the shirt was brimming with vermin that boiled over the hairs, we are told, like water in a simmering pot. After that, all knew Thomas must be a true monk and a probable saint.

Thomas was dead, and his death had won him greater love and veneration than any living act of his had ever done. The people canonised him at once, and scarcely more than two years after his murder Rome ratified what the people demanded. To a weaker King than Henry this blow would have meant the collapse of all his schemes ; Europe turned menacingly towards him, eager to revenge the martyr. Letters were sent to the Pope by Louis and Henry's other enemies demanding retribution ; Alexander was forced into a corner from which it seemed he could not escape. He imitated Henry and shut himself up for eight days. Henry could not shut himself up for ever. Doors and walls would not keep out the inevitable excommunication. He fled to Wales, hiding amongst those great hills and forests, and leaving strict orders that no strangers enter England lest they carry the papal interdict ; from Wales, Henry rushed to Ireland, where the Pope could not reach him, and began the great conquest of that country.

THE Irish wars do not concern us, important though they are to history. They gave Henry a breathing-space, they gave time for angers to cool ; when he returned to Normandy in May 1172, he met the papal legates and was able to argue against the terms they offered for a reconciliation with Rome ; he whittled the terms down until they were acceptable. On Sunday, May 21, in the cathedral at Avranches he swore publicly that he had neither commanded nor wished the death of Thomas. He added bravely that nevertheless he was the unwitting cause of the murder because of those reckless words of his. For penance he was told to pay for the support of two hundred men-at-arms in defence of Jerusalem, and he was himself to turn crusader unless excused by the Pope ; appeals to Rome by the English Church were to be allowed, although Henry could demand guarantees from appellants to prove that they were not intriguing against him ; all customs he had introduced against the Church were to be disclaimed, the possessions of Canterbury he had taken were to be given back to the see, and he was to promise to defend Alexander against his enemies. To all these Henry agreed, kneeling on a block of stone at the church door.

The absolution was given on the most extraordinary terms ; when one examines them, one finds that Henry had lost practically nothing by the murder. The Constitutions of Clarendon were ignored by the legates, and Henry had always insisted that these were in force during the reign of his grandfather ; therefore he could justly plead that he had introduced no new customs, he had only revived old ones. His situation with the Church was the same as it had been before Thomas began the quarrel. Subtle indeed must have been Henry to be able to stand against the horror aroused by the murder and to lose nothing by it. And, taking all blame, he would not have the murderers harmed. It would have been a simple matter for him to throw those four knights as a sop to the Church, but he would not harm them with royal justice. Perhaps he found secret pleasure in revealing that the very thing for which Thomas had fought—freedom for the Church to try its own cases—was a safeguard to Thomas's murderers. These men were ecclesiastical prisoners, and the worst that could be pronounced against them was merely excommunication, a deprivation of clerical privileges, the refusal of church ministrations.

Now it seemed that Henry had attained all that a man might aspire to, he was the most powerful king in Europe. Yet at the last was to come the greatest struggle of all, his conflict with his sons.

The eldest living son, Henry, was King of England, but he was a King in name only ; he might wear a crown and be given royal honours, yet he was the shadow of his father, he had no power. The second son, Richard, was Count of Poitiers and Duke of Aquitaine. The young Henry, living always in the background and darkened by his father's glory, despaired of ever becoming the true King, for that father was still a young and vital man not yet forty years of age. Besides, the lad's allowance was so small that he could barely keep up the position he demanded, while his wife, Margaret, Louis's daughter, was not even crowned. It is difficult to understand why Henry had not crowned Margaret, but presumably it was an act of sheer malice against his overlord, the King of France ; now, forgiven by the Church, he decided that he would also win Louis's friendship by arranging the coronation. Even here his meanness defeated the splendour of the ceremony, he grudged the spending of money that could be better used in the hiring of mercenaries. Instead of calming Louis's resentment and his son's jealousy, Henry only inflamed them both by the paltry show he put on. The young King openly plotted with Louis ; no longer was there any concealment, the two Kings of England were enemies.

Henry sent to Louis, hoping to break the intrigues. " Who sends this message ? " asked the King of France. " The King of England," said the messengers. " It is untrue," cried Louis, " behold the King of England is here and he sends me no messages by you. If you call his father by that title, he who was once King, then know that as a King he is dead." Ambitious and envious barons did homage to the young Henry in Paris, he gave them lands and promises ; and his mother spurred him on, she enticed her other sons, Richard and Geoffrey, to join the rebellion. Herself hastened to Poitou, dressed as a man, but was captured by her husband and imprisoned. Aquitaine was ready to fight for its independence, hating the Normans ; and Normandy itself, heavily taxed, was eager to join in any attempt that might rescue it from the elder King's hard just rule. Britanny, too, declared for the younger party, while Maine and Anjou simmered in preparation for the war, seeking an opportunity to rebel. Even England was not content under the elder Henry ; the people could not forget the murder of Thomas, and the barons were always on the look-out for an excuse of striking at the throne, of bringing anarchy into the land.

The elder Henry remained calm while his enemies leagued themselves together. Unshaken even by the treachery of his sons, he did not at once rush into war ; he cautiously strengthened his position, consolidating his friendship with the Church and appointing men he could trust to vacant sees. Then in April, 1173, rebellion flared, the traitors rushed from their castles ; from every side they came, pillaging, darting with sword and flame into the elder Henry's lands. Yet they had one weakness that made their cause a lost one before it started ; amongst them was no leader, no man able to bind them to an army and to inspire them with the courage needed for victory. The young Henry was unlike his father in almost every way save for the charm of his manners ; he was handsome and tall and generous and weak. Louis was cunning, but he was a coward and untrustworthy. Richard the second son was young, he was brave and powerful, yet his qualities were those of a soldier-of-fortune, not of a leader.

" The whole rebellion was crushed in a few months," it was

a matter of rapid sieges, of forced marches, with no decisive battles. When it was finished and the elder Henry had shown himself too strong and wary to be deposed, he yet was generous, wishing to have his children's love and not their hatred. With Louis he bargained to entice young Henry and Richard from their resentful enmity, but Louis was a peacemaker who did not want peace. He was himself the mainspring of the whole affair, he had goaded the young King and his brothers into rebellion, and he was determined that they would not now give in. The war continued. The Scots came down from the north, barons in England unsheathed their swords, and the sons again openly defied their father in Europe. The elder King darted from country to country, chasing his sons, besieging castles, scattering enemy troops. He was everywhere, men marvelled at the swiftness of his marches. Yet he could pause amidst the campaigns to seek penance at the magnificent tomb of the martyr Thomas at Canterbury. Barefoot, dressed only in a woollen gown, he walked from the west gate of the city to the cathedral, and at the porch, he knelt and prayed. When shown the spot where Thomas fell he kissed the pavement, weeping, and afterwards he lay beside the tomb and prayed in an agony of repentance. Then he bared his shoulders while each prelate struck him five times with a rod and each of the eighty monks struck him three times.

The martyr showed his gratitude almost immediately ; news came that the King of the Scots was a prisoner. The coincidence of Henry's repentence and this victory probably did more for his cause than any battle could have done. It revealed to the people that not only had the saint forgiven Henry for the murder, he was actively fighting on his side. The King was in bed, ill after the scourging and fasting, when the news reached him, and the messenger forced his way into the royal bedchamber. Scarcely daring to believe the news, Henry sprang up, weeping and praying, while the bells of Canterbury pealed the joyous tidings.

Only Richard now remained to be brought to reason. Although but seventeen years of age, he was courageous and a brilliant fighter. Henry had to chase him from castle to castle, harrying him through Poitou, until, alone and desperate, Richard was forced to surrender. The sons were now apparently united and at peace with their father who treated them generously.

WHILE Louis lived in hatred and jealousy of the King of England, there was small chance of the young Henry ever loving his father. For the moment he was quiet and submissive, but he merely awaited the opportunity for a second rebellion. It is difficult to understand why this fighting should have been ; the third son, Geoffrey, in particular is a peculiar person because he had little to gain and much to lose. Why he sided with his brothers can be explained only by the sheer love of mischief. They were strong lads, lovers of battle, who when at peace with their father were eager to turn their swords against each other like dogs snapping and snarling, knowing that themselves suffered little risk. Their father would always forgive, they knew ; and they might fight together, yet brotherly affection—although they had little of it —would always save them at the last moment from the *coup de grâce*.

Later, Geoffrey was to tell one of his father's messengers : " Do you not understand that it is our nature, planted in us by the heritage of ancestors, that no one of us should love the other, that brother should fight with brother, son against father ? I would not have you take from us our hereditary right, nor vainly seek to steal our very nature." Descendants of a demon, as themselves boasted, they joyed in evil like children on holiday. They were brutal and thankless, squabbling and killing for the love of war. Tragically alone, the elder King strove to settle disputes, to make his children love him. There was only the youngest, John, whom he could trust—John, and his illegitimate son, Geoffrey, his chancellor.

Richard had his personal troubles for a while, fighting in Poitou, then his resentment was further aroused by the elder Henry's refusal to let him marry his betrothed Alais. This was Louis's daughter, and as was the custom, she had been bred at the court of her affianced's parents. The elder Henry was not a wencher as his grandfather had been, but he loved the young princess. She usurped in his bed the position of the famous Rosamund Clifford, who died at about this time. The pretty stories of the maze, of the thread tied to Henry's spurs, and of the poison-bowl are all unfounded, we know very little of the real Rosamund except that she was buried at Godstowe nunnery where St. Hugh of Lincoln saw her tomb and " commanded that she be buried out of the church with other people, saying that she was a harlot." After her death, the elder Henry turned to the little Alais, and now when Louis asked that she be given to her betrothed Richard and when the Pope threatened an interdict unless she were surrendered, Henry had trouble in wriggling out of the net of their demands.

Louis died. He had not been an adversary worthy of the King of England. He had been cunning enough, but feeble in many ways, a worshipper of relics rather than of the sword ; his son, Philip Augustus, however, who became sole heir in September 1180, was almost a great man. He was brave and clever and ambitious, and he hated Henry. The plots of Henry's sons did not cease with Louis's death, they became more subtle.

For a time the brothers fought amongst themselves. Richard was fortifying castles that were rightly the young Henry's, the young Henry was conspiring with Richard's adherents in Aquitaine, while Geoffrey was eager to do any mischief he could. Helplessly the elder King watched his children snarling at each other over the lands he had built with such care. The troubles reached a head when young Henry insisted that Richard take an oath of fealty to him. Richard scorned the request, crying that if the first son were given his father's inheritance, the second should have his mother's. The father had to take the eldest's side. He dispatched Geoffrey and the young Henry to quieten some Poitevin rebels, they immediately joined them and defied both father and brother, and Richard murdered any prisoners who fell into his hands. When the father, trying to make peace, marched to Limoges, the young Henry and Geoffrey fired at him, and his jupon was torn by their arrows.

Treachery, lies, deliberate disobedience : Henry had indeed much to contend with. While his eldest son again pretended contrition and ate with him, trying to calm his suspicions, his other son Geoffrey was gathering troops. The young Henry, in penance, swore to go on a crusade when his treachery was discovered, his father tried to stop him, then giving in, promised him the necessary men and equipment. Young Henry instead rode to Angoulême to see what trouble he could make ; he captured one of Richard's towns and sacked Grammont, a house of religion especially beloved by his father, who wished to be buried there. Finding good booty at Grammont, the young King fell on other religious houses until at last he was gripped by fever and laid to rest in a blacksmith's hut. Dysentery followed fever. In pain, with sudden remorse, he implored his father to come to him, but the elder Henry had had enough of his son's treachery. He did not go himself but sent a sapphire ring—a magic stone of great curative value—and the Bishop of Agen who arrived in time to deliver the last sacrament. The dying King begged that his father forgive him, and he asked to be given the cloak that carried his crusader's badge : this he presented to his faithful comrade, William Marshal, commanding that he wear it to the Holy Land in his stead. Then, at the age of twenty-nine, he died at Rouen, in June 1183, after being dressed in a hair-shirt and having a rope placed about his neck. His last request was for the clergy to push him out of bed and lay him amongst ashes. Kissing his father's ring, he died.

The rebellion seems to us an act of pointless cruelty, of an ungrateful son turning against an affectionate father, but that is because we judge by twentieth and not twelfth century standards. The modern conception of sentimental filial love did not exist then, save rarely. Children were bred by strangers and they had little use for parents except as stepping-stones towards the attainment of power. Henry II, like William I, had been selfish, hating to share any of his glory with his children. He had been mean with money and lands, he had driven his children to rebellion, for men were not patient in the twelfth century, they were quick to see the faintest insult against their dignity, they were trained to fight, to conquer. Even John, who had most cause to love his father, eventually turned against him. The only son who remained loyal to the end was the chancellor, Geoffrey, but disloyalty would have brought him nothing because of his bastard birth.

RICHARD and Geoffrey and John remained. Eager to give power to his favourite, Henry suggested that Richard surrender to John his duchy of Aquitaine and that himself assume the vague kingship left open by the death of young Henry. Richard had fought to hold his lands and he did not intend to give them up now that they were comparatively at peace under his rule. Henry lent troops to John and fraternal war broke out again, Geoffrey rushing in, eager to fight anybody, but siding with John who was only fifteen at the time. A desultory war was the result, with no battles, merely a harrying of lands, a robbing of castles and of religious houses : the joy of fighting kept the brothers at it, probably none of them wanted a decisive victory and they therefore avoided each other. They submitted at once when their father told them to, and all three journey to England, evidently the best of friends.

There was trouble in the Holy Land. Baldwin, King of Jerusalem, hard pushed by the great Saladin and himself dying of leprosy, offered the crown to Henry II. Henry adroitly escaped the honour, although in his penance for the murder of Thomas he had promised to lead a crusade. But he dared not depart from his country while his three sons were eager to leap at each other's throats.

Loving John above all others—John whom he nicknamed Lackland because he had no possessions to offer him—Henry decided that he must give his favourite some honours. He knighted John and promised him Ireland. It was not long before he had to recall his son. John, resentful at being given this half-savage land, tweaked the beards of the chieftains when they came to offer homage and spent all his money on merry living with his friends.

WAR with France was the next vital problem Henry had to face. His third son, the treacherous Geoffrey, Count of Brittany, died of fever, and Philip, as overlord, demanded the wardship of Geoffrey's daughter and of Brittany. The war came to nothing except to make Richard a fast friend of Philip's and to give him an opportunity to steal his father's treasury at Chinon. Satisfied with the plunder, he did homage to his father at Angers.

The Holy Land was in a perilous condition for Saladin had now captured Jerusalem itself. The news struck all Europe with horror. Private wars ceased before this calamity. The tidings killed Pope Urban III : he died, it is said, with shame and despair. Richard, eager for any fight, took the cross at once without asking Henry, but Henry was forced to follow his example. Philip, too, could not avoid promising to rescue the Holy City. So many were the recruits that, to mark the difference of nationalities, it was decided that the English should wear white crosses, the French red, the Flemings green. To lead a crusade one had to have money, so Henry and Philip began at once to tax their already over-taxed subjects. Then Richard embroiled himself in a private war with Toulouse, and Philip took the opposite side ; Henry had to rush from England to help his son. The crusade for the moment was forgotten. The old squabbles, the insurrections, had begun again, men were slitting each other's throats on a paltry question while the Holy City was being broken by the triumphant hordes of Saladin.

At last the quarrel was patched up, then Philip demanded

the immediate marriage of Alais and Richard, to which Henry could not agree, for evidently he adored the girl. He was growing weary of these continual bickerings, exhausted in spirit at being made to fight those whom he loved. When Philip asked that Richard be recognised as Henry's heir, Henry refused. His sons had proved themselves traitors—Henry, Geoffrey, Richard —he no longer trusted any one save John, and without doubt he intended to disinherit Richard in John's favour. He tried to pass off Philip's demand by saying that it would injure his dignity to acclaim Richard, but at that Richard strode forward and, throwing away his sword, knelt at the feet of Philip, giving him homage for all his continental possessions except for those held from his father.

No longer was Henry's court crowded with men seeking favour. It was obvious that the King's health was failing, and Richard, the reckless open-fisted duke, was drawing men to his side. The continual wars and the Saladin-tax had drained England of money ; Henry was forced to remain passive, alone with John and the bastard Geoffrey, watching his eldest son with a suspicious eye. He was ill, a fistula was gradually killing him, and it was thought that he should confess lest he suddenly die. With his courtiers deserting him, with his vast empire dissolving before the schemes of Philip and the selfish ambition of Richard, the future could have held little promise for Henry. He had spent a furious life, he had built and fought and dreamed, only now at the end to see the greatness of his achievement decay before the jealous hatred of his sons.

United, Philip and Richard fought against him. He had little money, he was dying, his men fled from him to serve the stronger party. In Le Mans he was cornered, only to be driven out by a fire his own soldiers started to clear the land, and which a sudden wind drove backwards. In the terrible June sun Henry rode, sick and exhausted, for twenty miles to Fresnay-le-Vicomte on the way to Alençon. For the first time in his life he had been forced to fly, and as he turned on a hilltop to gaze back on the burning city, he lifted his arms and cursed God. " The city I loved best in the world," he cried, " the city in which I was born and reared, where my father lies buried and where lies the body of St. Julien—this, O God, to the heaping up of my confusion and to the enlarging of my shame, have You taken from me so basely ! I will reward You as best I can, I will rob You of the thing in me that You love best ! " As he rode, cursing and in despair, he was once almost captured but the collapse of a bridge held off pursuit. Exultant, joying to see his father run before him, Richard galloped after Henry. It was hot, and presumably for that reason, he threw aside his hauberk. He pressed on while the King's men fell by the wayside in the frightful heat, broken by hard riding. Dying, tortured by the fistula, cursing God, the poor King struggled forward with his raging son at his back. His rear was held by William Marshal, the friend of young Henry, and it was William who saved his King. Richard spurred forward triumphantly, thinking that at last Henry was at his mercy. William lifted his spear, and when he saw that hero of innumerable tournaments barring his way, Richard cried in sudden terror, " God's feet, Marshal, don't kill me ! I have no hauberk." " Kill you ? " answered William coldly. " No. I leave that to the devil." And he lowered his spear so that the point, instead of striking down the rider, slew the horse.

HENRY changed his objective, he decided to seek refuge in Anjou. His hatred for Richard was overpowering and he made his followers swear to deliver their castles to nobody but John. Richard must not have them, he swore, Richard would be disinherited. Yet he could do nothing. Seeing that their King was doomed, that his body was failing, and his power broken, his men deserted to Philip and Richard. It was impossible for him to hold out against such young and mighty enemies. He had to surrender.

Philip demanded that he come to meet them in a field near Tours. For the greatest King in Europe, he who but a few years since had seemed unconquerable, to be thus ordered about was too humiliating. Henry would not have gone if William Marshal had not counselled him to obey, and in truth patience was the one weapon he had left. He set out on this last journey, but his body was too racked with pain to carry him the full distance. At the house of the Templars at Ballan, such agony gripped him that he could not stand, and he had to lean shivering against the wall until his friends helped him to a bed. The faithful Geoffrey was not present, he had stayed away so that he would not witness his father's humiliation, only William Marshal was there of those who loved him, and it was to him that Henry called in his anguish. To proceed was impossible, and messages were sent to Philip and Richard asking for a short respite, but they refused to believe his plea of illness. Richard jeered at the tidings and Philip commanded that the dying King appear before him on the next day.

Sick unto death though Henry might be, although his body might drag him to a bed, the old proud spirit remained. It forced him to his feet, it made him clamber on to a horse and grimly, lurching in the saddle, ride to the place of meeting. When Philip and Richard saw him coming they knew at once that he had spoken truth, for death was written too plainly on the ashen face for them to doubt. With sudden contrition, Philip laid a cloak on the ground so that the dying King might sit in comfort. Henry scorned the shame of revealing his weakness. He would not get from his horse, he sat and told them that he had come only to hear what the French King asked of him and to learn why his lands had been stolen. Philip put aside his own compassion and spoke direct, he said that Henry must do homage and must give himself wholly to the mercy of France, Richard must be acclaimed his heir and be given the fealty of the barons on both sides of the sea ; Henry must pay Philip 20,000 marks, and they were to sail together on a crusade. All Henry's barons must swear to see that he kept these terms.

Henry did not speak for a moment. He had to accept whatever they asked, and it was not easy for him to swear away his kingdom. Then in the silence, while Philip and Richard waited, a crash of thunder was heard although the hot July sky was naked of cloud and of a bright blue. Both Kings started back at this unexpected peal that was like the menacing groan of some god, of perhaps the old Angevin demon turning in fury over the skyline. As the Kings recovered themselves and rode forward again, there came a second sudden crash out of the clear unbroken sky. Henry, his nerves already pitched to their highest, nearly fell from his horse, and his friends had to hold him upright. No longer was the oath kept back ; in terror, tormented in body and soul, he agreed to whatever Philip demanded, and —most humiliating act of all—he was forced to give the kiss of peace to his traitorous son. For the last time he held Richard in his arms, and as he held him he whispered fiercely, " May I live long enough to take revenge on you as you deserve ! " The threat did not trouble Richard, he laughed and jested about it afterwards.

For only one thing did Henry ask—a list of those who had transferred their allegiance from him to Richard.

As the dying King lay in his bed at Chinon that night he bade his vice-chancellor, Roger Malchat, read to him the names of the traitors. Roger took up the paper only to lay it down again with a sigh. " May Jesus Christ help me, sire," he faltered, " the first name written here is Count John's, your son." " Say no more," groaned Henry, unable to bear this last most terrible blow. He was silent a moment until, in mental agony, he cried, " Can it be ? John, my darling child, my very heart, for love of whom I have brought upon me all this torment, has he forsaken me ? " He sank back on the bed, then turned his face towards the wall. " Let things go as they will," he muttered, " I care no longer for myself or for the world."

He did not die at once. He became delirious, for days groaning and weeping and shouting curses on himself, on his sons and on God. The bishops tried to quieten him, but it was his bastard Geoffrey who at last brought a little peace to the tortured mind. It seemed the King slept when he leaned his head on Geoffrey's shoulder, his feet being stretched across the knees of a true knight ; then when he wakened, the marks of delirium were gone from Henry's face ; he gazed up at Geoffrey who was brushing away the flies, and spoke quietly. " My dearest son," he said, " you indeed have always been my true son. So help me God, if I recover from this sickness I will be the best of fathers to you and will place you among the highest in my kingdom. But if I do not live, may God grant you the reward you deserve for your unchanging loyalty to me." " Oh, father," cried Geoffrey, " I want no reward but your recovery to health and power," and the tears rushed to his eyes so that he had to run from the room lest he break down utterly.

Delirium returned. Henry tossed on his bed and groaned. Again and again he muttered the same words—" Shame, shame on a conquered King." Once more the madness passed, and once more he spoke plainly to his bastard son, telling him how he longed to reward him for his loyalty. He slipped off his gold finger-ring that was engraved with a leopard [1] and bade

---

[1] This is of interest as it is often stated that Richard I introduced the leopard into the royal coat of arms. Matthew Paris gives the young Henry a shield " per pale gules and sable, three golden leopards." Probably the elder Henry bore a red shield with the three gold leopards, but there is no proof of this ; Richard I bore three leopards. In heraldry a lion passant guardant was usually termed a leopard. It has been suggested that our lion springs from the fact that Henry I was called the Lion of Justice, but that seems rather far-fetched, it is more likely to have been derived from the arms of the dukes of Normandy—two leopards on a red field.

Geoffrey take it to the husband of his daughter Eleanor ; he told him where to find a second ring that he must keep for himself. Then he asked to be carried into the chapel, where he confessed and took the last sacrament.

For seven days the fever had lasted, and at the end Henry was quite sane and died peaceably. Immediately followed the usual uproar, the servants pillaged the castle, and everybody fled save a few faithful ones ; the body of Henry was stripped to the skin and tossed aside. During the last three days, when his recovery was hopeless, the castle had been robbed of everything of value. It was useless trying to stop the thieves, the King's friends had to stand aside and see their master's last hours made a mockery. They had not a few rags with which to cover Henry's nakedness until one of the knights took off his cloak and wrapped the corpse in that. William Marshal searched until he found a golden crown, a golden ring, a sceptre and sandals. In semi-regal state the great King was then carried on the shoulders of his barons to his grave at Fontévrault. He had wished to be buried at Grammont, but William Marshal did the only thing possible in taking him to nearby Fontévrault to " be shrouded amongst the shrouded women," thereby fulfilling a prophecy that for the last few months had spread through Henry's kingdom.

To this had Henry's glory descended, to a grave amongst women.

VI

KING RICHARD THE FIRST

1189-1199

RICHARD HAD BEEN WARNED about his father's death, and those who had remained faithful to the old King waited in terror for his coming. Many pleaded with William Marshal to escape while he had the chance ; so beloved was he that his comrades wished to give all their possessions and their own lives to protect him from Richard's vengeance. Calmly he answered, " Sirs, I do not repent me of what I have done. I thank you for your offers, but so help me God, I will not take what I cannot return. Thanks be to Him Who has helped me since I was made a knight, I do not doubt that He will help me to the end." Richard came late, riding in the dusk, and evidently quite alone. Without a word, while the frightened men strove vainly to read their future in his eyes, he walked into the quire. And it was said that the corpse spurted blood through the nostrils as he entered. Still silent, apparently unmoved, Richard stood beside his father's body and gazed into the uncovered face, then he knelt and prayed for a brief time. When he rose he called for William Marshal. With a friend, William came to the quire and Richard ordered him to follow him into the church. There he turned and said, " Fair Sir Marshal, you had like to have killed me. Had I felt your spear-thrust it would have been a bad day for both of us." " My lord," answered William, " I had the power to kill you, but I only killed your horse. And for that I do not repent me." Richard had no malice in him and he was touched by the bold reply. " You are pardoned, Marshal," he said, " I will hold no resentment against you."

He spoke the truth. William was dispatched to England to free Richard's mother, Eleanor—who had been more or less a prisoner since Henry had captured her in man's attire stirring up Richard and Godfrey against him—and for the rest of his life he proved himself a loyal subject. The bastard Geoffrey returned his seal of office to the new King, but later he was nominated

to the see of York, as Henry had wished upon his death-bed.
Other wishes of his father, Richard carried out as best he
could, and confirmed John in the countship of Mortain and in
four thousand pounds' worth of English land. Men who had
been loyal to Henry were received into favour, for now that he
was King, Richard needed true men at his side as his alliance
with Philip ceased automatically. Philip proved this by demanding that much-disputed strip of land, the Vexin, and Richard
avoided a direct answer by promising to wed Alais and by the
gift of four thousand marks. He was installed as Duke of Normandy
and received absolution from the church sentences passed against
him during his recent rebellion ; these sentences were evidently
not passed because he fought his father but because being a
crusader he had fought another crusader. He gave a series of
royal grants as if he were already crowned King of England,
and arranged for William Marshal to marry a wealthy heiress,
Isabel, who possessed great territories in south-west Wales, in
Ireland, and in Normandy : the bride was about seventeen,
William was between forty and fifty. Nevertheless he managed
to produce five sons and five daughters from her before he died.

The only one of his father's adherents on whom Richard's
anger fell was the seneschal of Anjou, because he failed to deliver
the treasures in his care. He failed not for any disloyalty,
he merely had no treasures to deliver and he was soon pardoned and taken back to favour. Then, secure in his continental possessions, Richard sailed for England on August 12,
1189, taking John with him. The first thing he did on landing
was to rush to Winchester to seize whatever was in the Treasury,
and then continued on a progress through the land so that the
people could see with their own eyes what kind of a man was
their new King.

IN appearance, Richard I must have seemed the perfect King.
He was tall and well built, being over six feet, and had a reddish
face and golden hair and beard. He was broad-shouldered
and long-limbed, his head was small, the nose firm and straight,
the thin underlip pushed out arrogantly, the eyebrows seemin,
curved slender lines. He was of great energy, but it would seem
when we remember that he was often a sick man, that his energy
was nervous rather than physical. A soldier who loved the
gusto of fighting, his life so far had been spent in continual war,
in petty forays, in burnings of towns and villages and religious

houses. He was always to be a warrior rather than a leader, loving more the thrill of hand-to-hand encounters than the careful planning of strategy and tactics. Yet, as shown in the retreat from Acre, he could plan well when necessary. His courage amazed even the hardy men of those times, Christian and pagan alike spoke almost with veneration of this King who had the heart of a lion. Brutal and insolent, yet quickly turned to good humour, he was a jovial if dangerous comrade but a worthless ruler. He liked the outward glory, the crown, the rich robes, the sceptre ; he did not share his father's contempt for regal trappings. The description of his coronation is without precedent ; it did, in fact, create a precedent to be followed by later Kings. He was generous and could forgive his enemies if the whim took him, but equally if the whim took him he could be harsh and merciless, seeking vengeance on the conquered. Lacking all sense of responsibility, he considered his people merely as so much cattle to be flogged into giving him money with which to fight ; and he could break a solemn treaty without a thought. Nevertheless it does not seem that he deserved the nickname of " Yea and Nay," which the troubadour Bertrand de Born gave to him ; but Bertrand was a malicious man who might have given it in a moment of pique. He was religious and never spoke during mass even if somebody spoke to him. All the same, he was not blind to the clergy's faults. Once when a prelate told him to marry off his three daughters, Richard retorted that he had no daughter. " Yes," said the prelate, " for you have Pride, Avarice and Luxury." " Hear ye me," cried the King to those about him. " Pride I give to the Templars, Avarice to the Cistercians, and Luxury to the Benedictines." He was a troubadour, a maker of songs, and during a service in the chapel he would walk through the quire waving his hands in time to the music.

Outwardly he must indeed have seemed to England the ideal King, with his proud golden head, his long limbs and charming manner. But he cared nothing for England. Normandy was to him the centre of his kingdom, he could not speak the English tongue, and only visited the land when his presence was vital to peace or needed for the gathering of money. The story of his reign has little to do with England, it is the tale of an heroic crusader and then of a man fighting his overlord in brave efforts to grip an empire that was gradually decaying.

The tale, therefore, of Richard is split into two : first, we see him in the Holy Land ; secondly, we watch his conflict with cunning Philip Augustus.

IT was a gorgeous cortège that set out from the King's apartments to the abbey on Sunday, September 3, 1189. Richard did not sit upon the throne, he sat first upon a chair probably in front of it, on a raised platform. The oath was the usual one, to keep justice with mercy, to guard Church and people. His robes were slipped from the broad shoulders, and in shirt and breeches, the duke stood for the anointing, the holy oil being placed on his chest and on either shoulder, slits being made in the shirt for the purpose. Over his golden head was poured the chrism, that mixture of holy oil and balsam used only for baptism, confirmation and ordination ; then the head was bound and was to be kept covered for eight days.

Richard was now the anointed King of England. Tunic and dalmatic were drawn over his shoulders, the cap of maintenance was pulled on to the chrism-cloths, gold-laced sandals were put upon his feet. Spurs, sword, stole and mantle followed, then he was led to the altar and took up the crown, passing it to the archbishop who placed it on the cap of maintenance. The archbishop, before giving Richard the crown, told him in the name of God that he must not accept it unless he was determined to keep his oaths ; with God's help, said Richard, he would keep them. The crown made him the complete King, but he must yet take the ring, the sceptre and rod before, to the deep chanting of the Te Deum, he was led to the throne of England.

While this great ceremony and the feasting that followed were taking place within Westminster there was a massacre outside its walls. Richard had ordered that no Jews should be allowed inside the abbey or hall, but some wealthy Jews had dared enter with gifts. They were immediately seized, robbed and thrown out, some of them were even murdered. Any excuse was enough for a Londoner to attack the usurers : the best way to pay your debts was to use a sword or a club. Seeing the unfortunate men being thrown out of Westminster acted as a signal to the populace. The people " up with staves, bats and stones, and laid on the Jews and made them to flee. Hereof sprang liking [*delightful*] tidings into all the city, as though the King had bidden, and up with staves to destroy the Jews. And the people, raving and crying, brake up the house where the Jews were y-flown for dread, and burned and spoiled and took what they might." The " liking tidings " spread through England. In each great city, save Winchester, there was a pogrom. Everywhere Jews were " y-beaten, y-slain and y-spoiled." At York occurred a ghastly tragedy. Over four hundred Jews took refuge in one of the castle towers, and finding themselves besieged and without hope, their offers of ransom being refused, they decided to die rather than have their women ravished and themselves suffer torture. They cut the women and children's throats and burnt the building on top of themselves. The few who remained were torn to pieces by the mob.

For months the massacres continued. Richard strove vainly to stop them, more in anger at losing the wealth of the Jews than for any love of them, and at last the fury burnt itself out and the people of the various towns were fined for their insubordination.

THIS was no good omen at the outset of a reign, but Richard did not intend to stay in England. He was eager to set out for the Holy Land. He made his old comrade William Longchamp chancellor : Longchamp was a wizened little lame man of fearful ugliness, he was of low birth and rapacious and cruel, if loyal ; for vice-chancellor he appointed Hugh of Puiset, a well-bred man, clever and cultured, in every way the antithesis of Longchamp. The true ruler of England, however, was to be Richard's mother, Eleanor. John remained, and of John Richard was quite rightly most distrustful. He tried to bribe his affections by grants of land, although he insisted that he keep out of England for three years, and for a while he considered taking him crusading to the Holy Land. Foolishly, he did not take John with him, but instead showered him with honours, at the same time giving him no appointment of power in the government.

First money must be collected before Richard could set out on his crusade. It was gathered by every possible and slippery means of taxation, by the selling of offices, by bribery and threats. And at last, on June 24, 1190, Richard started the adventure at Tours, receiving there the holy scrip and staff of the pilgrim.

AT Vézelai the two Kings met, the King of England and the King of France. They swore to stand together in all things and to divide equally any conquest or plunder. They marched to Lyons and there parted, Philip travelling to

Genoa *via* the Alps, Richard making for Marseilles, where he discovered to his rage that his fleet had not arrived. Richard was an impatient man and he probably wished to reach Genoa for a last talk with Philip. At any rate, after idling for a few days, he hired twenty galleys and ten busses—much larger ships—and made a slow but pleasant voyage along the Mediterranean to Genoa where he had a talk with Philip and an argument with Rome. When the bishop of Ostia came on a friendly visit, Richard insulted him, declaring that the papal taxes were too heavy and that the Church had no right to drag money out of England. Naples was the next stop, and here Richard so enjoyed himself that he lingered for ten days before continuing his slow pleasure-trip to Salerno. He did not always stay on board, when the seascape grew tiresome he travelled on land, and once while riding from Meleto to Bagnara he was stoned and chased by the peasants for stealing a hawk. At Messina he again met Philip, sailing in gorgeously with trumpets blowing and banners waving, Richard himself in regal dress standing on the prow of the highest ship.

At Messina he decided to embroil himself in a family affair. His sister, Joan, widow of William II of Sicily, had been imprisoned by King Tancred who claimed her husband's throne. Richard at once commanded that she be freed, he also asked for supplies for himself and the return of Joan's dowry. Tancred gave him Joan but ignored the other demands. Then Richard infuriated the inhabitants by throwing the monks out of a Greek monastery and giving their home to his sister ; affairs might have stayed at simmering-point if the crusaders had not treated the Messinese with insolent contempt. Richard tried to keep peace, but the outraged inhabitants at last could tolerate their guests no longer, and fighting broke out. The King, running to stop the tumult, was caught in a mob who jeered at him, asking where he kept his tail.[1] An insult such as this could not be ignored. Richard rushed home, put on his mail-shirt, and had

---

[1] It was a common belief on the Continent that Englishmen had tails, and various explanations have been given for the birth of so peculiar a legend. The insult remained for centuries, continuing through thé Hundred Years' War. Caxton's *Golden Legend* tells us that St. Austin damned the English to this penance for rejecting Christianity. " It is said commonly that this fell at Strood, in Kent, but blessed be God at this day is no such deformity." Polydore Vergil also mentions Strood, saying that God tailed the people for cutting off the tail of St. Thomas's horse. See Dr. George Neilson's *Caudatus Anglicus* (Edinburgh, 1896) for an interesting analysis of the subject.

his trumpets blown to call his men to arms. The city gates were barred, but Richard smashed through a small postern at the rear, charged down the streets and opened the gates to his men. " In less time than a priest could say matins Messina was taken." The booty was large and the women attractive : everything, including the women, was shared by the victors. Philip objected strongly to the slaughter, and then demanded a half-share of the plunder as had been agreed on at Vézelai.

It was the stormy season and therefore Richard and Philip decided to pass the winter at Messina, Richard negotiating with Tancred and promising him his nephew Arthur as husband for Tancred's daughter. Then Queen Eleanor arrived from England with complaints about the rule of Longchamp and with a bride for Richard. This lady was Berengaria, daughter of Sancho VI of Navarre. It is said that Richard had seen her many years ago and had been attracted to her, yet presumably she was not beautiful as he never cared for her after the marriage. Some chroniclers suspect Richard of homosexuality, but we have the names of two mistresses at least : perhaps he was bisexual. The arrival of Berengaria at Messina made it plain that Richard had no intention of marrying his betrothed Alais. Philip objected furiously, but Richard gave him the plain answer that he would not marry his father's mistress, and he bought himself free of the engagement with 10,000 marks.

Philip left for Acre on March 30, and soon Eleanor also departed. Berengaria remained with Richard and his sister Joan ; the two royal ladies were then sent in advance to Acre, and Richard followed, to meet storm after storm until his battered ships reached Limasol in Cyprus, where he found the ladies too terrified to land, for the inhabitants had imprisoned the ship-wrecked knights and sailors. Isaac Comnenus was Emperor of Cyprus, and it was believed that he was an ally of Saladin ; certainly, and with justification, he dreaded the coming of these Frankish pilgrims with their swords and haughty manners. He apologised to Richard for his subjects' defiance, offered to return all prisoners, and invited the ladies to disembark. Richard was suspicious of the courteous Greek, particularly when he noted that Isaac was slowly filling the city with armed men ; he demanded restitution for all damage in so insolent a fashion that Isaac very stupidly replied with equal haughtiness. Richard immediately blew his trumpets and manned his boats. Within a short time the city was his and the ladies were comfortably lodged, horses were landed and booty gathered. But Richard's dignity was hurt too cruelly for him to remain satisfied with so small a conquest ; he noted the beauty and richness of the land, and the next day he charged out and defeated the Cyprian army, chasing Isaac into his capital, Nicosia, in the centre of the island. Isaac for the first time realised what hornets he had kicked to life. He remained as quiet as he could and as far away from Richard as possible.

Meanwhile men were whispering about the virginity of Berengaria. She was now Richard's betrothed and as the chaperonship of Joan was not sufficient to protect her from slander, it was decided that the marriage must be solemnised at once. On Sunday, May 12—the black month for marriages—1191, Richard, " happy and splendid, laughing and pleasing everyone," wedded Berengaria, and the hopes of the wretched Alais were gone for ever. Feasting followed ; and negotiations were opened about the vacant kingship of Jerusalem. Guy had been King only through his marriage with Sybille, daughter of King Amalric, and as Sybille was now dead it was uncertain if he could continue to reign. His rival was the Italian, Conrad Marquis of Montferrat, whose elder brother had been Sybille's first husband. Philip on his arrival at Acre endorsed Conrad's claim, Guy therefore rushed to have Richard endorse his. This, Richard promised to do. He then, now that he was reinforced by Guy and his troops, decided to capture all Cyprus for himself. Isaac, in terror, tried to make peace, and a conference was arranged outside the walls of Limasol.

Richard dressed himself in his brightest at the least excuse. When he came to meet Isaac he wore a rose-coloured satin tunic belted at the waist, a mantle of striped silver tissue brocaded with silver half-moons ; his sword of Damascus steel had a hilt of gold and rested in a sheath of silver scales. He carried a truncheon and he wore a scarlet cape embroidered with golden beasts. He rode a Spanish palfrey, sitting in a saddle of gold that was inlaid with jewels ; instead of a crupper this saddle bore two gold lions with paws raised as if to scratch each other. Isaac did homage to the tall golden-headed King, promised to follow him to Jerusalem with five hundred horse, to surrender his castles and to pay 3500 marks indemnity.

Richard wanted more than money and castles, he wanted the entire island. He gave the Emperor the kiss of peace, then despite the feudal laws of overlord and vassal, he kept him as an

14

honourable prisoner. Isaac escaped, which gave Richard the excuse he needed. He swore that this was a breach of the treaty that himself had already broken, and he hounded the poor Emperor from corner to corner of his own island. Messages came from Philip pleading for Richard to stop fighting against Christians and hasten to kill the enemies of God ; Richard's reply was so direct that the scribe dared not write it down. Isaac was chased over Cyprus—Richard meanwhile accusing him of shooting poisoned arrows—until he had no more bolt-holes in which to hide ; then he crept to Richard, imploring only that he be not bound in iron chains. Richard agreed, he bound him in silver ones.

After this refreshing interlude, with the plunder of Cyprus aboard his ships, with his wife and sister to amuse him, and with a captive Emperor and an Emperor's little daughter as prisoners, Richard at last set sail on the great adventure. He began splendidly by capturing on the way a large pagan ship carrying reinforcements and munitions to the besieged garrison at Acre. Richard himself reached Acre on Saturday, June 8.

IT was impossible for Philip and Richard to remain friends ; it was impossible that as joint-commanders they could lead an army to victory. French and Anglo-Norman detested each other, and those modern writers who insist that there was no nationalism in the Middle Ages need only study the crusades to see how tireless were the bickerings, how deep was the hatred of one nation for another. Philip demanded from Richard half of Cyprus, appealing to the treaty of Vézelai, while Richard claimed half of Artois that had recently become Philip's owing to the death of its count. Little things showed the growing resentment between the two commanders. Philip had given each of his men-at-arms three gold pieces a month, Richard raised the price of his to four, and a great many of Philip's troops deserted to the English standard.

Then Richard fell ill, and after a repulsed assault on the walls of Acre, Philip also fell ill. The garrison tried to negotiate a surrender, but the Christian demands were so high that at first the Moslems dared not grant them without Saladin's permission ; their situation became so desperate that eventually they were forced to give way. They agreed to surrender Acre and the True Cross, to free their prisoners and to pay a ransom of 200,000 gold besants. The Christians kept all the garrison as hostages to make certain that the terms would be ratified by Saladin.

Meanwhile the various commanders were quarrelling amongst each other, suspicious of the faintest possible slight : Leopold, Duke of Austria, raised his flag as an independent prince within the captured walls, Richard pulled it down, and although Leopold was for the moment made to submit, his opportunity for revenge was yet to come ; he retired to sulk in his own quarters. Then Philip, weary of body, exhausted by quarrels, outraged by Richard's haughty bearing and afraid that events in France might turn against him, decided to go home. Guy and Conrad were still arguing with each other, Guy backed by Richard, Conrad by Philip, each claiming the throne of Jerusalem. The question was at last settled by giving the crown to Guy, with Conrad as his successor. Philip left, but before he would permit his going, Richard insisted that he swear publicly that he would not interfere with Richard's kingdom during his absence. Philip swore the oath and quickly forgot about it.

The unfortunate Acre garrison might, in its terrible extremity, promise anything for relief, but their promises were too vast for Saladin to endorse. The negotiations dragged on, and when it seemed that a compromise would never be reached, the Christians began to lose patience. Their 2600 hostages were taken out before Saladin's distant scouts and beheaded, half of them by Richard and half by the Duke of Burgundy who had taken Philip's place as commander of the French.

ACRE was a pleasant town and the Frankish knights—as the Christians were indiscriminately termed by the Moslems—did not wish to leave, for they had " good wine and girls, many of whom were very pretty. They gave themselves up to the wine and the women until the valiant men were ashamed of the rest." When Richard led his troops towards the capture of Jerusalem he had to pause in his march while men were sent back to drag malingerers from wine-cups and women. The women who had followed the troops were chased away, save those who could carry baggage, and each man was given ten days' supply of biscuit, wheat, wine and meat. The great standard, a dragon on an iron-hooped pole in a cart, was pulled forward, and the Christians set out determined to rescue the Holy Sepulchre.

The heat was frightful, the men in their steel shirts gasped and floundered amongst the dry brush and sand by the shore,

for Richard had determined most wisely to keep by the coast
where the sea could protect one flank. The distance was sixty-
five miles as the crow flies, but over a hundred by the sea-route,
and the men could not march quickly. In the heat and glare,
with the sun flaming on the sand-dunes and limestone cliffs,
and having to carry their heavy packs and wear their armour,
they were forced to stop and rest every now and again,
and only a few miles were covered each day. Saladin struck as
they marched, and the army had to be split into two : one
half being kept in battle-array to the left while the other with
the baggage hugged the sea-line. The country had been devastated by the Moslems, there was little to eat. Men fell in the
sand, exhausted, and could not rise ; they lay in their armour,
dying, prey to the enemy. Yet Richard pushed on, hampered
by the non-combatant pilgrims who followed so as to be first
to enter the Sacred City. " Holy Sepulchre, aid us ! " was the
constant wail, " Holy Sepulchre, aid us ! " The Moslems
charged from the hills, slashing at the rear, at the stragglers.
Richard drew up his men into a strong formation, in twelve
squadrons each of five lines. The Templars made the van,
followed by the Bretons and Angevins, then came the Poitevins
under King Guy, then the Normans and English with the
standard, while the Knights Hospitallers formed the rearguard.
The French were evidently kept as shock-troops, as a flying wing
to the left to hold back any sudden attack.

At nine o'clock in the morning of September 7, Richard
saw the Moslems barring his way to Arsuf. He was at a strong
disadvantage, being badly outnumbered in cavalry, yet the
Saracens could not resist admiring the courage with which these
exhausted Christian soldiers prepared for battle. " We had to
admire," a Moslem tells us, " the patience shown by these people
who suffered the worst fatigues without possessing military skill
or with any advantage on their side." Richard commanded
that his men keep their ranks, that they march stolidly forward,
smashing through the enemy in an unbroken wedge ; with his
lack of cavalry here lay his one chance, for he realised that
Saladin would try to lure his troops into disorder by driving them
to fury. This was what Saladin succeeded in doing. His men
swept on to the Christian rear that had to protect itself while
marching backwards. They thundered down and struck " as if
with mallets, for having no space in which to use the bow they
fought hand-to-hand, and the blows of the Turks [*the Christian*

name for Moslems] echoing from the metal shirts resounded as if
they had been struck upon an anvil. They were tormented by
the heat and no pause was allowed them." Patiently, striding
slowly backwards, the Hospitallers tried to withstand the flying
dashes of the Moslems, the quick dives of horsemen who were
unarmoured and agile, swift with the spear and bow and the
scimitar. They pleaded with Richard to sound the charge, but
he told them to stand firm, saying that he could not be everywhere
at once. They struggled backwards, gasping in the heat that
dashed into their faces with the malignancy of a living demon,
while the lightly dressed enemy, inured to the sun, felt no
fatigue and could charge and charge again without pause. Two
Hospitallers, stung beyond patience, spurred their horses, and
alone plunged straight at the enemy, yelling, " St. George !
St. George ! " At sight of this, their comrades forgot Richard's
orders, they broke their ranks, and, shouting, charged. They
were followed by the others. Even Richard could not withstand
the excitement. He turned his steed and drew his sword. " Then
might be seen numbers fallen to the ground, horses in swarms
without riders, many trodden underfoot by friend and enemy.
O how different is war from the thoughts of those dreaming by
the columns of the cloisters ! " The Moslems were swept back,
were pushed into the sea and many drowned. Richard was in
the forefront. " There the fierce King, the extraordinary King,
cut down the Turks, where he turned he slashed a broad path
for himself like a reaper with the sickle. Warned by the sight,
he was given wide room." The battle became confused, a mêlée,
neither side seemed certain of victory, banners were wrenched
from the hands of the bearers and flung to the sand. Many
Moslems fled, some crawled under corpses, others scrambled
into the trees and were shot down by bolt and arrow. For two
miles nothing but fugitives could be seen with exultant Christians
slashing at them. Richard so far forgot himself that he chased
the flying enemy and deserted his own standard. That standard
was in danger. The English and Normans had remained firmly
about it while their comrades charged to the fight, and now seven
hundred Moslems swept down. These were Saladin's own household troops carrying yellow banners, and only at the last moment
did help come and rescue the royal dragon.

The enemy was repulsed for the moment, but the exhausted
Christians had no sooner reached the walls of Arsuf than the
Moslems struck again. With only fifteen men, Richard charged,

and reinforcements swiftly followed, crying, " Aid us, O
Sepulchre ! " That was the last engagement. Sleep followed,
save for those who stole back to the field in search of plunder or
to find the bodies of dead comrades.

IT had taken the Christians nineteen days to cover those hundred-
odd miles, and when they found themselves in the gardens of
Jaffa they forgot dangers and wounds ; crowned with flowers they
made merry with the women who—despite Richard's ban—had
followed the army from Acre. In council, Richard argued that
it would be well if they captured Ascalon, which was being
destroyed by the Moslems, but the French insisted that they stay
and rebuild Jaffa. For about three weeks the rebuilding went on,
then the march was commanded to begin again, this time
directly towards Jerusalem which Saladin was fortifying in a
frenzy of haste, himself, although sick and old, lugging great
stones to the walls and toiling like a common man.

Richard was once almost captured. He fell asleep after
skirmishing in the hills and was awakened just in time to leap
upon his horse as a troop of Moslems galloped up. Luckily he
was not recognised, and " William of Préaux, one of his knights,
a loyal man and proud, shouted, ' I am the *malic.*' That is to
say, the King. The Turks seized him at once." On another
occasion he charged to aid a troop of outnumbered Templars
who were fighting the enemy. He had only a few men at his
back and they strove to make him turn, saying, " It is better
they die than that you die with them." " I sent them there,"
cried Richard, flushing, " I told them to go. If they die without
me may I never again be called King ! " And he galloped at
the Saracens so that " they fled like beasts."

The advance on Jerusalem turned back to Jaffa. Richard
had lost too many men to attempt to assault so strong a city,
and he decided to remain in Jaffa until reinforcements came.
Meanwhile he negotiated with Saladin. These two great men
were never to meet, Richard at first had pressed an invitation
on the Sultan, who had parried the request. His brother,
Al Adil, acted as go-between, and he and Richard became very
friendly ; they feasted each other on the strange foods of their
respective countries and exchanged gifts. Richard argued for
peace on one side, but on the other, Conrad was bidding against
him, each offering Saladin different terms. Richard even went
so far as to suggest that Saladin's brother marry his sister Joan, but

he could not have been serious ; undoubtedly Richard had a queer sense of fun, a cruel arrogant humour, and Saladin was not deceived by the offer although he pretended to discuss it gravely.

Further attempts were made to reach Jerusalem, and this time it was the French who suggested turning back. They resented serving under a King of England, and when Richard refused to lend them further money, they deserted and returned to Acre. Richard, too, was wearying of the conflict, he was afraid that while striving to win the city of God he might lose his own inheritance. Philip Augustus was home and was plotting with John, warnings came to Richard that John might steal his crown, yet he could not leave the East while Jerusalem remained unconquered. Then Conrad was murdered, stabbed by two assassins. He was killed at exactly the wrong moment, when Guy's followers were tired of his rule, when Richard had agreed to accept Conrad as King of Jerusalem and while himself was plotting successfully with Saladin. Both Saladin and Richard have been blamed for the murder, but there can be little doubt that neither had anything to do with it. The terrible Old Man of the Mountain [1] had sent his assassins, for he and Conrad were enemies and Conrad's election would have been dangerous to the Old Man's power. With Conrad put out of the way dissension ceased. A nephew of both Richard and Philip, Henry of Champagne, accidentally arrived at the very time when he was needed ; he came to Tyre and discovered that he was elected the new King of Jerusalem, and he was a choice that all parties could accept. The only dissatisfied person was Guy, but Richard consoled him with the kingdom of Cyprus to be held as a fief of England.

[1] Hassan ibn Sabah—called by the crusaders the Old Man of the Mountain—is so romantic a figure as to seem almost incredible. He began as a dissenter from the Islam faith and preached a doctrine that " nothing is true, all is permitted." Around him he gathered a secret order of young men who dressed in white save for red girdle and red slippers. He gave them opium in wine and taught them the joys of hemp-eating until they became automatons of his will. On an impregnable mountain he constructed a walled garden and filled it with things of beauty, with flowers, musicians and girls. The lads, drugged by opium or hemp, would be carried secretly here and would awake to find themselves for a few days in paradise ; this garden they were taught was actually heaven. Each was therefore eager to die so that he could return for ever to the garden, and the Old Man built an empire of terror, sending out his drugged fanatics to slay the great men of Islam. These murderers were called *assassins* from the Arab *ḥashshāshīn*, literally " hashish [hemp]-eaters."

WITH the kingship at last settled, Richard renewed his campaign. Before attacking Jerusalem he decided to clear the way by leaving no strong garrison between the city and the coast : he charged on Darun, and although the fort was called impregnable, he captured it within four or five days and took the garrison for slaves. Smaller forts were then demolished before he hurried back to Ascalon.   Now his path was open to the Holy City, but Richard yearned to be home, for he was continually worried by messages telling of John's treachery and of Philip's intrigues.   His followers pleaded with him to remain with them, and against his will he gave in to their importunity ; he announced before the city walls that nothing would make him turn back before Easter and that the army must instantly prepare to attack Jerusalem.   The men shouted with delight.   " Now," they cried, " we shall see the Sepulchre ! "

On June 7, 1192, Richard set out once more for the Holy City only to give way suddenly with the walls in sight.   The task was no simple one, Jerusalem was well built and well garrisoned, and the Moslems were continually breaking down the Christian army's communications.   One magnificent success Richard had during his retreat.   He captured a great caravan on its way from Egypt to Jerusalem, after a battle with five hundred guards sent by Saladin.   The booty was huge—gold, silver, silk, tapestries, embroideries, clothes, pavilions, shirts of silvered mail, spices, drugs, chessboards, plate, and fruit. Besides horses and asses, 4700 camels were taken, with five hundred prisoners to lead the animals which were roped with the plunder.

Richard's task was far more difficult than at first glance it would appear.   He had to march through hostile territory in ghastly heat and with little water, and his march was probably retarded by numerous non-combatant pilgrims and the inevitable prostitutes ; he also had the French, who were eager to frustrate him at any point.   The Duke of Burgundy was writing insulting songs about him, and Richard was answering in the same form. All the while he strove to make terms with Saladin, offering to give up Jerusalem and the hills if the Christians could keep the coast-line with free access to the Holy City.   Saladin agreed if Richard would pull down Ascalon and Toron ; Richard pulled down Toron but he refused to demolish Ascalon.

Any hope of retaking Jerusalem was now remote.   Richard, before the capture of the caravan, had already turned back after seeing in the distance the dreamed-of walls. He had gazed on the Holy City then turned away while the French had demanded an immediate attack. Richard had argued with his council, pointing out that Saladin had stopped the springs, filled up the wells and broken the cisterns so that no water was to be had outside the walls of the city. He was answered that the army could be divided, that while one half fought the city the other half could seek water. Richard answered that with a divided army the garrison could " sally out and attack those who stayed, and that will end it." When pressed further, he said, " You will not have me as leader when it would be folly to push on and disgrace to me. If you want to go to Jerusalem I will go with you as comrade but not as commander. I will follow, but I will not lead."

The Crusaders turned back after their one glimpse of the city in the distance ; they captured the caravan, but that was small gain compared to the relinquishing of Jerusalem.

ON July 26, 1192, Richard was in Acre preparing to leave for home. Then came news that the moment his back was turned, Saladin had struck at Jaffa. Richard acted at once. " As God lives," he cried, " I will go ! " He sent the Templars and Hospitallers overland to the relief and himself took ship. For two days the winds held him back off the Carmel headland, but on July 31, at night, his galleys reached the beleaguered city. It was dark and impossible to land. Impatiently Richard waited for the dawn to show what was happening on shore ; then as the mists dissolved and the sun flared over the hills, he saw only hordes of Moslems between the sea and the city. No sign of life in the city, no banners to be seen save Moslem banners. " Sir knights," he asked, " what shall we do? depart or land ? " They said that it would be best to turn back, for it seemed that without doubt Jaffa had fallen. The galleys stood off from the shore, the men watching the uncountable enemy, seeing the blank walls of Jaffa half a mile in the distance. It seemed that they were too late.

A priest from the city stole through the Moslem army and swam to the galleys. He was brought before Richard and told that the garrison was at that moment arranging terms with Saladin, forty-nine men with their wives and horses having already surrendered : Saladin's troops were pillaging the city, they were beyond the Sultan's control and were running through the streets half-insane with lust. Richard turned to his knights.

" Sirs," he said, " if God wills that we die with our comrades, damned is he who hangs back." His galley was first to touch the shore and he was the first to jump into the water that reached to above his waist. He was dressed in helmet and hauberk, he had not waited even to change his sea-slippers for fighting-shoes. Wading through the water, he lifted his crossbow and shielded his troops as they disembarked. As he strode forward he fired again and again into the densely packed enemy ; his men followed, and at sight of the red-gold head and flushed face of the demon *Malic Ric*, the Moslems scattered in terror. A barricade was built around the ships as the sands crunched under their keels ; but Richard did not pause, he charged straight towards the city, his knights about him. He knew a small door in the house of the Templars, and he rushed in so suddenly that the Moslems who were plundering the place were too startled even to fight. Richard was now in the city and his banner of the Lion was hoisted, to give heart to the garrison which sallied out at once. " Then the gate was so clogged by the fleeing that many died." The city that a brief while since had been in the hands of the Moslems was suddenly, by the mere appearance of the splendid King, again reconquered by the Christians. " This all happened under my eyes in less than an hour," writes a Moslem who had been trying to reorganise his plunder-crazed men.

Richard had arrived at exactly the right moment, while Saladin was discussing terms with envoys from the garrison. Saladin pretended that nothing was amiss, hoping to cheat the envoys into submission before they knew the truth, but the fugitives told everything. He was forced to retire, taking the envoys with him, while Richard, keeping away from the city that stank with blood and corpses, camped where Saladin's own tents had stood.

The suddenness of Richard's arrival and his courage in landing before a great army so astonished the Moslems that some of the chiefs that evening came to gaze upon the Lion King. Richard greeted them friendlily and laughed, saying, " Why did the Sultan leave when I came ? By God, I did not come armed for real fighting. Look, I still wear only ship-sandals." Then, becoming serious, he tried to make a bargain with the Moslems, sending them with messages to Saladin.

THAT night, realising that he would never take this King save by surprise, Saladin sent his troops secretly to the Christian camp.

They were seen just in time for Richard to leap from bed and to trumpet his men into formation. The front line knelt behind its shields with lances pressed into the ground and pointing outward ; behind it stood crossbowmen, with a second rank to pass re-loaded bows. Between the beach and the field, the army spread in sickle-fashion so that communications could remain open.

The Moslems charged. These were Saladin's crack troops, his Mamelukes and his own Kurdish bodyguard. The English stood firm, swiftly releasing the strings of their crossbows, passing back the empty weapons to be rebolted, and snatching loaded ones from the second rank. Before that fire, the cavalry swerved, the horses shied from the steel-points of the lances. Unbroken, the Christians kept their places while without a blow being struck, the Moslems turned and scattered ; they re-formed and charged again and again. Always the steady crossbow fire, the lance-tips glittering in the dawn-light, terrified the horses, sent them back before the curved Christian line could be even pierced. Richard was not able to remain inactive. His fingers itched to wield a lance, and with but ten horsemen, he galloped at the enemy. He smashed right into the Moslems, then turned to cleave his way through the mass, back to his own lines, using his battle-axe. The Earl of Leicester was down, tumbled from his horse ; on foot he stood at bay while the King charged to his rescue, and stamped and slashed a path through the Moslems, then he held his shield over his friend until he could remount. Another comrade was captured, Richard beat off the Moslems and rescued him. It seemed that nothing could kill this tall King, he remained unhurt, as fresh as ever ; and the Moslems, cowed by the savage splendour of one man, drew back.

While the armies paused to reform, a Moslem rode up leading two horses, a gift from Saladin's brother to Richard, for Richard's steed was not strong, as had been noted by Al Adil. " Sire," said the knights, " do not take them. There is evil in them and they will ride with you to the Moslems." " If Satan himself sent me a good horse," said Richard, leaping into the saddle of one of the beasts, " I would ride him."

The fight continued. The Moslems, realising that mounted men could not break the Christian lines, used their bows instead of lance and sword. The knights and men-at-arms did not flinch before this new attack, but the sailors fled with some of the Genoese. Where they left a gap, the Moslems broke through and again entered the city. Richard turned his horse and dashed after them. He struck down two of the enemy, then was himself in the city, calling to the fugitives and making certain that his ships were well guarded. Then he returned to the battlefield and with twelve knights—the only mounted men he had—scattered a charge of Moslems. One enemy, jeering at his comrades, spurred at the King. "Make way!" he yelled. "Oh, dogs, make way for a man!" Richard waited for him and struck as he came near ; so strongly did he strike that his sword peeled the man in half, it broke through the shield and lopped an arm and the head. At this, the Moslems turned, and fighting ceased. Scared, disheartened, they drew back ; they were rallied once more, but the gusto had left them. They were afraid of the demon *Malic Ric* who it seemed nothing could kill. There were arrows and javelins sticking in his hauberk, yet he remained unhurt, he was as strong as ever. The Moslems gave in, they could not fight with devils, and sullenly they drew out of range.

In the open space between the armies Richard rode alone. From end to end of the Moslem line he went, slowly, defiantly, lifting his lance, and none dared venture against him. An army stood at bay before one man. Saladin cried for his troops to charge, and his son alone responded ; but Saladin, a very loving father, dared not lose his son and therefore held him back. He gazed upon his troops and on that truculent King trotting up and down ; then despairingly he gave the order to retreat.

RICHARD fell ill. He was so ill that they carried him to Acre away from the pestilent city of Jaffa. No longer for a time could he lead the Christians, and news came that Saladin was gathering another mighty army. " Tell Al Adil from me," said Richard, " to arrange what terms he can. Anything but the surrender of Ascalon." Saladin, an honourable enemy, sent Richard gifts of snow and peaches when he asked for them, while negotiations went forward. Ascalon was the stumbling-block : Saladin demanded that it be demolished, Richard refused at first, but at last he had to give way, and the treaty was concluded. Ascalon was to be destroyed, but from Jaffa to Tyre the Christians were to hold all coastal towns with right of entry into Jerusalem.

An enormous amount of money had been spent and little had been gained. The crusade was a gigantic and magnificent failure, and the blame must be taken by Richard. Historians continue to argue about the cause of the collapse, some blaming Richard's incompetence, others the treachery of the French. It is true that Richard had insubordination amongst his men, but Saladin was facing the same problem ; besides, Richard was young while Saladin was old.

The basis of the failure was Richard's weakness as a leader. He came to the Holy Land in a mood of bravado ; it is difficult not to believe that from the first he was determined to be the sole commander and that he consciously angered Philip, Leopold and Conrad. His belief in himself remained until the battle of Arsuf; from that moment he seemed to lose his nerve, to vacillate from corner to corner, leading courageous forays but shirking the real objective, the capture of Jerusalem. Arsuf had taught him a great lesson : he was the finest hand-to-hand soldier in the world and little else ; war in the east was different from the wars he had known in the west. The fighting in Normandy had been a matter of petty sieges, of well-staged combats ; now he had to face organised troops, he had to plot strategy, to be able to think quickly and to remain calm. He tried to remain calm at Arsuf, but when the enemy fled he lost control of himself and joined in the pursuit, as no leader should have done. Hand-to-hand fighting was to him irresistible, yet when necessary—as Arsuf and Jaffa showed—he could plot and arrange his men in perfect formation. He was a leader until the battle started, then he became merely a fighter. His own sense of this weakness must have troubled him during those futile marches towards Jerusalem. When he suggested that he fight as a comrade but not as a leader, he was undoubtedly sincere, and the statement proves that he was not blind to his own faults.

" If I should be fated to lose the Holy Land," said Saladin, " I would rather lose it to *Malic Ric* than to any other." And a warrior capable of making so intelligent and brave a man as Saladin use such words must have been great indeed. For years his memory remained. Joinville, who in 1248—over fifty years after Richard—sailed with St. Louis for the Holy Land, remarks that " when the Saracen children cried, their mothers called out, ' Wisht ! here is King Richard ! ' in order to quieten them. And when the horses of the Saracens and Bedouins started at tree or bush, their master said to the horses, ' Do you think that is King Richard ? ' " Yet terrible though his memory might have become, he had failed in the great adventure.

He had failed simply because he lacked that one quality of leadership, and the tragedy is that he realised the truth.

ON September 29, 1192, the Queens Joan and Berengaria with the Cypriot princess sailed from Acre and eventually arrived in Poitou ; Richard followed on October 9 and was shipwrecked near Aquileia in the Adriatic. Disguised, he tried to steal through the country, for he had enemies on every hand : the Emperor Henry VI hated him because he had taken the side of Tancred in the dispute about the succession to the Sicilian throne ; Leopold of Austria hated him because he had torn down his banner from the walls of Acre. Exhausted by hunger and exposure, Richard was found by the men of Leopold in a cottage in the suburbs of Vienna. His servant had unwittingly betrayed him when buying provisions by offering gold besants in payment.

RICHARD was needed in England. While he had been fighting in the Holy Land, his chancellor William of Longchamp had driven the country to rebellion. He was an upstart who could not resist showing the power he had attained by patience and cunning. At first he had been friends with John and had absolved him from his oath to Richard not to return to England for three years, but when it was discovered that Richard declared that Arthur of Brittany—son of the scoundrelly Geoffrey, Henry II's fourth son—was to be his heir, John naturally decided to do whatever he could to steal the throne for himself. Those who hated Longchamp turned to John, and civil war broke out again in England, the King's brother fighting the King's chancellor. Longchamp won, he forced John to submit, and in his mood of triumph did an exceptionally stupid thing which made even those who had remained loyal to Richard turn against the chancellor. Henry II's loyal bastard, Geoffrey, had been consecrated Archbishop of York and now apparently felt that the Pope's pall—issued with Richard's approval—absolved him from his promise not to return to England. Longchamp tried to arrest him when he landed and then dragged him out of the sanctuary of St. Martin's priory, after besieging him there for days. This was an act of incredible recklessness, for the violation of a church gave his enemies a strong weapon, but Longchamp must have been almost insane with his own extraordinary power. He was deposed from the chancellorship by a grand council, and John was declared to be Richard's successor, failing issue from Richard.

Then Philip came back to France and turned greedily towards the realm of the absent King of England. He offered the unfortunate Alais to John with all Richard's continental fiefs. Queen Eleanor put a stop to these intrigues. Whatever had been her behaviour towards her two husbands, Louis VII and Henry II, she proved herself a sensible and loving mother. Her sons she had spurred against their father, she had urged them to revolt, but now that Henry was dead, all her efforts were to hold the realm together, to keep it secure for Richard. John was restrained from leaving England ; Eleanor forbade him to go.

Then came the news of Richard's imprisonment. The charming story of the troubadour Blondin recognising the King's voice as he sang a *chanson* is a tradition which is more than likely entirely baseless. All we know is that the news was sent to France by the Emperor Henry, who, as suzerain, not only demanded half-share in Leopold's prisoner, but also the possession of Richard himself ; he wrote merrily to Philip by a messenger " welcome above gold and topaze," that their common enemy was netted and safe at last ; Philip told John who instantly rushed to Normandy and did homage to the King of France, promising to marry Alais and to surrender the Vexin ; he then darted back to England to raise the standard of revolt, declaring that Richard was dead. He was surprised when very few believed him and he was made to truckle down and declare a truce after the French fleet had failed to land. While John was futilely invading England, Philip—who had vainly attempted to get the Pope to absolve him from his vow to Richard to keep the peace—was sweeping into Normandy. The Earl of Leicester, home from the crusades, held him off and at last pushed him back into France.

Meanwhile the Emperor was negotiating with Richard about the ransom-money, and it was settled at 100,000 marks, payable half by Michaelmas 1193 and half by mid-Lent 1194, to be shared with Duke Leopold ; and it was agreed that Richard's niece, Geoffrey's daughter, Eleanor of Brittany, was to marry one of Leopold's sons, while Isaac of Cyprus and his daughter were to be freed without ransom. To make the exchange of prisoner and money appear more or less legal, Henry arraigned Richard for supporting Tancred in his usurpation of Sicily, for

having stolen Cyprus, for having helped to murder Conrad, and
for having insulted the flag of Austria and ill-treated the German
crusaders. On and on dragged the negotiations, Henry arguing,
tumbling between offers from Philip and Richard, while envoys
came from England, and the country was drained of gold.
Longchamp was appointed to manage the ransom, but he was
still exiled from England and had great difficulty in wriggling
back, being first of all made to swear that he would attempt
nothing beyond the raising of money and choosing of hostages.
A tax of one quarter on all rents and movables was placed on
clergy and laity alike, nothing was excepted, not even church
furniture. When Longchamp came to England to gather the
money he merely infuriated everybody, no one would trust him
with his children to be sent as hostages to Germany, and Richard
was forced to recall him. The tax-collecting went on and on,
even without Longchamp : the first harvest was insufficient, and
a second and even a third had to be gathered. Then at last, on
Friday, February 4, 1193, after over a year's imprisonment,
Richard was released, but not until the German princes had
threatened to revolt against their overlord unless he gave way.
Henry had been receiving sums from Philip, and monthly payments of a thousand pounds were offered if he would only keep
Richard indefinitely behind bars. Henry would certainly have
agreed if his subjects had permitted him.

When Philip heard that Richard was to be free he sent that
famous message to John—" Beware, the devil is loose again ! "
John, in terror, hid at Philip's court, but Richard was not a man
to carry resentment ; besides, he was probably at the moment as
frightened of John and Philip as they were of him. He tried to
make peace with his brother, while John sent hurried messages
to his friends in England, bidding them keep his castles prepared
to fight the King. His messenger apparently got drunk : at
least, he talked so grandly during dinner with the Archbishop of
Canterbury that he was arrested and his letters were read before
the mayor and council of London. John was excommunicated
and his English fiefs were taken.

At this date, on March 12, 1194, Richard landed once again
in England.

Almost his first act was to demand more money, money for the
remainder of his ransom, money for war with France. He
confiscated offices and resold them, he demanded that a third of
the Englishmen capable of fighting were to enroll and the rest

were to pay a scutage—a bribe to escape military service—of £1 ; a danegeld of two shillings on the carucate—the name for the new land-tax—was levied, and the Cistercians were to surrender the whole of their year's wool-clip. England must have been practically penniless by this time.

PROBABLY to forget that Richard had done homage to the Emperor for the kingdom of Burgundy and to bridge the shame of his imprisonment, it was decided that Richard should be re-crowned. Once it had been the usual procedure for the King each year to wear his crown, but Henry II, despising the outward show of power, had formally sworn in 1158 never to wear his again in public, and the ceremony had not been renewed since. Richard, however, loved pomp—royal robes, the sceptre, the acclamation of the people, and the feasting. On the first Sunday after Easter, April 17, he wore his crown again at Winchester. Berengaria was not with him. He had apparently already tired of her, for he made no effort to seek her out.

Then, on May 12, two months after his landing, Richard again left England—this time, never to return.

PHILIP was driving his way into Normandy, striving to take the lands that John had promised him, but at the very mention of Richard's coming, he fled. John came forward, eager to win his brother's kiss of peace, and Richard met him a few miles from Barfleur. He forgave him at once, saying "Think no more of it, John! You were only a child left to wicked guardians. Their thoughts were evil to counsel you to evil. Rise, go and eat. John [*the host*], what can he have for dinner?" yet he did not trust John enough to grant him aught but dinner. He presented him with money but no lands, then he pushed on to the relief of Verneuil that was being besieged by the French. The enemy fled at his approach and he paused to repair the walls.

The fighting that continued was a feeble affair, of Philip slashing and running away, of Richard chasing him and once almost capturing him : Philip had left his men while he heard mass in a small church, and Richard rushed past, keeping to the road, never realising · that his enemy was so near and unprotected.

A year's truce was at last sealed, but it was a truce meant only for a breathing-space so that both combatants could fortify

15

their cities and gather money and troops. Richard now became reconciled to Berengaria, at least he took her back to his household, and he even reinvested John with many of his old honours. Philip was the first to break the peace, then a second treaty was agreed to, the lands being so famine-struck that neither King could fight, and according to this new arrangement Philip was ceded Gisor and the Vexin and the overlordship of Angoulême, while Richard got practically nothing apart from what he had already captured.

With the loss of the Vexin, Normandy became wide open to the French. The barrier was down and Philip whenever he wished could drive straight down the Seine to Rouen. To prevent this, Richard started building at a bend where the Seine was cut by a narrow stream, the Gambon ; the land he chose belonged to the Archbishop of Rouen who made a violent outcry at its loss and then fled to Rome to lay Normandy under an interdict. No interdict could stop Richard who was determined to hold that wasp of a Philip beyond his territory ; he built in stone his memory of the great walls in the Holy Land where the engineering skill of the Moslems far outpassed the Christians'. For over a year the work continued, and when finished it was the strongest castle in the west. Richard, proud of his masterpiece, called it his fair child, his Château-Gaillard or Saucy Castle.

While the castle was being built the war dragged on. Philip, considering Château-Gaillard a breach of the treaty, struck again and again into Richard's lands. There was trouble, too, about Richard's nephew, young Arthur, whom he had once thought to make his heir ; he wished to take the boy as a ward, but the Bretons gave him instead to Philip to look after. On and on went the struggle, Richard fighting the Bretons and trying to hold his enormous territories together against his treacherous overlord while calling endlessly for money until one is amazed to learn that England was capable of digging up another penny.

Richard turned to diplomacy, forming a coalition with the great men of the north against France. Philip, finding himself in a dangerous corner, suggested a conference with Richard, and the two Kings met on September 17, 1197. They agreed to another year's truce.

Pope Innocent III was determined to settle the question, seeking to lure the Kings into another crusade. He sent a cardinal to patch up the quarrel, and Richard and Philip again met just as the last truce was about to expire. Philip came on horseback, Richard travelled down the Seine by boat and stubbornly refused to land. He stayed in the river so that the two Kings had to shout at each other until they agreed—probably merely to get rid of the cardinal—to a five years' truce. This peace was broken almost immediately by Philip starting to build a castle on an island in the Seine, and when Richard furiously threatened revenge, Philip offered the most advantageous terms. But Richard was on his dignity and he would not listen. He adjourned the matter because he had had news of a miraculous find in the Limousin, at Châlus.

This was in the spring of 1199, and a peasant had accidentally discovered great treasure. His plough had ripped from the earth " an Emperor with his wife, sons, and daughters, all of pure gold, and seated round a golden table." That at least was the tale as it came to Richard, and it was more than likely a vast exaggeration. As this was treasure-trove it belonged to the overlord, and Richard was overlord of Adémar of Limousin, while Adémar in his turn was suzerain of the knight on whose land the gold was discovered. Richard therefore demanded the gold and Adémar sent him a share of whatever had been found, but that did not satisfy Richard. He wanted the lot, and he beseiged Châlus to get it by force.

In this petty quarrel, besieging an obscure small castle, bickering over the chance discovery of gold by a peasant, Richard received his death-wound. He settled about the castle with his army until Adémar became desperate, unable to hold out longer. Richard would grant his rebellious subject no terms whatever. When suggestions of surrender were made, Richard answered that he would hang the whole garrison, and Adémar with but six knights and nine servitors locked himself into the keep—the strongest part of a castle—and prepared to fight until death. He had few weapons with him and therefore had to pull the keep to shreds, hurling down stones and beams of wood while Richard's pioneers dug beneath the walls ; and on one occasion a rebel knight kept himself unhurt for hours against a shower of crossbow-bolts, using only a frying-pan for a shield.

At last, the pioneers were finished. The tower must fall. Richard came from his tent for the last assault and stood in the open without his steel shirt, wearing only an iron helmet for protection. A man in the keep saw that the King was open to a blow, and plucking a bolt out of the wall, slipped it into his crossbow and let fly. The King jeered as the man raised his bow, he shouted and laughed at him ; then the bolt hit Richard on the left shoulder, it struck downwards into his side. He did not seem to feel the pain, he merely told his troops to continue the assault and rode slowly back to his tent. Perhaps the surgeon was elsewhere, for in his impatience the King tried to draw out the bolt himself. The barbed head stuck fast and the shaft broke in his hand. Too late the surgeon was called and had to cut deep to take away the iron, for Richard was growing very fat. The wound became worse, gangrene set in, and Richard knew that he was doomed.

Until he knew the truth he had forbidden any one, save four barons, to enter his tent lest the men grow dispirited because of his wound. But when death was on him, impossible to avoid, he called to all his followers and instructed them in what they were to do. They must make John his successor, he said, and he forced them to swear fealty to John, and he bequeathed a fourth part of his goods to his servants and to the poor. Meanwhile the keep had been taken and all the survivors had been hanged save the man who had shot at Richard. They kept him for worse punishment and Richard commanded that he be brought to the royal tent. " What did I do to you," he asked, " that you should kill me ? " " You killed my father," said the man, " and two of my brothers with your own hand, and you would have killed me too if you could. Take what revenge on me you like, I will joyfully undergo the greatest tortures you can think of, for now I have seen you on your death-bed." Richard told the guard to free their prisoner and give him a hundred shillings, for " I forgive you," he said.

For eleven days he had lain in torment, the gangrene eating through his flesh, and now on April 6, 1199, he received the holy communion and asked that his corpse be embalmed and placed in penitence at the feet of his father at Fontévrault ; the heart, he asked to be sent to Rouen, and his brain, his blood and viscera he gave as a gift to the Poitevins.

" Shrouded among the shrouded women," Richard was laid at his father's feet at Fontévrault. His last wishes were fully carried out. He was buried in the robes he had worn at his second coronation, and with the crown on his head. And his heart, as he had requested, was placed in a thin silver box, covered with two leaden cases and taken to Rouen and there buried. Those who saw it spoke with awe of its greatness. for it was larger than most men's hearts.

In 1838, a French antiquary disinterred it and discovered that the great lion-heart had " withered to the semblance of a faded leaf."

VII

KING JOHN

1199–1216

FEW ENGLISH KINGS, save Richard III, have been damned so brutally by history as King John. It is true that he was extortionate and vindictive, licentious and cruel ; it is true that he was foolish and often lazy. But these are only the effects of character, and to understand John one must seek the cause for such effects, then having found them, sympathise with a man driven to extremes by a devil planted in him. It is simple enough to shrug John out of history, to dismiss him with a contemptuous epithet, or to stamp him as a blot upon the pages of a book. But that is not fair. No man is wholly evil or wholly good, no man can justly be charged with actions to the performing of which he was often driven by the heritage his fathers gave him. They were passionate men, these Angevins, they boasted of the demon who had bred them, who had flown out of the church when her husband had striven to hold her.

To find the key to John's character one must examine his childhood. From birth, he was regarded with pity, even by his father who nicknamed him Lackland because already he had sons enough to control his territories. To this, his fifth son, eighth and last child, born at Oxford on Christmas Eve day, 1167, Henry could give nothing, and for that reason perhaps he loved John best, as love is often given in greatest measure to a crippled boy or girl. John was politically a cripple, unneeded in the schemes of Henry.

This childhood must not be forgotten, the childhood of a boy who saw the gigantic power of his father and who knew that it was not for him. Deeply he must have resented the accident that placed him last of the brothers ; ambition demanded that he use the strength of his character and the violence of his mind in subtle ways, to become a traitor to gain what he could never get by open methods.

The statement cannot be too often repeated that most of our judgments of medieval men are inaccurate because they are based upon the morals of to-day. It is absurd to demand that a twelfth or thirteenth-century knight should behave in the decorous manner of a twentieth-century gentleman. The problems that faced a King like John are almost incredible to us, and our conceptions of loyalty are not always the medieval conceptions. Men who then seemed utterly noble shock us occasionally by their acts, for the character of a medieval knight was entirely different from a modern man's, he lived on the topmost peak of ecstasy, swinging from violence to violence, from tears to murder. King Richard in his excitement kissed the defenders of Verneuil, and William Marshal wept on provocations that seem to us ridiculous.

That John was a traitor cannot be denied, but his brothers also were traitors. Power was the ambition of a medieval man, there were so few other outlets for his energy. If he were a layman, he demanded power of territory ; if a priest, power for the Church and for his own aggrandisement. There can be no judgment made on John because he was ambitious and capable of treachery ; why he is judged and condemned is because of his methods in seeking power, his occasional stupidity, his arrogance, and his spite. He had these qualities, but they were inevitable in a lad brought up in such an environment as his, brought up as Lackland.

Between John and the throne stood Henry, Richard and Geoffrey, and even before he was born his father had divided the kingdom between the three, leaving nothing for him. Young Henry was crowned King of England, he did homage to Louis as Duke of Normandy, and Anjou would naturally become his property ; he was his father's shadow to turn substantial only on that father's death. Richard was given his mother's duchy of Aquitaine, and Geoffrey was betrothed to Constance, heiress of Brittany. All had been carefully parcelled out by Henry II lest he die ; he had no intention while he lived of making these grants separate from his own power ; they were merely a precaution against sudden death. Then John was born, and for John there was nothing. "Johans Sans Terre," King Henry sadly called him, "John Lackland," and the title was to stick through life, to be accepted almost as an ordinary surname. All that Henry could rake up out of his dominions for the baby was the county of Mortain, an unimportant and not very wealthy fief.

If he could not give John lands, Henry hoped to buy them for him by marriage, but his schemes were defeated by his eldest son who refused to surrender certain Angevin castles with which the King wanted to purchase a bride. This quarrel was one of the reasons for the young King's rebellion ; and Henry was able only to endower John with English revenues and castles and with splashes of lands in Normandy. Then he arranged another marriage, betrothing John to Isabel of Gloucester.

The young King died and it seemed that now was the opportunity for Henry to give his darling something of genuine value. He suggested that Richard as his heir take the place of the shadow-King while John should take Richard's place as Duke of Aquitaine. This would seem just enough, but Richard quite naturally objected. He knew that it was unlikely that his father after his recent experiences would crown another son as King while himself lived, and he had no intention of surrendering the solid power of Aquitaine for a flimsy honour. Besides, he had been for eight years struggling bravely to keep down his rebellious knights, and at last had quietened the duchy ; after those years of fighting and scheming he was not prepared to give his creation into the hands of his brother. As young Henry had declared war against his father when requests were made for John, now Richard declared war for the same reason.

Henry was still determined that his favourite would be given something. He decided that Ireland might satisfy John. The only thing that John strongly desired Henry refused. When the question of the kingship of Jerusalem was raised, as King Baldwin was dying of leprosy, the crown was offered to the King of England, and when he refused it, to any of his sons, even to John. Henry would not consider the question, his love for his youngest boy was selfish in its strength, and he could not bear to part with him, although John threw himself at his feet and implored consent. Instead, Henry sent him to Ireland, to a land that was half-savage, ruled by adventurous English lords only in small sections towards the east. John must have been furious. The crown of Jerusalem was denied him, and now he was given Ireland in its place ; angrily, he scoffed at the outlandish dress of the chieftains who came to offer homage, he pulled their long beards, and they left raging and determined to rebel. John did not want Ireland, he spent the money intended for his troops, he enjoyed himself with his friends, disdaining even to fight, and within five months he was back in England.

At every point John had been frustrated, had been made to feel his dependent position as Lackland. Even his full title as Lord of Ireland was withheld. The Pope, who claimed owner-ship of all Christian islands, sent legates with a crown of peacock feathers set in gold, but the legates infuriated the Archbishop of Canterbury by daring to don their mitres and to have their crosses carried before them in his own church ; to quieten the outraged archbishop, Henry had to send the legates away before the coronation could take place. At every point, it seemed that John was defeated, that fate was deliberately holding him in a condition of powerlessness.

It was inevitable that such continual disappointments must turn an ambitious youth into a scheming, arrogant man. John had only his own cunning with which he could hope to capture any prize, and he must have felt that all the world was his enemy, this world that seemed built only to frustrate him, to drag him back. His two brothers had refused to give him anything, his father had offered him only the worthless kingdom of Ireland, depriving him of the glory he desired as King of Jerusalem. The resentment aroused by such unceasing depressions must have made John loathe the world, must have made him turn even against his father. From birth he had been despised, pushed aside, pityingly offered gifts only to have them torn away as he was ready to grasp them.

The act of terrible treachery occurred when he deserted his father to stand beside Richard. It was this that gave the dying King his death-blow, and it is this—more than any other act—that has caused historians to detest him for centuries. Yet John had learned the painful lesson that he could trust to nothing save his own wits ; he had remained loyal to his father, but now that father was dying—and Richard would be King. He turned to Richard. It was treachery, an act which, according to modern standards, cannot be forgiven, yet even if we cannot forgive, surely we can feel pity for the youth who had seen the great power of his father given into the selfish grip of elder brothers and himself left utterly empty-handed ?

RICHARD, when King, rewarded his brother's treachery. John was " granted all the lands his father had given him, to wit, four thousand pounds' worth of lands in England and the county of Mortain with its appurtenances." He was then married to his betrothed, the wealthy Isabel of Gloucester, although the

Archbishop of Canterbury strove to forbid the wedding, John and Isabel being third cousins. Their lands were placed under an interdict which John managed to get the Pope to raise.

John was now an extremely powerful lord, far more powerful than ever he had been in his father's lifetime. Young Henry and Geoffrey were both dead, and although Geoffrey had left a son, Arthur, himself would undoubtedly succeed Richard ; and Richard showered his brother with lands, giving him vast tracts which, with his wife's dowry, made John master of Nottinghamshire, Derbyshire, Dorset, Somerset, Devon and Cornwall. He ruled like a petty King with no interference whatever from the crown. This taste of power only whetted his hunger for more. He waited eagerly while Richard prepared for the crusade.

The moment Richard's back was turned, John began to plot. Yet it is more than probable that he would have stayed content, hoping that his brother might never return, had not Richard decided for some peculiar reason to make Arthur his successor. We have already spoken of John's rising against Longchamp, of his lies about Richard's death, and of Richard's forgiveness on his return from captivity.

John, who for years had been the pathetic landless one, had tasted power, he saw that the throne was near and had tried most stupidly to seize it. Then suddenly, by the accident of a crossbow-quarrel, it fell into his hands, and John discovered that he, the despised, the landless one, was actually King of England, of the great empire his father had built.

ACCORDING to the modern rule of succession, Arthur should have followed Richard to the throne, but such ideas were only at this time struggling vaguely into form. Arthur, Duke of Brittany, was but twelve years of age while John was over thirty ; disloyal knights might wish for a minority during which they could do as they please, but true men like William Marshal dreaded a child upon the throne. We have the contemporary attitude summed up in the discussion between William and the Archbishop of Rouen. This conversation is recorded by William's squire and is therefore authentic. " My lord," began William who had arrived with the news of Richard's death, " we must hurry to decide whom to make King." " I think and believe," said the archbishop, " that according to right, we should make Arthur King." " To my thinking," replied

William, " that would be bad. Arthur is counselled by traitors, he is haughty and proud, and if we set him over us he will seek to do evil against us, for he does not love the people of this country [*Normandy*]. He shall not come here by my advice. Look rather at Count John, my conscience and knowledge both point him out to me as the rightful heir to the land of his father and brother." " Marshal," said the archbishop, " is that truly what you want ? " " Yea, my lord, for it is reason. Without doubt a son has a nearer claim to his father's land than a grandson. It is right he should have it." " So be it then," said the archbishop, " but mark my words, Marshal, never have you done anything that you will repent as you will repent what you are going to do." " I thank you," answered William ; " all the same, I believe that this is what should be."

When a man of the loyalty and uprightness of William Marshal declared for John, none could doubt that he was the true King. Besides, Richard on his death-bed had declared him his successor, and his mother Eleanor was ready to bring Aquitaine in defence of his rights.

John was with Arthur in Brittany when he heard of Richard's death, and he rushed straight to Chinon to seize his brother's treasure. For years he had waited, scarcely daring to believe that he would ever attain such power, and now that it was given him he acted in a manner that horrified his contemporaries. The crown, the glorious crown, was his, and he treated it with contempt, he jeered even at his own supporters, refusing to take the matter seriously. At first he pretended to be reformed, to have changed his habits of not communicating since childhood and of scoffing at noble things ; when the good Hugh of Lincoln showed him a sculpture of the Last Judgment as a warning, pointing ominously towards the damned, John dragged him to the other side and remarked, " Rather show me these whose good example I intend to follow." He behaved in so ridiculously pious a fashion that Hugh began strongly to suspect that it was all pretence, and he soon found his suspicions right. John refused to communicate, but nevertheless on Easter Day he attended high mass and stood idly gazing at some coins in his hand. " Why do you stand staring like that ? " demanded Hugh. " I am staring at these gold pieces," answered John, " and I am thinking that if I had had them a few years ago I should never have put them into your hands but into my own purse. However, take them now." Furiously, Hugh turned aside and would not accept the gift, telling John to throw the money into the bason and leave him.   So outraged was he by the insult that he preached a sermon on the difference between a good and a bad prince. Probably John did not object to the subject to the sermon, but Hugh kept on and on until John told him to stop because he wanted his dinner.   Grimly, Hugh continued, and John's dinner must have grown very cold that day.

Meanwhile, Arthur's friends were gathering : he had Brittany, Anjou and Maine behind him, and Philip was fighting his way as far as Le Mans.   Before defending himself, however, John must be recognised in his new power, and on Sunday, April 25, 1199, he was formally proclaimed Duke of the Normans at Rouen.   The ducal cap was placed upon his head, the sword was strapped to his girdle, but when the archbishop gave him the lance from which drooped the banner of Normandy, John turned to speak jestingly with his friends and the lance slipped from his fingers to clatter to the floor.   That was no good omen of the future—neither the scoffing at the ceremony nor the dropping of the lance ; John, however, seemed to take nothing seriously. The power was his, and now that he had it, he despised it.

England had yet to accept him.   He had sent William Marshal and Hubert, Archbishop of Canterbury, over the Channel to keep the peace and they had stilled the inevitable crime-wave that succeeded the death of any King.   On May 26, John entered London, and on the following day he was hallowed at Westminster.   We have no details of the coronation ceremony, only two points are noted by contemporaries—first, a protest from a bishop because they should have waited for the Archbishop of York, and secondly, the fact that John did not communicate afterwards as was the custom.

LIKE his father and his brother Geoffrey, John was a smallish, plump man, yet strongly built.   He resembled Geoffrey in other ways than physical, for both were cunning and reckless.   Apparently he was good-looking enough, with thick curly hair, although in later years he grew bald and fat.   His height, according to his skeleton, which was measured in 1797, was five feet six inches.

Cunning and cautious John might often be, but he was also foolhardy and brave, and he had that Angevin demon locked in his heart.   When he quarrelled with Longchamp on one occasion we are told that " he was more than furious, his whole body became so contorted with rage that it was scarcely recognisable, an angry scowl twisted his brow, his eyes flashed fire, his colour changed to a livid white, and I know what would have happened to the chancellor if he had come within reach of John's hands in that hour of tempest." He lacked the directed energy of his father and brother, he was usually slothful, although when occasion needed speed he could move as quickly as any man. There was nevertheless that core of weakness in John's character that crippled him, that turned a splendid soldier into a petty forager, into one who preferred lounging in bed all day to clapping his horse between his legs and his helmet on his head. He was a glutton and a lover of expensive wines, a dandy, a lecher, and seemingly most fond of music. He was also a traitor —he had destroyed his father by that ultimate treachery, he had schemed against his brother. Now that he was crowned he possessed all that any King could hope to possess, and he discovered that ambition was worthless, that power after all was a thing of little value compared to body's ease and body's satisfaction. If his childhood had not been so tragic, John might have become a great King, he was undoubtedly intelligent and a clever and brave soldier, but the years of striving had forced him to despise, not his own actions, but the goal itself. Through treachery he had conquered, and the conquest, he discovered, was ashes.

Crowned King of England and Duke of Normandy, with rebellion in his continental fiefs, with Philip ravaging his country, he yet did little to stem the decay of the empire. Richard, with his gigantic taxation, had started that decay, but if John had been stronger, less contemptuous of his power, he might have recovered all that Richard had lost. Instead, in his hands, the Angevin world of Henry II was to go for ever and England was to surrender itself to Rome.

Now was the moment to crush Philip, here was an opportunity such as Henry II had never known. Philip was declared the enemy of the Pope, and at a church council at Dijon, December 6, 1199, his lands were placed under an interdict to be proclaimed on the very day when his last truce with John would expire. Philip, usually so far-sighted, had let his desires master his intellect : he had already been twice married, his first wife had died in 1190, and his second, Ingeborg of Denmark, had been rejected by him the very day after the marriage on August 14, 1193 ; the unfortunate Queen then spent a miserable existence of being pushed into one convent after another; for Philip apparently abominated her for some reason, and her brother, Cnut VI, would not have her home in Denmark. The Pope tried to make Philip obey his vows, but poor Ingeborg must have been incredibly ugly, for Philip divorced her on the usual grounds of consanguinity. He extracted this divorce from the French clergy, but Rome did not consider it legal, and when in June 1196 he married Agnes of Meran, the act was taken as incestuous and after vain efforts to have it dissolved, the Dijon council declared Philip excommunicate and laid his domain under interdict.

Here was an opportunity for John, for Philip lay at his mercy, yet he made no attempt to take the least advantage of it. He carried on the old spasmodic border warfare, never trying to build strong alliances, or with a great offensive crush Philip for ever. Then Philip did another stupid thing, he seized and dismantled some Breton castles, the property of Arthur, for whom he was ostensibly fighting. Thus a second opportunity came to John and again he let it slip through his fingers. William des Roches, Arthur's seneschal for Anjou, in rage against Philip, declared for John, surrendered the city of Le Mans and actually placed his young duke in John's power. John evidently made some tactless remark, for the very night after he received his nephew and rival, the boy's mother and friends grew suddenly terrified and carried him off again.

These magnificent cards had been given to John and he calmly threw them aside, preferring to make an unnecessary treaty with Philip. By this treaty he arranged for his niece Blanche of Castille to marry Philip's son Louis, and for dowry he agreed to surrender large Norman territories and to pay 20,000 marks ; in return, Philip admitted him as heir to Richard's continental possessions, including the Norman Vexin, and relinquished the claims of Arthur. It seems a feeble act of John's when Philip was more or less in his power, but we cannot doubt that John's childhood had taught him to despise his father's greediness and lust for territory—the mainspring of great Kings. All that John wanted was to enjoy the sensual fruits of power, not to exhaust himself by reaching out in mightier ambitions. The cause of Arthur no longer existed when Philip withdrew. Therefore John had no rivals to combat, he could loll and wench at his ease, which presumably was all he desired —freedom to glut himself with the good things of which he had always dreamed, which had been so long and tantalisingly withheld. And he began to look wearily upon the woman he had married. Isabel of Gloucester had been a rich prize for the Count of Mortain, but to the King of England she was of little worth. Philip had rid himself of Ingeborg, and now John decided to do the same with Isabel. He was as yet childless although he had been married in 1189, ten years ago ; therefore it seemed likely that Isabel would never conceive— John was certainly not to blame, he had bastards enough—and a King, if he would keep peace in his dominions, must have a legitimate son to follow him. Either late in 1199 or early in 1200, he divorced Isabel on the grounds of consanguinity, appealing to the Norman or Aquitainian clergy for a dissolution of the marriage. The Pope's decision was not asked, and as Isabel did not appeal to Rome, he could not interfere. Isabel's silence rather makes one believe that the divorce was with her consent, that both were probably eager to be rid of each other.

As Isabel's successor, John decided to take the sister of the King of Portugal, and dispatched an embassy to ask her hand. Then suddenly he fell in love. It has been suggested that this abrupt change of plan was a matter of policy, and that Philip prompted it, yet the policy cannot be explained, it brought only harm to John. Besides, the fact that envoys were already in Portugal proves that this marriage could not have been premeditated. It was while John was on a triumphant progress through his lands, passing through Aquitaine, that he saw another Isabel and loved her. She was only about twelve years of age—just young enough for bedding according to medieval notions—and was the daughter of Ademar, Count of Angoulême. As was customary, she was being reared in the home of her betrothed, Hugh the Brown, son of the Count of La Marche of Lusignan. John with her father's help secretly stole her and married her at Angoulême.

It is difficult to believe that this marriage was a political one, although Miss Norgate [1] insists that the Portugal overtures were a blind to deceive the Lusignans and to put them off their guard. Surely there could be no necessity for this ? why should they suspect their overlord and Isabel's father of plotting to steal the girl ? and why should John go to such a dangerous extent as to infuriate the Portuguese ? It is true that the Lusignans were powerful enough to be almost a menace, yet John now deliberately stung that menace into action. The

[1] *John Lackland*, by Kate Norgate (Macmillan), 1902.

Lusignans naturally had to retort, but John hit at them first, hoping to catch them unprepared. He captured some of their Poitevin castles and drove his troops into their lands, meanwhile calling for men from England. But the barons had no interest in the quarrel, they refused to follow " unless he gave them back their rights," for John apparently had been pulling down their castles. He now threatened to pull down all their castles if they did not come, and having no leader to bind them to an army, they reluctantly gathered at Portsmouth for service over-sea. John thereupon sent them away again, demanding—in Richard's manner—an enormous scutage to pay for mercenaries. The barons gave the scutage, that bribe to escape service, and John left England, his Queen being sent ahead a few days before him.

PHILIP acted the peacemaker, and he and John met again and again to discuss the position, John at one time being lodged in the royal residence at Paris. He promised Philip that in his court as Duke of Aquitaine the quarrel between him and the Lusignans would be tried with justice ; but the Lusignans dis-covered that John's idea of a trial was ordeal by battle, a hand-to-hand fight which was already beginning to fall out of favour, and as John had bought every available champion they had little hope of making God prove that their cause was just. They refused to appear. Philip strove to bring John to reason, and John consented again to a legal trial, only this time he refused the Lusignans safe-conducts to the place of meeting ; once more Philip tried to make peace, demanding security for John's word. As the security was preposterously high, arguments continued until the two Kings agreed to meet ; they met, and nothing was decided. John was then cited to appear for his trial in Paris. He did not turn up, and at last Philip lost his temper. He unfurled his banner and set out to bring this contumacious vassal to submission ; and now he was no longer an outcast, Rome had forgiven him, for Agnes was dead and he had taken back Ingeborg as Queen.

The war was a feeble affair, neither army met, they contented themselves with captured small castles and towns. Philip knighted Arthur, betrothed him to his daughter Jeanne and invested him with Brittany, Anjou, Maine, Touraine and Poitou : Normandy he kept for himself, and Arthur was already Duke of Brittany in his mother's right. While Philip besieged

Arques, the young duke led his troops against Queen Eleanor and trapped her with a small garrison at Mirabeau. Eleanor had just time to send an appeal to her son before the enemy arrived and began battering on the walls.

John's dilatory tactics had earned him the nickname of Softsword, but he was now to prove, as he was to prove often later, that when needed he could be as swift and as cunning as ever his father had been. He was marching towards Poitou when his mother's message arrived, and instantly he charged to her rescue. It was beyond a hundred miles to Mirebeau, yet he sped over the distance within forty-eight hours. Arthur saw him coming and, contemptuous of John Softsword, galloped out to battle. It was no battle, it was a rout. All Arthur's men were either killed or captured, and himself with three Lusignans, including Isabel's betrothed, became John's prisoners. It was a lucky victory, for it placed in John's power not only his rival to the crown but his rival in love. He bound his prisoners in chains and put them into carts, then triumphantly he brought them to Falaise where Arthur was locked away under the care of Hubert de Burgh.

WE cannot be certain of Arthur's fate, he merely disappeared out of history, yet the conclusion is inevitable that John murdered him either with his own hands or by the hands of others. It was—in Fouché's reprimand to Napoleon—worse than a crime, it was a blunder, a blunder that lost John his most powerful allies and thereby the whole of Normandy. Yet we cannot be definite, we cannot point-blank accuse him of the deed. Men who knew the truth were naturally cautious, they dared not be explicit and wrote most vaguely, but John himself never asserted his innocence even when directly accused of the slaying.

We learn from one English chronicler that John's friends continually advised the killing or at least the maiming of Arthur, and that John resisted the temptation until Breton victories infuriated him into consenting. William des Roches, Arthur's seneschal, had thrown aside his allegiance to John when he could not make him free his master ; he was now leading the Bretons, forming them into strong armies, and this defiance awoke the old demon of the Angevins. It is difficult to believe that John could have been foolish enough to think that the maiming of Arthur would stop the Bretons, it would naturally only make their fury greater ; nevertheless he sent three men to Falaise with orders to blind the boy. Two of the men refused, but the third attempted to carry out his orders. Arthur's struggles, however, were so desperate that the garrison threatened to revolt if he was harmed, and the commander, Hubert de Burgh, was forced to save his prisoner's life. He lied to John, saying that his order had been carried out ; instantly the Bretons under des Roches went almost insane with rage ; to quieten them, de Burgh confessed that Arthur lived. This lesson, it might seem, would have taught John to let Arthur remain unharmed, and he was frightened enough to have the lad brought before him and to promise great honours if he would forsake Philip, an offer which Arthur rejected in a most insulting manner and was then imprisoned, not at Falaise, but at Rouen.

From this moment he disappears from history. We are forced to believe that John killed him, and one chronicler—writing about twenty years after this date—declares that John in a burst of Angevin fury, when drunk after dinner, murdered Arthur with his own hands, tied a stone about his neck and threw the body into the Seine where a fisherman netted it, recognised it, and had it buried secretly. A Breton poet in a panegyric on Philip, written *circa* 1216, gives more or less the same tale in a highly coloured and detailed romance, telling us how John rowed his nephew on the Seine one night, stabbed him with his sword, and threw the body into the river. Neither of these writers can be trusted, they do not attempt to give any authority for their stories, they merely relate them without substantiation. The truth seems to be that nobody really knew what had happened to Arthur : the first chronicler quoted above says that the murder took place on Maundy Thursday (April 3), 1203, yet we find Philip as late as October of the same year confessing his ignorance of the boy's fate. Other stories were circulated, and presumably rumour at the time vacillated between three theories —that John murdered Arthur, that Arthur was drowned by accident while trying to escape, and that he died of grief.

If John murdered Arthur—and I am afraid we cannot escape from the conclusion that he did—it must have been in a moment of temporary insanity. That Angevin demon was no myth : she had driven Henry II into speaking the rash words that doomed Thomas Becket, and it is likely that now she made John murder his defenceless prisoner.

The act brought John's enemies into the open, it leagued them against him. The Bretons demanded their duke's release, offering hostages in his place, and Philip summoned John to appear before his court. As John did not obey, the fighting continued although Philip as yet dared not accuse him of the murder. The Norman lords fell from John, many of them fought on the side of Philip, and gradually the empire of Henry II began to crumble, to disintegrate under the march of French troops. Desperately his followers pleaded with John to stir himself to action as news came day after day of Philip's ravages : " The King of France is in your land, an enemy, he is capturing your castles, he is roping your seneschals to the tails of their horses and dragging them shamefully to prison, he is taking your goods at his pleasure." But contemptuously John always answered, " Let him alone. Some day I shall take back all he is taking from me now." And while he idled, Philip pressed forward into Normandy until he crouched before the impregnable Château-Gaillard, that saucy castle built by Richard, the most powerful fortress in the west. High above the Seine it rose, sheer from unscalable cliffs, and it was commanded by Roger de Lacy, an Englishman with no bonds in France, a brave and loyal man whom John could trust completely. Philip pressed close to the walls, he smashed down the stockade that barred ships from coming up the Seine, and was therefore able to construct a bridge of pontoons. In the river was an island-garrison, and Philip could now concentrate on taking it before besieging the castle itself.

Again, when spurred to sudden action, John revealed how great a soldier he could be. The Château-Gaillard, that bulwark for Rouen, was threatened, and if it fell, all Normandy would lie open to the French. John plotted shrewdly, and his plan could not possibly be bettered, it failed by lack of knowledge on one point, by the most unfortunate miscalculation. Three hundred knights, three thousand mounted men-at-arms, and four thousand foot, under the command of William Marshal, with a troop of mercenaries, were to steal from Rouen along the left bank of the Seine and attack the French camp ; at the same time, boats laden with provisions and troops were to be rowed up the river, were to smash through the pontoons, co-operate with the land forces, and throw provisions into the beleaguered island-fort.

The scheme was superb and it would have succeeded easily if John had not been mistaken about the exact hour when the Seine would be navigable up-stream that night. Secretly, without the French one moment suspecting what was happening,

William Marshal led his men along the river-bank and just before dawn—after the cock had crowed three times—fell upon the enemy. Taken by surprise, the panic-stricken French rushed for the pontoons that collapsed beneath their numbers ; over two hundred were slaughtered before they were properly awake. Torches and fires were lit and showed the steel-shirts of the English and their banners in the glare ; then the French rallied, the bridge was mended, and a counter-attacked prepared. The darkness that had served William so well, now served for his own defeat. He in his turn was taken by surprise and driven from the camp. Then, too late to be of use, with the land-forces in retreat, the boats came rocking up the Seine to crash against the pontoons. The French were ready, they loosed their arrows and hurled stones and boiling oil and pitch, and threw great chunks of iron as the ships came steadily forward ; the first ship crunched her nose on the pontoons and the crew leaped down with sword and axe to cut her way through. The French held them off, and the Seine turned red in the dawnlight, it rippled about the corpses as they fell and about the desperate wounded trying to swim. A gigantic beam toppled down, it crashed on to the two front ships, broke and sunk them. At this disaster, the rest of the fleet tried to escape, struggling at their oars, knocking against each other. The French followed in boats, and two of the ships were captured.

John's great plan had miscarried simply because he had not known the exact hour when the Seine would be navigable. And he could not try a second time. The disappearance of Arthur had lost him many of his followers, he had neither money nor troops with which to attack Philip, who soon captured the Saucy Castle. In December 1203, John left Normandy and returned to England, furious at his defeat, blaming the men who had turned traitors or who had not followed him ; he taxed the country, including the Church, as it had rarely been taxed before.

WITH the fall of Château-Gaillard, Normandy was lost to England. Soon Philip had taken Rouen and the great Norman lords swore homage to him, throwing aside their allegiance to John. Maine, Anjou and Touraine were already Philip's ; then after Normandy, Poitiers became his. And now John lost his greatest ally, his mother. Eleanor, who had always kept Aquitaine strongly on his side, ended her life of eighty-two violent and courageous years at Poitiers on April 1, 1204. The hands of restraint were lifting from John; that great man Archbishop Walter died on July 13, 1205; he had been a loyal servant, a genuine patriot, yet when told of his death—according to a later chronicler—John merely shrugged and remarked, " Now for the first time am I truly King of England." Eleanor and Hubert gone, only William Marshal lived of those whom John could rely on utterly.

One cannot help considering the loss of Normandy with a sense of shame. England's possessions, within two years, had become French, and one's natural patriotism turns one to look with contempt and anger upon King John. Yet the loss was inevitable. Nations were growing towards modernity, nationalism was becoming more conscious. Normandy only hampered England, it made the King a foreigner who regarded his island as a sort of milch-cow from which to drain sustenance to keep the continental body living. And England itself, hammered into shape by the laws of the two Henries, would not have rested content under the rule of Kings more Norman than English. The loss of Normandy was a gain to both countries, both to France and England.

John must not be blamed too harshly. The difficulties with which he had to contend were greater than any that his predecessors had known. The English lords were no longer Normans with roots in the Continent, they had gradually become absorbed by their adopted country and could have felt little interest in the lands of their fathers. They were becoming united, self-conscious; Normandy gone, England began to grow, to unite ready to crush the unfortunate King who by his very dilatoriness had helped to build a nation.

THE next important issue in John's reign was his conflict with the papacy, and we find that while he was attempting nothing more than any of his predecessors had attempted, he was defeated by circumstances greater than they had faced. The trouble began, as usual, over the vacant archbishopric of Canterbury. The monks wished to elect Hubert's successor. John merely did what previous rulers had done, he wanted them to accept his choice. Other Kings had squabbled over the same question but now the monks were determined to prove their power; at a secret conclave they decided to agree on their own election, taking three names from which to choose their primate. The bishops of the province when they heard of this, protested vehemently, insisting that they, too, had a right in the election ; they appealed to Rome, the monks counter-appealed and then quietly elected their sub-prior Reginald, sending him secretly to Rome for confirmation. Reginald, however, was so excited that when he had reached the Continent he was unable to resist boasting that he was the elect of Canterbury, which so terrified the monks that they decided to have nothing further to do with him. They held a second election and John suggested Gray, bishop of Norwich ; the monks agreed and wrote to the Pope for confirmation.

The Pope was no weakling, he was one of the greatest ever to sit upon the papal throne, Innocent III. And he was eager to seize this opportunity of discord to press the claims of Rome upon the Church of England. He refused to ratify Gray's election because it had been made after the appeal of Reginald and he demanded that the monks, the bishops and the King all send representatives to Rome for a legal canonical election. The representatives were dispatched with bags of gold for bribery, and John told his envoys that they must consent to none but Gray. When the council met at Rome, Innocent stated that the monks alone had the choice of election and said that they had decided on a friend of his, an Englishman and a scholar, Stephen of Langton. Naturally John's representatives, having instructions to accept no one but Gray, refused to agree, and Innocent wrote to John asking his assent, at the same time pointing out that he asked only from politeness and whether John agreed did not really matter in the least. John, of course, refused, and Innocent after threatening him vaguely with damnation, consecrated Langton on June 17, 1207. John's Angevin-demon sprang to life and he raged against the monks, he seized their property and forbade appeals to Rome, and the terrified monks fled the country, running to hide in St. Bertin's Monastery at St. Omer. Now it was open war between John and Innocent. Like the Kings before him, John had attempted to maintain crown rights, but unlike those Kings he was faced by a truly great antagonist while his own country was in a state of prostration, taxed unbearably and broken in spirit by the loss of Normandy. During the squabble over the Canterbury election, John had made a feeble attempt to battle with Philip. Aquitaine was eager to join his standard and he fought his way to the Loire, Philip rushing back to France at his approach. Then when it seemed that a decisive battle would take place, when Philip had returned with a great army, John signed yet another treaty declaring peace for two years.

The quarrel with Rome and the discontented state of England were enough to absorb all John's energies. He had few men and little money, war was not easy under such disabilities, and he probably consoled himself as he had on a previous occasion by pushing the problem into the future. One day he would win back all he had lost ; until then it was necessary that he attend to other more pressing affairs. Half John's troubles were based in this amazing optimism ; he was a splendid soldier and a highly intelligent man, but his suppressed upbringing had forced on him the protection of arrogance. He knew his own abilities and he relied on them too thoroughly ; if only he were to expend all his strength, he realised that he could not fail. And being aware of this he sunk himself in present indolence, weakening his will, relying upon his own genius to rescue him from sloth at some undated hour—some time, any time that was not this moment.

INNOCENT threatened an interdict. It was the old threat and too often had it been abused, too often threatened and too rarely effective. Yet to the medieval man it was a terrible thing, for once a country was laid under interdict, the doors of all its churches would be locked and there would be no services, no preachings except in churchyards ; only baptism, marriages and ministrations to the dying would be allowed, while bodies would be pushed into unconsecrated ground, unsung, as if they were the remains of suicides, whores or malefactors. Faced with this calamity, John tried to quibble out of it, he strove to keep some of his rights, promising to obey the Pope " saving his prerogatives and those of his heirs," but Innocent would have all or nothing. He demanded from John complete obedience and John naturally refused ; he lost his temper, swearing by God's teeth that if the interdict were fulminated he would expel every ecclesiastic from the country and would tear the eyes out of any Italian who dared land.

On Passion Sunday, March 23, 1208, the interdict was fulminated. Its effect is rather surprising : instead of the country turning against a King who had deprived it of its spiritual rites, John's power became greater than ever. Church lands and property were seized by him at the moment when his exchequer must have been extremely low; nearly all the bishops left England and there was none to stand against him, for the barons, split by jealousies into isolated groups, could not unite, they had no leader. Now indeed was John King of England. " It was as if he alone were mighty upon earth," writes a chronicler, " and he neither feared God nor cared for man." The vastness of his power turned him almost lunatic, he taxed and passed strange laws, forbidding birds being killed, razing fences and filling ditches so that beasts fattened on crops, moving the exchequer from London to Northampton " out of hatred to the Londoners," mustering a fleet he did not use, then turning vengefully on the men of the Cinque Ports for no apparent reason, hanging, slaying and imprisoning them in chains. With the Church entirely at his mercy, its money flooding to his coffers, he made the free tenants of all classes above twelve years of age swear homage to him and his son : but this was obviously to make certain that they would not use the interdict as an excuse for revolt.

In the tales of John's tyranny, in the senseless acts recorded, there is probably much exaggeration. The stopping of the slaughter of birds might have been a humane law, and it is true that sadistic people often have a great fondness for animals and particularly for birds ; it is most likely, however, that John wished to conserve the birds for hawking purposes. The destroying of fences and filling of ditches cannot be taken seriously as it is obviously a malicious exaggeration : hedges were little used in medieval England, the serfs usually enclosed their meadowland—for hay—with wattle fences and their arable land with narrow lines of turf. That John should tear these down may seem tyrannical, but obviously he was only resuming royal forest lands illegally stolen for pasture, for very often forest lands enclosed numerous small holdings. His mustering of the fleet was for either an expedition or for defence, and we do not know what caused him to change his plans, nor do we know what the Cinque Ports had done to merit such punishment. For these acts we therefore cannot damn John out of hand, and he did try to lessen the pressure on his feudal tenants, for a few years remitting the detested scutage when he had church money with which to fill his treasury.

" All men bore witness," writes a contemporary, " that never since the time of Arthur was there a King who was so greatly feared in England, in Wales, in Scotland or in Ireland." Scotland he subdued, leading a great army that had no need to fight, a treaty being sealed almost at once ; Wales gave in without a blow being struck. John seemed secure with England at his mercy, but it was a false security, and his power was maintained by the mercenaries he kept at great expense. That he feared rebellion is shown by his demanding hostages from some of his greatest lords, even from William Marshal, who was then in Ireland. This unprecedented act of tyranny must have been forced on the King and it was a cunning move, although through it occurred one of the terrible episodes that have made John detested for centuries—the tale of the de Braoses. William de Braose was one of the wealthiest and most powerful men in England and at first a strong supporter of the King, then for some reason he quarrelled with John. In the statement given out by John himself we are told that de Braose failed to pay his yearly rent for some lands in Munster, and this is proved by the pipe roll. Nevertheless the quarrel must have been based on something deeper than a bad debt, and as de Braose had surrendered Arthur to John, it is safe for us to conclude that his conscience pricked him and he may have shown to John that he blamed him for the lad's death. This theory is borne out by the fact that when, as was his new custom, the King demanded de Braose's son for hostage, de Braose's lady declared that no child of hers should be placed in the hands of Arthur's murderer. At any rate, whatever the cause of the quarrel, de Braose fled to Ireland. John mustered a fleet and followed, chasing de Braose and his friends from castle to castle. He did not use all his time in seeking vengeance, he introduced English laws into the country and English administration. Meanwhile, Matilda, de Braose's wife, with son, daughter and grandchildren, had been caught in Scotland and she promised 40,000 marks for her freedom and the reinstatement of her husband in his lands. John sent her to Bristol, and as it was impossible for her to pay this vast sum—her property having been confiscated—she was deliberately starved to death.

John's cruelty always seems so futile, so tactless ; in him the Angevin demon was stronger than in father or brothers, and there must have been periods when he became almost lunatic. Except on this basis we cannot explain the murder of Matilda de Braose ; it was not only purposeless, it was foolish, for it horrified all England and John was later made to publish a statement explaining his behaviour. It is a shifty statement that tells us nothing, probably because John had nothing to tell. He had been mad for the moment and a madman cannot account for his own actions.

INNOCENT followed the interdict with a bull of excommunication, and, although this was not published in England, the people must have been aware of it. Nevertheless, during the Christmas festivities at Windsor, 1209, " all the great men of England " were present ; only the Archdeacon of Norwich rashly took note of the excommunication ; he was seized, chained, imprisoned, and crushed to death under a cope of lead. John was determined to hold his power by any tyranny. Once he met some officers leading a prisoner who, he was told, had robbed and murdered a priest on the highway. " Unbind him and let him go," said John, " he has killed one of my enemies." Those of the clergy who remained in England were taxed to the uttermost penny, and, probably to show how dispassionate he was, John placed a heavy hand on the money-bags of the Jews. Like the bishops and monks, many of the Jews fled from England, those who stayed were mulcted of nearly all they had. There was the famous Bristol Jew who lost a tooth a day until he paid 10,000 marks : seven teeth were extracted, but when the eighth was being jerked out he gave in and opened his coffers.

Papal envoys arrived in England in 1211 and met John during August, but negotiations soon broke down. Innocent wanted complete submission and naturally John could not agree. Then Innocent issued another bull, this time absolving from their allegiance all the vassals of the King of England ; in January 1213 he authorised Philip to invade the country and depose John. Here was the opportunity that Philip had hungered after, and swiftly he called a council to debate what best to do with England when it should be conquered : Philip's son, Louis, it was decided, should be King, while Philip should have John for his private mercy. The French fleet is said to have been 1500 ships, and the army, too, was huge.

John was not idle. He realised that many of his followers could not be trusted, and might desert him at the last moment; he therefore concentrated on the fleet, hoping to catch the French and to " drown them in the sea before they could set foot on land." His troops were so many that he was unable to feed them all, and he disbanded the more poorly armed, keeping the main force on Barham Down, between Canterbury and Dover. He raced from port to port, personally examining the fortifications and seeing that all was ready for a strong defence, and he did not rely only on defence. His ships destroyed some of the enemy fleet in the mouth of the Seine and at Fecamp, and they captured and burnt Dieppe.

Despite his enormous army, John was not safe. A contemporary remarks that although there was " no prince under heaven against whom they could fail to defend the realm of England," the men were not of one heart and mind, and there was the risk of disloyalty, of barons declaring for Philip. John had this continual threat to make him eager to avoid war ; besides, a hermit called Peter of Pontefract had declared that he had been told in a dream that John would reign fourteen years and no more, and that he would be kingless on Ascension Day, 1213. A prophecy, given by a hermit considered almost a saint, was a weapon that medieval men could not ward aside ; they were avid for miracles, eager to see God's hand behind the falling of a sparrow, in the tripping of a horse. When John heard of the prophecy, he had Peter arrested and examined : naturally the hermit could not prove his words, he could merely assert that they were true and offer to die if they were not confirmed. John locked him into Corfe Castle and waited apprehensively for the day to come and pass, the day on which he had been first accepted as King and which had now become a threat of doom. He darted about the coastal towns, fortifying the castles, mustering the troops. His situation was indeed perilous : his enemy of France was ready to invade the country, his own army might be large but it could not be trusted, and there was the prophecy of Peter to give strength to men's hatred. Ascension Day had to pass before he dared fight, and with traitors at his back, with his foreign enemy prepared to sail at any moment, John took the only possible course : he agreed to meet Pandulf, the papal legate.

John's submission to the Pope has made him appear a coward and a traitor to England, yet it is difficult to see what else he could have done. By submitting he took the power completely from the hands of his enemies, he robbed his barons of any excuse for treason, and he destroyed the hopes of Philip, who had spent great sums on his fleet. John was not the kind of man to let his personal dignity or the honour of his country block up the path of his ambitions ; his had always been the cunning stroke, the unexpected blow. He now gave in to Innocent because it was the sensible thing for him to do ; at Dover on May 13, 1213, he accepted the papal terms without reservation, he agreed to let Stephen Langton be Archbishop of Canterbury, and to reinstate all exiles, both clerical and lay, with full monetary compensation. Two days later he formally surrendered his kingdom to the Pope and received it back as a fief of Rome.

It is uncertain who suggested this amazing act. John said that it was a voluntary act of humiliation, his barons in after years, when appealing to the Pope, said that they had counselled it ; the truth is probably midway between the two—John surrendered his kingdom with the agreement of the barons, for it is scarcely possible that Innocent would have dreamed of suggesting so great a triumph. It must have been dictated by John's own cunning, that cunning which disregarded all, honour or dignity, to attain an end. And to the men of his time it certainly did not appear a very shameful thing for him to do, the barons when they revolted did not use it as a warcry ; and although one near-contemporary chronicler calls the submission " ignominious," he is careful to add that John was " very prudently providing for himself and his people, for matters were in such a strait, and so great was fear on all sides, that there was no other quick way of evading the imminent danger, perhaps no other way at all. For when he had put himself under apostolical protection and had made his realm part of the patrimony of St. Peter, there was not in all the Roman world a King who would dare attack him or invade his lands, for Pope Innocent was held universally in such awe that no Pope for many years past could equal him."

And the plan succeeded. The traitors, now that John was Innocent's friend, had no longer the excuse that he was excommunicate ; Philip lost his English allies and found himself deserted with a great and worthless fleet. He decided to use his ships in some way, and sent them to invade the lands of Count Ferrand of Flanders, the one vassal who had refused to attack England. Ferrand cried to John for help and John within a few days sent five hundred ships with a large troop of horse and foot under the command of his half-brother, Earl William of Salisbury. They found the French unprepared ; then " never came so much wealth into England since King Arthur went to conquer it." In fury at this disaster, Philip burnt whatever ships were left. England now was safe, John's fleet remained while Philip's was no more.

ASCENSION DAY came and passed. John, to vaunt his contempt for the prophecy, held a great feast in the open to show that he remained still King ; then men said that Peter had referred not to the ecclesiastical but to the lay anniversary of John's coronation. When this day, too, had passed and the hermit with his son had been dragged by a horse's tail from Corfe to Wareham and there hanged, the people found a new interpretation in the dream. Peter had meant, they said, not that John would die or be deposed, but that he would cease to be King by surrendering his crown to Rome.

Interpretations of any kind did not bother John. He decided to use his fleet not for defence, but for aggression, he would win back what Philip had taken from him, he would invade Poitou. His problems at home were many, but in his typical optimistic way he thought to shelve them ; at the last moment he was frustrated, the barons refused to sail, pleading that their money was exhausted by the long wait for Philip's fleet and adding unconstitutionally that their feudal tenure did not include oversea service. The northern barons in particular were outrageously frank, and it seemed that in his fury John would break the country into civil war, for he marched to the north. Stephen Langton, now the recognised archbishop, hurried after him ; and threatening ecclesiastical punishment, he made John turn back. For the moment there was peace but the King's temper was such that he could never forgive.

The main problem that John had to face was the restitution of church lands and money, and it seems that he had too depleted a treasury to fulfil his promises. He did his best, however, and negotiations dragged on until February 1214, when he decided again on a Poitevin invasion, landing at La Rochelle with a great army, although but few of the English barons sailed. At first the campaign opened splendidly, the Poitevins deserting Philip and swearing allegiance to John ; the Lusignans, still perhaps brooding over the theft of Hugh's betrothed, alone held out, and John swept down to bring them to submission. Within a few days they were suing for peace, and John arranged a peculiar marriage—a marriage in which there must have lurked a certain malice : he betrothed the son of Hugh to his and Isabel's daughter, Joan.

Soon he met his first check : when he marched out to battle with Philip's son, Louis, his Poitevin troops rebelled. John fled so rapidly that he left his baggage and tents and artillery, and

Louis pressed forward, recapturing all that he had lost. Deserted by his Poitevin barons, John turned to England, imploring help. His appeal was unanswered and he had to rely wholly on his continental allies ; soon came the final blow : at Bouvines, when with his allies he faced the French, he was defeated with terrible slaughter, and all hopes of rebuilding his father's gigantic dominions were gone for ever.

Not only had John lost his continental fiefs, but, while he had been fighting abroad, he had almost lost England as well. His absence gave the discontented barons the opportunity for plotting which they needed. Yet so reckless was John, so incapable of understanding the condition of the country, that on his return he demanded a large scutage from those who had not followed him to Poitou. This was the last touch to a people drained of money ; the discontented barons pretended to go on a pilgrimage to Bury St. Edmunds, and there they met and whispered of rebellion, swearing to demand a renewal of Henry I's charter ; it was time to take arms, they said, and they would prepare for battle after Christmas. All, however, was not done in secret ; some kind of open negotiations went on with John, who, in fear that clergy and barons should unite, strove to divide them by conceding a few privileges to the Church.

Christmas came, the date of action ; John was at Worcester, then travelled to London, lodging at the Temple. Armed, the barons appeared with the charter of Henry I, and John strove to evade a direct answer, shuffling the charter aside as well as he could ; he pleaded for grace until Easter, and reluctantly the barons agreed.

Until April, John was safe and he went swiftly to work, but he had overestimated his power. All parties were against him— barons, clergy and the commons. When he commanded that a fresh oath of allegiance be given and that Henry's charter be disclaimed, he did far more harm than good ; he brought to the notice of the ignorant that such a charter existed. Failing here, he tried to bribe the clergy, and again he failed. Then cunningly he swore to turn crusader, for a man who wore the cross could not be harmed. And he wrote to the Pope ; the barons also sent their embassy to Rome. Naturally Innocent was firmly on John's side, he reprimanded Langton for daring to have anything to do with insurrection and commanded that he instantly stop the barons from taking further action.

War was inevitable, both sides were rapidly preparing for
the conflict, John hiring foreign mercenaries, the barons calling
up their men. Attempts at parley were made, Langton and
William Marshal acting as go-betweens, but when Easter drew
near and John still showed no signs of reissuing Henry's charter,
the barons began their march on London. The city welcomed
them, and once it was in their hands, John knew that he could
do little although the Tower remained loyal. All he possessed
of England were castles garrisoned by mercenaries, the people
were firmly against him, both lay and clerical, lords and commons.
In his reckless arrogance, he had alienated all parties. He
had angered the English church by destroying its property
and recompensing it on a small scale ; both merchants and
peasant had felt his taxation. When he confiscated the goods
of the monasteries he took from the poor their one place of
sustenance. Yet he was only reaping what his father and brother
had sown. Henry II's administration had been splendid and
successful, he had arrogated to the throne gigantic but necessary
powers ; instead of lessening these when they had served their
purpose, Richard had only tightened them, while John had
tightened them still further. The root of the trouble was the
Continent ; in striving to maintain that great empire, England
had had to pay and pay and pay. The people had suffered
much, but if John had been tactful, less fierce in his demands for
money, the rebellion might never have taken place. If he had
remained firm by the Church and the commons, as Henry II
had done, this conflict might have ended as the conflict of 1173
had ended, in more power to the throne. Even Stephen Langton,
the man who should have stood beside him, who had been commanded by Innocent to fight the barons, was sympathetic towards
them.

Practically alone, John for the moment had to make terms.
On June 8 he gave safe-conduct to the barons to meet him at
Staines between the 9th and 11th of the month. The barons
preferred Runnymede, a point between Staines and Windsor,
for John was then at Windsor. Here on this meadow by the
Thames,[1] they raised their tents on June 15 ; they came armed

---

[1] The myth still persists that Magna Carta was sealed on an island in
the Thames. This story presumably was started in 1834 when the lord of a
Buckinghamshire manor decided to steal the glory of the charter for his
county and erected a monument on what he called Magna Carta Island,
stating that here was the actual spot of sealing. The charter itself definitely

as if for battle, and a chronicler tells us that ". it is useless to enumerate those who were with the barons, for they included almost the whole nobility of England." John pitched his tents a little away from the rebels ; when the articles were produced he agreed to them at once, and Magna Carta was drawn up and sealed. John, in his typical way, would agree to anything because he had no intention of keeping his promises : all he wanted was time for revenge.

A GREAT deal of nonsense has been talked about Magna Carta, and to the average Englishman it remains as the safeguard of his liberties. To the men of the thirteenth century it represented only a padlock with which to chain down an unscrupulous King. Its clauses have been twisted by later writers to include almost everything from the creation of parliament to trial by jury. Actually it was a conservative document made by the barons to retain their personal freedom ; they had no conception of consti-tutional liberty, they merely wanted to escape unjust taxation and the tightening of the feudal laws. Its value does not lie in any clause or immediate result, but in its importance as a symbol to later generations. The barons considered it a reactionary docu-ment, which it certainly was ; they made no attempt to create new laws but to consolidate those honoured by time. All laws that John had violated were collected and placed on record to be sealed and kept as a bludgeon for future transgression. It is definitely a feudal document and to understand it one must understand the feudal ties, the form of service by which power and lands were kept. We have no space here to discuss the complicated questions of incidents and aids and such, but, broadly speaking, the feudal system was built on a series of payments—the serfs paid for their land by tilling the land of their lord and in various other ways, the lords paid their King by following him to battle and attending his court. This apparently simple system was con-fused by the medieval habit of keeping few records—payment varied according almost to the moment, for the old conception of actually following a lord to battle was now developing into a

contradicts this—it was on the meadow of Runnymede, in Surrey. Surrey for some peculiar reason placed an inscription in another part of the county, giving the honour to the caves under de Warenne's castle at Reigate. The true Runnymede is in the manor of Egham, which until the Dissolution was the property of Chertsey Abbey. It was the perfect place for camping, being midway between Staines and Windsor ; there was a bridge at Staines.

system of giving money with which to hire mercenaries. If a baron paid scutage he could stay at home—that is, if the King permitted it, the baron himself had no say in the matter and was unable to refuse to fight. Therefore when the northern barons pleaded that John was acting illegally when he called them overseas, they were definitely in the wrong according to feudal law. This scutage, originally only a payment to escape service, grew into a tax to be levied even in peace ; in John's hands, in particular, scutages became outrageous, being levied almost every year and at a higher rate than had been known before. Scutage was the main cause of rebellion, but there were other less important laws which John had overstepped. Henry II had fought to make the King's courts of paramount importance, and a source of revenue therefore was diverted from the seignorial courts to the royal exchequer : this had been a long smouldering cause for resentment, and added to it was the shame of a baron being judged no longer by his peers but by a tribunal of inferiors, the King's officials. Wardship was another abuse that galled the barons : according to this, lands when inherited by a child were kept by the crown and the revenues collected, and a large sum was amassed when the heir succeeded to his fief : Magna Carta demanded that these lands be returned undamaged after the child had come of age. Not only lay baronies, but bishoprics also were held in ward when sees fell vacant, and it was naturally in the King's interest to keep the sees vacant as long as possible so that he could gather the revenues. As we have noticed, this was a continual source of trouble.

Unfortunately we cannot examine Magna Carta clause by clause, but it was more or less a reactionary document, and the abuses it strove to rectify were in part a progress away from feudalism. Henry II had organised his administrative system so thoroughly that the power of kingship had become dangerous to the barons : he had increased feudal obligations and curtailed feudal privileges. In John's hands these reforms, already a root of resentment, were carried to unbearable extremes. Nevertheless, the barons might never have united if Stephen Langton had not been in England. He could have had small love for John, and he was an intelligent man with genuine sympathy for the oppressed ; one story tells that he discovered Henry I's charter and thereby gave the rebels courage, but that is obviously absurd. Henry's charter could not have been unknown. All the same, the tale shows that Langton, while pretending to negotiate

17

for John, was actually giving inspiration to the barons and that he suggested Henry I's charter as a model for Magna Carta.

Contemporary English writers take but little notice of the charter, but a foreign troubadour mentions four clauses as being of particular importance : the disparagement of heiresses, the killing or maiming for poaching, the royal court's encroachment on the seignorial courts, and the committee formed to see that John behaved himself. The first of these was a serious matter : as already noted, widows and minors became wards of the crown, and John could sell them to whom he liked in marriage. There was nothing objectionable in this, for love-matches were uncommon in the Middle Ages, betrothals being purely business affairs, but John had disparaged his heiresses, he had sold them to inferiors, and that was unforgivable. The women had only two ways of avoiding such a marriage : by becoming nuns (in which case they forfeited their fiefs, for they were then considered dead to the world) or by outbidding the suitors offered. The barons' objection was not to John's sale of heiresses, but to their disparagement, to their being sold to inferiors. Of the troubadour's second point, the maiming or killing of those who slew deer —forests were one of the continual sore points with the people, for the King was always striving to extend them, enclosing them around the lands of the commons. The wretched people thus enclosed were not permitted bows and arrows, they could not uproot trees or kill any beasts, even wolves, that might ravage their crops. The law that forbade the loss of life or limb for the killing of animals was actually passed in 1217. The third point, the encroachment of the royal court on to feudal courts, we have already discussed ; while the fourth, dealing with the appointment of a committee to control the King, is certainly astounding enough to deserve comment. Twenty-five barons were appointed to look after John ; unfortunately, these barons soon showed no public spirit. They behaved in a most outrageous fashion—on one occasion when John was too ill to rise they refused to visit him, and demanded his immediate attendance. Presumably he had gout, and he had to be carried to these " over-Kings," and when he arrived they remained seated as if he were a man of no importance.

BOTH sides knew that the charter would not be kept. If John had kept it he would have been ruined, he would never have been able to gather taxes enough to pay his expenses. All he desired was time, time for the Pope to interfere, for the barons to separate and leave themselves open to attack. In public he remained calm as if this humiliation had not affected him in the least, but in private his rage was truly Angevin, for he " gnashed his teeth, rolled his eyes, seized sticks and straw and gnawed them like a madman, or tore them to scraps in his fingers." Innocent came to his rescue. He excommunicated " all the men who were disturbing the King and country," and John started rearming, buying mercenaries and gathering what jewels and money he could. Seeing that the King had not the least intention of obeying the charter, the barons decided that if he could not be brought to reason he must be deposed. They offered the crown of England to Louis, son of Philip of France.

John began the attack ; relieving his castles that had remained loyal, he raced over the country, dealing terrible revenge, destroying his enemies' lands, dragging money from the towns, ransoming prisoners. He devastated the country, he left burnt castles and crops wherever he went ; while the barons' defence was feeble, they waited for Louis's coming. Innocent was trying to stop the invasion, he forbade the French attacking a papal fief but Philip retorted that no King could give away his lands without his barons' consent—rather a weak retort after the barons themselves had boasted that the idea was theirs. At any rate, Philip said that it was not his affair, it was Louis's, and nothing could stop Louis. He embarked at Calais on Friday, May 20, 1216, and landed the next day on the Isle of Thanet. The storms which held him back had broken John's great fleet. John himself was on the coast, but when he realised that the winds were against him, he moved to Canterbury. It was not fear of a battle that kept him inland—he was always a brave soldier—it was the knowledge that he could not trust his men, for these mercenaries were vassals of France and probably would refuse to fight the son of their overlord. He was forced to withdraw and leave the passage open to London, where Louis arrived on June 2, barons and citizens doing him homage.

John dared not fight, he drew back farther into the west while his enemies took the field ; even his friends began to desert him. It is difficult to understand Louis's policy ; instead of swinging round on John, he attacked castles here and there, eventually settling half his troops before Windsor and himself leading the other half to capture Dover.

John was on the border of Wales when he decided to take the

offensive by relieving Windsor. At the last moment he turned aside and swept in a whirl of rage through the eastern counties, slaying, ravaging. The barons left Windsor and raced after him. With Lincoln as a base, John destroyed whatever he could reach. He had become wholly demon and spared nothing ; the October crops were fired and flamed to ashes—farmhouses, towns, all were burnt.

Meanwhile for over two months Louis had been idling around Dover Castle and gradually losing the affection of the English by his preference for his own countrymen. He made no effort to pursue John, he left that to the barons and to his second-in-command, the Count of Nevers, but they rode no farther than Cambridge, for some reason then turning back to London.

For three days John stayed at Lynn where he had been welcomed royally and given rich gifts, then he journeyed north. There is something distinctly tragic in the life of John ; it is true that he had the temper of a fiend, that he was arrogant and a liar, but fate struck at him again and again. Now was to come the final and most unexpected blow of all, the blow that caused his death.

Already he was ill. He had over-eaten at Lynn and was crippled by dysentery when he reached the treacherous Wash. The details of what followed are not complete : apparently the army crossed without mishap—probably John had hired a guide—but his baggage-train pressed forward impatiently, then " the ground was opened in the midst of the waves, and bottomless whirlpools, which swallowed them all with the men and the horses so that not one foot escaped to tell the King of this disaster." As John very soon knew of the calamity, it is likely that he was on the opposite shore and watched his " waggons, carts, and sumpter horses with the treasures, precious vessels, and all the other things which he loved with so much care " being gripped by " the sand which is called quick." If so, it must have been an appalling moment. We do not know with what those carts were weighted, the plunder must have been enormous, but it is doubtful if the tale be true that his crown was there. Yet these things which, " next to his life, he held too dear in the world " gradually sank into the quicksands ; the great unwieldy carts with their iron-studded wheels, the frantic horses and men, all were caught in the tide. They were probably cut off, the tide would be sweeping in over the path they had traversed.

That night John reached Swineshead Abbey; broken with grief and illness, he flung himself into a deeper fever by guzzling peaches and fresh cider. Nevertheless, he could not stay in bed, he forced his tortured body on to Sleaford where he was met by messengers from Dover asking permission to surrender to Louis. This increased his fever and he was bled, yet still the body and mind could not find peace. He determined to reach Newark and dragged himself " panting and groaning " on to a horse to travel three miles before he slid from the saddle, exhausted and in agony. They placed him in a litter, roughly hewn by his men with their swords and knives from the willows by the roadside and with merely a horse-cloth thrown over it. The litter was even more painful than the saddle. " This accursed litter has broken all my bones and nearly killed me," cried John, and again he pulled himself on horseback, struggling forward until he reached Newark.

The end was close. He knew that he was dying, and all his thoughts were for his children; he declared his elder son Henry his heir, and sent to William Marshal saying that he placed the lad " in God's keeping and in his." He confessed and received absolution and then dictated his will. The will was never finished. It remains a fragment, broken suddenly as if the voice had died in the speaker's throat.

That night a terrible whirlwind struck Newark. The people thought their houses would tumble down, and as they crouched in their beds, the spirit of King John passed from this world. His servants as usual plundered what remained, and the uncovered corpse lay on its couch as the wind wrenched at the walls and screamed against the shutters. In a whirlwind of fury he had lived, and the demon-ancestress came at the last to take his soul from the broken body.

THEY embalmed the corpse as well as they could; they dressed it in royal costume, and put a monk's cowl over the head. Then they carried it to Worcester; they carried it as if it were something precious that might be stolen, for the men who rode at its side were fully armed, being mainly mercenaries.

" Forasmuch," wrote a chronicler, " as when he came to die he possessed none of his land in peace, he is called Lackland." Lackland at birth and Lackland at his death : that is the key to John's character. He was never to forget that nickname, and himself by his own insane arrogance proved it to be true.

VIII

KING HENRY THE THIRD
1216–1272

ON HIS DEATH-BED John had thought of nothing but his sons. His sons must succeed him, Louis must not take the throne; that was his continual torment—the fear that these boys might be sacrificed for his stupidities. Then he recalled to mind old William Marshal, the most true knight in the world, William who had saved John's father from the fury of Richard, who had secured John's throne and who had remained always loyal despite the strongest temptations. William must guard the boys. "Sirs," cried John to those around him, "sirs, I must die. For God's sake, pray the Marshal to forgive me the wrongs I have done him. He has always served me loyally and has never returned me evil for any evil I have done or said to him. Sirs, for God's sake Who made the world, pray him to forgive me; and since I am more sure of his loyalty than of any other man's, I beg you that he may have my son in his charge and for ever keep him and guard him, for the child will never be able to hold his land through any one but the Marshal!"

William was now about seventy-three years of age, and in all those seventy-three years he had kept his honour unstained. Even his enemies respected him, no man could help but admire this knight of whom Philip Augustus was to cry—"The Marshal was the most loyal man I have ever known in any place where I have ever been!" He typified the perfect knight of the thirteenth century, and it is interesting to see how the chivalric ideas had grown from the days of Rufus, how the crude eleventh-century knight had become refined to this perfection. Perhaps in modern eyes William would not seem so perfect as he did to his contemporaries, he would seem narrow-minded with a trifle of the bully in him. Yet for his period he was an ideal, and certainly amongst the innumerable shifty scoundrels of the Middle Ages he shines with noble splendour, a relief against the darkness of treachery about him.

He did not want this burden which John passed to him, for he was old, nevertheless he rode into the fields outside Malmesbury to meet the nine-year-old lad who was carried on horseback by a retainer. " Welcome, sir," said little Henry, " truly, I commit myself to God and to you, that for God's sake you may take care of me, and may the true God who takes care of all good things grant that you may arrange our affairs so well that your wardship of me will be prosperous." " Fair sir," replied William, " loyally I tell you, as I trust my soul to God, I will be in good fealty to you and will never forget you so long as I have power to do anything." Henry wept, and those around, including William, wept " for pity."

To judge by this pathetic scene one would believe that little Henry was the most guileless and charming of boys, but the poet who records the tale is acute enough to call him a " welltrained child," and it is more than likely that the words had been carefully rehearsed. There is little in the facts of his later life to make one consider Henry charming. He was an entirely worthless King. Men of the type of Rufus and John one might dislike, yet it is impossible not to realise their power and their huge vitality, even though it be the vitality of evil ; they are great figures on the heroic scale, men of strong will and fine intelligence, eaters and drinkers and blasphemers, definite personalities by whom one cannot help being fascinated. Henry was merely worthless. The one good quality in his character, his piety, was carried to such an extreme that if he had had his way England would have become completely bound by the papacy, with poverty-stricken churches, with few bishops in the country, but with money flooding out continually to bishops in Rome. Even his piety one grows to suspect, for he stole his handful of the Roman taxes, yet perhaps that is not altogether fair, he may have felt himself under an obligation to the Popes because they had been more or less his guardians, and his devotion does appear genuine. He attended at least three public masses a day and very often went to others in private, and when on a progress he never failed to visit any church and " he always used to kiss lepers." The people of his time mainly believed in him, they regarded him as a kind of pious child : Dante, for example, in his travel through purgatory saw Henry amongst flowers and perfumes in a narrow valley, in the portion reserved for children. And perhaps Dante saw aright, for Henry was rather like a spiteful child, like a bad-tempered, stubborn and reckless child. He had the same quick rage, the same sentiment, the same fears, sulkiness, malice and cruelty as some boys. And also, the same fantastic imagination. It was this imagination that really made him dangerous. A dream would send him off on a lunatic venture, such as seeking the crown of the Holy Roman Empire, without a penny in his pouch ; he never looked into the future, the dream was sufficient. He had that much of his father in him, he had John's faith in the present, his belief was to-morrow.

Examining Henry's reign one has the impression of a naughty boy surrounded by desperate elders all of whom are driven insane as they struggle to control him. Cajoling, beatings, threats, nothing can bring the child to reason : he might be frightened, he might whimper and cower, but the next moment all was forgotten save the lust for revenge.

Matthew Paris tells us that Henry had a " heart of wax." Paris is an amusing but a malicious writer, nevertheless he shows the King most vividly with those words. His heart could easily be moulded by the person next to him, but it had to be manipulated very subtly, for in the centre was a core of stubbornness, of that awful stubbornness which maintains what it says or thinks whether it be right or wrong. You could mould that heart until you felt quite certain that it was shaped as you desired, then you would touch suddenly that core of unbreakable obstinacy ; or perhaps you would find that a second man had been manipulating the other side and that he was more cunning than you. Because of this, because he was weak, and violent as only a weak man can be violent, Henry was dangerous ; he could not love anyone, and the friend of to-day was often the enemy of to-morrow. Spiteful and treacherous, avaricious yet extravagant, Henry was one of the most futile of all English Kings. Behind that plump face with the drooping eyelid was a mean sly mind, the mind of a traitor, of one almost insane with ambitions so idiotic that they could scarcely be argued away. Except for that drooping left eyelid we have few facts of Henry's personal appearance, save that he was of medium height and fattish. The eyelid drooped so heavily that it almost hid the pupil.

His reign is no simple one to examine in this short space. If we keep to our conception of having personal biographies of the Kings, there will be almost nothing to tell, for Henry's kingship was merely one frantic wail for money in all those fifty odd years :

he was ruled first by guardians and later by his son, the cunning Edward. But during those fifty years we meet one of the greatest figures of medieval history, Simon de Montfort, and he must take first place. During the exciting and important episodes of this reign, Simon stands as the heroic idealist, as one doomed by his own reckless genius to betrayal and death, to a death splendid and tragic. The story of Simon's life is one of the great tragedies of man, it is the story of an enthusiast bound always by honour and faith yet firmly advancing towards a dim goal which he alone can distinguish, and being continually dragged back by the petty spite and hatred of jealous creatures. He was beyond his times, seeing into a future where tyranny would live no more and where the oppressed would be unburdened ; he could see so clearly that he was impatient with others because they also could not see. It seemed so simple to him, this righting of wrongs, this balancing of justice ; one sweep and he felt that he could clear all wickedness away to build a fine new England. He should have realised, of course, that man does not want justice when injustice can gratify ambition, that power is man's chief desire. But Simon, like all fanatics, could not see beyond the pinpoint of his own ideals ; he believed so surely in his dreams that he was astonished when others did not also believe in them. Sincere to the edge of madness, he brought his doom upon himself. Yet he had his followers—the inarticulate people, the leaderless hordes of England, knew him, trusted him and revered him. While he lived they could do nothing, but when he was dead their love and faith turned him to a martyr. And truly, if nobility and honour and faith make saints, few have been as worthy as Earl Simon de Montfort.

THEY had no time in which to get the royal crown. Henry III, on October 28, 1216, was crowned with " a sort of chaplet " in the abbey church at Gloucester. Louis was still at Dover, struggling to break the walls so bravely held by Hubert de Burgh, and the Marshal's first task as regent was to rid England of this enemy. He played a waiting game, pointing out to the rebels that now that John was dead they had no enemy to fight ; he waited until Louis stupidly visited France, then the rebels began to dribble to him, and although Louis returned with further men he discovered that a great many of his English forces had deserted.

The war kept on for a time, the French were defeated at Lincoln, then a fleet of reinforcements was scattered by Hubert de Burgh in the straits of Dover, and that finished Louis. A treaty was signed at Lambeth on September 11, 1217.

William Marshal had done his task cleverly, but he had not long to live. He died, old warrior, in his bed on May 14, 1219. As he lay waiting for death, he was continually worried about the future of the little King. " Let God give you a guardian who will do you honour," he said to Henry when the lad was brought to him some days before the end. Peter des Roches, Bishop of Winchester, who had been Henry's personal guardian, suggested that he take the Marshal's place, but he was a Poitevin, one of John's old friends, and few trusted him. " Never," said William, when des Roches asked for the power. To whom could he give the lad ? what man could be trusted in this island of ambitious traitors ? " There is no land where opinions are so divided as in England," said William next day when alone with his wife and family ; " if I give the King to one, the others will be jealous," and he decided that in only one man could safety be found, in the Pope ; therefore when Henry and Pandulf the legate came to him, William took Henry by the hand and, leaning on his side, said to the legate, " Sir, I have thought long about what we spoke of yesterday. I wish here, in the presence of all, to give the King to God, to the Pope, and to you who represent him."

It was not a wise choice, for Pandulf was an overbearing prelate, but it was the safest one, as it at least gave Henry the protection of the Pope. Soon, however, Pandulf was recalled to Rome, and the honest Hubert de Burgh remained in joint control of England with Peter des Roches : Hubert as justiciar, Peter as the King's guardian. They had much to contend with—there were still rebels to subdue, castles to raze, the great Welshman Llewelyn to fight, and Poitou to keep loyal. In Poitou the question was complicated because England had to rely almost completely on the treacherous Lusignans, and now John's widow married Hugh X, Count of la Marche, son of the man from whom John had stolen her many years ago. It is rather a degrading marriage—and there are suggestions that Isabel when Queen of England had not been without her lovers—and she strove to explain it on the most noble terms, making herself appear almost a martyr for England, pointing out that her new husband's betrothed—her own daughter—was " of such tender age," while the threat that Hugh might wed a French princess was so perilous to England that rather than risk it she had married him herself, " and let heaven witness," she added to her son, " we did this rather for your sake than for our own." After which, she suggested that Henry might give Hugh her own previous dowry and also her daughter's.

Then Philip Augustus died. It is difficult to understand how Philip attained such greatness, how he managed to build France to such enormous power, winning nearly all the English continental fiefs. He was cunning yet a coward, he was a lecherous glutton but he was usually faithful to his word, he was a man of quick temper but he was also quickly calmed ; he was treacherous but he was resourceful ; there was nothing actually great in him, he had points of good and bad woven so closely together that they built his character to one of strength. If he had struggled against a Henry II or an Edward I it is doubtful if he would have attained so much ; it was more his good fortune in being faced with adversaries like the careless Richard and optimistic John than any genius in himself which caused him to become more or less the creator of modern France. His son, now King Louis VIII, had not long to live ; he died on November 8, 1226, while fighting the Albigensian heretics,[1] and was succeeded by a boy of twelve, Louis IX. There was now no longer any risk of a war between the two countries, already the French King's guardians were taking bribes from Hubert de Burgh and were ready to strangle each other in the fight for power.

NOT only in France, but also in England the guardians of a boy King were ready to spring at each other's throat. Hubert won the battle here. In January 1227 he declared Henry of age

[1] It is difficult to know what the Albigensian doctrine exactly was, for our knowledge of it is almost completely derived from their opponents, but apparently it was merely an anti-Roman movement although its centre, the Cathari, had a definite set of beliefs. The actual Cathari were probably very few ; their doctrine was to reject the water-baptism as Jewish, and to believe that purgatory was the world and that hell was the inward man, and that unless peace was made with Christ before death the tortured soul flung itself back to earth to enter the first living dwelling it could, whether beast or human. That gives small conception of the complications of the theory, but it was strongly anti-Roman and its broadest principles at least were believed all through the south of France during the twelfth and thirteenth century, not only the people but the lords accepting it. Innocent III began the great crusade of 1209 which continued until 1229 and wiped out the glorious Provençal culture ; over a million lives are said to have been taken by the Church. "Kill all ; God will know His own," said the papal legate, Arnold Bishop of Cliteaux.

and dismissed Peter as being no longer necessary. Peter's retort was to accuse Hubert of treachery and to entice Henry's young brother, Richard—now just turned eighteen—to attack the justiciar ; but Hubert quickly bribed the lad, and Peter left England with his enemy in sole command. Young Henry was now nineteen and he was determined to govern. His ideas of government were crude enough, they consisted mainly of grandiose ideas not only impossible to perform but abhorrent to the people and exasperating to any honest councillor. He decided to attack France.

The French bogy did not exist any longer in England. The country had had enough fighting, and little interest was taken in its old continental dominions ; nevertheless, young Henry was determined to win them back, he was going to be as great a builder as his grandfather. Things were not so simply arranged as he believed, it was one thing to declare war and a different affair to make it. When in Michaelmas 1229 he prepared to embark at Portsmouth he discovered that there were not enough ships, and he turned in such fury on his justiciar, calling him traitor, that he would have murdered him had he not been held back. As it was, he drew his sword, and Hubert would certainly have died that day if his friends had not been quick enough to seize the King. And the Patent Rolls prove that the charge was unjustified : Hubert had done everything possible to collect a fleet, the Cinque Ports promising to send double their usual amount. All the same, Hubert was probably only too pleased to have some respite from the wasteful and futile invasion, even at the risk of his life, but the King would not be put off. Next year he sailed for Poitou. There was no fighting, the soldiers " in the manner of Englishmen " drank " as if every day were Christmas," and Henry and his brother Richard soon pleaded illness and returned to England. The war continued in their absence—if war it could be called—to an inglorious end.

Meanwhile, Hubert de Burgh was nearing the climax of his power. That climax was inevitable, no honest man could stand long beside Henry, only a fawning rascal could have borne the policy of such a King. Hubert fell in a noble cause, as the victim of Henry's spite against the Englishmen who were fighting to snap the Roman chain riveted by his father John. Innocent III had long since died, he had been followed by a kindly old man, Honorius III, who in his turn was succeeded by Gregory IX. Gregory had all Innocent's strength, but not his genius, he was a learned ascetic with little tolerance for the human failings he did not understand, but he shared with Innocent huge ambitions for the Church. He was eighty when he came to the papal throne, and he turned ragingly on the Emperor of the Holy Roman Empire. This was the brilliant Frederick II of Hohenstaufen, a man cold and brave, learned, charming and arrogant, who lived in pagan splendour, contemptuous of religion. With Honorius in Rome, Frederick had had everything his own way, but now that Gregory was Pope there was immediate war. Gregory insisted that Frederick carry out a promised crusade. Frederick carried it out as well as he could, but the heat was so terrific we are told that the armour actually melted on the knights' backs. Frederick, almost dead with fever, had to return to Naples. Now was Gregory's opportunity ; he excommunicated the sick Emperor for daring to come home, being determined to break him at any cost, but Frederick was not the man to give way to a curse. " I hold my crown," he said, " of God alone, and not the Pope nor the council nor the devil shall rend it from me. I who am the chief prince of the world, yea, who am without equal ! " Innocent, driven to greater furies by this defiance, preached a crusade against Frederick, and his own chaplain, Stephen of Agnani, came to England to levy a tax towards this holy war. For the second time Rome tried to tax the English church, but in 1184 Henry II had soon put a stop to any such question ; Henry III, however, was a pious King and he thoroughly endorsed the tithe. Having reaped the money with such ease, Gregory quite naturally decided to extract more, and he commanded the English clergy not to fill vacant benefices ; he filled them instead with Italian friends so that absentee bishops drew huge revenues from the country and gave nothing in return. It was useless appealing to Rome against itself, so the English clergy and patrons formed a secret society that burned the harvest of absentee bishoprics and attacked foreign clerks. The rioters on one or two occasions showed letters under the royal seal authorising their behaviour. There were about eighty of them led by Sir Robert Twenge who called himself William Wither, and to show that they were not merely thieves they ostentatiously gave alms to the poor, sometimes throwing coins in the air and telling the people to pick them up. Peter des Roches was now back in England and he seized this opportunity to drag down his old enemy ; he accused Hubert of forging the warrants and of inspiring the rioters.

There was probably some truth in the accusation, but there was probably much less in Peter's second attack that Hubert had been misappropriating the King's money. Henry was always in need of gold, being childishly extravagant, and he turned instantly on Hubert, only too eager for a scapegoat and for a chance of getting the treasury into his own hands. Hubert was dismissed and a long list of charges against him quickly put on paper, some of them—such as his having seduced his wife before marriage—being merely ludicrous. His efforts to explain away the accusations were suspiciously feeble, and at last he ran to sanctuary in St. Edmund's. Here he should have been safe for forty days, during which time if he carried no weapon he stayed under the Church's protection and no man would dare interfere with him ; even after the forty days he could not be harmed so long as he remained inside the church, he could only be starved out. Henry, pious though he might be, had Hubert dragged from the church and brought to London with his feet tied under a horse's belly. But he had gone too far. All men took the side of Hubert—the clergy because sanctuary had been outraged, and the barons and the Londoners because they hated Peter ; the Bishop of London insisted that Hubert be returned to sanctuary, and when a common smith was ordered to fetter him, he refused, saying that he would not touch the hero who had saved England at Sandwich. Hubert was put back into sanctuary and starved out after the legal forty days, being then sentenced to lose his chattels and his grants from the crown, although he was permitted to keep in peace all else beside.

With Hubert out of the way, Henry must have thought his power was absolute, and he probably had real affection for Peter who had been his tutor for many years. Under Peter's influence he grew to fear or hate nearly all Englishmen, and the hungry Poitevins came quickly to see what honours they could seize while their countryman controlled the King. They were offered almost every important position ; only one Englishman, an obscure knight named Stephen Segrave who was made justiciar, was given real honour ; and the English watched with jealous rage their country's wealth spilling into the hands of aliens. For leader they had Richard Marshal, second son of William, and in the name of the barons he demanded that all foreigners be dismissed ; Peter answered for Henry, he said that the King needed foreigners to protect him from his subjects' treachery. Richard then formed a league of defence, and he escaped capture just in time, flying to the Welsh border to make an alliance with Llewelyn and to call out his men in Pembrokeshire. Henry pursued him, beseiged Usk Castle and devastated not only Richard's lands but the lands of any he supposed might be his supporters. When Richard and his friends offered to stand their trial if they might be judged by their peers, the answer was that they would be judged by royal justices, which meant Poitevins, so they naturally sprang to arms. As usual, Henry had not considered the consequences of his actions, he never thought of the people's wishes but merely of his own desires ; the commons were firmly against him and the barons remained at least neutral, while Richard and Llewelyn captured Shrewsbury. Henry was forced to retreat and to suffer the humiliation of seeing his justiciar's lands being burnt before his very eyes. Richard Marshal next sailed for Ireland, where he possessed great estates, and he had scarcely landed before he was killed in battle. Instantly he became a martyr to the people ; but even before the news arrived, Henry had been forced to surrender, promising to dismiss his Poitevin councillors. He only gave in under the threat of excommunication from Edmund Rich, Archbishop of Canterbury, but once he had decided on a course, no matter how distasteful it might have been a moment since, Henry threw himself into it wholeheartedly. He not only dismissed the Poitevins but he assured Peter des Roches that had he not been a clerk he would have torn his eyes out. Peter never again meddled in politics ; Henry told him " to go to his diocese and attend to the care of souls and never again to interfere with the King's business." Peter took the advice, he fought for Gregory against Frederick, returned to England in 1236 and died two years later.

NOTHING could teach Henry a lesson. He had one of those elastic minds that take any form and are never punctured, that can be kicked yet will always return to the same serene shape. After his trouble about the Poitevins one might naturally conclude that he would have had enough of foreigners, or at any rate, that he would realise that England had had enough of them. Yet within a short time, Segrave was back in power—but Henry might plead that he was English, although of the Poitevin party— and friends of Richard Marshal were either banished or forced to surrender office.

Soon came a second influx of foreigners, and of foreigners

even more greedy and dangerous than the Poitevins, for they were led by one who could not be undermined, by Henry's Queen, Eleanor of Provençe.

IT was impossible for Henry ever to realise that he had no gold. He had that simple faith of the old woman who, possessing a cheque book, believed that she necessarily possessed money : Henry owned England, England was wealthy, therefore Henry must be wealthy. He forgot the Great Charter torn with such travail from King John, the charter which himself had ratified again and again in amended forms, all that he could understand was that he was King and that a King must possess money. Extravagant in his pleasures yet miserly in his justice, he would dip his hands to the wrists in the exchequer to fling away gold on some insensate pastime while yet demanding more and more from England and giving nothing in return.

His sister Isabel he married to the Emperor Frederick II, the Pope's great enemy, and although the alliance was politically worthless, he celebrated it with gorgeous pomp. It was followed next year by his own marriage to Eleanor, the beautiful twelve-year-old daughter of Raymond IV, Count of Provençe, and again all available wealth was poured out in celebrations. He was married on Sunday, January 20, 1236, and Matthew Paris, after setting out to give a detailed description of all he saw that day, suddenly throws his pen aside in exhaustion ; he gasps that it is useless to continue, that there is too much—too much to recount. London could not hold the mobs that swarmed to see the couple ; Henry had met his betrothed at Canterbury, and when the pair neared London, the citizens, in holiday attire, rode out to greet them and chased each other about the fields to show their horses' speed. The houses were hung with flags and banners, with wreaths and hangings and candles and lamps, while the streets, in honour of such a day, were swept of their muck, of sticks, stones, dirt and refuse. The young Queen went through her coronation, we are assured, with " incomparable solemnity."

BEHIND the beautiful Eleanor came a horde of relatives, of Savoyards and Provençals, who soon made themselves as detested as ever the Poitevins had been. Her four uncles were the most hated : William, Thomas, Peter, and Boniface of Savoy. William was to die within three years, Thomas was rarely in

England until 1244, but Peter and Boniface remained from the first. Peter became Earl of Richmond in 1241, and Boniface succeeded Rich as Archbishop of Canterbury in 1243. Together with these came William's clerk, Pierre d'Aigueblanche, a most cunning rascal who later was made Bishop of Hereford.

The horde rapidly surrounded the King, cutting him off from the English barons and clergy. Apart from Boniface, none cared for their adopted country, they were eager to filch what they could from its treasury and to use it merely as a rung on the ladder to Roman preference. Therefore they were always on the side of the Pope, every papal exaction was greeted kindlily and urged on to the King. The unfortunate English stayed outside this barrier of foreigners, they were unable to edge into the council and remained helpless, clamouring futilely for reforms and for the ousting of these hungry Savoyards. They had no leader, the King's young brother Richard, while feeling the shame as deeply as they, was himself of the Angevin dynasty and dared make no move that might imperil it. There was one man who might yet rescue England, but he was as deeply hated as the others, being also a foreigner. That was Simon de Montfort, Earl of Leicester.

He was a Frenchman who had come to England to ask a lost inheritance. His grandfather had acquired by marriage the Leicester estates, which had become forfeited with the loss of Normandy; Simon, a penniless second son, had sought their return from Henry III, his request was granted and he was also appointed a councillor. Naturally the English distrusted this tall Frenchman, the beloved of the King, and he as yet made no move to show that there were noble ambitions in him. He remains hidden from record until 1238 when he married Henry's sister, Eleanor. We know, of course, of his existence before that date, we know that his father was so zealous an avenger on the Albigenses that when he captured the castle of Brom, he cut off the noses and plucked out the eyes of a hundred of the garrison, mercifully leaving a man with one eye to guide the wretches to some dark and forlorn destination, for they were considered already spiritually blind, being cut off from the faith; we know that young Simon when in England tried twice to marry French heiresses and failed; but of his genius we receive no hint. He is merely one of the foreigners, apparently like them, dipping his fingers into England, until he steps forward as the husband of the twenty-six-year-old Eleanor, widow of William Marshal, younger.

18

Henry had helped on the wedding, which it appears was a necessary one ; it was performed on January 7, 1238, " in the King's little chapel which is in the corner of his chamber. The King himself gave away the bride to the said Simon, Earl of Leicester, and he received her gratefully, partly for her beauty, partly for the rich honours that went with her, and partly for her royal and distinguished birth." Immediately when this became known, there was a furious outcry led by Richard who vaguely threatened his brother because he had dared consent to the match without consulting the great council, for Henry as yet being childless, Simon's, a foreigner's son, might succeed to England ; shortly afterwards, Richard dropped the quarrel, and the only immediate result of Simon's marriage was to deprive the barons of their leader, for they spurned Richard as a traitor when he forgave his brother. Then Henry and Simon quarrelled. They quarrelled, of course, about money—the only subject that could really hurt the King : Simon had given Henry as surety when he bought a dispensation for his marriage from Rome, and now suddenly Henry objected. (This dispensation, by the way, was necessary, as Eleanor, on the death of her first husband, had taken a vow of widowhood.) The quarrel occurred shortly after the birth of Henry's first son Edward on June 16, 1239 ; on August 9, the Queen was about to leave for a monastery to attend her purification—the ritual cleansing that was customary after childbirth—when the King refused to allow Simon or his wife to attend the ceremony because he had " clandestinely defiled " her before marriage. Confused and ashamed, Simon withdrew and travelled by water to his lodgings at the palace of the late Bishop of Winchester, in Southwark ; from here he was forcibly ejected and when he visited the King, he and his wife were met only by insults. " You seduced my sister before marriage," cried Henry, " and when I knew of it I gave her to you to avoid scandal, although it was against my wish. And so that her vow might not stop the marriage you went to Rome where, by rich gifts and mighty promises, you bribed the curia to let you do what was unlawful. To crown your evil, without my advice or knowledge, with false witnesses you made me your surety ! " Simon took the only course of demanding a trial, which was refused; Richard saved him from imprisonment but nevertheless he was ordered from the King's presence, and left the country, raging in his humiliation. He set out for the Holy Land to fulfil an old crusading vow, Richard and many others travelling with him

The barons tried to stop Richard from leaving England, pointing out that if he deserted them they were utterly alone. Weeping, he answered, " Truly, even if I had not taken the cross, I would go all the same, so that I might not behold the evils of our nation and the desolation of the realm, which men think I have the power to prevent, though I have it not."

WHILE this personal quarrel was taking place, the country was being broken even more heavily under the constant hammering of the Pope. For some reason, Henry invited a papal legate to England, and the Cardinal Otto was sent in 1238. When the truth was known about his coming there was terror on every side, but the cardinal on his arrival was extremely charming and he calmed suspicion by at first refusing gifts ; nevertheless, England was alert for treachery. Everything remained quiet until the cardinal visited Oxford on April 23, when his Master of the Cooks, who was also his cousin, threw a pot of hot water into the face of an Irish scholar who was begging a meal. A Welshman shouted, " Shame that we should put up with this ! " and drawing his bow, shot the cook dead through a grille in the door. The city bell was tugged awake, the scholars trooped out to avenge the honour of the university, and they stormed the cardinal's lodging, yelling, " Where is that usurer, that simoniac, that plunderer of revenues, that thirster for moneys ! " Hearing of the uproar, Henry sent a guard to rescue the cardinal, but he could not unloose his vengeance on Oxford. When some of the students were taken to the Tower, that brave old scholar, Grosseteste, rose in his wrath and threatened to excommunicate without exception any man who dared lay hands upon a clerk. All that the cardinal could extract were masses for his cousin's soul and a public penance from the university. Probably driven out of his diplomatic calm by this outrage, the legate no longer pretended to be gracious and disinterested, he called for exorbitant taxes from the bishops and religious houses, and concluded by demanding a fifth part of all the English clergy's rents and movables. At about the same time another Roman, Pietro Rosso, was also extracting money for the Pope who was so grateful for the sums squeezed out of England that he promised the next three hundred vacant benefices to his Italian friends. This was too much for that wise old archbishop, Edmund Rich ; he was not a strong character, being a good and kindly man, yet the spectacle of his broken Church being gradually destroyed by the indifference and cupidity of Rome, drove him to action. He asked permission to visit the Pope and plead the case of England ; Henry avoided a direct answer, but all the same, Rich set out on the long journey. He died on the way and was buried at Pontigny, leaving absent the greatest benefice in the country.

HENRY again suddenly decided to attack France. His mother lured him to it. Louis had sent his brother Alphonse to be Count and suzerain of Poitou, and Hugh de la Marche visited him to do homage ; afterwards Isabel upbraided her husband for a coward and a traitor, shouting, " Out of my sight, am I a waiting-maid that I should stand before them while they sit at ease ! " Her dignity was so outraged because she, Queen-Mother of England, should have had to stand before the brother of the French King that she bullied her wretched husband into rebellion and called on her son for aid. Henry would have started at once if the council had not jolted him from his dream. They refused a subsidy because he had not consulted them on the matter. When Henry tried to be diplomatic and tamper with them one by one, they showed a list of all the taxes they had submitted to since his reign. There was no answer to that, so Henry lost his temper : " he burst into a violent rage, and with an oath he called the saints to witness that no terrors should stop him, that no quibbling speeches should turn him from his resolve· of embarking " for France. He kept his word. He landed in Gascony on May 19, 1242, only to be nearly captured by the enemy at the threatened battle of Taillebourg, July 20 ; his brother Richard—now returned from the Holy Land—saved him at the last moment by imploring a day's truce. The truce was granted although the French must have known that it was only asked to give Henry the opportunity to escape, which Henry promptly did ; he would have made an awkward prisoner, however. As it was, he was fighting, not as King of England, but almost as an adventurer ; had he been captured, the honour of England would have demanded instant war.

Henry crawled back to England after lurking for some time in Gascony because he was ashamed to face his subjects.

INNOCENT IV became the next Pope and he had no intention of altering the methods of his predecessors, he was a scholar, cunning and mean and treacherous. In 1243 he despatched " a new extortioner, Martin by name," to suspend all English bishops from the right of offering benefices until his relations and friends had been given a fat church each. This Martin appears to have been the most tactless of all the papal messengers ; at any rate, he inspired Matthew Paris to reach his highest flights of malice. Matthew loathed Martin. He shows us the sprightly little Roman darting at the religious houses, dragging gifts from the prelates, " particularly desirable pafreys," he shows us Martin before the King trying to entice Henry to back him. But even the King was beginning to tire of endless taxation, and Martin left without the protection he wanted. That was at first, but Henry later gave way and " protected him against all parties, perhaps from hope of remuneration, therefore the state of England became most wretched." But England had stood enough. With triumph and joy Matthew tells of the end of Martin, of how Fulk Fitz-Warin strode into Martin's chamber and said, eyeing him with a scowl, " Go and leave England at once." When Martin asked who was Fulk's authority, Fulk threatened to cut him into pieces and left the chamber shouting " terrible oaths, and Martin, breathless with alarm," rushed to the King. The King could do nothing, and when Martin asked for a safe-conduct, Henry, who was very excited and angry, cried, " The devil take you and give you a conduct through hell ! " His friends soothed his rage, and at last he agreed to see that Martin was escorted safely to the coast ; Martin rushed off at once, crouching amongst his guards, trembling in awful terror whenever a mounted man drew near.

For a short while after Martin's departure, Henry put up a feeble resistance to Rome, but gradually it dwindled. Nothing ever troubled him except the present ; the past was gone and the future would solve itself. He lived, like his father, in a mist of optimism, but he had not his father's strength to meet danger when it came nor his father's skill in battle. He now hid in his palace, afraid to show himself because his creditors were so many and so vehement, yet he could not curb his extravagance, he could not resist flinging away money on luxurious pomp or giving it to worthless friends and relatives. His mother died in 1246, and her five children, four sons and one daughter, rushed to England to live on their royal half-brother : more foreigners in the country—there had been Poitevins, Provençals, Savoyards, and now further Poitevins. Henry gave what honours he could to the four men, and he married the girl to the young Earl of Warenne. William of Valence was the worst of the brothers : Henry gave him a wealthy heiress and later created him Earl of Pembroke.

In an effort to live splendidly and to maintain these needy relatives, Henry sold his plate and jewels and every grant and privilege on which it was possible to raise money ; he called for New Year gifts from the Londoners and actually extorted some cash on the excuse of another war with France. From his council he could squeeze nothing and was reduced almost to begging from individual magnates and bishops, while his unfortunate servants took to highway robbery as the only method of getting paid. He pressed heavily wherever he could, straining every statute to extract money out of it, enforcing in all their severity the forest-laws, the laws against encroachments on royal preserves and the chasing of royal beasts. These tricks were not enough ; there was a leak, and a large one, in Henry's coffers—whatever went in went out again almost with the same gesture. Frantically he schemed, seeking new ways of getting cash, when all he had to do to raise money was to surrender his absurd pretentions to divine kingship ; if he had accepted John's charter and agreed to a council of English barons money would have been quickly found. But he was unable to surrender one shred of royalty ; better, he felt, to starve in a palace than to be a well-fed prisoner with a crown. Grimly the barons watched, noting each rush of the trapped animal towards the money he could not steal, each scream of outraged fury because England could sweat no more gold when he stamped upon it. Then Henry grew cunning, he recalled how Louis of France had been offered gigantic sums when he set out on the crusade in which he was still absent ; Henry decided that he, too, would turn crusader, and demanded that the English Church give him a tithe of its rents and movables for the next three years as the French Church had done for Louis. But Henry was no Louis, and England knew it ; Grosseteste advised the Church to refuse unless Henry swore to a confirmation of the charters and promised faithfully to spend the money on crusading. Henry, of course, would do neither, and he remained as poverty-stricken as before.

SIMON DE MONTFORT had returned from the crusade. So well had he acted in the Holy Land that the barons, knights and citizens of Jerusalem wrote to Emperor Frederick asking for his appointment as governor in Palestine during the minority of young King Conrad. We do know what answer Frederick gave, but he already knew Simon personally and—being of so brilliant a mind himself—he must have recognised the other's genius and perhaps for that reason would refuse the appointment. At any rate, it is unlikely that Simon would have accepted, but the offer shows that already men recognised in him a leader and a soldier. His genius, however, was only realised abroad ; in England he remained of little importance, scarcely ever at court, a country baron tending his estates and living mostly at Kenilworth with Eleanor his wife while their sons grew from sprawling babyhood to youth, and then were passed into the care of Simon's great friend, the superb old scholar, Robert Grosseteste, Bishop of Lincoln. Probably many of the ideas that Simon later tried to put into action were learned from Grosseteste, who was a teacher of the Franciscans at Oxford. At this stage, soon after their inception and when they were first introduced into England, the Franciscans were a truly noble order and struggled sincerely to carry forward the message of their founder. They believed in poverty and the true Christian virtues, and as yet corruption had not stolen into them ; they went amongst the people, amongst starving wretches shivering in their hovels with the cattle, amongst lepers with their melancholy clappers warning the healthy that living death approached, amongst those who had no hope, who had no money with which to buy services of the Church, who were doomed to unending hell because they could have no masses to waft them through purgatory to paradise ; amongst these walked the friars, cheerfully and bravely, and they taught a new lesson of hope that the world, exhausted by an avaricious Church and gradually losing its beliefs, needed most tragically.

The teachings of the great St. Francis, brought to him by Grosseteste, must have affected Simon very deeply. Until now he had been a man of little importance, a mere adventurer living on the risky hazard of a King's affection ; these talks with the courageous quick-tempered scholar of Oxford could not have failed to mould his character towards a definite purpose, and he must have gazed with horror and disgust at the simony-rotten Church and tyrannous court, and felt within him mighty ambitions gradually stir to life. Soon he was called to action, but not to the action that was to make his name a symbol of freedom for centuries. Henry commanded him to go to

Gascony. Since the fiasco of Henry's invasion there had been peace on the Continent, England and France having signed a five years' truce. Those five years were now over, and the English power in Gascony scarcely existed ; Simon was sent to restore order. He agreed on condition that for seven years he be given an entirely free hand and control of all the Gascon revenues. This was agreed to.

WITHIN a few months Simon had reduced the rebels to submission and was thanked by King and council, but soon rebellion rose again and he struck mercilessly at those he could not conciliate. Before long, Gascony was at peace and he was ringing it with royal castles when his enemies pounced. The furious Gascon lords, finding that their system of tyranny could not continue under Simon's strong rule, rushed to Henry with complaints about " vexations, spoilings, frauds, and oppressions, continuing in this manner to push their evil with the most shameless madness, both secretly and in public." Henry's waxen heart could be impressed most quickly with terrors and hatred, and he suddenly turned on Simon, abusing him " before many great people with immoderate shoutings."

Simon actually stood his trial, and although it was proved that he had behaved with extreme severity, he cannot be blamed for it ; Gascony, after all, was a rebellious fief, and rebels must be taught their lessons harshly. He had also exceeded the forms of law, being an impatient man who always judged swiftly—even in England, when administering his estate, Grosseteste had once rebuked him for this, pleading with him to be " a pattern of mercy and forgiveness rather than a master of cruelty "—and in Gascony, although his law was just it was too often informally given. Simon was acquitted, but Henry would not return him the money he had spent—there was no obligation to traitors, he said ; and the earl retorted that he lied in calling him a traitor, and added : " Were you not shielded by the dignity of the royal name, it would be an ill hour for you when you said such things. Do you call yourself a Christian ? Who would believe you to be one ? " Henry lost his temper, Simon lost his, and only the intervention of friends closed the uproar. Simon went back to Gascony to complete his term of seven years.

The Gascons were waiting for him, believing that Henry was on their side, but Simon was eager to clear his name, to shame the King and to "avenge his defamation." His term was almost over, and he wished to end his rule with one great feat that would prove him no traitor and would humble his enemies. He beat the rebels so thoroughly that he captured five of their leaders and sent them to Henry, then all was wrenched from him. He was told to cease fighting and to surrender his command, as the King's eldest son, the Lord Edward,[1] was to take his place. This blow, coming in the midst of his triumph, was almost too much for Simon : he expostulated, but was granted no favours save the repayment of his expenses and a gift of 7000 marks. In rage he turned from England and entered France, the country was at the moment leaderless—its King away crusading and his mother just dead—and Simon was offered the highest possible honour, the barons wishing to make him their seneschal and regent, but he refused. Although by birth a Frenchman, he had grown to love England and to dream with Grosseteste of cleansing its wounds, of cutting out the canker of a tyrannical court, and of severing its Church from the poison of Rome's exactions. Inactive, he remained in France until Henry, who had himself visited Gascony, called for his return when he saw the truth and realised how maligned the earl had been. Honours might be found in France, honours he could never hope to get from so fickle and jealous a King as Henry, yet when the call came, Simon had his horses saddled and he rode away from the land of his birth as if drawn towards the splendid destiny that was to bring to him only despair and death but to England a glorious future.

WHILE the King stayed in Gascony, England was ruled by Queen Eleanor and Richard. They did their best to entice money from the barons, and it is now that for the first time we see Simon as the defender of liberty. He rose in council and attacked a proposed subsidy that was to be raised to carry on a useless war, and the subsidy was not voted. When Henry came hurrying back, he found he could do no better than his regents. They had pleaded with the barons that Alfonso X of Castile was preparing to attack Gascony, but that argument

---

[1] It is difficult to know what to call Edward. The word Prince in its modern sense was not used until hundreds of years later, and the old English Ætheling had disappeared from the language. Men of his own time called him "the Lord Edward," or more fully, "the Lord Edward, the firstborn son of the King." I have thought it safest to follow them in this.

was no longer of any use as Henry had betrothed his son Edward
to Alfonso's half-sister Eleanor, giving him as a marriage-portion
everything he possessed except England—Gascony, the Channel
Isles, Chester, Wales, and Ireland. And in this passion of
giving things away, he accepted Sicily from the Pope for his
second son, Edmund Crouchback, a boy of nine. Rome had
for long been trying to find a prince stupid enough to accept
Sicily, because it entailed having to fight the Hohenstauffen
who owned the island and Henry, with his usual reckless optimism
promised to send an army and to pay £90,000 towards the
expenses of the war. He then asked the great council to give
him the money while the papal nuncio Rustand tackled the
clergy ; both council and Church refused, they had sweated
gold enough for the King's mad schemes, and for two years
Henry danced in an agony of rage and humiliation, bounding
from terror of the barons to terror of the Pope, afraid to push
too hard for the money, afraid to confess that he could not
fight the Hohenstauffen. But the barons were firm ; they
would not produce a penny with which to steal Sicily, and at
last the King had to crumple up and agree to send commissioners
to Rome to rescue him from his promise. Simon and Peter of
Savoy were two of the commissioners chosen, but at the last
moment Henry's optimism rescued him from shame ; he thought
that with Rome to back him he could yet wring some money
from the land, and decided to keep his hold on Sicily. The
papal court, still furious at the memory of the luxurious paganism
and culture of Frederick II, was determined that the whole
line of Hohenstauffen should be dragged, not only from Sicily,
but from every possession. It arranged that at the election to
the throne of Emperor, the votes should be cast for Richard,
who therefore left England in 1257 to accept his uneasy crown.

In 1256, the Welsh rose again, the petty princes being bound to
some semblance of unity by Llewelyn II, grandson of Llewelyn
the Great, and Scotland sealed a treaty with him ; Henry and
his son Edward rode to the marches as if to war, but turned back
suddenly without a blow being struck. This was the final
humiliation for England, its King was not only an avaricious fool,
he was also a weakling. When the great council met on April 28,
1258, the barons were determined to take action, to see that the
foreigners were sent packing from England. On to the foreigners
they threw all the blame, for it was difficult to attack the King

directly ; they could only hope that by ridding him of his bad advisers they might put good advisers in their places. Simon was at the council, as determined as any of the others to make a firm stand. His old friend, Grosseteste, was dead, and undoubtedly Grosseteste had kept a gentle restraining hand upon Simon's impatient idealism. Now that he stood alone, a leader without an army or a comrade, Simon's temper continually broke his control. There was a quarrel at this council. William of Valence, most hated of the aliens, finding that the English were banded strongly against his party, turned on them when the King hinted that he should help pay for the Welsh war ; he cried that the war was lost by English treachery, that the barons were in league with Llewelyn, and at last definitely he called Simon " a traitor of old standing." Simon would have grappled with him at once, " for anger is a brief madness," if he had not been held back. Despite this inauspicious opening and the barons' jeers at the Welsh fiasco, Henry had to ask for money. The barons agreed to grant a subsidy on condition that he expelled the foreigners from court, and that he appointed a committee, half from his own party and half from the barons, to govern and reform the kingdom and to control the exchequer. Leaving their swords outside but dressed in full mail, the barons gave this answer to the King. When he saw them enter dressed as if for battle, Henry shrank aside, wailing, " Am I your prisoner ? " but on being reassured, he agreed at once to anything they asked, and the committee was appointed, twelve—including Simon— being chosen from the barons, twelve from the King's party.

The barons had no intention of creating good laws, they only wanted to redress bad ones. All they wished was to surround the King with advisers of their own party who would see that their feudal rights were not interfered with. Complete power was to be given to a council and a parliament—the word was not used in the modern sense in any way whatever, it was borrowed from the French *parlement*, and here it meant twelve barons who were to represent their party to save the enormous cost of all the barons attending court. The council consisted of fifteen members, chosen from court and baronial parties, who were to control the administration of the country. These agreements, called the Provisions of Oxford, were as feudal as the Great Charter ; we find in them no hint that the people, or even the Church, were to gain—all power was to fall to the barons. Simon, it is said, agreed to them with the utmost reluctance, for they by no means embodied his ideals ; they were purely a reaction to feudalism, a monopoly of power as dangerous as unbridled kingship ; all that Simon could do was to force the barons to consult London, beyond that they would not go. Nevertheless, they put up a feeble pretence of being on the side of the commons ; they introduced clauses into the provisions guaranteeing good sheriffs, bailiffs and escheators, and they swore to give their tenants rights equal to those that the King had given. Magna Carta was sent to every shire-court to be preserved in the records, and as the copies were made in English it was read publicly at each of these courts.

Henry and Edward swore to the provisions, but the King's half-brothers, naturally, " scorned to take the oath," and were told that whoever refused would be considered an enemy. Realising that in war rested their one hope, they raced secretly to Winchester, but were pursued and taken and were forced to promise to leave the kingdom.

THE barons had complete power, the cabal of the aliens was smashed and both Henry and Edward had given in, yet the council could not agree together. Each man considered the restrictions valuable for his neighbour but not intended for himself. Richard de Clare, Earl of Gloucester, was the first to show defiance ; he refused to let royal officers interfere with the working of his estates, and Simon attacked him in the parliament of February–March, 1259, saying : " I do not want to live or talk with men as fickle and false as you. For we have made promise and oath together about these matters. And as for you, my lord Earl of Gloucester, the more you excel all men in rank, the more are you bound to keep good statutes." As Gloucester still remained defiant, Simon in disgust threw aside the cause and left for France, but the barons, finding themselves without their strongest member, threatened Gloucester that they would unite against him if he did not give in. Sullenly Gloucester gave in, and Simon returned.

With Grosseteste dead, Simon must have been a lonely man, for he could not help but realise that his ideals were different from the barons'. The King detested him. It was in July 1258, the month with its " scorching dog-star whose deadly barking commonly disturbs the atmosphere," when Henry decided to eat in the open, and was therefore rowed in his barge down the Thames from Westminster. Suddenly came thunder and lightning. The King was terrified of thunderstorms, and he commanded the rowers to land him anywhere at once ; the nearest steps were at the palace of the Bishop of Durham where Simon was then lodged. As the King rushed inside from the lightning, Simon greeted him courteously, saying, " What are you frightened of? The storm has passed." Not in jest, but seriously, Henry answered : " The thunder and lightning I fear beyond measure, but by the head of God, I fear you more than all the thunder and lightning in the world ! " " My lord," answered Simon quietly, " it is unjust and unbelievable that you should fear me, your true friend, who is ever faithful to you and yours and to the kingdom of England. It is your enemies, your destroyers, the lying flatterers whom you should fear."

The King might be direct in his hatred, but the King's son Edward was subtle. He realised that to resist further was to fail. The only method of defeating the barons was to lull them by pretence of acquiescence, to learn their plans, to bribe the disgruntled, then to strike when they were divided and unready. He made friends with Simon who welcomed him eagerly to the cause, although Edward had been the most flagrant of the court offenders, outstripping even the foreigners in his insolence and contempt for law. But Simon was only too delighted to find some one on to whose shoulders he could slip the responsibility of government, and there could have been no fitter person than the young lord, the King's eldest son. We can only be astonished at Simon's credulity, but it is the credulity of a man so entirely noble that he preferred to trust rather than to mistrust. Edward's reputation was of the worst, and the future of England under his rule seemed hopeless ; he led a band of noble rascals about the country, despoiling what he could, robbing and maiming at his will. He was exactly the type of lord to whom Simon was most strongly opposed, yet now, at the first hint of reformation, he welcomed him with joy. The handsome young man played his part well, then he spurred on the bachelors of England to appear at court with a list of grievances. It is doubtful whom these bachelors really represented, but they were apparently the lesser knights speaking on behalf of all free men. Before the King they complained that although he might have given power to the barons they did nothing but abuse it and took no heed of others' rights. Edward supported them in their complaint and asked an answer from the council, and a second list of reforms was then drawn up—the Provisions of Westminster. These

swept from the baronial courts half their revenue, enacting that
tenants—unless expressly sworn to do so by the terms of their
enfeoffment—could not be made to attend the feudal courts,
and that appeals should always go before royal justices. The
feudal courts were killed from that moment.

Edward kept so secretly at work that he deceived his own
father. Henry had been in France negotiating a treaty by which
he surrendered nearly all his continental claims in return for
money, and when he was about to return to England news
reached him that his son was about to rebel. So terrified was he
at these tidings that he dared not leave France, and only his
brother Richard, now King of the Romans, could calm his fears
enough to induce him to cross the Channel. On reaching
London he refused to see Edward, who was lodging with Simon
outside the walls. He pleaded that he dared not meet him. " Do
not let my son come before me," he cried, " for if I see him I
shall not be able to stop myself from kissing him." Within a
fortnight father and son were friends again, but only after Henry
—his suspicions sharpened by the lies of Gloucester—had locked
himself into the Tower and called upon the citizens of London
to arm in his defence. Edward was now exposed ; by confessing
the truth to his father, he had shown also the truth to Simon and
the barons.

HENRY had sent to the Pope for absolution from his oath to the
provisions, and when this arrived, he deposed the ministers
foisted on him at Oxford and appointed others on May 2, 1262 ;
and on August 16 he issued a proclamation stating that to choose
officials and ministers was a right inherent in royal power. After
that, England was split into two, having two rulers and two sets
of officers ; particularly amongst the sheriffs was there trouble,
and the people stood by the baronial ones—the guardians of the
peace, as they were called. The council summoned the knights-
of-the-shires to meet at St. Albans ; Henry counter-summoned
them to meet at Windsor. Before this determined front the barons
began to lose courage, and although Simon remonstrated, they
agreed to revise the Provisions of Oxford ; almost at the same
moment Gloucester ceased shifting from side to side, and flung
down his gauntlet on behalf of Henry. In this muddle of
frightened barons and traitors, Simon stood alone, unable to
direct because the people did not wish to be directed. Wearily
he left the country and journeyed to France, and with their

leader gone, the barons discovered that they were helpless.

Then Gloucester died, and with that ambitious traitor out of the way, Simon thought he might be able to build once more. He returned to England while the King was in France and tested the feelings of the barons, only to realise that they were too cowardly to be open ; but, at last, sheer self-defence made them call for Simon to direct them, and he accepted the post with joy. The King's brother Richard was on his side with Gloucester's young son, and they had gathered a mighty army. It was the time for action. Too long had Simon negotiated, trying by words to force the King to realise his responsibilities ; now he would show the strength of his followers. It was decided to treat as public enemies all who opposed the provisions, and Simon led his troops over the Welsh marches, he destroyed the lands of his enemies, he seized the estates of aliens and gave them to his comrades. Henry was back in England and he hid in the Tower with his Queen, unable to stem the torrent of armed troops riding over the land. London particularly was on the barons' side ; the wealthy burghers were naturally royalists, but the commons were staunch for Simon. Isolated from the city yet dangerously close, Henry watched from the Tower battlements and saw the gathering of the enemy. He thought to rescue Eleanor from this perilous situation, to send her to Edward at Windsor, and she was rowed down the Thames. Henry might be pitied as a weak, extravagant and avaricious fool, but the headstrong Eleanor was loathed as chief of the aliens. When her barge tried to pass under London Bridge the people yelled at her and threw down stones and muck, and she was only rescued from their hatred by the mayor.

Simon was approaching London. Richard, who seemed to veer day by day from party to party, tried to negotiate but Simon would not listen. Now that the King was cornered and the country seemed prepared to follow him, it would have been weakness to seal a treaty and thereby give time for the enemy to gather and his own troops to disperse. As Simon drew near the city, Henry surrendered utterly. He agreed to any terms, he offered all castles to the barons, he promised to banish all aliens that remained and to keep the provisions in every word.

Now that terms were sworn to by both sides and enthusiasm had slowly burned itself away, the inevitable reaction drew supporters from Simon. Edward, the cunning handsome lord, was always present to suggest, to hint, to lie. He did not attempt to conceal his attitude ; from the first he was strong against the treaty, and while Simon had marched on London he had been at Windsor trying to collect an army, having stolen the King's treasury at the Temple. Now he refused to stand by the treaty, and gradually by promises and bribes drew men from Simon, until at last the earl found that he was almost at Henry's mercy and was made to agree to abide by the arbitration of Louis IX of France. Louis's decision was foregone, he stood, of course, by Henry ; while the question was being discussed in Amiens, Simon started to re-gather his scattered troops, knowing exactly what would be the verdict. He did not trouble to explain why he broke his word in not abiding by Louis's decision ; there had been broken words enough not to need explaining any further lost oaths. Henry had rejected the provisions after solemnly agreeing to them, Simon now rejected the Mise of Amiens. But many of his barons felt that right had left them, that they had become definitely rebels, and gradually his troops thinned. " I have been in many lands," said Simon, " and nowhere have I found men so faithless as in England. But even though all forsake me, I and my four sons will stand by the just cause."

The barons might turn away, but the cities of England knew that they could trust the earl ; in him they saw their champion, a rebel who did not rebel for gain or for his own sake, but for freedom for all. An army came to him, an army of untrained citizens, without leaders or men fledged in war, but they were enthusiastic and loyal and brave. London led them, the chief city in the realm, but other great cities despatched their troops, and Simon found that he had a vast if unorganised mob behind him. He did not strike at once ; he waited while he tried to bring these raw troops to discipline and to gather further reinforcements, and at the same time he negotiated, being perhaps a little wary of deciding all on one battle when his men were unskilled. He offered to stop the offensive if Henry would rid himself of the aliens ; Henry refused and sent his troops to Northampton where the earl's son, young Simon, was captured ; the earl was on his way to the rescue and had reached St. Albans from London when the news came, then realising that it was useless to continue, he drew back. Enraged at the disaster, his followers vented their spite upon the London Jews,

Jews being under royal protection ; " they inhumanly killed old men with those yet older, the suckling with the aged, lads at play and babes not weaned, nearly four hundred Jews of both sexes and of all ranks being murdered." Some bought their lives and others escaped by undergoing baptism. It is a dark stain on Simon's career, but it must be remembered that he was the pious son of a fierce killer of heretics.

He marched to Rochester, and while in the midst of the siege, when the city was almost taken, news reached him that the royalists were descending on London. Simon darted to the rescue only to find that it was a false alarm, the royalists were actually making for Tunbridge, which they took, and were preparing to capture a fleet at the Cinque Ports. In this they failed. At news of the army's approach, the sailors put out to sea and stayed there until the royalists left. Simon was determined to stake everything on a battle. His brave impatient temper could not bear this indecision, this medieval hole-in-corner warfare. He chased the King as far as Lewes and caught up with him on May 12, pitching his camp about nine miles north of the town in the village of Fletching. Next day was wasted in negotiations that came to nothing, and on the night of May 13 Simon knew that battle was unavoidable. He did not sleep, he prayed and called upon his men to confess their sins, while the Bishop of Worcester " absolved them all." Then they sewed white crosses on their armour and shirts, for the white cross was always the badge of the English crusader ; besides, it was grimly necessary on this day, when families were divided and fighting against each other, in the press it would be impossible to know your friend unless he bore some mark. Before dawn, the whole army had set out on the march to Lewes, and so badly kept was Henry's watch that Simon had almost reached the town before his advance was even noticed. He was now on a height and stopped to dispose his troops in battle array. The standard and baggage were left in charge of a small guard with his personal carriage, and himself took command of the reserves so that he could direct the battle and choose the vantage moment for attack ; his sons, Guy and Henry, commanded the right wing, Gilbert de Clare, the young Earl of Gloucester, the centre, and the Londoners were placed on the left. Before giving the final command, Simon spoke a few words. " O, my beloved comrades and followers," he cried, " we are about to fight for the government of England and to

19

keep our faith. Let us implore the Lord of all that if it be His
pleasure He will grant us strength and help so that we might
show grateful service by our knightly belt, overcoming the malice
of all enemies." The men lay on the ground, stretching out
their arms to make a cross, and cried, " Lord, give us victory in
Your name."

Meanwhile the royalists were pouring from the town and
were forming into the usual three divisions : Edward had the
right wing facing the Londoners and was slightly ahead of the
rest of the army, the King held the centre almost as reserves,
and Richard commanded the left wing. Around Henry gathered
the more important nobles and above him was unfurled the
royal standard. Then the trumpets screamed and Edward led
the charge. He was determined to revenge himself upon the
Londoners who had insulted his mother ; generalship was
forgotten in this fury when he charged blindly forward, he
" thirsted after their blood as the hart pants for cool streams."
In his fury he did not pause, he thrashed the Londoners, he chased
them far from the battlefield, pursuing them in his madness for
four miles, and then was lured in the wrong direction by Simon's
standard on the hill, thinking to capture the earl. While Edward
charged impetuously away, Simon remained calm, swinging his
men to concentrate upon the left which was held by Richard, King
of the Romans. " Now flashed the lightning courage of the
barons fighting for their country with breathless zeal." The left
broke before them and Richard fled to a nearby mill ; Simon
then swept down with all his force on Henry, on to that dragon-
standard with its sapphire eyes. Henry fought well, he proved
himself no coward when facing a foe in battle ; his horse tumbled
down, hamstrung by Gloucester, and he was forced to take
sanctuary in a priory.

" Oh, miserable sight ! " cried a chronicler, " when the son
tries to conquer his father and the father the son : kinsman
against kinsman, fellow-citizen against fellow-citizen, with their
swords lifted on either side, drunk with the blood of the dead,
felling, maiming, trampling their foes under their horses' hoofs
or binding them alive in tightest bonds."

Richard was caught in his windmill. The barons shouted,
" Come down, come down, you wretched miller. Come out,
unlucky master of the mill, come out ! " The royalists' one hope
was Edward. He galloped back, deceived by Simon's carriage
and standard, then found the battle over and was forced to

withdraw to Lewes Castle. From here, when he saw the barons spreading about the priory in which his father was hidden, he wished to sally to the rescue, but it would have been a hopeless attempt. By his own recklessness he had already lost the battle, too late now he learned caution.

That night a treaty was concluded—the Mise of Lewes, it was called—between Simon and the King.

WE do not know the details of the Mise of Lewes, it has come to us only in summaries, which is a great pity, for it is the most important of all the treaties sealed in the conflict. It would have given us the exact intentions of Simon, we would have known completely what were his ambitions. As it is, we have the broad outline, and his demands appear to have been by no means sweeping. He wanted the Provisions of Oxford revived and expanded ; the council he demanded was to consist only of Englishmen chosen by a board of arbitrators, it was to manage the King's expenses until his debts were paid, and was to guide him in his choice of officers and administration of justice ; also, the charters were to be kept in every word. The difficulty here of course lay in choosing the board of arbitrators. Two suggestions were put forward : first, a committee might be formed composed of the Archbishop of Rouen, Hugh the Despenser, the Bishop of London, and one of the chief ministers of Louis IX. If the four could not agree on any question, a casting vote would be given by the legate, Guy Foulquois. Simon's mistake was to bring the legate into the question, he evidently did not know—as the royalists knew— that Foulquois was strongly anti-baronial. When he learned this, he hurriedly altered his plan and forbade the legate entering England. The second alternative was then discussed, that of forming a committee of French nobles, but Simon knew that the French were on the side of the King. Again and again he postponed his final decision, being unable to discover a perfect medium which could control Henry, and which he in his turn could control. A new committee was at last decided on, formed of two English and two French nobles with the Archbishop of Rouen—a safe neutral—to give the casting-vote.

While these arguments went forward, Simon was working on a fresh idea which he produced before the parliament on June 22, 1264. This was "A Form for the Government of the King and Kingdom," and it suggested that three men should be chosen who in their turn should nominate the royal council of nine members. Without this council's agreement the King was to do nothing and it could act in his absence on a two-thirds majority. The King could choose his ministers only on the council's approval. All councillors must be born Englishman. This scheme was approved, and Simon with his friend the Bishop of Chichester and his young follower the Earl of Gloucester was appointed to the chief power, to the committee of three above the royal council.

Now that success was his, with the King and the Lord Edward in his hands, Simon became a complete dictator. He scarcely bothered to ask his colleagues' opinions ; being so certain of his own nobility and of the justness of his aims, he hurried measures through on his personal responsibility. Many of the royalists were still defiant and had to be smoked out of their castles, while the north and the Welsh marches were in a state of anarchy where every baron snatched what he could and barricaded himself behind his walls at the first scent of danger. And there was the continual threat of invasion. Queen Eleanor was in France with the King's foreign brothers, and with the help of Louis mercenaries were being bought. Simon prepared to meet them. The Cinque Ports had always been his firm allies, and now he gave the barons permission to detain all foreign vessels entering or leaving English ports. This was the kind of order that those trained pirates, the English sailors, loved, they threw themselves into it with gusto, grabbing not only foreign but even native ships in their zeal. The crews they pushed overboard and the cargoes they stole, with the result that the prices of imported goods leaped to such a height that they were almost unobtainable. When the people objected to this, Simon retorted that the country should be self-supporting and refused to relax his vigilance. Soon fear of invasion passed ; the Queen did not have money enough with which to pay her mercenaries, and the troops deserted.

With the passing of this danger, another took its place. Simon was impatient and arrogant, he wished to grip all the power, and his sons lacked the nobility of their father. They were rowdy grasping scoundrels, and Simon cannot be rescued from the accusation of giving them and himself nearly all the revenues of the crown, appropriating confiscated lands, wardships, marriages, castles and ransoms. We might perhaps excuse Simon himself, he was administering these things, and naturally kept them under his control ; that, however, does not acquit him of showering them upon his sons. It was stupid as well as dishonest, for it infuriated his friends, and soon the Earl of Gloucester openly accused him of peculation. The young earl was not acting under any noble motive, he was furious because he had been kept away from the good things. The quarrel began over a petty matter. Gloucester and Simon's sons had proclaimed a tournament, which was not only a sin against the Church but was illegal according to the laws of England. Simon forbade it and threatened that " if they did not obey his orders he would put them in such a place that they should no longer enjoy the light of sun or moon." Scarcely had Gloucester recovered from his indignation at this insult before Simon refused to deliver up his prisoner, Richard, King of the Romans, and certain other important men captured at Lewes. The taking of prisoners was one of the vital points in medieval warfare, and many a knight supported himself on ransoms obtained from captives ; this is one of the reasons for the small death-roll of knights ; when a man alive was worth a goodly sum of money, it was sheer waste to kill him. Richard, being the King's brother, would be a most valuable prize, and Simon's refusal to part with him infuriated young Gloucester : from that moment the two, once friends and allies, became enemies. Gloucester was determined to hold the banned tournament, and Simon marched out with troops to see that he was obeyed ; Gloucester was warned in time, he fled to his estates on the marches where shortly he was raising the standard of revolt.

Meanwhile, on January 20, 1265, parliament met. This is the first hint we have of a parliament even remotely resembling our modern one, for to it were summoned " all the bishops, abbots, priors, earls, and barons of the whole realm, and many from the Cinque Ports, and from every city and borough four men." It is true that Simon wanted this parliament packed and therefore drew from among those classes on which he knew he could rely, hoping to form a strong opposition to the royalist magnates, nevertheless he must be given every honour—an honour often placed wholly to the credit of Edward I—for being the creator of our modern conception of a parliament where commons and nobles join to administer the laws of the realm. Once this privilege had been granted the towns, once this precedent had been created, it would have been difficult to leap back to the old baronial monopoly of power. Whether Simon intended this parliament as a precedent does not matter ; it became a precedent, one of the greatest steps of progress of the century.

Taking the King and the Lord Edward with him so that he could keep them securely under his eye, Simon rode to Gloucester to bring the young earl to reason. He entered the city without a fight, and negotiations were opened. There was something very childlike in Simon's nature, with the naive honesty of a just man, he was always prepared to take an opponent at his word, to accept an enemy as friend without question. He now drew to the west of the Severn, cutting himself off from England, and quietly set about quelling a few of the more rebellious lords marcher, thereby leaving Gloucester free for any treachery.

Then Edward escaped by the simplest trick. He was at Hereford in the care of Gloucester's brother, Thomas, and naturally the two plotted together. One day with Thomas and some knights, Edward rode outside the city for exercise and under the pretence of testing their speed, he rode each horse in the party until he had discovered the fleetest. Then he dug his spurs into its flanks and was off beyond hope of recapture. Shortly afterwards he was with young Gloucester and swore that if his father were restored he would keep to the old customs of the realm and would expel all aliens. With the King's son to lead it, the rebellion took definite shape, and Simon found that he was trapped, cut off from England. Somehow he had to cross the Severn and he thought to pass by the Bristol Channel, Edward however was prepared for just such a move. While Simon waited at Newport he saw his expected transports in the harbour either sunk or captured by the royalists. As he trooped back to Hereford, Edward closed in behind him, ringing him in gradually, not pouncing but waiting until his prey was truly cornered. Simon also waited, he stayed in Hereford while Edward camped at Worcester ; neither side wished to take the offensive : Edward knew the quality of his opponent and, remembering how himself had failed at Lewes, he did not dare fight openly with the crafty earl. Simon was outnumbered, but he was hoping for reinforcements from his son, young Simon, who was bringing the Londoners to his aid. Young Simon did not have his father's genius, he kept poor guard at Kenilworth. It was a hot August night and his men undressed ready for a swim in the morning ; naked they lay in Kenilworth while a woman called Margot slipped on man's hose and stole from the town to warn Edward, thirty miles away. The naked troops could not defend themselves and were slaughtered easily : young Simon managed to barricade himself with a few knights in the castle.

Edward had moved quickly and had acted with cunning, but he had left the path to England open for Simon. Simon hurried to use it, crossing the Severn four miles below Worcester, at Kempsey, so that when Edward returned from his raid he discovered that the enemy was already on the way to Kenilworth. He moved quickly and by daybreak had reached Evesham where Simon had camped the night.

It is difficult to understand why Simon had chosen Evesham. In every possible way it was the worst ground for a battle, and he must have underrated Edward. Otherwise so clever a soldier would have moved forward and not have let himself be trapped hopelessly, for on three sides Evesham was bounded by the Avon, and there was only one bridge across the river. Evidently he thought his enemies were still at Worcester and that young Simon would be prepared to join forces with him at any moment, for when, after mass on Tuesday, August 4, 1265, Edward's army was seen approaching with young Simon's banners displayed, the earl was certain that it was his son. Then when the truth was known it was too late for him to escape ; he was outnumbered and trapped with the river around him and with a great army ahead. " By the arm of St. James," he cried bitterly, " they come on well, but it is from me that they learned that order." He watched the enemy approach, no longer headlong and reckless—Edward had learned his lesson—but orderly and in soldier-like formation. There was not the slightest hope of breaking through. " May the Lord have mercy on our souls," said Simon, " for our bodies are theirs." His son Henry told his father to keep heart, and Simon turned sadly to him. " I do not despair," he said, " but it is your presumption and the pride of your brothers that have brought me to this pass. Now, I believe, I shall die for God and the just cause."

To die. . . . There was no other end. Trapped, he sat his horse and watched the horde swelling before him through the valleys. He had fought for liberty and was prepared to die for it : he faced young Edward, and neither knew the debt he owed the other—Simon because through Edward would be carried out his ideas and ambitions, and Edward because he had learned the secret of government from Simon. When Edward's army came through the hills, Simon had cried that Edward had learned the art of war from him : Edward had learned far greater things than the art of war. Uncle and nephew, they faced each other at Evesham, enemies for the moment, yet in truth they were brothers, brothers in ambition. Simon was prepared to die, and he could have died with a good heart had he but known it : his destroyer was the creator of his dream, of the government of England hand-in-hand with the people.

Simon led the charge. Up the hill to Wye he rode, leading his small force, a handful against that sea of steel, against that un-breakable living wall which held him from freedom. He had five thousand Welsh, but they did not follow the doomed army, they fled while the courageous little force galloped at the gigantic enemy. Simon cried that his friends might leave him if they wished, that it was his doom that was upon them and not theirs, but not one follower left. They rode to die with their leader.

His friend fell around him. Man after man was struck to the ground as the enemy pressed forward and closed about them, tightening the steel and deadly girdle of soldiers. " Never will I surrender to dogs and liars, but to God alone ! " cried Simon. His horse was on the ground, and, badly wounded though he was, he kept his feet and swung his great two-handed sword. If there had been only eight others like him, cried one who watched, the enemy would have been shamed for ever. He held them off, one man against thousands with only that red two-handed sword in both his fists. They could not reach him for a final blow, they could not creep under that sword, they lunged and sprang out of reach while panting and triumphant alone Simon held them at bay. Then one crept behind him and stabbed him in the back, and all the others closed in to slash at him whom they had feared as death a moment since.

In their blind hatred of the earl, the royalists almost killed King Henry as well. He wailed as they surged about him, " I am Henry of Windsor, I am your King, for God's love strike me not, I am too old to fight." The Lord Edward saw him and sent him from the field.

A thunderstorm had risen during the short battle—it had lasted only three hours—and men noticed with wonder that at the moment when Simon fell there was nearly full darkness over the earth. They did not spare the dead earl, no more than they had spared the living ; they tore the hair-shirt from his nakedness—for like a saint he had lived, in continual penance —and they carved the hands and feet and legs and head from " the old man " ; and afterwards the monks of Evesham piously gathered what remains they could and, wrapping them in an old cloth, buried them in their abbey. It was not long before the people of England were trooping to that abbey to pray beside a martyred saint.

" As the news of his death ran through the land there was a stopping of laughter, and a universal lamentation arose until later the sighs changed to hymns of praise and joy because of the numerous miracles said to have been caused by his unconquerable inflexibility and patience and purity of faith, and thereby was hope aroused of escaping from the oppression of the wicked." The people of England prayed at the tomb of Simon de Montfort ; they did not need the church to canonise him, he was the people's saint, their defender who had died in their cause. Many are the miracles that have come down to us, said to have been worked at his tomb. We may scoff like the modern catholic, or smile like the modern sceptic, but whether these miracles really occurred does not trouble us. They were worked at the tomb of every saint, and one grows tired of reading about miracles in the annals of the Middle Ages ; but what interests us and touches us is this revelation of a country's faith in a true martyr. They might hack the body to pieces, they might damn the man in records, yet they could not pluck him from the hearts of the people. Their sighs, their tears and prayers were a requiem he would have treasured and which in truth he deserved.

WITH the death of Simon, the reign of Henry III virtually ends. The King was old and incapable and the Lord Edward plucked the reins of England from his feeble hands and took control. Soon there was peace on all sides, for he was clever enough not to press his victory. When possible he accepted the submission of the rebels. London gave in, and after a brief struggle, the Cinque Ports surrendered. The young Simon kept the royalists at bay for a time in the isle of Axholme, but was later pardoned and surrendered, only to escape to his mother in France. Kenilworth held out for months although Edward maintained a fierce siege, and eventually it agreed to terms ; the rebels on the Isle of Ely held out even longer before giving in.

Gloucester demanded that Edward keep his promises, that he expel the aliens and swear to the Provisions of Oxford. As

Edward would give no definite answer, being busy attacking
Ely, Gloucester charged on London, captured it and held it for
two months before he surrendered. Edward realised that it
was useless to try to keep up the autocratic rule of his father,
it was time that he humbled himself a little and, by letting slip
some of the royal power, make the throne yet more secure. The
Statute of Marlborough of November 18, 1267, is not quite so
sweeping as the Provisions of Oxford, it did not deprive the
King of his rights, but it assured good government. Simon had
not fought in vain ; his ideals lived after him.

The remainder of Henry's rule is of little importance. Peace
was signed with Wales, and Edward, feeling that England was
quiet at last, joined Louis on a crusade. He returned only to
discover that while he was on his way home from Palestine,
his father, King Henry, had died on November 16, 1272, at
Westminster.

HENRY was sixty-five—very old for those days—and apparently he died of senility. He was lying in Westminster when
there was a riot in London, a quarrel over the choice of mayor,
the people fighting the magnates about whose candidate should
be elected. They yelled, " We, we are the commune of the city ! "
and their voices rose about the dying King—the shouting of the
people, of the people he could not suppress and who were defiant
to the last. To that triumphant roaring of the commons, the
feeble Henry died.

He was the first King of England to be buried concealed in a
coffin, to be hidden from the people who were shown, instead of
the usual bedizened corpse, a wax effigy " adorned with the most
precious robes, and the royal crown . . . shone with greater
splendour of glory when dead than it had ever appeared when
living." He was buried before the high altar of Westminster
in the same grave in which St. Eadward's body had lain before
its translation. That had been his wish, for he had always particularly revered St. Eadward and had called his son after him.
There was much likeness between the Kings, both were pious
and weak and foolish, and both lived on to a gentle death while
braver men died violently around them.

IX

KING EDWARD THE FIRST

1272–1307

EDWARD WAS RETURNING from the crusade when news came of his father's death. He was in Sicily or Italy when the tidings arrived, and as he continued on his way to England, " the people of all the cities came out to meet him, with processions and trumpets, and with loud shouts of ' Long live King Edward ! ' " His. training, as we have seen, had been a hard one, whatever of the father had been in the son was whipped out of him by circumstance : he had struggled and schemed and learned the lessons of Earl Simon. He reached the throne of England a man in every sense—a soldier and a statesman, one prepared and able to build a shattered country back to power.

The crusade had been an utter failure. It was Louis's second attempt. His first, in 1249, had ended in his defeat and capture at Mansura ; for four years he had remained in Syria, a prisoner of the Moslems and had been rescued only on payment of a huge ransom. The shame of this had stayed with him until nearly twenty years later he determined to go back to redeem his honour ; he asked Edward to accompany him, and the young man agreed at once. Edward took the cross in 1268, but two years were to pass before he was able to set out. Gloucester was making trouble in England, yet even more important than this was Edward's lack of money. The civil war had dragged the country into terrible debt and Henry in his multitudinous extravagances had borrowed every penny it was possible to borrow ; therefore, Edward had to seek money from Louis, offering to follow him as his vassal as Duke of Aquitaine. He set out in August, 1270. Louis had already started, and instead of making for Palestine, had paused at Carthage to battle with the Mahommedan Sultan of Tunis, whose proximity to Sicily had always been a menace to Europe. On learning of the altered plans, Edward sailed for Carthage and arrived only to discover that the King had died of fever and that his son

Philip had declared a truce with the enemy. " By God's blood,"
cried Edward when he heard, " even if all my fellow-soldiers and
countrymen desert me, I will go to Acre with Fowin, my groom,
and keep my word and oath to the death ! " With only thirteen
ships he followed the French fleet to Sicily ; then it seemed to
the pilgrims that God showed His hand, for a great storm swept
down on the sea and twenty-eight ships were struck to the
bottom, but of all the English fleet not one was harmed. Edward
had sworn that he would land in Palestine and he lingered only
while the mournful French sailed off with the corpse of their
saintly King. Henry of Germany, Richard's son, went with them
as Edward's seneschal of Gascony ; he never lived to take up his
duties. The sons of Simon de Montfort stole upon him as he
prayed in a church at Viterbo, and murdered him.

Edward remained at Sicily until the stormy season had passed,
then in the spring he unfurled his sails, thrashed his rowers
awake, and made for the Holy Land. Antioch had recently
fallen to Sultan Bibars, and of the great Christian kingdom in
Palestine of two hundred years ago, almost nothing was left save
a few coastal towns of which the most important was still Acre.
After touching at Cyprus, Edward made for Acre and was
greeted joyfully by the exhausted garrison that lived in hourly
terror of a siege ; but Bibars was at the moment fighting the
Mongols and the coast was open to Edward, who led a few forays
into the immediate interior. His men were killed, not by Moslem
spears and arrows, but by the heat, the fever, and their own
intemperance. The whole crusade was a miserable failure, and
a truce was arranged in April, 1272. To this truce Edward
refused to place his seal. His dignified attitude, his refusal to
treat with unbelievers, was intensely stupid ; it by no means
delayed the truce, which, as a matter of fact, was the only
solution to the problem, all it did was to satisfy Edward's own
preposterous vanity. He could not bear the thought of failure,
and even after his presence was no longer needed, he clung to
Acre with his wife Eleanor as if unable to leave, as if in some way
he still hoped to prove himself an old-time errant knight. Bibars
grew angry at his persistence and decided to make quite certain
that Edward would leave the Holy Land for ever. One of his
officers, the Emir of Jaffa, pretended a sudden interest in the
Christian faith and continually sent a messenger to Acre to
discuss the question. Edward interviewed the man who could
talk French, never suspecting that he was one of the followers of

the Old Man of the Mountain. On June 17, 1272—Edward's birthday—the assassin arrived in the evening and asked to see the English lord. He was admitted at once and found Edward dressed in a light tunic, for it was very hot, and sitting on his couch. The assassin gave him a letter, and bending low in answer to a question, suddenly drew a poisoned dagger from his sash and swung at Edward's heart. Quick as he was, Edward was quicker, he struck the weapon aside with his arm and kicked the Moslem, then as the man fell, he leaped on him, wrestled with him and stabbed him with his own dagger. Servants ran to the rescue, and his minstrel picked up a stool and smashed the assassin's skull as he lay prostrate. Edward spoke sternly, asking what use was it to strike a dead man? In warding off the blow he had gashed his arm on the dagger-point, and within a few days the poison had swollen and blackened the flesh, and Edward was so certain of death that he signed his will. " What are you whispering about ? " he demanded of the surgeons, as with solemn faces they consulted ; " can I not be cured? Tell me, do not be afraid ? " An English surgeon answered, " You can be cured, but only with intense pain." " Are you certain of the cure if I submit ? " asked Edward, and the surgeon told him— " I will answer for it." Edward immediately gave himself wholly to their skill, but first he was asked if he had any with him whom he could trust, and on his remarking that he had several, including his brother Edmund, they were told, " Then take this lady away and do not let her see her lord again until I say." Weeping and half refusing to go, the lady, Eleanor, was led outside. " It is better, lady," she was told, " that you should weep than the whole of England." In the morning the flesh was cut from the poisoned arm, and although Edward became well again, he was for many years to suffer recurrences of sickness that could be traced back to this night in the Holy Land.[1]

---

[1] A romantic tale assures us that Queen Eleanor with her own mouth sucked the poison from Edward's wound. This is sheer fiction ; the legend is an old and popular one, and was first attached to Edward by Rodericus Santius, Bishop of Valencia, who, writing a history of Spain in the latter half of the fifteenth century, cites the story as an example of the virtues of Spanish ladies ; and Camden took it from Santius. Contemporary allusions to Edward's wound are silent about Eleanor. In a French chronicle believed to have been written by Baudoin d'Avesnes, who died in 1289, we are told that Edward was cured by the help of God and by a certain stone given him by the Knights Hospitallers. The story related above seems the most probable and authentic.

WHEN Edward was on his way home to England news came that his eldest son John was dead, and this was quickly followed by the tidings of Henry's end. His host was surprised to see that Edward's grief was greater at the second news than at the first, and on mentioning this to his guest, he was told by Edward that while he could produce more sons he could never find a second father. And whatever stupidities Henry and Eleanor had committed, no matter how one may dislike or despise them, they were without doubt the ideal parents. We have no suggestion of scandal about the couple, they were arrogant and foolish, they gathered money only to fling it on empty pomp, yet in those corrupt times, when mistresses were an accepted part of a man's establishment and when children were reared and educated from home, Henry and Eleanor set a truly beautiful example of loving parenthood, and Edward was always to revere their memory. When he was a lad, and Henry had sailed for Gascony in 1253, so great was Edward's love that he had remained at Portsmouth " sobbing on the shore, and he refused to leave as long as a sail could be glimpsed."

Edward had been a sickly child. He was born at Westminster on June 17, 1239, and was named after the Confessor, Simon de Montfort standing as one of the sponsors at his baptism. For years, the people had feared that Eleanor was barren and that the sons of Simon might succeed to the throne of England, but whatever joy they might have felt at the birth was soon soured by the King's energy in dragging gifts from them. " God has given us a prince," people said, " but the King sells him to us."

In 1246, when Edward was seven, he fell dangerously ill at Beaulieu Abbey and lay for three weeks with his life almost despaired of ; and his mother, the arrogant greedy Eleanor, refused to leave the monastery but sat by him constantly to the horror of the stern Cistercians, the most strict of all the orders. Next year Edward was again ill, this time in London, and his father implored all the religious houses in and near the city to pray for his recovery. That was the last we hear of sickness ; Edward was now growing into an exceptionally handsome lad, tall and well built, with hair so flaxen that it seemed like burnished silver, although gradually as the years went on it darkened into yellow, and from yellow to black, then to white.

Henry dreamed of splendid ambitions for his son and looked about him for gifts to shower upon the lad. There was Gascony.

Richard, Henry's brother, was at that time governing Gascony, but that did not bother Henry. He pushed Richard aside and, together with almost every fief he possessed, gave Gascony to Edward as a marriage portion. Edward was fifteen, and his betrothed was much younger than he when first he met her at Burgos. She was Eleanor, sister of Alfonso X of Castile. Although the marriage was purely political, designed to keep Alfonso out of Guinne, it became one of the happiest of any of our Kings'. The example that Edward and Eleanor set their people was even more beautiful than the example his parents had set. For thirty-five years they lived contentedly together, and when she died his grief almost killed him ; he was never the same man afterwards, becoming more impatient and harsh.

On August 5, 1254, Edward and his mother arrived at Burgos to meet his betrothed, and Alfonso, after examining his son-in-law on his knowledge and military ability, knighted him and presented him to the bride. They were married two months later in the monastery of Las Huelgas, and then set out for Bordeaux where King Henry waited eager to throw away whatever gold he could collect in empty pageantry and feasting.

THE King's marriage gift might have been generous but it was troublesome. In 1257 the Welsh spread over the marches and when Edward—he was eighteen—asked his father's advice, Henry cried petulantly, " What's it to me ? The land is yours. Take action, win fame when you are young, make your enemies fear you. As for me, I am busy with other affairs." With little money and few men it was no easy matter to win fame and make your enemies fear you ; Edward could do almost nothing to stem rebellion, yet he learned tricks of war and studied Welsh tactics —the ambuscade and sudden attack.

The people of England watched their young lord suspiciously. He gave no promise of worthiness ; rather his reckless, cruel manner presaged a reign as tyrannous as John's. Then when Simon was killed at Evesham, Edward became King in all but name, and in his hands the country was quietened, the rebels were chased from their castles. Responsibility brought to the young lord an unexpected strength ; all the same, his love of adventure was still powerful enough to lure him to that futile crusade.

Eleanor had travelled with him to the Holy Land and she came back with him to England. He paused to speak with Pope

Gregory X, a good and simple man, and as he passed through
Lombardy the people crowded cheering about him, for already
he was famous as a jouster and as the crusader who had stayed
to the last in Palestine. Gifts and honours came to him at every
city ; the doctors of Padua elected him a member of the legal
faculty ; the Milanese gave him horses caparisoned in scarlet ;
and having passed the Alps, he was met by English nobles
who had come to do him homage as their elected King. With
this small army of over a thousand lances he entered French
territory. The French were jealous of his fame, resentful probably
because their own King had turned aside while Edward continued
the crusade, and now the Count of Châlon, a vassal of the Duke
of Burgundy, challenged Edward and his comrades to a tournament, a game of skill at which Edward was most expert.

The count had double the English troops and he soon showed
that he fought in earnest. As leader of the Burgundians he
singled out the leader of the English, and they fought with
swords, but there was no chink in Edward's swift defence, no
opening into which the count could lunge ; then suddenly losing his
temper, the count threw away his sword and, seizing Edward by
the neck, strove to pull him from the saddle. Edward calmly
struck his spurs into the horse, the beast sprang forward and
jerked the count from his seat, flinging him to the sanded ground.
The English force at last defeated the Burgundian, but so outraged was Edward at the count's unknightly attack that he
refused to accept the man's sword. He made him surrender it
to a simple knight. The English had won the little battle of
Châlon, but the spectators were so angry at their champions'
defeat that they attacked the victors, and Edward only managed
to still the riot by threatening to burn the town.

From Châlon, Edward rode to Paris, which he reached on
July 1274, and did the King homage for his continental fiefs,
but subtly he refused to agree to all that his father had given,
or to the loss of certain fiefs then in dispute owing to the death
of the Count of Poitiers and Toulouse ; when rendering homage,
Edward said : " Lord King, I do you homage for all the lands
I should hold of you."

It was not until August 2 that he crossed with his Queen to
Dover to be crowned on the 19th at Westminster.

EDWARD was thirty-three when he became King of England.
He was exceptionally tall and slim, " erect as a palm," and his

active life kept down any disposition to obesity. He had long strong arms and lean legs that earned him the nickname of Longshanks. Erect in bearing, oval-faced, broad-chested, wide-browed, he looked indeed a King with his curling golden hair and beard, his dark eyes, his prominent nose raised a little in the middle, and his strong teeth that remained whole until his death. Like his father, his left eyelid drooped, and he stammered badly except when thrilled by his subject, then he could so move his hearers that they were ready to weep or to die for him.

His enthusiasm alone thrilled people, for unlike most medieval Kings he never tried to outdress his court. Being rather miserly in many ways, he could never understand the value of outward show, particularly of dress ; besides, great men do not need robes and crowns and well-cleaned linen to reveal their greatness : it is seen flashing in their eyes, deepening in their voices, it is felt by the presence of genius living within the body. He was not miserly when it came to gifts for those he loved ; nor in the horses he kept, for horses were necessary things ; nor in the largesse he distributed to needy knights and to the poor. Only on matters of personal vanity, such as clothes, did he grudge money, for he lived frugally, not caring for food or drink so long as enough was in his belly to feed the terrific energy of his mind and limbs. Only once did he wear his crown—at his coronation—like that other great King, Henry II, who also despised dress, he put the crown aside, for outward show did not interest him. " I would not be a better man no matter however gorgeously I dressed," he once told a hermit who questioned him about his plain attire. And he would not have been a better King if he had weighed his head continually with the crown or kept the sceptre in his belt. He usually wore a simple short-sleeved tunic bordered with fur, always of a uniform colour. Yet he would never degrade his royal dignity as Henry II had done, he kept aloof and remained kingly, few daring to pluck his sleeve or whisper in his ear. By this simplicity of living, and by his love of sport—hunting and jousting and tournaments—Edward kept his body healthy and lived to a great age, despite the assassin's poison and his own unhealthy childhood.

When a youth he had been violent and unprincipled, leading a gang of young rascals about the country, two hundred lads ripe for mischief, from whose wanton sport no man or woman was safe. Wherever they went, they left only empty larders, broken pates and girls no longer maidens. Even monks were

20

robbed and thrashed if they fell into their hands. There is one particularly horrible story about Edward : out of sheer brutality, he lopped an ear and plucked an eye from some unfortunate lad whom he met by accident. The people of England, therefore, watched their young lord anxiously, and perhaps their very anxiety tended to exaggerate the tales. It is difficult to believe that the chaste, sober and just King could have sprung from so ignoble a youth, yet often conversion is sudden, and responsibility will sometimes cause the drunkard to desert his bowl or the wencher to forget his ladies ; Henry V was a wild lad, but the moment he was crowned King no man could have been more serious and pious than he. Perhaps Edward was from the same mould. When he realised fully the desperate situation of his father, he may have put for ever behind him the irresponsible drunken days of youth.

He was always an adventurer at heart. From the earliest times, from the moment almost when he could first sit a horse, he loved the tournament and the chase, and he was a famous swordsman. He had a vile temper which he strove to keep in harness. Once he was hawking on the banks of a river, probably seeking a heron, when one of his comrades awkwardly unloosed a hawk that had made a stoop on a duck amongst the osiers. Edward rebuked him in anger, and the man replied insolently : " It is lucky for me that the river is between us." Driven to fury by this impertinence, Edward spurred his horse into the river, reckless of its depth, and struggled on to the opposite bank. The man fled and, sword in hand, Edward pursued him ; realising that escape was hopeless and knowing his lord's temper, the man knelt upon the ground, pulled off his cap and bared his neck, humbly imploring mercy. Quick as was Edward's rage when his dignity was hurt, it went as quickly when the offender confessed his fault and asked pardon. He now slipped the sword back into its sheath, and soon the two men were again at the river, trying merrily to recapture the strayed hawk. He found delight in forgiveness, considering himself almost divine in the administration of justice. In later days, when one of his judges remarked that he might show mercy in a special trial, Edward cried indignantly, " *May* show mercy ! Why I would do that for a dog if he sought my grace ! " Yet that was not always true. Sometimes the Angevin temper broke its bonds and the lion of justice became the avenger. A squire was clumsy when attending the marriage of Edward's daughter Margaret ; the King caught up a stick and so thrashed the lad that later in remorse he gave him the large gift of £13, 6s. 8d. And he " was pleased " to snatch the coronet from his daughter's head at her bridal and throw it into the fire. A most expensive act, for the coronet held a large ruby and an emerald.

There is another and more pleasant tale that shows his recklessness, his courage and his sense of justice. When he was pursuing the rebels after the death of Simon, he chased one particular offender, Adam Gurdan, who was lurking in the forests of Hampshire. He caught him near Alton, and in his excitement rushed single-handed at the outlaw and his men although his own troops were separated from him by a wide ditch. It became a duel between the two, the others did not interfere, and at last Gurdan fell wounded. So delighted was Edward by the man's skill and bravery that he pardoned Gurdan, had his wounds dressed, and treated him like a comrade and not an enemy. All of Gurdan's followers, however, who were of low degree were hanged on the spot.

Brave and reckless he was, yet also he was cunning and, when necessary, could play the traitor as he had with Simon. " When he is cornered," writes a contemporary, " he promises whatever you ask, but as soon as he escapes he repudiates his promises." That, according to Edward, was statecraft, for he was one of those arrogant men incapable of conceiving themselves in the wrong. He knew that the end was good, and therefore he justified to himself whatever means he took ; this peculiar moral blindness, common amongst extremely pious people who believe that God is ever on their side, was a great help to Edward. It kept him unflinchingly to the path that he thought best. There was little genius in him, he lacked the furious inspiration of a Simon de Montfort, but he was sane and calculating, a plodder who went forward to his goal, undeterred by anger or jealousy. In this lay Edward's true greatness, in this one-sided humourless outlook, in this astounding faith in himself. Without the work of Simon on which to build, it is doubtful if he would have achieved any extraordinary works. Simon failed because he had the impatience of genius, because his ideals were beyond the conception of the men of his time ; he could see that the King was but an appointed governor, that he should live for the people and not the people for him. Edward was naturally incapable of such a thought, he looked upon the country as his personal property, he drilled it into shape at his whim. Parliament had been born from the dreams of Simon, Edward could not sweep it away, but he did his best to curtail its power, to use it purely as something that could vote him taxes and not as a chosen committee to legislate for the people. Yet he was sane enough to realise that he must not exceed his limits as his father had done ; within his narrow world he saw things very clearly, undisturbed by passion. He could see exactly what was wrong and was quite certain that he could set it right. He commands our admiration and our respect, but, unlike Simon, he does not call for our love. A great King, the English Justinian, a brave soldier, and a confident ruler—he was all that, but as a man he stands cold and brutal, without real love for his people, without true mercy, because he did not deal it from the heart.

He had been brought up religiously, for Henry had been a good churchman. All his life Edward kept this faith, he was ever eager to travel on pilgrimages and was constantly at mass, being charitable and a founder of religious houses. The love of architecture is a genuine artistic touch to be found in his character, together with his love of music, but love of music was almost universal in the Middle Ages. It was part of one's training to learn to sing, and a knight who remained dumb while others chanted would have been considered as much a boor as would a modern man who could not read his newspaper. Yet Edward's love for music was very deep—that was his only artistic weakness, other than his love for architecture and its brother sculpture, as can be seen in the flower-like crosses he raised in memory of Eleanor and in the superb tombs built for his father, wife and brother in Westminster Abbey. Otherwise his culture was apparently small. He knew English, French and Latin, yet had no interest in literature and was no patron of men of letters. He liked only to read books of chivalry, religion and agriculture, but he was always very careful to preserve the national archives.

Firstly, he was a man of action with little time for reading. He was a man of action with a deep reverence for the Church and with an amazing belief in himself, a belief that almost bordered on the divine. He felt that he was marked out by God, an appointed officer sent to dragoon the men of his land and to settle the complicated affairs of the western world. Playing chess one day he suddenly got up and went to the other end of the chamber, when a gigantic piece of masonry fell from the roof and crushed the chair on which he had been sitting. For this escape he thanked our Lady of Walsingham, and for ever afterwards he held her in especial reverence. Such an accident would not surprise Edward, it was almost what God existed for—to ward danger from him ; therefore he would throw himself recklessly into the forefront of battle, knowing that God was a buckler no arrow or spear could pierce. And like so many soldiers of this type, secure in his own amazing faith, he died at last quietly in his bed.

His faith in himself did not lead him to appreciate the faith of others. When a beggar shouted that his blindness had left him after praying at the tomb of Henry III, Edward pushed him away and cried furiously, " My father would rather have blinded such a lying rascal than have given him back his eyes."

Although in himself he is not an attractive figure, although he was arrogant and very often cruel, the fact remains that in his hands Great Britain was nearly drawn into one, and the English constitution first was built. He had learned from Simon, but fools cannot learn great lessons ; he had around him wise councillors, but only wise men know how to chose wise friends. Although not brilliant in his own conceptions, he was intelligent enough to recognise brilliance in others and to comprehend the ideals of greater thinkers. There is little else one can demand from a King. Genius is too erratic, too dangerous a lamp, to be placed upon the throne ; it is better and safer to have a solid, sensible King like Edward than a quick-tempered, impatient man like Simon to lead us towards the future. Edward avoided disaster, he never leaped without counsel. Therefore he was indeed a great King, perhaps of our Kings the greatest.

In this short space we must ignore much of his long reign and it is natural that we should ignore that part of it dealing with the Continent. He became truly the arbiter of Europe, and managed, despite the fiery partisanships of the Popes and the hatred of France and Castile, to bring peace at last, hoping to unite the nations for a great crusade. He never set out on that crusade, no sooner had he settled the European affairs than he had to hurry back to England after nearly a three years' absence so that he could settle the problem of the Scottish succession. It is this question that must take up most of our space, together with the war with Wales and his legislation in England.

Edward's reign is so important in its effect on England that it can scarcely be dealt with chronologically. We will forget the importance of various facets if they are separated, scattered between wholly divergent episodes. Edward's legislation, for instance, if examined as it occurs here and there in history, would become confusing and would lose a great deal of its effect. It is best to compress it into a few pages so that we can see it in its entirety.

Undoubtedly the most important of all Edward's schemes was the creation of parliament. This was no sudden arrival, it evolved gradually from the ideals of Simon de Montfort, and Edward himself never fully realised the greatness of the innovation ; to him parliament remained merely a larger council, a larger gathering of vassals to produce money at the flick of his fingers. He had no conception of parliament as a representation of the people's wishes ; to him, the people should have no wishes except his own. All he desired, roughly, was to devise a method of taxation which would efficiently keep the exchequer overflowing without the necessity of having to argue the point with a few powerful barons and churchmen. To bring the tax-payers closer to the throne without having to reach them through devious channels, he enlarged the old council that had been attended purely by crown tenants into a parliament to which were invited representatives of every class. From this small beginning, as a gathering of tax-payers, parliament grew, legislation was soon added to taxation, and its powers seeped gradually until the throne floated on them and could be capsized if ever a storm burst, as at last it did burst in the days of the Stuarts.

It was not immediately that Edward summoned these re-presentative parliaments. He dodged for a while amongst various forms, first calling the knights-of-the-shires, and the next year summoning the barons and bishops, then rushing into ancient history by sending a treasurer round the boroughs and communes to see what he could scrape out of the people by individual requests. Finding that this failed, Edward took another jump and called on both knights-of-the-shires and borough representatives to gather with the clergy at two assemblies. Again this did not suit his needs and he decided to deal directly through the local courts, then he called nobles, knights and burgesses without the clergy. Evidently the form of parliament varied with the people he wished to tax, and each of these assemblies was of equal authority. Matters would probably have stayed in this muddled condition, parliament remaining a fluid gathering at the King's whim, if necessity had not forced Edward to rely more directly upon the people. In 1293 and 1294, more or less representative parliaments, while agreeing to heavy taxation, decided that no taxes should be placed upon the country without the consent of clergy and commons ; then in 1295, the first real parliament assembled. To it came of course the barons, but with them were two knights chosen by every shire and two citizens and burgesses from every city or borough town. The clergy were present, not only important ecclesiastics but also representatives from each chapter, and two proctors from the parochial clergy of each diocese. For the first time the people of England met under one roof, for the first time the nation looked upon itself and found that all classes spoke with the same tongue and to the same ends. The three estates were there— the barons, the clergy, the commons. This set a precedent ever after to be followed, a precedent of unity. And Edward has always been glorified because of this splendid creation ; but there was a man long dead, struck down by the hand of Edward himself, from whom the dream had taken shape. Only the people remembered Simon de Montfort and revered him as a martyr.

EDWARD has been called the English Justinian, and it is true that he codified the laws of England ; he did not make new laws, he fixed and brought up to date the laws of the past. In this he was fortunate to have as chancellor Robert Burnell, son of a Shropshire squire, a most cunning lawyer and diplomatist. Burnell's greed and wanton habits caused him to be detested by the people, yet he remained always a firm friend of the King, and it was undoubtedly by his advice that many of Edward's most famous statutes were brought forth. The future King and his future chancellor met during the war with Simon, they were of about equal age and became friends at once ; already Burnell, a second son with no hope of succeeding to his father's estates, had distinguished himself in civil and canon law, and now he became chaplain and a kind of private secretary to the Lord Edward. Later, even while his father was alive, Edward tried to make his friend Archbishop of Canterbury, and the moment he became King he appointed him his chancellor and made him Bishop of Bath and Wells.

Burnell was not the only intelligent adviser of Edward, there were also John Kirkby, Bishop of Ely ; Henry Lacy, Earl of

Lincoln ; Anthony Bek, Bishop of Durham ; and Walter Langton, Bishop of Lichfield. All these men, and particularly Lacy, helped Edward in innumerable ways, while Langton as treasurer, although a man of lax private life, was faithful and extremely clever.

Burnell, however, must stand at the forefront of all Edward's ministers—at any rate, for the early years ; Langton's power comes afterwards—and he it was who introduced the famous First Statute of Westminster, the product of the parliament of 1275. This statute is of great importance, it covers in one huge sweep almost the whole of English law. Its fifty-one clauses rush from question to question, protecting church property from spoliation, giving freedom for elections of sheriffs and others, stopping too great fines that might imprison a man in perpetuity, correcting numerous abuses such as the marrying off of wards, and the levying of excessive tolls, and bringing the act of rape down from its position as a capital crime to one of lesser importance.

To follow all Edward's statutes in detail would be tedious and out of place. In none of his enactments do we find a great advance on feudal ideas, they were all either a restricting or an enlarging of existing laws. At one time, in 1278, he thought to pass a statute that would deprive the barons of much of their power by stopping many of the smaller baronial courts—already given their death-blow by Simon—but at the first hint of such a thing the barons rose threatening rebellion. One of Edward's most powerful adherents, the Earl of Warenne, took the lead, and when a King's lawyer tapped at his gate and asked to see the documents that gave him his authority, the earl pulled out an aged rusty sword and cried—" Here is my warrant. My ancestors came over with William the Bastard and won their lands with the sword. With my sword I will hold them against all usurpers." After such defiance from so loyal a follower, Edward very sensibly forgot about this statute.

He then turned against the Church's power, in 1279 passing the Statute of Mortmain which prohibited land being granted to corporations being held in Mortmain—*in mortua manu*, by " the dead hand "—without the King's consent, and in 1285 forcing church courts to deal only with ecclesiastical affairs ; but the causes and results of both these attempts will be dealt with more fully in the narrative.

Judicial questions absorbed much of Edward's interest. He tried to see that the country was well policed, reinforcing the ancient military obligations that were dying because of the constant civil wars and the Kings' greed in taking a scutage instead of arms ; he attempted to reform the law courts, even the small baronial ones, and three times a year he sent judges about the country to try nearly all kinds of civil law cases, and later these judges' powers were expanded and they could also sit on criminal trials ; and he cut the land up into definite circuits. There had been itinerant justices since the days of Henry II, but their visits had been spasmodic and their powers so limited that often years passed before the particular court needed was held in the correct district. Edward changed this, he made everything move according to rule, for he had the soldier's mind that desires all to go by routine. He was by no means a great administrator, there was no vision in his work ; he tightened what was too loose, and loosened what was already too tight. In fact, he fully deserves the name of the English Justinian, for Justinian, finding Roman law enormously involved, became more a codifier than a legislator. And Edward was little more than a codifier. This does not detract from his greatness ; the civil wars had broken the administration of Henry II, and although the barons had produced their Magna Carta and Henry III had continually sworn to ratify it, little progress had been made on the administration. Magna Carta, however, had not disappeared : Henry III migh ignore its provisions but Edward could not escape them. He had his father's example as a warning before him, and therefore in its essentials he stood by Magna Carta. Unconsciously Edward became the instrument of forces which he did not comprehend, through him the aspirations of a people took shape, he drew the country firmly together and led it towards a sane and prosperous government. His ambitions destroyed his administration to a great extent, he kept England at almost continual war, while he strove to bend Scotland and Wales to his will, and he died practically penniless. All the same, in his hands the country became—to use a stupid but unavoidable term—" modern," it ceased to be purely feudal, and the conception of a nation governed by the three estates—the nobles, the clergy, the commons—became more than the dream of a Simon de Montfort, it became a truth that could never afterwards be demolished.

We have discussed enough of Edward's administration, and it is time that we took up the threads of his life to see him as his contemporaries saw him—as a just yet brutal king, as a brave soldier, good husband, ambitious conqueror, and fearless leader.

UNTIL after his wife's death in 1290, Edward's reign, except for his quarrel with the Church, was more or less peaceful. He strove to avoid wars, dreaming of a great crusade and wishing to bind the western nations into one Christian army that would flood the East. Therefore he spent years on the Continent, patching up quarrels that had really nothing to do with him, and when there was the threat of rebellion in Wales, he did everything possible to avert bloodshed. Llewellyn II, Prince of Wales, was a brave ambitious man who swore to make actual the prophesies of Merlin that told of the coming time when the Saxon race would be swept away before the avenging forces of old Britain. He was determined never again to do homage to England for his own country, and he intrigued to marry Eleanor, Earl Simon's only daughter. He wriggled out of every demand Edward sent asking him to render homage; for years Edward tried to entice him to England and always Llewellyn managed to excuse himself until at last the King lost patience. In 1277, Edward led his troops from Chester.

Wales was no easy country to conquer; in those huge rolling hills and sudden gorges the natives could lurk and could pounce upon an unsuspecting army as it passed through the valleys. Henry II had driven great roads across the ridgeways, Henry I and Rufus had never penetrated far into the north, their successes were mainly in the south. It was a nation impossible to conquer, the poor soil could not produce food enough to keep an invader living, while the great mountains were a protection that could never be scaled by men in armour. All that England could hope to do was to force its way slowly over the marches and build strong castles to be given into the hands of powerful Englishmen called the lords marcher. These lords were often cruel, but they lived a dangerous life and only by striking terror into the enemy could they hope to maintain their grip. Once already Edward had tasted Welsh fighting and he knew that it was useless to try to conquer the land by war. He carefully bought the disaffected to his side, and he had those chieftains under his standard who were jealous of Llewellyn's greatness, and amongst them was Llewellyn's own brother David. Edward moved cautiously; from Chester to the Conway he drove wide roads through the forests, and he sent a fleet along the coast-line with provisions, knowing that he could not rely upon the barren principality to feed his troops. If possible, he wished to avoid marching into this dangerous land where hidden Welsh with terrible long-bows could strike down men from incredible distances ; his idea was to starve the enemy into surrender, and the plan worked perfectly. Llewellyn retreated into those mountains that were then vaguely called Snowdon, but Edward did not follow. He ringed in Snowdon, cut off every possible communication, and by winter-time Llewellyn was too exposed and hungry to hold out. He signed the treaty of Conway on November 10, according to which he ceded certain districts between Chester and Conway, paid 1000 marks a year for the island of Anglesey to be held only during his lifetime, paid further sums towards the cost of the war, and gave ten hostages as surety for good behaviour.

Edward did not wish to press his advantage, he wanted peace' on as friendly a basis as possible, and therefore he remitted both rent and fine and sent back the hostages. He did all he could to win Llewellyn's affections. Before the outbreak of war some Bristol seaman had captured a ship that bore Simon's son Amaury and his daughter Eleanor ; they had been making for Wales where Eleanor was to marry Llewellyn, and when they were sent to him, Edward imprisoned Amaury and kept Eleanor in the Queen's household. Now, after Llewellyn had done homage at Westminster during the Christmas festivities, Edward gave his Welsh vassal permission to marry the girl and himself condescended to attend the wedding.

For the next five years he struggled to govern the principality, and it was because of that peculiar narrow-mindedness of his that rebellion eventually broke out again. He had made laws for England, laws that seemed to him so just that he thought the whole world should submit to them ; he did not realise that the Welsh had a culture of their own which was to them more perfect than any he could superimpose. His own laws appeared to Edward so perfect that he could not conceive any country not wishing to adopt them, particularly a country like Wales that was split into numerous kingdoms and ruled by small despots. He offered the wisdom of England, and to his amazement the Welsh preferred their own barbaric administration, even when— as he said—their laws broke the Ten Commandments. Those ancient customs which appeared to him just, he permitted to remain ; those he thought unjust, he swept aside and replaced with English ones. The Welsh have always been a violent people, furiously nationalistic, proud and courageous. It hurt them not only to be conquered but to have their most treasured beliefs trampled upon and denounced as uncivilised.

Edward's determination to change Welshmen into Englishmen drove even his supporters to the other party. David became reconciled with his brother Llewellyn, and the proud nation lay ready and eager for the call to arms.

MEANWHILE, Edward had begun the inevitable conflict with the Church. Like his father, he was extremely pious and at the first opportunity he always dashed off on a pilgrimage or plunged his fingers into his pouch to help build a church ; yet even before religion, stood his kingship, and although he might be ready to bow at the feet of the Pope, he was equally ready to defend the rights of the crown against any encroachment. And he could not help looking upon the English Church almost as his own property ; wishing to use it to reward his friends, he insisted that Burnell be made Archbishop of Canterbury, and just before he had started on his crusade he had gone to the extent of breaking down the doors of the cathedral when the monks were deliberating in the chapter-house, hoping to terrify them into nominating his favourite. This show of force did not affect the monks' decision, they were not going to have a lecherous secular clerk raised to the greatest ecclesiastical power in the land. When he became King, many years later, Edward made a second attempt to get Burnell raised to the primacy, and although the monks were prepared to accept him, Pope Nicholas III would not be bullied. He appointed a Francisan, John Peckham, to Canterbury. Peckham was a sincere, humourless man, a fiery scholar who lived according to the strictest rules of his order ; he would never ride a horse and he fasted seven lents a year. He took the task of archbishop most deeply to heart, and immediately on his arrival he summoned a council to pass strong canons against pluralities, and he ordered the clergy to display a copy of Magna Carta in all churches and to denounce every offender against it as excommunicate. Edward could pass over the canon against pluralities—a genuine evil, for bishops often held numerous appointments and were therefore unable to attend to any of them—but the command to denounce any offender against Magna Carta was an obvious insult. Peckham, by this rule, could have referred to no one but Edward himself, and the King retorted at once. Before parliament in 1279 he made the archbishop retract all the canons he had passed at Reading contrary to the rights of the crown, and he also decreed the Statute of Mortmain, According to this statute, the Church was not to inherit lands or wards without the King's consent. Peckham, a Franciscan, could scarcely reply to this, and being a genuine ascetic, he must have realised that the enormous fiefs held by the Church were at the base of its corruption ; from being spiritual helpers the clergy had degenerated into the most grasping landlords of the people. Rents and such paid to a lord who was often needy and lax in his accounting were as nothing compared to the rents paid to a corporation that no death could stop, that continued for perpetuity. The Church owned quite enough land according to Edward, and Peckham in his heart must have known that he was right. Nevertheless, as the leader of the Roman Church in England, he had to stand against any law that interfered with ecclesiastic power. He could do nothing at the moment, but in 1281 at a church council he decreed that all suits concerning patronage and the property of the clergy should in future be dealt with in ecclesiastical and not in royal courts. Edward instantly quashed the decree and Peckham had to give way before the King's fury. The quarrel after that remained for a time in abeyance ; so far, Edward had won, then both King and archbishop forgot their personal troubles to unite against a common danger. Wales was again in rebellion, in both north and south the people rose, led by David and Llewellyn who were allies for once. David captured Edward's justiciar and Llewellyn led his troops to the very walls of Chester.

Edward was probably astounded at this rebellion. He had tried to be just to the Welsh, he had been as kind as was permissible to royal dignity, and now the people rejected his rule, they had taken down their long-bows and cleansed their swords for killing. From the mountains and the valleys they came, fierce and eager to avenge the insult England had placed upon their ancient laws.

Peckham excommunicated Llewellyn, and Edward rode out with his troops. He used again the tactics that had proved so efficient before ; he enclosed Snowdon, cutting his enemies off from relief or food, and Llewellyn was forced to creep out almost alone before the coming winter would force him to submit. He stole through the English lines and was soon on the marches, trying to gather allies. He was met at Builth by an English troop and in the skirmish was speared by a man who did not recognise him, who thought him but a simple knight. A leader saw the corpse and realised what luck was his ; he chopped off the head and sent it to Edward who passed it on to London to have it ivy-crowned and spiked above the gates of the Tower.

The death of Llewellyn broke the rebellion. David hid in the mountains, living a wretched outlaw's existence until some of his own countrymen betrayed his hiding-place in the bogs of Snowdon. He pleaded to see Edward but the King refused ; David was a traitor, an English subject who had defied his lord, and he was treated as such. A special parliament at Shrewsbury on September 30, 1283, sentenced him to be drawn, hanged and quartered.

Wales was now completely subdued. For a year Edward stayed in the land, seeing that his reforms were carried out, and in 1284 he decreed his Statute of Wales which declared the principality annexed to the English crown as shire-ground. He had learned his lesson and did not force too harshly his laws upon the people, retaining as many of the old customs as he possibly could. And as he strove to administer laws and build castles, Peckham was busy reforming the Church, ferreting out married priests, and seeing that the clergy were better educated.

While in Wales, two of Edward's children were born. The King was at Rhuddlan Castle, busy with affairs, when a Welsh gentleman arrived with the tidings of the birth of a son. Edward knighted the messenger at once, and gave him a grant of land, so overjoyed was he to have a second boy ; he was soon to have only one, for the elder, Alfonso, died within a few months. The story that the King offered the baby to his new subjects as their Prince is without any foundation ; little Edward—born April 25, 1284—was not created Prince of Wales until February 7, 1301.

In August, to celebrate his new conquest, Edward held a great Round Table tournament at Nevin in Carnarvonshire. Here gathered " the knights of England with many foreign nobles," and in the forests of Snowdon, between the huge swell of mountains, the knights fought chivalrously together : little figures they must have seemed, glittering like glass in their hauberks, amongst those trees and hills, in that gigantic landscape. At the same time were discovered the body of Constantine the Great and the crown of King Arthur—opportune relics, for the crown of the great British conqueror was now placed in the hands of Edward, and " thus the glory of Wales was passed on to the English."

FOREIGN affairs kept Edward busy in the years succeeding his conquest of Wales, but in 1285 he revived his quarrel with Peckham. In his typical manner he gave in half-way, conceding powers to Peckham and at the same time giving himself yet greater powers. He passed a statute that defined the jurisdiction of ecclesiastical courts, limiting them purely to spiritual affairs. Peckham could not fight against this, mainly because his own tactlessness and frenzied zeal had made him detested by his own party. Churchmen who sympathised with his aims were so repelled by his methods that they were unable to stand beside him. His lust for reformation had made him burrow into every church and quarrel with almost every bishop, including even the saintly Thomas of Cantilupe. Peckham hounded the unfortunate Thomas to his death, involving him in expensive and complicated suits at the papal court, and even when Thomas was no more he carried his malice to such an extent that he tried to forbid Christian burial to the corpse. Edward seized this as a stick with which to belabour Peckham ; he almost forced the curia to canonise Thomas.

Although King and archbishop might quarrel over the powers of the Church, they yet respected each other enough to unite when threatened by a common enemy. They had united against Wales, and now they united in a less laudable war, in a persecution of the Jews. Henry III, like most Kings, had always protected the Jews, for they possessed enormous wealth ; slowly by lending money at terrific interest they had managed to control all banking and many were the estates mortgaged to them beyond redemption. Edward had forbidden them to own property, he had forced them to wear their national dress, and had banned usury. By taking usury away, Edward made the Jews desperate, for they had no trade left to which they could turn ; money-lending had become their particular province, as the Church strongly forbade its people charging interest on any loan. The idea that money could breed money was rightly repugnant to good Christians, and they therefore let the Jews, who were in no peril of losing their already lost souls, manage banking, and the lowest interest they ever charged was 30 per cent. Now and again debtors were driven to such straits that they raised the old cry that Jews were crucifying Christians, and evaded paying back by the simple expedient of murdering their creditors. But the Jews were under the special protection of the crown, being able to bribe the King and his officers. Hated both as usurer and as

the murderer of Christ, the Jew lived nevertheless in comparative safety in England ; the people shuddered from him in the
street, yet they crept into his house to borrow money ; they
longed to kill them, both for economic and religious purposes,
but were afraid to draw their daggers lest the King's officers seek
quick revenge.

Edward, a deeply pious man, watched the Jews with disgust
and horror. Besides, they were outliving their usefulness, for
Christian money-lenders from Cahors in Guinne and from north
Italy were replacing them as bankers. It was now the time to
strike, to clear them from the country. Already Edward had
banished them from Guienne ; he decided to do the same for
England. Early in his reign he had forbidden usury, and the
Jew, deprived of his one trade, had been forced to seek less
reputable methods of making money. He clipped the coinage,
and he clipped with such a will that English money became wellnigh valueless abroad. Edward thereupon captured about
three hundred Jews, imprisoned them in the Tower, hanged about
two hundred of them, and confiscated their goods. Many Christians should have been hanged as well, for the goldsmiths were
the worst clippers of all ; they were arrested, but almost every
one was released, for no Christian jury would convict. With the
Jews it was different, it was a pious act to kill them ; those that
escaped hanging were imprisoned in 1287 and made to pay
gigantic fines to get out again ; in 1290 they were all expelled from
the kingdom.

Again we see that peculiar justness of Edward. He might
decree most brutally, but always he added a pinch of mercy to
satisfy his conscience. After forcing the Jews out of the country
he showed his justness by permitting them to carry their portable
goods with them, and when some were murdered as they crossed
the Channel, being robbed and put on a sandbank at low tide,
Edward hanged the murderers.

In the spring and summer of the same year, 1290, two of Edward's
daughters were married—Joan on April 30 to Gilbert de Clare,
the powerful Earl of Gloucester, and Margaret on July 8 to John,
Duke of Brabant. Another daughter, Mary, had turned nun
while under seven years of age, and was in the monastery of
Amesbury ; her grandmother Eleanor had insisted on her taking
the veil, and Edward, a most dutiful son, had surrendered to
his mother's pleading ; Eleanor herself lived a semi-monastic

existence in the same convent and had turned so pious that she had been one of the most fiery hunters of the Jews during their persecution. In contrast to this, we find that other Eleanor, Edward's Queen, protecting the Jews, for which Edward strongly rebuked her, pointing out that she was letting her love of money outweigh her religion. It was not often that he had cause to speak sharply to her, they were a most happy couple, and sometimes the stern King would make merry with her household. In Easter this year we have a pretty picture of him being hoisted in his chair by five frolicsome ladies and only purchasing his liberty at the cost of forty shillings to each maid ; and there is another tale that gives a charmingly intimate portrait of the great King. At the palace of Waltham one day when he was preparing for the hunt, coupling the hounds, mounting the horses, he noticed his Queen's laundry-wench amongst the lookers-on. Laundresses, for some reason, had the reputation of whores in the Middle Ages, and probably this lass, Matilda, was a hulking wench. Edward bet that she would not ride with them and be in at the death of the stag ; he had to redeem his wager at the cost of forty shillings.

At this time the question of the Scottish succession was interesting the King. Alexander III had died in 1286, and his only remaining descendant was a granddaughter, Margaret of Norway, not three years of age. She was proclaimed Queen, and a commission of regency was nominated to manage affairs during her minority, until Edward decided that it would be a good plan to marry her to his son, Edward of Carnarvon. All his elaborate plans, however, were wasted ; Scotland agreed to the union, but while Margaret was being carried from Norway to England in a Yarmouth ship she died, and the Scottish throne was left empty. From every side claimants sprang up, all producing good causes to show that they had rights to the crown, but the question was at last reduced to two men—John Balliol, grandson of the eldest daughter of David, Earl of Huntingdon, the brother of William the Lion, and Robert Bruce, son of David's second daughter. The regents dared not settle the problem, and passed it on to Edward, who, proud of his reputation for justice, was delighted at the opportunity and took full advantage of it, making the Scottish barons swear fealty to him as their suzerain. Once the oath was given he was satisfied and demanded nothing further, reappointing the former regents and adding to them an English border baron. He then, after long consultations, decided

21

that Balliol was the true heir ; Balliol was crowned at Scone as King John, and gave homage to Edward at Newmarket.

But before this settlement was reached, Queen Eleanor had died. Apparently she died slowly of some fever—" autumnal fever "—at the village of Harby, in Nottinghamshire, near Lincoln, on November 28, 1290. Edward was with her at the end ; after her heart had been sent to the church of the Black-friars in London, her embalmed corpse was taken to Lincoln, and from there on December 5 it set out on one of the most melancholy yet beautiful funerals in history. Wherever her body rested on its way from Lincoln to Westminster—which it reached on the 17th—Edward raised a cross of rare beauty, of Caen stone and marble, sculptured and marked with the heraldic shields of his dead Queen. There were twelve of these crosses—three of which still remain, at Geddington, Northampton, and Waltham—the last and most beautiful being built on the road from London to Westminster at the village of Charing.

This was a tragic year for Edward, the turning-point in his life. He found himself suddenly alone ; not only was Eleanor dead, but his treasurer Kirkby too was gone, and it was not long before his mother and Burnell also died, and were followed by Peckham. Edward remained alone, growing old amongst young men who did not understand his ideals, who were impatient of the past and eager to begin their own world of fresh dreams and ambitions. With the passing of Eleanor, Edward lost some of his greatness ; until now, he had succeeded at everything to which he turned his hand—the Continent was pacified, Wales subdued, the Church beaten, and Scotland at peace. All this was suddenly to go, as if the Queen had been some angel protecting him from defeat. " I loved her dearly during her lifetime," he wrote sadly to a friend, " I shall never stop loving her now that she is dead."

Over her tomb in Eadward the Confessor's chapel in Westminster he placed a splendid metal statue at the feet of Henry III. One hand upon her breast she lay and faintly smiled. Her long hair rippled to her shoulders, falling from a circlet made of trefoils. The metal effigy was thickly coated with gold. In that tomb the great King buried all he loved, and remained alone to face a world that was young and was contemptuous of his stern ambitions ; alone, with his son giving no promise of following his path, Edward faced a people who no longer really understood him. He was of a past generation, and soon he was to realise it, soon when the troubles gathered about him and he held with both hands to his throne, trying to bring sanity into a world gone suddenly mad.

KING PHILIP IV of France was determined at the first opportunity to make the King of England surrender Gascony. The opportunity came when in April 1293 the men of the Cinque Ports and the Gascons defeated the French fleet off Saint-Mahé in Brittany. Sea-fights were mainly personal affairs in the Middle Ages for there was little difference between a sailor and a pirate. But Philip seized this chance of humbling Edward and demanded that he indemnify the defeated French who had lost huge cargoes of wine and a great many seamen in the conflict. Edward naturally refused : he was a sovereign Prince, he said, and he would be subject to no man ; his courts were open to all nations, if any one had suffered injustice, let him plead there. Actually Edward was in the wrong, for being Duke of Gascony he was the vassal to Philip and the knowledge of this probably made him climb down a rung of his majesty. He suggested that the trouble might be ended by arbitration or by a personal interview between himself and Philip. Philip, however, was determined to press the question to extremity : he cited Edward to appear in Paris and when Edward stayed away he declared him contumacious and his duchy forfeit.

The last thing that Edward desired was war with France. His ambition had always been to lead a second crusade ; Acre had recently fallen, and Pope Nicholas IV had called upon him to sail to recapture it and to stamp the infidel out of Syria. The moment, it seemed, had arrived, when Philip suddenly denounced him. Edward strove to keep peace. While sending the brave John of Saint-John to defend Gascony against invasion, he dispatched his brother Edmund of Lancaster to Paris to try to calm Philip. Edmund was no match for the crafty Frenchman ; Philip led him on, apparently agreed to a treaty, and then denounced it, saying that he had never consented to its sealing. Even his own barons were horrified, for while Philip was within the law—the treaty having been arranged by his Queen—it was known that she had only acted at his orders. But Philip ignored their protests, he rushed his army into Gascony, and took the duchy almost without a blow, for Edward, accepting the treaty, had withdrawn his troops.

This treachery must have come as a great surprise to Edward.

He was a man who did not lie openly, if he swore an oath he kept to it until he found a trick of morally wriggling out of it ; Philip had lied, he had pretended to agree to all that Edmund had proposed and he had only waited until Gascony was undefended before he seized it. Even his noble rage, however, did not sweep Edward into war. Cunningly he tried to ring France in with enemies, forming alliances with Adolf of Nassau, King of the Romans, with Count Guy of Flanders, and with the Counts of Holland and Brabant ; Count Amadeus the Great of Savoy, the Count of Bar, and the King of Aragon were also drawn into the alliance. Not only did he seek foreign allies, but Edward was busy raising an English force. Here he found difficulty, for as yet there was no hatred between the nations—that was to come later, in the days of Edward III—and the English had little or no interest in Gascony. They did not care if it turned French, they were satisfied to remain snug behind the Channel and to spend their money on their own affairs. Edward strove to bully them, and at least the war did this good—it created a permanent parliament of the three estates, for the King's urgent need for money made him call on all classes. He sent his officers to squeeze every penny from the land, and in their zeal they broke open churches, ferreting in towers and belfries, smashing moneycoffers, and even forcing their way into miserable lazar-houses to strip the lepers. Money. . . . Edward must have money, and the clergy who did not follow him to war must pay the heaviest tax. Luckily for him, Peckham was dead and the primacy was vacant, therefore the clergy had no leader. He demanded half a whole year's revenue from every beneficed ecclesiastic, and his fury was so gigantic when they quibbled that the Dean of St. Paul's dropped dead from sheer terror.

At last, by stealing and threatening and raging, Edward gathered his army and prepared to embark. Then rebellion flamed in Wales and he had to turn his men away from France to use them against the principality he thought was at peace. Again he cut the enemy off on Snowdon, but his own troops suffered almost as greatly as the Welsh. During Christmas, 1294, while the snows lay like icing over the mountain-tops and the cold winds lashed the steel-clad men, the English were reduced to eating only a little bread and salted meat and drinking water sweetened with honey. Once when a cask of wine was found, it was put aside for the King's use ; Edward refused it, saying, " No, when all are hungry all things should be common, we will eat alike until God gives us release. I who led you into this pass shall have no preference." When spring came, the Welsh were driven by starvation to surrender, and in May 1295 Edward was back in England.

John of Saint-John had led an army to Gascony while Edward fought in Wales. The war fluctuated with victory on neither side ; it continued all through 1295, and in 1296 Edward's brother Edmund, when repulsed from Bordeaux, died of a broken heart, being suffocated with rage at his own defeat. And the alliances were crumbling, the Count of Flanders turned traitor, the Count of Holland was murdered, the King of the Romans forgot his obligations and began a private war in the east of Germany. Edward found that, despite all his care and planning, Philip possessed most of Gascony and himself was still unable to leave England. Wales might be subdued, but Scotland was rising, having sealed a treaty with France.

It was that peculiar narrow-mindedness of Edward that drove the Scots to rebel, as before it had driven the Welsh. In his treatment of both nations, Edward showed a tactless side of his character ; one feels that, although a sane and just man, he often let his sanity be over-mastered by his arrogance. He must have known, and he showed he knew, that the only way he could keep the Welsh and Scots as loyal vassals was by not interfering with them and by not forcing upon them the realisation that they were conquered peoples. In his dealings with John he made the poor King feel that he was a vassal who was to obey on the instant, and the whole country was outraged by his allowing Scots to appeal from their local courts to Westminster. Edward, how-ever, went too far altogether when he summoned the King of Scotland to appear in England on a charge of debt contracted by his predecessor and when he had the summons served by the sheriff of Northumberland as if John were an ordinary subject. The Scots intrigued with France—beginning that alliance which was to continue through centuries—and probably aware of this, Edward, in June 1291, called on John to meet him in London with eighteen of the magnates of Scotland to help in the war with Philip. John ignored the summons, which was about the only thing he could do, and Edward commanded that all his lands and goods in England be seized, together with those of all Scots-men who remained in Scotland. From this direct attack John could not escape ; he took the defensive and both countries made ready for battle. With the sacred banner of St. John of

Beverley waving above his host, Edward marched over the
border and made for Berwick. He summoned the town to surrender, and after waiting twenty-four hours received his answer
—a refusal. Then he trumpeted for the assault. We are told
that the English were driven to fury because of the insults shouted
by the besieged. Certainly, whatever the cause, they did a
bloody task that day. The Scots fell before their charge " like
leaves in autumn." When the Earl of Cornwall's brother lifted
his visor to see the clearer, an arrow struck him on the forehead.
Noticing his comrade fall, Edward shouted, " No quarter ! "
and no quarter was given. From seven to eight thousand Scots
were slaughtered and the massacre did not cease until Edward
saw a pregnant woman about to be murdered. He shuddered
and turned aside with the cry, " Laissez, laissez ! Let be !
Let be ! "

Berwick having fallen and the inhabitants being put to the
sword, Edward remained there a month to strengthen the broken
walls, himself actually trundling a barrow as he helped in the
work ; then a herald came from King John, renouncing his
homage. " The false fool ! " cried Edward. " If he will not
come to us we will go to him ! " and he called his troops to
pierce deeper into the country. On the heights around Dunbar
the Scots waited, but stupidly they left their position, thinking
the English were retreating, and charged down into the plain
to be beaten hopelessly by Earl Warenne. There was little
fighting after that. Towns gave in without an arrow being
strung, and on July 10, 1296, the wretched John surrendered.
Edward took him back to England, together with more valuable
booty—the Coronation Stone of Scone, which he removed to
Westminster. This was a small block of sandstone studded with
pebbles, but legend said that Jacob had used it for a pillow ; the
Scottish Kings were always crowned on it, and when Edward
carried it to England he was probably hoping to fulfil the prophecy
that the monarchy of Scotland would follow the Stone of Destiny.
He had a throne especially built for it and in future this was
used as coronation seat for the Kings of England.

After a progress through the defeated land, Edward called a
parliament of the nobles of both realms, intending to have himself recognised as King of Scotland. On August 28, 1296, the
barons, the clergy, the landowners and the burgesses swore
allegiance to him as " Sir Edward by the grace of God King of
England, Lord of Ireland and Duke of Aquitaine." By omitting

Scotland, Edward wished it to be understood that he did not consider it merely as a fief but as an integral part of his realm, as much England as Northumberland or any other county.

AGAIN Edward had to fight the English Church. The new Pope, Boniface VIII, forbade the clergy to pay taxes to any lay authority without papal permission. This outraged every King in Europe, and Philip of France retorted by forbidding gold or silver leaving the country ; he did not mention the Pope, but this law could be aimed only at Rome. Boniface was forced to give in, and hurriedly tried to explain what he had really meant by his bull. Edward had the same problem to face as Philip, yet he remained silent, letting the trouble run its course until it flamed before him. He was never a man to anticipate conflict ; when it arrived he tackled it with all his energy.

On January 13, 1297, convocation met in St. Paul's, and after eight days of discussion concluded that it could grant nothing to Edward without the Pope's licence. When the King was told of this decision, he replied curtly : " If you keep not your homages and oaths for your baronies, neither am I bound to you in anything," and he placed the clergy beyond royal protection, virtually outlawing them, for he forbade them to sue in his courts and took whatever lands they held by lay tenures, and if a layman met a clerk riding a horse he could take the horse ; this actually happened to the new Archbishop of Canterbury, Robert Winchelsea, when he hastened to try to soften Edward's rage. The King's officers took not only his horse but the horses of his followers ; and after all, his mission came to nothing. Edward would not be moved from his purpose, and the archbishop was forced to give back a little ; he decreed that every clerk could follow his own conscience. Most of the clerks rushed at once to free themselves from outlawry, but Winchelsea, a stern brave man, refused to pay a farthing. Edward took his lands away and never forgave him.

STILL the continental question remained undecided. Each time he had thought to leave for Gascony something had frustrated the King, and now he was determined to send an army to drive Philip finally from his lands. He called a parliament at Salisbury ; the clergy were not invited to attend for they were still considered outlaws, and, as the commons had already paid their tax, only the nobles were present. To them Edward told his

decision : he would go to Flanders to inspire his allies while the
barons could lead an army into Gascony. The barons refused.
Now that Gloucester was dead, the leaders of the baronage were
the Earl of Norfolk and the Earl of Hereford, and they spoke for
the others. " Willingly," said Norfolk, " will I go with you,
O King, and fight before you in the front rank, as is my hereditary
duty." " You will go with the others," said Edward, " and
without me." " I am not bound to do it," replied Norfolk,
" nor will I go abroad, my lord, without you." Edward lost his
temper. " By God, sir earl," he shouted, " you shall either go
or hang." " By that same oath, Sir King," answered the earl,
" I will neither go nor hang."

Norfolk was ready to prove his words. He and Hereford
retired to their estates and sent the arrière-ban amongst their
dependants, calling out the vassals sworn to fight with them.
Edward would not be daunted ; if the barons refused to fight in
the war, he would make them pay for it. He seized wheat and
oats, beef and bacon, and commanded all the wool in England
to be made ready for shipping overseas. Not only did he press
upon the baronage, but he turned also against the people, he
ordered that all persons owning land valued at £20 a year or
upwards to be ready with arms and horses for service either
abroad or at home ; a little later he summoned them to appear in
London by July 7 for an expedition abroad.

All classes were now prepared for rebellion. When the
King's officers entered the lands of Norfolk and Hereford to
seize wool and hides, they were ordered away under threat of
death or mutilation. Edward would not give in, and as he
cunningly worded his command for the levies to come to London
so as to make it seem a favour and not a demand—" affectionately requiring and asking them "—Norfolk and Hereford condescended to appear. Edward realised that his rage had driven
him beyond reason, and he spoke in an apologetic fashion, asking
pardon for his sins. Even Winchelsea was affected by his speech,
and Norfolk and Hereford, while remaining silent, made no
threatening move. " For your sakes," cried the King to his
people, " I am going to face danger, and I implore you, should
I return, to receive me as you have always received me, and I
will give back all I have taken. If I should not return, here is
my son, accept him as King."

Having satisfactorily smoothed over the danger, Edward
now asked for more money, and Winchelsea put him aside by

promising to call a council ; Norfolk and Hereford refused to serve abroad, pointing out that Scotland had risen again, that the country was penniless, and demanding that the King never take his subjects' goods by force and that the charters be reissued and confirmed. Edward could not evade submission, so he decided to ignore the trouble, to leave it behind him while he embarked for Flanders. Times had altered since the days when a King like John could defy the nation, for Magna Carta had done this good—it had created a precedent and had proved to all that a King was purely the guardian of his people and that he must not betray his sacred trust. Edward might fling his troubles aside by running from them, yet he was cautious enough in these more democratic times to write a letter to his people, speaking to them in a man-to-man fashion, remarking that the illegal taxation hurt him as greatly as it hurt them, that he had not inflicted it for personal profit, not to buy lands or tenements or castles, but to defend the nation against its enemies.

While at New Winchelsea overseeing the embarkation of his troops, Edward was nearly killed. The town was protected from the harbour by an earthen wall, and he was riding along this wall so that he could watch the ships moving in the tide, when the swishing of a windmill's sails terrified his horse. The beast sank back on its haunches and would not move, and Edward whipped it, struck it with his spurs, when suddenly it slipped and tumbled into the road below. It was thought that he was killed, for the fall was deep, but luckily the ground was mushy with recent rain and the horse fell upright on its hoofs.

On August 22 or 23 Edward sailed for Flanders, and he had scarcely left the country before Norfolk and Hereford appeared before the barons of the exchequer and offered their complaints in the name of the people of England, forbidding the collection of a tax that Edward had imposed. The regency, led by young Edward, could not stand against this force, to which was added the Archbishop of Canterbury ; all it could think to do was to summon a parliament to meet in London on October 6. Hereford and Norfolk arrived with small armies and took command of the gates of the city ; they showed Magna Carta and the Charter of the Forest, demanding that these be reissued. Young Edward was forced to give way, for news had come that the Scots had routed the English at Stirling. The King, who was at Ghent, could do nothing except endorse his son's act, and a great victory was won by the people.

Norfolk and Hereford were probably thinking only of themselves, they were not Simon de Montforts, but nevertheless their confirmation of the charters was of the greatest importance to England's constitution. They made no effort to plan redress, they produced the well-worn charters made with the skill of men long dead, and had them ratified. And this victory they tore from the fingers of the strongest of medieval Kings, from no reckless impatient John or feeble Henry III, but from a man who prided himself upon his statecraft and his courage. It is true that they waited until Edward's back was turned, yet Edward would have had to give in even if he had been in England at the time. After this concession, parliament was definitely formed.

THE barons were not the only ones taking advantage of Edward's absence ; Scotland too had risen, and now it had for leader a truly great soldier, William Wallace. Of Wallace's antecedents we know practically nothing, although songs and ballads have built for him the inevitable romantic childhood ; his name " le Waleys " means " the Welshman," but that he was actually Welsh is doubtful. He may have come from Strathclyde, which formed a part of ancient Cumbria or Wales, while a near-contemporary states that " although among the earls and lords of the kingdom he was looked upon as low-born, yet his fathers rejoiced in the honours of knighthood." To our knowledge, he had never sworn allegiance to Edward, and his ambitions must have been purely patriotic as he had no grudges to be revenged and sought nothing for himself. How his rising started we are not certain, for the various stories contradict each other, but it began just as Edward was about to sail for Flanders. Wallace was as yet not leader when Scots and English met at Irvine, and although the Scots had the greater army, they came to terms ; in disgust, Wallace drew back, and with a small force hid in Selkirk forest and from there defied the enemy. Then came the battle of Stirling, where the English were defeated and their leader, de Cressingham, was flayed, his skin being divided amongst the Scots, " for he was comely and too fat." It was an amazing victory, for Wallace led an undisciplined horde against trained soldiers, but the English stupidity lost the day. Instead of crossing the river by a ford, they pressed over a narrow bridge and were suddenly slaughtered before they could draw up in formation. Wallace's name rang through Scotland, the defeated country had at last a leader, and men of all ranks took down their swords and rode to fight beneath his standard. He chased the English, he flooded Northumberland and Cumberland with his avenging army, and the raw levies murdered and ravished at their will.

Edward was coming home. His efforts to inspire his allies with fresh courage had failed. The whole expedition, from beginning to end, was a series of failures ; when his troops disembarked at Sluys on August 27, the men of the Cinque Ports and the men of Yarmouth began a brawl in which twenty ships were burnt, and one of Edward's treasure-ships had to put to sea to keep out of danger. Then at Bruges Edward found that the burghers were in alliance with Philip. It was obvious that the war would only drag on with victory to neither side, and a truce was sealed declaring peace for two years.

Now Edward was free to tackle Wallace ; but first he had to fight his own troops who, chiefly the Welsh and Irish, began a private war against Ghent and for two days there was fighting in the city streets. Edward himself was once nearly killed ; a cross-bow was aimed at him and the bolt struck a man riding at his side. He had to pay heavy compensation for the damage done, and then set sail for England, landing at Sandwich on March 14, 1298.

BEFORE opening his war with Scotland, Edward went upon a pilgrimage to St. John of Beverley, whose banner had already once brought victory to him against the Scots, then he mustered his army at Roxburgh. He had few foot-soldiers, and those he had were chiefly Welsh and Irish, but, like all medieval generals, he relied mainly upon his chivalry. Wallace retreated beyond the Forth as the English army swept into Scotland, plundering as they went. Edinburgh was reached, and the invaders camped at Temple-Liston to the west of the city. Here Edward waited for his ships, as he was hard put for stores, Wallace having carefully wasted the surrounding country. Contrary winds kept his fleet from running up the Forth, only one ship arrived and it carried nothing but wine. This cargo Edward with extraordinary lack of foresight gave to his troops, with the result that civil war broke out between the Welsh and the English, and the Welsh, in their drunken fury, even talked of deserting to the Scots. " What does it matter if enemies join enemies," said Edward when this was reported to him, " Welsh and Scots are both our foes. Let them go where the like, for with God's blessing in one day we shall get our revenge on both nations."

News came that the Scots were at Falkirk and were making ready to attack, believing that Edward's movement towards Edinburgh was a general retreat. " As the Lord lives," cried Edward, " there is no need for them to follow me, I will march this very day and meet them face to face." His trumpets called his men together to proceed to the east of Linlithgow where they encamped on the moor. They slept with shields for pillows and with their horses tethered at their sides, and " the horses tasted naught but cold iron as they champed their bits." Suddenly in the middle of the night there was a shriek in the English camp and men sprang to arms, thinking the Scots were on them. The King was hurt, his horse had trampled on him, breaking two of his ribs, yet he refused to let the pain hold him from the battle. At dawn he mounted his horse with the others, and as he rode through the streets of Linlithgow he saw the lance-points of the enemy rimming the hills with silver. It was July 22, 1298, the feast of St. Mary Magdalen, and when Edward had reached the banks of the West-Quarter Burn, he called a halt so that mass could be celebrated. As the English approached, the spear-points disappeared ; Wallace retreated, then, realising that fight he must, he drew up his raw undisciplined troops in as strong a formation as possible. Wallace was a great general, and if his material had been better, his career would have been more glorious ; as it was, he departed from the usual medieval formation of three battles or divisions, and anticipated the tactics of later years by roughly drawing his men up into what to-day we might call " squares." He was on a gradual slope, his right touching Falkirk church, and before him was a swamp that the English must cross. He had few cavalry, and the footmen he massed in four rings or circles, the front ranks kneeling or crouching with raised spears behind a wall of stakes roped together. Between each circle he placed his archers ; these were not the dangerous archers of England or Wales, for the Scots in those days relied mainly upon the pike, and we are told that instead of drawing the string to the ear or shoulder, they drew it only to the hip. In the rear Wallace placed his scanty cavalry. This formation shows the brilliance of Wallace, his courage in attempting new ideas of war and it was his ill-fortune in having troops of untrained men that really lost him the day. Gazing upon his soldiers, Wallace briefly addressed them : " There," he cried, " I have brought you to the ring, hop [*dance*] if you can."

Edward did not wish to attack at once. After mass he thought to rest his troops awhile and serve out what provisions he had, but the barons were eager for the fight and argued that to dismount would leave them open to a sudden attack. Edward gave in to their demands. " Be it so," he cried, " in the name of the Father and the Son and the Holy Ghost," and he gave the signal to advance. He used the traditional formation of three battles, himself keeping command of the rear. The Welsh were placed in the front ranks, but they had no heart in the battle, being still in a state of mutiny, and the English men-at-arms led the charge. The swamp held them back, their horses fell in the mud and wet, and the first division had to wheel round towards the Scottish right, while the second division wheeled to its left. The Bishop of Durham, leader of this second division, thought his men raced too quickly, and he would have called a halt to await reserves if Basset of Drayton had not jeered at him. " To your mass, bishop," cried Basset, " leave us to fight."

The Scottish cavalry in the rear was struck on either side by the converging battles, and it fled. Then the English turned upon the rings. These could not be broken by charges, but arrows and slings soon smashed a path through the packed men ; and once a path was made, the fight was over. Wallace called together a small force and retreated into the woods at Callander while the English chased the fugitives for miles.

The battle of Falkirk destroyed Wallace, it wrenched from him the prestige he had gained at Stirling, yet he had performed his task bravely. With a disciplined army he might have rescued Scotland from the English, and his achievement was great. He had bound a broken nation together, he had given it courage and unity, preparing the way for Robert Bruce.

EDWARD had won the battle but Scotland was unsubdued. After desultory fighting and valueless marches, lack of provisions at last sent him from the country, and Christmas 1298 was celebrated at Cottingham, near Beverley, in Yorkshire. After Christmas he turned south.

On March 8, 1299, he met his parliament at Westminster to discuss the continental question. Pope Boniface was trying to arrange peace and had suggested that Edward marry Margaret, Philip's sister, and that Edward's son marry Philip's daughter Isabel. To this Edward agreed. His barons now reminded him of the charters, particularly of the Charter of the Forest, which took from the King many of his absolute rights over forest lands. These rights had been a strong grievance since the days of the Conqueror, and Magna Carta had tried to curtail some of them, taking from the King his monopoly of hunting, his fierce laws against interference with wild beasts, his treatment of those poor wretches whose lands were enclosed by forests, and the brutal punishments and heavy fines inflicted upon poachers. But the forest rights were dear to the hearts of Norman Kings— Edward, who adored hunting, would rather have surrendered anything except these ; he shifted his ground before the council's attack, he even left town on the excuse of illness, but the people were determined. They had suffered too long from this tyranny, the worst of all tyrannies. At last, on April 3, Edward was brought at bay, he was made to reconfirm the charters ; even now he would not give in utterly and he added a lawyer's clause, " saving the rights of the crown," which deprived them of their strength. They were read in St. Paul's churchyard, and " when the people saw the charters with their seals they blessed God and the King, but when they heard the ending their blessings changed to curses." Even his narrow legal tricks did not save Edward ; the people were united and they refused to help him in his Scottish wars unless he gave in completely ; raging at the parliament of May 3, he confirmed the charters without the cheating proviso.

Scotland was still unsubdued ; before Edward could lead another army northwards the continental question had to be settled and Philip was haggling about the terms of peace, not wishing to part with Gascony. Edward had dropped his alliance with Flanders and he expected Philip to drop his with Scotland, and at last reluctantly Philip agreed not to demand that Scotland be included in the peace. On August 3, 1299, negotiations were finally settled at Chartres, and on September 3 Margaret landed at Dover to be married to Edward on the following day.

The old widower might reverence the memory of Eleanor, all the same he was not above being enchanted by Margaret. She was apparently quite beautiful, although her elder brother and sister so dazzled contemporaries that they had few words left with which to speak of Margaret. Edward made certain that report did not exaggerate her qualifications for his bed ; he asked for the most intimate details about her person, and his ambassadors had to report not only on her obvious charms, but on the size of her foot and the width of her waist. She was twenty, Edward was sixty, and unfortunately we have no details of her person ; in character she was pious and charitable, " good withouten lack." When she married King Edward, her niece Isabel was also betrothed formally to her stepson. From Canterbury, after a month, the royal couple entered London, passing through streets hung with cloth-of-gold and down Chepe in which two conduits splashed out wine.

Margaret was sent to the Tower while Edward rode north to fight with Scotland. The Westminster apartments had been recently burnt and the Tower was the only royal palace suitable for a Queen ; besides, there was a plague in London and any city residence would have been dangerous. As it was, Edward forbade any petitioner from the city entering the Tower walls lest he bring contagion on his breath or in his clothes.

PHILIP and Pope Boniface were both on the side of the Scots— Philip because he wished to keep Edward out of France and Boniface because he wanted to show his power. Edward was told to cease fighting because Scotland was a papal fief, and if he had any quarrel with the country he was told that he could bring it to be heard before the curia. When the Pope's commands reached England, Edward was already in the north. It was winter, and with bad communications and the difficulty of transport, the season was rarely used for fighting in the Middle Ages. But Edward was impatient, stung to fury by the continual rebellions. With his son he reached Berwick in December to review the troops. It was a gorgeous gathering of knights in polished armour and heraldic surcoats, their shields blazoned in rich colours, with horses gaily caparisoned. Yet the army did not move. Edward had sworn to reissue the charters, but he had made no attempts to carry out his promises, he had not interfered with one forest law. Now he had again to turn his back on Scotland to meet a parliament where he was forced once more to confirm the charters. It was not until June that the glorious army gathered again, this time at Carlisle. " The blaze of gold and silver and the shining of the rich colours of the embattled host illuminated all the valley " as Edward led his men to the siege of Caerlaverock Castle. " The English knights were dressed, not in coats and surcoats, but were mounted on expensive and powerful chargers, and were well and strongly armed against surprise. There were many rich caparisons embroidered on silks and satins, there were many beautiful pennons on lances, and many a banner shown." Poorly garrisoned though it was, Caerlaverock held out bravely. When the English tried to escalade, they were tumbled off their ladders by huge stones, and their coloured coats were torn and dirtied while the men inside them were slain. Edward had brought with him the latest siege-engines, battering-rams and catapults, and after a week a white flag fluttered from the castle gate-tower. The man who raised the flag had his hand pinned to his face by an arrow as he waved it.

Edward progressed into the country only to be faced by the old problem—lack of food, and the rains this year were particularly heavy ; by August 30, 1300, he was back in England, where, pressed by Philip, he agreed to a truce to last until May 21, 1301. The Pope was also pressing him hard, demanding that he stop invading a papal fief. Winchelsea, as the Pope's representative, showed the letter he had received from Rome, and it was read aloud in Latin and French before Edward and his son and the leaders of the army. " By God's blood," cried Edward, " I will not keep peace for Sion nor silence for Jerusalem, but with all my strength I will hold my right which is known to the whole world." He had the barons beside him, yet he dared not quarrel openly with Boniface. He sparred for time by sending envoys to Rome giving details of his claim on Scotland, and he made it quite clear that he would not surrender his conquest, stating that " by God's blood " he would defend his rights.

Parliament at Lincoln on January 20, 1301, demanded that the charters be carried out. Edward, while reissuing these charters, had done nothing whatever to hold to his oath, and now again, with various shifty evasions, he swore to see that his promises were kept. The barons, on the King's submission, stood at his side in his dispute with Boniface.

For the sixth time Edward invaded Scotland, and again there was no definite battle. The disorganised Scots could not gather an army capable of meeting the English. Then Edward, who had such persistent ill-fortune in all his dealings, had a stroke of luck. Philip and Boniface quarrelled and Boniface hurriedly dropped the cause of Scotland, fearing to have Edward turn against him, and for the seventh time Edward prepared for an invasion. On April 22, 1304, he besieged Stirling, the last important fortress to stand against him. It was built high on a precipitous rock, difficult to capture, impossible to escalade, and it had remained in Scottish hands since 1299. Edward was now going to make quite certain of success ; he brought with him every available siege-engine, with balls of metal and stone that weighed from 100 to 300 pounds. He even wrenched lead from the roofs of churches to add to his store of missiles—although he paid compensation for it later—and he had with him a supply of the terrible " Greek Fire," a Byzantine weapon, a mixture, it is believed, of nitre, saltpetre, sulphur and carbon stuffed into clay vessels which either exploded on contact or were fired by a slow-match. They burst into flames that could not be extinguished and which stifled you with awful fumes. Besides the bomb-kind, there was also a liquid " Greek Fire," made of some preparation of naphtha which was either syphoned or pumped up a hose : it could burn through almost anything.

For three months the siege continued and " the King showed himself as freely as any of his men." His Queen was with him, and a special oriel window was knocked into the King's house inside the town so that with her ladies she could watch the fighting as if it were some knightly tournament. Probably the knowledge that her eyes were on him inspired the King to be so reckless with his person. A quarrel struck him once, it went through his armour but did not pierce the flesh. Edward had it pulled out, spat upon it, then shook it at the man who had fired the crossbow. " I will hang you for that ! " he shouted. And on another occasion a great stone was flung from the walls and struck down his horse. His men dragged him from under the beast and implored him not to expose himself to such dangers. " As the Lord lives," cried Edward, " I will not desert you, no matter if you go to life or to death."

At last the garrison surrendered unconditionally, and Edward, knowing that his lady watched, decided to stage a degrading show. He made the captain of the garrison with twenty-four of his officers kneel before him dressed only in their ungirdled shirts.

All the Scottish castles were now English but the brave Wallace was still free ; he had been hiding in the forests and hills, where we do not know, and he was active during the siege of Stirling, cutting off the English convoys. He then left the country and was captured at Amiens, only to be freed by Philip and sent to Rome. Soon he returned to Scotland, although there was a heavy price upon his head. A traitor told the English of his hiding-place and he was captured and chained and dragged to London, which he entered on August 22, 1305. The trial

22

was hurried through in a disgraceful fashion at Westminster Hall. Crowned with laurel because " he had said in times past that he ought to wear a crown in that hall," he was arraigned as a traitor, a murderer, a robber, a fire-raiser, and worse.   To the accusation of traitor he quite rightly objected, although he admitted the other charges.   He had never sworn allegiance to Edward and therefore, as he pointed out, he had never committed treason. Sentence was passed at once and executed immediately.   At the door of the hall Wallace was roped to the tail of a horse and, on a hurdle, dragged to the Tower, from the Tower he was dragged to Aldgate, and from Aldgate to the Elms at Tyburn. As murderer and robber he was hanged, as outlaw he was beheaded, for sacrilege " in burning churches and vessels containing the body of Christ and relics of the saints " his entrails were scooped out and burnt, and as a traitor his parboiled head was spiked on London Bridge and the four quarters of his body gibbeted at Newcastle-on-Tyne, Berwick, Stirling and Perth.

The sentence was barbaric, nevertheless had Wallace been guilty it would have been legal ; where Edward is to blame lies in the fact that Wallace was not guilty.   He was a soldier defending his country, and if in that defence he had killed and pillaged and broken open churches he had done nothing worse than the average medieval soldier, nothing worse than Edward himself had sometimes done.   He was no traitor or rebel, he had never sworn allegiance to England, and he should have been treated honourably as any conquered enemy was treated.   But Edward had decided that Scotland was not a separate country, that it was a part of his realm, and therefore any man who fought against him was fighting his rightful lord.   It was a legal quibble, typical of Edward, and it is unforgivable.   Wallace was a brave and noble patriot and he deserved a better end.   Others who definitely were traitors, who pledged their faith and then rebelled and afterwards submitted, tasted none of Edward's vengeance. Edward, after all, desired only the moral effect of Wallace's death, hoping to terrify future patriots.   In this he did not succeed, although at first it seemed that Scotland had given up all hope of breaking from its conqueror.   On September 15, 1305, a grand council of the two nations met and drew up regulations for the government of Scotland.   John of Brittany, the King's nephew, was appointed warden or lieutenant with the usual officers of state under him and with a council of twenty-two

Scotsmen to help in national affairs. Judges were chosen with sheriffs, coroners and other officials, both Scots and English. The old laws were abolished and English laws put in their place. Edward might rest satisfied, thinking the country subdued, but he had forgotten the hatred he had sown in a proud nation which, like the Welsh, was never to forget the humiliation of defeat and of seeing its ancient Celtic laws swept contemptuously aside.

At last Edward had the opportunity to take revenge on his own barons. Hereford was dead and Norfolk's spirit was broken. The King plotted to get into his hands the great fiefs that were capable of holding out against him. He was lucky when, in 1300, Cornwall fell to him by the death of his cousin, Edmund, and in 1306 when the Norfolk's estates escheated to the crown owing to lack of an heir. With the growth of his territories, Edward felt himself powerful enough to fight the Archbishop of Canterbury ; he had never forgiven Winchelsea for standing with the Pope on the question of taxes. His chance came when Philip arranged for Bertrand de Goth, Archbishop of Bordeaux, to become Pope as Clement V. Clement was a Gascon subject of Edward and he was so grateful at being elected to the papal throne that he was only too delighted to do anything that either King asked him. At Philip's command he even transferred the see from Rome to France, beginning the " Babylonish captivity " of the Church which placed it for years entirely in the grip of French Kings. Edward seized the chance to ask absolution for his oaths to observe the charters, and Clement agreed at once ; he absolved Edward from almost everything he had sworn. Armed with this bull, the King repudiated those clauses of the forest charter that had most annoyed him, and then he turned on Winchelsea, dispatching to Avignon a long list of the archbishop's alleged crimes, including treason. Clement suspended Winchelsea, summoning him to appear before the papal court, and the archbishop in a fury rushed to Edward and upbraided him, demanding permission to leave the country. " Permission to go," said Edward, " right willingly we give, but permission to return you shall never have. We know your craft, your subtlety, your treachery, and your treason. The Pope will deal with you as you deserve. Favour at our hands you must never expect. Merciless have you been to others and no mercy shall you get from us." On May 19, 1306, the arch-

bishop left England and he did not return until after the coronation of Edward II.

Then again started the war with Scotland. Robert Bruce,
eighth Earl of Carrick, was leading the revolt against Edward.

ROBERT BRUCE—or de Brus, to be exact—was the eighth male
descendant of a Norman baron who had come to England with
the Conqueror. He had become head of the family on the death
of his father in 1304 and owned great estates on both sides of the
border. These divided lands explain much of his fumbling in
the early days, his continual shiftings from the cause of Edward
to that of Scotland, and vice versa. A list of these fluctuations of
loyalty becomes monotonous and makes one at first despise the
man as a traitor to either side. Whatever were the sins of
Bruce's early years they were completely atoned for by the heroism
of his later days. One cannot compare him to Wallace, for
Wallace was a true patriot who desired everything for his country
and nothing for himself, Bruce had a claim to the Scottish
crown and his ambition was to become King. There were only
two really important claimants now that John was out of the
way—Bruce himself and the Red Comyn of Badenoch.

The opening of Bruce's career is dark with a terrible deed.
We have conflicting stories of this in detail, but they agree in
essentials. Although at the time he was strongly in favour with
Edward, Bruce suggested to Comyn that one of them should
make a bid for the crown, saying, " Support my title and you
shall have my estates, or give me your estates and I shall support
you." On February 10, 1304, he was at Dumfries where the
Red Comyn met him in the church of the Minorite friars, and
after a long talk they quarrelled ; perhaps Comyn threatened to
tell Edward of Bruce's meditated treachery. At any rate, Bruce
stabbed Comyn with a dagger and rushing from the church met
his two attendants, Kirkpatrick and Lindsay, outside the door.
They asked how things went with him, seeing his haggard face,
and Bruce cried, " Ill, for I doubt I have slain the Comyn."
" You doubt ! " said Kirkpatrick, " then I will make sure,"
and he ran into the church to stab the dying man with his dagger.
Red Comyn was surely dead after that.

Bruce hurried to Glasgow, away from the dangerous Comyn
lands, where Bishop Wishart absolved him for the murder and
arranged for coronation robes to be produced. He was crowned
at Scone on March 29, 1306, the bishop giving him not only the

robes, but the banner of the King of Scotland which he had kept hidden in his treasury.

EDWARD was not well, he was at Hyde near Winchester, enjoying the air and the sunlight, when news of the murder reached him on February 23. Quickly he made ready for a new campaign and Clement authorised the excommunication of Bruce. The King was too ill to ride, he was carried in a litter all the way to London where with great ceremony he knighted his son, the Prince of Wales, and during the banquet afterwards, when two swans in nets of gold were placed before him, he swore a most solemn oath that by God and the swans he would set out immediately for Scotland to avenge the wrongs done to Holy Church and the realm by the murderers of John Comyn ; and he added that when Bruce was defeated, he would never again bear arms against Christian men but would voyage to the Holy Land to die fighting the infidel. The Prince of Wales and the two hundred and sixty-seven new knights swore to the same oath, the Prince adding that he would not sleep two nights in the same spot till he had reached Scotland, while the King implored them not to bury him " until the Lord had given victory over the crowned traitor and perjured nation."

After this rather theatrical scene—for Edward, realising he was growing old, undoubtedly wished to inspire his son and the younger generation with his own ambitions—he gathered some more money by marrying off two of his granddaughters to young lords and by receiving a grant from parliament. In the excitement nobody seemed to notice that Edward had revoked his oath to the charters, having just received absolution from the Pope, together with Bruce's excommunication.

The King was too ill to travel, so the Prince led the army, following Aymer de Valence, Robert Clifford, and Henry Percy, who were already at Perth. The Bishop of Glasgow was caught on the way ; he was shackled and sent to England to await the Pope's sentence. Then on June 19, 1306, Bruce came hammering on the walls of Perth, and Valence told him that he would fight on the morrow; as Valence did not appear, the Scots withdrew for about six miles to Methven where they disarmed and sought for food and lodgings. It was not a strong army. Bruce had not had time to gather, equip and discipline troops, and when Valence, having again changed his mind, suddenly appeared, the battle was quickly over. The Scots ran to put on their armour and after a brave stand were quickly scattered ; Bruce himself was unhorsed and captured, but a friend recognised him and let him go.

It was not a great battle, it was little more than a skirmish, and its effect on Scotland was tragic ; when shortly afterwards Bruce was again defeated, it seemed that the national cause was doomed. Bruce managed to escape and hide in the Island of Rathlin off the coast of Ireland, and many of his followers were taken and treated brutally.

Again it seemed that Scotland was subdued.

IN asking absolution from his oath, Edward found that he had placed himself in the hands of Clement. Having given a favour, the Pope naturally thought it should be returned. He sent an agent, William Testa, to take control of Canterbury, now vacant after Winchelsea's suspension, and to demand the first-fruits of all other vacant benefices for the next three years. Edward was furious at this insolent demand, but although he might swear that no one should interfere with his kingdom, he dared not break openly with Avignon. He owed the Pope a great deal of money, and he compromised by ignoring the first-fruits and letting Testa seize all the temporal revenues of Canterbury while it remained vacant. Parliament was even more outraged than Edward when Testa put forward his claim. It addressed a petition to the Pope in the name of the clergy and people of England objecting strongly to these new exactions and it sent a similar protest to Edward. Testa was brought before parliament, forbidden to carry on his work, and made to deliver whatever coin he had already collected, while the Act of 1305 forbidding money leaving England was confirmed and published.

But the Pope was not to be got rid of quite so easily. There was trouble about the Prince of Wales's marriage, as Philip was not carrying out his agreement in surrendering certain castles. Clement interfered to settle the question, and his agent enticed from Edward three writs—one reinvesting Testa as administrator of the Canterbury revenues, another giving Testa power to act as papal nuncio, and a third permitting him to levy the first-fruits of all vacant benefices. When Testa came exultantly to Westminster, however, the council told him that although the King might give a dozen writs, he had not overruled the prohibitions of parliament and Testa must cease his exactions at once. This legal chicanery must have delighted Edward, it was exactly the kind of trick he liked to produce himself, and he quickly agreed to it. Testa was left as he was before, the writs being worthless without the backing of parliament.

AND now, for the last time in Edward's reign, Scotland rose in rebellion. Bruce had come from his hiding-place, he besieged Turnberry Castle; he had not men enough to withstand a relieving force from Carlisle and had to retreat. Then his comrade, James Douglas, surprised the English in his own Douglas Castle, and being unable to defend the captured walls, had to pull the place to scraps and destroy the provisions. Bruce was chased from bolt-hole to bolt-hole. Bloodhounds were used to track him down, and he eluded them by wading for a time through water, then he ventured back to the plains and men came flocking to serve under him. Aymer of Valence had long been jeered at for his inaction and, driven desperate by taunts, he challenged Bruce to battle. Bruce accepted the challenge and drew up his men across a field at the foot of Loudon Hill, with a marsh on each flank. The English could not break the sturdy line and were at last forced to retreat.

King Edward was very ill and he chafed with rage as messengers came telling of the weakness of his lieutenants. He could not send the Prince as he was away preparing for his wedding; there was nothing for it but to lead the army himself, old and sick though he was. Apparently he suffered from the medieval soldier's common complaint of dysentery, but his will was as strong as ever and he knew that without his presence to inspire the troops Bruce might yet reconquer Scotland. Therefore the old man stood upon his feet and offered up in the cathedral church of Carlisle the litter that had carried him from the south. Then he sat his horse and unfurled his banner and rode north to strike terror into the armies of Bruce. Yet, for all his courage, he could not ride more than two miles that first day, and scarcely farther on the second. On the third day he rested, and on the fourth he gritted his teeth until he had reached Burgh-on-the-Sands, barely six miles from Carlisle. He could ride no longer, and realising that he was dying, he sent his farewell to his son, insisting that the Prince continue the invasion of Scotland, and that he keep away from worthless favourites, and he begged him to carry his bones into Scotland so that even when dead he might lead his armies to victory, and he asked that his heart should be sent to the Holy Land with a hundred knights to fight the infidel.

Then quietly he died, on Friday, July 7, while his attendants were lifting him up on his couch so that they might give him his morning meal.

To the last his thoughts winged to those two ambitions he had never fulfilled—the conquest of Scotland and the conquest of the Holy Land. And even his dying requests were not carried out ; his bones did not go to Scotland nor his heart to Jerusalem. The Prince reached Burgh on July 18 to gaze upon the embalmed face of his great parent, then the corpse, after resting at Waltham, was carried slowly to Westminster where, on the feast of St. Simon and St. Jude, October 27, it was buried under the high altar to the north of St. Eadward's shrine. There it remained until busy antiquaries disinterred it on May 2, 1774, to discover that the face " retained its exact form, although part of the flesh appeared to be somewhat wasted. It was of a dark-brown, or chocolate colour, approaching to black ; and so were the hands and fingers. The chin and lips were entire, but without any beard ; and a sinking or dip, between the chin and under-lip, was very conspicuous. Both the lips were prominent ; the nose short, as if shrunk ; but the apertures of the nostrils were visible."

Over the tomb was raised a simple slab of Purbeck marble with a base of Caen stone, and at a later date was carved the inscription : " Edwardus Primus Scotorum Malleus hic est MCCCVLIII. Pactum Serva." The date of course is incorrect, but the words might have pleased Edward in one of his less splendid moments. " Here is the first Edward, Hammer of the Scots. Keep Covenant."

Hammer of the Scots ! That was his proudest achievement and the one in which he was to fail. But to-day he is remembered more because of the justness of his laws than for his continual invasions of Scotland. A great King—like many great Kings, he bequeathed to his son only a worthless heritage.

X

KING EDWARD THE SECOND

1307–1327

IT IS THE USUAL THING to dismiss King Edward II's reign with contempt, and it is significant that he is one of the very few English Kings whom no historian so far has considered worthy of being given a complete biography. He is usually hurried over, pushed aside as "worthless," as the futile and cowardly son of a great King. To-day he is beginning to be treated with a little more understanding, but so many historians put on their olympian spectacles before contemplating the Middle Ages that an unfortunate King such as Edward II has almost no hope of being studied with sympathy. In the first place, like William II, he was undoubtedly homosexual, and that is enough for most writers of the past to have considered him a man of bad morals and weak character. The morals of Edward we have no right to judge ; our concern is to see him purely as a man, and to try to understand through the cold phrases of old records and the biased comments of chroniclers what kind of a human being he was and why he behaved in the fashion he did behave.

The average man's knowledge of medieval and Tudor history is based upon literature—he turns to romantic writers to find what happened in the past, and, much as they may chafe at this, most historians have brought it on themselves by rarely bothering to see Kings as people moved by loves and hatreds, shaken by fears, bent by too human furies ; they have preferred to judge them by the loftiest standards of kingship. From birth these wretched Kings are supposed to wear haloes, and if they should fling the haloes aside to reveal their failings they are usually damned. Yet like us they lived tragic lives, they too dreamed weak dreams of happiness and were exposed to cold and heat, could feel the prick of love and the damp terrors of despair. And they were lonely, tragically lonely, seeking friendship amongst bullies and sycophants. Jealous nobles clustered about the throne, clenching fists in menace or holding out their palms for favours. To whom could a King turn during those awful moments that come at times to every man, those moments of helpless despair when all the world seems an enemy forest gradually creeping in to suffocate you? He was utterly alone with the heavy sceptre in his hand and the crown pressing upon his head ; watched on every side, if he sought merriment in simple fashion it was noted and whispered about ; if he loved, all men knew of it ; if he hated, revenge was too easy to take. And above everything lay the threat of rebellion, of the time when these grasping nobles might push him from his throne and seize all England. To be a King. . . . It is not passing brave, as Marlowe's Tamburlaine might think ; it is to know at their highest pitch the most damnable of all emotions—terror, rage, despair and loneliness.

To understand the Kings as they were, as human beings, the average reader turns to fiction, to be misled by the feverish action of Dumas, by the gigantic melodrama of Ainsworth, or to be gently cajoled by the wise Sir Walter Scott. And even stronger than the influence of fiction is the influence of the stage, and in particular of Shakespeare. The terrific hatred of Richard III to-day is without doubt based in Marlowe's drama—which bears the name of Shakespeare—and also the average man's conception of Edward II comes again from Marlowe, from one of the most splendid chronicle-plays in English but also one of the most inaccurate.

BEING the son of a great man, Edward II could scarcely become a great man. From childhood he had had this godlike figure before him of a strong brutal humourless father who would caress him with one hand and whip him with the other. To be the son of Edward I, of a King so certain of his own perfection, is enough to cripple ambition in any child. As the boy grew he realised that he was expected to carry out his father's wishes ; he was to be a third Justinian, a second Hammer of the Scots. Rebellion was inevitable.

Edward's childhood could scarcely have been a happy one with a father to whom justice was the only ideal. When he was six, his gentle mother died and he was reared by nurses for whom he always retained the deepest love. Of his childhood we have few details : when he was nearly ten he and his sister Margaret were ill with the tertian fever ; they were cured, as the physician himself proudly informs us, by being wrapped in scarlet cloth and having bed and furniture turned to a bright red. So delighted was the physician by this treatment that he used " the red system " on the sons of the noblest houses in England, " and made good cures of all."

Brought up in this stern household, drilled like a soldier into the ways of kingship, Edward yet found one comrade whom he was ever to love and whom history has treated with almost entire lack of sympathy—the Gascon, Piers or Peter de Gaveston, called affectionately Perrot by Edward. It has often been said that Gaveston came of ignoble stock, but his father had stood high in the affections of Edward I and had served him so faithfully that as a reward his son was placed in the household of the heir-apparent. From that moment—probably in 1299—the two boys remained the closest friends and it was Gaveston's insolence that gave the new King's enemies their opportunity to rebel. For Gaveston was insolent : he had a cruel tongue and an impudent manner ; he might be grasping, seizing money to help his Gascon relatives, yet he did not meddle with state affairs. He was the King's friend, never his adviser.

Edward himself rarely meddled with state affairs. His father's complacent belief in himself and in his own destiny had bred in the son a contempt for statecraft. He deliberately turned aside from the dead hand that the King in his last moments had forced upon him. Edward I had not thought of England as he lay dying, he had not thought of his son, he had thought only of his own ambitions and, like a curse, had laid their fulfilment on the Prince of Wales. Selfish and arrogant to the end, the great King gave to the future King a bankrupt exchequer and an apparently endless war.

Naturally, the son did not carry out his father's last commands. Because a parent whom he could never have loved had ordered him to continue a policy in which he did not believe, why should young Edward have kept on with futile attempts to annex Scotland? He was almost penniless and had to face not only war with Scotland, but also the threat of war with Wales, the possible loss of Ireland and Gascony, and a collection of outraged barons and clergy. It was not an attractive prospect. Edward I was probably our greatest King, yet in his greatness he had stretched to their most dangerous extent every royal prerogative, and now the unfortunate son was made to face the chaos.

EDWARD II was exceptionally handsome, he was tall and graceful and powerfully built. " God had given him," says a chronicler, " better advantages of birth and nature than any other King " ; and another writes, " He was a man of fine person, of great physical strength, but of no settled character." He was over twenty-three when his father died and those twenty-three years of subjection to a powerful will that could never bear contradiction had not destroyed Edward's character as they might have destroyed the character of a weaker man ; he was when necessary capable of action and of thinking for himself, but his childhood had robbed him to a great extent of real initiative, making him despise the things which his father had revered—statesmanship and war. That he was no coward he proved in the Scottish campaigns, only he could find no pleasure in killing. One chronicler complains that " if he had spent as much care on fighting as he spent on farming, very prosperous would England have been and its name very glorious upon earth." Tournaments he despised, perhaps because his father had loved them so greatly that he had even defied the edicts of the Church in holding them. Young Edward, all the same, was not lazy, for he was a keen huntsman and fond of dogs and horses ; he liked also driving and rowing. In every possible way he strove to be unkingly ; despising the friendship of men of his own caste—with a few exceptions like Gaveston and Despenser—he associated with jesters, jongleurs, singers and actors, and amused himself by toying with metalwork and by staging plays. This passion for lowly tasks, or rather this detestation of noble ones, drove him even to digging ditches and thatching roofs. He was familiar with common people and fond of jests, yet his temper was quickly roused if he were offended. Particularly " he liked too greatly the vile company of sailors " and was fond of wine and food, and when drunk he " would let out his secret thoughts and quarrel with bystanders for feeble causes." He did not trust himself and perhaps therefore he drank the heavier to create the illusion of a greatness he knew he lacked, for when drunk a man is every inch a King unto himself. And often those who are conscious of their own inferiority, shy and aware of their weaknesses, seek wine to escape from themselves until the morning brings the terrible reaction when alone and in despair the repentant drunkard looks into the foulest of mirrors. This inferiority made Edward distrust his own opinions ; although he was intelligent, he was eager to believe the promptings of others, doubting so tragically his own thoughts. Witty, generous, hospitable, yet unlucky in every way, the second Edward is really one of the most pathetic of our Kings, one of the most intensely human. His lack of moral courage found in the insolent Gaveston the counterpart it needed —a man of resource, a carefree adventurer who accepted life who laughed at and despised the things which serious people valued. Gaveston also is pathetic. Intelligent enough to see through the illusions that drove ambitious men towards a worthless goal—the lust for power—he could stand aside and cover his own despairing futility with a jeer and a boast. As handsome as Edward, he was loathed by the English who accused him of having robbers and murderers in his train and of taking blank charters with the King's seal attached ; yet the scanty records of his brief administration in Ireland show that, although he was absurdly extravagant, he fought bravely and did attempt to rule the country with moderation.

Amongst the armed barons these young men sauntered with a curiously modern air. They were disillusioned and young and brave. They liked the coarse and jolly things of earth, wine and food and merriment and songs and music ; they drank with sailors and sweated with working men. There is a feeling as of tragic laughter about them, of the desperate laughter of men determined to suck what joys they could from a brutal and meaningless world. It is the laughter of the condemned who await the inevitable moment of sudden death.

WE possess some of Edward's letters when Prince and they reveal a gentle kindly soul. We see him again and again attempting to help poor friends and retainers ; little do we find of cruelty save in a request that a certain thief be hanged because " he has taken such a spite against us and ours that we would not willingly have grace or favour shown to him." His casual manners were of course blamed on his friends. Twice had the old King banished Gaveston from his son's court, once because with the Prince he had returned from the Scottish campaigns without leave—he had not returned out of cowardice, both young men had distinguished themselves in the actual fight, but apparently they left Scotland from sheer boredom, being weary of slaughter ; and he did not leave England in disgrace, for the King gave him a pension of one hundred marks a year, which was a goodly sum. This was the second banishment, in 1306 ; the previous one had been caused by the Prince's desire to create him Count of Ponthieu.

Gaveston did not stay abroad for long. When the Prince of Wales, on July 20, 1307, was proclaimed King of England, he quickly sent to Gascony to recall his friend.

WITH his magnificent schemes, Edward I had exhausted almost every right of the crown. He had antagonised the barons and had broken up many of the ancient earldoms, and he was in the midst of a quarrel with the Church when death took him ; the exchequer was empty and the revenues both of England and Gascony had been pawned to Italian bankers. Young Edward must have felt horror deepening about him as he contemplated the gigantic task ahead and felt the weight of his father's dead hand on his back. There was, first of all, the war with Scotland ; and Scotland, like Wales, was no easy land to conquer : the soil was poor and supplies could not be gathered, while the enemy naturally preferred to use guerilla fighting rather than pitched battles. There was also Wales ; and Wales was only held in comparative subjection by the harsh lords marcher—the border lords—who kept great armies behind the walls of their castles and sought brutal vengeance at the slightest hint of rebellion. Ireland, too, was only held by the same methods, by isolated lords, foreigners, building impregnable castles. Continual vigilance was needed to keep down these three nations. Philip of France was still trying to steal Gascony, and the barons of England were waiting their opportunity to take vengeance on the crown for the continual humiliations put upon them by the great King who had seized and kept to himself any earldoms and baronies that were escheated—left without an heir—and who had persistently evaded the commands of the charters, particularly the forest charter, when in his hour of need concessions were dragged from him.

The prospect might have terrified a stronger King than Edward II, and he merely ignored it. Realising his incapability, he preferred to amuse himself. At Carlisle he accepted the homage of the English lords ; then at Dumfries those Scottish lords who were not with Bruce swore fealty to him. He made at the moment no pretence of carrying on the war—his father's corpse gave him an excellent reason to journey south. The body was sent to Waltham where for nearly three months it lay near the bones of King Harold while young Edward faced a parliament at Northampton on October 13. Meanwhile he had sent to Gascony for his comrade Peter Gaveston, and had pre-

sented him with the earldom of Cornwall, one of the most powerful in England, which had been reserved by Edward I for one of
his younger sons. The new King—although not yet crowned,
Edward II dated his reign from his father's death—turned upon
the old ministers, wishing to make a clean sweep of the past, to
institute a young world that had no connection with the ideals
of a dying generation. Barons of the exchequer, royal justices—
nearly all were dismissed from office ; on examination we
discover that what Edward actually did was to turn the Prince's
household into the King's, to keep his old officers in the same
positions although raising them to a more exalted rank. The
loyal treasurer, Walter Langton, Edward's friend and adviser,
was imprisoned and had his property confiscated ; this was a
stupid act for Langton was Bishop of Chester, Coventry and
Lichfield, and his clerical status should have kept him immune
from lay justice. He was replaced by Walter Reynolds, a clerk
who has often been called illiterate, his elevation being explained
by his skill at theatricals ; this is untrue, Reynolds may have
been a clever actor or stage-producer but he was certainly not
illiterate. Edward I had appointed him tutor to his son and had
given him the post of keeper of the Prince's wardrobe—in other
words, making him his treasurer. Reynolds, therefore, like many
others of the Prince's household, retained his old position when
he became the King's treasurer.

Parliament having voted a good round sum, the new King
carried the old King's corpse to Westminster where it was buried
to the north of St. Eadward's shrine and next to the tomb of
Henry III. Edward's one desire now that he had freedom was
to amuse and honour his beloved friend, and on October 29
Gaveston was formally betrothed to Margaret, the King's niece.
If he had worked to destroy his comrade, Edward could not have
gone about it in a subtler fashion. By creating Gaveston Earl
of Cornwall and by bringing him through marriage into
the royal circle, he antagonised almost every English noble,
for they were outraged to see such honours showered upon a
young Gascon adventurer. The terrific hatred felt for Gaveston
is rather puzzling, for apparently he did not interfere in state
matters and he held no royal office, although several chroniclers
mistakenly call him the King's chamberlain. His influence
was probably exaggerated ; he may have had incalculable power
over Edward, but that he used this power for any evil purpose
has not been proved even by his most violent enemies. On one

point he must stand convicted : he was greedy for money and undoubtedly he used his influence to amass a fortune, and was the friend at court of the Guienne moneylenders. Edward I, unable to tax his subjects further, had surrendered the revenues into the hands of Italian and other bankers, letting them collect the monies in return for large advances. What the father had begun, the son was forced to continue. Amerigo dei Ferscobaldi was the English representative of these bankers, he received the customs duties and handled the royal exchange, and he also controlled the financial administration of Gascony. Little of the money he gathered ever found its way to the royal coffers, most of it stuck to his fingers in the process ; yet although he was the most powerful, he was not the only foreigner controlling English revenues. With the expulsion of the Jews, the moneylending business became the property of North Italians and of usurers from Cahors in Guienne. Writing of 1235, Matthew Paris tells us that " in those days the abominable plague of the merchants of Cahors grew so great that there was scarcely any one in all England, particularly among the prelates, who was not trapped in their nets. For they took advantage of the necessities of the poor, hiding their usury as trade and pretending they could not understand that whatever is added to the principal is usury, no matter what else it is called." Grosseteste, complaining on his death-bed against the ways of Innocent IV, gives us an example of their methods : " I borrow a hundred marks for a hundred pounds and am forced to execute and sign a deed by which I confess that I have received a hundred pounds which I will repay at the end of the year. And if perhaps within a month or less you repay the papal usurer the principal of the money you now have, he will refuse to take it unless you give him the full hundred pounds. This is worse than a Jew's conditions, for the Jew will accept the principal courteously whenever you return it with just enough interest to cover the time during which you have had it in hand." It was useless to fight these Caursini —or Lombards, as they were sometimes called, and it is interesting to note that the three balls of the pawnbroker was originally a Lombard badge, probably being flat like coins, on a shield —for according to Grosseteste, Pope Innocent " had raised them up and protected them in high places, and if any man speak against them he is exhausted by loss of labour."

The Italians, the Lombards and the Caursini were perhaps the strongest of the usurers, and the Gascons were not far behind—

and were probably included with the Caursini as Gascony and Guienne were usually spoken of as one nation—and chief amongst these was Betrand Calhau, Gaveston's nephew. Calhau often acted as the King's financial agent, arranging foreign loans, and on one occasion he travelled on a royal mission to Avignon. Therefore the barons when at last they rose against the favourite had at least one piece of mud to throw that would stick ; but it was the only piece they could find, and that is undoubtedly to Gaveston's credit. With the enormous power of his complete influence over the King, he did nothing with it except to help his relations in usury ; he was accused of transporting huge sums through Calhau to Gascony, but we have no proofs of this. He went little further than many medieval ministers and much less than most in accepting, probably with Edward's knowledge, what to-day we would call " graft." This graft is not enough to explain the detestation in which he was held by the English nobles. There was something in the man himself that was loathed, something in his flamboyant restless personality ; he was insolent and he liked to show his power, to strut in splendid clothes before his enemies, and, most unforgivable of all, he had a cruel tongue. He nicknamed the great men of England with names that hurt. These great men, the strong nobles, were Thomas of Lancaster; Guy Beauchamp, Earl of Warwick; John of Brittany, Earl of Richmond ; John of Warenne, Earl of Surrey ; and Aymer of Valence, Earl of Pembroke. Of these five, Lancaster was the most powerful, a vicious, selfish creature, a traitor, and in many ways a stubborn fool ; Warwick was almost of the same type, his treatment of Gaveston is unforgivable, although he is redeemed at least by his culture, for the chroniclers accord him a knowledge and love of letters wellnigh unique amongst the harsh nobility ; Richmond was a vague creature, a turncoat ; Surrey was a savage animal with scarcely a decent quality; and Pembroke remains the only one for whom we can have any respect, he was honest and rather simple, one feels that he was rarely led by any self-seeking motive, he fumbled clumsily to discover a string to lead him on the right path. For each of them, Gaveston had pet names that appear to have varied from day to day : Lancaster he would call " Fiddler," " Player," and " Old Hog " ; Pembroke he named " Joseph the Jew," because he was tall and swarthy ; Warwick was " The Black Dog of Arden "— " Does he call me dog ! " cried Warwick, " let him take care lest I bite ! "—and even his young brother-in-law, Gloucester, a lad

23

for whom he should have had affection, was called "Whoreson" and "Cuckold's bird," and in these last insults Gaveston was jeering at the honour of the King's sister, Joan of Acre. Evidently he was possessed of that cruel wit which cannot be restrained, which in its malice will sting even a friend to show its cleverness.

In his exultation at the great honours given him, the favourite proclaimed a tournament at Wallingford, and he was tactless enough to win, to defeat some of the most powerful barons. Humiliated at being made to bite the sand and dust of the tilt-yard, at being struck down by the arm of an upstart Gascon, the nobles gathered together, united in hatred, waiting for an opportunity to destroy their King's dearest comrade.

PROFESSOR TOUT argues that Edward had every intention of carrying out his father's wishes and that he was frustrated by the selfish ambition of the barons.[1] This is true enough : Edward again and again wished to fight the Scots but if he had been really determined he would have made stronger efforts. Nor do we find him sending the old King's heart to the Holy Land or keeping his bones to carry into Scotland. Being a kindly soul, Edward probably suffered acute attacks of conscience in which he spurred himself to carry on his father's work, then when frustrated, he gave in easily. His rebellion could not have been a conscious one, he most likely revered his harsh father's memory, yet never do we discover in him any sustained ambition to fight the Scots or to obey Edward I in eschewing unworthy councillors. The first thing he did on his father's death was to recall Gaveston.

With Gaveston at his side, he was prepared to face the fury of all England, and there is real courage in these two young men. They knew the storm they roused, they knew its dangers fully, and they did not flinch. When leaving to bring his bride to England, the King made Gaveston his regent, and therefore yet another point was scored by the magnates against the Gascon. A further point was added when, after his marriage to the twelve-year-old Isabel in Paris, Edward at his coronation appointed Gaveston to bear the crown.

It was a most gorgeous coronation. The state ride from the Tower to the abbey was on February 24, 1308, the coronation being performed next day, on Sunday 25. Originally it had

[1] *The Place of the Reign of Edward II in English History*, by T. F. Tout (Manchester University), 1914.

been planned for a week earlier and the delay can only be explained by the nobles' objection to the great honour given to the King's friend ; if this were so, their resistance came to nothing as Gaveston bore the crown. A thousand barrels of wine were sent from Gascony for Edward was determined to make the ceremony a jolly one, but even wine could not soothe the outraged dignity of the magnates. Lancaster carried curtana, the pointless edgeless sword of state, Lincoln and Warwick carried the other swords, Lancaster's brother Thomas bore the rod with the dove, and Hereford had the sceptre with the cross ; Despenser—soon to be hated more than Gaveston—with Arundel and two others upheld a checkered table on which lay the royal robes ; while the barons of the Cinque Ports lifted the embroidered canopies over the heads of the royal couple ; but none could avoid seeing the insolent figure of Gaveston strutting with the crown in his hands and dressed in robes more gaudy than the King's, in purple sewn with pearls.

Everything tended to make the ceremony a failure. So enormous was the crowd that a brick wall around the quire was pushed over and crushed a knight to death ; and when the banquet was served, it was badly managed, the servitors being either lax or under-staffed, and although the kitchen was full enough, many an aching belly remained empty. Numerous French knights had come to England in the train of Isabel ; Philip's brothers, Charles of Valois and Louis of Evreux, were present with other foreign nobles. All were disgusted by the ill-served dinner and the arrogant manners of Gaveston. The Queen's two uncles left the country, feeling that Edward's love for his favourite was an insult to their niece ; the interpretation that naturally enough they placed upon the relationship between King and favourite is, however, against both the historic and psychological evidence. Edward and Gaveston loved each other purely as brothers, having been reared almost as such.

IT is really most puzzling to explain the hatred aroused by Gaveston. There is a link here that we do not possess and that link must have been something in his manner, an insolent air which the chroniclers were unable to express in words. Other favourites have been hated—it is the lot of most favourites—but few in history have been detested as Gaveston was detested and with such apparently little cause. After the coronation there were threats of rebellion on every side, there were secret meetings of the magnates ; Winchelsea had been recalled by Edward, and he showed his gratitude by immediately joining the King's enemies. Matters came to a head at the grand council of March 3 when the Earl of Lincoln tried to force Edward to agree to anything that the barons might propose without his even knowing what the proposals were. The only lords who sided with Edward were the elder Despenser (both father and son were named Hugh), Gaveston's brother-in-law the Earl of Gloucester who was more or less neutral, and—most surprisingly—the Earl of Lancaster. The council broke up, civil war seemed inevitable, and when on May 30 a parliament of magnates again assembled, the barons arrived fully armed—" for self-defence "—and demanded that Gaveston be exiled. He had, they said, seized royal monies for his own pleasure and had turned the King against his rightful advisers. A paper was then executed that propounded the doctrine that homage was due not to the wearer but to the crown itself. We are told that the younger Despenser drafted this clause.

Edward, even with Lancaster at his side, could not withstand such united enmity. He agreed to dismiss Gaveston by Midsummer Day and Winchelsea swore to excommunicate the favourite if he stayed an hour beyond his time. Edward did what he could to evade his oath, he wrote to Philip for help, he pleaded with the Pope to forbid the ban of excommunication, and he heaped on Gaveston greater possessions. But he could not twist aside as the appointed day drew near ; Gaveston had to go. Edward created him lieutenant of Ireland and personally escorted him to his ship at Bristol. The barons were not satisfied ; having tasted success they made Edward dismiss yet other officials, including the elder Despenser.

On April 27, 1309, a parliament of the three estates gathered at Westminster. Edward needed two things : money and the recall of Gaveston. His second request was not listened to, but money was promised if he would agree to certain reformations including the abuse of purveyance—the taking of food-stuffs without payments by the King's servants—the heavy customs duties, the depreciation of the coinage, the tyranny of royal officials, the taxes on fairs—the most essential part of medieval trade—and the sale of pardons to criminals. Edward pleaded for time to consider these matters and was given until July 27.

He had been pushed too far. Suddenly he determined to

assert his royal dignity, to defy the barons. He recalled Gaveston who hurried back at once, for the Pope had agreed to annul Winchelsea's threats. Together the two comrades faced parliament at Stamford on July 27. They were now not so completely alone for Edward had intrigued and won the Earl of Lincoln to their side, with the Earl of Surrey. Gloucester was still with them, although Lancaster was shifting towards the magnates. At Stamford little was arranged except the continuation of war with Bruce. In the court, all was peace again, Gaveston being even allowed to hold his earldom of Cornwall, but he could not quieten that tongue of his, he could not restrain his quick and insolent intelligence from infuriating the barons. Soon he had lost his new friends : Lancaster definitely sided with the magnates, and Lincoln and Surrey followed. Gloucester alone made no move, he was young and unsure of himself and therefore remained neutral.

When on February 8, 1310, a grand council met in London the barons came armed despite the King's order that swords must be left at home. They came truculently, determined to bully Edward into reason, and they refused even to meet him if Gaveston were present. Gaveston was therefore ordered into retirement and Edward alone had to face the storm. The barons' demands had grown since the previous year ; they now not only wanted the banishment of Gaveston but they wished to steal from Edward all power. They began by offering a petition in which they gave a list of the present abuses, and they ended by demanding the formation of a committee to control the King. This was purely a baronial measure, the existence of the rights of the commons was not even thought of, perhaps because it was unnecessary : the commons would have agreed had they been asked. So long as he could keep his Gaveston the King would agree to anything and twenty-one members were elected to form a committee : the bishops elected two earls, and the earls two bishops,· these four elected two barons, and so on until the full complement was reached. The members of the committee were called the ordainers, because they swore to keep such ordinances as were " to the honour and advantage of holy church, to the honour of the King, and to his and his people's advantage according to the oath taken by the King at his coronation." Winchelsea was included amongst the bishops, and Lancaster, Warwick, Pembroke, Hereford and Arundel amongst the earls. with the more moderate Gloucester, Lincoln and Richmond.

Two days after their election the ordainers issued six ordinances dealing with the more pressing questions such as the farming of customs-dues by foreigners and the King's taxing of the people without their consent.

Realising that the farther back he stepped the stronger would grow the attack, Edward decided to leave the south. In the vain hope of keeping Gaveston he had surrendered his power, but even greater than the ordainers' desire to remedy corruption was their hatred of the favourite. Edward, to escape their pressure, might plead the excuse of war with Scotland, yet no matter where he fled he could not escape the malice of his friend's enemies.

The Scottish war had never really died. On his accession, Edward had sent detachments to hunt down Bruce ; nothing of importance took place, mainly because Bruce was ill. In the spring of 1308, however, he was lifted on to his horse and, sick man though he was, he defeated the English at Old Meldrum and took revenge on the Comyns in brutal fashion. From now on he found nothing but success, the quarrels of King and magnates keeping the English within their own borders until in September 1310 Edward, who had ridden north to escape the bullying of the ordainers, reviewed his troops at Tweedmouth. Gaveston was with him, and of all the earls who had been summoned, only Gloucester and Surrey appeared. On September 16 the army crossed the Border and reached Roxburgh Castle, and on the 21st with astonishing recklessness it penetrated Selkirk Forest where, if Bruce had been prepared, he could have massacred it. But he had decided very wisely that his game was a waiting one ; he drove all cattle from the path of the invaders and destroyed the crops, leaving no food whatever for Edward and his men. Spies brought news that he was encamped on a moor near Stirling, but the hopelessness of keeping on into a foodless country made Edward retire to Berwick and open negotiations. He was back in London on August 13, 1311, having stayed away as long as possible, Gaveston he left at Bamborough. Parliament sat at Blackfriars on the 16th and Edward went, knowing full well that he would have to fight with all his strength if he would keep his friend.

THE barons had not followed their King to Scotland. All love of country was put aside in this consuming and terrible hatred of Peter Gaveston. To drag down Gaveston the magnates would turn traitors, murderers ; nothing counted with them except the destruction of one man, of this insolent witty Gascon adventurer. He must have been a great man indeed to have aroused such fury for so apparently small a cause ; his quick wit had hurt these slow-minded brutal lords who found themselves stung and yet were unable to retort. The " player " Lancaster and the " black dog " Warwick were the leaders, while the " pale Jew " Pembroke was, against his inclinations, fighting his King, and the " cuckold's bird " Gloucester tried to be peacemaker. The ordainers gave their ordinances to Edward and demanded that Peter Gaveston as a " public enemy of the King and kingdom be forthwith exiled for all time and without hope of return," and they made certain that Edward could not again trick them by sending him to Ireland, for they insisted that his banishment must be from all royal dominions. This was the one article with which Edward was really concerned, the others dealt with numerous abuses and strove to tear power out of his hands. Nothing troubled him so long as he could keep his friend at his side, and he had no hope of withstanding these determined lords. If he did not surrender it would mean civil war, and he had not the money with which to fight. He decided that it was better to temporise than to lose everything. On October 5 Gloucester and Despenser announced to the people that Edward had accepted the ordinances.

These ordinances were too violent, they snatched everything from Edward, not only his dearest friend but all his power. He was forbidden to leave the realm without permission, or to wage war. These restrictions did not matter, it was the twentieth article Edward hated, the article which banished Gaveston. To explain Gaveston's banishment the magnates must have scratched their heads for days in order to charge him with particular crimes ; they failed, they were able only to use vague phrases about the organisation of factions for illegal and constitutional influence, which, of course, meant nothing. The favourite's hands must have been clean indeed if nothing worse than this could be raked up against him. He was brought to London surrounded by armed men, then placed in a boat and sent down the Thames to Edward's brother-in-law of Brabant.

EDWARD had given way on every point. He had lost all and gained nothing. In fury against his own weakness and against these callous lords, he spurred north, and on January 7, 1312, called for the great seal to be sent to him at York. With the great seal he became King again, for no royal mandate could be passed unless the ribboned wax was pressed between those metal covers. It was whispered through England that Gaveston had returned, that he was lurking in the royal castles in defiance of the ordinances. Then the mask was thrown aside, Gaveston stepped boldly into the open before all men, and on the 18th Edward announced that he had recalled his " good and loyal " Peter Gaveston who had been exiled contrary to the laws of England ; on the 20th Gaveston's forfeited estates were given back and an order was sent countermanding a parliament that had been summoned to meet on February 13. Historians have puzzled over Gaveston's return and over Edward's " infatuation " in bringing him to England. A story, doubtless untrue, tells us that Edward tried to entice Bruce to give Gaveston refuge in Scotland and that Bruce refused, saying, " If the King of England will not keep faith with his own people, how then will he keep faith with me ? " But Edward would surely not bring his friend all the way from his safe lodgings in Flanders merely to pass him on to a dangerous enemy like Scotland ? Again, as with so much in this puzzling period, we lack a key to open the truth, and the truth is probably so simple that we disregard it as impossible. It seems to me that these two young men were fully conscious of their weakness, that they deliberately brought doom upon themselves ; with the peculiar delight some men take in danger, in the ecstatic orgasm of risking death, they wished to face together the greatest peril. Such types are by no means unknown, they are plentiful enough to-day ; there is, to some young people, a joy in danger that can equal no other pleasure. And it is more than probable that Edward did not recall Gaveston, that Gaveston came of his own will, wishing to stand beside his comrade and if necessary to die with or for him. That would be typical of Gaveston, of the sharp-tongued adventurer—to choose a quick death rather than to linger in peace and with the humiliating knowledge that he had been chased out of England by men he despised. That Edward called his friend to his death is to me incredible, for he was a kind man ; that Gaveston deliberately came to die, to make the last valiant magnificent gesture, is perfectly in keeping with his character. It was an heroic if foolish act ; he knew that he could not escape, but with the flippancy of a man who covers his own despair with laughter, he surrendered his body to the malice of enemies, perhaps because he knew that only by dying violently could he help his friend.[1]

THE magnates prepared for war. Winchelsea excommunicated Gaveston, and five of the eight lay ordainers swore to kill the favourite ; these were Lancaster, Warwick, Pembroke, Hereford and Arundel ; Gloucester, as usual, fought shy of any direct action, he promised to agree to anything decided by the others. England was then split up between the magnates, and tournaments were proclaimed to excuse the gathering of armed men ; Gloucester, of whose loyalty they were not certain, was given Kent to control. The others concentrated on the north.

Edward had feebly made some attempts to withstand his enemies. He had ordered London to guard itself for his cause and had proclaimed that he intended to keep the old laws and those of the recent ordinances that were not " prejudicial " to the crown. He was trapped and he must have known it ; he was cornered with the Scots above him and the barons below, and he had few followers, for even the people were against him : there was a ballad they sang,

> *The charter of the King's word is made of wax,*
> *it was held too near the fire and is molten all away,*
> *I understand.*

With Gaveston, the wretched Edward had to face unnumbered hordes. Desperately he sent to Gascony for troops ; he had not even money enough with which to feed his household. Lancaster was riding north with all speed, he reached Newcastle on May 4, and dashed into the city and almost captured Edward, Gaveston and Isabel, who fled to Tynemouth. In their hurry they left their baggage behind, their jewels and clothes and their horses. Raging at having to fly, Edward sailed with Peter for Scarborough, leaving the Queen behind, as she was soon to bear a child. Edward was not worrying about Queen or crown, he feared only for the life of his courageous friend, and therefore put him in Scarborough while himself

[1] This theory of Gaveston's self-sacrifice was first suggested to me by my friend, Mr. Hugh Ross Williamson, whose play, *Rose and Glove* (Chatto & Windus, 1934), while in many ways almost as factually inaccurate as Marlowe's *Edward II*, is nevertheless historically true because it gives one the colour of the period and explains the motives of many of the puzzling episodes in the early part of this reign.

hurried back to York to try raise an army. Scarborough was one of the strongest castles in England, it was built on a rocky peninsula and had the north sea for a moat on three sides, but Gaveston lacked men and provisions. When Pembroke, Surrey and Henry Percy arrived and began to dig at the walls, Gaveston had to surrender within a fortnight. On the gospels, the three magnates—Pembroke, Surrey and Percy—swore to protect him until August 1, by when parliament would have decided upon his fate ; if he disagreed with its verdict he would be at liberty to return to Scarborough with fresh supplies. The terms were extremely honourable, and Gaveston surrendered. Pembroke and Percy escorted him south, intending to lodge him at his own castle of Wallingford. They reached Deddington in Oxfordshire on June 9, and Gaveston slept at the home of the rector of the parish while Pembroke visited his wife in Northants.

It was sunrise when Warwick strode into the bedchamber, the black dog prepared to show that he could bite. His armies filled the streets as he shouted at Gaveston, " Get up, traitor, you are taken ! " The favourite was dragged from his bed and amidst the jeering mob carried to Warwick Castle.

When Pembroke heard of this outrage he did his best to rescue Gaveston : no one would support him, not even Gloucester. He was an honourable man and he had sworn upon the Gospels to protect his captive, his conscience hurt him to think that the oath was broken ; Warwick had not personally given his word, yet as one of the five leading earls he was a partner in whatever any of the others should pledge. With Lancaster and Hereford he talked the subject over, he had done enough in the cause of hatred and it was time that the others took a hand. Lancaster and Hereford accepted the prisoner and carried him a mile and a half from Warwick Castle, to Blacklow Hill, which was on Lancaster's estates. They were followed by crowds eager to witness the favourite's destruction, yet even these people were moved by the sight of Gaveston and by the sound of his pleas for mercy. Lancaster had no mercy, he was a pitiless stubborn animal, he gave the captive to two Welshmen in his service, and while one stabbed Gaveston with a sword, the other hacked through his neck. They left the body to lie and bleed on the grass while they carried the severed head to where the three earls waited to make certain that the insolent tongue was stilled for ever.

There had not been even the most informal trial. Personal

vengeance and not justice killed Gaveston. His corpse lay under the sunlight, headless and bleeding, until four shoemakers placed it on a ladder and bore it to Warwick. The earl refused to have it on his land, for it had been found on Lancaster's estates, and the body was carried back to the hill to lie in the pools of its own drying blood. There some Oxford Dominicans found it and took it to Oxford, yet even now the corpse had no rest ; Gaveston had died excommunicate and therefore could not be interred in holy ground. For two years the body stayed unburied until the King removed it to a new Dominican friary at King's Langley, to a friary raised in memory of his poor friend.

EDWARD was never to forgive this murder. He had not the strength to fight, he waited his chance while the brutal Lancaster with his bloody hands pushed his way into the centre of affairs. At first Edward tried to seek vengeance openly, and Pembroke and Surrey, furious because their word was broken, stood at his side. He called on London to guard its gates on his behalf, he sent out writs to bring levies to his standard, himself travelling in Kent to enlist the Cinque Ports. Gloucester meanwhile tried to bring peace, and negotiations were opened. Then the Queen bore a son at Windsor Castle on November 13, 1312, and the child brought a gentle influence into the hurly-burly of threatened war. With this pledge that his throne would not die with him, much of Edward's fury lessened, and his enemies felt that they dared not force their claims while England's sympathy would lie with the King. Edward, as a matter of fact, had won a certain affection from his people by refusing to call the child Louis as the Queen's uncle requested, he called him Edward after his own father.

On December 22, an agreement at last was reached, and civil war was for the moment averted. Those concerned in Gaveston's murder, it was decided, were humbly to beg pardon from the King, the jewels and horses captured at Newcastle were to be returned, and the barons were to try make parliament give a subsidy towards the Scottish wars ; in return, the King offered a free pardon to anyone concerned in the death of Gaveston. It was not until October of the following year that Lancaster, Warwick and their friends could bring themselves to receive the kiss of peace in Westminster Hall.

With England again at rest, men's thoughts turned to Scotland. Bruce had been rushing his troops over the border, and it was time that some attempt was made to defeat or capture him. Edward found that his barons were too intent on arguing about the government of the country to think of defending it. When he called on them to join him they objected that he had no right to levy war without the agreement of parliament, and when the troops mustered on June 11, 1314, at Berwick, Edward found that Lancaster, Warwick, Arundel and Warenne stayed away. Nevertheless he had Gloucester, Pembroke, Hereford and Clifford on his side with particular friends like Despenser. It was a large army, but evidently the numerous carts containing food and weapons hampered it when it began to move. Edward gave the command and started blithely into Scotland, going, we are told, not as if to war, but as if he led a pilgrimage to St. James, the fighting saint of Compostella.

OF the ensuing battle we have many versions, and modern research has upset the old belief that Bruce remained passive behind his barrier of pikes on a ground previously chosen by himself.[1] It is true that Bruce did choose this position, but he altered his plans at the last moment after he defeated the English advance guards. The actual battle appears to have been somewhat as follows. Bruce, wishing to bar the way to Stirling, encamped in the Torwood between Stirling and Falkirk. Hearing that the English were on the way to Falkirk, he then drew up his troops about two miles south of Stirling on the old Roman road. Edward meanwhile was rushing with absurd haste towards the battle ; he went so quickly that he left " little time for food and less for sleep," and men and horses were exhausted when on Sunday afternoon, June 23, they reached Torwood. It was painfully hot, yet desultory fighting took place at once. Gloucester, dashing forward with the van, was unhorsed, and Sir Henry de Bohun, the Earl of Hereford's nephew, outdistanced his men. Bruce, on a grey palfrey, " little and jolly," darted to cut off his retreat. In his hand the Scottish leader wielded a battle-axe and he wore a basinet of cuir-bouilli ringed with a tall crown, while Bohun was mounted on a war-horse and was fully armed. Bohun raised his lance and pressed it to his side and charged, but Bruce's nimble pony slipped away ; then

[1] See *Bannockburn : A Study of Medieval Warfare* by W. M. Mackenzie (MacLehose, 1913), and his *The Real Bannockburn* in *Transactions of the Glasgow Historical Society* (1910) ; also the notes to his edition of Barbour's *Bruce* (Black, 1909).

lifting himself in his stirrups, Bruce raised his axe, and struck. So powerful was the blow that it sliced through Bohun's helmet, cutting him open from skull to chin and it broke the shaft of the axe and hurled Bruce himself from his saddle.

Clifford with three hundred men was wheeling to the right, hoping to outflank the Scots and relieve Stirling. Bruce's nephew Randolph was hiding in a wood at this point, and when Bruce noticed that he made no move he sent a curt message telling him that " a rose from his chaplet had fallen," and Randolph instantly moved out with his footmen to face the enemy. " Wait a little," cried Henry of Beaumont as he saw the Scots appear ; " let them come on, let them come out on the plain." " Sir," said Sir Thomas Grey, " I fear they are too many for us." "Look you ! " retorted Beaumont, " if you are afraid you can go." " Sir ! " cried Grey, " it is not through fear that I shall go this afternoon," and he dug his spurs into his horse and charged. Randolph was prepared, his men drawn up in the Scottish oval, and before those pikes the English horsemen scattered : Grey's horse was impaled and he was captured. The Scots remained, their lines unbroken, seeming " like a hedgehog," with their bristling pikes.

The English retreated a little and encamped amongst the mudflats and pools beside the little stream of Bannockburn, with the plain on which the recent fighting had taken place immediately in front of them. Here they were caught in a river-bend, as Earl Simon had been caught at Evesham. Bruce was on the other side of the burn, almost on the same ground that he had previously chosen to withstand the English attack. He was thinking of retreating, feeling that he had won enough for one day and dreading an open fight with his infantry against the mounted English ; then a deserter came and said that if ever he wished to be King of Scotland now was his moment for " the English have lost heart and are uncertain, they are dreading a sudden assault." Bruce decided to stake all hopes upon one battle.

While the Scots stayed quietly in their camp, the English spent the night in revelry, drinking, and " shouting wassail and drinkhail with astounding noise." It was, however, usual for soldiers to drink hard the night before a battle and customary for the leaders to serve plentiful wines ; the silence amongst the Scots might not have been so much because they were " burning with love of their country and of freedom," it was probably because Bruce was too poverty-stricken to give them anything to drink.

When it was morning on Midsummer Day, Bruce led his men from the ridge and marched into the carse, forcing the English to take their stand on the level ground to the north-east, nearer the Forth ; this cut them off almost wholly from retreat, they could only move back towards Stirling over treacherous ground, for the Forth was to their right and curved to the rear, the Bannock was on their left ; the ground was narrow and marshy. Bruce pushed forward, facing the enemy and driving them to battle. He drew up his troops into the Scottish rings, the schiltrons, with the dreaded pikes forming hedgehogs. The men knelt to pray. " They kneel, they kneel ! " cried Edward, " they beg for mercy." " Sooth, sire," answered young Ingelram of Umfraville, " they beg for mercy, but not from you ! Those men will never give in, they will conquer or die." " Be it so," said Edward ; " we shall see."

It is uncertain who started the offensive, but Bruce would have been foolish to break the shelter of his hedgehogs. Probably the English charged and the Scots forced them back into the river-bend. Covered by archers, they strove to smash the schiltrons. Gloucester was killed, it is said that his horse was disembowelled upon the pikes. That morning when he had suggested that they wait until their weary men recovered, he was called liar and traitor, and had cried, " To-day it will be clear that I am neither traitor nor liar ! " It was made clear enough. His recklessness brought his own doom, for in his hurry he forgot to don his jupon and therefore was unrecognised and killed. The English, caught between the rivers, could not deploy over the mushy ground ; they were at a disadvantage and could rely only on charges. They were jammed together, driven back by the frightened horses that sheered from the glitter of sharp pikes. Then Bruce charged, and the Scots sank into the enemy as if " plunged into the sea," they scattered the English who had no way of escape. Some managed to fly in the direction of Stirling, and the rivers Bannock and Forth were brimmed with their corpses. " On them, on them, on them ! " yelled the Scots, " they fail ! " Edward was nearly captured, he was guarded by Pembroke and a famous Hospitaller, Giles of Argentine, each of whom gripped an end of his bridle ; seeing the rout, they tugged Edward's horse towards Stirling and dragged him from the press, Edward having to fight his way with his mace. Then brave Giles, a warrior of the East, drew back and said, " Sire, I was placed in charge of your rein, seek your own safety. There is your castle of Stirling where your body will be safe. For myself—I am not used to running away, nor shall I do it now. I commend you to God ! " He turned his steed and galloped to his death, charging into the midst of the Scots and yelling, " Argentine ! Argentine ! " until they cut him down.

Edward reached Stirling, and its commander implored him not to enter. He could not hold out, he said, and for the King to seek refuge here would be but to surrender to Bruce. Edward pressed on to Linlithgow, and from Linlithgow reached Dunbar, where he took ship for Berwick.

EDWARD was too ashamed to appear in public. He felt most deeply the disgrace of that defeat which placed Scotland utterly into the hands of Bruce and himself into the hands of his enemies. Exultantly, Lancaster, who had stayed in England, declared that the defeat had been caused by the King's refusal to uphold the ordinances. He had the King completely in his power, and he insisted that Edward dismiss his ministers and sheriffs, particularly the younger Hugh Despenser, whom Edward now loved almost as much as once he had loved Gaveston. Despenser went into hiding for a time and Edward was forced to submit to his truculent cousin. He wanted to carry on the war with Scotland, and could not bear the thought of making peace; the memory of his father, that Hammer of the Scots, must have risen before him and shamed him. But the earls would not follow, they were more eager to humiliate him than to waste energies on war. At a London parliament held on January 20, 1314, Edward was treated like a disobedient small boy—his friend, the younger Despenser, was dismissed from his council, and himself, the King, was put upon the miserable allowance of £10 a day—a tiny sum to cover the gigantic expenditures of a royal household.

Through the years of Lancaster's administration the country reached almost the rock-bottom of misery. Edward might have been a careless ruler, Lancaster was a stupid sullen suspicious one whom everybody grew to loathe. There was trouble in Wales and continual petty warfare over England in which Lancaster himself was one of the worst offenders—his wife ran from him and he wreaked his vengeance on the Earl of Surrey because he had connived at her escape—the Scots took Berwick, and even invaded Ireland where Bruce's brother, Edward, almost made himself a petty King. In fact, Lancaster's rule was far worse than ever Edward's had been, and he lived suspiciously, half the time refusing to meet parliament or the King. His domination continued until 1318 when on August 9, at Leake, he was forced to surrender.

The dilatory, feeble, yet brutal manner of Lancaster had alienated his friends and had split the baronial power. Pembroke then formed what one might call a moderate party, and he was the first to break with Lancaster, perhaps because he had never forgiven him for the murder of Gaveston after he had plighted his oath for his prisoner's safety. Warwick was dead but Pembroke soon created a cabal—a party between Edward and Lancaster. He had Surrey, now Lancaster's bitterest enemy, and Lord Badlesmere and Roger of Amory, one of the Welsh marcher-lords who shared through his wife a third of the Gloucester estates that were soon to cause so much evil. Faced with these allies, Lancaster had to give in as before he had forced the King to give in. He was suspected of being in the pay of the Scots and it was certainly rather peculiar that Bruce in his raids always avoided Lancaster's estates ; if he had wished to be brutal, Pembroke could have arraigned Lancaster on serious charges, and he was lucky in receiving a full pardon for all offences against the peace. A standing council was then formed with Pembroke at its head. Despenser returned to the King's household, becoming chamberlain.

The Despensers were a queer couple, they had fought on opposite sides during the rebellion : the elder being with the King, the younger with the magnates, and the younger it was who presumably invented the theory that reverence was due purely to the crown itself and not to the man under it. Now he had sided with the King. It was not uncommon in the Middle Ages for a family deliberately to fight against each other so as to be on the safe side ; whichever party won did not really matter because one of the family would necessarily be in at the spoils. Yet the younger Despenser's volte face is rather sudden when one recalls his ingenuity in thinking of that trick against the King—a trick that was later to be used with strong effect against himself. It is difficult to estimate his true character. He was ambitious and foolish, and he was also intelligent. If only his ambition could have been curbed he might have made a wise councillor and lived an honoured life. But he was greedy for power, he wanted to become too great for England to hold him, and, unlike Gaveston, he used his influence over the King with strong effect. He had married Eleanor, eldest of the Gloucester heiresses ; the other two girls were Margaret and Elizabeth. Margaret, Gaveston's widow, had married Hugh of Audley, and Elizabeth had married Roger of Amory. When on Gloucester's death the vast estates were divided in 1317, Despenser was given Glamorgan, Audley the town and castle of Newport and the country of Gwaunllwg, and Amory was given lands on the Wye.

The lords marcher, the guardians of Wales, held a peculiar position. In their small way they had complete power, and if they had united they could have fought the King himself. They maintained armies, they lived in almost continual warfare, trying to break the spirit of the stubborn Welsh. They held their lands by the sword and kept laws of their own—the " customs of the march." Subjects of England, they were nevertheless powerful enough to be free if they wished ; they dared not break away, they needed the weight of England behind them to keep order. They spread into Wales, conquering gradually, brutally, and they stayed roughly united, hating each other often enough but bound together by common fear of a rising of the Welsh. Personal hatreds were forgotten when one lord marcher called to another for help.

Despenser through his marriage now became one of this band, but he could not stay satisfied. Restlessly he moved in his estates, gazing on the lands of his brothers-in-law with jealous desire. He wanted to exceed his powers and he outraged the customs of the march by taking a pardoned rebel, Llewelyn Brent—he had only rebelled against the tyrannous behaviour of one of Edward's officers—escorting him to Cardiff, and there executing him as if himself were already King of Wales. Edward gave him every fief he could, and the Despenser estates began to grow rapidly, yet they could not grow rapidly enough for the new ambitious lord marcher ; soon he was ruler of almost the whole vale of Towy and of all the hills and dales between Towy and Teivi. Yet his longing grew until he managed to twist from his brother-in-law, Audley, the castle of Newport-on-Usk and its nearby lands, and later to make him give up Newport and Nether Went. He turned also on Amory, but Amory refused to be bullied ; Despenser, however, managed to get a grip on Lundy Island, important as commanding the Bristol Channel. He decided next to steal from the great house of Braose, and would probably have bought Gower if Braose had not died to be succeeded by the

24

strong John Mowbray. Mowbray took possession of Gower immediately on his father-in-law Braose's death, without bothering to ask royal licence. Despenser seized this opportunity; he insisted that the King's law in Wales was the same as in England and that no tenant therefore had the right to take up his inheritance without the crown's permission. To this Mowbray retorted that he acted according to the customs of the march, but his protests did not save him. Despenser declared the Braose estates escheated and prepared to take them for himself.

He had gone too far. Already he had outraged the marcher lords in every way, and they watched with apprehension the growth of his estates; if, as seemed inevitable, he were given Gower, he would become lord of South Wales from the Teivi to the Wye. Hurriedly the lords marcher met, they called to arms against a common enemy. Only Pembroke and Arundel did not answer the summons, every other great marcher joined the coalition, and Lancaster, eager to seek revenge for his loss of power, gave them his support. They made no move until Edward ordered Gower to be seized, then they marched to defend Mowbray. There was war again in Wales. Edward commanded the chief marchers, Hereford, the two Mortimer brothers, Giffard, Thomas and Maurice of Berkeley, to appear before him at Gloucester; Hereford replied that he would never come to court so long as the younger Despenser was there, and suggested that the favourite be given into the custody of Lancaster. Edward, as usual, found that he could do nothing; he made a threatening move, marching as far as Bristol, but he had no troops, and royal authority without the backing of arms was helpless. The marchers defied him, they led their men into Despenser's lands, they robbed his castles and stole his goods.

Then Lancaster did an amazing thing: he held a private parliament of his adherents as if the King were no longer of any importance. It was held at Pontefract on May 24, 1321, and Hereford appeared to represent the lords marcher. Lancaster agreed to help rid the King of evil ministers, and all swore to support the marchers against the Despensers. Having given his oath, Lancaster did nothing further; he was satisfied to sit behind the thick walls of his castle while others did the fighting and dragged into his lap the fruits of power. Edward, by surrendering so utterly to his new favourite, had lost the support he had won against Lancaster; even Pembroke slipped away and remained at least neutral while the magnates marched on London ; the citizens refused to let them enter and they had to camp in the suburbs.

Since July 15 a parliament of the three estates had been sitting at Westminster and now solemnly eleven articles were produced damning the Despensers. They were accused of accroaching to themselves royal authority, of estranging the King from his people, of absorbing full government and of keeping the other magnates from the King, of removing ministers appointed by the ordainers, of inciting civil war, of usurping jurisdiction, and in every way of perverting and hindering justice. Against the younger Despenser, particular grievances were added : he had tried to form a league to control the King and he had taught the doctrine that it was to the crown alone and not to the King that allegiance was due. It is certainly rather peculiar to find the barons dragging up this old charge, this theory which they had welcomed when they had found it useful to their own ends.

Edward could not bring himself to pass sentence on his favourite. For a fortnight he held out while the younger Despenser, in a burst of arrogant lunacy, borrowed an armed ship from the King and sailed up and down the Thames ; nor would he stop his defiance until the magnates threatened to burn all the royal building from Charing Cross to the abbey. Edward at last gave in, with the moderate Pembroke urging compliance, and with his Queen on her knees before him ; he entered Westminster Hall on August 14, through ranks of mounted men who crowded the building amongst those on foot. And with this fierce horde around him, the poor King once again surrendered a friend to the malice of his enemies. On the 19th, both Despensers were condemned to forfeiture and exile and were forbidden to return to England without the assent of full parliament. And while the Despensers were sentenced, the lords marcher were pardoned for any breaches of the peace they may have committed while bringing the accused to justice.

WITHIN a few weeks luck favoured Edward. When Queen Isabel was on her way to Canterbury, she reached, on October 13, Leeds Castle in Kent ; this was a royal castle held for the King by Bartholomew Badlesmere as constable. Badlesmere was away when the Queen arrived, and his lady refused point-blank to let Isabel enter. Isabel in person went to the gates to assert her authority, and still was refused entrance ; she then lodged in a nearby priory and ordered her companions to force their way into the castle, but after five or six of them had been killed, she had to call them back. Isabel was a proud and arrogant girl, bitterly resentful of her husband's casual treatment and continually watching for any slight upon her royal dignity. She demanded that Edward take vengeance, and as he was eager to catch at any straw to help him against the opposition, he called for levies. The response was immediate, and soon with a large army he was encamped outside Leeds; on October 31 it surrendered, Lady Badlesmere was imprisoned in Dover and thirteen of her garrison were hanged.

The whole episode is most peculiar, but Badlesmere was a rather peculiar man. He had begun as a strong partisan of Lancaster, and had withdrawn from the baron's party when Lancaster, during his tenure of power, had revealed his incompetence and stupidity. Evidently the two quarrelled violently, as afterwards they detested each other; Badlesmere next joined Pembroke's moderate party and became a member of the standing council, he then, during the quarrel with the Despensers, threw aside his allegiance with the King and joined the magnates. By this act he became lost between two sides; he was the enemy of Lancaster and the enemy of Edward. This shifting of allegiances, however, does not explain his wife's discourteous behaviour towards the Queen; Badlesmere, being with the opposition, perhaps considered himself right in humiliating Edward; if so, he had behaved most stupidly, for he was well-nigh completely friendless : Pembroke sided with the King, at least on this question, and while Lancaster remained the King's enemy, he was also Badlesmere's enemy. Badlesmere ran to the only allies he could get, to the lords marcher, and joined Hereford and Roger Mortimer at Kingston-on-Thames. They dared not fight for him, they could only offer to mediate, and when their overtures were curtly dismissed, Edward seized his opportunity with both hands. He called on men in Wales to muster for the defence of the country and he urged his friend, Walter Reynolds, now Archbishop of Canterbury, to force the clergy to reverse the sentence of banishment on the Despensers. Convocation agreed, and Reynolds proclaimed their verdict at St. Paul's. Already the King, not waiting for convocation's reversal to be published, had recalled his comrades. He marched with an army into the west, keeping Christmas at Cirencester, then proceeding towards the Severn. The marchers were helpless, for Lancaster, in his blind hatred of Badlesmere, let his chance slip and did not go to their help ; if he had risen with them then he could have captured England : petty hatreds bound his hands and he stayed quietly behind his castle walls. On January 22, 1321, the two Mortimers surrendered and were sent to the Tower ; Audley followed their example and was sent to Wallingford ; Badlesmere knew that he could find no mercy : with Hereford, the younger Audley and Amory, he ran to join Lancaster in the north.

EDWARD had not forgotten the shame of Bannockburn. For the son of the Hammer of the Scots to be chased from a battlefield before the troops of Bruce was a humiliation that only victory could wipe out. He called for a general muster on February 28 at Coventry, but he did not lead the troops against Bruce, he turned them on Lancaster. There is no doubt that Lancaster was a traitor as well as a fool ; Bruce had always spared his lands when he ravaged the north, and soon it was discovered that he was actually intriguing with his country's enemies. On December 16, 1321, Black Douglas, " the Good] Lord James," had granted a safe-conduct to an emissary of Lancaster's, and a similar safe-conduct was given to the same man by Bruce's cousin Randolf on January 15, 1322. Conferences were held in February between Randolf, John Mowbray and Roger Clifford, and letters were sent to Lancaster—in which he was called " King Arthur," scarcely a tactful name to give a man whose wife, like Queen Guinevere, had fled from him—and a treaty was at last arranged, between Lancaster and his allies and the Scots, in which it was agreed that Bruce would help the English rebels and would yet claim nothing in return.

Edward turned his army against Lancaster who at the moment was besieging the royal castle of Tickhill ; on hearing of the King's approach, he immediately advanced to Burton to hold the bridge against the royalists. The Trent was flooded, but nevertheless after a few skirmishes the King managed to cross and, through Lichfield, marched on Burton. Lancaster made ready for battle, then suddenly he lost heart ; he turned and fled with the King at his heels. Edward, following his enemy, reached the castle of Tutbury where Roger of Amory was captured. He was badly wounded and was tried immediately and condemned, but " because the King loved him much " he was respited, only to die within three days. Edward pressed on after Lancaster ; for once he was the pursuer and not the pursued ; for once he was powerful with strong allies, he was seeking vengeance for the blood of Gaveston and for years of humiliation. Proclamations were issued declaring Lancaster and his adherents to be outlaws. Swiftly, Lancaster raced to the north, probably hoping to link with Bruce ; he sped so quickly that he could not pause even at his chief castle of Pontefract ; on March 16 he reached Boroughbridge, where he found the crossing over the Ure barred by a force of Cumberland and Westmoreland men under Andrew Harclay, the King's constable of Carlisle. Caught between the advancing Edward and Harclay's troops, Lancaster had to fight or be massacred. He decided to fight, to force his way across the river.

Harclay had learned his lessons from the Scots. He dismounted his troops and placed a strong shiltron at the ford, his men standing in Scottish ovals with pikes outthrust, supported by a band of archers ; and at one end of the wooden bridge, he posted a band of men-at-arms and spearmen. This bridge was long and narrow and could not be used by horsemen, and Hereford and Clifford courageously offered to fight their way across on foot while Lancaster and his mounted knights concentrated on the ford. The bridge could never be passed, it was almost certain death to tread upon it : Hereford with three knights and his standard-bearer were struck down, a Welshman jabbed his spear up through the planking and horribly transfixed the earl. Clifford was nearly killed, he was dragged away sore wounded. Lancaster did not even touch the water at the ford ; under the shower of arrows he sprang back and pleaded for a truce until the morrow, which Harclay granted.

Lancaster's stupidity is really amazing. He had now ahead of him a night of freedom in which he could have stolen to Bruce. Instead of that—although a great many of his followers were wiser than he and sneaked off—he calmly sat down with his friends and waited until dawn, when the arrival of an army under the sheriff of Yorkshire cut off any hopes of retreat. He surrendered with the other leaders. The merciless earl could expect no mercy, the brain that in cold blood had given the command to strike down Gaveston was to know the same treatment ; Gaveston had died without even the pretence of a trial, Lancaster at least was given that. He was arraigned at Pontefract on March 22 before the King and magnates, and charged with being a rebel. The evidence of his treaty with the

Scots—found in Hereford's baggage at Boroughbridge—was produced ; the King refused to let him speak, he treated him almost as harshly as Gaveston had been treated. Without an opportunity to defend himself, the earl was condemned as a rebel taken in arms. No further time was wasted, he was dragged off immediately to execution through a jeering mob that called him " King Arthur ! " As he came of royal blood they merely chopped off his head without cutting out his bowels and hacking off his limbs. Six of his allies suffered with him, but Audley was reprieved. Clifford and Mowbray were drawn and hanged at York, and Giffard at Gloucester. Badlesmere, enemy and fellow-rebel of Lancaster, was hanged at Canterbury, having been captured at Stow Park. Of the others, twenty-five barons and knights were executed, fifteen were released and seventy-two were imprisoned. Edward made a clean sweep of his enemies now that he had the chance.

Lancaster was a brutal stupid rogue, but the people did not realise that. They remembered only that he had stood for their rights against the King, they did not know him for a proved traitor, for a sullen murderous brute. He became a symbol in their wretchedness, they thought of him as a second Earl Simon and believed him a martyr. A chapel was built above his grave, miracles were worked there, and the rogue became a saint. It was at least something to win a heavenly halo even if he had missed a crown of jewels on earth !

PARLIAMENT met at York on May 2, and the ordinances were repealed as prejudicial to the Crown, and it was decreed that " matters which are to be established for the estate of our lord the King and of his heirs, and for the estate of the realm and of the people, shall be treated, accorded, and established in parliaments by our lord the King, and by the consent of the prelates, earls, and barons and the commonality of the realm, according as hath been heretofore accustomed." Although the ordinances had been repealed, the King had given in a big step by agreeing, of his own accord, that no legislation was valid unless it was passed by the three estates. This was announced in full parliament, in a parliament indeed so full that it was the only medieval one to which the Welsh were ever summoned.

Edward seemed utterly secure. He had executed his enemies and had repealed the hated ordinances. Enough retribution had been exacted, now was the moment to reward those who had remained faithful. Harclay was created Earl of Carlisle, and the elder Despenser, Earl of Winchester. Then Edward again had his opportunity of fighting Bruce, for the Scots were raiding the north from Carlisle to Preston. He rode to seek revenge on August 19, 1322. Bruce retreated, not wishing to battle in the open when starvation and guerilla-fighting could more safely defeat the English. Edward soon found that the commissariat was the most important section of an army, the only food he discovered was an aged cow in a corn-field at Tranent. " The dearest beef I ever saw," growled Surrey—it cost him a thousand pounds. Edward found neither man nor beast and at last had to turn back. Bruce struck at once. Black Douglas was sent to harry the rearguard, and on October 1 Bruce himself crossed the Solway and dispatched troops to desolate the Cleveland Hills on the east coast. He then darted forward to try to capture the King. Edward was in Rievaulx Abbey, and on news of Bruce's coming he sent Richmond to bar the way. Although the English were formed in a strong position on a ridge and terrified the Scots by rolling huge stones on top of them as they struggled uphill, they were nevertheless badly defeated and Edward escaped just in time. Had it not been for his precious baggage he would probably have been caught : the Scots paused to grab their booty and thereby let the prize escape.

This was the final blow. Edward was weary of the whole question, he would neither fight nor make peace, and Harclay —hero of Boroughbridge—in desperation decided to act on his own. It was a brave and reckless gesture and it cost him his life, but he could not remain quiet while the Scots plundered at their leisure. He drew up a secret treaty with Bruce, according to which it was decreed that each realm should have its respective King and that Harclay would aid Bruce against his enemies ; if Edward should agree to this within a year, Bruce swore to found an abbey in Scotland for the souls of those killed in the war and within ten years to pay an indemnity of 40,000 marks, and he also promised to give to Edward the disposal in marriage of all his heirs-male. It was a sensible and honest treaty, but to Edward it seemed the act of a traitor. Harclay was no traitor, he did not attempt to hide the truth, he openly laid the facts before a gathering of lay and clerical Cumberland magnates and wrote to the mayor of Newcastle. Edward, on February 1, ordered his arrest. He was trapped while sitting unarmed at his table dictating correspondence, and was tried on March 3. The trial was unnecessary, for Edward had already ordered the judges to convict and had given minute details of the sentence. Harclay, said Edward, was to be stripped of his earl's belt, and was to have his knight's spurs hacked from his heels ; he was then to be drawn to the gallows, hanged, beheaded and quartered. He died very bravely, telling the people the truth of his intentions, and declaring himself no traitor.

And after all, Edward had to make peace. On May 30 he signed with Bruce a thirteen years' treaty. He could not bring himself to call his enemy King of Scotland, but as Bruce used the title when he signed the document and as Edward made no protest, the subject was quietly dropped.

THE Despensers now had complete power, and the fact that they kept it for so long shows, not that their rule was just, but that there was no man capable of fighting them. They were intelligent, yet power drove them to such extremes of arrogance that whatever sympathies Edward might have had amongst the magnates was soon lost for ever. Drunk with power, the Despensers went out of their way to humiliate the Queen, and she was not a woman to countenance anything that touched her dignity. She stayed silent, waiting her chance, even when the King took her lands from her and fed her the miserable pittance of a pound a day ; she became almost a prisoner, the younger Despenser's wife being placed on guard, and under her quick eyes Isabel could not even write a letter without having it read by her unacknowledged jailer. They treated her " like a maidservant ! " cried the Queen, yet she hid her wrath and strove to appear meek before the insolent favourites, even smiling upon them. We may well commiserate Isabel in this painful situation, although she very likely deserved it. Of her behaviour until now we know little, but when later we see her, powerful and guiding affairs, she is revealed as possessing every feminine vice—malice, cruelty, spite and arrogance—with not a feminine virtue to save her. Edward, it is suggested, was considering a divorce, and it would have been well for him if he had gone further than merely considering it.

Then Roger Mortimer escaped. So far Mortimer has appeared only as a lord marcher in arms against the Despensers, he is shortly to take a large space in history. The Bishop of Worcester, Adam Orleton, rescued him from the Tower by

drugging the gaolers' wine ; Mortimer scrambled somehow on
to the roof of the kitchen and climbed down a rope-ladder into
the inner-ward.   A boat was waiting on the Thames and he was
rowed to Bermondsey where horses were ready saddled.   From
Netley he sailed for Flanders.

Edward at this time was having trouble with France.   The
new King, Charles IV, demanded the customary homage from
the King of England as Duke of Aquitaine, and Edward dared not
leave his country.   Already there was the possibility of war with
France owing to the zeal of the Gascons who attacked a fort
that the French had built on their land ; and in this perplexity,
with Charles growing more truculent every moment, Edward did
not know where to turn.   The act of homage was degrading for a
King and he could not face the prospect, while the Despensers
were determined not to let him go.   He was their one protection,
for they knew well how they were hated.   Then Edward did a
most astonishing thing—he let Isabel go to her brother Charles
as his representative.   Undoubtedly he detested her, but he must
have realised that she was his enemy.   She promised to calm
her brother if Edward would agree to let their son—then about
thirteen years of age—become Duke of Aquitaine and Count of
Ponthieu.   Isabel's scheme was so transparent that it is difficult
to understand how Edward could not see through it ; and even
if Edward was deceived by her sly blandishments, surely that
cunning pair, the Despensers, could not have been fooled ?
Nevertheless, Isabel was actually permitted to leave England
and, most crowning folly, her son was dispatched after her to do
homage to Philip for the dukedom and countship.   Isabel, of
course, had no intention of returning to England—at least, as the
wife of Edward—she had her eldest son safely with her, and in
France she was the King's respected sister.   Edward's bed could
remain cold so far as she was concerned ; not so her own bed.
Soon Mortimer became her lover and the intrigue grew so
scandalous that the Pope interfered, ordering Charles not to shelter
the adulterous couple.   Isabel therefore had to move, going first
to Ponthieu and then to the Flemish border.   Meanwhile she
kept up an absurd pretence of innocence, writing that " she could
wish for nothing better than to live and die in the company of
her dear lord," adding that she feared for her life because of
the enmity of the younger Despenser.   Edward wrote at once to
Charles when he heard this fable, flatly contradicting it, and
showed in his missive a lamentable ignorance of women by his

expressions of amazement when he remembered her charming deportment before the Despensers ; he repeated this in a letter to Isabel, writing, " We cannot marvel too greatly when we recall your flattering behaviour towards each other in our presence, so friendly and sweet was your manner," and he added that he could think of nothing that might have offended her except some remarks he had let slip about her " pride," which is rather peculiar coming from a husband who had virtually imprisoned his wife and degraded her at every opportunity. Unfortunately we do not possess Isabel's answer.

Isabel was not satisfied with her freedom and her lover, she wanted revenge as well, and began to intrigue with the disaffected in England. Also she promised to marry her son to Philippa, second daughter of William II of Avesnes, Count of Holland, Zeeland and Hainault, in return for help in the invasion of England. Her doings were no secret, but Edward was distracted by threats of a French landing and he spent his time on the south coast and thereby left the rest of England open. On September 24, Isabel sailed up the Orwell and landed on the Suffolk side of the river while Edward, who was at Westminster, fled to the Tower. He was utterly alone, not a man came to stand beside him except Surrey and Arundel ; even the Tower was not safe, and he decided to make for the Despenser lands in Wales. He reached Tintern on October 14, and did not stay long, deciding to seek refuge in either Ireland or Lundy. At any rate he set sail for somewhere, only to be driven back by storms into Cardiff.

Men flocked to the standard of the Queen as she hurried after Edward, determined, now that the chance was hers, to seek full reparation for the years of shame. As in running away the King was considered to have abdicated, his son was proclaimed warden of the realm, and at Oxford, Adam Orleton, Bishop of Hereford, preached before the university, taking his text from Genesis : " I will put enmity between thee and the woman, and between thy seed and her seed," an allusion, as afterwards explained by Orleton, to the Despensers and not to the King. The Queen continued with her forces towards Wales. At Bristol she paused to capture the elder Despenser who was in command of the town. He was too old to run, too powerless to battle ; he surrendered on October 26, 1326, and was condemned as a traitor and straightway executed.

The King, being foiled by the winds in his efforts to reach

Lundy or Ireland, now wandered desperately over Wales. For six days he disappears from history, then he was captured—by what means we do not know—on November 16 at Llantrissaint. With him was taken the young Despenser.

Now that Edward was with his wife again he should automatically have become King of England ; instead of that, Orleton took away the great seal, and sent him, in the custody of Lancaster—brother of the late earl—to Kenilworth where he stayed until the April of next year and was looked after in royal fashion—in too royal a fashion to please Isabel.

Now Isabel had her enemy the younger Despenser at her mercy. He was arraigned before a high commission on November 2, and was charged with being a condemned traitor banished by parliament who had returned without permission. After his return, it was stated, every miscarriage and calamity that had befallen the country was due to his influence. They would not let him reply to the indictment, as they had refused to let his father reply when charged with the same crimes, because Lancaster had been condemned without permission to defend himself. " Withdraw, traitor, renegade traitor ! " they shouted. " Go and receive judgment, malicious and attainted traitor ! " Fifty feet high was the gallows on which they hanged Despenser, and a follower who had jeered at the Queen's behaviour was hanged with him, ten feet lower down.

We cannot pity the Despensers as we can pity Gaveston. They were able men but they were also self-seeking rascals. When Orleton, because of that sermon preached at Oxford, was later accused of instigating the people to seize the King, he tried to wriggle out of the charge and stated that " it is public and notorious that the said lord the King, captured with the said lord Hugh the Despenser, who himself was holding the King captive, came of his own will to the Earl of Lancaster, his kinsman." And there may be some truth in this. It is, of course, absurd to consider Edward actually in bonds and dragged as a hostage over Wales, but he was the Despensers' captive in the sense that he was unable to desert them. They were the only friends he possessed, and he remained loyal to the end. He was their captive because he must have known the true worth of the couple and must have realised that they would only bring doom upon him. Yet he remained firmly beside them to the end, the prisoner of love.

PARLIAMENT met in London on January 7, 1237, and, following

the example of the York parliament of 1322, it was made so complete that even the Welsh were summoned to attend : Mortimer probably arranged that. Since the beginning of the struggle London had been in tumult and now the citizens fought their way into the hall so that they could watch the proceedings. Bishop Orleton led the Queen's party and he stated that Isabel's life would be in danger if she returned to her husband, and he asked the assembly to consider whether they would have the father or the son for King. Parliament took all night to think it over, and next day it had little opportunity to give an answer ; the crowd of Londoners, probably drunk and out for mischief, yelled that they wanted the son for ruler. Before this clamour the friends of Edward remained silent ; they dared not speak.

A deputation of bishops waited on the King at Kenilworth to ask him to abdicate in favour of his son. Edward would not listen, he cursed them as traitors. Later he gave way when it was pointed out that he would continue to live honourably if he surrendered to his son, while if he refused, his whole line would be blotted from history. Weeping, dressed in sable, he faced the deputation, and as he gazed on the stern unfriendly faces, he fell sobbing, swooning, to the floor. Leicester and Stratford lifted him to his feet and the cruel Orleton repeated the threats that all his lineage would disappear if he refused to abdicate. Again poor Edward wept and groaned when he realised how his people hated him, and he told them that they might have his son for King if that was their wish.

In his submission he had sealed his doom.

HENRY of Lancaster was too kind a jailer, and therefore during the night of April 3–4, 1327, the deposed King was taken from Kenilworth by Thomas of Berkeley and John Maltravers the younger. Berkeley was Mortimer's son-in-law, and Maltravers was Berkeley's brother-in-law ; it was therefore quite a family matter. Edward was moved from castle to castle, and always at night ; evidently it had been arranged that his two jailers were to take it in turns to guard him. From castle to castle went the poor King : first he was lodged at Lantony Abbey near Gloucester, then he was hurried to Berkeley, from Berkeley to Corfe, from Corfe to Bristol, and from Bristol again to Berkeley. Always at night, with armed men around him, Edward moved over the country, being taken from secret place to place so that no one could tell where he was at a given moment.

While Edward lived, Isabel would never be safe. She dreaded lest the Church damn her for her adulterous love and send her back to live with her husband ; and always there was the possibility that the fickle easily swayed populace might turn against her and rescue Edward. Therefore Edward must die, he must not be murdered, he must die presumably a natural death. At first they thought to kill him by inches, horribly. It was ordered that he should not see or be seen by any one, that he ride bareheaded and lightly clad, that he be disturbed in his sleep and given bad and unpalatable food. His jailers argued with him, contradicting every word he said and swearing that he was insane. They treated him like a rebellious child, bullying him with jeers. When they came near Bristol and were afraid that the citizens might rescue him, the jailers plaited a crown of hay and stuffed it on to Edward's head. " Advance, Sire King ! " they laughed. Then as they approached Berkeley they thought to disguise their prisoner by shaving his head and beard. They pulled him from his horse and placed him on a mole-hill while they brought ditch-water to shave him with. When Edward protested at this, they answered that cold water was good enough for him. He wept and cried, " I shall have hot water whether you will or not."

They could not kill him. He was very strong and was only forty-three years of age. Next they tried to suffocate him with the stink of putrid meat, and when he resisted even this, they knew that violence must be used. They feared to mark his body, it was the body of a King, so they devised a cunning plan to circumvent this danger ; but all their cunning could not stifle the awful shrieks that woke the people in Berkeley Castle and the peasants without the walls. The murder was one of the most revolting in history, for they pressed the King under a door so that he could not twist aside, and then they pushed a drenching-horn into his anus and inserted a red-hot spit that burnt him internally to a ghastly death.[1]

[1] In *Archæologia*, vol. 50, Mr. Stuart A. Moore threw doubts upon this story of Edward's murder, alleging that poison would have been simpler and that, if murdered in such a brutal way, his features would have shown " unmistakable marks of agony," while " historians have said that the face was peaceful in its expression." The argument that poison would have been simpler is not an argument at all, and as a matter of fact the crime was committed in a most cunning fashion : the ox-horn deprived of its tip and inserted into the anus as doctors use a speculum would prevent the skin from becoming burnt or scorched. The instrument used was most likely thin, probably

For a month the body remained at Berkeley Castle and was then covered with black canvas and placed in a chariot and taken to St. Peter's, Gloucester, where it was buried on December 20. Soon the tomb that the son built over his father's body became almost as popular as the shrine of Thomas of Lancaster, " so that within a few years," writes the chronicler of Gloucester Abbey, " the gathering of people was so great that our city of Gloucester could scarce contain the multitudes which flocked thither from divers cities, towns and villages of England, and the abbot completed St. Andrew's aisle [the south transept] from top to bottom, within the six years of his prelacy, from the offerings at that tomb." This completion of St. Andrew's aisle was actually not the building of an unfinished work, it was the covering of a crumbling Norman wall with a tracery of perpendicular Gothic, the first time, it appears, that this lovely delicate architecture was used.

From the money offered to the soul of Edward by repentant sinners who implored his intercession to help them into heaven, the warm intricate curves of this new Gothic was born, enfolding, like a young budding tree of stone, the shrine of a pathetic and brutally murdered King.

a kitchen-spit. We don't know how long he took to die, but some time apparently lapsed before the body was shown. If the instrument was very thin he might, my friend Dr. Barton tells me, "linger on for forty-eight hours or even longer. If so, his end might be very peaceful. Death is a great relaxer of muscles, a smoother of wrinkles, a bringer of peace even to the tormented."

XI

KING EDWARD THE THIRD

1327–1377

WITH THE DEATH OF EDWARD II, Roger Mortimer became the uncrowned King of England although the Duke of Aquitaine, now fifteen years of age, was proclaimed King Edward III on January 24, 1327, and was crowned on February 1. A council of regency was appointed, consisting of four prelates, four earls and six barons, with Henry of Lancaster as president, supported by the Earls of Norfolk, Kent and Surrey. Orleton, of course, was among the prelates, together with that professional traitor, Walter Reynolds, Archbishop of Canterbury. Mortimer was cunning enough to remain in the background. taking no seat on the council but retaining his place in the bed of the Queen. All power was his, and he found when he held the destinies of England that they were heavier than he could manage. The Scottish question remained unsettled although Bruce was a sick man ; it is believed that he suffered from some form of leprosy, but this we may doubt as in the Middle Ages all skin diseases were roughly classed under that most horrible scourge. Ill he might be, yet Bruce would not remain on his couch, he kept on ravaging the north until Mortimer was forced to take action. In the invasion of England Mortimer had brought large bodies of Hainault mercenaries and he called for fresh troops of foreigners to help against the Scots. This was tactless, for when the Hainaulters joined the muster at York on May 29, they fought with the English archers over a dicers' quarrel. In the morning, we are told, three hundred and sixteen bodies were found in the streets. With an army prepared at any moment to turn upon itself, the campaign become a fiasco. Negotiations were opened for a lasting peace.

Meanwhile young Edward was married to his betrothed, Philippa of Hainault, the bride being not quite fourteen years of age. The ceremony was performed on Sunday, January 24,

1328, in St. Peter's Minster, York. With the marriage of the young King, peace was made with Scotland, the formal treaty being sealed by Bruce at Edinburgh on March 17, and it was agreed that his four-year-old son David should marry Isabel's daughter Joan, who was then seven years of age. On Sunday, July 17, the pair were formally betrothed.

Bruce was soon to die, but he had lived long enough to see Scotland separated from England. As King Robert I he ended his splendid life at Cardross on June 7, 1329, at the age of fifty-five, and twenty-three of those years had been spent almost continually in the saddle or at the council-table. On his death-bed he asked Sir James the Black Douglas to take his heart to the Holy Land because, in penitence for the blood he had shed, he had sworn to lead a crusade when opportunity should come ; that opportunity now would never come, and like his old adversary, Edward I, Bruce wished to die with the knowledge that his heart might go where the body could never venture. Douglas carried out his King's wishes as well as he was able, but on the voyage he died in Spain, charging magnificently into a host of Moors and dying without the support of the Spaniards who remained idly watching a foreigner being butchered in their quarrel. The heart of Bruce was carried back to Scotland to rest for ever in Melrose Abbey.

All that the average Englishman recalls of this great man is a stupid fairy-story about a pertinacious spider teaching him to try-try-try again, a tale that has no authority whatever in history. The abominable habit of schoolmasters trying to wring moral lessons out of the past has resulted very often in the truth being forgotten and only the lies remembered. Bruce deserves a better memorial than a tale which is an insult to the courage of a man who never dreamed of turning back, who never became so discouraged that only a spider tumbling on a thread could inspire him to fresh efforts. He built Scotland into independence and he taught England a lesson it was never to forget, a lesson in war tactics—the importance of stolid infantry and its power over horsemen. He began as a shiftless traitor, vacillating in his loyalty, and he seized Scotland by a most brutal murder : those early days were fully redeemed by his courage, by the heroism of the long and stubborn war he carried on for twenty-three years.

ANOTHER important death had taken place in the previous year.

25

Charles IV of France had passed away on January 21 and left as his successor a fourteen-year-old daughter, a widow about to have a child. Isabel suggested that the vacant throne be given to her son who was Charles's nephew, but the French magnates would not have an Englishman for King ; they elected Philip of Valois, son of Charles's uncle. Isabel and Mortimer protested violently, they argued that although women might be excluded from the monarchy, surely they could bridge the way for a successor ? and was not a nephew closer in kin than the vague relationship of an uncle's son ? From this pretension later grew Edward's claim to the throne of France. When Charles's daughter produced not a boy but a girl, Philip who had been regent after his uncle's death, was proclaimed King Philip VI and Edward was commanded to do homage to him for Guienne and Ponthieu. Isabel answered this demand with, " My son, who is the son of a King, will never do homage to the son of a count," but when the French threatened to sieze Gascony, she was made to humble her pride, and Edward, on June 6, 1329, performed homage in the quire of the cathedral of Amiens. There were a great many arguments about the exact form of Edward's oath and when at last it was given it was made as vague as possible.

ENGLAND had not forgiven Mortimer for the " shameful peace " with Scotland, and the people contemptuously dubbed little David's bride as " Joan Make-Peace," while Edward had been so ashamed of the treaty that he had not signed it. Mortimer had no love for England, he stayed in the background and manipulated his tools like Orleton while trying to throw the weight of all responsibility on to Henry of Lancaster, the cousin of Edward II, who was president of the Council ; Mortimer's interest was in Wales, for above all, he was a lord marcher. Gradually he absorbed the lands that were escheated to the crown, imitating the Despensers in trying to gain control of Wales, and he took to himself the title of Earl of the March which " was until then unheard of in England." And as the Earl of the March he acted as if he were a King, maintaining a larger retinue even than Edward and holding almost royal banquets and tournaments. His behaviour and his notorious liaison with the Queen at last drove Lancaster to action. He formed a strong party and took London as his centre. A meeting was held at St. Paul's on January 2, 1329, and it was decided that young Edward should be captured from Mortimer and that those who had negotiated the " shameful peace " with Scotland should be impeached. But all the plans and determinations came to nothing. Mortimer ravaged Lancaster's estates in the King's name, and when the earl rode to battle, he found himself deserted by some of his strongest allies and was made to submit.

With Lancaster humbled, Mortimer decided to rid himself of Edward II's half-brother, Edmund, Earl of Kent who had taken an active part in the invasion of England and the capture of the King. Probably Kent had never realised that Mortimer and Isabel would seek such vengeance as to seize the throne from Edward, for he now lived in miserable remorse, being uncertain if his brother were alive or dead. The rumour was very strong that Edward was alive and Mortimer deliberately played upon the tale to lure Kent to his doom. He was a feeble creature, this Kent, who had joined Isabel in France, had landed with her and had then taken the side of his cousin, Lancaster, in his vain attempt at rebellion ; the vanity of that attempt was mainly the result of Kent's treachery, as he deserted at the last moment and left Lancaster to the mercy of their enemies. Yet for all his weakness he brooded on his shame, and when Mortimer's agents hinted that Edward II still lived, he grasped at this opportunity to redeem his manhood. Mortimer arrested him at once for conspiracy, and the cowardly earl confessed everything, in his desperation he accused anyone he could think of as his accomplice, even adding the Pope's name to the list, but this final treachery could not save him. His confession was laid before parliament and he was condemned to death. March 19 had been decided on as the date of his execution, at the last moment no man could be found who would perform the deed. The wretched earl had to wait for hours before an executioner agreed to put him out of his misery.

Mortimer had gone too far. No man felt safe, and Lancaster in particular realised that he would be the next to follow Kent to the scaffold. His one hope was to stir Edward to action, and Edward did not need much prompting. The young King detested Mortimer as his mother's paramour and probably had only restrained his anger because by dragging down her lover he must expose Isabel's shame to the world, and already it was rumoured that she was with child. The situation was unbearable for a lad of Edward's spirit ; while Mortimer and Isabel seized what wealth they could, dividing between them the

Scottish indemnity, the crowned King's wife had to live on a tiny pittance. Then Philippa on June 15, 1330, gave birth to a son, Edward of Woodstock, whom later generations were to label the Black Prince. The responsibility of fatherhood and the important status it brought him, decided the King to rebel ; he was now seventeen, fully a man, and he talked the question over with the youth of his household. It was decided that Mortimer should be captured during the great council at Nottingham on October 15 ; there was a leakage among the conspirators, and when the council met, Mortimer accused Edward of plotting against him. Faced with this direct attack, the King could only plead innocence while his comrade, William Montagu, leaped to his feet and defied any man to call Edward a traitor.

Edward had to act quickly, before Mortimer followed his own advice that it was " better to eat the dog than to be eaten." The Queen and her lover commanded the castle that was well guarded by Mortimer's Welsh troops, but Edward managed to win the constable, Robert Holland, to his side. He suggested that Holland open the gates secretly in the night ; the constable explained that this was impossible, and instead he showed the King a subterranean passage through the sandy rock on which the castle was built. Through this passage crept Montagu with twenty-four friends at midnight, October 19, and was met by Edward fully armed before his mother's door. There was a scuffle and some of Mortimer's attendants were killed as the conspirators forced their way to the favourite's chamber which as usual was next to Isabel's. Mortimer was consulting with his chancellor when the lads burst in and captured him. Hearing the scuffle, Isabel ran to her lover's rescue. " Fair son, fair son," she wailed, " have pity on the gentle Mortimer ! " Her cries were ignored. The favourite was bound and carried off, and next day the King announced that in future he would govern alone, while Mortimer was locked into the Tower.

In the indictment brought against the Earl of the March there is no reference to his liaison with Isabel ; he was charged with having usurped royal authority, with having " murdered and killed " Edward II, and with numerous other offences, the most startling being the accusation that he had dared question the King's word at Nottingham when the King denied intending to harm him or the Queen ! As usual in such cases, Mortimer was not allowed to defend himself, he was not even taken before his judges ; on November 29 he was drawn on an ox-hide to the

Elms at Tyburn and was there hanged upon the common gallows. Isabel was treated gently. She hid in terror when her lover was captured, donning the habit of the Poor Clares, a sister order of the Franciscans ; but apart from taking away the money she had stolen during her reign, Edward took no reprisals for his father's murder. He gave her a large income and often visited her. She died in 1358.

With the death of Mortimer, Edward III became truly King of England.

HE was a handsome lad ; although not so tall as father and grandfather, he was nevertheless strongly built and well-proportioned. The effigy on his tomb in the quire of Westminster Abbey— reproduced here—is probably a very good likeness, as we know that a wax portrait was modelled from the corpse before burial. We see a beautifully bearded man with firm delicate nose and unruffled forehead. One chronicler, Adam Murimuth, describes Edward so completely and gives so just an estimate of his character that it is best to quote his words in full. " This King Edward," he writes, " was of infinite goodness, and glorious among all the great ones of the world, being entitled the Glorious *par excellence*, for that by virtue of grace from heaven he outshone in excellence all his predecessors, renowned and noble as they were. He was so great-hearted that he never blenched or changed the fashion of his countenance at any ill-hap or trouble soever that came upon him ; a renowned and fortunate warrior, who triumphed gloriously in battles by sea and land ; clement and benign, familiar and gentle even to all men, both strangers and his own subjects or dependents ; devoted to God, for he held God's Church and His ministers in the greatest reverence. In temporal matters he was not too unyielding, prudent and discreet in counsel, affable and gentle in courtesy of speech, composed and measured in gesture and manners, pitiful to the afflicted, and profuse in largesse. In times of wealth he was not immoderate ; his love of building was great and discriminating ; he bore losses with moderation ; devoted to hawking, he spent much pains on that art. His body was comely, and his face like the face of a god, wherefrom so marvellous grace shone forth that whosoever openly considered his countenance, or dreamed thereof by night, conceived a sure and certain hope of pleasant solace and good-fortune that day. He ruled his realm strictly even to his old age ; he was liberal in giving and lavish in spending ; for he was excellent in all honour of manners, so that to live under him was to reign ; since his fame was so spread abroad among barbarous nations that, extolling his honour, they averred that no land under the sun had ever produced a King so noble, so generous, or so fortunate ; and that, after his death, none such perchance ever be raised up for future times. Yet he controlled not, even in old age, the dissolute lusts of the flesh ; and, as is believed, this intemperance shortened his life."

Such hyperbole, even when brought to earth by a confession of Edward's carnal nature, has often made later historians look upon him with a certain distrust. In their reaction against contemporary worship they too often slide off in the other direction and underrate his achievement. And he was undoubtedly a great King, a King who concentrated on the navy, who was the father of English commerce and the patron of the vital wool-trade. Like his grandfather he preferred to lurk behind legal quibbles rather than come out openly with his demands, and that was typical of the medieval mind with its casuistry and insane passion for logic. As a soldier he cannot be spoken of too highly, and as a diplomat he was cunning and successful. It was the soldier in him that appealed to the world ; he dazzled contemporaries, he became to them the personification of chivalry.

It is necessary to pause a moment, because we have reached the heyday of the chivalric notions, and they have changed since the era of Rufus—or rather, they have expanded. The crusades with their hysterical passion for martyrdom had wrought chivalry into a religious form : the knight set out with the ideal of God before him. Joinville expounds this attitude again and again in the pages of his magnificent chronicle of St. Louis's crusade, he tells of knights deliberately throwing themselves on the swords of the Moslems so that they could win to heaven ; then in the fourteenth century, Froissart shows us the new form of chivalry in which love had usurped religion. Women had entered the world of masculinity, the old knight of chivalry forgot his wife or mistress the moment armour was placed over his body and the sword—that living sharp-edged cross—was gripped in his hand. And I feel that this change, or this development, was to a great extent the result of the gigantic wave of Mariolatry that swept over Europe in the twelfth century and was in full swing in the thirteenth when the Blessed Virgin's acts were written out and when almost a new gospel was created. The early Christian Church did not consider Mary of importance, and the first collection of her acts dates from the eleventh century; from then on, her worship became the most vital part of the Church, God the Father was almost completely forgotten, Christ took His place, and Mary became the semi-human mediator between her Son's inflexible wrath and miserable sinners. Her cult spread with astounding rapidity, for it was a cult that was needed, the old religion being too harsh, and man will always require the worship of the Great Mother. Into the love of Mary was fused memories of Venus, Isis, Diana, Ceres; she became the Virgin-Mother-Wife, the threefold woman containing in divine flesh all the perfections of femininity—the mystery of the unsoiled terrifying Virgin, the companionship and humanity of the Wife, with the tender self-sacrifice of Motherhood. No goddess has exemplified so perfectly the ideal woman, and the western world immediately became her slave. Men did not place her amongst the clouds as an unapproachable cold goddess, they brought her to earth and made her compassionate and childlike. Her relics were shown on every side, churches exposed for reverence her hair, her milk, her clothes, her gloves and slippers, her comb and veil, her sweat, her girdle, her handkerchief. So greatly was she adored that men could look back upon their fall from paradise as fortunate, because through it she had been born. And with the growth of the Mary cult the attitude of chivalry changed until love entered it. So important became love to the medieval knight, the outward show of love—the swooning youth, the kissing of finger-tips and the reading of poems aloud in little walled gardens—that Froissart, seeing the too-too-human love-making of Edward III, was forced to invent a pretty tale to make his hero perfect. The tale, which could not have happened according to the dates given, tells of Edward's chivalric passion for the Countess of Salisbury and is of interest as the basis for that charming myth about the Countess of Salisbury's garter being picked up at a dance by Edward and his ready retort of " Honi soit qui mal y pense " when the bystanders naturally sniggered. This Order of the Garter was created by Edward in an attempt to revive chivalry, for to every period chivalry is more or less a thing of the past. The garter itself probably represented Arthur's Round Table, as Edward built the Round Tower at Windsor to house a similar Table. And it is rather typical of the exalted outlook of knights that, while ideals should remain perfect amongst gentlefolk, the wretched villeins could be thrashed without mercy.

To build this Round Tower, workmen were impressed throughout six counties, and at one time seven hundred and twenty-two of the poor wretches were toiling to erect a monument to chivalry. The Tower was built in 1344, the Garter was instituted in 1349, and Froissart sees a connection between the two. Those words—" Honi soit qui mal y pense "—to explain which a legend has been created, probably had no dark meaning whatever. Very likely they were a jest with which to retort on jealous wives who asked embarrassing questions about what their husbands did when they were alone together.

Edward consciously tried to ape the perfect knight, and he succeeded, he was looked upon as the hero of chivalry in his own time. The modern student is apt to be repulsed by his ostentatious manners, he is liable to consider Edward as showy, vulgar. But " vulgar " in the Middle Ages did not have the insulting meaning that snobbery has placed upon it, it kept its real meaning of " the people," and was never used as we use it to-day. Edward III, like most great medieval Kings, was vulgar in the modern sense, and he deliberately made himself vulgar, that being the attribute of royalty—to parade your clothes, your wealth, to make sweeping gestures, to pin your palpitating heart on your sleeve. A King must not do good by stealth, he must boast and fling largesse, he must stage his triumphs with jewels and dancing-girls, with conduits bubbling wine and with streets carpeted with flowers. The world must see him and reverence and fear him. The elaborate and to us degrading show that Edward put on after the surrender of Calais, when he made the burghers walk out with ropes about their necks and had his wife ready to play a part and implore mercy, actually would impress Europe. The people were liable to forget that an important town had been captured unless it was captured with a grandiloquent gesture.

Because of this—because by his very vulgarity Edward became the perfect medieval King—modern writers too often see him through icy spectacles. We must judge him, not by present-day standards, but by medieval ones ; and except for that itch of lechery and the shame of his last years, Edward was the ideal knight.

HE could be merry when he wished and condescending to inferiors. He gave a glorious banquet and he placed the wives of London citizens next to the perfumed ladies of court ; he could be gentle and devout ; or he could leap into battle "like a wild boar, shouting, 'Ha Edward St. George ! Ha Edward St. George !'" ; or he could lead the merrymaking at Windsor Castle, dressed in white buckram tinselled with silver, his tunic and shield worked with the motto :

Hay, hay, the whité Swan !
By Goddés soul I am thy man !

Lecherous though he was, it seems that his marriage was a love-match, despite it having been arranged for political purposes. In 1327, Isabel formally asked her son if he would marry one of the four daughters of the Count of Hainault, "and he began to laugh, and said, 'Yes, I am better pleased to marry there than elsewhere ; and rather to Philippa, for she and I accorded well together excellently ; and she wept, I know well, when I took leave of her at my departure.'" The dispensation had to be bought from the papacy—for they were second cousins—and when at last Philippa landed at England she travelled to York where Edward was in the midst of his feeble campaign against the Scots. "And all the lords of England who were in the city came forth in fair array to meet her, and with them the young King, mounted on an excellently-paced hackney, magnificently clad and arrayed ; and he took her by the hand, and then embraced and kissed her ; and so riding side by side, with great plenty of minstrels and honours, they entered the city and came to the Queen's lodgings." Froissart adds, "Tall and straight she was ; wise, gladsome, humble, devout, free-handed, and courteous ; and in her time she was richly adorned with all noble virtues, and well-beloved of God and men." This was no exaggeration from the adoring clerk, it was the truth, for Philippa appears to have been a kind, good woman. There is a description of her dated 1319 in the official register of Bishop Stapledon of Exeter, transcribed by Dr. G. G. Coulton,[1] and even these cold emotionless letters cannot hide the sweetness of Edward's Queen. "The lady whom we saw has not uncomely hair," runs the entry, "betwixt blue-black and brown. Her head is clean-shaped ; her forehead high and broad, and standing somewhat forward. Her face narrows between the eyes, and the lower part of her face still more narrow and slender than the forehead. Her eyes are blackish-brown and deep. Her nose is fairly smooth and even, save that it is somewhat broad at the tip and also

[1] *Chaucer and his England*, by G. G. Coulton (Methuen), 1908.

flattened, yet it is no snub-nose. Her nostrils are also broad, her mouth fairly wide. Her lips somewhat full, and especially the lower lip. Her teeth which have fallen and grown again are white enough, but the rest are not so white. The lower teeth project a little beyond the upper ; yet this is but little seen. Her ears and chin are comely enough. Her neck, shoulders, and all her body and lower limbs are reasonably well-shapen ; all her limbs are well set and unmaimed ; and naught is amiss so far as a man may see. Moreover, she is brown of skin all over, and much like her father ; and in all things she is pleasant enough, as it seems to us. And the damsel will be of the age of nine years on St. John's day next to come, as her mother saith. She is neither too tall nor too short for such an age ; she is of fair carriage, and well taught in all that becometh her rank, and highly esteemed and well beloved of her father and mother and of all her meinie [*household*], in so far as we could inquire and learn the truth."

And the cautious bishop's measured praise is borne out by the Queen's effigy in Westminster Abbey which, like Edward's, may be taken as an actual portrait. Here she has fattened since the time when Stapledon peered at her, and the " reasonably well-shapen " figure has coarsened until there is small difference between breadth of shoulders, waist and hips. Yet in the plump face remains a humorous charm and she seems a good-natured, motherly creature.

WHEN, on the death of Mortimer, Edward found himself truly King, the problems that confronted him were mainly ways of straightening out the anarchy of the past years. Despite the dissensions under his rule, the people in Edward II's reign had been fairly prosperous, and he had exhausted the exchequer not by private extravagance but by the alienation of crown property, by giving rich lands to favourites. Slowly under his son, the country was brought back to peace and gradually the crown became more powerful, until Edward III started to itch on his throne out of sheer idleness and to dream of military glory. He had not forgotten the " shameful peace," and he longed for an excuse to start another war with Scotland. In England were many Scottish magnates—the disinherited they called themselves —who had been dispossessed of their estates over the Border. Edward, who always wished to stand by the letter of the law in the manner of his grandfather, could not openly take up their cause, but he could and did shut his eyes when they prepared for an invasion, led by Edward Balliol, the son and heir of King John whom Bruce had succeeded. At the battle of Dupplin Moor, the disinherited defeated the loyal Scots, and Balliol occupied Perth, where he received the homage of many of his enemies while struggling to fortify the old walls. In late September or early October, he was crowned King of Scotland at Scone and sealed an agreement with Edward, giving Scotland as a fief to England. Within a few weeks he was running from the country and appeared as a refugee at the court of Edward. This was Edward's chance. He sent Balliol back for a fresh invasion, and himself followed, reaching Newcastle on April 22, 1333, and immediately setting out to help besiege Berwick which for the last six weeks had been holding out stubbornly against Balliol and Montagu. A fierce assault in honour of the King's arrival was beaten back by the besieged ; the walls raised by Edward I were too strong to break and the only way of taking the castle was to starve the garrison to surrender. Its captain, glumly tightening his belt, agreed, in the usual medieval fashion, to capitulate if help did not arrive within fifteen days.

At last young Edward had his opportunity to fight. So far, he was comparatively unskilled in war and was eager to prove himself his grandfather's equal against the shields and swords of enemies. But his hopes at first came to nothing. The Scots marched forward as if for battle, then suddenly turned aside and attacked Bamborough, where Queen Philippa was lodged, hoping to lure Edward from the siege. Not only had they avoided a battle, but by forcing some kind of a relief into Berwick, its commander insisted that the clauses of the treaty were satisfied and refused to surrender when the fifteen days were up. Edward immediately hanged one of his most important hostages and the Scots hurriedly gave in ; they once more promised to surrender if not relieved by a certain date. This time Edward had it down in writing to make quite sure that there could be no argument about it afterwards, and the Scottish army instantly deserted Bamborough and rushed to rescue Berwick. On July 19, at midday, their banners could be seen rising over Halidon Hill to the north of the city ; on another hill, Edward drew up his men ready for battle. He had taken precautions against a sally in the rear from Berwick, and he formed his troops into the usual three battles, and he flanked each battle with a body of archers bearing the terrible quick-firing long-bow of the Welsh, the weapon that was soon to make the English feared throughout the western world. Horses were sent to the rear—a lesson learned from the Scots—and the men-at-arms stood on foot.

The Scots were at a disadvantage because they had to desert their strong shiltron formation and attack, having to fight their way through the English lines and somehow reach Berwick. According to the treaty, if not less than two hundred men entered the castle it would be considered technically relieved. Before nightfall, as the hour of vespers approached, the brave foolish Scots galloped to the desperate assault. They rushed downhill and into the swampy hollows, and here they were trapped, floundering in the muck while the English archers picked them off with their deadly rapid longbows. " As thick as motes on the sunbeam," the arrows came. The Scottish right made a brave attempt and actually reached the English left under Balliol, there they were tumbled back, shot at, clubbed. The slaughter was ghastly, and later the English boasted that the Scottish question was settled once and for all, as they no longer had a man living who was able to lead or govern them in fighting.

The next day Berwick surrendered and became hereafter the most important of the English Border towns. Balliol was again King and young David was hurried to France with his little English bride. Edward demanded not only Berwick, but all south-eastern Scotland, and the wretched Scottish King found himself detested by his subjects and despised by the English. Amongst the disinherited themselves quarrels developed into warfare ; a country like Scotland could never be taken, it might be defeated in pitched battles, yet there were always the Highlands in which to lurk, and the scattered troops fought here and there like out-laws, bravely, stubbornly.

FRANCE had continually helped Scotland in the trouble and now Edward turned to demand his revenge. We have not the space to follow his cunning diplomacies, his gathering of allies who took his money to desert at the last moment, his interference in French affairs, in the Netherlands, and in the Breton succession. There is, however, one battle that cannot be ignored, for because of it England gained her supremacy of the seas, and this is the battle of Sluys. For many years the seamen of England and the seamen of Normandy had watched each other with jealous hatred, between them the Channel was disputed territory, they fought their personal duels, murdered each other, stole each other's cargoes. Now they were to meet to decide the question of supremacy. The Norman fleet was waiting in the harbour of Sluys to intercept Edward when, on Thursday, June 22, 1340, he sailed from the Orwell with an invading fleet so great that many of the offered ships had to be refused. He left against the advice of his ministers who knew that the enemy were prepared to attack him in the Channel. "I will go in spite of you," cried Edward, "and you who fear where no fear is can stay at home."

It was almost noon on the 23rd, when the English saw " a very forest of masts " in the harbour of Sluys. They did not attack at once, for as one story tells us the King refused to fight on a Friday, the day on which Christ had suffered ; the King himself however, made no reference to such piety, he explained that the tide was against him. He anchored off Blankenberg, ten miles to the west of Sluys, and sent troops overland to reconnoitre the enemy's position. Their report was that the French fleet was 190 ships manned by over 35,000 Normans, Picards and Genoese, a formidable host. We are uncertain of Edward's exact numbers, for we must grope carefully through medieval figures : it appears that he had just under 150 vessels. He was, however, superior in troops, for it seems that the French commander, Pierre Béhuchet, had economised by enrolling men of low status, while the English were mainly " gentlemen."

At dawn of the next day, both sides prepared for battle. The French wisely stayed on the defensive, they sailed to the harbour-mouth and drew up with the largest ships in front, the rest trailing behind in three or four ranks deep ; to make the mass as solid as possible, and as like a besieged castle as they could, they chained and roped the vessels together. Medieval sea-tactics were the same as land-tactics, men besieged ships as they besieged castles, having few cannons, and victory depended on archery or on hand-to-hand fighting. Here in the harbour-mouth the French waited while the English manœuvred in the open until wind and sun and tide were in their favour. Then the trumpets were blown, " well after midday," and with the tide the English fleet unloosed their sails for Sluys. In the front rank swayed the larger ships, in the rear was a squadron to guard the ladies who were travelling to join Philippa at Ghent ; for every ship manned by men-at-arms there were two filled with archers, and there was also a squadron of archers who were to act as occasion suited. To the trumpets and the kettledrums, the

viols and the tabors, the English sailed forward and they yelled
as the first ship crunched against the enemy. Grappling-irons
were thrown ; the archers pulled the strings to their ears, and
their deadly fire wiped out the massed French ; the Genoese
crossbowmen found themselves defeated, unable to load their
mechanical weapons in time to retort. Then the English men-
at-arms leaped the bulwarks and with axes, spears and swords
they cleared the decks. Edward was wounded in the leg but he
refused to go below ; he stayed on deck until the last arrow had
flown, the last blow struck. Then in the rich sunset, with the
golden light flooding the blood-soaked water, the French ships
were broken hulks, while triumphantly the embroidered and
painted English lions amongst the lilies lolled with drooping
tongues from the mast of every vessel.

THE victory made Edward famous as a soldier, it brought England
to the forefront of affairs, but the King could not follow it with
greater victories. He was almost bankrupt and was only able
to escape foreign creditors on one occasion by having to run
away ; his inability to pay his debts almost destroyed Florence,
and some of the greatest banking-houses, like the Bardi and the
Peruzzi, were forced to go into liquidation. Lack of money held
Edward from his great achievements, from his dream of capturing
France, to the throne of which he considered himself the true
heir through his mother, Isabel.

Except for Sluys, the opening battles of the Hundred Years'
War had been indecisive, mere sparring-bouts in which neither
side had dared stake everything upon one blow. Edward
possessed such little money that he was unable to begin a campaign
on a large scale, then in 1346 he made a particular effort. He
called for a return from the counties south of the Trent of the
names of all those who owned 100 shillings' worth of land or
upwards ; persons worth 100 shillings were required to provide an
archer, persons worth £10 a hobeler—a light horseman, rider of a
hobby or pony—and those worth £25 a man-at-arms—a heavily
mounted horseman—and so on up the scale of feudal military
exactions. Actually this was a revival of the worst forms of
scutage, for the people taxed did not send the men demanded, they
gave money instead—20 shillings being offered in lieu of an archer,
£3, 6s. 8d. for a hobeler, and £6, 13s. 4d. for a man-at-arms.
The protest raised by this was so great that little of the money
was collected ; all the same, the army, when at last Edward

had got it together, must have exceeded 10,000 men. On July 11, 1346, he set sail upon the great invasion.

Caen was the first point at which he found any resistance. Until then his march through Normandy was unopposed, he tramped over country made desolate by his enemies, and had to build bridges where old ones were smashed ; there was no fighting until he came to Caen, an unwalled city, we are told, that was "larger than any in England except London." It was at the junction of the Odon and the Orne ; the castle was on the north-west, in the Grand Bourg, and a bridge held it to the Île Saint-Jean, in which quarter the defenders gathered, the castle being left to look after itself. Edward Prince of Wales—whom we had best, for convenience sake, call the Black Prince—entered the Grand Bourg, while the Earl of Warwick, son of the Black Dog, with the Earl of Northampton, attacked the island "without orders or array." The bridge was well defended and there were boats in the river manned by crossbowmen ; the English archers soon wiped these out and captured the boats, and the Welsh swam and forded their way on to the Île des Prés that jutted out between the Grand Bourg and the Île Saint-Jean. After that, defence was hopeless ; and the constable and chamberlain in the bridge-house, luckily recognising a one-eyed knight with whom they had fought in Granada, surrendered their swords and Edward gave the city up to pillage, the inhabitants being ruthlessly massacred.

For three days Edward stayed in Caen and reached Lisieux on August 2 where he was met by the inevitable legates sent by the Pope to settle the question peacefully. Edward told them that he was only too delighted to make an honourable peace, then was forced to prove his words a lie when they offered him the duchy of Aquitaine "as his father had held it." On refusing this, Edward continued his march until he found the bridge to Rouen broken down and was forced to repair one at Poissy. From here he could wellnigh see Paris, as it was only fifteen miles away. His men raced to the walls of the capital, and the citizens gazed in terror at the western sky that was red with flames as if with a perpetual sunset. They cried on their King for help, and Philip could think of nothing better than to send absurd challenges to Edward, which, of course, were ignored. Edward's one desire was to get out of the country, he had not enough troops to remain longer or to consolidate his conquests, and it seemed that he was trapped. There was not a bridge he could use across the Somme, and every moment Philip's army was growing larger, more formidable, and his own was weakening. Desperately he offered rewards to anyone who would reveal a path over the river, and a traitor, one of the prisoners, led him to a ford across the estuary, a reef of chalk called the Blanche Taque, and, crossing that night, Edward and his men slept on the edge of the forest of Crécy, the Somme passed at last.

Edward swore that he would retreat no farther, he would stand on the earth that was his by right, in Ponthieu, and he would battle with the French. Carefully he examined the countryside to find the ideal ground, then on Saturday, August 25, he was up early and at mass. The field he had chosen was past the village of Crécy, next to the road to Wadicourt—it was on a slope, so that his men had the forest at their backs and the village to their right beyond a little valley. The only way the French could attack would be uphill, either in front or to the English left. Edward drew up his army in the usual three battles, and the men-at-arms dismounted. The Prince of Wales was given the right, and he was placed in the care of Warwick and other lords. The left was commanded by Northampton and the Earl of Arundel, while the King himself commanded the centre which was slightly behind the other two divsions. The archers were flung out as a series of split triangles between each division. To make the approach yet more difficult, Edward commanded that pits be dug on the slope to trip the horsemen, as Bruce had ordered at Bannockburn. He had three cannon, awkward machines cast in one piece and as liable to blow up as to blow out, and these were given to the archers. Then all being drawn up to his liking, the King rode to the extreme right of his men and stood beneath a windmill from where he could oversee the complete field. This was to be his position, but during the painful wait, during that suspense most heart-breaking to men expecting a fight, Edward sat his palfrey and, with a white staff in his hand, rode through the ranks with a smiling word for everyone, with a cheerful mien and ready laughter. Nine o'clock came and the French had not appeared, so he dismissed his men for dinner; they were soon recalled to hold their positions, to sit idly on the ground with their weapons and helmets before them.

We do not know the exact numbers of the French, but they were certainly far superior to the English : Froissart, writing from hearsay, calls the English " a mere handful " in comparison with the enemy. Philip led his men under the oriflamme of St. Denis ;

they were formed in three divisions, and when he neared Edward's camp he called a halt to give his troops a short rest. His officers refused to obey, they were eager for battle. " Tarry and abide here," cried Philip, " in the name of God and St. Denis," and while the front ranks paused, the rear marched forward, so that " without order or good array " they came in sight of the English.

It began to rain, a thunderstorm had gathered, and the lightning flashed into the faces of the advancing French, while crows flew past scared by the noise, the light and the black clouds. But the storm soon went, and the English, who had been lying down, slowly rose to their feet and waited, taking their bows out of cases and wrappings which had protected the strings from the rain. The Genoese crossbowmen had not been so cautious, their strings were wet and slack and almost useless. " Make the Genoese go on before," cried Philip, " and begin the battle in the name of God and St. Denis." Grumbling and weary after their long tramp, the Genoese led the host, marching into a brilliant sun that had come out after the storm. Then the English drew back the strings of their longbows ; they had a greater range than the Genoese and were quick - firing. Blinded by the sun, killed without being able to retort, the Genoese could only jump and yell in the vain hope of frightening the enemy who " stirred not for all that." They kept on firing, and their arrows fell so thick " that it seemed snow." The wretched Genoese threw away their bows or in their rage cut the strings and tried to run, but the French would not open their ranks to let them pass. " Ride down the rascals ! " they cried, and they turned their horses upon their own allies. All was confusion, arrows came quicker than ever, and the Welsh crept out with long knives to prise apart the joints in armour of fallen men, thereby killing knights who would have brought good ransom. Again and again the French lumbered forward, trying to break those stolid ranks, and again and again they were sent helter-skelter down the slope. Fifteen times it is said that they charged. The Prince's division stood the severest attacks. He called for reinforcements and when the messenger told of his plight to the King who stood upon the windmill-hill under his banner of the Wessex Dragon newly draped with the lilies of France, " Is my son dead or hurt," asked Edward, " or on the earth felled ? " " No, sir," replied the messenger, " but he is hardly matched ; wherefore he hath need of your aid." " Well," said Edward, " return to him and to them that sent you hither,

26

and say to them that they send no more to me for any adventure
that falleth, as long as my son is alive : and also say to them that
they suffer him this day to win his spurs ; for if God be pleased
I will this journey be his and the honour thereof, and to them
that be about him." The message heartened the Prince and he
fought more courageously than ever, but Edward was father
enough to send a little help—twenty men-at-arms.

It was scarcely a battle. The English kept their lines and the
French charged without formation, without plans or tactics.
Philip was struck in the face by an arrow, and the blind King
of Bohemia was killed during the retreat.[1] It was a rout, the
dispirited French were massacred. Edward would not let his
men pursue, he bade them keep their places on the battlefield,
and when dawn came they saw another enemy approaching—
reinforcements who were unaware of the result. These were
easily defeated ; then was the moment for the gathering of
booty, for the stripping of the dead, for the killing of the wounded,
and the counting of prisoners. Edward had won a splendid
victory, he had wiped out many of the greatest men in France,
and with almost no loss to himself.

On August 28 he continued his march, and was before Calais
by September 4. This was a most important city, strongly walled,
and with a double moat that was filled with every tide, and
Edward was determined to capture it. Too long had it been the
centre for Genoese pirates, and it would be invaluable to England

---

[1] Legend states that the Prince of Wales's ostrich feather badge was borne
by this King of Bohemia with the motto *Ich Diene*, and that Edward of Woodstock chose them in honour of the battle. Although ostrich feathers apparently
had nothing to do with Bohemia, the old King did wear them at Crécy and
Anne of Bohemia had them for a badge. The feathers, as a matter of
fact, were used by some of the Prince's brothers as well as himself,
and it appears that one of Queen Philippa's coats-of-arms was black with
three silver ostrich feathers, probably an allusion to Ostrevans, a fief of the
Counts of Hainault. The Black Prince's father, grandfather and greatgrandfather had all taken badges from their mothers' devices, and it is likely
enough that he followed their example and borrowed from Philippa for his
shield-for-peace ; his shield-for-war would naturally be the royal coat-of-arms
differenced by a silver label. Both shields can be seen on his tomb in Canterbury Cathedral, the shield-for-peace being surmounted by a scroll with the
motto *Ich Diene*, German for " I Serve." It is strange that Edward should choose
a German motto and it seems more probable, as he was Prince of Wales, that
these words were actually a corruption of the Welsh, *Eich Dyn*, " Your Man."
As for the question of the queer nickname, the Black Prince, that still remains
a mystery, but it might have originated from his shield-for-peace—that is,
silver feathers on a black field.

as the stepping-off place for future conquest. Exhausted though
his army was, Edward settled down before Calais, writing to
England with news of the victory and requests for further supplies ; as the medieval commissariat more or less did not exist,
an army lived on what it could forage from the country it invaded.
A town of huts grew around Calais, winter was approaching ;
it was called Newtown the Bold and had streets and shops as
well as living quarters ; it was surrounded by earthworks, and a
market was held in it twice a week. Months passed, and Edward
lived in his huts while Philip, apparently demoralised by the
defeat of Crécy, made no move to rescue the beleaguered city.
Meanwhile King David had returned to Scotland and, prompted
by Philip, invaded England. He was badly defeated at Neville's
Cross and was captured and sent to the Tower. It seemed that
everything was working well with Edward, for Calais was growing
desperate, with English troops on the land and an English fleet
in the Channel ; to stop even small boats sneaking through the
blockade with supplies, Edward built a jetty of piles that could
not be passed. The inhabitants were starving, dogs and cats
and horses were eaten, until at last, on June 27, 1347, Philip
arrived ; he dared not move, he stayed out of reach and sent
fruitless challenges to Edward who naturally was not going to
desert his strong position to fight in the open at Philip's convenience. On August 2 Philip burnt his camp and retired, and the
last hope was taken from Calais ; it could do nothing now except
surrender. Edward, however, had wasted too many months to
let the garrison walk off without harm ; it was impossible according to the rules of chivalry to hang the besieged or to slaughter
them in cold blood, as they had surrendered, therefore he staged
a pageant in which his vanity was satisfied and the enemy humiliated. A deputation of soldiers and burghers was made to walk
barefoot from the city, ungirdled, bareheaded, and with a rope
about each man's neck. They were to carry the keys of town
and castle and were to lay them solemnly at the King's feet and
implore mercy. The pageant was unfortunately a little marred
because the captain of the garrison suffered from gout ; Edward
was kind enough to let him sit a palfrey. On the appointed day
out they came in their penitential garb and knelt to Edward.
First they offered him " a sword of war," then the keys, then
" a sword of peace." With lowered brow, Edward watched and
pretended anger until Philippa knelt with the deputation and
implored him to give these people to her mercy. Everything

being satisfactory to his honour, Edward granted the deputation to his Queen and served out provisions. His largesse did more harm than good ; after their long privation, many of the people so over-ate themselves that they died.

With the capture of Calais, Edward ended this opening phase of the Hundred Years' War. He had won a splendid victory and, far more important, he had captured a seaport that was to remain English until the days of Queen Mary I. He was determined to use Calais as a commercial centre, as the banking-house of English merchants exporting their goods to the Continent, therefore he declared it the sole staple for all tin, lead, feathers, cloth and worsted leaving England, and merchants were made to promise to use no other gateway for their goods and produce.

Having been fifteen months abroad, the King at last landed at Sandwich on October 12 after a stormy crossing. " Holy Mary," he cried, " why is it that when I go abroad the weather ever smiles on me and frowns when I return ? "

It was time that Edward called a halt in his conquests. His allies had deserted him and he had no money left ; at Calais he had signed a truce on September 28 which included Scotland and Brittany as well as France, and which was to last until July 9, 1384. His success seems to us small enough. All that effort, that waste of men and money, and with only one town to show for it, yet that town was of vital importance and Edward's military skill won for England a place in the world it had not known for many, many years. A war such as this, in which small numbers of professional soldiers only were used, must not be compared with the present massacre of civilians bullied into uniform. While Edward was fighting abroad, England was able to settle down peacably and correct its own troubles. After the treaty of Calais, the King might return penniless but England was comparatively well off ; wages were low, but then, so were prices, and unemployment scarcely existed. One could not call it an era of prosperity, it was an era of well-being, for the merchant was beginning to take first place in the nation's affair ; war in Flanders had brought Flemish refugees to England and they set up their looms in this country, while the victory of Sluys had placed English shipping beyond the Italians, the Netherlanders and the Germans in the race for foreign trade.

Then suddenly, while Edward was considering how to continue the war, and as the merchants were gazing on their books and tally-sticks with a new complacency, the Black Death came to Europe. It rose from the East, like a " dark stinking mist," evidently from the highlands of Persia, the earth appeared to have spat it out in earthquakes, it reached Cyprus, and from Cyprus rushed in 1347 to Provençe and almost depopulated Avignon where Pope Clement VI shuddered to see his cardinals dropping about him. From Provence it went to Guienne to kill Edward's daughter Joan, and on July 7, it touched England, reaching first the Dorsetshire coast. There had always been plagues throughout the Middle Ages and they continued until long afterwards, but none could equal this. It was evidently bubonic [1] and any one who has lived in a city struck by this pestilence will realise how terrifying must have been its effect in medieval times ; to-day, with modern skill to fight it, the effect is ghastly enough, to walk a crowded street of masked people and suddenly to find it empty save for a crumpled corpse on the ground, to lie in bed unable to sleep and fearful even of breathing lest you drew contagion through your teeth. . . . It must have been the most incredible hell in the Middle Ages. Yet astonishingly we find little panic, for there was a curious fatalism, a belief in predestination, in the medieval man ; he accepted everything, good or evil, because everything came from God : a blessing was a reward, a scourge was God's revenge. All the same, as the plague at last gradually died, we discover a quick reaction, an hysterical religious mania as with the flagellants, or a passion for debauch as shown by Boccaccio's tale-telling in his walled Florentine garden. Boccaccio, as a matter of fact, gives us one of the fullest descriptions of this plague which struck down Petrarch's beautiful Laura. " It showed itself," he tells us, " in a sad and wonderful manner, and different from what it had been

---

[1] To identify diseases of the Middle Ages is extraordinarily difficult and medical men still argue about the Black Death. I have asked many doctors to decide whether it was plague, typhus or influenza, and none care to be definite. Their attitude is best summed up by Dr. Saxon Barton who states that it is impossible to prove that the Black Death was " either pneumonic or bubonic plague or a mixture of both, but it would seem probable that it was a mixture of both. The bubonic variety affects the lymph glands of the body while the pneumonic sets up in the lungs a kind of plague pneumonia. The mortality of the bubonic form is about 75 per cent. and of the pneumonic form about 95 per cent., the bubonic being spread by the rat-flea, while the pneumonic may, in addition, be spread directly by the expectoration of the patient. It is likely that typhus fever might have behaved in somewhat the same way as the Black Death. The possibility of it having been influenza is evidently very slight.

in the East, where bleeding from the nose is the fatal warning ; here there appeared certain tumours in the groin or under the armpits, some as big as an apple, others as big as an egg, and afterwards purple spots in most parts of the body, in some cases large and few in number, in others less and more numerous. . . . They usually died the third day from the first appearance of the symptoms, without fever or other bad circumstances attending." Giovanne Villani, the historian of Florence, himself later a victim, contradicts Boccaccio : " It generally took men in the head and stomach," he wrote, " showing first on the groin or under the armpits in little knobs or swellings called kernels, boils, blains, blisters, pimples, or plague-sores, being usually attended with devouring fever, with occasional spitting and vomiting of blood, whence for the most part they died presently or in half a day or within a day or two at the most."

The plague struck London early in November, and soon it had spread through the whole country, invading even Scotland which had boasted of its immunity and called the plague " the foul death of the English." In the terror of this time, when men healthy one day were dead the next, the chroniclers exaggerate the figures of mortality almost beyond hope of our discovering the truth : no one man in ten lived, we are told, and the survivors were so few that they could not bury the dead which lay festering in the streets. It was a scourge from God, a judgment on the pride and debauch of the magnates and their ladies, on the cupidity and cheating of the merchants, and on the worldliness of the Church. " Man's iniquity and sins of every kind had so multiplied upon earth that their stench and the cry thereof came to the just ears of the Almighty." The Pope " shut himself up in his own chamber with great fires continually lighted, and gave access to no man," and many of the clergy refused to act unless given an excessive salary so that the dead were often buried without church offices, while other clergy finding their parishes diminished, fled for lack of money and others for fear of death. All the clergy, of course, were not of the same type, there were many good Christians amongst them, priests who sacrificed their lives to bring consolation to the dying. England had not sufficient burial-grounds and special plague-pits had to be dug into which the bodies were thrown indiscriminately by the hundred. There was harvest enough in the country and no hands to reap it, there was cattle enough but no herdsmen to tend the beasts. In London, although the records are scanty, the mortality appears to have been great, as would be expected amongst those crowded streets and lanes, those wooden houses with refuse stinking outside their doors. Gentle and simple, all were struck down, although it appears that more men died than women and that the magnates escaped more often than the poor ; within twelve months there were three Archbishops of Canterbury.

No sooner had the first visitation gone than fresh waves of death struck the country : 1348, 1349, 1362, 1369, were all plague years of particular vehemence. The economic effect of these visitations was very great. They gave the death-blow to the ancient manorial order by the scarcity of labour they created and the consequent rise in wages. To the simple medieval mind these conditions could be remedied by laws, and in 1351 was passed the famous Statute of Labourers which demanded that prices and wages return to what they had been before the Black Death. This, an attempt to force the workmen to submit to the demands of the narrow gilds—those organisations of the employers to control monopolies—at first hit the employers as hard, if not harder, than the employees, although it was eventually to culminate in the Peasants' Rebellion of 1381. Employers were forbidden to pay high wages under threat of heavy fines, while labourers were imprisoned until they promised to accept the ancient payments. The labourers had the whip hand, however, for statutes cannot dominate a nation, and that was particularly so in the badly organised Middle Ages. It was impossible to imprison all the labourers in England, but it was possible to fine the merchants and farmers, and therefore the weight of the statute fell mainly on the employers who were trapped between the King's courts and the labourers who moved to better pastures at the first hint of a drop in wages. That was at first, then as the population equalised, the labourer discovered that the employer too often adhered to the statute so far as wages were concerned, and ignored it when it came to prices. At least the plague did this good ; it brought in time better conditions to a class living under oppression inconceivable even in these days of economic tyranny towards the unemployed. The poet Gower, like the great Langland, could sympathise with the peasant yet both had class-prejudice enough to be horrified when the peasant asked for something more than wheaten bread, corn, beans and water to live on. Langland, who had the courage to create a peasant-saint and could show the misery of the time, believed nevertheless, that the labourer should remain content with yesterday's cabbage, penny-ale and a slice of bacon, he implies that it is preposterous for him to dare to ask for hot fish or meat. Gower is even worse, but then of course he was a landlord as well as a poet, and the two professions are diametrically opposed. " The shepherd and the cowherd," he cries, " demand more wages now than the master-bailiff was wont to take, and whithersoever we look, whatsoever be the work, labourers are now of such price that, when we must needs use them, where we were wont to spend two shillings we must now spend five or six." Even such intelligent men as these were blind to any conception of real freedom, although Gower was awake enough to realise that such oppressions could not continue, and he blames the lords for their self-satisfied weakness, warning them that " this impatient nettle will suddenly sting us before men do justice upon it." His warning was proved in 1381. It was all very well to sentimentalise about the peasant—as even modern novelists attempt to do nowadays—to see him as a picturesque toiler tipping his hat to the gentry : he had grievances and he had learned to use the scythe and the reaping-hook while poets had given him a warcry that was later to be shouted by John Ball :

When Adam delfe and Eve span, spur if thou will speed,
where was then the pride of man that now mars his mede?

What the Black Death did was to make the wage-earner realise that he was not a slave and that wages could be no more stable than prices. The whole weight of this sudden change descended upon the landowners, and therefore in particular upon the monks, the greatest landowners of all. Rents fell to nothing and crops perished for lack of cheap hands to reap them, tenants moving to where wages were higher and where few questions were asked in that dearth of working men, while the villein no longer could be made to keep his bond, he won his freedom by packing his rags and walking to another district. The lords were forced to commute the feudal idea of service into the payment of a small rent. This was the end of the old land-tenure systems, the yeoman replaced the villein, the serf disappeared to make way for the farmer who kept his freedom so long as he could grub up enough coins to pay for roof and earth.

The plague left behind it a passion for founding religious houses. In penitence the wealthy strove to avert the anger of God by offering Him the thing they valued most—gold. Gold was offered to churches and monasteries, and if the monks attempted to shut infection out by barring their gates, offerings were flung over the walls. Others discovered relief in wine and debauchery, they talked merrily and ogled each other in Boccaccio-gardens while men and women rotted in the streets outside. Then came, too, the usual outbursts of religious lunacy such as the Flagellants who, I am delighted to say, were looked upon very coldly in England. About one hundred and twenty of them arrived from Holland in 1349 ; preceded by singers wailing for repentance, they marched through the streets with linen cloths about their loins and wearing some sort of hat—probably a hood—marked with a red cross behind and in front. Each carried a knotted iron-pointed whip and flogged the back of the man before him. They did this twice a day.

DURING the plague there was of course no fighting between France and England, so Edward kept himself amused by founding the Order of the Garter and by dedicating a chapel to St. George at Windsor in which the knights were given stalls. On June 24, 1348, a great tournament was held at Windsor for the churching of the Queen—her Feast of Purification after the birth of her fourth son William. Edward was a man of action. At the first opportunity he gripped his sword in his hand. There was a French plot to recapture Calais and he was warned of it. King and Prince hurried over at once to join the fun, and on the night when the French were to enter the city, the royal couple hid behind a mock-wall. Then as the first detachment of the enemy rode into the ward, a great stone was hurled down, smashing the drawbridge and cutting off retreat, while Edward and the Prince galloped from gates on opposite sides of the town and charged the remainder of the French. " Ha, Edward St. George ! " yelled the King. " Ha, Edward St. George ! " It was of course unnecessary and perhaps foolish of him to risk his life in this way, but such adventures made him beloved. On another occasion he set out to fight the Spanish fleet in 1350, and with his two sons, Edward and John of Gaunt—the English way of spelling Ghent, his birthplace—the King piped and danced to the wharves. There followed another victory for England. Edward sat on his ship cheerily, dressed " in a black velvet jacket and a beaver hat that well became him " ; then when the enemy was sighted, with his knights he drank a cup of wine and put on his armour. Archery, as usual, won the fight, and the Spanish sailors had to skulk in terror behind their bulwarks, afraid to show their faces while the English drifted close enough to grapple.

EDWARD's claim to France might seem rather absurd to us to-day, but it did not seem absurd to his contemporaries. When Charles IV died and left no heir save an unborn grandchild that turned out to be a girl, Edward as Charles's nephew had more right to the throne than Philip as the son of Charles's uncle. If he had been a Frenchman it is more than likely that Edward would have been accepted, as an Englishman of course he had no hope. There were many reasons for the invasion of France, and the claim to the throne was at first merely a pretence that Edward himself began eventually to believe in ; France had aided the Scots and by her piracies and an alliance with the Netherlands had interfered with England's wool-trade. All the same, had Edward not been a born adventurer the troubles would most likely have been patched up by treaties : but Edward loved fighting, he loved to imagine himself as an errant-knight in a story-book, and this chivalrous attitude he passed on to his son, Edward of Woodstock, the Black Prince.

After the plague had gone, Edward continued the war in a desultory fashion, for he had not money enough to muster a great army and he could only lead raiding-expeditions that were politically and financially worthless. King Philip was now dead ; he died in the flush of passion, for he had fallen deeply in love with his eighteen-year-old cousin Blance, had married her in January 1350, and had ended his life suddenly in August of the same year at the age of fifty-eight. He was succeeded by his son John, a courageous and stupid fellow who showed no desire to end the war, who in fact seemed determined to carry it on although France was in a desperate condition. Adventurers from all corners of Europe took the broken country for their battlefield, they fought on either side or on any side, their one desire being plunder and a violent life. These free-lances did as they pleased, and one of them, a Gascon nicknamed the Arch-deacon, held Avignon for ransom and made the Pope ask him to dinner and give him absolution for his sins. The peasants left their fields, they lurked terrified in pits or churches, afraid to venture into the open lest they be killed, and it became a jest of the time to say when speaking of their patience, " Jacques Bonhomme has a broad back and can carry anything." This

evil of the " free companies " was just beginning, and as the war
continued it was to grow until France became almost utterly
despoiled and the wretched peasants at last took revenge into
their own hands. Their new King was even more absurdly
chivalrous than our Edward ; to the true knight the people were
not worth considering, they were looked upon as lower than
animals, for there was sport to be found with dogs and horses
but none with serfs. King John ignored the state of his country,
he would not listen to a peace with England. " I will have in
France no master but myself ! " was his continual cry.

Therefore the war continued. Then came the glorious
victory of Poitiers when on September 19, 1356, the Black Prince
with a tiny force defeated the chivalry of France and captured
its King. Again it was the foot soldier against the mounted
knight, the longbow against the awkward crossbow. And it is
interesting to note the anger of the French because the English
possessed a weapon superior to theirs ; it was taking an unfair
advantage, they cried, it was—one might almost say—unsporting.
Girard de Vienne summed up his country's attitude in two lines :

On the first archer an hundred curses be !
T'approach the foe he was too cowardly !

Always an advance in weapons is hailed with protests from
the other side ; such was our own outraged dignity when
the Germans produced poison gas ; such was the howl of the
French when the English wiped them out by standing off and
pulling the string of a longbow to their ears. It was against the
rules of chivalry, cried the French, against the old-fashioned
honourable conception of a battle being a series of personal
combats in which only the common soldiers were slaughtered,
knights being taken for their ransom and always treated
courteously. Now these treacherous English killed noble knights
as impartially as they killed base villeins : it was definitely unfair,
cried the defeated French.

When the news of Poitiers reached England, bells rang, the
conduits flooded wine, bonfires were lit, and Edward remarked
that heaven was obviously on his side as with a mere handful of
foot-soldiers his son had not only won a great battle, he had
captured the King of France. Soon the royal prisoner was
brought to England and entered London on May 24, 1356. Over
a thousand citizens rode into Southwark to greet their returning
Prince, the members of the gilds being tricked out in all their

newest liveries. Young Edward sat a little galloway, a small black palfrey, while his prisoner rode a great white charger richly caparisoned. For hours the triumphant procession edged its way through crowded streets from the Bridge to Westminster Hall, passing the houses bedecked with cloths and flowers and showing as many weapons as could be dragged from garrets or borrowed for the martial occasion. In Westminster Hall, King Edward waited and courteously rose from his throne as John entered ; he took his son's prisoner in his arms and embraced him as a cousin and a guest. John's imprisonment was rather a gay affair, he was fêted and taken to tournaments ; there was a tournament held by torchlight at Bristol on New Year's Day, 1358, and one particularly gorgeous affair on St. George's Day which was said to be more splendid than anything since the time of King Arthur. It does not seem that his imprisonment troubled John, he was the perfect knight of chivalry to whom courtesy-rules were of greater importance than statecraft. While Edward haggled about his ransom and while money was thrown away on feasting and tournaments, France was in a desperate condition. The free companies did what they liked, they ransomed any man they could capture, they treated the peasant as a slave. King-less, led by the weak Dauphin, France could do nothing against these organised ruffians. On the peasant—poor Jacques, as he was called, probably because of the jacque or short jacket that he usually wore—lay the deepest suffering, for he was taxed to raise John's ransom and was bullied by his own lords and slaughtered by the free companies. Unable to bear their torments any longer, the peasants rose on May 28 and attacked the nearest castles. All over France, once the initiative had been given, poor Jacques shouldered his scythe or reaping-hook and sought revenge for years of most ghastly oppression. The chroniclers speak with horror of this rising—called the Jacquerie—but the peasants behaved in a most restrained fashion, preferring to pull down castles than to kill their enemies ; there was less damage and fewer killings in this rebellion than in the private brawling of the nobles and in the justice they gave him when poor Jacques had been defeated. The peasants were not executed, they were slaughtered.

John, being a true knight, naturally wanted a large ransom to be paid for his royal person, and Edward's demands were so huge that war started again. The King and his sons sailed on October 28, 1359, to begin a futile campaign that reached to the very walls of Paris, and which settled nothing. It was a gallant army that landed in France, but none of the names—names of brave men, great lords—come to us with the same thrill as the name of one obscure valet in the service of the King's son Lionel. It is with a shock of delight that one reads of Geoffrey Chaucer, a youth as yet unfledged in fighting and unfledged in art, but soon to become one of the very greatest poets England has ever known. The campaign was disastrous and Chaucer himself managed to be captured by enemy skirmishers ; the King, however, was intelligent enough to think of him worthy of a £16 ransom. Chaucer won no glory in the field of battle but, as with most poets, we may be certain that he was no coward and that when the moment arrived for fighting he used his sword as agilely as any knight. Edward reached the walls of Paris and sat before the overcrowded city that was filled with shivering refugees ; it was " a foul dark day of mist and of hail, and so bitter cold that sitting on horseback men died. Wherefore, unto this day it is called Black Monday, and will be [for a] long time hereafter." For seven weeks the English blockaded the city, but the walls were too great for assault, and a treaty was sealed at Brétigny on May 7, 1360, according to which Edward renounced his claim to France and his overlordship of Normandy, Anjou, Maine, Touraine, Brittany and Flanders, being given in return Gascony and Guienne, Poitou, and numerous outlying districts. King John's ransom was agreed on at the gigantic price of three million crowns of gold, each crown being worth 3s. 4d., a sum that could never be paid.

FROM now, the King moves into the background, while his sons, Edward the Black Prince and John of Gaunt, take the leadership. Therefore, although these latter years are of vital importance to English history, they are small concern of ours. The treaty was followed by a recurrence of the plague, but details are lacking, as the chroniclers had written enough about it already. Having more or less surrendered his claim to France, Edward began to interest himself in family affairs, plotting rich marriages for his children. His eldest son, the Black Prince, wedded his cousin Joan, who was called the Fair Maid of Kent. This description refers to her personal charms, her character was by no means unblemished ; it was, in fact, of such sort that in later days men seriously believed that her son Richard might not be the child of her husband.

There was inevitable trouble about the treaty and the Black

Prince was sent to govern Aquitaine which he did with such zest that the people soon grew to loathe him. Then came the absurd war in Castile when Prince Edward took the side of Pedro the Cruel against the King of Aragon. Pedro was a demoniacal creature who from the age of sixteen apparently murdered everybody he disliked, including his wife, his father's mistress, two of his half-brothers and a great many of his chief nobles ; even worse than this, however, he had actually loved a Jewess ! The Black Prince took his part while that great and ugly soldier, du Guesclin, fought on the other side ; and about the only good result of the wars was that they drained France of many of the free companies, although they came back as furious as ever when fighting ceased. The Black Prince returned with an army broken by dysentery, with everything lost except English prestige. Unconquered, yet in despair, the English soldiers withdrew, and none dared strike at them as they went.

Meanwhile King John had returned to France, but he was soon back in England. Four princes of the blood-royal had been left as hostages for his ransom and one of them escaped ; this so hurt the King's knightly honour that he hastened to take his son's place, although there were those amongst his subjects who whispered that it was not his honour so much as weariness of statecraft that sent him from his country, that he preferred to be a fêted prisoner rather than a distracted prince. He did not live much longer : landing at Dover on January 4, 1364, he died in the Savoy on April 8. Edward sent his body to France in royal state while four thousand torches and four thousand tapers were lighted at his obsequies in St. Paul's.

Parliament, with the French problem merely simmering instead of boiling, decided to fight the Church. The papal prestige was very low, the Babylonish captivity at Avignon had made England suspicious of French influence, it had brought the Pope from his exalted throne amongst the traditions of old Rome and had placed him as a pawn in the hand of France. During 1351, when the statute of labourers was passed, parliament also enacted the first statute of provisors which denied the Pope's right to elect provisors to English benefices and decreed the arrest of all such appointed by Avignon. In 1353, this was strengthened by the first statute of præmunire which enacted that all who carried their complaints to foreign courts—which could refer only to Avignon—should be liable to forfeiture and outlawry. Finding that these statutes were more or less ignored, parliament in 1365 decreed a second act of præmunire, making it stronger, tighter. Then came the old question of King John's tribute, his rent to Rome for the possession of England ; this tribute, in 1366, had not been paid over for thirty years, and Pope Urban V was growing persistent in his demands ; infuriated by England's new statutes which were gradually clipping the papal cords that dragged such gold to Avignon, he formally asked that the arrears of rent be paid at once and threatened to take proceedings in his own courts if delay occurred. Edward passed the problem on to the peers, and after deliberation, lords both spiritual and temporal, answered that no King could give away his realm without their consent. That finished the problem. Parliament swore to resist the Pope to its full powers if he kept on asking for the tribute, and Urban had to give way.

THE Black Prince ruled Aquitaine with a cruel hand ; his troops were made up of soldiers-of-fortune who put gold before loyalty, and to pay them he had to squeeze all money he could from his subjects until the Gascon lords appealed against him to his overlord, Charles V, the new King of France. Charles demanded his appearance before parlement and the Black Prince cried, " We will go to Paris if the King wishes it, but it shall be with bascinet on head and with sixty thousand men ! " He might threaten, his temper might be as courageous as ever, but his body was so weak that he could not sit upon his horse. Evidently he suffered from dropsy. All that he could do, apart from bold speaking, was to fling into prison the lawyer and knight who had brought Charles's citation.

This was to be the Black Prince's last fight. John of Gaunt was sent to his aid, but Gaunt lacked the genius of his father and brother, he was a weak and easily thwarted soldier, and when fighting against a man with the brilliance of du Guesclin he was beaten before he struck a blow. If the Black Prince could no longer fight, he could, however, seek revenge, and the sack of Limoges remains as the most brutal passage in his brutal career. He was carried to the siege in a litter, and as the walls were too strong for assault he had to mine beneath them. Gunpowder was not used for these operations, the pioneers dug under the foundations and then propped them up with beams. The beams were lighted and when burnt through they dragged down the walls, causing a breach to be opened. After six days of sapping the command was given for the torch to be applied, and

at dawn on September 19, 1370, the great wall of Limoges
shuddered and crumpled, and a huge gap showed in the stone.
Only clergy and knights were spared ; otherwise man, woman
and child were murdered. Through the smoke and carnage
the Black Prince was carried in his litter, shouting to his men,
spurring them on to yet bloodier work, and there was no pause
until the streets were thick with blood and piled with white
corpses horribly slashed.

Sated with killing, the Black Prince resigned himself
to the commands of his physicians and was carried back to
England to live almost the whole of his short remaining life in
Berkhampstead.

EDWARD III, pattern of chivalry, had forgotten that his steel was
rusting, that his sword remained clenched in its sheath, that his
helmet hung on its perch from the wall. He had discovered a
softer bed than blood-soaked earth, a merrier sound than the
yelling of men and the clattering of steel to the twang of long-
bows. Arms toughened by the weight of armour were no longer
lifted to deal strokes of death, they were raised to clasp the unre-
sisting body of a woman ; the fingers that had moved in awkward
gauntlets now toyed with woman-hair, felt woman-flesh. The
courtesan, Alice Perrers, Lady Windsor, ruled England and
its King.

Queen Philippa had died of the plague on August 15, 1369,
but even before her death it seems that Edward loved one of the
ladies of her chamber—this Alice Perrers. Unfortunately, our
main facts about Alice come from an anonymous and spiteful
enemy who can scarcely bring himself to mention her by name,
calling her " the often named harlot," " the harlot scarce worthy
to be named." We can distrust many of his statements : for
example, it seems unlikely—although, of course, by no means
impossible—that she won her hold over the King only " by
fortune (being neither beautiful nor fair), she knew how to
cover these defects with her flattering tongue." And we can
safely dismiss the statement that she was " of a base kindred, for
she was a weaver's daughter of Hunneye, beside Exeter." Actually, she was the daughter of a Hertfordshire squire and therefore
of good family. It was also, inevitably, said that she had be-
witched Edward, and we are told that she learned the tricks of
love from " a certain fool that used with his hands to carry water
from the conduit to men's houses for necessary uses." Whoever

may have given Alice her education, she must have been a woman of great charm to capture Edward so completely. She abused her power, she seized all she could—lands, jewels, clothes—and " was not ashamed to sit in the seat of judgment at Westminster, and there, either for herself or her friends or the King as his promtrix, was not afeared to speak in causes and presently to ask of the judges different sentences in her matters, who, fearing the King's displeasure, or rather more truly fearing the harlot, durst not oftentimes judge otherwise than she had defined." Her wealth was enormous, few suits prospered without coins being slipped into her little grasping hands, and one is only surprised that she did not force Edward to make her actually his Queen. There was no need for the crown, she flaunted her position, and Edward meekly yet proudly showed to all the chains of desire in which she bound him. At a great tournament in Smithfield in 1374 she came to be worshipped as the Lady of the Sun, and rode from the Tower to the tilt-yard in a triumphal chariot, lolling there with the adoring old King beside her. She was dressed gorgeously, and wore a cap of tanned leather embroidered with gold thread and bound with gold ribbons furred with ermine—all from the royal wardrobe. Ahead of the chariot rode noble ladies each of whom held captive a knight, gripping him by the bridle of his horse. Shamelessly Alice paraded her position, proudly dominating the King and country.

The King was old according to medieval standards, and this sudden burst of lechery destroyed both body and will. Alice " demolished his honour, and not only with her pleasant entice-ments craftily entrapped him, but (as it is said) by evil arts had so much drawn him to the unlawful loving of her that his old heart dried from [him] his natural moisture by such lusts of Venus, and weakened his whole body, and so she brought a double damage unto him, for she made him reproachful of all nations near and almost void of all strength."

WITH the old King caressing his sweet demon and with the Black Prince writhing impotently on his bed of pain, the nation felt in despair, leaderless, facing a future of anarchy. The great possessions won at Crécy and Poitiers were going, and the naval power that had made England's coast safe and her trade secure was stolen by the united fleets of Spain and France. The haughty English, who, Froissart tells us, were " affable to no other nation than their own," found themselves pushed aside, their own country invaded, their seaports burnt, their armies defeated, and their ships captured or sunk.

John of Gaunt controlled England and he was no scrupulous man. We must ignore much of the venom spat at him by the chroniclers, for he stood beside Wycliffe in the battle with the Church and was therefore hated by the monkish writers ; nevertheless, like most other statesmen of the time, he preferred to fill his own pouch rather than fight for England's honour or help the oppressed. He and Alice ruled England, and in their selfish hold on the old King they were foolish enough to antagonise the great lords who drew sulkily away, envious and angry. The lords, however, could do little without the help of the commons, for in this brief time parliament had become the one medium through which the country could be taxed and thereby through which the King could be humbled. Alice and Gaunt postponed calling a parliament as long as they were able, but the exhausted exchequer forced them at last to summon one for April 1, 1377. This is the gathering that history has rightly honoured as the Good Parliament.

Knowing that the Black Prince was sympathetic towards it, parliament opened bravely only to find that its patron died in the midst of the session. Nevertheless, it continued its task fearlessly, impeaching minister after minister. The death of the Black Prince came at the most unfortunate moment, when the moral strength of his backing was desperately needed. For six years he had been ill, his body racked with continual pain, and for him, for a man of action, to be forced to lie on his back like an overturned beetle, futilely cursing his own weakness, the weakness of flesh that spirit cannot subdue, must have been greater agony than the sickness of his body. He had seen his brother, Gaunt, lead hopeless campaigns in war and then ignore conquest to squeeze money out of a corrupt court ; arrogant and merciless the Black Prince might have been, yet he was nobler than his brother, being strong even in his weakness. Embittered, he lay at Kennington, unable to move. One of Gaunt's friend, Sir Richard Stury, called to ask how he was. " Come, Richard," jeered the Prince, " come and look on what you long desired to see ! " But jeers could only mask the sullen despair of a man who knew that he was doomed, that he must leave his life-work incomplete. For nearly six years, as the chronicler tells us, " continually was he visited with a great and incommodious disease of his body ; for all that time, commonly every month, he suffered the flux both of seed and of blood, which two infirmities made him many times so feeble that his servants took him very often for dead ; notwithstanding, he bore all these things with such patience that he never seemed to offer unto God one mutinous word." Even at the last, when taken from a life that was splendid because of his own courage and still rich with promise, he bit the fury back and made a pious end.

Yet the death of its protector could not quieten the Good Parliament. Through its Speaker, Peter de la Mare, it refused a grant of further taxes because the King was impoverished only through the greed of his " privy friends." Then on the following day it began to enumerate these " privy friends," and to impeach them. It was useless for Gaunt before this united front of lords and commons to protect his comrades ; he did the wisest thing by acting the enemy and by taking a forefront in the impeachment. Thereby he remained safe and was able later to rescue those who were condemned : these were chiefly Lord Latimer the chamberlain, and Lord Neville of Raby the steward, together with various London financiers, particularly Richard Lyons, a great merchant. On Lyons came the first assault, and unable to escape the accusations, feebly protesting that he had only acted by the " command of the King and his counsel," he thought to bribe justice. He sent a barrel of gold to the Black Prince, but it was refused ; a similar gift to the King was accepted at once, Edward merrily remarking that as it was his anyhow, he didn't see why he shouldn't take it.

With Lyons, fell Latimer and Neville ; Lyons was sentenced to forfeiture and to imprisonment at the King's pleasure ; Latimer received the same sentence, but was merely deprived of his offices, as was also Neville. Others fell with them, and Parliament, excited by its victory and not deterred by the death of the Black Prince, struck at Alice Perrers, the Lady Windsor. It passed an order that no women should appear in court to support causes ; this behaviour of Alice, this forcing of judges to arbitrate in her favour, was by no means the crime that it appears to us to-day : it was then the custom of all magnates to enter court with an army so as to have their own justice administered, and it was a common cry of the times that no man could win a suit unless he had a great lord to stand beside him. Parliament used subtle weapons against Alice, weapons suited to a woman : it told the King that she was married and that therefore she was living with him in adultery. This was perfectly true, she was the wife of William Windsor, a north-country baron then acting as the King's lieutenant in Ireland, but the news could not have been so surprising to Edward as he made out it was. He pretended to be horrified, yet pleaded with the commons to deal gentle with her because of his love. Finding themselves defeated on this point, the commons sought for other weapons. As they could only explain the King's love on the theory of magic, they searched for a magician and found one in " a certain friar of the order of St. Dominic [preachers] who in outward show professed physic." It is an interesting sidelight on medieval illnesses that the only way the commons knew whereby to trick this friar into believing that two of their members needed attention was to have them call on him with " urinals in their hands." The friar was immediately captured and Alice was sentenced to forfeiture and banishment if she dared approach the King, while the bishops agreed to excommunicate her if she broke her oath.

The commons had done their task worthily, and amidst the impeachments had found time to repudiate a suggestion from John of Gaunt that England should introduce the Salic law which banned females and the descendants of females from reigning. As the Prince of Wales was dead and the King might die any moment, the question of succession was an important one, the Prince's heir being little more than a child, and in the Middle Ages children had a perilous path to manhood. Between Gaunt and the throne, should little Richard die, stood Edmund, Earl of March, the husband of his elder brother Lionel's daughter, Philippa. Naturally Gaunt thought that he had more right to the throne than the husband of his niece, but he wished to make quite certain. The commons left him in little doubt by rejecting his petition.

PARLIAMENT was in an unfortunate situation—the moment it was dissolved it no longer existed, and it was even rare for the same members to be returned twice running. Therefore, when the commons and lords had ridden from Westminster to their different homes, Gaunt set immediately at work to undo what they had enacted. His friends were returned to power, and, having learned his lesson, he began carefully to bribe the strong lords to join his party. They were only too delighted to have a hand in the corruption. Lord Percy—soon to be Earl of Northumberland—had been one of the strongest supporters of the Good Parliament, yet when Gaunt offered him the post of marshal, his old loyalities were at once forgotten. The only lord who could not be bribed was the Earl of March ; so Gaunt tried to send him to Calais : he refused to go, fearing poison or the assassin's blade. Having won powerful allies, Gaunt took vengeance on the speaker of the last parliament. Peter de la Mare was seized and without trial imprisoned in Nottingham Castle.

Feeling perfectly safe, with Alice Perrers still wantonly cajoling the King and with Percy and others ready to fight for him, Gaunt summoned another parliament, packed it cunningly, and enacted that all the statutes of the Good Parliament should be reversed. Convocation, the assembly of the clergy, was not so easily defeated. It refused to grant the taxes until abuses were redressed. Its main grievance was Gaunt's behaviour to William of Wykeham, Bishop of Winchester, who had been so hounded about the country that he was penniless. He had been dismissed from his office of chancellor in 1371, then when Latimer and Neville were impeached, Gaunt thought it would be a good idea to impeach the previous ministers if only to prove that his friends were no worse than their predecessors. It is impossible to be certain if Wykeham was guilty of the charges brought against him ; they were never really proved, although Gaunt behaved as if they were ; while parliament could only ask the King to deliver justice, Gaunt could force him to deliver it, and the wretched Wykeham was treated abominably. Convocation now determined to see that he was given his rights and refused to decide anything until he joined the assembly. He was afraid to appear because the King had forbidden him to, but the Archbishop of Canterbury commanded him to come, and none dared stop him. Flushed with this success, convocation took a further step forward and summoned John Wycliffe to appear for trial.

Now this scholar of Oxford appears before us for the first time, and it is impossible for us not to devote a certain space to the effect of his teachings. To understand the great changes that were sweeping through England in the fourteenth century we must look at Wycliffe, for in many ways he created those changes. They would have come inevitably, but Wycliffe brought them quickly to a head. When we read his works we are struck at once by their modernity. It is difficult to realise that such extreme freedom of belief could have existed in a period of church domination, and it says much for the tolerance and fearless attitude of Englishmen that it was from this country grew the thought which was taken up by John Hus—who was burnt for thinking it—and which later spread into the Reformation. At this stage, Wycliffe's theories were mainly political, he had not reached the point where he judged the dogmas of the Church and put forward the terrible heresy that the wine was not actually blood and the bread not actually flesh when taken in the eucharist. He was, in 1377, merely a famous scholar at Oxford, and was of the realist school—which means almost exactly the opposite to modern realism : medieval realism dealt mainly with abstractions, with what were termed " universals," a subject far too complicated to be examined here. By gradual metaphysics, working from abstractions, Wycliffe evolved a very concrete doctrine and decided that the Church had no right to interfere in temporal matters ; its task was the cure of souls, and therefore the temporal state had every authority to deprive the Church of its property if only for the sake of the Church itself.

John of Gaunt had no knowledge of scholastics, but this argument of Wycliffe's suited him too thoroughly to be ignored. England was being crushed under the exactions of the Pope, and parliament was continually trying to force action, to make the King put a stop to plurality of benefices and to absentee clergy ; also it was remarked that the Pope, being in Avignon, gave English cures to Frenchmen so that English money was being used against English troops. Edward III had passed the statutes of præmunire and provisors already mentioned, but he had taken almost no notice of them. He needed the Pope and the Pope needed him. Before a candidate could be installed in the Church, his appointment had to be ratified by the curia, and as Edward kept bishoprics for cheap rewards to give his friends, he did not mind surrendering other benefices to the Pope so that he could give them to his friends. Either way, the people suffered. There was another very powerful grievance against the Church—non-residence. Gradually advowsons had been absorbed by the large monasteries, most of them being bequeathed by great sinners desperate at the last moment and eager to bribe God's pardon with eternal masses. The monasteries took the advowsons and the parsonages as well, and then paid ignorant clerks a miserable pittance to look after them, while quite often they did not even bother to do this, they merely gathered the tithes—heavily fining anybody who refused to pay, as their courts had supreme command over such spiritual matters as tithes, probate of wills, marriages, burials, divorces, etc.—and giving the parishioners no vicar in return.

These were the abuses against which Wycliffe stood, and it was for his attacks on the wealth of the clergy and for his doctrine that a bad priest could not administer grace that he was called to his trial at St. Paul's on Thursday, February 19, 1377. Gaunt protected him, being eager to break the wealth of the Church if only for his own pocket. With Percy he tried to force a path through the mob of Londoners who had gathered in the cathedral. The aisle was blocked with sightseers, and Percy—great lord that he was and contemptuous of commoners—jostled the people aside. William Courtenay, Bishop of London and son of the powerful Earl of Devon, called to Percy to cease hitting his flock, adding that he would not have let him enter had he known that he would go on in such a fashion. Gaunt answered that Percy would behave as marshal whether the bishop like it or not. Argument began once more when they had reached the Lady Chapel where the conclave was waiting. " Since you have much to answer to," said Percy to Wycliffe, " you will need all the softer seat," but Courteney cried that Wycliffe would have to stand during the proceedings. Gaunt lost his temper, he swore to drag down the pride of all the bishops in England and told Courteney that he need not rely on his parents to protect him, for they would have a hard time of it looking after themselves, which gave Courteney his opportunity to retort that he trusted in God and not in his relations. Gaunt whispered that he would drag the bishop out by the hair, and the trial ended in a riot, with Wycliffe free but with the Londoners prepared for any devilment. It was not that they resented Wycliffe's doctrines— they were shortly to rescue him in a moment of similar peril— they were infuriated by this insult to their bishop and were desperate because of a rumour that Gaunt intended to deprive them of their mayor. Then news came that Percy had imprisoned a man in the official residence of the marshal, thereby usurping the functions of a magistrate, and that was enough to drive the mob temporarily crazy. They rescued the prisoner and almost tore Percy's house to pieces in their lust for revenge ; they then made for the Savoy, Gaunt's palace, and on the way they met a priest who was foolish enough to remark that Peter de la Mare—the speaker of the Good Parliament—was a traitor ; they beat him to death. The Savoy would probably have been burnt to the ground had not Courtenay rushed to its rescue and quietened the mob.

Meanwhile, Percy and Gaunt had been dining with a friend

in the city when news came of the riot. Gaunt "leaped so hastily from his oysters that he hurt his legs against the form," and the pair ran to the river, rowing furiously to seek refuge with the Prince of Wales's widow at Kennington.

THEN Edward died. He died " almost suddenly " on June 21, 1377, at Sheen—now Richmond—being sixty-five years of age. Until the last moments he felt in good spirits, talking merrily of hunting and hawking with Alice Perrers and his courtiers. While he talked, his voice began to falter and slowly to fade ; those around saw in the frightened eyes and pallid face that death was on him, and they fled at once, for always Kings die in loneliness, their friends running to hide when the protecting hand is no more. We are told that while Edward lay gasping, Alice tore the very rings from his fingers.

He was quite alone now in his chamber save for one nameless priest who implored him to think of God. The dying King found voice enough to whisper through his sobs the one name, " Jesu," and although he could scarcely pronounce it, the sound yet gave him strength enough to gasp a short prayer and to pardon offenders. The priest then showed a crucifix, and Edward caught it in his hands " and with tears and sighing he put it to his mouth, devoutly worshipping and kissing the same, and within a little while after, he yielded his spirit unto God."

OF King Edward III's funeral we know practically nothing. The chroniclers were too eager to record the coronation of the new King to remember the death of the old. " Le Roi est mort. . . ." Yet after all, Edward perhaps deserved the neglect of writers who once had spoken with ecstasy of his achievements. Few men have begun life with such splendour only to end it so wretchedly.

XII

KING RICHARD THE SECOND

1377-1399

RICHARD OF BORDEAUX, son of the Black Prince, became King the day after his grandfather's death. At Sheen he took the great seal into his hands ; Gaunt, March and William of Wykeham were all three present, which shows how rapidly the outward show of jealousies had gone now that the ten-year-old King replaced the lecherous dotard. Further show of peace was made when a deputation of Londoners came to the manor to offer their allegiance, and young Richard said that he would help to reconcile them with his uncle. Gaunt no longer intended to suppress the mayor of London, the riot had taught him his lesson, and he was delighted at the opportunity for peace. A formal reconciliation between the city and John, Duke of Lancaster, was proclaimed in St. Paul's on June 27 ; then when William of Wykeham, too, was reconciled with the duke, and Peter de la Mare was released, the nation felt content, believing that at last it had a gracious sovereign, the worthy son of its beloved Black Prince.

Therefore the coronation was acted with such enthusiasm that the obsequies of Edward III were wellnigh ignored by the chroniclers. On July 15, Richard entered London on his state-ride from the Tower to Westminster, and the city was decorated as it had not been decorated since Richard's father brought in triumph a French King for prisoner. All the houses spread their richest and gayest coloured hangings, their cloths-of-gold and silver out of windows or threaded them on ropes across the streets ; the great conduit at the east end of Chepe—where the Poultry joined that wealthy merchant's highway, the widest in London—rippled wine for the three hours that the procession took to leave the city ; and on the little conduit towards the west, opposite Foster Lane—also rippling wine—a castle was built with four turrets and a central dome ; in each of these turrets stood a little girl of the same age as the King, and each girl blew a shower

425

of gold leaf upon him as he approached, and threw down imitation gold florins for his horses' hoofs to trample. With leaf and florins gone, the maids darted downstairs and offered the King wine in a golden cup. From the dome a gilt angel was jerked over on wires, and as the King paced forward, the angel held a crown above his head. The men of Bayeux rode first in the procession, and were followed by liveried members of one of the city wards, by a troop of German mercenaries, by members of another ward, by the Gascons, and by further Londoners with the great men of the kingdom. All were dressed in white to symbolise the boy-King's innocence, and—a Welshman who saw him tells us—Richard seemed as " fair among men as another Absolom." Gaunt and Percy rode ahead of Richard to clear a way for him, but their manners were different from the insolence they had shown in Paul's, they were gentle and smiling and careful not to hurt even a child. Westminster reached at last, Richard drank a cup of wine and retired to his chambers to eat and to undergo the ceremonial bath, the washing away of sins before he entered upon this almost divine phase of monarchy.

It was usual for coronations to be held on a Sunday, but Richard was crowned on a Thursday, July 16, 1377. The reason for this change is clear enough, for the 16th was the eve of the feast of St. Kenelm the boy-King, a good augury for the reign. When the ceremonies, exhausting for a child, started on that day, the cathedral was crowded. From the hall Richard walked to the abbey and was met by the clergy. Gaunt carried the pointless sword curtana, March the second sword, Warwick the third, while, as was their ancient right, the Barons of the Cinque Ports lifted on silver rods a blue silk canopy over Richard's head ; Richard walked barefoot a long carpet of striped worsted towards the high altar where he knelt in prayer before being led to his throne.

The tedious ceremonies dragged on : the singing, the sermon, the administering of the oath—and it is interesting to see the advance in theories of monarchy, for instead of asking the people if they would accept Richard as King before administering the oath, the archbishop now asked them after it had been administered, thereby making it purely a traditional matter of form—the chanting, the prayers : it must have been most wearisome to little Richard. A curtain of cloth-of-gold was lifted to hide him and the archbishop as his upper-garments were taken off ; the shirt was specially made, being cut in certain places and held together with silver links, these links were now unclasped, and the archbishop hallowed the King, touching him with chrism or holy oil on the hands, the chest, the shoulders, the elbows and the head. So that this symbol of grace should not too quickly evaporate, the King's head was afterwards bound in a chrismale or linen coif. Then followed the ceremonial robing ; the crown was blessed and placed over the chrismale, the spurs were clipped on to Richard's heels, the ring slipped on his finger, the sceptre placed in his left hand, and the cross and ball in his right. Then he was led to the throne to listen to the Te Deum and to receive homage from his great barons.

When all was over, Richard was lifted in the arms of his tutor, Simon Burley, and was carried to the palace. As his small, tired body lay in those strong arms, one of the consecrated slippers fell from his foot and was lost in the mob. The feasting that followed was so crowded that Gaunt and Percy, as seneschal and marshal, had to stamp a passage with their horses so that the servitors could carry food to the tables. In the courtyard had been built a tall marble pillar topped with a gilt eagle, and from the four sides of the pillar bubbled four different kinds of wine, and every one could drink—the very poorest could have their bellyful of luxury for an hour or two.

ALL was. at peace. The little King, innocent and helpless, had because of his very weakness drawn parties together, had soothed hatreds for the moment. Quarrels were laid aside as men knelt in homage to the small slippered feet, and knew that here was a will that they could not bend, for there was no will as yet with which to tamper. Despite the English losses abroad and the continual threat of invasion, the people gazed hopefully into a future that was to become as black as ever they had known it.

Yet we cannot entirely blame Richard for the futility of his reign. He inherited from his father courage and ruthlessness, love of friendship and luxury, from his mother great beauty of face, feminine cunning and swift anger when frustrated. He had terrible problems to face, and he had three powerful and ambitious uncles with whom to contend. Besides, he must have been aware that he was only the son of a Prince while those uncles were the sons of a King. To appreciate Richard's helplessness we must understand something of the isolation of a Kind in the fourteenth century. He was desperately alone, poiseg between the commons and the lords ; only the inevitable hatred of the two classes kept him from being crushed. But when the commons struck at the King, the barons forgot their hatreds and joined with him. That was his one protection, to keep these parties continually in opposition to each other—to terrify the commons by the strength of the lords, and to frighten the lords by the persistence of the commons. A standing army was unknown at this date, and Richard in a moment of danger had to rely purely on the goodwill of his lords, for they were the leaders of armies, able to trumpet hordes of men-at-arms and archers to follow their standards. Unless the exchequer was full, and it most certainly was not full when Edward III died, the King could not purchase men to fight. Therefore he had to work cunningly, to rouse jealousies in the powerful nobles lest they united.

Brought up in the grip of his uncles, bullied into manhood, Richard naturally sought revenge when he was old enough to seek it. He had no armies to call to him, he had to work by underhand ways, striking with treachery. He could never love these nobles; he felt small amongst them, being merely the son of a Prince, and perhaps for this reason he often chose his favourites from among the lower nobility. To these favourites he rarely surrendered his will as Edward II had done, there was in him a hard and selfish core which made him usually secretive even to the best of comrades. He was, in his own time—as shown by the parliament of 1386—considered in many ways to resemble Edward II, but the resemblance is only on the surface, lying mainly in his great affection for men favourites and in his tragic death. He had not the kindness, the simplicity, and pathos of Edward II, for he was wilful and bad-tempered, capable of falling into childlike pets or into the most violent tempers. He vacillated: one moment he was strong and the next he was weak, veering from kindness to cruelty, from independence to complete dependence. His favourites apparently were honest men; the one against whom the strongest hatred was aroused was Robert de Vere, Earl of Oxford: we know very little about him, certainly nothing to his actual discredit.

After his death Richard was nicknamed the Redeless—the Shiftless—and the name suits him to perfection. His life was one shifting of ideas, of hatreds and affections. He could stay true to nothing except to a few friends and to his wife. Her he adored, and it is likely that she had a certain, if small, influence upon him. After her death he became even more shiftless, if that were possible, even more vindictive. We might, in fact, cut his reign into three : into his minority when he scarcely existed, into his efforts to shake off the power of his uncles, and into the period when he sought revenge and found only retribution. One cannot pity him as one can pity Edward II. By his personal spite he lost his throne ; to calm his own wounded vanity he would have thrown all England aside ; yet he suffered much in his youth, and perhaps we can find a little tenderness for a lad brought up in an atmosphere of intrigues and bullyings to occupy a bankrupt throne, brought to rule a country taxed beyond endurance and in a state of national disillusion and despair.

Courage he possessed, at least in youth, and in a high order— he faced the rebels at Smithfield and challenged the King of France to a duel—but moral courage was needed more than physical bravery. That, Richard lacked. He was will-less, driven by the storm of his passions, blind in a moment to all consequences only to awake like a repentant drunkard to the shame of his actions, as on the day he thrashed Arundel in Westminster Abbey. This same Arundel, Richard FitzAlan, summed up the nobles' attitude to Richard when he cried during his trial that he objected to " government by boys and widows " ; the people objected even more to the King's extravagance and to the horde of violent retainers he maintained who did what they wished with the country : he " kept in his following four hundred unruly men of the county of Chester [*a hotbed of murderers*], very evil ; and in all places they oppressed his subjects unpunished, and beat and robbed them. These men, whithersoever the King went, night and day, as if at war, kept watch in arms around him ; everywhere committing adulteries, murders, and other evils without end. And to such a pass did the King cherish them that he would not deign to listen to any one who had complaint against them ; nay, rather he would disdain him as an enemy." But this was towards the latter part of Richard's reign, when the abuse of liveries—of which we will hear a great deal—had become unbearable. At first he was the idol of his people, especially of London. His physical beauty, his helplessness, his charm of manners, the glitter and luxury of his court, his interest in art and music and literature, dazzled the people. For the oppression of the country they blamed the nobles—Gaunt in particular. England might be in a state of anarchy, yet men looked towards the little King and dreamed that if they could only steal him from the hands of Gaunt he would set all right again—dreams soon to be harshly broken.

It was a colourful period, and the King dressed himself as gaily as any one, for he liked the good things of life. One of his coats, fiery with jewels, was valued at thirty thousand marks—a large fortune.[1] He was a patron of the arts, and he is the first King of whom we have authentic portraits, the beautiful painting in Westminster Abbey reproduced here, and the rich altar-piece executed for him in 1381 that shows him kneeling in gold embroidered robes, clean-shaven, faintly smiling, with, standing near, St. John the Baptist, St. Eadmund and St. Eadward worshipping the Virgin who comes with angels in a flood of blue— the Wilton diptych in the National Gallery, London. The copper effigy—once gilt—in Westminster Abbey, which shows him as he was in later years—the portraits could not have been painted after he was twenty—still with a little forked beard and with more plumpish face, was cast, together with his wife's, under his personal direction. Not only painting but architecture too, interested Richard; the raising of the walls of Westminster Hall were examined by him. Music and literature were also under his patronage. Froissart gives us a charming portrait, telling how " the King desired to see my book that I had brought for him : so he saw it in his chamber, for I had laid it there ready on his bed. When the King opened it, it pleased him well, for it was fair enlumined and written, and covered with crimson velvet, with ten buttons of silver and gilt, and roses of gold in the midst, with two great clasps of gilt, richly wrought. Then the King demanded of me whereof it treated, and I showed him how it treated matters of love ; whereof the King was glad and looked in it, and read it in many places, for he could speak and read

---

[1] In *Archæologia*, vol. 62, Mr. W. Paley Baildon gives us a charming description of one of Richard's costumes in his *A Wardrobe Account of 16-17, Richard II, 1393-4.* It consisted of doublet and hanselyn, but what a hanselyn means remains more or less a mystery except that it was some kind of loose outer garment. The white satin with which to make these cost 5s. 9d.—if you multiply the sums given by five you might approximate their value in modern coin—and nine yards were used. The hanselyn cost 14s. to make and the doublet 4s., and £6 was paid to embroider the hanselyn with leeches, water and rocks, and it was sewn with fifteen whelks and fifteen mussels of silver gilt and with fifteen cockles of white silver. To embroider the doublet with gold orange-trees cost £5, and it was also sewn with 100 oranges of silver gilt weighing 2 lb. ½ oz. Troy. The total cost for both equalled £24. " Probably connected with the costume," adds Mr. Baildon, " were thirteen pairs of hose, of black and white, and green and white, made for Christmas, green and white silk fringe, and possibly a gown of green damask embroidered with a band and cuffs of hops, which cost £4."

French very well ; and he took it to a knight of his chamber, named Sir Richard Creadon, to bear it into his secret chamber."

OF Richard's early days as King we need speak very briefly, as he was only a minor, a toy in the hands of others. With the coronation, Gaunt disappears from the scene for a time ; he was loathed as the oppressor, and he and Percy were excluded from the council elected to guide the new King. Percy retired to his vast unruly estates in the north, and Gaunt wandered off amongst his numerous castles—first of all, however, giving Richard a quiet hint that he possessed the largest army in England. The war with France continued, for the nation was too proud to bow before defeat ; money was wasted and men were slaughtered to keep alive a cause already doomed. Alice Perrers still lived with her reward of harlotry, and parliament sentenced her to forfeiture and banishment : Gaunt took a nice handful of her possessions when they were seized.

THE main problem at this moment was a quarrel with the Church over the rights of sanctuary, precipitated by the court party dragging two enemies out of Westminster and murdering one of them in the abbey itself. All churches in medieval days were considered beyond the power of temporal law. A murderer, a thief, an escaped debtor—anybody except a heretic or sorcerer—could run to a church and be safe so long as he entered unarmed ; he would be permitted to remain for forty days, after which he would be starved out. If before that time he wished to abjure the realm he called to the coroner and solemnly swore to leave England, and the coroner told him what port he must leave by. He was then stripped of his clothes, which became the perquisite of the clergy, and was dressed in a shirt—in this, the fourteenth-century breeches were also allowed—and was to carry a cross; he was directed to a port, very often so far away that it was impossible to reach it in the time allowed, and on arrival he was to embark on the first outgoing ship ; if there were no ship ready he was every day to walk into the ocean up to his knees to prove that he did want to leave the country. After forty days, if no ship had left, he was to run to a church, call for the coroner, and all was to begin again. The punishment was heavier than it might seem ; he was, while walking to the port, " to go not out of the King's highway, neither on the right hand nor on the left," at the risk of becoming an outlaw, and in medieval times it was stated that " an outlaw and weyve [*female outlaw*] bear wolves-heads, which may be cut off by any one with impunity, for deservedly ought they to perish without law who would refuse to live according to law." In the badly policed Middle Ages, it might seem to us a simple matter to wander to another town and begin life afresh, but it was not so simple ; they had their pass-ports. Any suspicious-looking stranger could be made to tell from where he had come, and if he could not show a letter from his gild or sheriff, inquiries were made and he was soon un-masked. A statute enacted in the reign of Edward III shows fully the hopelessness of trying to hide anywhere except in forests, it commanded that if " any stranger pass by the country in the night, of whom any have suspicion, he shall presently be arrested and delivered to the sheriff, and remain in ward till he be duly delivered." The powers here are so enormous and the charge so vague, that an honest man could be seized by an enemy and locked away indefinitely, as was often done.

The right of sanctuary, the right to protect a fugitive for forty days, was held by all churches, but some had also the extra right of " perpetual sanctuary," which meant that criminals could live around them for ever. Westminster Abbey was one of these perpetual sanctuaries, and London possessed one in St. Martin-le-Grand. This right was a great evil, as it protected debtors and criminals from justice, yet it was to continue until the reign of James I ; parliament in October 20, 1378, tried to abolish it, hoping to strike first before the bishops sought revenge for the violation of Westminster when a fugitive was murdered by King's officers. It failed lamentably, and disgusted at the weakness of the commons, Wycliffe retired from public life ; he had been one of the disputants at this parliament, proving that sanctuary was illegal. It is the last we hear of him for some years ; just before this time he had faced the bishops on his second trial for heresy. The widow of the Black Prince instructed the bishops that they were not to dare sentence their prisoner while the Londoners rushed in a mob to save him, pulling him out of the archbishop's chapel at Lambeth, and " in this way," says the bitter monkish chronicler, " that slippery John Wycliffe deluded his inquisitors, mocked the bishops, and escaped them by the favour and care of the Londoners, although all his propositions are clearly heretical and depraved."

The world had need for a Wycliffe in that age ; now was beginning the Great Schism, the war between rival Popes—one at Rome, one at Avignon — which was to continue until the next century and in which, it was calculated, two hundred thousand Christians slaughtered each other. It was started by Pope Gregory XI who left Avignon in 1376 to return to Rome. France was furious at this loss of political strength and therefore had Gregory deposed and Urban VI put in his place. Once crowned, Urban showed no gratitude ; he refused to go back to Avignon, and France thereupon deposed him also. He was braver than Gregory, however, and would not be deposed, so France erected a rival as Clement VII who became " the Pope of Avignon and France."

England was naturally on Urban's side.

THE great event of Richard's minority was the Peasants' Rising. It was a splendid effort, entirely different from the jacquerie in France ; Poor Jacques merely rushed in a disorganised mass upon his oppressors, the Englishmen marched with a definite grievance, with a policy and a faith, and in more or less disciplined ranks. There were many causes for the rebellion, and it may at first seem strange that it should come at a time when the country was more or less prosperous, when food was cheap and the prices of wool and cattle high, but it is at such times that the worker begins to wake from his sloth and realise that after all he is a man like his masters, a man with a birthright of freedom. The peasants had a faith, they were swung into life to the chant of

> *When Adam delfe and Eve span*
> *who was then a gentle man ?*

and they had the moral backing of great scholars like Wycliffe, whose words were twisted by the wandering friars — those socialist menace to the well-fed monk—until they included the dispossession of all property. Wycliffe preached that the Church should be dispossessed of the vast lands it had been given by frightened sinners when at the point of death they thought to buy their way to paradise ; he did not mean that property should be divided on a communist basis, but friars and poor parsons of the type of John Ball forced such a meaning from his words. They wandered about the country, the only sort of clergy who would deign to enter the hovels of the poor, and many of them preached this amazing doctrine of human brotherhood. The doctrine was no new one. Jean de Meung, author of the second part of the *Romant of the Rose*, had spoken it two hundred

28

years before ; it had gradually seeped into the half-savage minds of the peasants until continual oppressions, the cries of John Balls and the attacks on the Church by Wycliffe, made it conscious. Most historians deprecate the socialist tendencies of the revolt, but without doubt they were the mainspring. It is argued that when the people's demands were put forward there was no request to share everything equally : such an argument is absurd. The fire that started the outbreak had naturally burnt itself out a little ; in the first enthusiasm of a popular movement the people go almost insane, the mob-mind dominates the individual and turns him to an unthinking automaton ; when the King was ready to discuss terms it was natural that the first conceptions of a communistic state must fade before reality.

The peasants had abuses enough to be redressed without asking for what was impossible. For centuries the serf had been a chattel of the lord without a will of his own : to marry he must pay a fine, to die he had to pay a fine. When a peasant left a life of unceasing toil, the lord took his best possession while the Church took the second best, leaving the widow and children almost destitute. Naturally such extreme laws as these were not always enforced, as it would have been stupid of the lord and Church to cripple their beast of burden beyond hope of his working for them again. The Black Death brought a certain relief because it put the price of workmen up and made them more independent ; it flooded the towns with countrymen who have always dreamed of the pleasures and easier work to be found in streets. Here in the towns they soon discovered that the gilds were as tyrannous as had been the lords-of-the-manors and the monks ; to enter a gild was a most difficult and costly process, and the capitalist kept the monopoly of trade, often refusing to let apprentices join the companies so as to keep them as journey-men—piece-workers paid a miserable salary. These journeymen tried to form gilds of their own, trade unions under the guise of religious fraternities, but they were always repressed ; sometimes they did become powerful enough to declare a strike : that was rare, owing to excess of workmen.

And there was the agricultural problem. Now was beginning the grievance that was to continue for centuries. Sheep were eating the labourers out of the land. The unfortunate peasant seeing his living going from him, sweated by lord and monk, taxed unbearably, listened open-mouthed to the preaching of men like John Ball, poor parsons who were paid tiny salaries to hold a cure while their tithes were gathered by absentee bishops and by monasteries. The thought of freedom came to the labourers, and the long war with France had taught them to use weapons and had shown them the strength of discipline. When the time to fight arrived, they were ready with bill-hook and scythe, with rusty sword and cudgel, and with bows " that had hung so long in the smoke as to be browner than old ivory, with one arrow apiece, many whereof had but one wing " and therefore could not be aimed truly. Nevertheless they were determined ; mad with dreams of freedom, they formed into ranks, into military battles, and when they marched, they marched like an army, and " if they caught any man thieving, they cut off his head, as men who hated thieves above all things."

The spark that lit the flame of rebellion was the poll-tax of 1380. To carry on the stupid war with France, the government taxed every man in England, graduating the fines according to the wealth of the people. The third tax of 1380 was to be assessed at a shilling a head, and " the rich were to aid the poor," one pound was to be highest payment from a married couple, fourpence the lowest. Every one over fifteen was made to pay, and the collectors' methods of discovering if girls were truly over fifteen were sometimes dictated by other desires than pure business. This was a most gigantic tax, and as the collectors were to produce a shilling for every poll in the district, the weight fell heaviest on the poor. To understand how drastic this was, we have only to remember that the average wage of a carter, ploughman or shepherd was merely 13s. 4d. a year. The returns were so small that the King's council could only explain them by declaring that the officers had been bribed or were careless, and they sent out a new commission to examine the lists of inhabitants in all parts of the country. That was the final touch. The people believed that they had come to raise another levy, and revolt broke out.

It began in Essex and soon spread to Kent. The peasants rose, many of the poorer gentry rose with them, and naturally numerous outlaws left the forests to take arms. They had a leader, a mysterious man named Wat Tyler. Evidently " Tyler " was not a surname : in the medieval fashion, it referred to his trade ; he was from Essex but was living in Kent at the time of the rising. We are told that he was intelligent and that he was an excellent speaker, although Gower damns him as a chattering jay ; but then, Gower was a landlord and spent his time during the rebellion lurking in forests where his poetic soul remained blind to the charms of nature. His temporary sufferings brought with them no sympathy for the peasants whose whole existence was scarcely better than his brief and loudly lamented privations ; Gower was a lawyer as well as a landlord, and lawyers, landlords and John of Gaunt were the three enemies of the commons.

About Tyler we know sadly little. He appears suddenly on June 10 after the movement had already started, and our efforts to know something about him are frustrated by the fact that there was more than one Tyler in the rebellion. There is a story that he turned leader because one of the tax-gatherers had pulled up the smock of his daughter when trying to discover her true age ; that is an Elizabethan fable, it first appears in Stow and was probably suggested by the methods of some of the tax-gatherers as given by the contemporary Knighton. Whoever he was, Wat Tyler soon made himself the leader of the movement and marched at the head of the people to Canterbury where they sacked the archbishop's palace and vowed to chop off his head if ever they caught him. The next day they broke open Maidstone jail and released that other great man of the movement, "the mad priest," John Ball. It has been asserted that Ball was a disciple of Wycliffe, and although he may have learned something from Wycliffe's teachings, his ideas in many ways differed from the great scholar's. It was probably now, after his release from Maidstone, that he composed the famous watchword to be sent through the country, calling the oppressed to join the standard of the commons : "John Schep, sometime St. Mary's priest of York, and now of Colchester, greeteth well John Nameless, and John the Miller, and John Carter, and biddeth them that they ware of guile in borough, and stand together in God's name, and biddeth Piers Plowman go to his work, and chastise well Hob the robber [? *the new treasurer, Robert Hales, Prior of the Hospitallers*], and take with you John Trueman, and all his fellows, and no more.

> " *John the Miller hath ground small, small, small :*
> *the King's son of heaven shall pay for all.*
> *Beware or ye be wo'* [worse],
> *know your friend fro your foe,*

have ynough, and say hoe *!*
and do well and better, and flee sin,
and seek peace and hold you therein,
and forbiddeth [pray for] *John Trueman and all his fellows.*"

There were other catch-phrases of the same type, in almost schoolboyish cryptograms yet rather typical of the medieval mind and obviously based on Langland's great poem. " Jack Trueman," runs one of these catch-phrases, " doth you to understand that falseness and guile have reigned too long "; and another : " John Ball greeteth you well all and doth you to understand that he hath rungen your bell." Apart from these messages circulated over the country, the rebels had a countersign. You would be asked : " With whom hold you ? " and if you did not answer, " With King Richard and the true commons," off would fly your head.

Comparing this revolt with the French jacquerie one is amazed at the little damage committed by a disorganised army of peasants and yeomen. But they did not consider themselves rebels, they were true men armed to rescue their King from the clutches of John of Gaunt. The enemy-classes such as landlords and lawyers were murdered on sight, records were burnt, and monasteries— as the most oppressive of all landlords—were sacked ; otherwise the rising was quite orderly, and when the Princess of Wales returned from visiting her husband's tomb at Canterbury she was respectfully allowed to go through the rebel-lines and join her son in the Tower of London.

The same orderliness prevailed even when London opened its gates, despite the temptations in so great a city. The Savoy, of course, was burnt to the ground as being the home of John of Gaunt. Yet even when this rich palace was sacked the order went that not a thing was to be stolen. Rich tapestries and carpets, cushions such as these poor wretches had never dreamed of, were heaped in the Savoy hall, with precious clothing, and all was burnt to ash, the hall itself being then blown up with gunpowder and incidentally imprisoning thirty-two drunkards who had been exploring the cellar and who now perished in the midst of plenty. " We are not thieves, we are true commons ! " cried the wreckers, and one man who thought to steal off with some plate was caught and hurled living into the bonfire. A jack—a quilted war-shirt sometimes woven with steel—was lifted on a spear and made a butt for the archers as a symbol of the absent

Gaunt, for they would have " no King named John," they swore. To be connected in any way with Gaunt meant death, and his followers tore his livery-badge from chest and sleeve and hid it away, while a friar, the duke's physician, was murdered when found later in the Tower. The Savoy was burnt, and the commons also wrecked that lawyers' stronghold, the Temple, and the homes of various enemies : otherwise little harm was done this first day.

The government was helpless. The great men hid in the Tower with their King while the city was owned by the mob, and the mob now threatened to capture the Tower as well and to kil the ministers. So far the leaders had kept order, but the crowd, swelled by London apprentices, was growing out-of-hand when luckily the King promised to meet it at Mile End. On Friday, June 14, young King Richard and his nobles rode from their stronghold to face the commons in the meadow that the Londoners then used for sport in summer-time. The King was very brave as he sat his horse before the standards of the commons—their two banners of St. George and their many pennons. Wat and the other leaders treated him with great respect, and the people cried, " We want no King but thee, O Richard ! " The demands made were : firstly, they must be surrendered all traitors ; secondly, villeinage must be abolished ; thirdly, manoral courts and all other private courts must be abolished ; fourthly, rent must be fixed at a groat—fourpence— an acre ; fifthly, freedom must be allowed the worker in every condition of service. Richard granted all five demands on the proviso that the traitors must first be legally proved as such.

The " traitors " who had been left behind by the King were surrendered to the mob. Wat led his horde to the Tower ; the drawbridge was down and the crowd swarmed into that great palace and prison. The " traitors " were waiting for them in the chapel, prepared for death ; the Archbishop of Canterbury was dragged to Tower Hill and there beheaded, with the treasurer and others. Their heads were pushed on to lances and carried in triumph through the city. In the great Tower the rebels did as they wished, the bewildered and frightened guard pressing against the walls to let them pass. On the 15th the King called for another meeting with the commons who were now almost entirely out-of-hand. He met them in the market-square of Smithfield, outside the walls near the New Gate. It was the hour of vespers, of evening prayer, when he rode through the stinking cattle-market and faced Wat Tyler and his army. It is difficult to disentangle truth from lie about this meeting ; if we accept the royal chronicler's Wat behaved in an incredibly insolent manner, growling that he was thirsty, calling for beer, rinsing his mouth with it, and then spitting before the King. This seems scarcely credible in a man who had kept a disorganised mass of peasants together ; besides, his behaviour at Mile End was respectful and it is absurd to think that he could suddenly lose all sense of courtesy and act the boor. This, however, we do know as truth : Wat drew aside with Richard and talked with him and treated him with more familiarity than was rightful with a King, but it must be remembered that Richard was a boy of fourteen and it is likely enough that Wat forgot his position and affectionately touched him in a way that outraged the King's haughty attendants. What caused the quarrel it is impossible to know. The story that a valet—a page—swore that Wat Tyler was " the greatest thief and robber in Kent " and that Wat then attempted to kill him can surely be dismissed ? In so perilous a position a valet would scarcely whisper such dangerous words, and there is no reason whatever to suppose Wat a thief and robber. I feel that the description of what happened that day in Smithfield has been deliberately distorted. Something had to be written to explain the murder of Wat, and most likely all became so confused that very few knew the truth, and those who did know naturally lied about it afterwards. William Walworth, mayor of London, with a baselard—a short sword—struck Wat Tyler in the neck and head while a valet stabbed him in the chest. Shouting for help and vengeance, Wat staggered on his pony for a few hundred yards, to tumble to the ground, dead.

Then King Richard did a splendid thing. The commons were stringing their bows and the King's attendants were sneaking away when the King himself courageously rode forward and cried, " I will be your captain ! Follow me ! " and meekly the commons followed him until he had led them to Clerkenwell Fields, where they were trapped by mercenaries and by an army of citizens that had been hurried up ; they found the rebels in a field of corn " like sheep in a fold." " Fall out ! you wretches ! Slack bowstrings and begone ! " was the command, and the unfortunate commons—triumphant a few minutes since—fled from the field. They were given no mercy afterwards. The slaughter that followed is sickening to read and unnecessary to relate.

THE courage of a fourteen-year-old boy in thus riding before an armed enemy is truly amazing. All the same, a boy of fourteen in the Middle Ages was a youth capable of going to war and he would be looked upon almost as we look upon a lad of seventeen or eighteen to-day. But few men would have had the heart to do what Richard did that evening in Smithfield. A moment's delay and all would have been lost ; he acted upon a sudden impulse and by sheer audacity did what brutal force could never have done. It was Richard's moment, a moment of superb courage ; the tragedy is that it is the one glorious moment in a lifetime of pettish bad temper and selfishness.

It is rather curious that he did not take control of the government now that he had proved himself a man. He contented himself with gradually building a narrow court party that was in time to oust his uncles and advisers. Chief amongst his friends were Michael de la Pole, a renegade from Gaunt's side, and the de Veres. Yet at first Richard took no active part except to seize all the money he could to give to friends or to waste in luxury. Then on January 20, 1381, he married " the excellent virgin, the damsel," Anne of Bohemia. After great difficulties Anne reached London on January 18, and it is a pathetic sidelight on the decay of England's power when we learn that she dared not cross the Channel until twelve French ships had left the passage free.

It is difficult to estimate Queen Anne's character. She did little to interfere with England, and unlike Edward II's Isabel, apparently remained the best of friends, not only with Richard himself, but with his men favourites. The King adored her, and his despair at her death was extraordinary. We are told that she was beautiful, and when one looks upon her effigy in Westminster Abbey, built under Richard's supervision, it is perhaps difficult to believe this, although there is something attractive about Anne's face as she lies beside her lord—beside his burly figure with the plump cheeks, little beard and long coronation robes. Richard looks so solemn and she so impish, one feels almost that she is mocking him, watching him from the edges of her closed eyelids and ready at any moment to burst into laughter. That under-lip is pushed up beyond the rather long upper, it seems ready to tremble with amusement ; one feels that the straight lovely nose must in life have been a nose that crinkled at the corners suddenly with quick intelligent amusement. It is true, as Miss Strickland's feminine eye sharply noticed, that the effigy has " a narrow, unintellectual forehead, a long upper-lip, [and] cheeks whose fullness increased towards the lower part of the face," yet beauty is not a thing perfect in every feature, then it becomes mere prettiness ; real beauty is something in which every feature, whether ugly or perfect, unites to form a whole of inexpressible charm. I feel that Queen Anne had something of that beauty— although in this effigy the sculptor has swamped her features in too much flesh—and it is to be regretted that Richard, a patron of painting, did not command her portrait to be limned. Yet we must not be ungrateful : he has given us at least this coarsened monument and placed her for ever beside him with her little hand in his.

RICHARD did not shake off the grip of his tutors suddenly, he merely replaced them slowly by his friends, and within four years of the Peasants' Rising he was isolated from the old nobility. In the parliament of October 1383, matters reached a head when the peers tried to force him to give up his councillors. The King lost his temper and swore that he would save his kingdom from the misgovernment of the old nobility. Matters rested at that, until the next year's parliament of April 1384. Gaunt had been more or less out of affairs for some time ; he had married Constance, the Infanta of Castile, and had then tried to take her kingdom for himself, only of course to fail. He was now back in England, and had discovered that during his absence Richard had alienated those who had once been his enemies while his bitterest foe, the Earl of March, was dead. Yet with the power of his vast estates, never do we find a suggestion of real disloyalty in Gaunt, although Richard continued to detest him and try to drag him down.

War was the main discussion of the '84 parliament. England was weary of continual defeats, exhausted by the drain of men and money, but discussions were forgotten in the jealousies of the nobles. The Earl of Arundel insisted that the country was being ruined by Richard's worthless administration and extravagance. " If you say my government is at fault," cried Richard, white with rage, " you lie in your throat ; go to the devil ! " Gaunt came to the rescue and soon the King appeared to have forgotten the outburst. But it was not in his nature to forget, he was a man who could wait patiently for nothing except vengeance, and soon we learn that an Irish Carmelite had told the King that Gaunt was conspiring to murder him. Whether the friar invented the story or whether Richard prompted him to say it we cannot tell, we only know that the tale was a lie. Richard pretended to believe it and, we are told, he would have killed his uncle immediately without trial if his friends had not restrained him. This was at Salisbury while parliament was still sitting, and when Richard did not appear at an important mass to be given for the safety, honour and welfare of the land, Gaunt went to find out what detained him. " There is the villain ! " yelled the friar the moment Gaunt entered the room, " seize him and kill him, or he will kill you in the end ! " He could not substantiate his story, he named men as witnesses but they soon proved their innocence, and Thomas of Woodstock, Gaunt's young brother, behaved in an insolent fashion, swearing to kill any man who dared accuse Gaunt of treason. That made Richard scream with rage and throw his cloak and shoes out of the window, but he could not protect the friar, who was taken away to be tortured in Salisbury Castle. We are told that no one could be found to do the torturing, which is certainly peculiar, and that the friar died revealing nothing. Later, miracles were worked at his tomb and Richard wept when informed of his tragic end.

There are so many lies in Richard's reign, so much plotting and whispering, that it is almost impossible to know what is the truth, on whom to place the guilt for certain actions. Gaunt, it appears, in the following year insulted the King by accusing him almost of cowardice in not leading the English arms to France. Either because of this or his chronic hatred of Gaunt, Richard began again to plot, and it was decided to capture the duke during a tournament : a pretence of legality was to be made, he was to be tried for treason, and executed. Some one told of the plot and Gaunt wasted not a moment. He rode to see Richard at Sheen—Richmond—but he rode dressed in steel and with a strong bodyguard. He did not tax the King directly with the plot, he lectured him for his misgovernment and told of the premeditated murder. Richard tried to charm him with vague promises, but Gaunt was not to be won ; he said that he would avoid the court until the King dismissed his ministers, and he would have kept his word had not Richard's mother besought him to make friends.

On every side, Richard darted at the men he hated. He had a violent quarrel with the Archbishop of Canterbury by insisting on fixing the day for convocation, which no King had ever attempted. The archbishop refused to attend, and when by accident the King's barge and the archbishop's passed on the Thames, Richard pulled out his sword and had to be held back from committing not only murder but sacrilege.

His reign was one of personal spite and extravagance. He lived only for himself, never for England, and it is difficult to find the least liking for him or to keep one's impatience in check as one studies his deliberate misgovernment, his selfish policy, and his feminine spite and arrogance. Only for one thing can we respect him—the thing for which he was most hated—his desire to end the senseless war with France. Soon he was relieved for a time of the man he detested most. Gaunt sailed again for Castile. But Richard had barely stopped exulting over this than he found himself bullied by an even more aggressive uncle, Thomas of Woodstock, Duke of Gloucester.

When parliament opened on October 1, 1386, Richard himself precipitated the storm by creating his favourite, de Vere, Duke of Ireland. When the commons and peers, unable to attack Richard directly, demanded the dismissal of his advisers, the King merely walked away to Eltham and told them to mind their own business. But it was their own business, and for the first time Richard knew what it was to face a united front of enemies. He threatened parliament with dissolution, he swore—most strangely—to take counsel with the King of France if they talked rebellion, and he was only brought to heel by a covert allusion to the fate of Edward II. The hint was enough. He raced to Westminster at once and promised to get rid of whatever ministers they asked and even agreed to the appointment of a committee of eleven lords to regulate the royal household and income. Many of Richard's deadliest enemies were on that committee, including Richard Courtenay, Archbishop of Canterbury. Amongst the others were Gloucester, Arundel, the Lords Cobham and Kent, Scrope of Bolton, and Devereux.

In many ways, Richard was an impatient man. The committee was only to last for a year, yet his proud spirit could not bear even a year's supervision. He asked legal advice about the committee's validity after parliament was dissolved, and legal advice obligingly answered that it was derogatory to the royal prerogative, and that those who instituted it were traitors worthy of execution. Richard did not make this decision public at once, he quietly gathered troops. There were threats of civil war, and once Gloucester, Warwick and Arundel actually rode

to Westminster and did obeisance to Richard, but it seemed that
the King was determined on his own doom. The stumbling-
block to peace was apparently de Vere. He was hated by the
barons as Gaveston had been hated, and like Edward II, Richard
would not surrender his friend. The ministers who had been
dismissed he reinstated, he proved that no threats could bring
him to reason, and the barons prepared for war. It was de Vere
they wanted, and they gathered at Huntingdon on December 12,
1387, to intercept him as he came from the north to London.
Gloucester was present, with Arundel, Warwick, Nottingham,
and young Henry of Bolingbroke, Earl of Derby, the son of John
of Gaunt—" a man of much greater cunning than his father."
There was not even a battle. The earls distributed their armies
so as to guard every possible road, and de Vere stumbled against
Arundel. He unfurled the royal banner and the banner of St.
George, but when Arundel cried that if de Vere's men fought
they would be fighting on the side of a traitor, they threw away
their arms and left the wretched favourite to take care of himself.
Somehow he managed to get away, to leave the country, never to
return.

This fiasco proved to Richard that he was alone, that the
nation which had welcomed his coronation was tired of him.
When the earls threatened, pointing out that the Earl of March
had left a small son, Roger Mortimer, now thirteen years of age,
Richard gave in at once and parliament made ready to impeach
its enemies. This has been nicknamed the Merciless Parliament,
and merciless indeed it was. The five lords appellant—as they were
called—Gloucester, Bolingbroke, Arundel, Warwick, and Nottingham, produced a bill of thirty-nine charges against five of
Richard's ministers, only one of whom was then in custody, and
he was soon condemned and executed ; they found a second
accused, and he too was executed. Cheated of their greater
enemies, the lords appellant turned upon the lesser and killed
them off with the briefest of trials. One of the accused was
Simon Burley, the man who had carried Richard in his arms
at the coronation, and who had been his tutor and a brave soldier.
The Queen implored pardon, she knelt to Gloucester, and Bolingbroke—Gaunt's son and himself one of the lords appellant—
strove to make his uncle show mercy. For over three weeks
Richard remained firm, he could not have Burley executed, but
Gloucester seemed insane with power, mad for blood. No matter
who bent to him for compassion, he refused to surrender his prey,

and on May 5 Burley was beheaded on Tower Hill, Richard saving him at least from the disgrace of hanging at Tyburn.

Having slaughtered those he disliked, Gloucester urged parliament to give its consent to everything that the lords appellant had committed. This was done, and the Bohemian attendants of Queen Anne were ordered to leave England within a month. Then Richard was asked to repeat his coronation oath.

RICHARD was beaten, and beaten badly for the moment ; but he had the patience of a true murderer who can wait until his victim is in a safe position for killing. He could wait for years. Soon came the English defeat at Otterbourne when the Scots sent the troops of Hotspur—Percy's son—helter-skelter back to England. Gaunt returned in 1389 and Richard welcomed him as a saviour, for he was the one lord powerful enough to withstand his brother Gloucester. Richard did his best to win Gaunt to his side, he was charming to all powerful men these days, trying to ring Gloucester in with enemies. The lollard question was growing out of hand, and pious Romans began to wonder what it was that they had nursed so long. Strangely enough, while Richard was a strong enemy of the lollards—on his tomb he had engraved as you can still read, " He overthrew the heretics and laid their friends low "— his beloved wife evidently favoured their doctrines, their demand for the dispossession of the Church, and their belief that in the eucharist the bread and wine were only a cloak to Christ's flesh and blood, and not the living flesh and blood. Even more important to England than Richard's vengeances and persecution of the lollards—the nickname, by the by, evidently meant to loller or mumble—was the signing of peace with France. Then suddenly, while Richard was apparently at ease with his enemies, the plague took Good Queen Anne from him. She died at Sheen. Her death drove Richard into a fit of lunatic grief. The royal manor-house in which she died he avoided, he demolished her apartments, and for a year he would never pass through a door into a house where they had been together. On August 3, 1394, she was buried in Westminster Abbey, her corpse with great pomp being carried from Sheen. The citizens of London, dressed in black with black hoods, followed the hearse. " Abundance of wax was sent for from Flanders for flambeaux and torches," so that the glare was such as had never been seen before. All the nobility of England, both male and female, were present ; Arundel, harsh and contemptuous of sentiment, came late and poked his head in at the abbey door, almost immediately asking permission to go home. Richard ran at him, seized a stick from a verger, and so thrashed the earl that he fell stunned to the ground and bleeding from the head ; he was then carried off to the Tower, to be released a week later. But by his fury, Richard had polluted the Church, he had shed blood and the ceremonies had to stop until the building was purified and reconsecrated. It was late indeed when the people hurried off, night was falling, but the hour did not trouble Richard. In that tomb in Westminster, he had buried all he loved. He was a more cruel and desperate man from that day.

To escape England, to fly from these scenes made torment by memories of happiness, Richard left for Ireland where he stayed for over seven months, returning in May 1395. He had decided to marry again, but the marriage was a political one, his desire being to consolidate peace with France ; it might also have been because he wished to infuriate Gloucester, for he betrothed himself to Isabel, the six-year-old daughter of King Charles VI, and Gloucester's desire was to maintain the war. At any rate, any marriage with France would seem to him a kind of treason.

To hurry the negotiations, Richard himself went to the Continent to meet the French King. Elaborate care was taken to see that neither should be murdered, and at last, on October 26, Richard under the escort of the Dukes of Berri and Orléans rode from Calais, while Charles under the escort of Gaunt and Gloucester rode from Saint-Omer. Tents had been pitched on the meeting-ground, the English tent being circular, the French square, and when the two Kings stepped into the sunlight they walked between unarmed troops of English and French, united for once. It was three o'clock in the afternoon. Richard wore a scarlet gown that reached to his heels and had his badge of the White Hart on his breast ; around his golden head was a coronet given him by Charles, and it glittered with gems. Charles's gown reached only to his knees and he wore red and white hose ; he had Richard's White Hart on his breast ; his hood was in the new fashion, being coiled up and peaked like a cap, and it also was bright with jewels. Step by step, neither pacing one inch faster than the other, the two Kings walked, smiling, towards the post that had been marked as equidistant between both tents. Richard took off his coronet, Charles his hood, as they held hands and kissed, and everybody knelt. Afterwards sweets and wine were served while the Kings took it in turn to visit each other's tent, and they parted with a kiss. The same ceremony was performed on the following day, and a truce was sworn to, an alliance both defensive and offensive. Then his betrothed was delivered to Richard ; the Dukes of Berri and Burgundy carried the little creature in their arms to the central post where she was surrendered to the King of England, who must have smiled sadly if he thought of Anne when he saw the wondering face of his new bride staring up at him.

THE coronation of the new Queen was performed on January 7 ; two days before, she made her first entry into London. The crowd was huge when she was brought from Kennington to meet the mayor and aldermen on Blackheath, then to be escorted over the Bridge, along Bridge Street to the Tower ; the Londoners were so eager to gaze upon the child that nine people were crushed to death.

Richard was living at such an extravagant rate that the exchequer could barely support him. He is said to have maintained ten thousand people at his court, while three hundred worked in the kitchen alone. His retainers, men wearing his livery, had power of life or death, and many a rascal worthy only of hanging lorded it because the White Hart swung from a chain around his neck, or was sewn to his arm. This system of retainers was one of the evils of the period, and Richard did no worse than other lords. In the old feudal tenure the retainer was bound to his lord by service, by the act of tilling his land or by fighting for him in war, but this new system was a matter of money, the retainers were paid wages, and they formed small—and often large—armies. Many of them were adventurers home from the French wars who possessed no trade other than the sword and the axe, they would have sold their masters and themselves for a handful of gold. Some of them were, of course, chivalrous knights, men who sought only an honest profession and who took their task seriously, but most were a cut-throat rabble who did what rascality they wished because they were protected by their lord's badge. They could steal, murder or ravish, and none dared complain lest an army of them should come at their comrade's shout and seek vengeance. They would tramp into law-courts and finger their swords menacingly until judges decided as they demanded ; if they liked a house they took it, if they didn't like it they very often burnt it ; if they liked a woman they pulled her over their saddlebows and galloped away with her ; and they stole heiresses, married them, then defied the parents to seek justice. This practice of liveries was called maintenance because the lord maintained a following. Statutes were passed trying to put a stop to the evil, but it was impossible to suppress when the King himself was one of the worst offenders. Langland describes the terror their name spread through the country, how at the whisper of " harts " or " hinds " men knew that they would have no mercy, for the " liverers " plucked the very plumage from the skins of the poor and showed their badges as warrant if they were questioned, then the questioner stayed silent, lucky if he kept his own skin unplucked.

It is more than likely that Richard's desire to outdo the great lords with his multitude of retainers was the result of his visit to Charles VI. France had not progressed so rapidly as England in many ways, owing to the continual war ; its King was not held as the English King was held by parliament, he was a despot. And probably Richard thought to make England accept him also as a despot, and therefore he tried to bully the people by a show of force ; he kept a troop of Cheshire archers with him, and Cheshire—lying next to Wales—was a country of desperate men, a land in which it was not safe to walk without a guard. When the King travelled, the curses of the people followed him— wives beside the corpses of husbands, and girls sobbing, wrenched brutally from maidenhood. It was like the passing of an enemy through hostile land.

But Richard had an even stronger protection than his lawless Cheshire archers. He had the friendship of John of Gaunt.

WHEN Gaunt returned from his second futile invasion of Castile he found, as we have seen, his young brother Gloucester in almost supreme power. With Gloucester were the Earls of Warwick, Arundel, and Nottingham, and Gaunt's son Bolingbroke. Warwick and Arundel were sincere simple men, crude and fierce, who probably did believe that the country needed a stronger hand than Richard's ; Gloucester was an ambitious rascal ; Nottingham—Thomas Mowbray, soon to be Duke of Norfolk—was a traitor and a murderer ; Bolingbroke was a fearless cunning man, a brave soldier, an adventurer, and a lover of legal arguments. There was true greatness in him. The arrival of Gaunt split this party of lords appellant ; Bolingbroke naturally sided with his father, and Mowbray was heavily bribed to turn a Ricardian. Gloucester, Warwick, Arundel and their supporters found themselves driven from the King's counsel. They decided to strike at Gaunt, to tear him from their path so that they could return to their old position, but they had miscalculated their strength and the unpopularity of Gaunt. The days were gone when he was hated, time had shown the people that he did not intend to usurp the throne, and it had proved that at least he was a no worse tyrant than Richard or the lords appellant themselves.

In the parliament of 1394, Arundel rose to indict Gaunt and his policy. He gave six articles : he said that it was presumptuous of the duke and contrary to the King's honour for the two to be seen continually arm-in-arm ; that the King degraded his royalty by wearing the duke's livery and by letting his retainers wear it ; that the duke in council and parliament had so bullied the lords that they were afraid to answer ; that it was to the King's disadvantage to have given his uncle the great duchy of Aquitaine ; and that the King had wasted public money to help his uncle conquer Castile. The indictments showed genuine cleverness. They began by working upon Richard's childish vanity, by hinting that he was still in tutelage, the toy of his uncle, and they appealed to the people against the destested habit of maintenance; the grant of Aquitaine, with which Richard hoped to bind Gaunt more strongly to his side, was unpopular in England, as many did not wish the royal power to be broken ; but the invasion of Castile was Arundel's most telling point. It had been a waste of men and money, of English blood and gold, to help the personal ambitions of one man.

Richard answered the charges. He said that it was not only with Gaunt but with all his uncles that he walked arm-in-arm ; that of his own will he had taken the livery collar from Gaunt's neck and worn it, and that he had commanded his men to wear it ; that he did not believe Gaunt had bullied the council, and if he had, the earls had equal right to answer back ; that parliament had ratified the grant of Aquitaine ; that it had voted 200,000 marks towards the Castile expedition and that Gaunt had merely borrowed the remainder and intended to pay it back. Parliament agreed that Gaunt was not to blame on any point, and Arundel was asked if he had anything further to say. He answered that he had nothing to say and Richard then told him to apologise. It must have been a terrible moment for the proud earl when he muttered his apology : " Sire, sith that it seemeth to the King

29

and to the other lords and eke that they have been so mickle grieved and displeased by my words, it forthinketh me and beseech you of your good lordship to remit me your mautelant [*displeasure*]."

Arundel was defeated. He retired from the council to sulk in private. Then Gaunt's second wife died and he scandalised the court by marrying Katherine Swynford who had been his mistress for over twenty years. She was the wife of Sir Hugh Swynford, nurse to Gaunt's children and later their guardian when their mother, Blanche, died. After Blanche, Gaunt married Constance of Castile and thereby started his insane wars for her crown, but the liasion with Katherine continued until after Constance's death in 1394—Sir Hugh had died in 1372—and in 1396 Gaunt married his mistress and the mother of four of his children, John, Henry, Thomas, and Joan, surnamed Beaufort. Richard declared these children legitimate. It was a brave gesture of Gaunt's to defy public opinion and marry the woman whom everybody knew to be his mistress, and it is rather a sad comment on medieval morals that the people were horrified by it.

It was now that Richard married little Isabel. The marriage could never have been intended as a real marriage, it was a political alliance ; already the King had declared his intention not to produce an heir by stating that the Earl of March, Roger Mortimer, should be his successor. This Roger Mortimer was the great-grandson—on the distaff side—of Edward III, his grandfather being Edward's second son Lionel.

RICHARD had waited a long time to take revenge on the lords appellant who had driven his beloved de Vere from England. Bolingbroke as yet he dared not harm, and Mowbray he had bought to his side : they could both wait until opportunity for vengeance came. A fortnight after the coronation of little Isabel, parliament met on January 22 and the King gave his reasons for summoning it—he intended to help Charles of France against Lombardy. To this the commons could not agree, hatred of France was too deeply rooted in England for such a volte-face of policy. Richard lost his temper and swore that if he wished he could " order his people to go to the support of his friends, and for that purpose to dispose of his own goods as and when he pleased." Despite this bad opening, parliament continued to an amiable end mainly because, for some peculiar reason, it almost grovelled to the King, and the easiest way to please Richard was to grovel to him. He had the most exaggerated ideas of royalty and insisted on obeisance at every point. He was now almost a megalomaniac, his vanity was so gigantic and his manner of showing it so insolent that one is astonished that men like Bolingbroke could tolerate him. He signed himself on one occasion "Full Emperor of England," and was actually—most amazing of prophecies—trying to have Edward II canonised. For this purpose he had a book of Edward's miracles transcribed and sent to the Pope.

The taxation was heavy, and when raised, it was mainly spent on luxury or in bribes to entice nobles to his party and away from Gloucester's. Gloucester fought to the last. When Richard restored Brest to France, England was furious, fully aware that the King had been given a huge bribe to break up his kingdom. Gloucester told him so, and the rumour spread through England that Gaunt had remarked—"Calais grieved more England and did more hurt thereto than profit, for the great expense about the keeping thereof." If Brest should go, why not Calais? asked the people.

Richard was ready to strike. Mowbray, twice-traitor, informed him that Gloucester, Arundel, and Warwick were conspiring, and Richard invited all three to a banquet at Cold Harbour near St. Paul's. There is no reason to believe that there ever was a plot. As Sir James Ramsay puts it—"There was, in fact, but one conspirator in England, and he was the King."[1] Only Warwick was simple enough to accept Richard's invitation, Gloucester apologised, giving that most dangerous excuse of illness, while Arundel did not even bother to answer. Warwick was sent to the Tower, and Richard with the young men who were his confidants galloped to Pleshy where Gloucester was lodged. The duke had retired to bed and came half-naked to greet his royal nephew, unarmed, and with none but his chaplains to attend him. With his own hand Richard arrested him jeeringly and ordered him to be sent to Calais under Mowbray's escort. He never returned to England. No man at the time knew how Gloucester died, for his plea of sickness helped the murderers, but when Henry IV was King, a certain John Hall, one of Mowbray's valets, confessed that Gloucester was taken to Calais Castle and from there to a house in the town called Prince's Inn where they smothered him with a feather-bed. Arundel surrendered himself, most foolishly.

[1] *The Genesis of Lancaster*, by Sir James H. Ramsay, 2 vols. (Oxford), 1913.

It was a packed parliament that met on September 17. Westminster Hall being half-dismantled at the time, the session was held outside on a wooden stage. Richard had taken every precaution to see that his vengeance did not miscarry. With his " juvenile council," the new lords appellant, he discussed all points, and summoned his great army of retainers and his Cheshire bowmen to ride with him. This was illegal, as no weapons were allowed at Westminster lest commons and peers be bullied by the wealthy. But Richard thought himself almost a god, above rules made to bind lesser men. He came as if he were a conqueror in a conquered land, and he placed his archers completely round the stage with bent bows, arrows strung. Gloucester was dead, yet that did not stop him from being declared a traitor so that Richard could steal his lands. Before impeaching his enemies, Richard carefully revoked the pardons granted in 1388 for their rebellion, and the first prisoner to be called for trial was young insolent brave Arundel. He showed no sign of fear, he scoffed at a government of " boys and widows." His earl's belt and his scarlet hood were taken from him. When charged with treason he appealed to the pardons he had been granted ; these were now revoked, he was told, by the King, lords, and faithful commons. " Faithful commons ! " jeered Arundel, " where are the faithful commons ? the faithful commons are not here ! " On one occasion during the proceedings he so infuriated the new lords appellant that the whole eight danced on the floor with rage ; Gaunt and his son were shouting with the others — " Traitor ! " " Liar ! " . . . " Traitor," said Gaunt who presided as seneschal," that pardon is recalled." " Truly you lie ! " cried Arundel ; " I never was a traitor." " Then why did you ask for pardon ? " demanded Gaunt. " To shut the mouths of my enemies," retorted the earl, " of whom you are one. And as for treasons, you need pardon more than I."

His insolence could not save him. Gaunt proclaimed sentence : " Richard, I, seneschal of England, do adjudge you traitor, and I do by sentence and judgment condemn you to be drawn, hanged, beheaded and quartered, and your lands entailed and unentailed to be forfeited." The King had at least the gentleness to commute the worst details, and Arundel was hurried off at once to Tower Hill, being led there by that rascal of a Mowbray, and surrounded by archers. He made a brave death. He flung his gold to the people, tested the axe-edge with his finger and asked the executioner to make quick work. The executioner obeyed. His head fell at one blow. Not long afterwards the people showed their hatred of the King by considering the dead earl a martyr, and the story went that his head had miraculously joined the body. Richard was scared by the rumour and had the corpse examined. He found that the head was sewn on.

Gloucester was called next before parliament, but being dead, as Mowbray swore, his estates were forfeited, then Warwick was condemned to forfeiture and exile to the Isle of Man. Richard was determined that his sentences should not be reversed. Both houses were made to swear that they would not attempt to reverse them, and at the next session—this time at Shrewsbury—his triumph was astounding. It is really impossible to explain the obsequiousness of this parliament, for it surrendered the whole nation to the King's whim, it gave England as a toy for Richard to do with as he liked. All that brave men had striven to win for centuries, what the barons in their callous way had accidentally aroused at Runnymede, what the great Simon de Montfort had died for—all this was swept away within four days. Richard was made absolute monarch.

Articles of high treason were produced. It was treason—parliament declared—to cause the death of or to depose a king, it was treason to renounce homage to him or to stir the people to rebel against him or to attempt to reverse or to annul " any judgment, statute, or ordinance rendered or made in the then parliament." Richard wanted these articles sworn to so that they could never be evaded ; oaths were given on the cross of Canterbury, and he even asked if there were no other formula more binding. On being assured that this was the most binding oath possible, he was forced to remain satisfied, although he remained troubled because he could not also bind his successors. This Shrewsbury parliament is horrifying in its servility. After passing these statutes it destroyed itself by granting the King an income for life, thereby frustrating the necessity of further parliaments. And now was passed the most suicidal act of all : the powers of parliament were delegated to a standing committee of eighteen lords and six knights, nearly all of whom were Richard's friends.

Richard had won more than any of his predecessors had ever won, he had made himself absolute, a tyrant. By cunning he had achieved this power, by remorseless hatred and by patience. He had waited, seeming so weak and characterless with his pretty face and feminine manners, fondling his council of boys and of elderly women who gossiped in the court and whom he had actually introduced into the Order of the Garter— probably only to the dinners—to the scandal of the conservative masculine knights. His childishness deceived strong self-centred men of the type of Gloucester or fierce young knights like Arundel. He stuttered when he spoke, blushed very easily, and did not like swords and tournaments ; the strong men scoffed at his boys and his widows, but they never realised that although women cannot fight with fists, they have subtler weapons in their malice and in the suppressed passion of their lusts. And in many ways Richard was a woman, with a woman's protection—delicate looks and physical frailty. He had realised his own short-comings, and with the greatest cunning had used the weapons he possessed but as with so many despots, power giddied him, it made him believe himself subtle enough to cheat and conquer men of the intelligence of his cousin-german, the heroic quick-witted Bolingbroke. Despite his outward friendliness, Richard had never forgiven Gaunt for those early years of oppression, nor Bolingbroke for being one of the old lords appellant.

Of the following story we do not know the truth. We possess only Bolingbroke's version, but it is logical and rings true. Between the parliamentary sessions, Bolingbroke was riding with Mowbray from Brentford to London in December when Mowbray in sudden agitation disclosed a plot ; he said that Richard intended to destroy them all, and in particular the house of Lancaster. This tale is not difficult to believe. Mowbray had been a traitor so often—beginning with Richard, running to the lords appellant, then back to Richard—that we can surely credit a further treachery ? It was at his command that Gloucester had been smothered under a feather-bed at Calais and he must have known that Kings fear men who carry dangerous secrets. After his success at Westminster, Richard was un-doubtedly plotting ways whereby to strike at Gaunt and Bolingbroke. They would inevitably be his next victims. And what more natural than that he should disclose his plans to the rascal Mowbray ? and that Mowbray, realising that he must follow Gaunt and Bolingbroke to the scaffold, should confess those plans to Bolingbroke, hoping to form a union strong enough to crush the King ? If this was his idea, he failed badly, for his confidant immediately informed his father, and Gaunt suggested that he repeat the tale to Richard, who, on being told, suggested that Bolingbroke impeach Mowbray formally in the Shrewsbury parliament. Bolingbroke obeyed, and as Mowbray was not present, writs were sent to demand his attendance within fifteen days under threat of forfeiture. In Richard's presence, the two dukes faced each other on February 23, 1398, at Oswestry, when Bolingbroke repeated his story and Mowbray answered that he lied. They were dismissed, and Richard commanded them to appear at Windsor on April 28 when the question was argued " according to the laws of chivalry." There was only one course to take—an appeal to the old-fashioned ordeal, to fight it out in the lists.

Ordeal by battle had never been popular in England, and the world was amazed to hear that Richard in the fourteenth century could allow two dukes to fight to the death. He had other plans, however, but he delighted in secrecy and told nothing, letting Bolingbroke order a suit of armour from Milan and Mowbray one from Bohemia. The contest was to take place at Coventry on Monday, September 16, and so great was the crowd on the appointed day that, besides the usual palisades, a wet ditch had to be dug to keep out the mob. At eight o'clock in the morning, the constable and marshal, dressed in their bright Garter robes, rode into the lists, and at nine o'clock, Bolingbroke arrived with six mounted men. Challenged as to his name and business by constable and marshal, he replied that he was Henry of Lancaster, Duke of Hereford, come to do his duty against the false traitor Thomas Mowbray, Duke of Norfolk. The oath was then administered that " Thou, Henry of Lancaster, this thy bill is sothe [*true*] in all points and articles from the beginning continued unto the end, and that is your intent to prove this day on the foresaid Thomas Mowbray, so with God's help and His halwes [*saints*]." Bolingbroke, having taken the oath, swung himself again on to his horse, crossed himself, and rode to the farther end of the lists where he sat in the chair prepared for him. This chair was hung with curtains like a tent and was draped with the arms of St. George. Richard came next with his friends and his bodyguard of archers, then Mowbray arrived to undergo the same formula of challenge and oath as his opponent. Fully armed, helmets on, the dukes waited at either end. They sat in their high-arched saddles that gripped belly and back, and each lance was measured and tested, each knight pushed its tip into the rest and pressed his gloved fingers up under the vamplate. The trumpets sounded. " Faitez vos devoirs ! " cried the heralds, " laissez les aller ! " Bolingbroke had dug the spurs into his horse when Richard suddenly stood to his feet and flung down his baton as signal that the combat must stop. For two hours he kept those knights fidgeting on horseback in the weight of armour until his decision was announced. So as to keep the peace of the land, Bolingbroke was sentenced to banishment for ten years and Mowbray to banishment for the term of his natural life.

RICHARD most likely thought that he had done something parti-cularly clever when he thus got rid of the two men he hated. He had made the most stupid act of a stupid life. Mowbray went on pilgrimage to Jerusalem, and died of plague on the way home ; Bolingbroke went to Paris. Scarcely had Bolingbroke left England than his father died. At the age of fifty-nine, John of Gaunt passed from a troubled ambitious yet futile life, with the realisation that all the sycophancy of his last years had come to nothing, that Richard had never forgiven him and never would forgive his son.

Richard was reckless ; made careless by his inordinate vanity, he seized Bolingbroke's estates when Gaunt died. That was sufficient cause, apart from the other degradations, to excuse Bolingbroke seeking justice. He had tried to remain loyal to an unforgiving and vindictive King. Now was his moment for revenge, and he was prepared to make Richard realise that success could be won by the strength of one's arm and by love of the people as easily as it could be won by treachery and by the maintaining of bought armies. With him was Archbishop Arundel who had been exiled by the same parliament that had sent his brother to execution ; together they prepared to invade England.

There comes a point in the lives of many men when it appears that they desire death, when they deliberately drag their doom upon themselves. The psycho-analysts may be able to explain it, I can merely state this truth which we discover again and again in history. Courage is a glorious thing, but it is not courage to seek death, it is very often cowardice, the desire to escape the stress of living ; it is some-times braver to hide and live than to face the glittering spears and throw away your steel as the shouting multitude bears down. Therefore martyrs are often robbed of their greatness, for there is nothing splendid in flinging yourself upon the naked swords of puzzled Romans as the ancient Christians commonly did. Apart from martyrs, amongst ordinary men not driven by hysteria, this moment sometimes comes when they step blindly towards an ambush which they must realise is there ready to destroy them. That moment had come to Richard. He had forced the most powerful man in England out of the country, he had infuriated him by stealing his heritage, and now he calmly sailed for Ireland and left his kingdom open to any adventurer !

He sailed for Ireland on May 29, 1399, to settle an unimportant squabble about some lands he had taken against his word. There was no actual rebellion, there was nothing whatever that needed his personal attention, yet he sailed, and on landing, he did what no sensible general would ever do : he attempted to fight the Irish who were lurking safely in a thick wood. In the meantime, while his pioneers were chopping down trees and the Irish were quietly slaughtering any laggards, he knighted amongst others the son of Bolingbroke, Henry of Monmouth, later King Henry V of England. It does not seem that Richard had taken little Henry as a hostage, he presumably had great affection for the boy and, we are told, was fond of repeating an ancient prophecy foretelling that a prince called Henry " will be born in England who, through the nobility of his character and the splendid greatness of his achievements, will illumine the whole world with the rays of his glory." After repeating this, Richard, we are told, would gaze fondly on young Henry of Monmouth and would say, " Verily do I believe that this young Henry here will be he ! "

Bolingbroke landed at the now disappeared port of Ravenspur, near Bridlington, on about July 4. His progress was not barred, royal castles opened their gates, nobles rode to his standard. He swore he did not come to take the throne but merely to claim his lost inheritance and to reform the government. He could scarcely state the truth : the people might be eager to depose Richard, but Richard's heir, little Roger Mortimer, was alive and was next in succession.

Richard still wasted his time in Ireland. When he heard of Bolingbroke's landing, he called Henry of Monmouth to him and said sadly, " Henry, my boy, see what your father has done to me ! He has invaded my land and put my subjects to death without mercy. Certes, I am sorry for you, since because of these unhappy doings you might lose your inheritance." " In truth, my lord," answered little Henry, " I am greatly grieved at these rumours. But I believe your lordship understands that I am innocent of my father's deeds." " Yes," said Richard, " I know you have no part in your father's crime and therefore I hold you excused of it." Even now, Richard had not lost all hope. But his courage milked from him when he landed in England. The bravery of the lad who had faced Wat Tyler's mob in Smithfield no longer existed. It was a weakling who fled through Wales in the disguise of a monk, wailing and pleading to the Virgin, cursing Bolingbroke, and sobbing like a girl. He had only the weapons left with which he had won power— duplicity and apparent helplessness. He thought that with these he might yet win, and started negotiating with the enemy, but he is reported to have said in private, " Whatever agreement or peace he may make with me, if I can get him into my power I will cause him to be foully put to death." No sign of his hatred showed when he met Bolingbroke at Flint ; the dinner beforehand was prolonged, none wishing to stop the meal, all being eager to postpone the meeting of the cousins. But the meeting could not be postponed for ever, and at last Richard and Bolingbroke faced each other in the castle yard.

The artist who illustrated Jean Creton's riming chronicle of Richard's last days has portrayed the scene, and as the likenesses in these miniatures are very exact, we may take the drawings as more or less authentic. Richard with his golden hair, plump face, and little beard droops before Bolingbroke ; he stands with straight arms, dressed in a red gown and with a black hood flopping to his shoulders ; before him kneels Bolingbroke, unhelmed, and in full armour : above the dark-brown jupon, the coif of blue mail pushes up his bearded chin, and the blue links reach to his wrists, and on his bent leg we see the plates of shining yellowish steel. Bolingbroke knelt very low when the King stepped from the castle into the yard ; then he bowed a second time, cap in hand, as Richard came close. Richard took off his cap and spoke first, in his quick stuttering voice, " Fair cousin of Lancaster," he said, " you be right welcome." Bowing yet a third time, Bolingbroke answered, " I am come sooner than you sent for me : the reason I will tell you. The common report of the people is that for twenty or two-and-twenty years you have governed them badly and most harshly, and therefore they are not well contented with you. But if it please our Lord, I will help you to govern them better than they have been governed in time past." "Fair cousin," said Richard humbly, "if it pleases you, it pleases us well." Creton adds, lest we doubt him : "And be assured that these are the very words that they two spoke together, without subtracting or adding anything : I heard them and understood them well."

For all the courteous words and the bowing and the doffing of caps, Richard was prisoner, and Bolingbroke soon made him realise it by placing him in the custody of the sons of two of his victims—the Earls of Gloucester and Arundel. In their custody Richard was brought to Chester.

PARLIAMENT had to be called. Writs were sealed in the King's name, summoning a session for September 30 at Westminster. Then with his royal captive, Bolingbroke rode to London. Once Richard tried to escape. At Lichfield, during the night, he climbed from a window in the tower where he was lodged, and reached the garden. He was seen and dragged back and afterwards was allowed no privacy, he was not even able to sleep, for always ten or twelve armed men were in his chamber.

England welcomed Bolingbroke. He was a strong man, brave and serious ; besides, any change was preferable to the misrule of Richard. At first Bolingbroke had intended to place Richard on his trial in parliament, but the experiment would have been too dangerous. Richard's plump girlish face and helpless manner might suddenly shift the balance, he would weep and implore mercy, and men are sometimes swayed by royalty in bonds. Wisely, Bolingbroke changed his mind and made every effort to force Richard to abdicate of his own free will. We do not know what arguments were put to him, but we do know that when Adam of Usk the chronicler called on the King on September 21 he found him in an highly excitable state, crying and muttering, reviling and praying. At last, however, he gave way, and apparently quite cheerfully. Bolingbroke had probably told him the most stupendous lies, for Richard insisted upon reading the whole of his deposition aloud as if he were struck by his own literary style, and he signed it with his own hand, even remarking that he would like Bolingbroke to become his successor, slipping his own signet ring upon the usurper's ready finger.

Parliament fully agreed to Richard's deposition, although Richard himself insisted that as he was an anointed King royalty

was like a halo and could never be renounced, which explains much
of his previous stupid behaviour. He had actually believed that
the hallowing imparted some godlike quality : a study of
the King he had wished to canonise, Edward II, might have
told him an entirely different story. He also remarked that he
hoped Bolingbroke would be good to him and give him a large
allowance.

At a secret sitting of the house of lords on October 23, it was
decided that to keep Richard on show was dangerous and would
incite rebellion ; it were best to imprison him secretly for the
term of his natural life. Bolingbroke, now Henry IV, objected to
the suggestion that Richard be murdered, and two days later " the
King that was " disappeared from the Tower of London to some
unknown destination in the country. And there he remained
until his friends destroyed him by rising in his cause. Henry IV
knew that so long as Richard lived there would be continual
disturbances, plots and insurrections. A privy council meeting
informed him that if Richard still lived he should be safely locked
away, if he were dead his body should be publicly produced.
The hint was enough, and reluctantly Henry agreed to the murder.

We are not certain about the way in which Richard was
killed. It was believed at the time and probably with truth,
that he was starved to death ; others said that he had deliberately
starved himself, but that is scarcely consistent with his character.
Another story tells of Sir Peter Exton trying to murder him with
seven men, and relates that Richard tore an axe from one of
the men's hands and defended himself with it so superbly that
he killed four of them before Sir Peter jumped on to a chair and
hit him twice on the head with another axe. This preposterous
story was finally exposed when some antiquaries examined
Richard's skull in the seventeenth century : it was found not to
have " any such marks of a blow, or wound, upon it, as would
at all warrant the commonly received history of this wretched
King's unhappy end."

£80 was paid from the exchequer to carry Richard's corpse
from Pontefract to London so that it could be viewed by all and
thereby stop for ever the rumour that he lived. From the bottom
of the forehead to the throat the face was exposed, and the
curious stared on the features of a King who could no longer
glare them to a sudden death. In the shadows of vast St. Paul's
the corpse lay for two days, and Henry himself attended the
service for the dead and offered twenty shillings to the poor.

From St. Paul's it was carried to the Friars Preachers at Langley, Hertfordshire, where it remained until Bolingbroke's son, Henry V, had it removed from its leaden covering and placed in a new elm coffin. With splendid pomp and crawling at the snail-pace that Richard had himself requested, on December 4, 1413, the body of the redeless King came to Westminster in the light of one hundred and twenty torches to lie beside the bones of his dear Anne in the tomb of his own design.

To lie—but not to rest. When the tomb was built, by some accident it was not made airtight ; there were five metal shields on its side, and these shields when dislodged revealed five holes through which vandals could reach their hands and play with the bones or push stupid momentoes into the tomb. These momentoes were all discovered, together with a fifteenth-century plumber's shears, when the tomb was opened in 1880.

Shameful as all this sounds, one nevertheless feels that it was a fitting end to the redeless King. He had designed a splendid tomb, had lovingly made effigies of himself and the Queen he adored ; he prepared for the great adventure of death with kingly pomp only to have it all stolen from him, to die wretchedly, to be exposed to vulgar eyes in the gloom of St. Paul's, and to be buried long after his time by the son of the man who had murdered him. Despite his efforts to be in every way a King, he failed ; his bones were played with by sacrilegious Protestants—descendants of the lollards whom he loathed—and a schoolboy stole his jawbone for a trophy. There is, however, this one consolation : his bones are mixed for ever with the bones of the person he adored above all others, his good Queen Anne, under their effigies lying hand in hand in the shadow of the Confessor whose tall shrine rises in the abbey above the Kings of England that encircle it.

XIII

KING HENRY THE FOURTH

1399-1413

WHILE RICHARD II WAS IN THE TOWER, Henry of Bolingbroke, Duke of Lancaster, faced a parliament in Westminster on Tuesday, September 30, 1399. He possessed Richard's abdication in which the redeless King absolved his subjects of all "liegance and obeisance," and confessed that he was "naught worth" to govern, and "not unworthy" of being deposed because of his demerits ; yet this document was not sufficient, it left Henry open to the accusation of having extorted it under pressure ; therefore he decided to throw half the guilt of his usurpation on to parliament by making it impeach Richard. He did not attempt to pack the parliament, Richard's friends were present as well as his enemies. At the lower end of the hall stood the vacant throne draped with cloth-of-gold, the throne on which the King should sit. It was now empty, its arms reaching out as if prepared to embrace the man who would dare take so dangerous a seat. Henry did not accept the embrace as yet, he took the chair that his father used to occupy.

Richard's formal renunciation was read aloud in both English and Latin, and the estates were asked if it should be accepted. Not one man dared shout—*No ! Aye, Aye,* went the ripple of voices in that gathering. Then were read the articles of objection against Richard, the reasons why he had himself agreed that he was "naught worth" to govern. First, the coronation oath was repeated, to be followed by thirty-three counts of accusation. These began by retelling the old abuses, they mentioned the King's injustice to Henry of Lancaster and the duke's illegal exile and deprivation of his inheritance. Mention was made of the grovelling parliaments of 1397 and 1398, of Richard's tampering with elections, his alienation of crown estates, his unlawful taxation and purveyances, his oppressive army of White Harts, his non-payment of debts, his extortions, and his rash words, such as his saying—and acting upon the saying—that the life of every subject, his lands, tenements, goods and chattels lay at the royal will. The charges seemed endless, and each man present, even Richard's friends, knew that they were justified ; when at last they were finished, the estates were challenged both individually and as a whole, and they agreed that there were sufficient grounds to depose the King.

Now was the throne vacant. It had stayed behind the pall of gold, its arms reaching out as if imploring a man bold enough to sit therein ; Henry of Bolingbroke, Duke of Lancaster, rose slowly in his place. He crossed himself on forehead and breast, and read aloud : " In the name of Father, Son, and Holy Ghost, I, Henry of Lancaster, challenge this realm of England and the crown with all the members and appurtenances thereto, I that am descended by right line of blood coming from the good King Henry the Third, and through that right that God of His grace hath sent me, with the help of my kin and of my friends, to recover it ; the which realm was in point of being undone for default of governance and undoing of the good laws." It was a well-thought-out statement, for Henry had to go carefully, his claim being actually very thin and the true heir, Roger Mortimer, being alive. We are told that at first he had thought to demand the crown by right of conquest, but that his friends calmed his impatience and suggested the statement given above. The claim of " line of blood " was rather vague, being based on descent from Edmund Crouchback, but Henry had created a most important precedent by throwing himself on the mercy of the people, by making election by parliament necessary to kingship.

Again the estates agreed without a murmur, and Henry showed the signet-ring that Richard had given him. Archbishop Arundel took him by the right hand and led him to the vacant throne before which he knelt for a few moments in prayer. When he sat on that uneasy seat, little realising the small peace it would bring him, the archbishop preached a sermon on the country's good fortune in escaping a " government by boys and widows," the theme of his collation being from the First Epistle to the Corinthians, " When I was a child, I spake as a child, I understood as a child, I thought as a child : but when I became a man, I put away childish things." Henry stood to offer thanks. " Sirs," said he, " I thank God and you spirituals and temporals and all the estates of the land, and I do you to wit that it is naught my will that no man think that by way of conquest I would disinherit any man of his heritage, franchise or other rights that he ought to have, nor put him out of that he hath and hath had by the good laws and customs of this realm, except them that have been against the good purpose and the common profit of the realm."

Parliament, after one day's sitting, was dissolved to reassemble the following week when the acts of the previous session were confirmed. The coronation took place on Sunday, October 12, the state procession as usual riding from the Tower to Westminster. Forty-five new knights, dubbed that very morning, went ahead of the King and were dressed in priest-like cloaks of green, Henry himself rode bare-headed despite the rain, and wore a German tunic of cloth-of-gold with the Garter on his left leg. Cloths were hung from windows, the Cheapside conduits bubbled wine, but there was little pageantry, all were acutely aware of the King-That-Was fuming and cursing and praying in the Tower and were wondering if the King-That-Is would seek vengeance on his supporters.

The coronation went according to formula except for the introduction of some oil given by the Virgin Mary to St. Thomas Becket while he prayed one night at Sens in the Church of St. Colombe. Mary had told Thomas that this oil was to be kept for future Kings of England who should recover Normandy and Aquitaine and kill a great many pagans in the Holy Land. All this was rather peculiar, as England had not lost Normandy and Aquitaine in the days of Thomas, but medieval men did not look too deeply into miracles, they were only too grateful to accept them. The Virgin had suggested that Thomas secrete the oil in the quire of the Church of St. Gregory at Poitiers, and it was poured into a crystal phial enclosed in a gold eagle. The whole apparatus, eagle, oil and phial, had been found in a leaden vessel containing the story of the miracle in Thomas's own hand ; John of Gaunt had brought it to England and given it to his brother the Black Prince, but the Black Prince was sceptical and sent it to the Tower, where it had lain until the devout Richard II discovered it. Now for the first time this most precious oil of Mary's was used, being sprinkled on the russet head of Richard's successor and usurper. Adam of Usk, who was evidently present, adds the interesting detail that Henry's hair was crawling with lice.

At the coronation banquet, the King's Champion, Sir Thomas Dymock, rode fully armed into the hall while the heralds cried that he would defend Henry's honour against all comers. " If need were, Sir Thomas," smiled the King, " I would in my own person ease you of this duty."

THE new King was a serious man, the type that England needed after the frivolous reign of Richard. He was no waster, the fopperies of life held no interest to him, he was careful and cautious yet brave. It is untrue to say that he was not cultured, for he liked music and could play upon that wooden flute-like instrument, the ricordo, with its low rather melancholy sound, so gentle, and so sweet ; and that he had at least a slight interest in literature is proved by his invitation to the poetess, Christine de Pisan, to visit England ; of architectural pursuits we find small mention except for a little work on Westminster Hall ; but at the same time we must remember that Henry's reign was a disturbed and worried period during which he could have found few moments to spare for gentle pleasures. We learn, however, that he liked to enter those involved discussions so popular in the Middle Ages about morals and law, all placed in a vague world of preposterous logic.

When with King Richard in France he had proved himself a brave jouster on the plain of St. Inglebert near Calais. A spectator tells us that his skill and strength made strong contrast to Richard's feeble efforts. From this tournament, he voyaged with the Duc de Bourbon and a troop of English knights to the siege of Tripoli where the Doge of Venice was leading a grand assault upon the Moslem pirates. We next see him fighting with German knights on the shores of the Baltic and in the Gulf of Danzig. After this he returned to England, only to rush off on a pilgrimage to the Holy Land. He sailed from Venice in a galley presented by the Duke of Austria, and within sight of Jerusalem had to turn aside ; alone he could not battle with the Moslem hordes that owned the Sepulchre. For the remainder of his life, Henry was not to forget that disappointment and was to dream continually of leading another crusade. It is likely, however, that he visited the Mount of Olives to see the Church of the Holy Sepulchre. His journey home was a succession of fêtes, and as souvenirs he brought with him a parrot, a leopard and a Saracen christened Henry. He would still have continued his adventures, uncertain whether to join the famous French jouster Marshal Boucicaut in an attempt to rescue the Emperor of Byzantium from the Moslems, or to fight with the Count of

30

Oostervant in Friesland, but his friends persuaded him to come back to England.

It is difficult to reconcile this young brawling Henry with the staid cautious King who gathered the broken throne of Richard together and made it secure for his son. Historians, I feel, have usually underestimated him, they have not taken into consideration the state of England when he became King and compared it with the state in which he left it.[1] His reign was violent and comparatively brief, there was nothing glorious in it, nothing despicable ; it was sound and honest. He came with small right to the throne yet he held that throne through troubled years and made it powerful. Aware that many of his subjects despised him as an upstart, he was always most careful not to intrude his kingly privileges and to keep strictly within the bounds of constitutional principle. He never lost his temper, he was always tactful and understanding although surrounded by jealousy and hatred ; yet undisturbed he walked the delicate tight-rope of diplomacy, towards the end of his life tortured by disease and by fear that his eldest son was a drunkard, a wencher and perhaps a traitor. There is one dark mark against King Henry : he introduced into England the statute against heretics, *De heretico comburendo*, and thereby brought the burning death to this country. But we must not expect medieval men to have the tolerance we have to-day, and it would never have occurred to Henry, true son of the Church, that he was acting in an inhumane fashion by burning to a ghastly death poor wretches whose opinions differed from his own. Lollardy had a powerful grip in England, and with its growth opposition inevitably came. Richard II had once shouted at a man who thought to introduce a lollard statute— " I swear to you that if you ever break your oath [to forswear lollardy], I will slay you with the foulest death that may be," and it remained to Henry IV to introduce that " foulest death "— slow burning.

WHEN little more than a boy, fifteen years of age, Henry in 1381 married Mary de Bohun, who was two years younger than he. It was evidently a splendid wedding, as the music was supplied by minstrels from the King's own court. To the little bride, Gaunt

[1] Since writing this, my friend, Mr. J. D. Griffith Davies, has published a biography of Henry (Barker, 1935), and I am gratified to find that he holds the same high opinion of him as I do. It is time that Henry was given his rightful place.

gave a ruby worth thirty marks and to his son " forty shillings for as many pence put upon the book on the day of the espousals." As the wedding apparently was in London, it is likely that the festivities were held at the Savoy or at the de Bohuns', Coldharbour. Then the young couple were put to bed, stripped and laid side by side while the priest censed them and blessed them and called for an auspicious future. During the following year, Mary produced their first child, a son who died at birth—which is scarcely more than could be expected at the mother's early age, at an age when girls to-day are still nursing dolls. Tradition states that a second still-born child arrived in 1386, but we do know for certain that at Monmouth on September 16, 1387, the first child to live came to earth and was to grow into Henry of Monmouth, later King Henry V. Babies followed with clock-like regularity : Thomas in 1388, John in 1389, Humphrey in 1390–1, Blanche in 1392, and Philippa in 1394. Philippa killed her mother—Mary dying in childbirth in July 1394.

Henry was a handsome man in youth, powerfully built and of middle height, but a terrible disease in later life so disfigured him that few dared look upon his face. His beard was reddish, as was proved when his tomb in Canterbury was examined on August 12, 1831. Antiquaries opened the King's coffin and found leather wrappings swathed five times round the body. " These wrappers were cut through, and lifted off ; when, to the astonishment of all present, the face of the deceased King was seen in complete preservation. The nose elevated, the cartilage even remaining, though, on the admission of air, it sunk rapidly away, and had entirely disappeared before the examination was finished. The skin of the chin was entire, of the consistence and thickness of the upper leather of a shoe, brown and moist ; the beard thick and matted, and of a deep russet colour. The jaws were perfect, and all the teeth in them, except one fore-tooth, which had probably been lost during the King's life. The opening of the lead was not large enough to expose the whole of the features, and we did not examine the eyes or forehead. But the surveyor stated that when he introduced his finger under the wrappers to remove them, he distinctly felt the orbits of the eyes prominent in their sockets. The flesh upon the nose was moist, clammy, and of the same brown colour as every other part of the face," but this dark colour would be the result of the embalming and must not be taken for Henry's complexion.

One can only regret that this exhumation was in the days before cameras, particularly as we have no authentic portrait of Henry except the figure on his tomb at Canterbury; but the miniatures in Creton so resemble this figure that I feel we can accept them without cavil. In these miniatures, Henry has a well-trimmed slightly forked reddish-brown beard, and evidently a liking for a tall fur-hat which he wears in the painting reproduced here. He is in these drawings stockily-built, with a downward droop to the mouth; and under curved brows, he has slanting eyes deeply pouched above, giving him a strangely eastern appearance, as also does his tomb.[1]

WITH the capture of Richard and his own election to the throne, the simplest part of Henry's usurpation were over, now was to begin the difficult labour of making the country accept him and of rooting out the inevitable rebellion caused by friends of the King-That-Was. First, parliament had to reverse the acts of Richard's parliaments, and Henry condemned the delegation of the powers of the lords and commons to a committee and asked that the law return to what it had been in the reign of " his noble grandfather King Edward the Third, whom God assoil." Then his son, Henry of Monmouth, was accepted as heir-apparent, and a new dynasty was founded; young Henry was created Prince of Wales, Duke of Cornwall and Earl of Chester. The great earldoms were slowly falling to the Crown : Derby, Leicester, Northampton, Lancaster, Lincoln and Hereford. Of the powerful nobles, the Percies were the strongest, the Earl of Northumberland and his son Hotspur; they looked with scorn and jealousy at this new King, at this upstart who was no better than themselves.

The commons insisted that Henry impeach those who had counselled King Richard in evil. They dared not seize the great lords immediately, they took a lesser man, Sir William Bagot, while the six survivors of Richard's lords appellant—Albemarle,

---

[1] There is a curious portrait of Henry in Elmham's *Vita Henrici Quinti*— B. M. Cotton MS., Julius E. iv. f. 8. The portrait of Henry V in the same MS. is excellent, and even that of Richard II reveals a likeness, yet the Henry IV seems entirely inaccurate, as he is shown clean-shaven. The mouth is long and harshly marked at the corners, and fluffy fair hair puffs out over each ear from under the beautiful flower-like crown. He wears his royal robes and carries the sword of state. But why clean-shaven ? Need it be added that the "portrait" of Henry IV in the National Portrait Gallery, London, is obviously the work of an artist some hundred or so years later?

Surrey, Exeter, Dorset, Gloucester and Salisbury—kept their uneasy seats in parliament and waited nervously for attack. Bagot tried to save his skin by turning traitor, he accused Albemarle of being the instigator of Gloucester's murder at Calais. Albemarle, in a highly wrought condition, lost his temper and challenged Bagot to a duel by hitting him with his hood; Henry—always temperate—ordered the challenge to be withdrawn. Fuming, Albemarle sat down while Bagot continued to gush his tales. He said that he had only acted under the late King's order, that his doings had been sanctioned by parliament. As Surrey and Exeter had sat in that parliament, they now sprang to their feet and gave Bagot the lie, swearing to prove their innocence in the field against him or any man. The unfortunate Bagot, fearing on one side the vengeance of his old comrades and on the other the justice of the King, now threw the weight of guilt upon a valet, one John Hall, then imprisoned in Newgate. Hall, on being produced, said that Gloucester had been murdered in Calais at Albemarle's command. Albemarle again leaped to his feet and pulled off his hood and Lord Fitz-Walter sprang up to accept his challenge ; Surrey defended his friend, but he only made matters worse by his confused details, and before long over twenty hoods were scattered on the floor, and the unfortunate Albemarle would have had a hard task of it to cleave his way to innocence.

The next day being a holiday, parliament adjourned to meet on the 22nd, when the commons now demanded even the impeachment of Richard himself. Henry was not a cruel man, he loved to temporise, to stave off petty vengeance, and at a secret meeting of the house of lords, he stood out strongly against the suggestion that Richard be executed. At last it was agreed to imprison him secretly for the term of his natural life.

When this sentence was made public, the commons, hungry like dogs at the scent of prey, made another rush at the old lords appellant. Before their determination, Henry could do practically nothing and the six accused each pleaded his cause. They all admitted a little guilt, Albemarle saying that he had acted under compulsion ; Surrey, out of terror—for he had been only a boy favourite of Richard's with little mind of his own— ; Exeter said that he had tamely followed the others ; Dorset, that he had been so surprised that he hadn't had time to object ; Salisbury, like Surrey, that he had been afraid of Richard ; Despenser, that he was simply amazed when he saw his name on the bill of attainder against the old lords appellant, but on seeing it written there, he said, he had not dared withdraw it. On November 3, the chief justice pronounced judgment on the lords, and in its leniency we can see the hand of the moderate King. Albemarle, Surrey and Exeter were deprived of their ducal titles, becoming again the Earls of Rutland, Kent and Huntingdon, the Marquis of Dorset becoming Earl of Salisbury, and the Earl of Gloucester the Lord Despenser, and they were ordered to forfeit all estates acquired since 1397 and to disband their armies. Salisbury, for some reason, was not harmed ; he was placed in the Tower and then released on bail.

Henry had been too gentle ; by restraining the fury of the commons he had given freedom to men who hated him and who would never cease hating him. Great lords such as these could only be executed or pardoned entirely ; the slightest censure they considered an intolerable insult, and now they conspired together to seek revenge. And the people, too, were dissatisfied, seeing their prey taken from them. Henry found an unsigned letter in his closet threatening rebellion if the guilty were not more fiercely punished, and hinting that justice had been bribed. It is difficult for a King to remain balanced between two strong parties, to try to please both, and soon Henry was warned that the degraded appellants, on the eve of Twelfth Night, 1400, were to capture him, taking advantage of a tournament—the old trick— to carry arms to Windsor. The conspirators were to meet at Kingston on January 4. We do not know who exposed the plot to Henry, but the evidence suggests that Rutland—recently Albemarle—turned traitor at the last moment. He did not confess to Henry until the very evening of the meditated rising. Henry could not have been surprised ; the friends of Richard had not concealed their hostility, openly they wore the White Hart and called themselves King Richard's Nurselings. All the same, he evidently had made no preparations ; with his sons he was spending a miserable Christmas at Windsor and was heard to remark that he did wish King Richard would die. The whole family became ill, King included, and, naturally, poison was suspected. He was very lonely, being despised by the nobility. Then came the traitor with tidings of conspiracy, how the degraded appellants were gathering at Kingston and how they had with them a priest called Richard Maudeleyn who was the double of Richard and who was to impersonate him until the ex-King could be rescued. Henry wasted not a moment. With his sons and two attendants he galloped to London, somehow managing to steal through the conspirators' small army, and was in the city by nine o'clock that night. The rebels reached Windsor twelve hours after he had left, and the gates were opened to their knocking ; finding their prey gone, they hurriedly decided to march on London, meeting at Colnbrook. Kent— recently Surrey—visited Richard's Queen Isabel at Sonning, near Reading, and proclaimed in a fit of boyish enthusiasm that her husband was again to be King of England, and he tore the badges of Lancaster from her servants.

Kent had been premature in his announcement. Henry was no coward to run when his throne seemed in danger, he was a soldier and probably welcomed a chance to fight in the open. With an army, he rode from London, and the conspirators seeing that the game was up, fled for their lives. They reached Ciren-cester only to be attacked by the citizens, who besieged them in their lodgings ; it was impossible to hold out against a town, and they surrendered and were locked into the abbey. Their friends tried to rescue them and merely infuriated the citizens into beheading Kent, Salisbury and Lord Lumley, and in sending the remainder to Oxford. Despenser, who fled to Wales, took ship at Bristol, only to have the crew mutiny and take him back to port where he was murdered by the populace. Huntingdon was beheaded by a mob in Pleshy Castle. The rumour that Rutland told Henry about the conspiracy seems to be justified when we discover that he was given the bloody task of trying his erstwhile friends, which he did with such gusto that he executed twenty-six or twenty-seven of them. Richard's double, Maudeleyn, was executed at Tyburn.

The rebellion had been a failure in every way, and it doomed Richard. It was now that he died and was more than probably murdered. On February 27, Henry had the corpse brought to London to put a stop to future conspiracies, yet the elaborate show did little good. Not so very long afterwards a man was impersonating Richard in Scotland and remained an annoyance to Henry for many years.

WITH Richard dead, Henry's one rival was the Earl of March, a minor, but he still had troubles enough. France would not recognise his title, and there was war with Scotland. It was not an important war and was soon over, and its main interest is in the King's kindness, his humanity ; for he did not burn and murder and ravish, he pardoned freely when pardon was asked. But more important than the Scottish war was the Welsh rebellion.

The Welsh marcher-lords were brutal men, for they had to rule by violence, there was no other way of making the conquered nation realise that it was conquered. Like the Scots, the Welsh were a proud people and deeply resentful of the high-handed manner of the English. This was the inevitable result of trying to rule the country by oppression, by giving it with almost royal rights to a few lords. One of these lords was Reginald, Lord Grey of Ruthin, and he quarrelled about some lands with one Owen Glendower—or Owen Glyn Dŵr, to give his name correctly, but I prefer to use the inaccurate spelling made familiar to us by Shakespeare and English historians. This Glendower was an educated gentleman, lord of Glyndyfrdwy and Cynllaith Owen, who had been trained as a lawyer at London and probably also at Oxford. He had fought with Richard in the Scottish campaigns of 1385 and had been an esquire to the Earl of Arundel and, it appears, to Henry IV during some of his errant adventures oversea. At the time of the rebellion, Glendower was forty-one years of age, a cultured hospitable man, at peace with England and with his own tenants. Welsh singers thought to build for him a royal lineage, and it does seem that he came of good family although not of noble descent. He had married Margaret, daughter of one of Richard's justices of the King's bench, and by her had children, but of their number we are uncertain, we only know that he had daughters and at least one son.

The rebellion began over a petty squabble. Grey demanded some lands that Owen possessed, and Owen, a true lawyer, took the case to court, while Grey, a true lord marcher, seized the disputed territory, " a piece of commons " called Croesau, that lay between the two estates. Already Grey had made trouble by his cruel bearing towards the " Welsh dogs," and particularly with a rascal named Gruffydd ap Dafydd ap Gruffydd, called by Grey " the strongest thief of Wales." For some reason Grey's spite settled on Owen, not only did he try to seize Croesau but he behaved in a really despicable fashion when Henry summoned his tenants for the Scottish war. Such a summons in Wales would go through the hands of the lords marcher, and Grey deliberately withheld Owen's, with the result that Henry accused him of treason. Owen could not explain the truth and he was already irritated beyond endurance ; he called to his friends in his manor of Carrog in Glyndyfrdwy, and rebellion was decided. But it could not be a rebellion of great armies, of pitched battles ; the people of Wales were scattered and had little money. To bring them together was difficult, but it would have been still more difficult to train their individualities to accept discipline, to control their quick tempers and enthusiasms. A Welsh rebellion had to be one of guerrilla warfare, of sniping with the long bow, of trapping the enemy in gorges and valleys.

In September 1400 the first blow was struck, an attack on Grey's town of Ruthin, probably on the 21st during the fair of St. Matthew's Day. The town was sacked, the people massacred, but the castle was too strong to take. With more booty than they could carry, the troops of Glendower left the place in ruins, and the tale of those burnt walls and gashed bodies ran through Wales ; through the hills and the valleys of Wales ran the message for which men had been dreaming as they sharpened swords and tautened bow-strings—the message of rebellion. To the outlaw in the forests, to the peasant crouching over peat-fires, to the gentleman of the manor, the message came that Wales was ready. She had been waiting years for the call, a broken people brooding on departed glory, and at last a man had come to bind the people as a nation, to unite them against the hated English—one man, a soldier and lawyer, Owen Glendower.

When the rebellion started it gained power swiftly, and Henry, just back from Scotland, had to turn his sword against other marches than the north. With the Prince of Wales, he charged at Wales, he charged into an empty landscape, not at a nation. In this land of mountains it was impossible to grapple an enemy ; besides, the new King's policy was temperate, he did not want wars, he wanted peace in which to have time to rebuild England. There were more pardons than hangings in this futile campaign, and at last he withdrew to leave the Prince nominally and Hotspur actually in charge, while a proclamation was given out offering pardon to all who would submit before the meeting of the next parliament. But the situation was far more serious than Henry realised. It was not a mere outbreak, it was rebellion.

He had his troubles in England, although they were beginning to quieten, and there was the problem of Richard's widow Isabel. Henry wished to marry her to his eldest son, but the French would not listen ; they demanded the immediate return of her person and dowry. Henry did not mind surrendering her person, the dowry was not so easy with an empty exchequer.

Rebellion kept on in Wales. Henry made another attempt at invasion only to turn back because, as he explained, the Welsh " were but people of small account." Nevertheless they brought him a third time over the marches, chasing a will-o'-the-wisp that drew him into hilly lands with not a living soul to be killed or captured. This time a Welshman offered to betray his leader, he led the King of England as far from Owen as he could, and then confessed his duplicity ; he was instantly drawn, hanged, beheaded and quartered. As Hotspur had to defend the marches almost wholly out of his own pocket he resigned from the council and returned to his lands in the north ; his place was taken by Rutland and the Earl of Worcester.

WHILE the Prince and his council were trying to corner Owen, Henry in England was pouncing on the lollards. Wycliffe himself was no more, he had died on New Year's Eve, 1384, of a paralytic stroke ; on the eve of the coming year, in the dawn of liberty, of the breaking of the chains that held England, economically and morally, in the grip of foreigners, Wycliffe ceased to lead the people. His doctrines lived and lived the stronger for persecution, they were to spread to Bohemia, from Bohemia to Germany, and from Germany back to England. It is during the age of Wycliffe and not of Henry VIII that the birth of Protestantism should be dated. In Wycliffe's early years the commons had been strongly on his side, but the Peasants' Revolt lost him many supporters, for it was felt that to stand by any revolutionary doctrine, particularly a doctrine affecting property, was dangerous. It was not, however, until after the death of Simon of Sudbury, Archbishop of Canterbury, that the persecution really began, for his successor, William Courtenay, was a powerful aristocrat who detested lollardy. In May 1382, he summoned a church council to discuss Wycliffe's doctrines : first, that most violent doctrine of all, the disbelief in the wine and bread turning literally and not symbolically into blood and flesh ; then the lesser heresies, the belief that a priest in mortal sin was unworthy of administering the sacraments and that Christ had not ordained the ceremonies of the mass, that contrition was more important than confession, and that confession was often superfluous, and that there should be no more Popes. All these doctrines were condemned as heresies, and Wycliffe noted with eager glee that God instantly vented His displeasure on the very afternoon this announcement was made by sending such an earthquake as England had not known for years. The bishops were terrified and would have fled the shaking building had not Courtenay insisted on them keeping their places.

This was the first open blow at lollardy, but real action was not taken until the reign of Henry IV when parliament in 1401 passed the terrible and famous statute, *De heretico comburendo*. It was not introduced by the commons but by the clergy's parliament or convocation which pleaded with the King for a statute to forbid unlicensed speaking and the preaching or teaching of opinions " contrary to the Catholic faith, or the determination of holy Church," and asked also that the prohibition should include writing as well as speaking, and to words spoken in private as well as in public. The King, an orthodox man, agreed, and the statute was passed. Courtenay was dead, but the new primate was an even more zealous anti-lollard—this was Archbishop Arundel who had returned from exile with Henry. Arundel is rather a pathetic figure, he was driven by a kind of fury into persecution, yet there was humanity in him and often he would weep at the spectacle of some poor wretch he had doomed to a revolting death. The statute was introduced at the right moment, for while Richard himself had been a most faithful papist, many of his courtiers, like Queen Anne, had been touched by lollardy ; it was therefore felt that while striking at the heretics, parliament was also striking at Richard's party.

The first victim was William Sawtree, " alias Chatrys," chaplain of St. Osith's, London, who, with John Purvey, an aged friend of Wycliffe's, was brought to trial before convocation. Sawtree was tried first, on February 12, and was charged with certain heresies, including the importance of preaching above church service, the adoration due to the True Cross, and— most vital of all—for having remarked " that after the words of consecration in the eucharist, the bread remains bread, and nothing more." Sawtree confessed to the charges, he said that a priest should preach rather than say " hours," and that, after all, " hours " might well be omitted for more important duties such as confession or the study of the scriptures ; he said that he would adore Christ crucified but not the cross itself except with " vicarious adoration " as a " memorial " ; he was equally straightforward about transubstantiation, saying that while bread and wine remained bread and wine after consecration they became symbolic. Arundel did his best to bring the man to reason, he argued with him, perhaps realising that a public burning would not destroy heresy but would rather strengthen it. Sawtree was no coward, although he tried to wriggle out of some of the lesser charges, muttering, " I do not know," " I do not understand ; " from the important question, his disbelief in transubstantiation, he would not shift. On February 26, convocation sentenced him to be publicly degraded in St. Paul's.

It was at this point that the power of the Church ended, and it is at this point that modern Catholic apologists shrug their shoulders and talk about their Church shrinking from the taking of blood. Such statements are mere quibbling of the worst kind. The Church commanded the temporal power to shed the blood, although the sentence was not passed in its own courts ; the Church never had had the right to condemn men to death, as we have seen with Thomas Becket's murderers who escaped scot free. When Sawtree was passed to the secular arm for punishment it was exactly as if the Church itself had condemned him, because the secular arm would not have dared to release him. On March 2 he was burnt alive at Smithfield, and the spectacle was enough to make John Purvey hurriedly recant. There were a great many recantations, which were exactly what the Church desired, and it might have seemed that lollardy would die for lack of martyrs, although by now it had a powerful grip on the people and it was said that if you met two men on any road in England, one was sure to be a lollard. The wealthy classes with the fall of Richard had soon hidden their beliefs or dropped all touch with the lollards, but with the poor and what we would call the middle class, it grew stronger every day, particularly in the cities. London was almost completely lollard.

At last Richard's little widow returned to France, with the dowry question not yet settled. The Welsh fighting died every now and again only to flare with redoubled violence, and at home Henry was having his troubles. He received anonymous letters, and a conspiracy was discovered in his household at Westminster which he preferred not to investigate. Then on top of it all came news that Richard II was alive in Scotland. None knew better than Henry that the rumour was untrue, but men swore that they had seen the ex-King and evidently there was another Maudeleyn impersonating him. Jean Creton the chronicler, when sent to investigate, swore that the " mummet " was not Richard, but men will believe what they wish to believe,

and quite a few Englishmen wished to believe that Richard lived.
Henry was ruthless on this question, he immediately executed anyone found spreading the rumour.

Owen Glendower was for once extremely fortunate ; he captured Sir Edmund Mortimer, uncle of King Richard's heir, the
little Earl of March. Later, it was suggested that Mortimer
allowed himself to be captured : that is difficult to credit, as
the battle in which he was taken was a very bloody one. Owen
treated his prisoner as an honoured guest and rapidly began to
undermine his loyalty.

Again Henry invaded Wales only to be defeated by the
weather. He was nearly killed by his tent falling on top of him,
and had it not been for the protection of his armour he might have
been stabbed with his own lance. The English swore, as wind
and rain swept down, whirling away tents and baggage, that
Owen Glendower was a wizard who could swing the weather to
his will with an incantation. Henry had to turn back without a
fight.

But while he struggled with the weather, the Percies, father and
son had struggled with living Scots, and had defeated them at the
battle of Homildon Hill. It is now for the first time that we see
Henry behaving in a tactless fashion. The Percies had captured
some valuable prisoners and Henry, against all rules of war,
demanded that they be surrendered to him. Probably he
wished to break the power of the Percies, already the strongest
nobles in England ; otherwise this act is impossible to explain in
the life of a man who showed himself always most careful to infuriate nobody. Hotspur refused to obey, but at last he agreed
to release his most important prisoner if Henry would ransom
Sir Edmund Mortimer from Owen. Mortimer was very friendly
with Owen, therefore Henry was suspicious, and would not agree
to Hotspur's arrangement ; he had every right to be suspicious,
as very soon Mortimer married Owen's daughter Katherine and
issued a circular to his friends and tenants in Radnorshire stating
that if Richard lived he would be rescued and returned to the
throne, if dead, the rightful heir, the Earl of March, should have
the crown ; and he got in touch with the great and truculent
Hotspur.

IT was the decisive moment. Henry had no one to stand beside
him except his young son the Prince of Wales, now fifteen years of
age and already a proved soldier in Welsh guerilla-fighting.

Yet for all the worries of that year, even when under the threat of rebellion, Henry could pause to wed Joan of Navarre, the widow of Duke John IV of Brittany. He had first seen her— at least, to our knowledge—just previous to his invasion of England, while he paused at the court of Brittany. When her husband died, Joan secretly procured a dispensation from the Pope giving her permission to marry whomsoever she liked, and she liked Henry. On April 3, 1402, she was betrothed to him by proxy at Eltham, and she landed in England on January 13 or 14 of the following year, after five days of seasickness in the Channel.

Henry met her at Winchester, where they were married on the 7th in the Church of St. Swithin. The bridal-feast was vastly expensive and included a " sootilte," which was either a sculptured confection or a play. London, as usual, made splendid preparations to greet its new Queen, the mayor and aldermen and sheriffs riding to Blackheath attended by the members of the different gilds in brown and blue and with scarlet hoods. Joan was crowned at Westminster on Sunday 25th.

It is naturally impossible to know whether Henry loved his second wife, but she had strong political alliances that induce one to think that he had reasons apart from love for the union ; besides, he probably felt that his family needed a woman's hand, and Joan had proved herself the good mother of six children. She must have been at this date in her early thirties and, judging by her effigy in Canterbury Cathedral, she was handsome enough. Her life had not been an easy one, we can therefore excuse her avariciousness, and we can also excuse her love for the children of her first marriage, a love that in later years was to cause her to be charged with witchcraft.

BUT Henry had little time to waste on nuptials. He arranged for tournaments to amuse and honour his Queen ; but more deadly tournaments were coming in which he would have to stake his life and crown against the fury of the Percies and the Welsh. There was a pretence of friendship at the moment, but Henry must have known that at any moment the mask of amiability would be thrown aside and helmets would be donned. He thought to take action before the Percies, perhaps to scare them by a show of force ; on July 4 he rode with an army from London, pretending friendliness, writing that he was coming to support " his dear and trusty cousins in the battle against the Scots, so honourably undertaken by them." While Henry rode north, Hotspur rode south to join Glendower, he entered Cheshire of which he was justiciar, and distributed White Hart badges to the people, telling them that Richard was alive. To Henry—whom he called " Henry, Duke of Lancaster "—he sent a formal defiance, stating that the King had broken all his promises, that he had forced his election by parliament to the exclusion of the Earl of March, and that he had murdered Richard by cold and hunger.

When he knew that rebellion had truly broken out, Henry called for levies and started immediately in pursuit. Hotspur rode south with his Cheshire reinforcements, trying to meet Glendower, and after about a forty-five mile march from Lichfield he came to Shrewsbury on July 21 ; the banner of Henry was on the walls and it did not flutter down to the trumpetings of rebels. The gates remained closed and wearily Hotspur had to lead his men three miles towards Whitchurch until he reached a small hill by the roadside. He drew up his men in a field known as Hayteley with a stretch of thick peas before them, and with mushy ground and scattered ponds below the slope on which he waited.

Henry was riding fast, he came to Shrewsbury, then hurried on, desiring combat. Early on the morning of the 21st he drew his army into three battles, giving the van to the Earl of Stafford, himself taking the centre, and Prince Henry the rear. Watching the enemy move into place, Hotspur called for his sword, and it could not be found. It was his favourite weapon, used in all his battles, and it seems that it had been left behind at the village of Berwick where he had slept the night before. Hotspur blanched when he was told, he cried, "We have ploughed our last furrow, for a wizard in mine own country prophesied that I should die at Berwick ! "

Henry did not wish to fight. Always it was his desire to temporise, and he sent the Abbot of Shrewsbury to offer terms. Hotspur, perhaps fearful at the loss of his sword, instructed the Earl of Worcester to see the King, but Worcester was a haughty man and he met Henry's peaceful suggestions with a taunt. "You rob the country every year," he cried, "and always say that you have nothing, that your treasurer has nothing, you make no payments, keep no house, you are not the rightful heir ! " Henry tried his best to placate him, but the earl retorted : "We cannot trust you." "Then on you must rest the blood shed this day and not on me," said the King.

Shortly after midday the fight started. " Suddenly blew the trumpets, the King's part crying ' St. George upon them ! ' the adversaries cried ' Esperance Percy ! ' and so the two armies furiously joined." The Prince, eager to win his spurs in battle, could not leash his patience, and even before the cry was given, he had begun the advance. He marched into a storm of arrows from Hotspur's archers, " than whom no better could be found in all Cheshire." Through the field of unreaped corn and tangle of peas the Prince charged gallantly only to have an arrow pierce his cheek. He would not turn to have it dressed, " lest his departure from amongst his men might haply have stricken some fear into their hearts." His friends besought him to retire. " My lords," he answered, " far be it from me such disgrace, as that, like a craven I should stain my novitiate in arms by running away. If the Prince runs, who will stay to end the battle ? Believe me, to be carried off before victory would be everlasting death ! Lead me, I implore you, to the very face of the enemy. I would never say to my comrades, ' Get you first to the fight.' It is mine to cry, ' Follow me, my friends ! ' " With blood-stained face, he led his men into the hail of arrows. His father swept round to his rescue, although rescue was not needed. So furious was his charge that the Prince crumpled the rebels' right against their own left, and the battle became so confused that you could barely tell friend from foe. Hotspur and the Earl of Douglas—whom he had captured on Homildon Hill, and whose ransom had started the trouble—would " fight neither with small nor great, but only with the King." Followed by thirty men they hacked a path through the medley of bodies until they reached the royal standard itself and ripped it from its staff. Douglas, using a mace, smashed his way along ; Henry he could not find, he killed only " the appearance of the King," never the King himself. Then suddenly Hotspur died, was struck down by an unknown hand ; he was killed " and no man wist of whom." His troops missed his great presence, they failed to see his bloodied sword flashing above the swords of lesser men, they cried, seeking to hear his answer, " Henry Percy King, Henry Percy King ! " and the King of England ran before them and with his own voice answered, " Henry Percy dead, Henry Percy dead ! "

Even now, with their leader killed, the rebels would not surrender. Stubbornly they died in heaps ; from midday until after sunset the battle continued. Only darkness brought an end. Men could not tell comrade from foe, they stumbled amidst the corn and peas and slipped in the ponds and on the blood, until at last exhausted they lay on the ground and slept " in mixed heaps, weary, and beaten, and bleeding." And dawn found them, enemies, comrades, lying on the wet and slimy ground, gazing into each other's startled faces amongst the tumbled bodies of the slain.

HOTSPUR was killed, the rebellion crushed, but the spirit of the dead Percy was almost as powerful as the living man. His reckless manners, his courage and violent death made the people treasure his memory. The King himself wept over the body of him who once had been his friend, yet sentiment did not make Henry sentimental, he dared not give honourable burial to the corpse of a rebel. He had the body dug from the church in which friends had placed it, he put it into a common cart and carried it to Shrewsbury, where, after being rubbed in salt as a preservative, it was pushed between two upright stones for a warning in the pillory. The head was sent to be spiked above the gate of York, while the heads of other rebels were taken to decorate London Bridge.

Only a few days after the battle—so strong was the perverse bitterness of the people at the death of Hotspur—the King was forced to send messages through England warning his subjects not to speak ill of the government, then he had to take horse for the north where Hotspur's father was prepared to start fighting. Henry calmed his rage and fear, pardoned him, and returned south.

It is difficult to understand why Owen did not join Hotspur at Shrewsbury. Tradition states that he watched the fight from a distance, but that can scarcely be believed. If he had rallied to Hotspur's aid, the Lancastrian line would have ended on that day. Yet he remained idle, and the only explanation one can offer is that he was so used to the Welsh tactics—the guerrilla-fighting on mountains and in valleys—that he dared not lead undisciplined troops into a pitched battle. Whatever the cause of his absence, it lost him an opportunity he was never to have again. The moment the victorious English left the country, he swooped down on one of his raids—and this act seems so feeble, so petty after the brave show of Hotspur, that one finds it difficult to forgive him for staying away while others died in a cause that was partly his own.

31

WHEN he had recovered from his wound, the Prince again took command in Wales, and did his task well despite lack of funds and inexperience. Owen continued his furious raids, his sudden rushes of bowmen and knifemen into undefended villages, or fell upon armies and towns when they were unprepared. Desperately the Prince held his own against heavy odds, even when French troops came to help the rebels.

The Earl of Northumberland, Hotspur's father, rebelled, but Henry crushed his rising before it barely started, and Northumberland fled to Scotland, from whence he managed to reach Wales. It was now, if ever, that the famous Tripartite Indenture was drawn up, the division of England between Northumberland and Mortimer, with Owen taking Wales for his share. Then the Prince led so brisk an attack into the country that Northumberland fled again, this time to Brittany. Young Henry decided that there was only one way of subduing the country, and that was to re-take Aberystwyth which Owen had captured from the English. The castle was deemed impregnable, so cannon were shipped from Bristol to smash in the walls, and as two of these clumsy creatures merely blew themselves up, the Prince preferred to starve the besieged into surrender. In a short time the famished garrison was asking for terms and agreed, according to medieval custom, to give the castle to the Prince if not relieved by a certain date. When Owen was told of this agreement, he swore to chop off the captain's head if he abided by it. The Prince, after a most severe winter, divided his forces ; while half squatted outside Aberystwyth, he led the remainder to besiege Owen's headquarters at Harlech. This was really the end of the rebellion. Mortimer died during the siege, and when at last Harlech fell—not long after Aberystwyth—the Prince took captive Owen's wife, his two daughters and his three grandchildren. They were sent to the Tower.

We do not know the end of Owen. He disappears from history, lurking somewhere in the mountains of his homeland and stubbornly refusing to accept any pardons offered, no matter how tempting. His rebellion had been a brave attempt, yet it lacked unity ; perhaps that was inevitable amongst scattered people like the Welsh. While giving Owen all praise possible, the thought persists—what was he doing when Hotspur fell at Shrewsbury ? It was the apex of the rebellion, his one magnificent chance, and he did not take it. Perhaps there is some simple explanation so far unknown. I hope that is the truth. Shrewsbury is the one mark one cannot rub out, the one smear on a record of courage and patriotism.

WHILE the Prince had been crushing Owen, and thereby learning the art of war that was to bring him such glory on the Continent in after years, the King had been struggling with problems of finance and with parliament's efforts to reform his household. Henry was not extravagant, but he was in that awkward position, so familiar to many of us, of never being able to catch his debts. Richard had exhausted the exchequer and Henry had to pay for it, he had to skimp and had even to withhold most necessary funds from the Prince during the Welsh campaigns. When he asked parliament for help, it insisted on his getting rid of the Queen's foreign friends and relations and on reforming his household, on stopping waste and expelling his " rascally " retinue. Henry inevitably had to give in, for parliament had the whip-hand. The people were not strongly enough on the King's side for him to dare speak for himself. He was a usurper and was never permitted to forget it.

Then began the tragic separation with his eldest son. This whole question is so vague and has been so distorted that it is now almost impossible to discover the truth. That Henry and the Prince ever really quarrelled I do not believe ; that there was a strong difference of opinion between them cannot be doubted. There were now two parties at court, one was controlled by Henry Beaufort, Bishop of Winchester, and the other—the royal—one by Archbishop Arundel. The Prince was with the Beauforts, the more or less reactionary group that wanted expansion for their youth, fighting oversea, the spreading of England's glory. The French question brought the parties definitely to opposite extremes.

Charles VI of France was very often a lunatic who foamed at the mouth and ate his food like a dog ; and with a madman on the throne, two parties fought for power—the party of Burgundy and the party of Orléans. Both had a grip on the court—Orléans because he was the Queen's lover, and John of Burgundy because his daughter was betrothed to the Dauphin ; then Burgundy had Orléans murdered in the streets of Paris, and most surprisingly the city welcomed him as a saviour. But the widow of Orléans was determined on revenge which she strove to make her easy-going son Charles swear to undertake ; when she died, Charles so little reverenced his father's memory that he swore peace with Burgundy. The peace was not kept, Charles's father-in-law, Bernard Comte d'Armagnac, forced him to action, and again France was split into civil war — Burgundians against the Armagnacs.

England thought to take a hand in the trouble, and then began the difference of opinion between father and son. While the King was unwell—he was a very sick man nowadays—the Prince controlled the council, and he sealed a pact with Burgundy, sending reinforcements that won a great and almost decisive victory. The King, however, favoured the Armagnacs and he objected to his son's high-handed act ; he sealed a treaty with the opposite party and sent men to Orléans' aid. But by the time they arrived, the two factions had embraced, and it cost the Armagnacs a large sum to bribe their too-enthusiastic allies to go home.

That is really all that can be made out of the quarrel between father and son. Perhaps, too, feelings were aggravated by the behaviour of Archbishop Arundel, who in his battle with heresy made a sudden descent on Oxford which he forced to condemn the teachings of Wycliffe. The Prince was a friend of Richard Courtenay, chancellor of the university, and he defended the rights of Oxford. This seems rather a peculiar attitude for young Henry, who was later to become a fanatical hater of lollardy, but in these early years he had not perhaps definitely formed his opinions. He was young enough and human enough to feel compassion for the oppressed. We see this division in him, this conflict between fanaticism and humanity, in his behaviour towards John Badby, a lollard burnt at Smithfield. The lollards had grown so strong that only force could hope to destroy them. In the provincial synod at St. Paul's, January 1409, Arundel republished his constitutions against the Wycliffe heresies. Preaching was repressed by this fresh edict, unlicensed clergy were not to speak without permission from their bishop, and this permission was only to be granted after the applicant had been cross-examined, teachers in art or grammar were not to discuss theology, no one was to translate the scriptures into English, or even to read them aloud under the penalty of excommunication, and no disputes were to be permitted on questions settled by the authority of Rome. With his re-publication of the constitutions, Arundel looked around for another example so as to impress upon the people the dangers of meddling with Church affairs. He fastened on one John

Badby, a tailor of Evesham, who had been tried by the diocesan court of Worcester in January 1409 where he had made the heretical announcement—" How could Christ, sitting at supper with His disciples, give them His living body to eat ? " He was brought before convocation in London on March 1, but nothing could shift his beliefs. Gamely he stood by his faith even when he was chained at Smithfield above the faggots smeared with brimstone to make them burn the merrier. The Prince of Wales was standing nearby and he was touched by the man's courage and devotion. He asked Badby if he would recant and he offered him threepence a day if he would only accept the Church's infallibility. As the fire was about to be lit, the Prince thought he saw weakness show in the poor tailor and commanded that he be unchained. Badby even then would not give in, and he " burnt was unto ashen dry."

Young Henry, who later was to win such magnificent battles, saw something in the calm heroism of the poor tailor that must have affected him deeply—a power that would not flinch from slow and painful death, a fanaticism that all the fires in Smithfield could never smoke away.

KING HENRY was a very sick man. He had a great tumour beneath his nose, and his flesh was rotting. The Parisians reported that his toes and fingers had dropped off, and the Scots—whose Prince had been taken at sea and was now an honoured captive in England—said that his body had shrunk to the size of a twelve-year-old child. A reputable authority tells us that his face was " so foul that leprous doth appear," while others were satisfied with a bare mention of leprosy, by which the modern scourge need not always be meant. In medieval times all skin-diseases, even eczema, were classed as leprosy. I owe to my friend Dr. Philip Nelson the suggestions that Henry's real disease was peripheral dry-gangrene due to eating rye-bread infected with ergot. According to Dr. Nelson this disease, " variously called St. Anthony's Fire, Ignis infernalis, or Igner sacer, was in early times not infrequently mistaken for erysipelas." [1]

---

[1] See *The Antiquaries' Journal*, July 1934. The actual disease was first noted, *circa* 858, at Xanten, in Germany, and was caused by the fungus *claviceps purpurea*. In his collection, Dr. Nelson has a gold signet-ring, *circa* 1500, which was worn as a protection against ergotism ; on each shoulder it bears a Tau cross. Dr. Nelson suggests that the shape of this cross—like our letter T—might be symbolic of a crutch. It was the usual sign of St. Anthony.

The disease, whatever it was, made the King often incapable of attending council or parliament. His latter years must have been agony with the rotting of his body and his fears for his son's loyalty. Special doctors were summoned from abroad, and Henry's one consolation was his friendship with old Archbishop Arundel. He often stayed with Arundel, visiting him for quite long periods, yet ever keeping by his side his Dominican confessor lest death leap suddenly and take him unawares. Ghastly to look upon, unable to sit a horse, he yet clung to power, trying to hold public affairs completely in his hands. Sometimes he was overheard muttering to himself, pleading with God to bring the end quickly, for life was terrible, too terrible to be borne.

Then God took pity on His servant, striking him during Lent, 1413, while he was making offerings in Westminster at the shrine of St. Eadward. He was seen suddenly to stagger and fall, and his attendants carried him through the quiet shadowed cloisters to the Abbot's Palace, and laid him on a pallet before the fire in the chamber called the Bethlehem or Jerusalem Chamber. As he lay gasping before the fire, the crown was brought and placed upon a cushion of cloth-of-gold at his side. That was the custom. Gradually his limbs became frozen as if he lay on ice that seeped into the blood, and the watchers could detect no breathing ; they thought him dead and covered his tragic ugly face with a silk napkin. News was sent to the Prince and he came at once, taking the crown from its cushion and bearing it off. Abruptly the King sighed and the attendants lifted the napkin and saw that he lived. He gazed wonderingly about him and noticed the empty cushion ringed by the weight of the vanished crown. The Prince explained that, being the eldest son, he had taken it for safety and Henry asked—" What right have you to it, my son, seeing that I had none ? " " Sire," replied the Prince, " as you have held and kept it by the sword, so will I hold and keep it while my life shall last." " Do as you will," said his father, " I commend me to God, and pray that He may have mercy upon me." He looked about him and, seeing his confessor, John Tille, asked what he did there ; Tille told him that he had come to administer the last sacrament. They lifted the dying King on his pallet while his confessor told him to repent for the killing of Richard and for his usurpation, but Henry answered that the Pope had absolved him, and as for the usurpation—his sons would never give up the crown even if he demanded it. He took the Prince into his arms and kissed him. Then he counselled the lad to do good, to pay his debts, to remain true to his friends, to seek peace with wise confessors and counsel from learned ministers, and to work always for the honour and glory of England.

Thus King Henry IV, having " made a happy end," died on St. Cuthbert's Day, March 20, 1413. And it was noted that he who in his youth had had to turn back with the sight of the Holy City in his eyes, and who in later years had dreamed of leading a crusade to the rescue of Palestine, now had his wishes granted— he died in the Chamber of Jerusalem.

His body was carried from Westminster by barge to Gravesend, and from there taken by road to Canterbury to be buried in the cathedral, on the north side of the shrine of St. Thomas Becket. It had been his wish to lie here, beside his uncle, " the Prince Edward," and that was only right. The usurper's bones should not be entombed amongst the bones of the rightful Kings of England in Westminster, that family gathering encircling St. Eadward's lofty shrine. He was carried to quiet Canterbury, as lonely in death as when he had lived.

And was there a desire to plead forgiveness, to propitiate that haughty tormented man, the Black Prince, in thus asking to be buried near him ? Did he wish to lie there for ever, eternally imploring forgiveness from the father of the King Richard whom he had deposed and, perhaps, murdered ?

XIV

KING HENRY THE FIFTH

1413-1422

THE NIGHT OF HIS FATHER'S DEATH, Henry of Monmouth stayed with a hermit in Westminster, preparing for the great part he was to play, a part that he was to play most seriously. From this moment he changed as suddenly as Thomas Becket had changed on becoming archbishop ; no longer do we hear tales of riotous nights in Eastcheap, few Kings have been so chaste, so single-hearted as King Henry V. The coronation was performed on Passion Sunday, April 9, 1413, Henry being then twenty-five years of age. On the previous day, he knighted young men of birth and rank, as was customary, but it is surprising to find amongst those admitted to his father's Order of the Bath—so called because one's feet were always washed before a great religious ceremony—Edmund Mortimer, Earl of March, and his brother Roger March. In this simple fashion did the new King announce that he did not fear rivals to the throne, that the Lancastrian usurpation was no longer a usurpation but the founding of a dynasty.

It was " a sore ruggie and tempestuous day," when Henry set out on his state ride from the Tower to Westminster. He was attended by the fifty new knights and by the great nobles of his kingdom. Again the oil given to Becket by the Holy Virgin was used to consecrate a King of England. Henry sat upon a scaffolding draped with cloth-of-gold and erected between the altar and the quire. Arundel officiated, and the watchers, standing in the august shadows of the abbey, gazed speculatively at the solemn young man who was to be their King and listened to the thudding of hail on the roof, the lashing of rain on the painted windows. Some whispered that this storm was a bad omen, others answered that it was a good omen foretelling that the evils of the past would be washed from England. It was impossible to read the thoughts of the King ; no light shone in his eyes, no smile was on his lips.

Humbly and devoutly he went through the tedious proceedings, and even afterwards at the banquet he sat mute, brooding perhaps on the sins of youth or dreaming of great conquests. He sat in a marble chair and looked " like an angel." The cooks had used all their art to make the feast a memorable one, the concoctions of sweet foods were enough to make a modern digestion wince at the bare thought, and many of them were moulded into the usual subtleties, into figures sprouting trite advice on government. Mounted servitors carried the food along the hall, and the gathering of minstrels was particularly large, perhaps because the young King was very fond of music. Dymock, dressed in full steel upon his destrer, made his customary challenge, and, of course, it was not accepted, not even by those who remembered sadly the days of Richard and who thought the Earl of March the rightful heir.

During the feasting, the toasting, the laughter, the new King never moved. Outside the painted windows snow fluttered down, it was a winter such as these men had never known before ; and in the lighted hall, with long tables drawn against the draughty walls and with the King on his marble chair upon the dais, with a great fire roaring in the open hearth in the centre and whirling up flames and black-grey smoke towards the hidden painted louvre, in all the warmth and merriment, the new King never smiled, he did not eat nor drink, he sat like a statue, unheeding what was spoken and staring before him.

For three days afterwards he did not eat. Like a hermit preparing himself for a holy vision, Henry V began his reign as if he would wash every sin from body and mind.

WE have stories about the wild youth of Henry of Monmouth, but they are mainly of late invention. The contemporary chroniclers are satisfied with a bare statement of lechery and brawling. " The Prince was in his youth an assiduous cultor of lasciviousness," writes Thomas Elmham who knew him well, " and addicted exceedingly to instruments of music. Passing the bounds of modesty, he was the servant of Venus as well as of Mars ; youthlike, he was fired with her torches, and in the midst of the worthy works of war found leisure for the excesses common to ungoverned age." Titus Livius de Frulovisiis (*circa* 1440) writes : " He exercised meanly the feats of Venus and Mars and other pastimes of youth for so long as the King his father lived." From Thomas Walsingham (*circa* 1422) we learn :

" As soon as he was made King he was changed suddenly into another man, zealous for honesty, modesty and gravity ; there being no sort of virtue that he was not anxious to display."

With this consensus of contemporary and near-contemporary evidence it is impossible to deny that Prince Henry of Monmouth was a wild lad although he became a chaste King Henry V. For once, Shakespeare was not far off the mark, but his creations of Falstaff and Bardolph—great literary figures though they be— are terrible libels on two honest and brave men. We have not the space to examine the stories about Henry's youth—I have gone into them in detail elsewhere [1]—but the verdict remains more or less an open one. All that can be stated is that he spent much of his time in the pleasure that most young lads desire above all others—in the arms of women. When we recall the fact that he was almost continually fighting from the age of fifteen, we can understand that the few months he could steal from war should be filled with every conceivable joy before the inevitable return to Welsh knives and arrows.

HENRY has been called with truth the perfect knight of chivalry. He is, in fact, so very perfect as to seem inhuman. When studying his reign, the feeling often creeps over one that this was not a man at all, that he was a machine acting a preordained part to the call of some medieval poet. We see him first as the reckless lecher in the stews of Bankside, then when the crown is on his head we find him change abruptly to a saint in armour, to a saint who slays the dragon of heresy, defeats giants and wins in the end the love of the woman he desires. It is perfect yet it is true ; the short life of Henry V remains one of the most exciting and inspiring tales in history.

[1] *King Henry V: A Chronicle,* by Philip Lindsay (Howard Baker Publishers), 1969, pp. 115–128. Also, for a defence of Henry, *The Story of Prince Henry and Judge Gascoigne,* by F. Solly Flood (*Royal Historical Society Transactions,* new series, vol. iii.), and for a discussion of the different Falstaffs, amusing but unconvincing, *The Two Sir John Falstolfs,* by L. W. Vernon Harcourt (*R.H.S.T.* 3rd ser. vol. iv.). Mr. Flood has also a strong defence of Henry in *Prince Henry of Monmouth—His Letters and Dispatches during the War in Wales* (*R.H.S.T.* new ser. vol. iv.). Reference should be made to *Henry V,* by J. D. Griffith Davies (Barker, 1935), pp. 83–95 ; *The Reign of Henry V,* by J. H. Wylie (Cambridge, 1914), vol. i. pp. 186–201 ; *Henry V,* by R. B. Mowat (Constable, 1919), pp. 60–85 ; *Henry V,* by C. L. Kingsford (Putnam's, 1903), pp. 80–93 ; *A History of England under Henry IV,* by J. H. Wylie (Longmans, 1898), vol. iv. pp. 91-99.

It is perhaps difficult to love Henry, but it is impossible not to admire him, not to be thrilled at least by the glories of Agincourt. To the men of his own time he represented the perfection of knighthood. " He was a Prince of high understanding," writes an enemy, " and of a great will to keep justice. Wherefore the poor folk loved him above all others. For he was prone and careful to preserve the lesser folk and to protect them from the violence and wrong that most of the nobles had done them." This side of Henry, his sympathy with the poor, interested his contemporaries because it was extremely unusual, but he was only following his father whose Scottish invasion is notable because so many lives were spared. We have seen how the Black Prince, that pattern of chivalry slaughtered the common people of Limoges and freed the knights ; Henry was never capable of that kind of act, save at Rouen, and his cruelty there was necessary. The only times that we discover a really brutal and vindictive streak in him is when his dignity was harmed. At the siege of Meaux, for example, he took vengeance after its capture on some men who dragged a donkey on to the walls and " made it bray by the force of the blows which they gave it, mocking the English, and saying that this was their King and that they ought to come and help him." After the same siege he also executed an unknown " man who blew the trumpet on the walls "—who apparently made unforgivably insulting noises at him. On this point, on the question of royal dignity, Henry was inflexible, he forgave everything else except this and disloyalty. One of his favourites, Bertrand de Chaumont, who had fought gallantly at Agincourt, was beheaded for accepting bribes to release prisoners. The Duke of Burgundy and Henry's own brother the Duke of Clarence went on their knees, imploring de Chaumont's pardon. " By St. George," answered Henry, " fair brother, had it been yourself we should have done the same." He was always just, and nothing impressed the medieval mind more than that rare quality ; his dearest friend he would execute if he thought he deserved it, his greatest enemy he would pardon if worthy of pardon.

There is one episode that reveals Henry most vividly, a cruel and rather extraordinary episode. During the siege of Louviers he was standing at his tent-flap talking with the Earl of Salisbury when a stone snapped the tent-pole into splinters. After the garrison had surrendered, Henry hanged eight of the gunners who had fired that shot. Such an act as this seems unforgivable :

we recall Richard I pardoning the crossbowman who killed him, and we feel that Henry was moved by personal malice in taking revenge. Yet there was in him a queer touch almost of lunacy that made him believe himself wellnigh divine. His ambition was to bring the western nations to unity under one ruler and under one church : it was the ambition of all medieval men, but Henry if he had not died so young might have achieved it for a brief space. He wished to hold back the growing power of the Turks, to re-take Jerusalem ; and a man with such ambitions, believing himself the chosen of God, is liable to look upon enemies as heretics worthy only of death. Henry did not execute those gunners because they had aimed at King Henry V of England, but because they might have struck down the pre-destined creator of a united western world. He was a crusader, and a crusader was always immune from attack.

Henry was a great politician, and in his hands the terrible Schism of the Church was to end, he was one of the greatest soldiers of the Middle Ages and he was a just ruler, the beloved of his people. The tragedy is that he came too late, that he was born into a period of flux, and all his efforts could not hold back inevitable progress—the freedom of the commons and of the English Church, the growth of the humanities and the fleshy idealism of what we call the renascence. When the medieval world was dying, flowering in decay, Henry V arrived and thought to stop a progress that could not be stopped because it was a progress of thought. Man had outgrown the serfdom of body and mind of the Middle Ages, he was beginning to believe that he could be free, that he could think for himself and act for himself. Henry came at this moment, the great reactionary who filled the western world with wonder at his achievements ; and he came too late. Already the power of the Church was doomed, the Schism had dealt it the final blow, turning Rome into a contemptible battle-ground for the personal ambitions of rival Popes. When France made Avignon the centre of the Roman Church it degraded the Popes for ever in the eyes of England.

Then came Henry with his great dreams, and he healed the Church, he won splendid victories, he made the hearts of Englishmen proud after the shameful loss of their continental fiefs. He was a hater of the lollards and was nicknamed the Priests' Prince, yet we do not find him persecuting to a particularly violent extent ; there was a certain pity in him which he tried to cloak. Rather consciously, I feel, he aped the stern unflinching crusader, masking his emotions, keeping his eyes cold, his lips unsmiling. The chief failing we discover in him was a lack of humour, but humour is often a dangerous quantity, it is liable to make ambitions seem tawdry, to belittle the petty things that great men must idealise if they would remain great.

We have four paintings of Henry, all in the one pose of the profile reproduced here. It is a slightly repellent face, the face of a dummy. From forehead to chin is practically a plumb-line except of course for the nose, which is a very straight sharp-pointed nose turned up a trifle at the tip. The nostrils are long and the ears large, while the mouth is beautifully formed and sensual. That mouth defeats the coldness of the hazel eyes, it proves that the passions of Henry's youth did not die with the donning of the crown, they remained to be held back by his iron will. His is not a pleasant eye, for the upper lid droops in an arrogant fashion, and the brow is curved into that expression of the schoolmaster who is assured of his integrity and doubtful of yours. In the jaw we see the strong will—it is a powerful jaw, the jaw of a fighter, a leader.

The chroniclers give us little worth adding to the painting. Henry, we learn, was handsome, taller than most men, and powerfully but slenderly built. " In wrestling, leaping, and running no man almost durst with him presume ; in casting of great iron bars and heavy stones he excelled commonly all men." His hair was thick and smooth and brown in colour, and it was usually cut into the efficient bowl-crop, being clipped round immediately above the ears and shaved below ; this would be the ideal cut for a soldier as the old-fashioned long tresses must often have swept into the way of the helm or got caught in armour-rivets. His eyes were hazel, and could be as quiet as a dove's, we are told, or as furious as a lion's ; the chin was cleft, the forehead broad, the shape of the face oval.

Being a good churchman he was no jouster nor was he interested in tournaments ; his sports were fishing, hawking, hunting, running and jumping. He was as quick as a hare, and often he would start a deer, chase it, and with the help of two others, bring it down without dogs. He did not spend his days wholly in fighting, sport and statecraft, when he could steal time from his devotions—at which he was most assiduous, never permitting any one to interrupt him at mass—he spent his hours in study, for he was cultured and could write well in the two necessary languages, French and English. When he captured a town he would seize the library as its greatest treasure, and he read practically everything, from books of sport to history and religious works.   We still possess a copy of Chaucer's *Troilus and Criseyde* stamped with his arms when Prince of Wales, and Corpus Christi College, Cambridge, has a translation of St. Bonaventure's *Life of Christ* which contains a charming miniature of Henry enthroned and in which a sixteenth-century hand has written : " This wass sumtyme Kinge Henri the Fifeth his booke." Also he was a patron of Hoccleve who dedicated to him his long and rather wearisome *De Regimine Principum*, and to Lydgate, whom he inspired to write his greatest poem, *The Life of Our Lady*.

A tradition exists that Henry once studied at Oxford, and for many years the chamber over the Queen's College gateway bore a Latin inscription to that effect.   But apart from this, the tradition has no foundation, except that Henry's uncle, Henry Beaufort, was chancellor of Oxford in 1398 when the Prince was eleven years of age—an age suitable for the university.

ONE of the first important acts in Henry's reign was a renewed—or rather the continued—persecution of the lollards, and we now meet the most famous of them all, Sir John Oldcastle, Lord Cobham.   When Shakespeare wrote his *Henry IV* he was actually refurbishing an old play in which the comic character was called Oldcastle, but it was impossible on a Protestant stage to make a jest of one of the most famous martyrs, and therefore Falstaff was born, and another but lesser man was maligned for eternity.

Archbishop Arundel had burned insignificant men, and now he wished to strike at lollardy on high, to drag down some of the great, and Oldcastle was the greatest.   A book he had commissioned was found at a limner's and was seized and passages from it were read before the King.   Henry was amazed to find that such heresies could be written, but Oldcastle had fought with him in Wales and he pleaded with Arundel to suspend proceedings until he could talk personally with his comrade.   Oldcastle repudiated the book, but on being pressed, he told the truth.   He was a lollard.   Patiently Henry argued with him, but no arguments could even dint Oldcastle's faith and he was surrendered to the Church.   The trial took place in St. Paul's chapter-house on Saturday, September 23, 1413, and the accused was first formally asked if he would renounce his beliefs.   Oldcastle said no, he had brought with him his profession of faith, and asked permission to read it loud.   On permission being

given, he read the following four articles : he believed that " the
most worshipful sacrament of the altar is Christ's body in the
form of bread " ; he believed completely in penance and that
to be saved from sin man should be penitent " with true confession " ; " as for images " he considered them a matter of
faith, being " calenders to lewd [*ignorant*] men to bring to mind the
passion of Christ and the martyrdom and good living of other
saints " ; he did not think pilgrimages essential to grace, for " he
that knoweth not, nor will not know, nor keep the holy commandments of God in his living here, albeit that he go on pilgrimage to all the world, and he die so, he shall be damned ;
and he that knoweth the holy commandments of God and keep
them to his end, he shall be saved, though he never in his life
go on pilgrimage, as men use now, to Canterbury or to Rome,
or to any other place."

Admitting that these four articles contained much that was
" Catholic and good," Arundel asked Oldcastle two vital questions:
did the bread in transubstantiation remain material bread ? and
was confession valuable if a man who could have gone to a priest
deliberately went to one who was not ordained ? These were
the two test-questions on which the Church was founded, and
Oldcastle tried to wriggle aside by refusing to answer, although
Arundel warned him that if he were not careful he would be condemned as a heretic—in other words, he would be burnt alive.
To us, to-day, weakened morally and physically by comfort and
tolerance, it seems incredible that men could face the most
horrible death in the world in defence of their beliefs. Such
courage is almost frightening, but undoubtedly men stirred to
martyrdom are in a condition of hysteria, they are armoured by
enthusiasm against physical hurt.

When convocation reassembled after a brief adjournment,
Oldcastle remained as firm as ever in his beliefs. He had
been given a statement containing the Church's attitude towards
the eucharist, confession, the authority of the Pope and clergy,
and pilgrimages which were " needful to a Christian man."
To these Oldcastle could not agree, he quoted scripture in
support of his faith, then he began to lose his temper ; he called
the Pope the head of Antichrist, the clergy his body and the
four orders of the friars his tail. He swung round towards
the lay spectators and shouted, " These men who are bent
on damning me, mislead themselves and you, and will drag
you down to hell ! Therefore beware of them ! " He was

condemned and passed on to the secular arm for burning. That was on October 10 ; on the 19th, he somehow escaped from the Tower of London, and the lollards felt that now was the time for them to prove their strength, that they must make some effort to withstand the organisation of Rome. Bills were fixed to London church doors declaring that 100,000 men were prepared to rise, and messages were sent to friends in the country, promising 50,000 London apprentices and servants in case of a revolt.

By taking arms in this fashion, the lollards shifted the question from a moral to a political one, and destroyed whatever hopes they had of undermining the Church. The great progress in thought since the days of Wycliffe should have made them realise that it would not be long before public opinion in England would itself defeat the Roman overlord. Yet they were afraid of the new King, whom they called the Priests' Prince. Force was decided on, and then some would-be murderers were arrested in the palace-grounds. The lollards arranged to meet in St. Giles' Fields, outside the city walls, on January 9, 1414. We are not certain what they intended doing, and probably they were not quite certain themselves, except vaguely to rebel against the Church and probably to seize Henry and force him pass some statutes decreeing freedom of religious thought and worship. Protestant writers have tried to make this gathering in St. Giles seem a kind of prayer-meeting, but it cannot be doubted that the lollards intended to rebel. When Henry was told—there is inevitably a traitor in all conspiracies and this could scarcely have been a secret as it was conducted on so large a scale—he acted at once. He was at Eltham, and on hearing of the St. Giles' gathering he rode with his brothers, with Archbishop Arundel and others, straight to Westminster, sending messages to London to have the gates barred so that sympathisers could not leave the city, and on the country roads he posted men to waylay lollards travelling to the meeting-place. He was a fearless man, and although his troop was small, he did not pause to gather reinforcements ; he rode direct to the ground itself. Suddenly a meteor flashed over the sky, a spear of flame that seemed hurled out of heaven ; to the lollards it appeared that God had spoken, proclaiming that the new faith would blaze through England ; to the Church also it seemed that God had spoken, telling them to smite with lightning. Henry accepted the omen, he would not listen to the councillors who begged him to wait until dawn, he faced the rebels in St. Giles, and his mere presence was enough to scatter them although his followers must have been greatly outnumbered.

Four new gallows were built on the highroad near St. Giles. They were called the Lollards' Gallows, and thirty-seven condemned men were drawn there to hang, and some had fires lighted under the soles of their feet so that they might suffer both for rebellion and for heresy. The swiftness of the King's justice, his courage and staunch orthodoxy, broke the power of the lollards for the time. They dared not openly rebel after this ; they were driven underground from whence they were dug every now and again for a public burning. The new faith was to stay hidden, but it grew more powerful because of that.

A PIOUS task remained. King Richard II had wished to lie beside his wife in Westminster Abbey in the beautiful tomb himself had raised, and King Henry prepared to fulfil this wish. Perhaps, too, he felt that by offering a splendid funeral to the dead King he was asking forgiveness for his father's act and was rendering homage to a man who had always been most kind to him. It was indeed a splendid funeral, and it crept from Langley at the mournful pace Richard had requested in his will. The body was taken from its lapping of lead, laid in a new elm coffin, draped with black velvet and borne on a horse-bier. One hundred and twenty torches flamed beside it, and by strange irony the banners and guitons of arms used at the funeral of Henry IV were taken from Canterbury and used now for Richard.

Henry attended the service of Westminster and distributed largesse. After fourteen years at Langley, Richard at last lay beside the wife he loved, the wife whose bones had waited for his under the gilt bronze effigies for nineteen years.

HENRY decided to invade France. The French themselves besought him to, for the country was broken into parties, into Burgundian and Armagnac, and each party desired his help. It is doubtful if Henry at this time really intended to steal the throne, he probably wished only to regain England's lost dominions, but the country lay open, and for a man of his courage and ambition it was inevitable that he should seize so great an opportunity. He pledged himself to the Burgundians on May 23, 1414, agreeing to share with them any territory " saving the rights of the King

of France, the Dauphin and their successors " ; he was at the
same time negotiating with the Armagnacs, lulling both sides while
he gathered an army.   There is a tale made heroic by Shake-
peare that the Dauphin offered to send Henry " little balls to
play with, and soft cushions to rest until what time he should
grow to a man's strength," and that Henry answered : " If God
so wills and my life lasts, I will within a few months play such a
game of ball in the Frenchmen's streets that they shall lose their
jest, and gain but grief for their game."   Although nearly contemporary, this tale is difficult to believe.   Had it been true,
negotiations would have been broken at once.   It is more than
likely that it was a recruiting-lure, a propaganda-tale spread
through the country to arouse the people.

At last, after weary months of preparation, Henry was ready
to sail when suddenly a conspiracy was discovered.   The Earl of
March confessed the truth ; he and others, including one of the
King's dearest friends, Henry Lord Scrope, had arranged to
murder Henry and to declare the " mummet " in Scotland their
new King—that is, if he were truly Richard II, if not, March was
to take the throne.   The conspiracy was quite far advanced,
and might have succeeded had not Oldcastle been drawn into
the net ; when Scrope heard that lollards were involved, he was
so outraged that he abused the earl who in terror ran to Henry.
The whole conspiracy seems rather pointless, although it is understandable that March, the true heir, should hunger for the
crown ; Scrope's treachery is truly mysterious and can be explained—as his contemporaries explained it—only by believing
that he was bought by the French.   Henry could not forgive
him ; March he pardoned, but Scrope suffered the full penalty
of treason—he was drawn on a hurdle to the place of execution,
half-hanged, cut down alive and beheaded.   Two other conspirators saved their dignity and were merely beheaded, and
although it might seem a trivial point to us whatever way we
died, it was a serious question to medieval men.   Death itself
they did not fear, they saw it too often and lived perilously,
scrambling always towards a peak of power from which a sudden
blow might at any moment strike them down ; to be beheaded
was almost a patent of nobility, to be hanged was a shame that
would besmirch your descendants.

After this one feeble effort to assert his rights, the Earl of
March gave in before the strong will of Henry.   Never again do
we hear from him any suggestion of treason.

WHEN Henry sailed for France, he told no one of his objective. Each party, Armagnac and Burgundian, had tried to win him, and now they realised that they had drawn a common enemy who might destroy them both. Burgundy made tentative offers to join the Dauphin, but his offers were rejected in terror ; France lay open to an invader, the great cities had to look after themselves, to man their own walls and lead their own armies, for the Dauphin John was a fat lazy creature who preferred cushions to iron-balls or winged steel. The coastal towns frenziedly rebuilt their walls, particularly Boulogne, which seemed the obvious point of attack; Henry instead swept round to Harfleur, the gate to Normandy.

During his negotiations with the Armagnacs Henry had revealed his ambitions—he had demanded from them far more than had been ratified by the Bretigny treaty with Edward III, he wanted all that Henry II had possessed, every strip of continental earth that had ever been owned by a King of England. The request, of course, was hopeless, as Henry well knew ; France could never surrender Aquitaine, Normandy, Anjou, Maine, Touraine, Brittany, Flanders, half Provence (which did not even belong to it) and the territory between the Somme and Gravelines. His ambitions soon became even greater than this. Not very long after his landing—which was conducted without the least opposition—he challenged the Dauphin to a duel, the winner to be crowned King of France. Such gigantic ambitions come as rather a surprise after the reigns of Richard II and Henry IV, but Englishmen could still recall the glorious times of Edward III when a King of France was prisoner in the Tower of London and when a handful of English could defeat huge armies. Nevertheless, this invasion was extraordinarily courageous when one remembers that Henry was the son of a usurper with no actual right to the throne, and while the lollards were waiting to rise and while in Scotland lived a false Richard whom many believed the true King. Despite these dangers, Henry soon after his accession had calmly turned his back on his country as if the land were at peace and as if himself came of a long lineage of hereditary monarchs. Perhaps he thought that war might distract the minds of the people and lure the disaffected abroad. That is very probable ; nevertheless, it was a dangerous act, and only a man of supreme courage and faith in himself would have dared attempt it. But Henry never doubted himself, that was the secret of his genius. He was indeed a god in flesh, a creature of

intense energy and of the noblest fanaticism, fanaticism after all
being only the outlook of a man who believes so utterly in one
idea—which is himself—that nothing counts beside it, that others
can die, that all can be destroyed so long as faith is sustained.
To the very end, when he had to be lifted on to his horse, Henry
kept living within him this divine flame, it never even flickered,
steadily it burned and drove him forward to an end of which
perhaps he was not completely aware—the binding of the western
nations into a united Christian world that could stand against
the rising tide of the insolent Moslems.   This ambition was never
spoken, yet one feels it beneath Henry's actions ; by waging war
actually he wanted peace, peace to attain his ends.   When he
fought with France he undoubtedly believed that he was merely
claiming what was his.   For this reason he did the least he could
to interfere with the people, he attempted to make them remain
in their homes, to continue to trade and to be as they were.
Slowly he won ; slowly with that unfaltering courage of a man who
never doubts himself or his great purpose, he attained everything he set out to attain, until death took him in the midst of his
triumphs.   We should be grateful that he died at that moment.
If he had lived he must have failed.   Like all men of political
genius, like Simon de Montfort, he overrated his abilities and did
not consider the malice of small egoisms.   For this reason utopias
must die, because man is an entity who fights for his own hand.
No matter how sane the government, how noble the dreams of the
leader, those beneath will envy or will squabble amongst themselves.   To have united Europe under one King was a glorious
dream, but its futility can be seen in the decay of the Holy Roman
Empire which had become an empty title for German monarchs.
Henry, with his genius, might for one moment, for one incredibly
splendid moment, have reached the peak of his ambition—it
could never have been for more than a moment.   If there is no
other way out, the jealous hatreds of small men will seek the
assassin's dagger or the poisoned cup.

And after all, the real battle of Henry was not against France,
nor even against living men, he was fighting time.   He stood
for the old world against the new, he wanted to stem the flood of
humanism that was to rise shortly in the renascence.   Like a
knight from the song of a troubadour, he defied dragons, but
dragons were out-of-date ; it was hopeless even for his smallest
ambition to be reached—the recovery of the continental fiefs.
They were gone, Edward III even had come too late.   Modernity

was rising, the people had struck against the old régime, they had risen in the Peasants' Revolt, they had risen as the lollards. New thoughts had taken the place of the old, new beliefs had come. In art, too, this could be seen ; Chaucer wrote in English and scandalised pedants like Gower ; the perpendicular architecture had replaced a purer Gothic ; and painting was no longer a miniature of decorative backgrounds behind prancing beautiful figures, it was becoming realistic under the brush of so great a man as van Eyck. Against all this movement, this growth, Henry V stood out defiantly, the perfect knight, the hero who amazed the world, last of the real medieval Kings.

IN Henry's methods of warfare, however, there was nothing reactionary. His greatgrandfather, Edward III, had always insisted that the primary rule was to avoid sieges, and the very first thing that Henry did when he landed in France was to besiege Harfleur. He had reasons enough. He did not come as the invader, he came as the disinherited claiming his own ; war with France was unavoidable, but he did not desire it ; his strategy was to go calmly from castle to castle, city to city, until either by force or by persuasion, he made each realise that it belonged to him. Unfortunately France would strike because France had stolen his property.

The siege of Harfleur was a long and miserable business, for it was a most powerful city and was considered impregnable. Patiently Henry sent his rams to break through the walls, he sent the pioneers to dig beneath, and his men died around him—not from war, but disease. Pestilence, as was common with medieval armies, broke out amongst the troops in the terrible heat, yet Henry himself showed no sign of fear as day passed day. He walked like any common man through the ranks ; dressed as an ordinary soldier, he personally inspected the walls. Calmly as if in his own palace of Westminster, he went about the routine of siege-work while his men died in scores and while the garrison, although starving, fought with great courage. The siege had begun on August 17, 1415, and it was not until exactly a month later that the captain of the garrison asked for terms. As these were too heavy to accept and the captain hesitated, Henry decided to deliver one concerted attack at dawn, and all night his cannon flamed and spat their great balls of stone and iron. This was too much for the besieged. They again besought terms and promised to surrender by the 22nd at one o'clock if not relieved.

The day arrived without the Dauphin, and the city keys were placed into the hands of Henry. He had won his first continental battle.

It was not a great victory, his army was broken by disease, the ranks thinned—and all for the sake of one city. As he rode through the gates and then walked barefoot to the Church of St. Martin, Henry must have felt that this was but a sorry conquest. Could he return to England and tell the people that all he had to give for money spent and men lost was one city ? Something greater must be achieved, something that would make all Europe look to England with new eyes. Yet before determining on the next adventure, Henry examined the conquered city. He obviously intended to create in Harfleur a second Calais, and while surrendering all movables as plunder to his troops, he divided the citizens into three classes : into those worth ransom, into those strong enough to remain after taking an oath of allegiance to him, and into those infirm or old who would be useless in a city that must withstand continual sieges. The knights he freed on condition that they submitted themselves to him at Calais on November 11 ; and the poor and weak were shepherded out of the gates with five shillings each, only to be robbed by their own countrymen as they sought refuge. And although Henry sent strong inducements to the London merchants to settle in the new Calais, the scheme never prospered.

It may appear a reckless act to have freed the knights on parole, but it was by no means unusual in the days of chivalry ; the ostensible reason was to give them time to collect their ransoms, Henry's true reason was to send them into the country so that they might entice other Norman lords to his banner.

OVER half the army had either died or deserted ; Henry's brave young brother the Duke of Clarence was so ill that he had to be shipped home, twelve hundred men were placed in Harfleur as a garrison, and it would therefore seem that the amount of troops left would be about nine hundred men-at-arms and three thousand archers. With this tiny army Henry declared that he was going to march to Calais. His friends were amazed ; they pointed out that the Dauphin was gathering men at Rouen and that his numbers must be hopelessly larger than Henry's ; yet the King would not listen to cautious advice. " I have," said he, " a great desire to see my lands and places that should be mine by right. Let them assemble their great armies, there is hope in God that they will hurt neither my army nor me,. I will not suffer them, puffed up with pride, to rejoice in misdeeds, nor unjustly, against God, to possess my goods. They would say that through fear I had fled away, acknowledging the injustice of my cause. But I have a mind, my brave men, to encounter all dangers, rather than let them brand your King with word of ill-will. With the favour of God, we will go unhurt and inviolate, and, if they attempt to stay us, victorious and triumphant in all glory."

Splendid boastful words ; from another soldier one might smile at their braggadocio, but coming from Henry, a man with no humour and few conceits, they came from the heart ; and soon he was to prove them no empty boast, no childish rhodomantade of a craven striving to turn away shadows by the reflection only of the sunlight on his sword. Henry was to prove them by the blade and was thereby to make his name one that all Englishmen would treasure for centuries. It was not only glory of this kind that Henry sought ; he knew too well the danger of returning home without a laurel, without even a worthless laurel like a victory in the open field, to lay before the people. He would march to Calais, he swore, through lands armed to withstand him ; defiant of troops gathering at Rouen, without communications, he would march through hostile territory, with a bare handful of men to fight a nation. It was heroic, there are few acts in history to compare with it, and to the eternal glory of Henry V it succeeded.

On Sunday, October 6, he marched with his small troop from Harfleur, taking his baggage with him, his crown, his sword of state, the chancery seals, and a strip of the True Cross six inches long and over an inch wide. He issued strict orders against pillaging, but the French had wasted the land and it was difficult to restrain the men from stealing what they could. There were a few small battles on the way, mere skirmishes, but the worst danger he encountered was in the castle at Boves, where a great store of wine was discovered. The men fought like demons for a drink, and all Henry's efforts to stop them were in vain. " What need ? " said a friend, " the brave fellows are only filling their bottles." " Their bottles ! " cried Henry in disgust, " they are making great bottles of their bellies and getting drunk." Day after day the march continued while the French gathered in force at Rouen. For the moment, disputes were more or less forgotten, although Burgundy still held off, while men rode to fight beneath the standard of their Dauphin. It was a gigantic army but it had no leader, for the Dauphin was a lazy wretch and the knights quarrelled with each other about precedence, old hatreds rising to drown patriotism, Burgundians refusing to serve under Armagnacs, Armagnacs refusing to serve under Burgundians. And while the French squabbled amongst themselves, the feeble army of Henry continued its painful march, half-starved, seeking a passage across the flooded Somme. Bridges everywhere were smashed, and Henry had to turn aside and continue inland. It seemed that he would never be able to pass until he reached the source of the river, yet amidst these dangers, with the continual threat of a huge enemy and with the despair of marching from broken bridges to damaged fords, he could nevertheless halt and refuse to continue until he was told the name of a thief who had stolen a gilt pax that looked like gold. The thief was hanged on a tree and the pax returned to the pilfered church. Then at last Henry heard news of two fords, one at Béthencourt and one at Voyennes, which the guards had deserted, thinking the English far away. Both fords were approached by causeways over a swamp, and the crossing was slow and dangerous. First it was discovered, after the men had waded up to their armpits through the muck, that the causeways were broken ; these had to be repaired, houses being pulled down and trees felled, and the labour wasted one whole valuable day, from eight in the morning until nightfall, and even then in parts the causeways were so narrow that two men could not walk over them abreast. One was given to the foot, the other to the mounted men and the baggage-train. Henry himself guarded one ford ; the crossing began at midday and did not finish until an hour after sunset.

It was the next morning that the French, having missed this superb chance of annihilating the English, sent Henry a challenge and suggested a meeting-place for battle. " Let all things be done that are pleasing to God," answered Henry, and on being pressed for a more definite reply, added that he would go "straight to Calais. And if our adversaries attempt to stop this road, they will do so to their own hurt and great peril. We indeed do not seek them, nor will fear make us move either more quickly or more slowly. Nevertheless, we do urge them not to hinder our way nor to seek so great an effusion of Christian blood." Then he dismissed the heralds with a present of two hundred crowns each, and calmly continued his march. Still no enemy came to meet him, and he marched as if through peaceful lands, until near Peronne he saw in the mud the tracks of a huge army, pad of man and hoof of beast, and he knew that the heralds had not lied. Calmly he continued, neither quickening nor slackening his pace ; he crossed the river again, at Blangy, and on the opposite bank he climbed a hill and stood before his men, staring into the valley to his right. Through the narrow neck was pouring a huge army, he saw the banners of the French, he saw their shining steel, their plates like strips of ice, their gleaming helmets, spearpoints glittering like dew in sunlight. He saw a host beside which his own army seemed infinitesimal ; he saw the French men-at-arms on horseback, and their archers on foot, he saw the baggage-carts, the cannon, the embroidered pennons and coloured jupons. One Englishman, Thomas Elmham, who was present, relates what was the effect on him of that great army ; it looked, he tells us, " like an innumerable host of locusts, with only a small valley between them and us." The moment had come, the moment when all the great dreams of Henry were to be staked upon a few hours of conflict ; he did not despair, he led his men down the hill.

IT was a peculiar battlefield that the French had chosen, for it gave no advantage to either side. Roughly it was triangular-shaped, being a field between three villages each of which stood within a small wood : to the north-west was Agincourt (to-day spelt Azincourt), to the north-east Tramecourt, to the south Maisoncelles ; the French were forming into the narrow space between Agincourt and Tramecourt, and the field widened towards Maisoncelles in front of which Henry had to make his stand. On either side of each army stretched the woods of Agincourt and Tramecourt. About the numbers of the opposing armies it is impossible to be accurate. Elmham says that the English were 6000—which is probably correct—and that the French were ten times stronger ; the lowest contemporary estimate makes the French three times stronger. If we place the odds at five to one we will perhaps hit somewhere near the truth.

The disparity was so great that for the first and last time in Henry's life we find a moment of doubt. He sent across the prisoners he had taken during the march on condition that they returned if he won the field, and offered to give up all conquests and to pay for all damage if the French would let him pass to

Calais ; if the offer was refused, he asked only that they would fight him the next day. The offer was refused, and he prepared for battle. Never again are we to see a flicker of weakness in Henry ; just for that moment, when he saw the locust-horde in his path and gazed upon the half-starved exhausted handful of men at his back, he faltered, he doubted if his destiny was so great as he believed. When the offer was refused, however, he made no comment, he formed his troops into line, ordering the knights to send their horses to the rear, while himself too dismounted. " Sire," said a friend, " I would that we had ten thousand more good English archers who would gladly be here with us to-day." "You speak as a fool ! " cried Henry. " By the God of heaven, on whose grace I lean, I would not have one more even if I could. This people is God's people. He has entrusted them to me to-day, and He can bring down the pride of these Frenchmen who boast of their numbers and their strength." Already the armour of arrogance was on him again, that jewel of courage shone once more in his heart ; he no longer feared, he remembered that he was God's anointed, a man different from others, one sent to fulfil a great and divine destiny. In the young autumn wheat he stood and spoke quietly to his men, speaking of Crécy and of Poitiers. Then all knelt and prayed while the chaplains confessed them and gave them the eucharist. Evening drew on, yet the French made no move. There would be no battle that night Henry realised, when he saw the French breaking their ranks, and he commanded his men to maintain utter silence—if a knight spoke he was to forfeit horse and harness, if a soldier spoke, he was to lose his right ear. It was beginning to drizzle, yet even in the rain and with soggy ground for mattress, the English could rest after their long march. The French did not rest, they shouted and drank and bet upon the amount of prisoners they would capture, they painted a cart in which they intended to draw the King of England through the streets of Paris and Rouen. The Dauphin was not with them, they had told him that his life was too valuable to risk, and therefore they were leaderless and confused, so that when in the morning of Friday, October 24, 1415, they made ready for battle every knight wished to form the van. In contrast to this hubbub and confusion, the English drew up in orderly fashion after mass, being drawn into one line, as Henry had not enough men for reserves. He commanded the centre, the Duke of York the right, and Lord Camoys the left. Archers were thrown forward on the flanks of each division in the shape of split triangles, thereby forming complete triangles when the divisions closed together ; these triangles were called the " herse " or " harrow," and had been used by the Black Prince at Crécy. On left and right flanks the herses were, of course, incomplete, but were protected by the woods. Each was four or five deep, and the Duke of York had suggested cutting long sharpened stakes that could be driven into the ground before each archer When all was in order, Henry donned his bascinet which was ringed with a gold crown flaming with jewels, and unspurred, he mounted his grey palfrey. Still there was complete silence as the men took their places under his stern eyes, and while above him waved the royal standard quartered with the arms of Our Lady, the Trinity, St. Eadward and St. George. He asked what hour it was, and was told that it was prime, six o'clock in the morning, the opening office of the day. " Now is good time," he said, " for all England prays for us ; let us, therefore, be of good cheer and go to our journey ! " For three further hours he waited while the French squabbled amongst themselves ; in their van the crush was so great that banners had to be furled and sent away, all the chivalry was here, the knights and men-at-arms, while the lowly archers were pushed aside. The men-at-arms were on foot with shortened lances, and there was a detachment of horse on either wing. Having no leader, the French had apparently no set plan except to charge, and the English waited, tense, silent. At last suspense grew unendurable. Henry crossed himself and gave the order—" Forward, banner ! in the name of Jesus, Mary and St. George ! " Each man kneeled three times, kissing the ground to prove that he would rather be slain than run away, and pressing the earth to his lips for a last earth-housel. Sir Thomas Erpingham threw his warder into the air and the cry went to the archers— " Knee ! Stretch ! " Trumpets and drums struck up, and the English gave three yells of defiance, " Hurrah ! Hurrah ! St. George and Merry England ! " and that tiny host strode slowly towards the huge enemy.

Amazed and ashamed that the English should dare strike the first blow, the French wings spurred their horses and charged. But the ground was muddy and slushy, and the horses staggered while the English stood firm ; they dug their stakes into the earth and aimed their arrows. The terrible long-bow wiped out the tumultuous French, it struck down horse and rider, and those who came close enough were impaled upon the stakes.

Numbers told at first, the English line sagged " a full spear's length," then it closed again and did not break. Before that calm and accurate hail of arrows the French were powerless, their maddened horses turned and dashed back into the on-coming ranks of plodding men-at-arms. Arrow after arrow was strung until arrows were exhausted, then the archers leaped from their places and stabbed at the heavily armoured French, darting in and out, hitting with anything they could find—with axes, poles, swords, spears, arrow-heads. All became confusion ; unable to form into ranks, able only to stand in isolated groups and try to beat aside the lightly armed English, the French were slaughtered, and when they fell they could not rise in the plate-armour. The English used the corpses, they jumped upon them so that they could reach above the tall knights and hit down-wards. " Nor was it ever seen in former times," wrote one who watched, " mentioned in chronicles of history, that so many choice and strong soldiers made so sluggish, so disorderly, so cowardly, and so unmanly a resistance. For they were seized with fear and panic ; there were some, even of the more noble, as it was said in the army, who on that day surrendered them-selves ten times over. But no one had a chance to make prisoners of them, but all of every rank, as they were thrown to the ground were put to death without pause, either by those that threw them or by those that followed." Henry did magnificently, we are told ; his brother Humphrey was struck down, and he stood across his body and defended him until he was rescued. Eighteen French knights had sworn to kill him or to die ; they knocked a fleuron off the crown of his helmet but did no further harm to any but themselves. They died, as they had sworn to do.

For three hours the slaughter continued, then between three and four in the afternoon the French gave up the hopeless struggle and fled while the jubilant English sought amongst the bodies for those worthy of ransom, killing those that were valueless. As they went about this slow but pleasant task, news came that the French had rallied and in the distance they heard shouts of men, the war-cry of " Brabant ! Brabant ! " Henry was trapped between these apparent reinforcements and his own prisoners, he gave the command which for so long has been considered a stain upon his honour—he commanded that all prisoners be murdered. We cannot blame him, he had no alternative, yet one feels a faint protest when one learns that dukes, earls and other important captives were spared. This was undoubtedly a part of the chivalric code, nevertheless such prisoners were Henry's personal property and this command leaves him open to the charge of deliberately saving his own pouch while emptying the pouches of his troops. There was almost a rebellion at first, the men objecting, not from humanitarian reasons but at such waste of ransom. Henry called a troop of archers to him to shoot down those who disobeyed, and the slaughter began. Most of the knights were already half-stripped of their valuable armour, and now their throats were slit and their heads smashed with pole-axes " in fell and cruel wise." Even the houses in which the wounded had been laid were burnt above them—and all for nothing. The French had not rallied. The Duke of Burgundy's son, the Duke of Brabant, had defied his father and had ridden hard to be in at the fight, he rode so swiftly that he outdistanced his men and baggage, and when he paused to don his knightly jupon he found that it was miles behind and therefore he had to wear his trumpet-blazon with a hole cut in it through which to push his head. He was killed by an English soldier who failed to recognise his ducal rank because of the tawdry blazon.

Historians have mostly either tried to excuse this slaughter or to damn Henry because of it, either attitude is absurd. You cannot blame Henry ; contemporaries never dreamed of blaming him, the English grumbled only at the loss of ransom, while the French vented their fury on the unfortunate Brabant whose futile charge had caused the massacre. Even on the count of retaining his own prisoners Henry must be acquitted, for these men were of the highest rank, and even if the articles of war had not decreed that they should be his, he would without doubt have spared them. In medieval times you did not murder the relations of Kings as if they were ordinary men, for the code of chivalry was in every sense aristocratic, it was built always to protect the noble.

When the slaughter and pillaging was over, Henry asked the name of the castle he saw in the distance. It was Agincourt, he was told. " Then," said Henry, " let this day be called the Battle of Agincourt." His camp he pitched on that bloody field, and was served by his more important prisoners, who included the Duke of Orléans. He was quite friendly with them, but he did not forget to mention that it was God Who had won the victory and that therefore England was God's country.

IN heavy sleet, the King's ship reached Dover on the night of November 16, after a particularly stormy crossing. Yet no matter how fierce the wind, how overtoppling the waves, Henry gave no sign of fear or sickness, and his calm manner astonished the French prisoners even more than had the victory of Agincourt. The Barons of the Cinque Ports waded to the ships and carried their King shoulder-high to land, through the sleet. The next day Henry stayed at Dover so that his prisoners could recover from the voyage, then he began the march to London. On Barham Down the men at the Cinque Ports were drawn up in battle-array to greet him. " What ! " cried the Duke of Orléans, " shall we go to war again ! " " Nay," answered Henry, " these are only children of my country come to welcome me home." The mayor of London with twenty-four aldermen in furred scarlet gowns and black-and-white striped hoods met him on Blackheath, and out came twenty thousand citizens in the bright liveries of their crafts. At ten in the morning of November 23, Henry, with his prisoners and attended by this gigantic crowd, rode towards London Bridge. On either side of the Stone Gate at the Southwark end stood a giant and a giantess, " as if man and wife " ; on a stick the giant proffered the city keys to Henry. " Hail to the royal city ! " cried the King. At the foot of the Bridge was a pavilion in which stood a figure of St. George in full armour save for his helm, instead of which he had a laurel wreath studded with pearls about his brow. Boys " dressed in white and with faces shining with gold " to represent cherubim, played hand-organs and sang. At the conduit on Cornhill the tower was covered with crimson cloth which was dragged out to form a tent, and from the tent at Henry's approach ran a company of prophets dressed in gold coats and mantles and with crimson turbans. From their cupped hands they unloosed a flock of sparrows that fluttered about the King and perched upon his shoulders. Entering Chepe, the procession was met by further old men, this time representing the twelve apostles, who chanted and offered leaves of silver-and-wafer and wine from the conduit ; Queen Eleanor's Cross was hidden under a wooden castle, and over the drawbridge danced " a chorus of most beautiful virgin girls, dressed gracefully in white and virgin dresses, singing with timbrel and dance, as to another David returning from the slaying of Goliath," while boys from the castle-windows threw down boughs of laurel and gilt bezants.

Never once did Henry smile, never did he turn his eyes upon the dancing maidens or upon the old men chanting of victory. He drew his purple cloak tightly about him and rode as if he disdained such petty triumphs of a grateful people ; he had refused to let his helmet and sword of Agincourt be borne before him, for the victory, he said, was God's, and not his. Unsmiling he rode through the excited crowds until he reached St. Paul's. . . . Here was the greeting he desired—the censing of the priests, the chanting, the singing, the clamour of the bells and the august darkness under the tall arch, while the altar shone with jewels before him in the candlelight.

HENRY knew that the victory of Agincourt was politically valueless except for the glory it gave to England and the fear it struck into France. He wished to carry on a war of subjection and not of slaughter, to take castle by castle, city by city, and not to fight armies in the open ; therefore he carefully prepared his second invasion. Before the time came for this, however, he had sealed the Schism which for so long had broken the western Church. We have not the space to detail the complicated moves he made with King Sigismund, the hereditary Emperor of the Holy Roman Empire : with great care and cunning he and Sigismund not only managed to subdue the three anti-Popes, but to have their own candidate elected to the papal throne as Martin V. France remained fighting internally and had it not been for Burgundy's intrigues, Armagnac would have recaptured Harfleur. The Dauphin Louis was now dead, and his brother John took his place as the centre of the plots, each party striving to control him, when he suddenly died, and Armagnac was accused of poisoning him. Everything was exactly in the state of uproar that Henry wished when, on July 23, 1417, he sailed from Southampton on his second invasion.

The castle of Bonneville surrendered without a blow, Lisieux fell with the minimum of fighting, then Henry marched on the great city of Caen. For over a fortnight he besieged the garrison, then on September 4 he commanded a general assault. It was said that over eighteen hundred Frenchmen died that day before the city became Henry's, and on the 20th the garrison submitted. After the capture of this famous city, the lesser castles lowered their drawbridges at the first blast of the trumpet ; gradually the land fell once more under English rule, and by the end of April 1418 the whole of lower Normandy had pledged itself to Henry. Undisturbed he had gone from city to city with his army while the French knights murdered each other. King Charles the insane in a moment of sanity captured the lover of his Queen Isabel, tied him in a sack and threw him into the river. Isabel he sent to Tours where she immediately joined forces with the Duke of Burgundy and together they almost captured Paris. This lack of patriotism is really amazing, but medieval men were ambitious creatures who fought usually for themselves, who could see no divine right in the crown, they felt that every man might snatch it if he dared. Patriotism, in the modern sense, did not exist even yet ; there were feudal loyalties, or at the most, heavy emotions of a vague race-solidity— the closest to patriotism and not strong with the cultured class who had an inarticulate Rome-loyalty, a mixture of superstitious reverence for the Pope and a feeling that the ancient Roman empire must some day, somehow, materialise again. Combined with this were the local feudal bonds which could change as rapidly as new oaths could be sworn. This explains how Henry captured France with such ease : loyalty was an oath more than a principle and fresh oaths could easily be made—and just as easily broken.

Castle after castle, city after city, fell to England, and England itself remained at peace under the wise rule of Henry's brother John, Duke of Bedford. The only important episode that occurred during this time in England was the taking of Old-castle. Badly wounded, he was carried to the Tower on a horse litter, and on December 14, 1417, was arraigned before parliament as a traitor and a heretic, being then sentenced to be drawn, hanged [in chains], and burnt. Apparently his sufferings had driven Oldcastle a trifle mad, for while he was being drawn on a hurdle to St. Giles' Field where he was to die, he called on Sir Thomas Erpingham, a recanted lollard, to speak with him after he had risen on the third day. Not a murmur came from him as the fire leaped up.

Henry, having captured lesser cities, now struck at Rouen ; this was, according to Henry himself, " the most notable place in France save Paris," and the citizens had had months of warning in which to repair the walls and gather supplies ; these walls that extended for five miles were so banked with earth that a loaded cart could be driven along the top, and the suburbs were cut down, houses demolished, gardens uprooted, to give no cover for the enemy. The Duke of Exeter led the advance-guard of the

English, he called on the city to surrender, and they "gave no answer but their guns"; then on August 1, 1418, Henry himself arrived. Outworks were captured, trenches dug, cannon were dragged into position, but the siege of so powerful a city was a wearisome task. It was impossible to mine such great walls, it was impossible to approach near enough to escalade, and the only way to capture the place was to starve the garrison into surrender. Henry cut it off from communications in every direction while his own supplies were brought from Harfleur down the Seine. Winter approached, and the people within the walls found their situation desperate, even their water was giving out; horse-flesh was soon exhausted; and dogs, cats, rats, mice, were eaten. The people scratched up roots, they licked the dew from grass, and all humanity was forgotten, was swept aside by this, the greatest of lusts, hunger. Messengers were sent for help, and none came. Men crept from the gates and were taken by the English, they told a ghastly story of hunger at its worst, of how maidens bartered their maidenheads for a scrap of food, of how men killed each other for lusts of the belly. "Hunger breaketh the hard stone wall" that guns could not smash. The garrison decided that what little store of food remained must be kept for the fighters and they herded the non-combatants out of the gates; Henry crushed whatever pity he possessed and would not let these people through his ranks. It was a cruel but necessary act; he dared not show mercy lest thereby he inspire other cities to hold against him. The starved creatures, crawling on hands and knees and wailing, "Have mercy on us," were fired at and made to return; the city gates were shut and they were therefore caught between two lines. They had no refuge except the half-dry moat and the space between the moat and the walls, and there they lay half-naked in the rain. Some women suffered childbirth in that misery, and the newborn babies were hoisted up to the city-walls so that the priests might baptize them while they died lest otherwise they go straight from hell to a greater hell. Children begged food from the English beside the corpses of their parents; in the muck lay living, dying, and dead. There could be seen, a soldier tells us, women holding corpses of babies in their arms and crooning to them, and living babies sucking greedily at the empty paps of dead mothers.

When Christmas came, Henry relented enough to offer a day of peace so that he could feed these wretches. They were placed in a row while priests served food, and they rejoiced because the

33

English were of more " tender heart " than their own countrymen.

On New Year's Eve, 1419, the garrison made overtures of
surrender, but at first Henry would not listen. The deputation
seemed very troubled—as well it might—about the wretches in
the ditch and besought the King for love of Jesus and the Blessed
Virgin to have pity on them. " Fellows," he answered, " who
put them there ? They lived in the city while they could. Let
them find what they have sought." He grew still angrier when the
deputation remarked that Rouen was a goodly city to capture.
" It is mine ! " he cried, " and I will have it ! Let those within
make ready, for men will speak of me till the day of doom ! "
After talking apart with his brother Thomas, Duke of Clarence
he pretended to relent and promised to listen to terms. At last
it was agreed that Rouen would surrender on January 13 if not
relieved. No relief coming on the appointed day, Henry passed
through the gates in silence. Before him had ridden Exeter and
a troop shouting, " St. George ! " and " Welcome, Rouen, our
King's own right ! " but there was no shouting, no music, no
tumult, when Henry entered on his black horse. Silent and
taciturn, he went direct to the cathedral, as was his wont, to offer
thanks to God.

After Rouen, only Paris remained for him to capture.

Two months were spent in the city, for Henry after taking a town
always tried to make life begin where his arrival had broken it.
He did not consider Normandy a foreign country, and he wished
to make the people realise this by setting up just laws and trying
to open trade. Meanwhile he negotiated with Burgundy who
was a shiftless cowardly creature, and at last it was agreed that
Burgundy should bring King Charles and the Princess Katherine to
Troyes on May 15, 1415, and would there discuss matters with
Henry. A large field was marked out for the meeting and was
bounded with palisades ; two trenches were dug, parcelling the
field into three—one for the French, one for the English, and a
central one for the royal parties. Henry arrived on May 30 ;
as the French King was suffering from one of his periods of
lunacy, he was represented by his Queen Isabel and the Duke of
Burgundy ; but it was not until June 1 that the Princess Katherine
appeared. She was apparently very beautiful, despite her heavy
Valois nose, and Henry loved her at once. As he bent to kiss her
hand in that first moment of meeting, she blushed most charm-

ingly and glanced aside. He was given that one day to look upon her, then she withdrew and he had to be content with memories of her beauty while he argued with Burgundy. Both parties must by now have realised that a settlement was hopeless. Henry openly accused the duke of treachery, saying, " Fair sir, we would have you to wit that we will have your King's daughter and all we have demanded, or else we will drive him and you out of his kingdom." " Sire," answered Burgundy, " you are pleased to say so ; but before you can drive my lord and me out of his kingdom I make no doubt that you will be heartily tired." The truth was that Isabel and Burgundy had grown afraid, they had overreached themselves and had arrogantly believed that they could do what they willed with France ; now they realised that by making peace with Henry they would throw their supporters on to the side of the Dauphin, and Burgundy, always treacherous, began to conspire with his own enemies, trying to make peace with the Armagnacs.

Henry had promised not to fight until July 29, and he kept his word ; on the very day after the treaty expired he struck a terrible blow suddenly. His troops assaulted the Burgundian stronghold, Pontoise, on the road to Paris, attacking at dawn while the garrison was at mass, and capturing enormous booty. Clarence followed the victory by leading his men to the very walls of Paris, shouting for admittance so that he could visit the shrine of St. Denis. When this was refused, he cried that he would come " some other day, whether you will or no ! " Spurred perhaps by the thought of Katherine and by rage at Burgundy's double-dealing, Henry struck fiercely, capturing town after town ; and meanwhile Burgundy had agreed to meet the Dauphin. So far Henry had fought isolated cities, each city defending itself, but if the Dauphin and Burgundy clasped hands, there might come another Agincourt—an Agincourt with perhaps a different climax. And Henry wished to avoid pitched battles, those futile and indecisive affairs which gave victory to neither party. He made no pause, however, in his conquests, relying on his destiny that so far had never failed him. And it was not to fail him yet. Personal hatreds were too strong in France to be forgotten even for the sake of the country, and the Armagnacs could never forget the body of Orléans in a Paris street, his hand chopped off and daggers in his face and belly. They would not make peace with Orléans' murderer, and therefore when Burgundy arrived at the appointed place of meeting they killed him,

they struck him down on the bridge of Montereau in the presence
of their master the Dauphin.

When Henry was told of the assassination he mourned the
death of Burgundy, yet he could not resist crying that now with
the help of God and St. George he would have the Lady Katherine
even though every Frenchman said him nay ! His vast ambitions
had become symbolised in the body of this woman, for she was
France. And almost immediately after the murder of Burgundy,
he was in touch with Queen Isabel and with Burgundy's son,
Philip. Yet he was strong-willed enough to mask his desires
and could gaze sternly on the messengers from Isabel and pretend
that he was unsure which side to take, saying that the Dauphin
was corresponding with him and that he feared to trust the son
of a traitor like the dead duke. He said that he would give help
to Isabel and Philip only on condition that Katherine married
him while one of his brothers married Philip's sister, and that he
become King of France on the death of Charles. These demands
were laid before Isabel and Philip, and in their lust for vengeance
and their terror of the Armagnacs, they could do nothing but
agree ; a formal treaty was drawn up and ratified at Troyes
on May 21, 1420.

Henry had attained all that he had set out to attain. He
was from now to sign himself the heir of France, and if, while the
Dauphin lived, there would be war in his possessions, he never
doubted that he must conquer in the end. Luck had been with
him, but only a great man knows how to use opportunity when it
comes. He was the heir to France and the husband of dear
Katherine ! He met her again when he called upon the mad
King the day before he sealed the treaty. Charles nodded on his
throne upon a dais at the end of the chamber and he did not stir
as Henry strode towards him. Henry bowed low and greeted
him, but Charles still took no notice, until he said suddenly
as if just roused from sleep, " Oh, it's you ? You're very
welcome since it's you. Greet the ladies ! " Quickly Henry
turned to greet the ladies, and with " great joy " he kissed his
Katherine.

They were betrothed the following day, then on June 2
Katherine was taken to the Church of St. Jean at Troyes in a
coach drawn by eight snow-white English horses Henry had
given her, and there she was married to the King of England
and Heir of France. Henry looked, we are told, " as if he were at
that moment King of all the world," and so he was indeed—the

conqueror, the lover who held by the hand the woman he desired, and who owned the country he had schemed and fought to win.

LITTLE time was wasted in merriment. When his followers wished to celebrate the marriage by a tournament, Henry told them that they would have tilting enough, but that it would be tilting in earnest. He had pledged his word to Philip that he would revenge the death of Burgundy, and even the beauty of Katherine could not hold him from his word. Sens was quickly captured, then the combined English and Burgundian army moved on Montereau, where Burgundy had died. Here the slaughter was ghastly, for Philip and his men could not restrain their fury ; the corpse of Burgundy was disinterred and re-buried with great honour, and all wept at the sight of the terrible gashes in the body. After Montereau, city after city fell to Henry and Philip, but there was little unity in the allied troops, and when Henry visited Paris the French were angered to see the royal state he kept while Charles lived almost alone, neglected and wellnigh penniless.

Henry decided to return to England. There was no real necessity for this return, as his brother Bedford had ruled wisely in his absence, but perhaps he desired to show the people their beautiful Queen and to relax a moment from the constant fighting of the last three years. After landing at Dover, he left his bride at Canterbury and galloped ahead to make certain that all was prepared for her entrance into London ; from there he sped to Eltham where he rejoined his Queen, and together the pair rode to the great city. As after Agincourt, money had been poured out to make pageants and statues, and that night, her first in London, Katherine slept in the Tower.

On Sunday, February 23, in Westminster Abbey, she was crowned Queen of England, Henry, of course, not being present, for it was against etiquette for him to preside over what was given purely in her honour. After the great ceremony of crowning came the banquet, and as it was Lent, the cooks had expended all their cunning in devising quaint dishes. We still possess the menu, and it is a wondrous and rather terrifying list. Brawn with mustard was apparently the only meat allowed, and there was every kind of fish and crayfish and eel that could be hooked or netted, and, of course, there were " soteltes." One represented " a pelican on her nest with birds, and an image of St. Katherine with a wheel in her hand disputing with the heathen clerks, having this reason [*maxim*] in her hand, ' MADAME LA ROIGNE ' ; the pelican answering ' C'EST ENSEIGNE ' ; the birds answering ' EST DU ROY PUR TENIR JOIE, A TOUT GENT IL MET SENTENT.' " That was in the first course, the second course also contained its " sotelte," and so did the third. If poor Katherine tasted a quarter of these dishes it is likely that she never forgot the feast, for she must have struggled to digest a conglomeration of every kind of spice with every kind of obtainable sea-creature—with pike, powdered [*salted*] lamprey [*a kind of scaleless eel-like fish*], powdered eel, trout, codling [*small cod*], fried plaice and merling [*whiting*], great crabs, leche lombard [*a concoction of almost everything mixed in a bladder*], jelly decorated with columbine flowers, bream, conger, sole, mullet, chub, barbel, roach, fresh salmon, halibut, roasted gurnard, fried smelt, lobster, dates in compost, cream motley [*parti-coloured*], carp, dory, turbot, tench, perch, fresh sturgeon, whelks, roasted porpoise, fresh-water crayfish, shrimps, roasted eels with lamperns [*river lampreys*], and, of course, those " soteltes."   And it must not be thought that if a dish were fried or roasted it was cooked in the modern manner : the ambition of a medieval chef was to disguise the food with spice and sweet-stuffs.   The equivalent of sugar—honey—was freely used, and so was wine.

AFTER the coronation and the feasting, Katherine set out with Henry on a progress through the country, then came sudden news of tragedy. Henry's young reckless brother Clarence had fought a battle at Baugé and had been killed ; he had been left in command in France and seemingly he had wished to fight another Agincourt, but at Baugé he was fighting disciplined Scottish troops and in his eagerness he did not wait for reinforcements, he disdained even the help of archers, and against the advice of his friends, he rode to certain death.   When the news reached Henry at Beverley he made not the least sign that he was affected. He continued his progress and it was not until the following day that he mentioned the tragedy, although he had lost his brother and risked also the loss of his conquests ; yet he did not hasten his preparations for a return to France, he went about his business as if there were no necessity for speed. On June 10, 1421, he sailed for the last time from Dover, and he did not take Katherine with him. She was expecting a child and remained in England.

THE moral effect of Henry's return was felt at once. The Dauphin withdrew ; whenever Henry struck at him he fled, and despairing of a pitched battle, the King decided to besiege the strong city of Meaux. Here he found the most difficult task he had yet encountered, for not only was Meaux powerfully built, it was garrisoned by the worst ruffians in France, men who knew that they would find no mercy at the hands of the stern Englishman. Therefore they fought like wolves at bay while famine and floods struck the besiegers. Yet famine and death and desertions could never turn King Henry from his purpose, he kept doggedly at the siege, building great engines that would overtop the walls, sending troop after troop to perish gallantly until at last he had a footing between the wall and the moat. It was a slow and painful task, but news came to gladden Henry in the midst of toil, he heard that his Queen at Windsor Castle had given birth to a son. He said that the boy must be christened Henry and that Katherine must at once hear a mass of the Trinity and offer the child to God. Then he struck again at Meaux, although illness was fast dragging him to his bed.

At last Meaux fell and he could hasten to Bois de Vincennes to greet his Queen. Together they rode to Paris where pageants were devised in their honour, although smallpox was deadly in the city ; they soon left for Senlis, and from there travelled to Compiègne. Henry was ill unto death but he refused to believe it ; he felt that his destiny could not strike him down whilst his task was unfulfilled. With Philip he had sworn to lead a crusade to the Holy Land, and he had actually dispatched a knight to reconnoitre the East. While Jerusalem was in the grip of Moslems, while France was still rebellious, destiny surely could not touch him ? Yet he was ill, perilously ill. Apparently it was dysentery that broke his strength—dysentery, that scourge of medieval soldiers—but Henry clenched his teeth and tried to shake the pain aside. He was needed, for he had sworn to join Philip who was about to relieve Cosne that was besieged by the Dauphinists. Reckless of the agony, defiant of physicians, Henry was determined to keep his word, yet even his iron will could not give him strength enough to sit a horse. Like a woman, he had to be tossed in a litter until even this became too painful, and reluctantly he resigned the command to his brother, Bedford.

They rowed him in a boat down the Seine towards the Bois de

Vincennes; his pride was so great that he could not lie help-less, he could not bear the shame, and he struggled to his feet, he swore that he would ride. For a few paces he kept his seat, then he would have fallen had not attendants lifted him and placed him in a horse-litter. Thus, in a litter, the great conqueror returned to Vincennes, and no longer could he hide from the truth—he knew that he was dying. He gave minute directions to those near him about how the war must be carried on—Bedford was to hold Normandy, his other brother, Glou-cester, was to be protector of England, and little Prince Henry was to be placed in the charge of Gloucester, the Earl of Warwick and Sir Walter Hungerford. Burgundy must be kept as a friend, he insisted, and the Duke of Orléans must remain in England. Then he talked with the brother of Gilbert de Lannoy, the man whom he had sent to reconnoitre the Holy Land, before he calmly asked the physicians how much longer he had to live. They faltered, they spoke evasively; he demanded the truth, and one of them said, " Sire, think upon your case, for it seems to us that, except by the favour of God, we judge not that you can survive two hours." He gave no sign of fear, he called for his confessor and other religious and asked them to recite the seven penitential psalms. When they had reached the verse, " Oh, be favourable and gracious unto Sion : build thou the walls of Jerusalem," Henry gestured for silence and said, " Good Lord, Thou knowest that mine intent hath been, and yet is, if I might live, to re-edify the walls of Jerusalem." Then he lay back, half-conscious, in the arms of his confessor until he stirred again and cried, " Thou liest ! thou liest ! my portion is with the Lord Jesus ! " He gripped the crucifix, and in a firm low voice muttered, " In manus tuas, Domine, ipsum terminum redemisti. . . ." Then with a feeble gesture he died a little after two o'clock on the morning of Monday, August 31, 1422, in the thirty-sixth year of his age, " for whose death the Duke of Bed-ford, his brother, and the Duke of Exeter, his uncle, and gener-ally all the other princes, lords, estates and commons of England made great lamentations and bewailings in right great anguish and heaviness."

THEY buried his bones in Westminster Abbey, and many relics had to be moved to make a space for him near the shrine of St. Eadward. His tomb was built of Caen stone and Purbeck marble, and Queen Katherine commanded to be made above it a beautiful monument with a body of oak plated with silver-gilt and with a head of solid silver. Head and sheathing were later stolen, but the glory of Henry's conquests, even when they themselves were lost to England, could never be taken. They remain the pride of Englishmen until this day, although the conqueror's tomb lies bespoiled in Westminster.

XV

KING HENRY THE SIXTH

1422–1461

ONE CAN SCARCELY CALL Henry VI a King. He began his reign as a minor and he ended it as a captive, while the middle period was more truly the rule of his Queen, Margaret. When he was only a few months old he became King and his guardianship was given to the brave old Duke of Exeter. The Queen Mother, however, held actual charge of the baby King, and when he was two years of age it was decided that he must make his first public appearance. Henry on this occasion showed far more spirit than he was ever to show afterwards ; he refused to sit on his mother's " chair "—which might have been a chair strapped on to a horse's back or one borne between two horses. He " shyrled " and wept, and " nothing the Queen could devise might content him," and he shyrled indeed with such gusto that the Queen feared he " had been diseased " and carried him inside again. Later chroniclers noted with satisfaction that already Henry was proving himself a saint because the day was a Sunday ; the next day he left the inn without a murmur, and when reaching London sat in his mother's lap in the chair and was quite content while carried through the cheering streets. In the following year, 1424, he was found to require a new nurse, and a solemn note was made in the proceedings of the privy council that " because of our youth and tender age it behoves us to be taught and to be instructed in courtesy and nurture and other matters beseeming a royal person," a certain Alice Botiller being " expert and wise " was given permission " to chastise us from time to time as the case shall require, so that you shall not be molested, hurt, or injured for this cause in future time."

In 1425, Henry opened parliament and " he went upon his feet from the west door [of St. Paul's] to the stairs and so up into the quire." Afterwards, he sat on a great horse and was taken through the streets of London, and men decided that he had " the very image, lively portraiture, and countenance of his famous father." In 1426, May 19, he was knighted by his uncle, Bedford, and then in his turn he knighted his playmates, who included Richard of York. In the same year Exeter died, but it was not until 1428 that another guardian took his place ; this time Richard Beauchamp, Earl of Warwick, being appointed. His instructions were simple enough, but the one Warwick appeared to take most to heart was that which enjoined him to " chastise " Henry " reasonably from time to time as occasion shall require."

In 1429, the year that Joan of Arc first led her troops to victory, little Henry was crowned King of England, mainly because it had been decided to crown him King of France and the English ceremony must naturally come first. The ceremony was a failure ; perhaps the youth of Henry—he was " not fully viii year old "—made his protectors feel that there should be no horseplay or drunkenness in the streets. The conduits that usually flooded wine were empty, being decorated instead with moral images of Grace and Mercy and such, while all the liquor given free was a miserly one cup per person, and even that had to be asked for nicely. Nevertheless the crowd was great and a few people were crushed to death and some cutpurses were caught, as was natural, and even a heretic was roasted alive on Smithfield. In the abbey, little Henry, wearing a suit of furred scarlet, was placed on the scaffolding between the high altar and the quire, and he sat there, " beholding the people all about sadly and wisely." Then followed the usual disrobing and dressing, the holy oil of the Virgin Mary was used for the third time, and the great crown of St. Eadward was placed over the boy's head. It was too large for him to wear, and he had to have " two bishops standing on every [*each*] side of him, helping him to bear the crown, for it was over-heavy for him, for he was of a tender age." One can only hope that he did not eat too largely of the banquet that followed, as it contained an appalling amount of indigestible dishes and the usual " soteltes."

The crowning in France was an even more dismal affair ; on the way to Paris Henry was lodged at Rouen during the trial of Joan of Arc, although it is more than doubtful if he ever met her ; if he had, he would, of course, have considered her a witch as his father would most decidedly have done. From Rouen he was taken by Bedford to Paris and was crowned in Notre

Dame on December 16, 1431. Everything possible went wrong with the ceremony ; English bishops officiated and thereby infuriated the Archbishop of Paris, and the English procedure was used which disgusted all the clergy in the country. Not a single French Prince appeared, and although Henry's own grandmother was in the city at the time she stayed away. Not a penny was given in largesse, not a prisoner was freed, no taxes were remitted. So utter a failure was the whole affair that Bedford thought it wise to hurry the King back to England. This was Henry's one trip abroad.

London welcomed him royally, the citizens offering him a golden casket that contained £1000, with this pretty address : " Most Christian Prince, the good folk of your notable city of London, otherwise cleped your Chamber, beseech in their most lowly wise that they now be recommended unto your highness, and that [it] can like your noble grace to receive this little gift, given with as good will and loving heart as any gift was given to any earthly Prince."

WE know very little of Henry's upbringing, and it seems likely that at this stage his uncle, the Duke of Gloucester, was gaining control over his weak mind. Somebody must have been interfering, for when the boy was nearly eleven, Warwick approached the council and asked for the right to dismiss officials about the King's person and " any person in his discretion suspect of misgovernance " ; he also asked for protection against the likelihood of the King growing to hate him because of the amount of chastisement he had given the royal person ; he wished that Gloucester and the Council should " assure him they shall firmly and truly assist him in the exercise of the charge and occupation that he hath about the King's person, namely, in chastising him of his defaults, and support the said earl therein ; and if the King at any time will conceive for that cause indignation against the said earl, my said Lord of Gloucester and lords shall do all their true diligence and power to remove the King therefrom." The council, of course, agreed, but Warwick repeated the same thing later, he asked that it made " known to the King that it proceedeth of the assent, advice, and agreement of my Lord of Gloucester and all my lords of the King's council that the King be chastised for his defaults or trespass, and that for awe thereof he forbear the more to do amiss and intend the more busily to virtue and to learning."

DURING these years of Henry's minority the English had been almost swept out of France. Bedford, a great man without the inspiration of his greater brother, did everything that was possible, but the adventure was absurd in the fifteenth century ; only the genius of Henry V could have conceived and carried it through. England did not have men enough to garrison the captured cities, and it had not money enough with which to buy mercenaries. Doggedly the troops fought to the last, even against the divine fury of Jeanne d'Arc—whom they called Joan of Arc—until they trapped and burnt her. She might die but her task was over, she had infused new spirit into France, she had taught the exhausted people that victories were possible even against England. Bedford did all he could, but he was hampered on every side and he longed for peace ; his brother, Gloucester, however, intriguing for power, ambitious and cunning, would not listen to any suggestion of closing the war : he wanted to keep Bedford in France while he could conspire in England. The fruitless conflict dragged on, kept living only by the absurd pride of the English who could not tolerate the bare conception of giving in. Bedford hurried to England in 1433 and almost made parliament agree to a final peace, but Gloucester—although there is not the least suggestion that he had any personal dislike of his brother—defeated the project, and back to France went Bedford to continue a war that he knew was doomed. Soon Burgundy tired of the struggle and negotiated with King Charles ; then he openly wrote to Henry stating that the alliance was at an end. When Henry read the letter and saw that he was not styled King of France, he wept, while the Londoners rushed on the Flemish residents and murdered them. From now the cause was hopeless, and in the following year, 1435, Bedford died at Rouen on September 15. His had been an honourable and tragic life, far different from his brother Gloucester's.

ALL this time the Queen Mother in some mysterious fashion had been carrying on a secret intrigue with her clerk of the wardrobe, a Welsh esquire called Owen Tudor. How the secret had been kept is really astounding, as she had borne her lover four children —Edmund, later Earl of Richmond and father of King Henry VII ; Jasper, later Earl of Pembroke ; Owen, who was to turn monk ; and Margaret—and it was not until the birth of Margaret in 1436 that the liaison was discovered. Her children were taken from the Queen and given to the Earl of Suffolk to rear, and her lover was locked in Newgate, but was afterwards released. Katherine retired to the Abbey of Bermondsey where she died the following year. It is really amazing that an affair such as this could have been kept quiet in so gossip-hunting a place as a royal court, and it was even said that the pair had married, although we have no proof of it.

We do not know the effect of such a discovery on the young King, but it must have horrified him, as he was extremely pious. At the same time he lost another friend, the Earl of Warwick, who took command of the army in France.

Then he was proclaimed fully King, being sixteen years of age, and no longer in need of tutors or governors or chastisers.

WE have three authentic portraits of Henry : the first at King's College, Cambridge—which he founded—shows him as a young man and is probably the least like him, for there is an air of insolence about the pose and in the heavy-lidded eyes and in the pursed mouth. The whole attitude, too, is insolent, the shoulders being thrown back a little and the head brought forward. The second painting, in the National Portrait Gallery, London, is undoubtedly an excellent likeness ; there is a timidity in the pale eyes and in the questioning eager-to-please attitude. The third portrait—reproduced here—in Windsor Castle shows him in later years, more wrinkled and lined. There is also a delightful sketch in the Stuttgart MS. of Jörg von Ehingen's diary ; [1] the costume shown by Ehingen is absurd, for he gives Henry a purple chaperon—a round hat that could be pushed aside and hung from the shoulders by a cloth called the liripipe, which can be seen dangling in the sketch—and a pale blue coat of the cut known as the houppelande, except that the houppelande usually had great baggy sleeves in the style yet worn by the Benedictine order, while Henry here has more or less narrow sleeves. Otherwise the gown seems a houppelande, being high-collared—the scarlet collar is unbuttoned and slides back—and falling almost to the ground in heavy folds ; the shoulders are thickly padded ; around the waist is a crimson girdle with a gold buckle, and the black shoes are not too long and pointed. If we dismiss the costume as being out-of-keeping, too showy, interesting

[1] This fascinating work, giving brief descriptions of the famous people of the time, has been published in England with most beautiful reproductions : *The Diary of Jörg von Ehingen*, trans. and ed. by Malcolm Letts (Oxford University), 1929.

though it is as an example of fifteenth-century dress, the countenance is obviously Henry's. We see the same heavy underlip and heavy eyelids, the usual gentle pose of clasped hands as if he prayed while he walked ; the head bends on the neck as he peers downwards.

That must have been Henry's common attitude, the attitude of religious meditation. We see it also in the three portraits, although in these he is dressed in his ordinary costume : in a dark gown with bands of ermine over shoulders and around neck, dark red sleeves, gold collar, and in each the same dark tightly-fitting cap with upturned brim, a shape popular amongst Princes at the time. He usually dressed, we are told, in " a long gown with a rolled hood like a townsman [resembling the chaperon, which was only an evolution of the hood rolled turban-wise], and a full coat reaching below the knees, with shoes, boots and footgear wholly black." In figure he was tall and slender and well-proportioned.

At first it may seem strange that the stern conqueror of Agincourt could be the parent of this good-natured characterless creature, but Henry VI must have taken after his mother, not after his father, and Katherine was the daughter of the mad King of France. Henry VI was not insane—except in spasms—he was simple, with no understanding of the world ; he was continually in debt, being unable to refuse a request, and before long he had given away many of the most important crown lands. When his great-uncle, Cardinal Beaufort, died and left him a legacy of £2000, Henry refused it because, he said, the cardinal had been so good to him when he was alive he could take nothing from him now. The amazed and probably scandalised executors suggested that he might give it to his two foundations, Eton and King's College, and to this he agreed. The truth was that he had not the least understanding of money, it was merely something that you gave away, and often his servants had to go without wages because he had not a penny with which to pay them.

He was most pious, and strictly forbade his courtiers to chatter during service, or to bring their hawks with them or to dress their swords in church. He knelt devoutly all through service, bareheaded, silent. Music he liked, and he composed a sanctus still preserved at King's College. He could not tolerate an oath, he was almost as strict as a lollard on that point, and he never swore beyond, " Forsooth and forsooth ! " and " St. John ! "

He was also most modest, and when he visited Bath he fled almost at once because of the nakedness or the near-nakedness of the bathers ; and at the same town when presented to some ladies in immodest costume he turned away and strode out of the room, muttering, " Fy, fy, for shame ! forsooth ye be to blame."

This piety brought out his one cruel side ; so strong was his hatred of lollards that he had no mercy for them, and during his reign there were continual public burnings. Although not brutal, he was also no coward, but during the civil war, when he put on his armour he found himself unable to kill Christians, an attitude that must have amazed the crude knights of the period. Nevertheless when he was caught in a battle he showed no fear and did not try to run away ; and when during his imprisonment a man wounded him in the neck with a dagger, Henry felt no resentment and pardoned his attacker when he was King again. Riding into Cripplegate one day from St. Albans, he noticed a blackening piece of something on a stake and on his asking what it could be, a companion answered that it was a quarter of a traitor " false to the King's majesty." " Take it down at once ! " cried Henry, " I would not have a Christian treated like that on my account ! " Unable to contain resentment of any kind, he was prepared to forgive his greatest enemy, and had it not been for the selfish policy of his wife he would without doubt have ended his reign in peace, but whatever the Queen demanded Henry gave because he loved her.

A gentle Prince, a man who should have been a monk, who would have been content to pray without ceasing or to meditate for hours in cloisters. Things of the earth had no value in his eyes ; when a great lord once brought him a beautiful gold-worked coverlid he scarcely bothered to examine the gift, to the great lord's indignation. He " ruled his own affections, gaped not after riches, and was careful only of his soul's health." For this reason, being able to despise physical matters, he never lost his temper and calmly suffered the most terrible privations or insults.

The people wearied of his extravagant charities, his meekness, and his misrule under the guidance of his wife, yet he was truly a saint. Had Henry VII lived a few more years we cannot doubt that his exertions would have led to Henry VI's canonisation : he did his best to have it brought about, however, not for love of the poor King, but because he wished thereby to make the Kings who had followed him seem murderers of a saint. In 1446, Pope Eugenius IV thought Henry VI deserving of the great gift of the Golden Rose, an honour kept for the most ideal devotees of the Church. It is true that the Pope had an ulterior motive in giving the distinction—at the time he wished to extract some money from the English Church—all the same he would never have sent the Rose to an unworthy Prince. It must have shamed poor Henry to the heart when he had to ignore the money question while writing with deep gratitude to acknowledge the gift.

Perhaps the noblest quality in Henry was his interest in education. Numerous grammar schools were founded during his reign, and himself founded King's College, Cambridge, and Eton. This Eton was vastly different from the modern school into which it has grown, for it consisted of a provost, a schoolmaster, ten priests, four clerks, six choristers, twenty-five poor and indigent scholars, and twenty-five poor and feeble old men, and schooling was to be given " freely, without exaction of money or anything else." It was founded in 1440, and in 1443 the number of poor scholars was raised to seventy, while the poor men were cut down to thirteen. Henry was very fond of this school, so close to the castle, and if he found any of the scholars in Windsor he always slipped a coin into their palms and told them to be good boys ; if he came across them inside the castle walls he sent them off briskly with the warning that a court was not the place for the young to visit.

A pathetic and charming creature, this Henry VI, who was doomed to an existence of such pain that it is astounding how he managed to live through the tragic years, but he " took all human chances, miseries, and afflictions of this life in so good part as though he had justly by some offence deserved the same."

AT the age of sixteen, Henry VI became truly King, but he was quite incapable of ruling. Gloucester was in power, a determined advocate of the war policy, and although Henry must have desired peace and had apparently little love for his uncle, he was too weak to withstand him. He could do nothing with his kingship except give away money, and very soon the council was scribbling minutes about the King's extravagance and reminding itself that it must speak to Henry about granting pardons, for one pardon alone had lost him 2000 marks ; the council also reminded itself of a stewardship worth 1000 marks which Henry had given away to somebody.

34

Gloucester for the moment was in power, but he had strong enemies in the Beauforts, those descendants of John of Gaunt by Katherine Swynford. They struck at Gloucester through his wife, Eleanor Cobham, who had been playing with magic ; her husband being next in succession if Henry died childless, Eleanor had thought to read the future and even perhaps to forestall it by making a wax image of the King and melting it in fire. She fled to sanctuary in Westminster, but the Church did not protect heretics or witches and she was dragged forth to trial. Her accomplices were executed, one man being drawn, hanged and quartered, and a woman burnt, while Eleanor was sentenced to perform a public penance—she had to walk barefoot through London carrying a taper weighing one pound—and later to lifelong imprisonment. She died some years afterwards. While the hunt was up, Gloucester remained very quiet, not daring to defend his wife lest he, too, grow entangled in the awful indictment, for he knew full well that the blow came from the Beauforts and was aimed at him, not at Eleanor.

It was decided that the King should marry, and Henry was eager to oblige. Saint though he was, he did not have any horror of women, and he was very particular about the personal appearance of his future bride. When it was thought that one of the three daughters of the Count of Armagnac might be suitable, he demanded a portrait of the girls, and instructed an artist to "portray the iii daughters in their kirtles simple, and their visages, like as ye see, their stature and their beauty and colour of skin and their countenances, with all manner of features ; and that one be delivered in all haste with the said portrait to bring it unto the King, and he to appoint and assign which him liketh." This venture coming to nothing, the same procedure was evidently followed when it was thought that Margaret of Anjou might make a pretty bride, for we learn that Henry soon had a portrait of her, and that he feel deeply in love with it, as well he might, for she was apparently most beautiful. Margaret was then about fifteen years of age and was already famous for her wit and her charms, her father being the lazy cultured Duke René, a true Provençal who loved the arts above war-harness. The marriage was a Beaufort suggestion and therefore was opposed by Gloucester, now rising out of the disgrace of his wife's downfall. Oppose it though he might, Gloucester no longer had any control over the King, and soon Margaret was on her way to England after a pathetic farewell from her friends and relations.

The Duke of Suffolk had been sent to escort her, and years afterwards the romantic fiction grew that he loved her and had sworn to make her Queen ; as Suffolk was fifty, rather an old man for those days, and Margaret was but fifteen, the story may be dismissed. He had had trouble over the marriage-portion. René was penniless but haughty, and although he could give no dowry, he demanded that his lands of Maine and Anjou be returned; Suffolk had full powers to treat, and he agreed to surrender the fiefs in exchange for Margaret. He realised the enormity of this and kept it secret ; later, it was to prove his downfall.

As there was now a truce with France, Suffolk, standing proxy for the King, married Margaret at Nancy. In England Henry was frenziedly trying to raise enough money for the wedding, and Margaret herself was little better off. Although she could afford to spend 4s. 9d. on fourteen pairs of shoes to be given to poor women, and at Rouen to buy some second-hand plate, she was made to pawn " divers vessels of mock silver " with the Duchess of Somerset for her seamen's wages. The voyage across the Channel was evidently abominable, for on reaching Porchester, Suffolk had to carry Margaret ashore in his arms and she stayed the night at a convent ; next day she was rowed in state to Southampton, with seven foreign trumpeters blowing at her from the decks of two Genoese galleys as she passed. At Southampton she became ill and was unable to leave the convent in which she was lodged. This illness is rather peculiar, for we learn from a letter dispatched by Henry to the lord chancellor that " our most dear and best beloved wife the Queen is yet sick of the labour and indisposition of the sea, by occasion of which the pocks been broken out upon her, for which cause we may not in our own person hold the feast of St. George in our Castle of Windsor." From this it has been deduced that Margaret had either chicken- or small-pox, but this is most unlikely as never afterwards do we hear of a single blemish. Pox was a general term for skin-eruptions in the Middle Ages and Margaret may have had some temporary rash. Her retirement she spent in gathering her trousseau, or rather in adding to it, with the help of one Margaret Chamberlayne, " tyremaker " or dressmaker, brought in great haste all the way from London.

The marriage, probably because of Margaret's indisposition, was quietly solemnised at Titchfield Abbey, nine miles from Southampton, on April 23, 1445, Henry being twenty-three and the bride barely sixteen.

When they approached London on May 28, King and Queen were met on Blackheath by the mayor, aldermen and sheriffs dressed in scarlet, and by masters of the crafts in blue gowns with embroidered sleeves and red hoods, who escorted them through Southwark to the Bridge. The usual pageants had been devised, and John Lydgate had been commissioned to write the pretty verses that were spoken or sung as the Queen rode past. The Londoners all wore daisies—marguerites—in their caps and hoods and greeted her merrily, not yet knowing of the loss of Maine and Anjou.

On May 30, Margaret was crowned in Westminster Abbey with such pomp that it is astonishing how Henry ever screwed out enough to pay for it, and a great tournament was held. Then the festivities died down and men had an opportunity to discover what sort of a women this new Queen was who had cost them so heavily. Gloucester was not long in discovering the truth. He had opposed the marriage, and Margaret was a vindictive woman who could never forget the smallest insult. Gloucester soon found himself jostled aside by the Beauforts and Suffolk, then when he rode to parliament at Bury St. Edmunds in February 1447 he was met by messengers from Henry who told him that he need not greet the King but had best go to his lodgings and dine. In the bitter weather, Gloucester turned aside, realising that his power was at an end. It must have been a doleful meal that night with the rain hammering on the shutters and horn-paned windows, when his enemies entered the chamber and arrested him, evidently for treason. And Gloucester died. We do not know how Gloucester died. Rumour, of course, swore that he was murdered, that he was " stranguled," that the inevitable featherbeds were made to stifle him, and even memories of Edward II produced the tale that " he was thrust into the bowel with an hot burning spit." Soon the legends of his bounty grew and men spoke of him as Good Duke Humphrey ; and selfish and ambitious though he might have been, Gloucester was also a patriot ; he is rather a pitiful figure whose dreams were always pricked, mainly by his own arrogance and violent temper. Now he was dead, and probably murdered, yet it is more than likely that the shame of his imprisonment brought on some kind of apoplexy, for he was physically not a strong man. If Suffolk and Margaret did actually murder him, they were to pay most bitterly for the deed.

Gloucester was gone, but the Duke of York still lived, and he was next in succession to the throne should the King die child-less, for the Beauforts, though made legitimate by Richard II, had been excluded from reigning by act of parliament in Henry IV's time. York, however, was of direct descent from Edmund of Langley, the younger brother of John Gaunt, while his mother Anne was the daughter of Roger Mortimer, Earl of March, descendant of Lionel, Duke of Clarence, the elder brother of Gaunt, whose children had been declared the true heirs by Richard II. Therefore from both parents York had a strong claim, stronger even than Henry's own. The Beauforts and Suffolk sent him as lieutenant of Ireland to get him out of the way, but they could not hide for ever the facts about the marriage-settlement, and soon it became known that in exchange for the Queen, England through Suffolk had surrendered Maine and Anjou. The fury of the people was so great that Suffolk asked for an opportunity to defend himself, which he did before the council in May 1447, and was completely vindicated. That did not save him from the hatred of the populace, and all misrule—the continual defeat of English arms in France, the non-payment of troops and overseas garrisons, Burgundy's embargo on English cloth, and the wholesale poverty of the country—was blamed upon him. Yet in this dangerous time, when the people's hatred was sharpening beyond control, Suffolk and Margaret could be stupid enough to take a monopoly of wool and thereby to turn even the merchants, those staunch supporters of the crown, against them.

Henry was penniless and his household had to petition parliament for their wages. Then war broke out more fiercely than ever on the Continent—Warwick was dead—and when the Bishop of Chichester arrived at Portsmouth with the long-overdue pay of the troops, they murdered him. The state of the country was too perilous to be ignored, and on January 26, 1450, parliament petitioned for Suffolk's impeachment. He was locked into the Tower while the commons prepared their bill ; they could not rake up very serious charges, but they were determined on blood, and Henry could only frustrate their vengeance by banishing the duke for five years. The Londoners were so outraged by this lenient sentence that they would have murdered him if he had not crept from his home in St. Giles by a different way ; as it was, the mob captured his horse and attacked his servants. His fate was merely delayed. On April 30, he sailed from Ipswich for Flanders, some ships intercepted his vessel and had him brought aboard one, the *Nicholas of the Tower*. "Welcome traitor !" said the master of the *Nicholas*, and told Şuffolk that he must die. They gave him the next day and night in which to confess, then he was rowed in a boat on which stood an axe and a block. One of the crew, an Irishman, "the lewdest [*most ignorant*] of the ship, bade him lay down his head, and he would be fair-fared [*fairly treated*] and die on a sword ; and took a rusty sword and smote off his head within half-a-dozen strokes, and took away his gown of russet and his doublet of velvet mailed [*reinforced with steel*], and laid his body on the sands of Dover."

The killing of Suffolk—"Jackanapes," as the people called him—was the prelude to rebellion, to an organised rebellion, carefully planned and superbly executed. The leader is known as Jack Cade and he was apparently a well-to-do gentleman of Kent. Some chroniclers state that he was an Irishman and others that he had been outlawed from England for murdering a woman. The Irish tale may have originated in perhaps a visit to the Duke of York in Ireland, but the murder is an obvious calumny. Whoever Cade might have been remains to this day a mystery, yet he was an intelligent brave man and a born leader ; at the time he gave himself the names of John Amend-all and of John Mortimer for propaganda purposes, Mortimer being a good rallying-cry, as it reminded the people that the Lancastrians were usurpers who had taken the crown from Mortimer, the chosen of Richard II. This was not a peasants' rising as under Tyler, the squires and farmers and artisans joined ; it was orderly and knew exactly what it wanted, and its claims were succinct and essential. These claims were : 1. The King had given away so many crown lands that he was forced to tax the commons oppressively while the stuff and purveyance for his household were rarely paid for, but were seized by his officers ; 2. The offices of the collectors of the revenue were farmed out to the highest bidders instead of the men being elected by the knights-of-the-shires—the local members of parliament ; 3. The knights-of-the-shires were not elected by the people who were bullied by great lords into electing the lords' nominees ; 4. Justice was corrupt, bail was too high, courts were too far apart, crown taxes were levied without warning, men were impeached by court favourites and were unable to defend themselves so that their lands were taken from them, men were arrested far beyond the jurisdiction of the justices and heavily fined, the Barons of the Cinque Ports should not be exempt from certain taxes ; 5. The King's lands in France were lost by mismanagement and the traitors walked unpunished ; 6. Offices were given only to favourites of low birth while lords of the royal blood were sent from the King (this, of course, referred to York being posted to Ireland). Such were the main grievances, and to rectify them Cade demanded : 1. The King should resume crown lands ; 2. Suffolk's ministers should be removed and replaced by the Dukes of York, Exeter, Norfolk and Buckingham ; 3. The extortions of the King's officers were to cease and justice be reformed ; 4. The provisions of the Statute of Labourers which enacted that certain wages be kept stable were to be repealed, for conditions had altered since the days of Richard II and Wat Tyler.

These demands were most moderate, and the men of Kent were ready to back them with the sword if necessary. They mustered like soldiers and in many hundreds they were called up by the constables themselves. Then the " army " marched on London, reaching Blackheath on June 1. When the King learned of the rebellion he dissolved parliament and hurried to London, lodging at the priory of St. John's near Smithfield, hoping to avert bloodshed in some way, although he had 20,000 men with him. Negotiations were opened, and Cade produced his petition which was examined by the council and rejected. Knowing that the royal army was far stronger than his, Cade withdrew towards Bromley and Sevenoaks so as to join the Sussex men who were preparing to rise with him. Henry, fully armed, led his soldiers in pursuit, then for some reason he divided his army—it is said, at the persuasion of Margaret, who did not wish him to ride into danger—and himself stayed at Blackheath while the remainder of his men followed the commons. They were met near Sevenoaks and slaughtered, and the Blackheath army mutinied at once, saying that they were now on Cade's side ; and Henry fled to Greenwich.

All over south and east England the rebellion spread. Men took down the harness they had used in France and clothed their limbs again in steel, old swords were buckled on, old pikes cleaned, old axes sharpened. The men of England rose to the call of liberty. In Wiltshire the Bishop of Salisbury was murdered, and the murderers " made boast of their wickedness." From Essex and Sussex men rode to stand beside Jack Cade, they came also from Surrey, and it seemed that at last the commons had a leader capable of fighting for their wrongs. There was no hatred of the King. He was still loved, but his ministers were blamed and hated, their heads were demanded. Cade moved to Southwark and lodged in the White Hart Inn while the Londoners debated what best to do, whether to admit him or to keep the gates barred. Only one alderman opposed his admittance, and he was at once imprisoned. Over London Bridge rode Cade, between the old houses that had seen so many victorious Kings returning from France, that had seen King John and the Duke of Orléans ride by as prisoners, that not so long ago had watched the beautiful Margaret beside her smiling husband ; now the walls gazed down on English gentlemen and farmers marching with rusty weapons, victorious after battling with the King's troops and prepared to die for justice. Cade cut the ropes of the drawbridge as he passed, slicing them with his sword, and as he rode down Cannon Street, with his sword he tapped old London Stone and cried, " Now is Mortimer lord of this city ! " He rode like a victor, like a man who knew his worth and was assured of conquering ; he wore the gilt spurs of a knight and a gown of blue velvet ; over the gown was a brigandine—armour of overlapping plates riveted inside a coat of canvas—and on his head was a gilt helmet. Before him was carried a sword of state.

Cade was no butcher as Shakespeare would make him. He was a gentleman, a man who had probably fought in France, and he held his troops in strict order, no easy task amongst a confusion of every class and every trade. During the march to London he had hanged one, Paris, for being insubordinate. That he could keep his men disciplined is proved by the battle of Sevenoaks, and now again in London, where at first there was no pillaging, where all went friendlily. His men camped in Southwark, probably to avoid disturbances that might jeopardise the cause, and the next day, July 3, Cade re-entered the city and sought vengeance. Lord Say and Sheriff Crowmer, two well-hated men, were dragged from the Tower where they had been hiding, and Say was brought to trial in the Guildhall. He demanded trial by his peers, but the mob lost patience and dragged him out and chopped off his head in Cheapside. Crowmer was beheaded at Mile End, without Aldgate.

It was now that Cade did the one act that doomed his cause, the one strange act that has made historians judge him harshly. He robbed the house of Philip Malpas, an alderman, but Malpas was warned and escaped with some of his valuables. The truth appears to be that the only things Cade took were some jewels belonging to the Duke of York which Malpas held in pawn ; they were found afterwards untouched. Yet somehow he had to find money if only to stop his men plundering ; at first he had levied on the Lombards, and the Londoners had not minded that in the least, now he wished from them enough to pay his troops, and the citizens hid their moneybags. Besides, it was natural that outlaws should seek an opportunity for plunder, that murderers should creep out of sanctuaries and mingle with the army. Whatever small looting went on one can only be amazed that there was not more. Cade was fighting a losing battle, somehow he had to feed his men and keep them contented, a difficult enough task for an officer with tradition behind him, but almost hopeless for a man who had to rely on his own personality and on the honour and faith of his soldiers. Honour and faith are infinitesimal beside the force of gold ; the Londoners were soon to prove that. They shouted lustily at the voice of freedom, but they were not prepared to pay for it. When Cade took money from a merchant called Curtis, the Londoners grew afraid and plotted together while the unsuspecting commons rested in Southwark. Troops were brought secretly from the Tower, and at ten in the night of July 4, they marched to the Bridge. All night the battle continued in that narrow space— about eight feet wide between the houses—until the houses began to rock and almost tumble into the river. Somehow a fire started —Cade, of course, was afterwards blamed, but it would have been a purposeless thing for him to do—" and some desiring to eschew the fire leaped on his enemy's weapon, and so died ; fearful women with children in their arms, amazed and appalled, leaped for fear into the river." The commons were eventually driven back into Southwark. Cade might be locked outside the city walls, yet he was still powerful enough to make the court party so afraid that they sent envoys who considered him " a subtle man." The envoys took the petitions, gave no answer, but promised a free pardon to Cade and all his followers if they would disperse ; and stupidly half the army trooped off with astonishing faith in the promises of men who had proved themselves rascals again and again. Cade knew the truth and kept as many followers as he could, warning them that their cause was not won until parliament had ratified the petitions ; and he soon proved his words. After leading a vain assault on Queensborough Castle he was attainted, and the pardon was declared invalid as it had been issued in the wrong name, in that of Mortimer and not of Cade. The court party dared rise now that it had to face a handful of men instead of a united commons, and a price of a thousand pounds was set on the head of Cade ; he was chased through Sussex into the woods near Lewes, and was cornered in a garden at Heathfield. He fought magnificently but was outnumbered, he fell beneath the swords of enemies. His parboiled head was spiked above the Drawbridge Tower of London Bridge, and Sheriff Iden who had killed him was given a comfortable annuity and was made keeper of Rochester Castle. Commissions went through the country, ferreting out the " rebels," eight of whom were executed at Canterbury ; Henry himself was present at the time, and also when a further twenty-six died at Rochester. They called it " the Harvest of Heads."

Yet Cade had not failed, no blow for freedom fails although men perish. His attempt had made England aware of the terrible abuses and had made men realise that another leader might yet come to save them. And they turned towards Ireland where the Duke of York was ruling so justly that ever afterwards the Yorkists were to be remembered there most lovingly.

York was a short plump man with a squarish face ; he was a brave and stubborn soldier without particular genius. And he was weary of being pushed aside while Margaret and her favourites—some of whom, men whispered, were her lovers—did what they willed with England. He decided to take a hand in affairs almost at the exact moment when Henry recalled from Calais the Duke of Somerset who was blamed for the loss of Normandy as Suffolk had been blamed for the loss of Anjou and Maine. When news came of York's return there was terror in the court and troops were sent to arrest him, but he eluded them and reached St. Albans where there was almost a fight. Then he kept straight on for London and demanded to see the King. Henry cowered before him and promised almost anything. What York wanted was the banishment of the " traitors," and he demanded it most truculently, after which he retired to his castle of Fotheringhay and waited until parliament met in November. The lords brought to it such armies that men found it almost impossible to get lodgings in the city, for all expected that there would be war between Somerset and York. York had the stronger claim to the throne, but if Somerset could reverse Henry IV's act that banned the Beauforts from reigning, he might with his power over the King and Margaret be promised the succession. In parliament men tried to discuss matters normally, each shrinking from opening the question of the King's advisers, while the livery-men of the rival dukes glared at each other. There was a brawl, Yorkists and Londoners attacked Somerset and he was dragged into a barge and rescued at the last moment. His lodgings at Blackfriars were plundered, as were also the houses of his friends and supporters. Henry strove to keep order by putting on his armour and riding through the city with a troop of knights, but affairs had reached a dangerous pitch. When parliament reassembled in January 1451, the subject was definitely opened, and the banishment of thirty court favourites was demanded, including Somerset. Henry promised to dismiss some of his advisers for a year, but, of course, he did nothing.

The year passed and still there were threats of civil war, and York, finding himself still kept from power, issued a manifesto to the men of Shrewsbury on February 3, 1452, saying : " I signify unto you that, with the help and supportation of Almighty God, and of our Lady, and of all the company of heaven, I, after long sufferance and delays, though it is not my will or intent to displease my sovereign lord, seeing that the said Duke [of Somerset] ever prevaileth and ruleth about the King's person, and that by this means the land is likely to be destroyed, am fully concluded to proceed in all haste against him with the help of my kinsman and friends." Which he immediately did, setting out for London and slipping aside from Henry who rode to meet him. Yet after all York did not enter London, he crossed the river at Kingston and camped at Dartford. Henry followed and drew up his men on Blackheath, and sent envoys to the duke. He promised a great many things and York was induced to believe him, but when after recklessly dismissing his soldiers he called on Henry he found Somerset present as strong as ever. York was now in the hands of his enemies and when the King entered London he made him ride ahead as if he were a prisoner, then at St. Paul's he forced him to swear that he would never again gather men without the King's command. After that York was permitted to go, as Somerset dared not imprison or execute so popular a man.

THE Hundred Years' War was at last at an end. In 1453, after

the capture of Bordeaux by King Charles, the English were permitted to sail home, and on October 19, the French formally
took possession. The long struggle was over, it had kept on since
the days of Crécy and Poitiers, lapsing until Henry V again
made the Englishman a conqueror ; but after Henry's death,
despite the courage of Bedford, the war had changed, the French
became victors, led by the Maid of Orléans ; when Bedford died, the
fighting degenerated into a series of painful campaigns in which
the unpaid English troops were gradually pushed out of France.

Now in England men could look after their own affairs, and
there was much fighting in the north between the Nevilles and
the Percies, but at last that was calmed, and then all of a sudden
King Henry lost his senses because of " a sudden and thoughtless
fright." For eighteen months he was to remain sunk in a
stupor like a man already lifeless whose body still perambulates
when the soul has gone. • He could not walk nor lift his head,
and even that momentous event, the birth of his first child,
a son, on October 13, 1453, had no effect upon the numbed
brain of the poor King. They tried to make him bless the
child, he did not stir in his seat ; again they tried to make him
understand that this was his son and at last " he looked on
the Prince and cast down his eyen again, without any more."
The boy was christened Edward, and although many said
that he was not Henry's child, his birth nevertheless made
a great difference to the political situation. York was dragged
from his perch as the heir-apparent, and no longer could he
lead troops except as a rebel against the present régime ; he
determined to lead instead a party in politics. Now that the
King was incapable, Somerset was at his mercy, and he soon
had him impeached and imprisoned while himself was appointed
Protector and Defender of the Realm until Prince Edward should
come of age. He carried out his duties with honour and wisdom
and did not seek revenge, he permitted Somerset to remain
unharmed in the Tower. His main trouble was to settle the
disturbances in the north, those continual battles between jealous
nobles, and on his side he had his kinsman, the strongest noble
in England, Richard Neville, Earl of Warwick. Warwick, who
had just come of age, was the son-in-law of Henry Beauchamp
and was to become famous in history as the Kingmaker, He was
brought into York's party through his father, the Earl of Salisbury,
York's brother-in-law ; the three united made a group that could
not, it seemed, be defeated by open war.

Unluckily, just as York was shaping the country back to prosperity, Henry showed glimmers of intelligence, and at last, " as a man who wakes after a long dream," he became fully conscious.   On December 28, 1454, Queen Margaret brought little Edward for his father to see, " and then he asked what the Prince's name was, and the Queen told him Edward ; and then he held up his hands and thanked God thereof.   And he said he never knew till that time, nor wist not what was said to him, nor wist not where he had be[en] whilse he had been sick till now."

Naturally York had to resign when Henry became sane, and the moment his strong hand was relaxed the country rushed to anarchy.   Somerset was released, York's captaincy of Calais was taken from him and presented to his enemy, while Salisbury was dismissed from the chancellorship.

MARGARET and Somerset were vengeful people, their private hatreds were to them of greater importance than the welfare of England ; they did not bother about the country, they were determined to destroy the Duke of York.   They summoned a council to provide for the King's safety " against his enemies," and they omitted to summon York, Salisbury, and Warwick. Immediately, these three nobles realised that they were threatened and decided to strike first, there was nothing else they could do ; all their efforts when in power had been honest and wise, they they had not let personal feelings in any way interfere with justice.   Now they were to be attacked and, for their own pro-tection, they had to take up arms.   They called out their tenants, and the first blow was struck in the long Wars of the Roses.   It might be mentioned at this point that the term " Wars of the Roses " is a late invention—the white rose of York existed at this date but the Lancastrian badge was the letter S which possibly stood for " Sovereign."   The Red Rose was not thought of until the next century.

Arriving at Royston on May 20, 1455, York, Salisbury and Warwick issued the usual manifesto in which they assured the people that they meant no harm to the King and that the army was only there " to keep ourselves out of the danger whereunto our said enemies have not ceased to study, labour and compass to bring us."   This manifesto they sent Henry, it never reached him : Somerset destroyed it, with a separate and more personal letter.   The two armies, the King's and the Yorkist faced each outside St. Albans, and Salisbury's brother-in-law, the Duke of Buckingham, was sent by the King to ask the intentions of the Yorkists, and they answered that they had come as " rightful and true subjects " who wanted Henry to deliver to them " such as we will accuse." When this bold answer was reported to the King he flew into a rage most unusual in so quiet-tempered a man, but always he was staunch to his friends and an insult at Somerset he felt as an insult directed at himself. " I, King Harry," he cried, " charge and command that no manner of person, of what degree, or state, or condition that ever he be, abide not, but void the field and not be so hard [as] to make any resistance against me in mine own realm ; for I shall know what traitor dare be so bold to raise a people in mine own land, where through [*whereof*] I am in great dis-ease and heaviness. And by the faith that I owe to St. Eadward and to the crown of England, I shall destroy them every mother's son ; and they [shall] be hanged and drawn and quartered that may be taken afterward, of them to have example to all such traitors to beware to make any such rising of people within my land, and so traitorly to abide their King and governor. And for a conclusion, rather than they shall have any lord here with me at this time, I shall this day for their sake and in this quarrel myself live and die ! "

Between eleven and twelve o'clock in the morning the battle started. York opened the attack, charging down a street towards the market-place in which the royal standard was raised. Lord Clifford barred his path and he could not break through, then Warwick charged over gardens in the rear of the city, and once inside the walls " suddenly they blew up trumpets and set a cry with a shout and a great voice, ' A Warwick ! A Warwick ! A Warwick ! ' " Soon the " whole street was full of dead corpses," and the royalists broke in terror. Down went the royal standard, it was trampled underfoot, and the King's men, " disliking the sight of blood, withdrew." Somerset and Clifford were killed, and Henry stayed alone beside his banner with arrows falling about him ; one barb pierced his neck, yet he did not stir until his friends besought him to take refuge in the nearby house of a tanner. Here he was found by York, Salisbury and Warwick, who knelt and asked forgiveness, " and therefore the King our Sovereign Lord took them to grace, and so desired them to cease their people and that there should no more harm be done."

AGAIN when in power York sought no vengeance on his enemies, he tried to rule with moderation. Henry's wound was for a while quite serious, then he fell into his second coma, although this time it lasted only for about four months. It was not until March 24, 1458, that any attempt was made to soothe the embittered feelings of those who had fought at St. Albans. On that day a proclamation was given out according to which York, Salisbury and Warwick swore to found a chantry in the city for the souls of those who had fallen in the battle ; York agreed to give five thousand marks to the widowed Duchess of Somerset, and Warwick to give one thousand marks to the bereaved Cliffords. And on Lady's Day a public reconciliation between all enemies was made in St. Paul's Cathedral, but it was an empty reconciliation. Once blood had been spilt more blood was demanded, feuds began, men once friends looked upon each other as enemies when they remembered the corpses of loved ones.

Margaret took the initiative in hatred. In April, 1459, writs, sealed by the privy seal and some of them even signed by Henry, were forwarded to various supporters commanding them to " be with the King at Leicester the x day of May with as many men defensibly arrayed as they might according to their degree, and that they should bring with them for their expenses for ij months." York remained quiet, refusing to be drawn into what was obviously a challenge, and slowly he gathered his forces. Then in September Salisbury was ordered to appear before the King, and he immediately wrote to his son Warwick at Calais, bidding him come to his aid. Again it meant civil war, and Salisbury hurried to join York at Ludlow, but he was intercepted by a superior force of Lancastrians at Blore Heath ; their superiority of numbers, however, did not save them from defeat at the hands of the brave experienced earl who arrived safely at York's castle. Warwick set out at once from Calais and, landing at Sandwich, marched to Ludlow. The three were united again and ready for battle, yet if possible they wished to keep the peace. They wrote to Henry, but as before, the letter never reached him, and a forged answer was sent, saying that the King would meet his enemies in the field. Sorrowfully the three prepared for the coming fight, digging trenches, bringing up cannon and hammering in stakes, but they were hopelessly outnumbered, for Margaret had had time to gather a huge force. Her men came to fight " for the love they bare to the King, but more for the fear they had of the Queen, whose countenance was so fearful and whose look was so terrible that to all men against whom she took a small displeasure her frowning was their undoing and her indignation was their death." York tried to maintain the courage of his small army by pretending that Henry was dead and he even went to the extent of having masses sung for his soul's happiness ; but when the enemy arrived there was no hiding the truth. The King was to be seen by all, cheering on his men when they camped on the other side of the river. That night Henry proclaimed that he would give free pardon to every man save the leaders who would join his standard, and the Yorkist desertions were so many that the duke fled with his second living son Edmund of Rutland and managed to reach Ireland ; Salisbury and Warwick, with York's eldest son Edward, made for the coast.

Now that the power was hers again, all that Margaret did was to drive the country strongly on to the side of the Yorkists. She did " as her liked, gathering riches innumerable. The officers of the realm, and especially the Earl of Wiltshire, treasurer of England, for to enrich himself, peeled the poor people, and disinherited rightful heirs, and did many wrongs. The Queen was defamed and slandered, that he that was called Prince, was not her son, but a bastard gotten in avoutry [adultery]."

Salisbury, Warwick and York's eldest son Edward, Earl of March, were the first to return. They landed in Kent and marched towards London, pausing at Canterbury to worship at the shrine of St. Thomas Becket. A herald was sent ahead to demand admittance to the city, and on July 2, 1460, the gates were opened, the drawbridge was let down, and Warwick and his friends marched over the old bridge into London. With them they had brought a most valuable friend, a papal legate, Francesco dei Coppini, Bishop of Terni, and he sent a letter to Henry ordering him at the peril of his soul to agree to the Yorkist demands, which must have troubled the pious King. As convocation was then sitting in St. Paul's, Warwick explained the situation to the bishops, and with his comrades swore on the cross of Canterbury that he meant no harm to the King. After which he began collecting troops and marched out to battle, Salisbury being left to subdue the Tower which remained defiant.

On Thursday, July 10, the Yorkists found Henry in a meadow outside Northampton, his army in formation behind trenches.

They made one last attempt to bring the King to agree to their demands, but as all efforts failed, at two o'clock in the afternoon Warwick's trumpets " blew up " and the fight began. It was scarcely a fight. There was a traitor with the King, one Lord Grey of Ruthyn : he held the van, and instead of attacking Warwick he attacked his comrades. Within half an hour all was over, the Yorkists were victorious, and they found the poor King alone in his tent " as a man born and predestinate to trouble, misery, and calamity." Warwick, his uncle Fauconberg, and young Edward of York knelt and begged forgiveness, then they led Henry " with procession " into Northampton.

Queen Margaret and her son were in Eccleshall Castle, and when they learned of the Yorkist victory they fled for Wales. Passing near Malpas, in Cheshire, they were robbed and even the Queen's life was threatened, but she struggled on, riding most of the time behind a lad of fourteen named John Combe until she found refuge with the King's half-brother, Jasper Tudor, in Harlech Castle.

YORK came from Ireland, and his duchess, travelling in a chair covered with blue velvet, met him at Hereford. He then rode to London in royal state, with heralds and trumpeters racing ahead and with a sword borne upright before him. He had five hundred men, and when he reached Westminster where parliament was then in session, he walked straight to the royal throne and laid his hands upon the cushions as if he would sit there. He paused while the lords and people " ran together and looked," then realising that the moment had not yet arrived, he drew back. It was then suggested that he speak with the King, but he cried, " I know of no one in the realm who would not more fitly come to me than I to him." In his rage at not being acclaimed, he went to the royal palace and actually broke open the doors of Henry's apartments, and " the King hearing the great noise and rumour of the people, gave him place and took another chamber."

York had been too open, he should have waited—perhaps in his hurry he thought that he had waited too long—Henry was yet loved and the moment had not come when he might safely be deposed. Until now York had behaved with restraint, staying silent under real provocation, and it is strange that he should thus suddenly declare his intentions. He should at least have tested the lords, have tried to gather a strong party about

35

him, before claiming the throne. As it was, he outraged his friends. The realisation that the crown was close appears to have driven him slightly mad with arrogance, and Warwick tried to remonstrate with him. With his brother Thomas Neville he strode into the duke's chamber which was crowded with men-at-arms. York was leaning on a sideboard and Warwick gave him many " hard words," when young Edmund Duke of Rutland entered and said, " Fair sir, be not angry, for you know that we have the true right to the crown, and that my lord and father here must have it." Only Edward, Earl of March, now eighteen years of age and extremely intelligent, realised the danger of angering Warwick. He interrupted Edmund. " Brother," he cried, " vex no man, for all shall be well." Warwick would listen to nothing further. He turned away and spoke to no man save to Edward.

On October 16, York formally claimed the throne, basing his right on direct descent from Henry III. The lords attempted to shuffle the problem on to the shoulders of the justices, but the justices refused to tackle so dangerous a question, and desperately the lords turned to the King's sergeants-at-law and attorneys, who also refused to answer, and the poor lords found that they must answer York themselves. Each man in turn gave his opinion, and York's claim was rejected on five points, but at last it was decided that Henry should keep the crown while he lived, after which it was to pass to York, who was then created Prince of Wales.

When Margaret learned that her beloved son was to lose his inheritance she started immediately to gather an army in Scotland, and York went north in a peculiarly indolent fashion. It is impossible to explain this sudden carelessness on his part, when the Lancastrians swooped down on his castle of Sandal he had few men with him. A truce was agreed to that was to last until after Christmas, but there was no keeping faith with Margaret's men ; we have two conflicting stories of the battle that followed, the contemporary writers state that the Yorkists were attacked when gathering provisions, while a later and usually reliable chronicler tells us that the duke was drawn from his castle by taunts and by the shame of skulking before a woman " whose weapon is only her tongue and her nails." Whatever began the conflict, this we know is truth : York was killed in the fight, his son Edmund was caught on a bridge by the Black

Clifford, son of the Clifford who died at St. Albans, and was there slain : another story tells us that Edmund was stabbed as he beat on a woman's door imploring admission, and that Clifford cried as he struck him down, " By God's blood, thy father slew mine, so will I do to thee, and all thy kin ! " Salisbury was later captured, taken to Pontefract and there beheaded ; another writer, however, assures us that he bribed his way to freedom but the " common people of the country which loved him not, took him out of the castle by violence and smote off his head."

The fate of York was indeed a tragic one. His corpse was set upon an ant-heap and crowned in mockery with a wreath of grass, while his enemies jeered and cried, " Hail, King without a kingdom ! " Then they beheaded him and set his head with a paper crown upon a spike above the Micklegate Bar of his own city of York.

EDWARD, Earl of March, took the place of his father in the Yorkist party. He was young and extremely handsome. With Warwick and Warwick's uncle Fauconberg he waited to intercept Margaret's army on its journey south. But first at Mortimer's Cross he defeated her allies. Before the battle he noticed three suns swimming in the heavens and he pointed at them and cried to his troops, " Be-eth of good comfort and dreadeth not ; this is a good sign, for those three suns betokeneth the Father, the Son and the Holy Ghost, and therefore let us have a good heart, and in the name of almighty God go we against our enemies." The battle was soon over, and Owen Tudor, the widower of Queen Katherine, was caught and executed. When he saw the axe he said, " That head shall lie on the stock that was wont to lie on Queen Katherine's lap," and died bravely.

Meanwhile Warwick was defeated at St. Albans. He tried to dam the Queen's great army, but the inevitable treachery lost him, not only the fight, but the person of the King. Henry was again with his beloved wife, he was found after the battle sitting under an oak tree and " smiling to see the discomfiture of the army." In Clifford's tent they brought the Queen and his son to him, and greatly rejoicing he took them in his arms and kissed them and thanked God. The boy was only eight, yet the next day he was dressed in a purple velvet brigandine as if about to march to war, and after being given his father's blessing was knighted. Then he was made to decide the fate of two prisoners, Margaret asking what kind of death he would like them to have. " Let them have their heads taken off," said little Edward, and one of the prisoners could not help crying in disgust, " May God destroy those who taught thee this manner of speech."

WARWICK joined Edward, and on February 27, 1461, the pair entered London. For some strange reason the Lancastrians did not follow up their success but instead marched north again ; one of the explanations given was that Henry was so horrified by the behaviour of the troops that he refused to let them advance ; the more probable reason is that the leaders dared not bring such an unruly mob to London which would have lost them the city for ever. As it was, they lost their King his throne.

No longer did Warwick stand in the path of the Yorkist claim to England. His father had been killed at Wakefield and, deeply embittered by the memory, he must have known that any reconciliation with such a woman as Queen Margaret was impossible. On Sunday, March 1, his brother, George Neville, the chancellor, addressed the citizens in St. John's Fields, Clerkenwell, with the Yorkist troops about him. He told them of Edward's right to the crown, a stronger right than Henry's ; afterwards at a council in Baynard's Castle in Blackfriars it was decided to make Edward King without delay. The populace had shouted their acclamation in St. John's Field, clapping their hands and beating their armour—" I was there," writes a chronicler, " I heard them "—and now on March 4, Edward and his friends made offerings in St. Paul's and rode to Westminster. In the great hall, Edward took the throne and spoke to the people, telling them of his right. The crowd shouted as they had shouted three days ago, and he was escorted to the abbey, where the clergy presented him with the crown and sceptre of St. Eadward.

From this day Henry VI became either a fugitive or a prisoner, but never King, save for a brief restoration of six months.

XVI

KING EDWARD THE FOURTH

1461–1483

ALTHOUGH NOT YET CROWNED, King Edward IV's reign was considered to have begun with the deposition of Henry VI. He did not usurp the throne as the Lancastrians had usurped it, this was actually a legitimist restoration, for his grandmother was the direct descendant of that Mortimer chosen by Richard II to be his successor, the Mortimer whom the Lancastrians had put aside. Edward was now nineteen years of age and extraordinarily handsome and tall : he looked indeed the ideal King.

After the hasty ceremonies, Henry VI being formally deposed, Edward set out for a final battle with Margaret whose badly disciplined army had retreated north. On March 16, 1461, he began his march, and on the 27th had reached Pontefract, close behind the enemy who were guarding the road to York where Margaret and Henry and their son were lodged. The Lancastrian army itself was at Towton, having the flooded Aire between it and the advancing Yorkists. The van, under Black-Faced Clifford the Butcher, held the Aire at Ferrybridge, and on the 28th Lord Fitzwalter was sent by Edward to force his way across. Apparently he kept a slovenly watch while he strove to erect a new bridge, for Clifford in the night suddenly darted down, smashed the makeshift bridge, and drove the Yorkists almost mad with terror. Fitzwalter, not fully armed, was slain as he stepped out of doors, and even Warwick became half-hysterical. He galloped to Edward's camp and killed his own horse, shouting, " Let him fly that will, for surely by this cross I will tarry with him who will tarry with me, fall back, fall edge ! " He was wounded in the leg, yet that did not keep him from joining in the ensuing battle. Edward, always sane and rather sceptical, refused to budge until the sun had risen and he could see exactly what had been the damage, he then sent Fauconberg to cross the Aire three miles off and to attack Clifford in the rear as he retreated. Fauconberg did his task well. Clifford was caught near Dintingdale and his men slain before they could seriously defend themselves ; Clifford himself had unstrapped and taken off his helm to ease his neck where the mail gorget had chafed the skin, and he was therefore easily killed. The Aire being now open, the whole Yorkist army crossed, and on Palm Sunday, March 29, Edward drew up his men to the east of Saxton, with Scarthingwell on his right and with the low valley of Dintingdale before him. One mile to the north the Lancastrians stood on Towton Hill, they were said to be the largest army put into the field during the entire wars, and Edward must have been outnumbered by almost two to one, besides having the disadvantage of being made to attack an enemy perched on a hillside. It was very cold, and between eight and nine in the morning he led the advance into an icy wind. His left wing, slightly ahead of the main body, was commanded by Fauconberg, Warwick held the centre, Edward himself the rear, Norfolk keeping the right wing in reserve. Then suddenly the wind veered, instead of beating against the Yorkists it beat against the Lancastrians. Snow began to fall and it fell so heavily that neither army could see the other. Fauconberg's archers took advantage of the wind and they were using a new " flight-arrow " which had extra emperons, or feathers, on the shaft and possessed a range forty yards greater than the Lancastrians' whose badly-aimed arrows— because of the wind " their sight was somewhat blemished and minished "—fell harmlessly into the snow until they had exhausted their quivers. They had then to charge, for being arrowless they would have been slaughtered had they remained impassive under Fauconberg's deadly aim ; the command was given, and they charged down the hill upon the Yorkists who stood ready with sword and battle-axe and the mallet of lead that could smash through the thickest helm. The men grappled each other in the piercing wind and scattered snow, and a part of the Yorkist left wing broke and fled, but Edward, with Warwick fighting like " a new Hector," rallied the men and brought them back over snow-deep fields that were " more red than white." Norfolk's reserves cut the Lancastrians off from Towton, driving them back upon the Cock, a small stream, in which many were drowned, for it was " not very broad but of a great deepness." The Yorkists gave no quarter, all night they chased the fugitives, killing them to the very walls of York. Young Somerset managed to escape, and with Henry, Margaret and little Edward raced for Scotland. The victory had been magnificent, yet Edward had not succeeded in capturing or killing his main enemies, and so long as they lived his throne would ever be in danger.

The next morning he rode into York and was met "with great solemnity and processions," and he took down the heads of his father and friends from the gates and put up instead the heads of enemies. Yet Henry was still at large and was clinging desperately to England. A certain Thomas Playters writes to John Paston : "I heard that Harry the sixth is in a place in Yorkshire called Coroumbe [? *Carham Castle, Northumberland*] ; such a name it hath or much like. And there is a siege laid about, and divers esquires of the Earl of Northumberland's gathered them together five or six thousand men to bicker with the siege, that in the meanwhile Harry the sixth might have been stole away at a little postern on the back side ; at which bicker [have] been slain three thousand men of the north. . . . Some say the Queen, Somerset and the Prince should be there." Edward did his best to catch them and gradually he drove them into Scotland, where Margaret did a most foolish act ; she surrendered Berwick to the Scots in exchange for help, and thereby infuriated the English. Even Henry tried to stop her, but at last he "was constrained thereunto in this extreme misery." And it was a useless gift, Margaret did not get the help she expected.

IT was time for Edward's coronation and the ceremony was arranged for Sunday, June 28. Two days before the appointed date he rode from Lambeth to the Tower with the mayor and alderman and four hundred citizens "well horsed and clad in green," twenty-eight Knights of the Bath were created that evening and five others in the morning ; amongst these were the King's little brothers, George and Richard, who during the festivities after the coronation were created respectively Dukes of Clarence and Gloucester. The ceremonies were prolonged as it was deemed unlucky to be crowned on Childermas or Innocents' Day which fell this year on a Sunday ; on the 27th Edward performed the usual state ride from the Tower with the newly created knights ahead of him "in blue gowns and hoods upon their shoulders like to priests " ; on Sunday he was hallowed ; and on Monday, St. Peter's Day, he went again to the abbey to avoid the risk of Childermas ; on Tuesday. as it was the commemoration of St. Paul's, he visited the cathedral and was welcomed with pageants, while an angel drifted down on wires and censed him.

FEW Kings have looked or acted the part so perfectly as Edward IV. He was " very tall of personage, exceeding the stature almost of all others, of comely visage, pleasant look, broad-breasted, the residue even to his feet proportionately correspondent, of sharp wit, hault courage, of passing retentive memory touching those things which he had once conceived, diligent in doing his affairs, ready in perils, earnest and horrible to the enemy, bountiful to his friends and acquaintance[s], most fortunate in his wars, given to bodily lust, whereunto he was of his own disposition inclined ; by reason whereof, and of humanity which was bred in him abundantly, he would use himself more familiarly among private persons than the honour of his majesty required." The people adored him, men would die fighting for one smile of commendation, women languished for his kisses. Like a jovial golden god he took the throne of England, quick to action when needed but preferring to drink a cup of wine or to fondle the little chins of ladies. For this reason he has been spoken of even by contemporaries as no politician, yet under his rule the feudal system definitely ended, the great baronies were broken up, ready for the Tudors to began their miserly reigns. His laziness conquered his intelligence, he was too good-humoured to take even politics seriously, and his lackadaisical manners show up in strong contrast beside his serious-minded noble brother the Duke of Gloucester, later King Richard III. These three brothers, Edward IV, George Duke of Clarence and Richard Duke of Gloucester, are a fascinating trio if only because of their extreme differences in character. Richard was more the dreamer, the believer in chivalry, in noble and high aims ; Edward was easy-going and liked the ripe things of earth, he liked women particularly, and few men's wives were safe within his reach ; George was a scoundrel, weak-willed, resentful, a man who could never stay satisfied, who must for ever grope for more splendid honours.

Edward was six feet three and a half inches tall, fair-complexioned and with long flaxen hair to his shoulders. Comines tells us that he " was not a man of any great management or foresight, but he was of an invincible courage, and the handsomest Prince my eyes ever beheld." Again we find this contempt for Edward's abilities, yet when we examine his reign we discover that his achievements were actually very great. They were not of the old-fashioned dazzling type ; when he invaded France he fully realised that money was of more importance than conquests—and does not Comines himself slyly assure us that honour is always on the side of the victor ? The world of chivalry was dying, and Edward was prepared to take advantake of new ideas ; the first glow of the sceptical renascence was lightening the West, and Edward was a renascence figure, pleasure-loving, tolerant, a patron of the arts and sciences. On the question of politics he showed himself astute by more or less keeping out of European affairs—except in vain efforts to marry off his children—by breaking the power of the great barons like Warwick, and by turning trader. He was a merchant-prince and struggled to escape from the grip of the Hanseatic League. This league, a federation of the German maritime towns, was a huge shipping organisation that carried the produce of nations unable to gather vessels numerous or strong enough for the task. The league became indispensable, and England granted it huge privileges, allowing it a guildhall in Thames Street rent-free. The Steelyard—as it was called—became an important centre of London, and the apprentices were continually in moments of national depression trying to tear down the walls and murder the inhabitants. The Hanseatic imports, according to Stow, were mainly wheat, rye and other grain, cables, masts, pitch, tar, flax, hemp, linen, wainscots, wax, steel and other " profitable merchandise." Under Edward the English merchant adventurers strove to wrest this trade from the league, and there were continual battles ; in Bergen the English merchants were murdered, and the Hanseatics attacked and pillaged the English coast. Edward would probably have broken their power had he not been made to run from England and seek their help.

Under his rule the merchants grew to strength until London seemed a second Antwerp, and the King himself liked to invest his money in trade. In this way he amassed a huge fortune, and the more he amassed the more miserly he grew.

A man who achieved all this from a country broken by civil war could have been no childish politician.

He was born in Rouen on April 28, 1422, and was therefore called the White Rose of Rouen. His portraits do not endorse the tales we hear of his dazzling beauty, but perhaps it was more his giant body and charm of manner than any facial perfection that made men and women look upon him almost as a god. He possessed numerous mistresses and "would say that he had three concubines, which in diverse properties diversely excelled —one, the merriest, the other the wiliest, the third the holiest harlot in the realm as one whom no man could get out of the church to any place lightly but if it were to his bed." The first of these was the famous Jane Shore ; of the other two we know nothing except that "they were somewhat greater personages than Mistress Shore." Jane has for some reason become almost as popular as Nell Gwyn, yet actually we have few details of her early life except that she was married to a prosperous " citizen and mercer of London, *alias* late of Derby, yeoman." In his numerous liaisons the King never forced his royal prerogative, he never bullied the woman by a show of power, he won their love either by his charm of manner or with the corruptive gold in his pouch.

When dealing with the Yorkist Kings most historians have accepted the spitfire Tudor chronicles as history, they have rarely attempted to sift them for the truth ; eagerly they have swallowed every tale spread by usurpers eager to blacken the memory of the true Kings ; Richard III has suffered abominably because of this, and even Edward IV has been besmirched. Yet he was really an honourable and kind man. He never refused a petition for pardon and continually forgave his strongest enemies. That he loved many women is true, but his personal affairs have nothing whatever to do with his abilities as King, while the women did little harm, and probably some good. Jane Shore, for example, " never abused " her power " to any man's hurt, but to many men's comfort and relief."

As a soldier it is literally impossible to rate Edward too highly. He was, like his brother Richard, a genius in war ; although he never refused a combat, he was never defeated. During the Scottish war of 1482 he instituted a posting system, having relays of horsemen every twenty miles so that news could be carried a hundred miles a day. He was religious but not fanatically so. Only one lollard was burnt during his reign ; this was John Goos who died on Tower Hill in 1474. Before going to execution Goos asked if he might dine, saying, " I eat now a good and competent dinner, for I shall pass a little sharp shower ere I go to supper." But perhaps the few burnings may have been for lack of men strong enough to abide by their faith rather than for any tolerance on Edward's part. He was the patron of Caxton and was deeply interested in alchemy, which stood to the intelligent medieval man somewhat as physics does to us to-day. In fact, he was the ideal cultured gentleman of the fifteenth century, a soldier, a merchant, a sportsman, a lover of books and alchemy and of women, a slightly careless politician, trusting perhaps too greatly, yet always prepared to reward loyalty and to forgive his enemies.

AFTER the coronation, parliament met in the Painted Chamber in Westminster on November 4, and it had two important matters with which to deal—the recognition of Edward's title and the attainder of the Lancastrians. It opened with an address from the commons to the King, thanking him for accepting " the reign and governance of the said realm whereunto ye be right-wisely and naturally born," and demanding the punishment of those who had stirred up disorders during the late reign. Next came a petition rehearsing Edward's claim to the throne, tracing his descent from Henry III through Richard II, the last true King, who had been put to death by " Henry, late Earl of Derby," and praying that his title be affirmed by act of parliament, as Henry IV, Henry V and Henry VI were usurpers. All this being agreed to, an act of attainder was passed against nearly one hundred and fifty Lancastrians as guilty of high treason against their liege lord King Edward IV. The " late King " Henry the " usurper " began the list, Margaret " late called Queen of England " followed, and " her son " Edward, " late called Prince of Wales," came third. It is interesting to note that the boy was referred to as " her son," and not as Henry's.

At the conclusion of the session Edward addressed the speaker and commons. " James Strangeways [speaker]," he said, " and ye that be commons for the commons of this my land, for the true hearts and tender considerations that ye have had to my right and title, that I and my ancestors have had unto the crown of this realm, the which from us have been long time withheld, and now, thanked be almighty God, of Whose grace groweth all victory, by your true hearts and great assistance I am restored unto that that is my right and title ; wherefore I thank you as heartily as I can, also for the tender and true hearts that ye have showed unto me in that that ye have tenderly had in remembrance the correction of the horrible murder and cruel death of my lord my father, my brother Rutland, and my cousin of Salisbury, and other[s], I thank you right heartily : and I shall be unto you with the grace of almighty God as good and gracious a sovereign lord as ever was any of my noble progenitors to their subjects and liegemen ; and for the faithful and loving hearts, and also the great labours that ye have borne and sustained towards me, in the recovering of my said right and title, which I now possess, I thank you, with all my heart ; and if I had any better good to reward you withal than my body, ye should have it ; the which shall always be ready for your defence, never sparing nor letting for no jeopardy, praying you all of your hearty assistance and good continuance, as I shall be unto you your very rightwise and loving liege lord."

MARGARET had not given up the struggle. For a woman proud and ambitious as she was, it must have been the most excruciating torment to see the son of her enemy upon her own son's throne. She sailed for France and made a treaty with the new King Louis XI who took from prison an old admirer of hers, a brave soldier, Pierre de Brézé, and gave him to her for captain. De Brézé raised about eight hundred men and sailed with Margaret to rescue her throne, but the attempt with so small a force was naturally a failure, and soon she was forced again to fly with her son, this time to Flanders, where she arrived almost penniless, living on de Brézé's charity, yet as determined and as revengeful as ever.

Margaret was out of England but Henry VI was in Scotland, and Somerset, son of the late Duke, was leader of the Lancastrians ; whatever danger threatened from the north was soon frustrated by the Earl of Montagu, Warwick's brother, who won the battle of Hedgeley Moor and quickly followed it with a great victory at Hexham, in which Somerset was captured and later executed.

At last it seemed that Edward would have peace. He was now accepted as King of England by the Pope, by Burgundy, Brittany, Denmark and Castile ; Louis of France was angling for his friendship, and he had signed a fifteen years' truce with Scotland. Yet there was one man within the kingdom itself who stood too high to please any King, and that was Edward's friend and benefactor, the Earl of Warwick. We have no details of the behaviour together of these comrades-in-arms, but it needs no strong imagination to believe that the haughty Warwick swaggered in the court and perhaps patronised Edward a little. A hint is given us in a letter from Calais to Louis in which the

writer maliciously remarks : " They tell me that they have but
two rulers in England : Monsieur de Warwick and another
whose name I have forgotten." Whatever Edward felt he did
not speak, and outwardly the two remained friends while
Warwick busied himself to find a bride for his protégé, casting
first in Burgundian waters, then in Scottish, then in Castilian
and finally in French. It seemed to him an ideal match for
Edward to marry Louis's sister-in-law. Edward thought otherwise : on his way to suppress a northern rising, on May 1,
1464, he paused at Stony Stratford and rode quietly to Lord
Rivers' house at Grafton Regis where Elizabeth Woodville
awaited him. He married her secretly early in the morning at
Grafton, and no one was present " but the spouse and spousesse,
the Duchess of Bedford her mother, the priest, and two gentlemen
and a young man who helped the priest to sing. After the spous-
ailles the King rode again to Stony Stratford, as if he had been
hunting, and then returned at night."

This Elizabeth Woodville was the eldest daughter of Lord
Rivers who had married the widow of John Duke of Bedford ;
as a wife she was far unworthy of the King for " she was not
the daughter of a duke or earl, but her mother, the Duchess of
Bedford, had married a simple knight, so that though she was the
child of a duchess and the niece of the Count St. Pol, still she was
no wife for him." She was a widow, her husband Sir John Grey
had fought for the Lancastrians and had died of his wounds after
the second battle of St. Albans. We cannot doubt that Edward
loved his Queen, he certainly dared a great deal to win her,
and was afterwards ashamed to confess the truth while men
" marvelled that our sovereign lord was so long without any
wife, and were ever afeared that he had not been chaste in
his living." The truth could not be hidden indefinitely and
Edward at last announced it to his privy council at Reading
in September, and on Michaelmas day Elizabeth was brought
openly into the abbey chapel by the Duke of Clarence and Warwick and was presented to the lords in council as their Queen.

Even now there was not a definite break with Warwick.
Although the earl must have felt deeply hurt after his vain negotiations with Louis, he still hoped to bind Edward to a strong
alliance with France, and he hurried abroad on an embassy
when the day arrived for the Queen's coronation. Elizabeth
had innumerable relations, most of them in need of money,
she had three brothers, five sisters, two sons, and a father and

mother. Edward began to marry them off into wealthy families, and before two years had elapsed the whole brood was settled. Warwick must have watched with apprehension this sudden rise of an upstart family, seeing the Woodvilles grow every day more insolent with power, seeing them build around the throne a new nobility that might become as powerful as his own great family.

Then Henry VI was captured. His life had been a miserable one since Margaret had left him. While Somerset fought at Hexham he had been lodged a few miles off in Bywell Castle and when news of the defeat reached him he had fled so quickly that he left behind his crowned helmet, his sword and other treasures. He took refuge in the Lake District, wandering disguised from Lancashire to Westmoreland, hiding secretly in the houses of friends, and being protected only by his chamberlain, Sir Richard Tunstall of Thurland. We have few details of this tragic odyssey. In the Liverpool Museum are preserved a boot, a glove and a spoon that Henry is said to have left behind at Bolton Hall, near Sawley, in West Yorkshire. Unfortunately these relics are of the sixteenth century, we know practically nothing of Henry's various hiding-places, but at Bolton there is a well that bears his name, because it is believed that it was enlarged so that he might bathe in it. Then in his wanderings Henry was trapped. He sought lodgings at Waddington Hall not far from Clitheroe on the boundary of Lancashire and Yorkshire, and the master of the house, Richard Tempest, bade him welcome. But a " black monk of Abingdon " recognised him and told Richard's brother, John Tempest, who rode at once to capture the royal prize. He did not wish to fill his brother's house with armed men and therefore he entered with only a few comrades. Henry was at dinner and when Tempest would have plucked him from his seat, the faithful Tunstall drew his sword and rushed to his King's defence so zealously that he broke John Tempest's arm. He was a brave man, this Tunstall, he gripped poor Henry's hand and fought a passage through the men-at-arms until he could run with him into the woods. But they were on foot and their pursuers were mounted, they ran helplessly amongst the trees with a few friends until they were caught on the stepping-stones over the Ribble.

Warwick met the royal captive at Islington probably to guard him against rescue, and poor Henry with his spurs taken from

him and his feet tied to the stirrups was led through Newgate
to the Tower where he was to remain for the next five years.
Evidently he was quite well treated, having wine sent him from
Edward's own cellar, and was allowed visitors " by licence of the
keepers." It was as if he were in a monastery, he had unending
time in which to doze and meditate and pray, and he was allowed
a chaplain, the kind of company he liked. Occasionally he
realised the truth in sudden gasps of shame and would weep
and moan and ask what sin he had committed that he should
be thus locked up. Some bad-mannered fool dared ask him how
he could justify his usurpation and poor Henry answered in a
puzzled manner, " My father had been King of England, possessing his crown in peace all through his reign ; and his father,
my grandfather, had been King of the same realm. And I, when
a boy in the cradle, had been without any interval crowned in
peace and approved as King by the whole realm, and wore the
crown for wellnigh forty years, every lord doing royal homage
to me, and swearing fealty as they had done to my forefathers ;
so I may say with the psalmist, ' The lines are fallen unto me
in a pleasant place, yea I have a goodly heritage ' ; ' My help
cometh of God, Who preserveth them that are true at heart.' "

THE friendship between Edward and Warwick was near break-
ing-point. At every elevation of one of the Woodvilles, Warwick
fumed yet dared not speak his mind, then Edward deliberately
insulted him. The daughter of the Duke of Exeter, Anne
Holland, was in the marriage-market and she brought a dowry
worth squabbling about ; Warwick wished to buy her for one of
his nephews, but Edward instead gave her to his Queen's brother
Thomas. Another strong point of anger was Warwick's determination to force Edward into a French alliance and Edward's
determination to stand by Philip of Burgundy and to marry his
sister to Burgundy's son, Charles. On October 23, 1466, Charles
signed a private treaty with Edward, and soon afterwards his
bastard brother Anthony visited England, ostensibly to fight a
pas d'armes, but actually to arrange the matrimonial treaty.

Rumour reached the King that his brother George Duke of
Clarence intended to marry Warwick's daughter Isabel. That
would have brought the Kingmaker too close to the crown.
Edward called both his brothers to him and demanded the truth.
Clarence denied it, although he could not resist saying that " it
would not be a bad match," on hearing which Edward " waxed

wrath and sent them from his presence." He must have realised
that George was lying and his fear of Warwick grew strong,
prompted undoubtedly by suggestions from his wife—those bed-
time suggestions in the dark which husbands may repudiate, but
which work mischief nevertheless. Edward was a brave man and
he knew Warwick well, he knew his ambitions and how he would
fight to advance his two daughters to the highest possible places
in the realm, and perhaps Edward had noticed that his second
brother Richard loved Warwick's other daughter. If George, Anne
and Richard married these two sisters, Warwick's position would
have become impregnable, and already he was powerful enough
to be a menace if he turned enemy. In an effort perhaps to
lessen that power, Edward now most foolishly took the great seal
from George Neville, Warwick's brother.

When Warwick visited him to ask an audience for the French
ambassadors in 1467, Edward paid not the least attention to
what he was saying, he gazed idly around the chamber as if no
one were speaking. Furiously Warwick left, yet the next day he
called again, this time bringing the ambassadors with him, and
Edward surrounded by the Woodvilles, behaved in exactly the
same insulting manner. This was too much for the earl. As
he was rowed in his barge from Westminster he cried suddenly,
" Have you not seen what traitors there are about the King's
person ! " The ambassadors attempted to calm him, saying,
" My lord, I pray you grow not hot ; for some day you shall
be avenged." " Know that those very traitors," cried Warwick,
" were the men who had my brother displaced from the office of
chancellor, and made the King take the seal from him ! "

What could Warwick do ? He dreaded to rise in open
revolt, but what other chance had he of asserting his strength, of
breaking down that barrier of enemies, the Woodvilles, which
hedged the King ? For five years he had fought for the Yorkists,
and here was his thanks—to have his advice rejected, to have his
brother dislodged from the chancellorship and himself insulted in
court ! He had helped to put Edward on the throne, pouring
out blood and money in his cause, his father and brother had
died for the White Rose, his mother and his wife had been driven
from their homes, and now he was rejected, cast off when no
longer useful while those upstart Woodvilles were creeping into
every estate, gathering money and lands. No wonder Warwick
fingered his sword and dreamed of unmaking a King himself had
made. He had no sons, only two daughters, Isabel and Anne,

and these girls loved the brothers of Edward, yet they were not allowed to marry ; probably if he died they would be pushed into the arms of some detested Woodvilles, made to mingle the blood of the Nevilles with the blood of upstarts. George and Richard were living with him while he brooded in Middleham and it is more than probable that he tried to draw them to his side ; with George he succeeded, even his passion for Anne, however, could not destroy Richard's loyalty to Edward.

As Edward refused to let George marry Isabel, Warwick decided to marry them without permission ; first he had to buy a dispensation from the Pope as they were cousins, and at the same time he tried to obtain a cardinal's hat for his brother, the dismissed chancellor. Edward frustrated him : the cardinal's hat came safely to England, but it was for the Archbishop of Canterbury, and Edward forwarded the Pope's letter to the disappointed George Neville. The dispensation did not come, Edward had arranged that with the Pope. All over England men were waiting, watching Warwick ; messages reached him from one calling himself Robin, and Warwick bade him " go home, for it was not yet time to be stirring." The sense of impending action, of imminent civil war, spread to all classes ; it was dangerous to travel, most dangerous to be abroad at night ; and Earl Rivers' manor in Kent was attacked and his deer killed. In the unruly north there were continual risings, and Edward decided at last that he must lead an army to quieten the rebels by a show of force.

Warwick, meanwhile, as keeper of the sea, had sailed with George of Clarence and Isabel from Sandwich. He had managed to bribe a dispensation from Rome and the lovers were married at Calais, after which, with George and his brother the archbishop, he signed an open letter stating that the King's true subjects had called on him to rescue Edward from the " deceivable covetous rule and guiding of certain seditious persons," adding that he would be at Canterbury by the coming Sunday.

Edward now found himself caught between two enemies, between the rebels in the north and Warwick in the south. He sent the Woodvilles to safety and marched south, hoping to join with Welsh troops led by the Earls of Pembroke and Devonshire. His men deserted as he marched, yet he kept on until he reached Honiley, three miles west of Kenilworth. At midnight he was awakened by a great clattering and shouting, and he leaped from bed to see in the streets the armed troops of Warwick. In the ante-chamber, George Neville greeted him and told him to dress at once. Edward refused, saying that he had not yet rested. " Sire," replied the archbishop, " you must rise and come to see my brother of Warwick, nor do I think that you can refuse."

WARWICK had won the first blow, he had captured the King, when suddenly he realised that his efforts had been for nothing. He could not execute or depose the King, although he did chop off the heads of two Woodvilles, the father Earl Rivers and his son Sir John. Yet what to do with Edward ? He could not even keep him prisoner. The plotting had been futile, it had attained only the marriage of George and Isabel and the execution of two of the Woodvilles. Warwick was almost in the same position as he had been before.

Soon Edward was back in London, as free as ever he had been and, John Paston writes, he had " good language of the Lords of Clarence and Warwick, and of my Lords of York and of Oxford, saying they be his best friends ; but his household men have other language, so that what shall hastily fall I cannot say." Nothing fell for a while, then Warwick started to intrigue again, although after the first failure, heaven alone knows what he expected to attain this time. He attained nothing. As before, he hoped to squeeze Edward between rebels in the north and himself in the south, but the King held as hostage the father of the chief rebel, and he threatened to execute him if the enemy did not disperse. Instead of dispersing, they charged in a desperate attempt at rescue, and against the military skill of Edward were soundly thrashed. But in the fight they exposed Warwick and George, for their battle-cries had been not " Henry ! Henry ! " but " A Clarence ! A Warwick ! " Even after that, Edward would have forgiven the two traitors, but they dared not trust him, they fled to Exeter where they stole a ship and sailed for Calais. Edward, however, had forbidden the garrison to let them enter, and although Isabel was expecting a child, she was not even permitted to land during her confinement. Warwick next sailed for Honfleur and threw himself on the mercy of the King of France ; Louis was delighted to receive him, he was delighted to have any guest who might stir up trouble in England.

Warwick no longer dreamed of placing George on the throne of England. His hatred was so enormous that it made him turn even to Margaret. The great earl could humble his pride and offer his fist to one-time enemies, to the slayers of his father, but Margaret's dislike of him was so intense that at first she refused to listen. For days she withstood all the arguments of Louis and her father René : they offered her the throne of England, Warwick would win it for her son, but she could not bring herself to accepting his friendship and, in particular, to letting his daughter Anne marry her son Edward. For a quarter of an hour, Warwick was forced to kneel to Margaret ; and at last, after weeks of arguments, threats and cajoling, she agreed to let her son marry Anne on condition that he remained in France until Warwick had conquered England ; after which, when Henry VI again should be King, Warwick was to be named regent and governor—Henry being unfit to reign—and on the Prince's accession he was to take the rather vague position of the Prince's guardian. On a piece of the True Cross Warwick swore to keep faith, then with men and ships from Louis he set out to finish Edward once and for all.

As before, Edward was drawn north only to find himself caught between two enemies when news of Warwick's landing reached him. He galloped for London, and when he had reached Doncaster the sergeant of his minstrels woke him in his bed to say that the enemy were only six or seven miles off, Warwick's brother Montagu having shifted his allegiance from Edward. With his brother Richard and a few friends, Edward raced for the coast ; he was nearly drowned in the Wash, but at Bishop's Lynn managed to hire a boat. So poor was he, so hurried was his departure, that he could give only his marten fur-lined gown as payment to the ship's captain when he reached Holland and sought refuge with his brother-in-law, the Duke of Burgundy.

Warwick had won without a battle so secret had been his plans, and on reaching London he took poor Henry VI from the Tower and lodged him in royal apartments. He dressed him in Edward's robes and escorted him through Cheapside to the Bishop of London's palace, and thus began the " readeption " of King Henry VI ; the long imprisonment had addled what little wits the poor King had possessed and " he sat on his throne as limp and helpless as a sack of wool. He was a mere shadow and pretence, and what was done in his name was done without his will and knowledge." On October 13, 1470, he was led through London in the hope of inspiring loyalty, and " all the people to right and left rejoiced with clapping of hands, and cried, ' God save Henry ! ' "

Edward was a soldier, not one to sit tamely under deposition. His sister Margaret helped him to raise ships and with but fifteen hundred Englishmen and three hundred Germans, and with his brother Richard and his friends Lords Hastings, Say and Scales, he sailed from Flushing on March 11, 1471, on this most desperate adventure. He had only a tiny force to range against Warwick with all England ; but a born leader, a great commander like Edward possesses that genius against which odds do not count. He landed at the same spot on which Henry IV had landed in his invasion, at Ravenspur. A terrible storm had wrenched the little squadron apart and when Edward landed he was alone in one ship. While his men eased their cramped limbs on the sands, the sight of banners and of steel glistening over a distant hill made them run to arms, but it was Richard of Gloucester riding to join his brother, his vessel having been driven five miles away ; soon the third squadron under Rivers appeared and the little army was united again. Edward burned his ship so that there could be no possibility of retreat, then he marched into the interior. He marched into a dead country where men neither fought him nor came to his standard. The people were afraid, believing his cause doomed, and Warwick was gathering a great army for the fight. Very sensibly Edward did not ride to London, he made for his own city of York and asked for admission. He did not say that he was the King of England coming to regain his crown, he called himself a simple duke wanting his inheritance ; this fiction saved the city's honour, the people were therefore not traitors when they opened the gates. To show how abrupt had been the change in his opinions, Edward clipped the Prince of Wales' badge to his helmet and shouted for King Henry and Prince Edward when he entered.

The campaign that followed is one of the most brilliant in history. Edward with the tiniest of forces invaded a country that was hostile, indifferent or afraid. Within three months from the date of landing he had out-manœuvred his enemies, he had won two battles and had recovered his throne. Against him stood Warwick with all fickle England, with troops and guns and money; Edward had less than two thousand men under his friends and Richard of Gloucester, a lad of eighteen who was yet to prove himself his brother's equal in war. With this little army he marched from York into England. Warwick was waiting at Coventry, Montagu was ready to pounce from Pomfret, the Earl of Oxford was riding from the east, Clarence from London. Calmly Edward rode against this gigantic force, then he swung suddenly to the west of Pomfret and reached Nottingham, leaving Montagu isolated and baffled. At Nottingham men trooped to join him ; his courage, his splendid presence as he sat his horse smiling like a god, drew men to him by that magic in the heart of all great leaders, that dauntlessness in the face of danger which brings courage to the most cowardly. Oxford and Exeter had ridden from the east to withstand him, but when they learned of his growing army they withdrew to Newark. He marched to Leicester, then he darted on to Coventry and defied Warwick, calling on him to leave his walls for battle. Warwick, completely outwitted and scarcely believing that Edward had achieved so much in so small a time—it was a fortnight since the landing— dared not sally with his seven thousand men, and Edward camped three miles off on the road to Banbury to await the coming of George of Clarence. Young Richard conducted the negotia- tions between the brothers, but George was probably already weary of the Kingmaker with his grandiose schemes from which himself derived nothing ; he declared for Edward, and the three brothers, having none to bar their way, made for London. On entering the gates, Edward went straight to St. Paul's, then he visited Henry VI. " My cousin of York," said Henry, " you are very welcome. I know that in your hands my life will not be in danger." He was put back into the Tower and merrily Edward rode to Westminster. During Henry's " readeption," Queen Elizabeth had fled to sanctuary and while living in that city of cut-throats and runaway debtors beside the abbey, she had borne Edward's first son—a charitable butcher keeping her in food.

But Edward had no time to pause, little time for anything except to gather men, for Warwick was riding to take vengeance. At Barnet the two armies met. They met in the dark and fumbled for position ; Warwick was drawn up on a slope behind a line of hedges, and when Edward's men arrived they could not make certain where he stood and in the night they camped far closer to him than they realised. Luckily, Edward's right wing over- lapped Warwick's left, and Warwick's right overlapped Edward's left, for all the cannon were on the Lancastrian right, with the result that they fired fruitlessly, wasting ammunition. The sun rose in a heavy fog and the men could barely see each other, armour glowing rather than shining, while they formed into line. As this was Easter Day, Edward knelt in the mists, unhelmed, and prayed for victory ; then he stood up and shouted for the advance. It was between four and five in the morning, with the sun burning dully through a leaden sky ; the hand-guns—those new inventions —were touched to life by the slow-matches and blazed redly through the mists. But axe and sword and lance were the safest weapons, battles were still hand-to-hand, man to man, as the two armies rushed together, steel thundering and clattering above shouted war-cries. Both right wings overlapping, the left wings were crumpled easily, and Oxford in the thrill of seeing the Yorkists give, chased them for miles. Richard who commanded the Yorkist right did not make the same mistake ; when the Lancastrians gave he swept them back upon themselves, charging inward towards the centre where his brother Edward was cleaving down " all that stood in his way " with his great battle-axe.

Neither army knew the truth about the broken wings, each thought itself winning, for the morning was so dark that it was impossible to see beyond a few yards. Then Oxford galloped back in triumph ; his badge was the blazing star of the de Veres, while Edward's badge since the day he saw the parhelion at Mortimer's Cross had been the sun-in-splendour, therefore when Warwick's men saw de Vere's blazing star coming at them through the fog they thought it Edward's sun-in-splendour, and they opened fire. " Treason ! " cried Oxford and fled. " Treason ! " cried his men, and the shouting echoed through the mists, reaching Warwick's centre. " Treason ! " In the confused darkness, it was impossible to learn the truth, and the Lancastrians began to run from the field. Warwick fought desperately but he could not stay the panic. His brother Montagu was killed, and he drew back slowly, fighting every inch, until at last he realised that he could do nothing more, that the day was utterly lost, and then too late he tried to run. He was killed as he ran. Edward shouted that he was not to be harmed, but his cry was unheard. The Yorkists cornered Warwick on the edge of Wrotham Wood and " killed him and despoiled him naked."

IN St. Paul's Cathedral, the face of the dead Kingmaker gazed blindly at the shadowed roof. People came to stare upon the bloodless flesh, to see the lifeless hair falling each side of the brow, to touch perhaps the dry skin of him who had made and unmade Kings. This rite was necessary so that " the people should not be abused by feigned seditious tales " that Warwick yet lived. He had been a great man struck down by a greater. We can pity him fighting against forces that were dimly felt, the forces of modernity, of strong kingship united with the people against tyrannical magnates. Neither Warwick nor Edward were, of course, aware of the struggle, they were symbols, they were men fighting for their own brave egoisms, not realising that they fought for greater things—Warwick for the old régime, Edward for the new. And the old must die some time : it died heroically in a whirl of battle, with blood spilt amongst the dull mists, with men screaming through a sea like smoke, screaming and falling, with the blazing sun-in-splendour, golden and victorious, brighter than the living sun in the fog, with the sun in splendour shaking its silken folds above a field of corpses, and of men coughing and bleeding gradually to death. An end such as Warwick would have desired—the end of a hero, to the shrieking of the trumpets and the subdued chatter of the drums, to the crash of cannon tearing red gaps in mist, to the clatter and clang of steel, to the zip of bowstring thudding on the bracer, to the animal-panting of men struggling for a death-grip and screaming when the sword struck home. It was an end worthy of Warwick, of this turbulent arrogant man, embittered by the treachery of friends, scheming for greater power, for more tawdry glories.

In St. Paul's he lay beside his brother Montagu. The coffin enclosed limbs that were still at last, the hands at peace, no longer groping for the sword, and the legs that could clench around a horse and spur to victory, drawn straight, unmoving. The Kingmaker, Richard Neville, Earl of Warwick, was dead, dead beyond doubt.

BUT Edward had living foes. Margaret had sailed with the Prince from France, with three thousand men under Wenlock, Langstrother and John Beaufort ; when she landed and heard of Warwick's death she would have fled at once had not her lords besought her to stay. Edward rushed to intercept her, he drove his men and gave them no pause even to eat, he harried poor Margaret, he chased her and gave her not a moment's rest. The Lancastrians grew panic-stricken before that continual pressure in the rear, before the knowledge that Edward the unconquered was following rapidly. Edward's own courage kept his men upon their feet ; the Lancastrians with no great leader were crushed by the sense of impending doom, by the thought that the sun-in-splendour might any moment be seen rising above the hilltops to the shrill crying of trumpets and the thudding of destrers' hooves. Some dropped and fell under the terrible heat and could not move, they lay by the roadside and saw the troops of Edward pass swiftly—the golden King upon his horse beside his brothers, Richard and the glowering George, with the arms of England and the sun-in-splendour curling above his flaxen head. The inspiration of a great leader, that indefinable genius that can lead men singing to a certain death, kept Edward's men upon the march and made them forget their weariness. The Lancastrians " knew well that the King ever approached towards them, near and near, ever ready, in good array and ordinance," and the knowledge drained all strength from their limbs. At last reaching Tewkesbury at four o'clock in the afternoon of May 3, 1471, they threw themselves on the ground after a forty-four-mile march in full armour and great heat. Some leaders had energy enough to stir the men into position for battle " in a field, in a close even at the town's end ; the town and abbey at their backs ; afore them and on every hand of them foul lanes, and deep dikes, and many hedges, with hills and valleys ; a right evil place to approach as could well have been devised."

ON the 4th, the battle was opened by Richard of Gloucester. He led his men across that " evil place " which had " so many hedges, trees and bushes that it was right hard to approach them near and come to hands." The Lancastrians, perched on the hillside, could have wiped out Gloucester's men without striking a blow, although Gloucester's fire was deadly, but their leader Somerset —brother of the executed duke—perhaps hoping to win honour by some great strategic move, left his position and brought his men from behind the ridge to attack the Yorkists in the flank. Such moves against a soldier of Edward's genius were foredoomed. He had posted a troop of three hundred spearmen in a nearby wood to the right of the enemy with orders to act as occasion demanded, and now, as Somerset's wild charge smashed into the Yorkist lines, the spearmen came to the rescue and caught him in the rear. In panic the Lancastrians tried to fight on every side, they were surrounded, while Richard led his men straight at the centre commanded by young Edward. The Prince fought bravely but the battle was already lost, the Lancastrian army was in retreat, while the King smashed his way through the gap left open by Somerset, and then it was his turn to be above the enemy. Prince Edward " was taken fleeing to the townwards, and slain in the field," and it is said that he " cried for succour to his brother-in-law, the Duke of Clarence." Tudor chroniclers invented a dramatic story of how Richard of Gloucester murdered the Prince after the battle : this has even less authority than most of the lies about Richard.

Those who escaped death in the field ran to the abbey church, which had no rights of sanctuary above that enjoyed by all churches, yet Edward pardoned them " at the reverence of the blessed Trinity, the most holy Virgin Mary, and the holy martyr St. George by whose grace and help he had that day attained so noble a victory." The leaders alone were beheaded ; soon Queen Margaret was caught and, with Anne Neville, dragged before the King. Edward did neither of them harm but kept them by him while he rode to London.

He entered the city on May 21 and either on this night or— which seems the more likely—two days later, King Henry died. It is impossible to know the truth, but it is difficult not to believe that he was murdered at Edward's command, although such an act is by no means typical of Edward, who was certainly no brutal King. All we know is that Henry died very soon after Edward's return and the official Yorkist statement that he died of a broken heart on learning of his son's death and his wife's captivity is scarcely convincing when we recall the vicissitudes he had already suffered without protest. Naturally the Tudor writers in after years declared that Richard Duke of Gloucester, murdered him ; there is no proof of this except one contemporary statement that he happened to be in the Tower that night : so were a great many other people, so was probably Edward himself and the whole court, for the Tower was a palace as well as a prison. At any rate, if Henry died on the 23rd as stated in a letter to Bruges, Richard could definitely have had no hand in the killing, as he was then at Sandwich. This date is also corroborated by the household accounts, which prove Henry to have been alive until the 24th. As usual, the Tudor falsifiers of history overreached themselves in their determination to vilify Richard.

That Henry was murdered seems more than probable, and when his dismembered bones were disinterred in 1910, we learn that " to one of the pieces of the skull there was still attached some of the hair which was brown in colour save in one place where it was much darker and apparently matted with blood." These bones, however, prove little as there are still doubts about their authenticity. The Tower officials to-day will obligingly show you a recess that was once an oratory in the Wakefield Tower, and they will solemnly tell you that Henry was murdered there by Richard Duke of Gloucester, while Eton boys lay a wreath of flowers on the spot every year. There is no basis for this legend, we have not the slightest idea how or where Henry died.

THE Lancastrian cause ended with Henry, now Edward could be at peace while his brother Richard could marry the girl he loved, Anne Neville, who was not quite fifteen. We may dismiss at once the idiotic stories glorified beyond redemption by the sobbing pen of Miss Agnes Strickland [1] that Richard pursued a girl who loathed him and forced her into marriage. Even Dr. James Gairdner,[2] no friend of Richard, is forced to confess that there is " reason to believe that she did regard Richard with favour." There is no reason whatever to believe anything else. As Richard had been reared in Warwick's household it is more than likely that they had loved each other since they had been children, but now when there was no bar to their marriage, Anne Neville suddenly disappeared. George kidnapped her. As he had married her sister Isabel, he possessed the huge Warwick estates, and if Anne in her turn were to marry, he would have to give up half his wife's dowry. For two years Richard searched for Anne, and soon George also was looking for her as she managed somehow to escape from him, and, being under an act of attainder because of her betrothal to Prince Edward, she hid from everybody until Richard by some unknown means discovered her in a cook-shop. Now was the opportunity for that malignant demon created by the Tudor writers to show the baseness of his lusts ; he had Anne in his power, he could do what he willed with her, and instead of behaving like a true romantic villain, he tamely took her to sanctuary in St. Martin's-le-Grand, where she would be safe from everybody, including himself. George, as her guardian and therefore the controller of her property, demanded her immediate return, but Richard

---

[1] *Lives of the Queens of England from the Norman Conquest,* by Agnes Strickland, 1850.

[2] *History of the Life and Reign of Richard the Third,* by James Gairdner (Cambridge University), new and revised edition, 1898.

placed her under the protection of her uncle, George Neville. Edward tried to make peace between his brothers, George would not listen : Richard, he insisted, " may well have my lady his sister-in-law, but they shall part no livelihood." Both dukes pleaded their cause before the council, and they pleaded with such effect that even professional lawyers were amazed by their eloquence. The dispute grew serious, there were threats of civil war, and men began to grease their weapons once again and to rub the pumice against the rust of peace. And all the while the brothers squabbled over Warwick's lands, Warwick's widow, hiding in sanctuary, was begging for justice. Richard took her under his protection, then defying George, he married Anne in Westminster Abbey in 1724, and to the fury of George was given her estates. George was not to forget, and England watched apprehensively when he swore vengeance. As Sir John Paston writes, " It is said for certain that the Duke of Clarence maketh him big in that he can, showing as he would but deal with the Duke of Gloucester ; but the King intendeth in eschewing all inconvenience, to be as big as they both, and to be a stiffler atween them."

PERSONAL feelings were for the moment forgotten when Edward announced that he intended to imitate Edward III and Henry V and lead an army oversea to recover the " old inheritance of the crown and realm of France and the duchies of Normandy, Gascony and Guienne." It is difficult to understand the reasons for this, although it seems that Edward, tired of internal squabbles, decided to bind the nation together in a war. It was an expedient that had worked under Henry V, and was likely to work again. Besides, he had doubtless promised support to his brother-in-law Charles the Bold of Burgundy in an invasion of the common enemy, but Edward was not stupidly honourable enough to have taken that seriously unless his own desires went with it. His situation was not a happy one, for he needed money, having lightened the coinage and borrowed more than he could ever repay ; this reduction of the weight was a common trick of medieval Kings, who deliberately lowered the value of money so that less silver should be used. Although his private income was gradually accumulating through various trading ventures, Edward needed further sums for the war and was voted huge grants by parliament which never voted money easily unless for an invasion of either Scotland or France. Then

Edward invented a cunning scheme—nicknamed sarcastically
" benevolences "—he borrowed money without paying it back.
Being an extraordinarily handsome man he either cajoled the
gold, or being a tall and lusty man, he bullied it from his subjects. A visiting Italian records with wonder how the King
plucked " out the feathers of his magpies without making them
cry out " ; and he tells us, " I have frequently seen our neigh-
bours here who were summoned before the King, and when they
went they looked as if they were going to the gallows ; when they
returned they were joyful, saying that they had spoken to the
King and he had spoken to them so benignly that they did not
regret the money they had paid." His trick was to welcome the
poor wretches with great familiarity and ask what they would
give towards the expedition ; if the offering pleased him, he had
it recorded immediately, if he thought it too little he would frown
and say, " Such a one, who is poorer than you, has paid so much ;
you, who are richer, can easily pay more." With women his
methods were simpler—he kissed them ; and once when an old
lady was asked what she would pay, she answered, " For your
lovely face you shall have twenty pounds " ; the King kissed
her with gratitude and, also with gratitude, she doubled the offer.
" Oh," cried Margaret Paston as Edward roamed the countryside in search of benevolences, " the King goeth so near us in this
country, both to poor and rich, that I wot not how we shall live
but if the world amend."

At last, when even Edward's greed was satisfied, the army
sailed for France.

THE war was a fiasco. Burgundy's troops had been so badly
defeated at Neuss that he could give no support save promises,
and Edward marched into France without a single battle. Louis
offered to pay him to depart, and he accepted the offer. Every
noble in Edward's army was bribed, save one, and that was
Richard Duke of Gloucester. Alone, feeling this stain on
England's honour, he would not touch the gold of France and
deliberately and ostentatiously stayed away when Edward and
Louis met on the bridge of Picquigny across the Somme. This
meeting was a sheer formality, both Kings wished to swear in
each other's presence that they would keep the peace for ten
years and that Louis's son should marry one of Edward's daughters.
A bridge was built over the river and was roofed in in case of
rain ; across the centre were strong bars except for a wooden

grating "such as is made for lion's cages," too narrow for a dagger to be thrust through. Louis approached from one direction, Edward from the other, and each was attended by twelve men and had with him four of the opposite nation to see that no treachery was intended.

Louis arrived first on the appointed day, August 29, 1475. He was dressed like a minstrel—that is to say, he wore cheap yet bright clothing—and as was his custom he had dressed a man exactly like himself to deceive assassins. The man chosen this day was the historian Philip de Comines, who has recorded the whole interview for us most vividly. Louis was leaning on the barrier when Edward arrived, and the English King paused as he stepped on to the bridge and he pulled off his cap and bowed almost to within half a foot of the boards. He was dressed in splendid if rather old-fashioned clothes : his cap was of black velvet and had on it a huge fleur-de-lys of precious stones, and his gown was of cloth-of-gold. "He was a Prince," writes Comines, "of a noble and majestic presence, but a little inclining to corpulence. I had seen him before when the Earl of Warwick drove him from his kingdom ; then I thought him much handsomer and, so far as I can remember, my eyes had never seen a more handsome person." Through the bars of the grating the two Kings embraced, and when Edward had made another low bow, Louis said, "Cousin, you are heartily welcome ; there is no person living I so desired to meet, and God be thanked that this interview is upon so friendly an occasion," and Edward answered in very good French. After a tedious speech from the English chancellor, the treaties were shown and each King endorsed them. Louis then merrily suggested that Edward should have a jaunt in Paris with the ladies, adding that Cardinal Bourbon, who was present, would willingly absolve him. Edward was delighted with the suggestion, "and made his highness several good answers, for he knew that the cardinal was a jolly companion." After further talk of this kind, Louis ordered the others away and the two Kings whispered alone through the barrier ; what they said we shall never know.

It was a pleasant interview, and Edward prepared to go home with a well-stuffed pouch and with the promise of Louis's son for one of his daughters, yet he must have dreaded facing an indignant England who had seen its honour sold when it expected further Crécys and Agincourts, and it was noticed that on the voyage home he kept his brother George Duke of Clarence always at his side. If England should rebel, he did not want George far away.

ENGLAND did not rebel and Edward settled down to a quiet and pleasant reign. If no one had been killed in the expedition, Edward himself had apparently caught a tertian fever and he was growing fat and lazy and avaricious. It was George who woke him out of his lazy contentment. Isabel had died in December 1476, and George was looking for another bride when Charles the Bold was killed at Nancy. He left only a daughter, Mary, and Louis immediately sent his troops into the land, declaring that it was a male fief which must revert to the crown. Poor Mary with her mother Margaret, Edward's sister, waited for a prince to rescue her from the French ogre, and it occurred to George that he would make a perfect prince. Edward thought otherwise, he forbade his brother even to consider such a thing ; frustrated here, for Mary soon married Maximilian of Austria, George thought he might marry the sister of King James of Scotland, and again Edward put a stop to any such schemes. He did not want his treacherous brother to be King anywhere, as he was quite capable of invading England. George sulked and waited for his chance of revenge. It would seem that he had some kind of a persecution mania, as he now arrested a former servant, Ankarette Twynyho, and accused her of having poisoned Isabel, while a certain John Thurseby was taken on the suspicion of having poisoned George's child. Both the accused were hanged. This little episode deserves no mention except that, by trying, sentencing and executing people, George was usurping royal justice, he was deliberately insulting Edward. The King, probably feeling that it would be degrading to accuse his own brother of treason on so flimsy a cause, retorted in a roundabout fashion by arresting an Oxford clerk, Stacy, and a man of George's household called Burdett, and accusing them of witchcraft. They were both executed, while a third accused was pardoned. George, on hearing of this, rushed to Westminster with a certain Dr. John Goddard, whom he forced to read aloud a declaration of innocence made by Stacy and Burdett. This was too deep an insult for Edward to ignore, George appealed from the King's judgment to the King's council, and to make the insult deeper, he had brought Dr. Goddard with him, the man who at Paul's Cross had expounded Henry VI's right to the crown during Warwick's control of England. Edward had to take action or his lunatic brother would have made him appear despicable before the people. To a medieval King nothing was so important as dignity, he must keep that sense of godhead even though he mingle with the commons as Edward mingled with them and proved himself too human far too often with the wives of citizens. Henry V had hanged men who jeered at him, William I had destroyed a city because of a jest, and even easy-going Edward IV had to do something when his crown was becoming a contemptible thing under the stupid insults of his brother.

Even then perhaps Edward would have concealed his rage had not Louis's ambassador remarked that there was a rumour abroad that George intended to help Margaret of Anjou invade England. Edward summoned George to Westminster and " with his own lips " he accused him of conduct " derogatory to the laws of the realm, and most dangerous to judges and jurors." George was committed to the Tower and remained locked away for months before Edward could bring himself to the final, that utterly final, act of impeachment. It could not be postponed for ever. George has brought before parliament in Westminster on January 16, 1478.

No one save the King would dare accuse the King's brother. The bill of attainder was brought forward and read to its dreary end by Edward. No one else dared speak. Only the King's voice was heard in that great room ; all was silence except for the voice of the man who feared to lift his eyes from the paper and meet the mocking furious gaze of the accused, his brother. It was a very long attainder ; we possess it in full, and one cannot help wondering how Edward managed to read to the very end. He spoke of treasons, of treasons most diabolic and unnatural, and at last— did it stick in his throat ?—the name, George Duke of Clarence. " Wherein it is to be remembered that the King's highness of tender youth, unto now of late hath ever loved and cherished him, as tenderly, as kindly as any creature might his natural brother, as well it may be declared, by that he being right young, not born to have any livelihood but only of the King's grace ; he gave him so large portion of possessions, that no memorial is of, or seldom hath been seen, that any King of England heretofore within his realm gave so largely to any [of] his brothers. . . ." Repetitions of gifts : he had given him this and that, and that and this, he had given him everything, and what was the return ? . . . . " The said duke nevertheless, for all this no love increasing, but growing daily in more and more malice, hath not left to consider and conspire new treasons, more heinous and loathly than ever afore, how that the said duke falsely and traitorously intended and purposed firmly, the extreme destruction and disheriting of the King and his issue. . . ." At this, perhaps Edward's voice might grow stronger, memories of gifts and of a happy past would be forgotten as he thought of present treacheries. Yet the treacheries produced are very vague, there is nothing definite about them, they are a muddle of words that seem, by their very emptiness and confusion, to be trying to mask the truth, one feels that there was a deeper, more secret treason which Edward dared not confess lest it destroy him. George must have done something more tremendous than such trifles if Edward was determined on his end. He was accused of declaring openly that Burdett " was wrongfully put to death," of unlawfully assembling people, of producing an exemplification of the deed made between Margaret and Warwick, according to which he would inherit the throne if the Lancastrian line were to die, of enacting secret oaths of allegiance to himself and enlisting men for an immediate rising.

At last Edward finished, and George cried that he was not guilty, he offered to fight the King, he offered wager of battle. In that " sad strife not a single person uttered a word against the duke except the King ; not one individual made answer to the King except the duke." There was a makeshift trial, witnesses who were accusers were brought forward, and George could only declare his innocence. He was sentenced to death as a traitor.

EDWARD could not bring himself to a public execution ; did he fear the secret that George held, the treason that can be sensed although not spoken ? did he fear lest in his last moments George might shout it to the multitude ? Their mother, the old Duchess of York, wept that brothers should kill each other, and Richard implored Edward to forgive George, but Edward dared not do it. George was murdered.

It was rumoured at the time that George was drowned in a butt of malmsey. Peculiar though this death may sound, it may be accepted if only because of the consensus of opinion amongst the chroniclers. Jean Molinet adds the charming touch that George was offered any death he liked and chose the malmsey-butt.[1]

---

[1] Need I add that the Tudor chroniclers accuse Richard of murdering George ? There is scarcely any prominent murder that they do not blame him for. The truth is that he did his best to make Edward forgive their brother.

WITH the death of George, Edward had nothing to fear, and he lived the remainder of his life in what tranquillity his conscience and his fat and feverish body would allow. Fighting he left to Richard, who did splendid work against Scotland. No longer the debauchee he had been, Edward's energies now went into the gathering of money and into subtle schemes to marry his daughters into the reigning houses of Europe. Then as he locked away his money and dreamed of seeing a crown on the head of every child, news came that smashed his world. Mary of Burgundy was killed, thrown from her horse, leaving two children, Philip and Margaret. As Maximilian was not the hereditary duke, being only Mary's husband, the Burgundians seized the children and offered them to Louis. Louis did not want to fight, treaties were always to him of more importance than the sword, and he suggested that little Margaret marry the Dauphin.

Edward went almost mad when he heard. His most treasured dream had been the marriage of one of his daughters to the Dauphin as Louis had promised at Picquigny, and now the rascally Frenchman dared forget his promise. Edward called a parliament and demanded war on France. His fury was so terrific that it killed him, it pushed him into his bed, and he lay there, suddenly realising that he was about to die, that the incredible at last had come to pass.

During Easter, 1483, he first took to his bed in Westminster and on April 9 he died. But first he called to him the quarrelling nobles and made them swear friendship, and in his will he left the care of his son's person and his kingdom during the minority to his brother Richard. He named no one else. Richard alone was to be protector and regent.

For ten or twelve hours the dead body of the King lay covered only " from the naval to the knees " so that all the spiritual and temporal peers then in London might see it, together with the mayor and aldermen. Flabby and white the young god had grown ; the sun-in-splendour was very dim as the soft flesh was embalmed and lifted into the coffin.

XVII

KING EDWARD THE FIFTH

1483

ON HEARING OF HIS BROTHER'S DEATH, Richard's first act was to attend the obsequies in York Minster. He then proclaimed his nephew King of England as Edward V, and wrote consolingly to Queen Elizabeth before he set out for London, riding with six hundred men in deepest mourning. He would have ridden straight into a trap had not the Duke of Buckingham galloped hard to warn him. The Queen and her relations were determined to resist Richard's protectorship, they held the young King and were conspiring to steal the power. Richard acted with a promptitude worthy of his brother. He was at Northampton when Buckingham arrived on April 29, and he learned that the little King had been taken by Lord Rivers to Stony Stratford to avoid meeting him. Then Rivers dared to brave his treachery by joining the Protector, hoping by false smiles to lull Richard's suspicions while the Woodvilles got all ready for rebellion. In council it was decided that Rivers be arrested and that Richard should push on to Stony Stratford to seize the person of the King. This Richard did, and he arrived just as Edward was about to start for London ; finding themselves leaderless, the Woodville army surrendered while the Queen ran to sanctuary.

London, hearing strange rumours, would have barred the gates on Richard, until they were told the truth and shown the " barrels of harness "—armour and such—captured from the rebels, then their terrors changed to rejoicing. Richard, still dressed in mourning, entered the city on May 4, the day that had been chosen for the boy's coronation which was now necessarily postponed. Edward was lodged in the Bishop of London's palace while Richard took up his residence in the family home of Baynard's Castle on the Thames.

A council was called and the Protector was commended for his swiftness in repressing the rebellion and an oath of fealty was given to him. It was then decided that Edward should be sent to the Tower as a more appropriate residence for a King, Richard, when Anne came to town, moving to Crosby Place.

THE council was still sitting when, on June 8, Dr. Robert Stillington, Bishop of Bath and Wells, made an astounding revelation. He said that Edward before his marriage to Elizabeth had been betrothed to the Lady Eleanor Butler. In those days, a betrothal was as legally binding as a marriage-ceremony and therefore, if Stillington spoke truth, Edward's Woodville marriage was bigamous and his children were bastards incapable of reigning. This must have been the secret which George had held and for which he had been murdered, and it is significant that at the very time when George had been attainted, Stillington had been arrested for " uttering words prejudicial to the King and his state." He had soon afterwards been released, probably on oath to remain silent, and Edward had given him numerous important posts. Now he came forward with the truth, having held his tongue while Edward lived, but fearing lest under a minority civil war would break again. He had witnessed the betrothal, he said, and afterwards Lady Eleanor had turned nun in the convent of Norwich where she had died on July 30, 1466. To prove he was no liar he produced " instruments, authentic doctors, proctors, and notaries of the law, with depositions of divers witnesses." The council listened fearfully to the old man, for the news in its suddenness was numbing ; they refused to decide, they passed the question on to parliament which was to meet on June 25.

RICHARD stood in a perilous place. He could not hide the truth about his brother's marriage even if he wished, and he must have dreaded the inevitable war that must break out. The Woodvilles would do everything they could to discredit Stillington, they would not pause at murder. And he stood alone with Buckingham against heaven only knew what dangers. Soon he was told of plots against him, and wrote at once to York to send troops to his aid, then he decided that rather than wait for the blow to come, he would face the conspirators. What happened that day in the White Tower of London we do not know, we have only the story given us in the so-called history that bears the name of Sir Thomas More, although without doubt More did not

write it.   It is Tudor propaganda, exposed as lies by the ingenuity
with which it twists dates, if not by numerous other details.

On June 13 Richard went to the White Tower, he faced the
conspirators and arrested them.   Lord Hastings, who evidently,
with Bishop Morton, was the leader, was condemned and executed
on the 20th.   It is difficult to understand how Hastings, a true
Yorkist, had involved himself in the conspiracy, and even Richard's
greatest enemy confesses that " undoubtedly the Protector loved
him well, and was loth to have lost him."   Yet after all, Hastings
was Edward's friend, and it is quite possible that misguided
loyalty, if not personal ambition, had made him join Bishop
Morton and the Woodvilles in an effort to take the power.   They
had all been looking forward to a jolly time under a minority,
for they realised that Richard, who had proved himself an honourable and brave soldier, would countenance no peculation.   The
conspiracy was definite enough, a *supersedeas* had actually been
sent out forbidding parliament to meet.

Meanwhile Rivers and the others were tried at Pomfret and
sentenced to death, and it shows the faith that even these men had
in the Protector when Rivers appointed Richard supervisor of his
will.   Only Hastings suffered for the conspiracy in London.   Like
his brother, Richard pardoned too easily, and because of this weakness he was eventually destroyed.   Bishop Morton was arrested and
given into the care of the Duke of Buckingham ; Lord Stanley was
pardoned and actually rewarded ; Archbishop Rotherham was,
after a short imprisonment, permitted to go back to his diocese.
Jane Shore had also been involved in the plot, probably drawn
into it by her lover, the Marquis of Dorset, Elizabeth Woodville's son by her first marriage.   Richard has often been condemned for his cruel treatment of Jane, yet he behaved towards
her extremely well ; he did not charge her with treason, as well
he might, he passed her over the Bishop of London's court in
which she was condemned to public penance as a common
harlot.   The Woodville's opposition disappeared, they realised
that it was useless to fight any longer, and the Queen in sanctuary
surrendered her second son to bear his brother company in the
Tower.   It is usually said that Richard forced Elizabeth to give
up the boy, but there is no evidence of this, nor do we find that
Elizabeth ever afterwards regretted her act.   Far from it.   She
remained friendly with Richard to the end, and even conspired
to marry him to her daughter—scarcely the behaviour of a
mother towards the murderer of her children.

Those two boys disappeared into the Tower. For generations it has been said that Richard slew them, although almost immediately after the death of the last Tudor, Queen Elizabeth, men whispered the truth, stating that Richard's hands were clean and that the actual murderer was King Henry VII. This question cannot be examined here, and I have written largely of it already.[1] It can only be said that the tales about Richard having killed the boys are from Tudor sources. The problem remains insoluble, but it can be summed up in these words—If neither side can be proved either innocent or guilty, at least the weight of evidence is against Henry VII.

The *supersedeas* which the conspirators had sent did not stop parliament from meeting, although the fact that it was sent, turns this gathering into what would later have been called a " convention." It met on Wednesday, June 25, and proofs of Edward IV's bigamous marriage were produced. As the Duke of Clarence had been attainted of high treason, his children were disabled by law, and therefore the crown automatically descended to Richard.

He was in Baynard's Castle when on the 26th the lords spiritual and temporal and the commons arrived to ask him to accept the throne. They told him that if he refused, they would seek a King of a different lineage, passing over the children of Edward and George, and Richard consented. " King Richard ! " shouted the people, " King Richard ! King Richard ! "

[1] *King Richard III: A Chronicle*, by Philip Lindsay (Howard Baker Publishers), 1969. In a pamphlet, *On Some Bones in Westminster Abbey* (Ivor Nicholson & Watson), 1934, I examined the evidence produced from the alleged bones of the Princes disinterred in Westminster Abbey on July 6, 1933. The arguments given there appeared to be of so little interest that only one paper, *The Times*, to my knowledge even bothered to notice the monograph's appearance. The defence of Richard is very rarely given a hearing, while the prosecution is offered all the space it needs in nearly every English newspaper. Why this should be it is impossible to understand. Those interested should also consult that most valuable work, *Richard III : His Life and Character Reviewed in the Light of Recent Research*, by Sir Clements R. Markham (Smith, Elder), 1906.

XVIII

KING RICHARD THE THIRD

1483–1485

ON JUNE 26, the day after the offering of the petition that besought him to accept the crown, Richard sat upon that marble chair, the King's Bench, in Westminster Hall. He took the coronation oath and, calling the judges before him, gave them "straight commandment" to be just and punctual in their duties ; then proceeding from the hall to the abbey, he was met by the clergy, and the abbot gave him the sceptre of St. Eadward. After offering at the Confessor's shrine, he rode to St. Paul's, and then returned to Westminster, to his lodgings in the palace. That night he was proclaimed King Richard III, and the coronation was fixed for July 6.

Two days before the appointed date, Richard and his Queen were rowed in the royal barge to the Tower, and on the 5th they set out on their state ride through London to Westminster. Richard was dressed splendidly in blue cloth-of-gold and with a purple cloak trimmed with ermine, while Buckingham as the new Kingmaker was almost as gorgeous, his horse's trappings being bright with "burning cart-naves of gold." Anne was in a litter, and she wore "a kirtle of white cloth-of-gold, and a mantle with a train of the same white cloth-of-gold," all tipped with ermine, while her women followed either in chairs or on horseback, lolling sideways on saddles hidden under crimson velvet.

The next day was the coronation day, and the usual scaffolding had been erected and was draped with red worsted tacked with gilt nails. After the crowning, the royal couple left the abbey for the banquet which started at four o'clock in the afternoon. The challenge was delivered, Dymock—whose family held the hereditary right—trotted into the hall, armed cap-a-pie, and with white harness. He cried that he had come to defend King Richard's claim, "and when he had all said, anon all the hall cried King Richard all with one voice."

WHAT was this new King really like? We know the tales repeated in every schoolbook, we have heard guides at the Tower and Westminster Abbey speak with histrionic horror of his crimes, we have seen him with crooked back upon the stage mouthing of diabolic crimes in Marlowe's play—that Tudor work given the authority of Shakespeare's name. These tales were spread by the paid writers of Henry VII who, through a bastard-branch, revived the claims of Lancaster and therefore strove to discredit the Yorkists as the slayers of Henry VI—whom Henry VII vainly tried to have canonised to give force to his arguments —and of the two Princes in the Tower. As Bishop Stubbs remarks : " Richard III yet owes the general condemnation, with which his life and reign have been visited, to the fact that he left none behind him whose duty or whose care it was to attempt his vindication." [1] He left the opposite, he left a miserable King, a miser who instituted in his fear a standing army and who more than probably had the Princes murdered to bolster up his own weak claim to the throne. There was no reason for Richard to kill the boys. As we have seen, they had been declared illegitimate by parliament and there was no danger to him in their living ; but Henry VII married the daughter of Edward IV, hoping to make his claim stronger, and as he declared Elizabeth legitimate he automatically declared her brothers legitimate, and therefore they should have taken the crown before him. Why should Richard kill them? Henry VII had every motive for the deed, and he treated the men named in the " More " life as the murderers with kindness, although he tried to make them live outside England. Sir James Tyrrel, in particular—the man who is usually damned as the villain—Henry fondled and showered with gifts, while during the latter end of Richard's reign we hear nothing of him. Henry made him a knight of the King's body and presented him with a general pardon for unnamed crimes, he appointed him constable of Guienne and sent him abroad as ambassador, he made him steward of the King's lordship of Ogmore in Wales, although he was not permitted to enter Britain ; he had to stay in Guienne while he drew the revenues. Then at the first opportunity Henry pounced on him, dragged him to the Tower, and executed him without trial, without giving him an opportunity to tell the truth. The person he had most to fear was, of course, the boys' mother, Elizabeth

[1] *The Constitutional History of England in its Origin and Development*, by William Stubbs, 3 vols. (Oxford University), 1874-78.

Woodville, and he pushed her into a nunnery and seized her goods ; in Richard's reign we will find that he and Elizabeth remained the best of friends, and surely if he had murdered the boys the mother at least could never have forgiven him ?

We have no space to continue further, and I have already devoted two books to the question. Frankly, the blank wall of enmity that is before any Ricardian becomes occasionally depressing, and one falters, not in one's love for Richard, but in one's helplessness, one's inability to beat aside this strange hatred. I feel that Shakespeare—or rather Marlowe—is most to blame. Ranted on the stage, repeated in schoolbooks, the lie continues, and until that play is smiled at as history and the schoolbooks rewritten, nothing will make the people realise that one of our noblest Kings has been traduced for centuries.

WHEN he became King, Richard was thirty years of age and was slim and short. Henry VII invented the lie of his crouchback for which there is no contemporary evidence ; apparently one shoulder was slightly higher than the other, otherwise he had no other deformity whatsoever. Stow, the Elizabethan, tells us that he had talked with old men who had known Richard in their youth, and they said " that he was of bodily shape comely enough, only of low stature." It is impossible to believe that sharp-eyed historians like Comines would not have noticed any deformity, particularly as Richard was hated in France because of his insult to Louis in refusing the bribe and not appearing at Picquigny.

His short reign gives us little opportunity of judging his character, but even his greatest enemies confess that what little we know of his rule shows him to be one of the most just Princes England has ever known, and Lord Campbell—no friend of Richard's—says of his parliament that " we have no difficulty in pronouncing Richard's parliament the most meritorious national assembly for protecting the liberty of the subject, and putting down abuses in the administration of justice that had sat in England since the reign of Henry III." [1]

When we examine his recorded actions, trying to forget the Tudor lies, we find that very few Kings—if any—can measure up to Richard's standard.

[1] *Lives of the Lord Chancellors and Keepers of the Great Seal of England,* by John Lord Campbell, 7 vols. (Murray), 3rd ed. 1848.

ALWAYS he had been most loyal to his brother. *Loyaulté me lie—* " Loyalty bindeth me "—was his motto, and it was no idle phrase, it was Richard's creed. Although he loved Warwick's daughter Anne, and although his brother George had proved that he could marry her if he wished, Richard took the hard path of honesty and faith, and even put aside his desires to abide by his conscience. His behaviour in France shows in strong contrast beside the other nobles who jostled each other to scoop up Louis's gold. As a soldier he had proved himself at least Edward's equal, while his administration in the north had made the Yorkshire people remember him always with love, and until then his family had not been popular amongst them. His battles with the Scots were always successful. There is not a single authentic act of Richard's that does not prove him upright and just and noble and brave.

Rivers before execution could appoint him his executor, and Elizabeth Woodville was to prove by her schemes that she respected and perhaps loved him. And he was happy with his wife. Never is there any suggestion of scandal. It is true that he had three illegitimate children, but they were born before marriage.

Queen Anne was evidently beautiful, fair-headed and blue-eyed. " In presence she was seemly, amiable, and beauteous, and in conditions full commendable and right virtuous, and according to the interpretation of her name, Anne, full gracious." They had one child, Edward, born some time in 1473.

AFTER the coronation Richard set out on a royal progress to show the people what kind of a make was their new King. These progresses were necessary to medieval lords, otherwise they would have starved. Food was mainly powdered—salted— and perhaps for this reason medieval recipes seem to us revolting. A diet of salt meat and fish would have become tedious, and as salted meat usually tastes of almost nothing except salt and sawdust, to make it palatable the cooks brought into use all known spices and herbs and sweets. Honey and wine were often added to meats—eggs in honey was a common dish, and flowers such as violets and marigolds were baked in pies. Ambergris, too, was used, and various sweet waters, ginger, pepper, figs—although " they do stir a man to venerous acts . . . and also they do provoke a man to sweat : wherefore they doth engender lice "— saffron, raisins, tansy : all were in the cook's spicery, brought overseas, and were stewed, fried, or baked in the open medieval kitchens ; the food was rather sloppy, as there were no forks : [1] a man used his hands and his own dagger. With great hordes of followers, Kings and other nobles could not live for long in one castle ; they exhausted the larder in one place and then moved to another.

Richard left on this progress a fortnight after the coronation, and Anne joined him at Warwick. It was a most triumphant progress. " He contents the people where he goes best than ever Prince did," wrote Bishop Langton who accompanied him, " for many a poor man that hath suffered wrong many days has been relieved and helped by him and his commands in his progress. And in many great cities and towns were great sums of money given him which he hath refused. On my truth I never liked the conditions of any Prince so well as this. God hath sent him to us for the weal of us all."

Then in the midst of the merry-making, while Richard was endearing himself to the people, came sudden news that Buckingham had revolted. We have few details about the causes of this revolt, but obviously Buckingham intended to steal the crown. His claim was quite good. He was a descendant of the fifth son of Edward III, Thomas of Woodstock, Duke of Gloucester, and of the third son, John of Gaunt, through the illegitimate Beaufort branch. But why had he not thought of it earlier? why crown Richard, then try to steal the crown? The answer is not so difficult as it might appear, for Richard had placed in Buckingham's custody one of the conspirators, Bishop—later Cardinal—Morton. This Morton was a complete rascal. He had been a Lancastrian pardoned by Edward after Tewkesbury and had sailed to France to accept Louis's bribes. To understand the man we had best run a trifle ahead and examine his subsequent career. He was one of Henry Tudor's advisers and after the usurpation became chancellor in 1486 and Archbishop of Canterbury in 1487, and he revealed to the King " the confessions of as many lords as his grace listed." He was also the inventor of the

---

[1] Forks in the Middle Ages were occasionally used for eating fruit. We find one mentioned in the inventory of Edward I, while Gaveston possessed two or three for pears. It is most likely that they had only two teeth. They arrived in England to be used with meat in the first half of the seventeenth century. Coryate tells us how surprised he was because the Italians had these queer instruments, although he was not above introducing them into England " to th' sparing o' napkins "—Ben Jonson tells us—it being now no longer necessary to keep on continually washing your hands during meals.

notorious Morton's Fork, a trick of taxation by which it was argued that a man who spent little must have saved much, while a man who spent much must have much. There can be little doubt that if he did not actually write, he inspired the so-called " More's " history of Richard. Sir Thomas More's name has become attached to this party-pamphlet because a portion of it was discovered in More's handwriting after his death. It needs no strong imagination to believe that More was only copying the work or, as he was in Morton's household when a lad, taking it down by dictation. There are parts of this book that More could not have written, as they are obviously described by an eyewitness of a time when More was too young to understand what was happening. Only Cardinal Morton could have had recourse to information for many of the details, and it is impossible not to believe that he wrote most of them. This work is the great enemy to Richard's rehabilitation, for people still believe that Sir Thomas was the author and feel that a man of such probity and beauty of character could not deliberately have been lying.

Our details of Buckingham's revolt come from this source and are therefore tainted. It is absurd to accept, as Morton insists, that Buckingham intended to give the throne to Henry Tudor, to a Welsh adventurer whose claim was by no means as good as his own. Although we may dismiss this part of Morton's narrative, he is obviously telling the truth when he boasts of having inspired the rebellion. Undoubtedly the prisoner worked upon the vanity of his jailer until Buckingham, in a moment of drunken arrogance, decided to take the crown for himself.

He failed, of course. Richard did not even need to use the troops that came to his aid. Buckingham was cut off from England in Wales by a sudden violent storm that overflowed the Severn and which drove Henry Tudor back to Brittany, for he had sailed to unite with the rebels. Starved and exhausted, Buckingham was caught before he could put up a fight and was tried and sentenced to death. Morton escaped to work further mischief, he joined Henry Tudor.

This Henry Tudor now begins to step upon the stage. He was a thin partially bald man, a coward and a miser, but was the only branch of Lancaster remaining to which the malcontents could turn. The Lancastrian cause had become the Tudor cause after the death of Henry VI. Tudor's claim was a meagre one based on descent from Henry V's widow and from John of Gaunt through his mother Margaret Beaufort. This second claim was so weak that even Henry scarcely dared to produce it except in a vague fashion, for not only were the Beauforts debarred by parliament from reigning, and while his mother lived, the claim did not devolve on to Henry. His only hope of bolstering his demands was by a promise to marry Edward IV's daughter Elizabeth. This promise he gave, but by marrying Elizabeth he declared her brothers legitimate which meant that after all his trouble he had only stolen the crown for one of the detested Yorkists to take. For this reason it would seem that he murdered the Princes.

At the moment, however, after the defeat of Buckingham, no one would have thought Henry Tudor had the least chance of stealing Richard's crown. The country adored its young King, for he had been generous and forgiving, eager to put a stop to all crime and to see that justice was given impartially.

Parliament met in January 23, 1484, at Westminster. The first question was, of course, the settlement of the crown, and this was passed on every point, Richard being acclaimed the true heir, the " very and undoubted King of this realm of England," and the bill added that the King's title was too clear even to be discussed in parliament, although the settlement was necessary to remove " occasion of all doubts and seditious language." Richard's title being made clear, Buckingham's adherents were attainted, and the Countess of Richmond, Henry Tudor's mother, was declared incapable of holding or inheriting any estate or dignity. The sentence was never carried out. The merciful heart of Richard did not permit him to harm a woman, and she was allowed to retain her goods during the lifetime of her husband, Lord Stanley.

This parliament is of real interest, as it shows us Richard's profound care for the condition of his people ; he tried by enactment to keep up the standard and quality of certain cloths and to stop interference with exported wool. Tariffs were placed on foreign goods except, it is refreshing to note, on " books, written or imprinted." In passing we might remark that Richard was one of Caxton's patrons, and that Caxton had dedicated his *Order of Chivalry* to him. Other important acts of legislation were attempts to put a stop to underhand land deals and to declare that suits-at-law should be brought within five years, and that justices of the peace should be empowered with the same rights to admit prisoners to bail as justices sitting in sessions, while officers were forbidden to seize the goods of prisoners before conviction. The main act, however, was the abolishing of those detested benevolences of Edward IV, that " new and unlawful invention " which had brought dire poverty to many. Then a solemn oath was taken to ensure the succession of the Prince of Wales, and parliament was dissolved on February 20.

ELIZABETH WOODVILLE had been lurking in sanctuary all this time, and Richard felt the shame this placed upon him. He promised to protect her and her five daughters, and she came from her hiding-place. One would naturally expect that a mother deprived so long of her sons would ask how they were and would wish to see them. According to the " More " life, Richard had murdered the Princes during his progress north, and therefore they were already corpses when Elizabeth came with her daughters from that vile city of thieves nestling against the abbey. Yet we do not find her accusing Richard of the crime ; from this moment she remained his staunchest friend. It is difficult to conceive any mother loving the murderer of her sons, yet we are expected to believe that Elizabeth Woodville was so degraded a creature that she actually strove to make the slayer of her sons the husband of her daughter ! Surely that is not credible, even to the prejudiced mind of the most violent Tudor supporter ?

Few Kings have suffered so terribly as Richard suffered. In those brief years during which he ruled the country he was doomed to lose everything he prized, he was to find himself alone with all the power a man could desire but without the affection he needs. First his son died. This little Prince of Wales, Edward, died at Middleham Castle on April 9, and Dr. Barton has suggested to me that according to the small evidence we possess, it seems more than likely that he died of appendicitis, as he was attacked suddenly with violent pains in the stomach. For some reason, probably from fear, the news was kept from Richard until the 20th, when he was told at Nottingham. " You might have seen his father and mother in a state almost bordering on madness because of their sudden grief." Edward was their only child and it seems that they would have no others, for Anne, like her sister Isabel, was delicate. Ever afterward Richard was to call Nottingham, where the news reached him, his " Castle of Care," and he avoided visiting it. The child was buried at Sheriff Hutton in the chapel on the north side, which was dedicated to St. Nicholas, the patron saint of children. To-day the tomb can still be seen, pathetically worn, the alabaster face with broken nose as if some giant hand had crushed it. In the windows were placed coloured glass ; to-day all that is left except a few odd pieces is the sun-in-splendour high in the arch, blazing dully above the little child.[1] It has often been wondered why Richard should have chosen this Yorkshire church in which to bury his son ; but surely it is understandable that he would like the bones to lie close to his castle, the centre of the lordship of the north ? York might have been a more worthy setting, but he had no private residence in that city.

With his son dead, Richard had now to arrange the succession if he would keep the Tudors out of England. Clarence's son was under his father's attainder and was only nine years of age, nevertheless Richard declared him his heir, no doubt intending to reverse the attainder when parliament next sat. There was much to be done before England could be settled, and the King had small time to linger on his grief. In September he met the Scottish ambassadors at Nottingham, and a three years' truce was arranged on the promise that King James III's eldest son should marry one of Richard's nieces. Then Richard removed the body of Henry VI from Chertsey and interred it in the nearly finished St. George's Chapel at Windsor, to the south of the altar. His enemies have naturally taken this to show his bad conscience, and they may be correct, but it does not mean that Richard killed Henry. His conscience would have been equally troubled if Edward had commanded the murder.

ONE feels that fate might have tired of tormenting the poor King, yet now he was to lose his beloved wife. Christmas was kept at Westminster, and on the surface it was a most jolly affair, the King's niece Elizabeth being dressed in a gown very like the Queen's, which the traducers of Richard have eagerly seized on as proof that he intended to poison his wife and marry his niece. It proves only the gentleness of his heart, showing that he wished the children of Edward to forget the bâton sinister and to realise that they were a part of his family and would be treated with all love and honour. Anne was

---

[1] The enemies of Richard even go to the extent of trying to prove that Edward was not buried in the tomb of Sheriff Hutton, but their arguments have been fully answered by the researches of Dr. Saxon Barton and Captain T. B. L. Churchill. See *Proceedings of the Yorkshire Architectural and York Archæological Society*, vol. i. No. 3, for the essay, *Some Notes on the Royal Monument in the North Chapel of Sheriff Hutton Church*, by Capt. T. B. L. Churchill.

evidently a delicate woman, perhaps consumptive : she died on March 16, 1485, and was buried in Westminster Abbey. Richard wept openly as she was lowered into the grave, for now he had no one left for him to love save a few old comrades ; his brothers, his father, his son, and his wife . . . all dead. Of that ill-fated house of York he alone remained to keep the sun-in-splendour. And he was tragically alone, with that spiritual loneliness of a man who has no one to love. He had his palaces, he had courtiers and women to fawn upon him, he had all the riches, the power that royalty gives, yet of what value were they compared to the body of the woman in that grave ? For man is a beast who needs a mate, he needs the solace of her silence, the comfort of her presence, and the spiritual quickening given by her kisses, the consoling touch of her hand, and the whisper of her voice. Richard now tasted the most morbid and crushing of all emotions, loneliness ; he had to walk through chambers made vivid with her memoried presence, to lie abed at night and stretch his hand across the empty pillow, never to feel again her crinkling golden hair between his fingers. There is no escaping a ghost, a ghost in your heart, for it runs with you, it chases you when you ride from it, it follows, torments you ; when you believe it banished, it catches you suddenly unprepared and rushes tears into your eyes. The house of York was doomed, its banners falling in the dust, the sun was fading in its splendour ; only the silver boar remained, driven and stabbed by fate yet snarling and ever ready for the last great fight. Let fate take everything he loved from Richard, it could not destroy him. Tragic and lonely he awaited the final blow.

ELIZABETH WOODVILLE was one of those women who must be continually plotting. She now decided to marry her eldest daughter to Richard, and when Richard heard of the rumour he formally and publicly repudiated it. His enemies, of course, fully believe that he intended to marry the girl ; in the first place, Richard was a most devout Catholic and would never have been able to bring himself to marry his niece ; in the second place, such a marriage would have been entirely pointless and would have alienated the country. We have definite proof, however, that Elizabeth had every intention of pushing through the marriage if she could, and her daughter was apparently eager for it—strange behaviour of the mother and sister of two murdered boys towards their murderer ?

This trouble was small compared to the ever-threatening invasion of Henry Tudor. Richard took up his position at Nottingham and issued commissions of array. The treasury was impoverished—for he did not touch a penny of Edward's private fortune, he had it put under ecclesiastical sequestration in the care of the Archbishop of Canterbury—and he was forced to borrow money without the sanction of parliament. It has been said that this was a return to the abolished benevolences, that is not true. Richard gave " good and sufficient pledges " for all he took.

HENRY TUDOR set sail from Harfleur and landed at Milford Haven in Pembrokeshire, his own country, on August 8, 1485. He brought with him a few Lancastrian exiles and some French troops. Altogether he had about two thousand men, but there were many traitors in England, and the Welsh would naturally fight for him. His mother did good work : she enticed her husband, Lord Stanley, her brother-in-law, Sir William Stanley, and Sir William's son, Lord Strange, to his cause. Henry had a great many friends and he bought others with promises ; when he raised the standard of Cadwallader on Welsh soil, the Welsh naturally took down their bows and spears to fight for their countryman against the hated English.

When Richard was told of Tudor's landing he was at Beskwood Lodge on the edge of Sherwood Forest, quite close to Nottingham, and he was so eager for the fight that he could not wait for reinforcements ; he left Nottingham on the morning of the 17th. With him were his friends from childhood, Viscount Lovel and Sir Robert Percy. The Duke of Norfolk and his son the Earl of Surrey were galloping from the eastern counties, Lords Ferrers and Zouch rode from the Midlands, Sir Robert Brackenbury—the man who, it is said, was so revolted by Richard's command to kill the Princes that he refused to obey—now flogged his horses from London so that he might join his King in battle ; the Earl of Northumberland was coming from the north. The list of those who were preparing to ride with Richard is long, but foolishly, bravely, he disdained to wait. England had conquered often against great odds, and Richard did not fear, he did not pause for reinforcements. Life held little for him, and he was eager to fight ; he had forgotten one thing —too trusting, he did not realise that there were men who could be bought, and that Henry Tudor's mother was a woman who would do anything to help her son.

On August 21 Richard rode from Leicester with his army. He was dressed in the armour of polished steel he had worn at Tewkesbury and there was a golden crown about his helm. We also know that his steed, that gallant creature, was named White Surrey. The countryside near Bosworth where the battle was to be fought rippled on every side into little hills, and narrow streams flowed west to join the Anker. Richard's first camp was in a field near Stapleton called the Bradshaws, and about two miles to the north Norfolk encamped at Cadeby. The traitor, Lord Stanley, fresh from a conversation with Henry Tudor, came as if he retreated before the rebels and settled near Stoke Golding, facing Richard ; Sir William Stanley, traitor, drew up his men nearer Norfolk before the town of Market Bosworth ; Henry's army was on White Moors, beyond the swamp. It is difficult to know what were the exact numbers of the opposing forces, but it seems that the Stanleys had about 8000 men, Norfolk 4000, Richard 8000, while Henry had 2000 French and about 6000 Welsh and English. Everything therefore depended on the Stanleys, and they were already bought, hoping for great honours under the rule of their relation by marriage. It is refreshing to learn that these hopes were never satisfied.

Richard altered his position, he moved north to join Norfolk, and drew up his men on a small hill called Sutton Fields. He drew them up in two lines, archers and artillery under Norfolk in the van, horse on the flanks, and billmen in the rear. Stanley followed. He wanted to be close, ready for the moment of treason. Richard by now must have known that he was sold ; others knew of it. Northumberland was warned, and although he arrived in time, he remained inactive. He was later murdered by the Yorkshiremen when trying to gather some of Henry's excessive taxes ; Yorkshire always remained most loyal to Richard. When Norfolk arose that morning he found a paper pinned to his tent with these words on it :

> *Jock of Norfolk, be not too bold,*
> *for Dickon, thy master, is bought and sold ;*

the rime did not affect his loyalty. Brave man, he stayed to die with his young King although he knew that he was doomed.

BEFORE he charged on that tragic morning of August 22, 1485, Richard sent word to Lord Stanley that he would execute his hostage, Stanley's son, unless he fought with him. The threat

38

did not succeed, neither did Richard fulfil it. The lad was found after the battle, unharmed. Down the slope rode Richard before his men, and then Lord Stanley struck. He swept down on Richard's flank.

The battle was lost in that moment, yet with the courage of despair, Richard charged with his cavalry, hoping to capture Henry ; but that cautious man hid safely within his bodyguard behind the battle. He did not fight as Richard fought, he lurked in terror while others died. Richard swept down, lifting his heavy battle-axe for the blow. Men fell before him, none could withstand the heroic rage of that young King. We are told that his comrades, seeing that all was lost, besought him to fly and offered swift horses, and " he answered that that very day he would make end either of war or life, such great fierceness and such huge force of mind he had." He slew all who dared oppose him as he sought the coward Henry. Norfolk fell, smashed to death, but Richard charged on ; he met Henry's standard-bearer and struck him down so that the red dragon on green and white sarcenet was stamped into the mud. Richard's standard-bearer kept the lions of England above the head of his brave King. His name was Sir William Parker, and although both legs were cut from under him he held aloft that standard while bleeding horribly to death. The giant Sir John Cheney charged at Richard, and Richard knocked him from the saddle.

For one glorious moment it seemed that England might conquer as the frightened Tudor gaped up at the avenging King ; for one moment, then the traitor, Sir William Stanley, rushed his three thousand men between them, and Richard was surrounded. His friends strove to make him fly, but he cried, " Never, I will not budge a foot, I will die King of England," and he rushed forward to his death, " fighting manfully in the thickest press of his enemies."

As they clubbed him down and struck at his slim body, he kept on shouting, " Treason, treason, treason ! . . ."

THEY stripped the poor King naked, for Henry's spite wished every degradation to his enemy. They tossed the broken body over a horse behind a man stated differently as Blanc Sanglier— Richard's personal pursuivant—and as " a pursuivant called Norroy," but there never was a pursuivant called Norroy and this must refer to Norroy King-of-Arms. No matter who the rascal was who carried the dead King that day to Leicester, when he passed over a bridge he went too near the wall and bruised the face against the stone. And thus King Richard " despoiled to the skin . . . all besprung with mire and filth, was brought to a church in Leicester and there lastly irreverently buried." This church was the Grey Friars, and it has long since been demolished. Richard, last of the English Kings and the first since Harold to die in battle, was treated like some beast too vile for decent burial ; and the treatment of his memory has been no better as the centuries passed.

How different from the Tudor tales is the simple statement given in the York register when the news of his death arrived— " He was piteously slain and murdered to the great heaviness of this city." I prefer to believe those few words, written in a moment of great sorrow by men who had seen and who could iudge the King, to all the lies that have been printed since Henry VII began to destroy old records and to rewrite history.

Last of the English Kings, the most hated and the most noble ! Poor Richard, he has no grave where we can mourn for his passing, but his recorded deeds stripped of their lies are a greater memorial than any carving in stone or alabaster. For all his cunning, Henry VII could not destroy the truth.

Vincit veritas.

XIX

HAIL ! AND FAREWELL

AFTER BOSWORTH they found the crown of England under a hawthorn bush. It was the gold chaplet King Richard had worn around his helm, and now one of the traitor Stanleys placed it over the narrow half-bald head of Henry Tudor. The crown of England was given to a Welshman, the crown for which so many men had struggled and schemed and fought and died. . . . And after the Welsh—Scots, Dutch, German Kings ; the true English line died with King Richard on the field of Bosworth. And with him died not only the race of Plantagenets, but medieval England itself. Modernity first really began in England with the crowning of Henry VII ; not that it was a sudden lightning-flash, it was a gradual dawn that had brightened by the time the Tudors took the throne. They have been honoured for much that was not their doing, under the Yorkists the dawn would still have come, and perhaps more splendidly.

We have watched this dawn slowly rise, we have seen the Middle Ages pass as the renascence was born, for we have travelled through many centuries. Richard III's was the first parliament to publish its statutes in English, men were forgetting that the nation was born from foreign seed, from a confusion of Saxons, Danes and Normans. England was truly England by this time, it was ready for the self-centred tyrannical rule of the Tudors who reigned quietly by the simple expedient of murdering anybody who might have a claim to the throne beside themselves. If the Yorkists could have been as brutal, the Tudor usurpation would have never come.

IT is with genuine reluctance that I conclude this book. If only such a thing were possible I wish it could continue for ever, and there are enough details ignored or slurred to fill a dozen volumes of this size. But the cover must fall some time, the gates must shut finally upon the printed letter ; the gates here are shutting upon that which I love more than anything in all the world—

medieval England. We have not seen a great deal of medieval England, the Kings have stood too largely in the foreground for us even to peep behind them and glimpse the merchants in their counting-houses with notched tally-sticks, the villeins ploughing the earth, and the monks browsing in shady cloisters. Behind the Kings there was a busy world, people like you and I were living their secret enormously important lives, they were working and cheating and gossiping, dancing, singing, weeping, drinking too heartily of wine or ale, and making love and going to church—doing all the things that men and women do until this day and will until the world shall end. Above them stood that great man, their King, and there was a queer loyalty towards him, inarticulate, yet living ; he may have been a bad King, nevertheless he was theirs, and they would fight for him or, if a stronger came forward, fight against him. Yet one feels that there was always a sense of loyalty towards the crown. Most Kings began by being adored and most of them forfeited their people's adoration by truculent selfishness. He must have appeared a strange creature to ordinary men, this King of theirs, they saw him in processions, they gossiped about him in taverns, yet they rarely doubted his right to rule. The holy unction made him a saint in a small way ; to the very last, Richard II believed that this aura of semi-divinity could not be stolen by swords or legislation.

But take the crown away, rob these Kings of their purple cloaks, see them as men, and they become tragically human. Before we dare condemn them, we must realise the huge temptations that lay on every side, the ease with which they could kill or ravish or steal. Kings must not be judged as ordinary men are judged.

NINETEEN KINGS have passed before us—for we can scarcely include Edward V—nineteen Kings from the Confessor to Richard III. Each has worn the crown, has felt that weight of gold, yet few have found true happiness—Harold and Richard III slain on the field of battle ; Eadward on his death-bed watching visions of a disrupted England ; William I and Henry II despairing as they fought against their own blood that strove to tear the crown from their living heads ; William II struck down by an unknown hand in the New Forest ; Henry I, gripping his belly sick with lampreys, his mind sick at the memory of a dead son and of a crown he could pass only to a woman ; Stephen—perhaps he was contented, at least he was King when he died even if another man did rule the country ; Richard I with poisoned flesh on a bed of agony ; John in the tempest seeing the world crumble about him and remembering his baggage and his troops struggling amidst the quicksands ; Henry III, old and ill with the commons yelling their independence outside his window ; Edward I, like Henry V, dying as he clung to the saddle and felt his body give before the brave spirit that would not die ; Edward II and Richard II both foully murdered ; Henry VI after a life of pain also perhaps murdered ; Edward III with the wench he loved pulling the rings from his fingers as he tried to croak the name of Jesus ; Henry IV eaten by disease that made him appear so foul that men dared not look upon him, and haunted always by the ghost of Richard and of ambitions unfulfilled ; Edward IV, perhaps the happiest of them all. . . .

They had suffered much to hold that crown. All of them knew treachery and hatred, some even grew to doubt the ones they loved, and all at times despaired. For the crown, for that symbol of gold and jewels, how much blood has been spilt, how many men have dreamed and have woken from dreams to find that actuality was hell on earth ! The crown . . . and to fall at last beside a hawthorn bush and to be fitted around the skull of him who least deserved it !

For these Kings it is difficult to feel hatred, one can only feel pity or admiration. None of them were cowards and some were heroes. It is not a record of which England need be ashamed. It is a great heritage. What those men built is the nation in which we live ; they are our ancestors, common in our fathers, and we should look back upon them with love and feel pride at their achievements. Even if they failed, if like Richard II they were spiteful and giddied by the unction on their heads, if they were simple like Henry VI, nevertheless they were our fathers, and even for the worst of fathers we cannot feel utter loathing. We may sometimes dislike them, we may not respect them, yet after all, even in their weaknesses, we must love them.

INDEX

39